Western Heritage | *A Reader*

# Western Heritage | *A Reader*

EDITED BY THE HILLSDALE COLLEGE HISTORY FACULTY

**Hillsdale College Press**

Hillsdale, Michigan

HILLSDALE COLLEGE PRESS

*Western Heritage: A Reader*
©2010 Hillsdale College Press, Hillsdale, Michigan 49242

Printed in the United States of America.

*Cover design*
Hesseltine & DeMason, Ann Arbor, Michigan

Library of Congress Control Number: 2009936706

ISBN 978-0-916308-27-8

# CONTENTS

# PREFACE

Humans are historical beings. Our identity, our sense of purpose and meaning, all depend in some measure on a remembered past—a heritage. The past is always with us, always shaping, enabling, and limiting our freedom no matter how informed we are about the past. We may know little about the specific origins and evolution of ideas like liberty, but these ideas—developed, altered, expressed by myriad individuals—have supplied us with a range of beliefs that enable us to make sense of ourselves and our world. We inhabit these ideas and beliefs since they provide us with our intellectual, moral, and spiritual homes, no matter how much we may remodel them.

Of course the past is with us also in the form of beliefs upon which we act. Our ignorance of World War II does not change the fact that people, following ideas strongly held, sacrificed themselves and thereby shaped the future. In countless ways, individuals long since forgotten made decisions small and large, courageous and cowardly, noble and base, that altered the environment in which they lived and thereby the ages to come. The one inescapable conclusion from a serious study of history is that all humans are obligated to act freely, to make choices about the mundane and the momentous; and that these decisions necessarily shape the world we inherit and the world we pass along.

Through historical inquiry we come to understand the past and its purchase on our lives. In this sense, then, history constitutes a form of self-inquiry, because these stories about the past tell us something of the universe of meanings we inherited and which shaped our own perspectives. Ignorance of one's history necessarily leads to intellectual, moral, and spiritual disorientation, a loss of identity and purpose. Disorientation leads to disorder, because in the absence of a clear identity one is incapable of discriminating, of making meaningful judgments. Without a remembered past—stories told and internalized—a society has no direction. Heritage anchors a person and a society, investing in each an inheritance worth protecting and a purpose transcending the needs or desires of the individual. The remembered past connects members of a society together as heirs of a common tradition, however large and diverse. Rooted in the same intellectual and moral soil, they participate together in a story much larger than themselves, but one in which each individual must play his part.

*Western Heritage: A Reader* is an integral part of a course designed to acquaint students with the historical roots of the Western Heritage, and, in particular, to explore the ways in which a modern people are indebted to Greco-Roman culture and the Judeo-Christian religious tradition. Both the reader and the course examine dominant themes of this extraordinarily rich and varied heritage.

Beginning with Hebrew civilization, the course emphasizes the development of political cultures in Europe to about 1600, including classical Greece, the Hellenistic world, republican and imperial Rome, the spread of the Christian Church, the gradual development of a synthesis of the classical, Christian, and Germanic traditions that formed medieval Christendom, and the eventual breakdown of the political, social, intellectual, and religious consensus of medieval civilization in the early modern period.

The primary role of *Western Heritage: A Reader* in this course is to supply rich sample documents from the periods we examine. These primary sources provide portals into distant civilizations. By reading them, one escapes the provincialism of one's own time and culture, while also noting the early manifestations of beliefs or ideas that one recognizes as part of one's own, often unanalyzed, belief system. As artifacts of the past, these documents do not convey information, but they are the sources historians interpret to make sense of the past. Consequently, students are invited to engage in the same enterprise, to handle, examine, and interrogate these fragments of the past as the primary means of better understanding those civilizations from which they emerged as well as their own civilization. The jarring task of viewing sympathetically something alien—a puzzling through a different way of understanding the world—is an important and exhilarating part of a proper education in which one seeks to make sense of oneself as a human, who by definition is a historical and acculturated being. Properly understood, then, this book is a means toward self-understanding, with all of the pride and shame that attends any such exploration.

Careful reading of and reflection upon the documents in this volume will highlight an inescapable fact about the Western Heritage. Its political and cultural order, however varied in form and expression, grew from a shared understanding that humans are religious beings subject to an order of Divine origin. People are able to live, to work, to worship, and to play together only when they share a sufficiently common culture as the ground of their social order and stability. What are the sources of that order? While reading this book, the student should consider the following questions. What do shared cultural assumptions, traditions, and institutions have to do with obtaining and securing political stability? In what ways have societies appropriated the cultural components of earlier civilizations? In what ways do such social structures as the family, religious institutions, and local communities contribute to political stability? How is political stability fostered when law and custom function to limit the power and scope of government? To understand the answers to these questions is to grasp key themes of the Western Heritage's political culture.

This heritage also became the inheritance of those American colonists during the seventeenth and eighteenth centuries who laid the foundations upon which our republic would be built. To comprehend the Western Heritage, then, is to begin the task of understanding the American Heritage, because the American founders did not create the United States ex nihilo or from their colonial experience alone. Rather, they drew from a rich body of sources that included the political thought of the Greco-Roman world, the Bible and Church history, knowledge of English common law, and European political custom.

Many twenty-first-century students may be tempted to ask about the utility of such an immersion in documents penned by men long dead and gone. The answer remains disarmingly simple. The highest things, the most noble ideals—the well-ordered soul, the furnished and disciplined mind—are valuable for their own sakes, not just for the alleged practicality they may have for getting a job or earning a dollar. In a world where so many see education as mere job training, too few tend to the purposes for which we work and live. Too few see education as preparation for living worthy and virtuous lives in which flourishing can be measured in nonmaterial ways. Consequently, too many colleges and universities have become places for focusing on means, and not upon ends—and, as such, places where the confused and bewildered of the next generation acquire techniques and tools, but graduate having gained neither direction nor order to their souls. Such students become clever but not wise. They can make a dollar but have not the wisdom to spend it well. A liberal arts education is an education in those things that are worth studying for their own sake, because they are beautiful, good, and true, because they help make us wise and prepare us to live well. The Western Heritage is part of a liberal education. While the practical utility of the documents in this book may elude immediate detection, the inheritance they offer is beyond price.

Just as the Western Heritage unfolded over time and was the product of many minds, this book issued from the collective efforts of more than a dozen colleagues from the Hillsdale history faculty working and teaching together for over a decade. Some who began work on this volume at its inception have moved on. John Willson, who has retired from full-time teaching, and Ted McAllister, now at Pepperdine University in California, played important early roles, John as the senior member of the department in the early days of this project and Ted as the original author of this

Preface's first six paragraphs. Others, new faculty when we began, have matured into tenured and seasoned professors while teaching the documents of this volume. Although these documents were written by others, the process of their selection, editing, and in some cases translating was our own labor. Further, each document opens with an introduction written by a member of the history faculty as does each section of the book. Recognition for such effort is owed to Thomas Conner, Lucy Moye, Paul Moreno, Paul Rahe, Harold Siegel, Burt Folsom, Richard Gamble, David Raney, and especially to Bradley Birzer and David Stewart, whose tireless enthusiasm and remarkable organizational talents were conspicuous and invaluable.

MARK A. KALTHOFF
Chairman
Department of History
and Political Science
HILLSDALE COLLEGE
Hillsdale, Michigan

# I
# THE ANCIENT NEAR EAST
# AND THE HEBREWS

The study of history rarely allows us to pinpoint the precise origin of any people, or culture, or idea, or form of government. Finding the true beginning of a chain of cause and effect can be impossible. More often, history permits us merely to observe a gradual transition from one state of affairs to another. How difficult, then, would it be to find the starting point of something as complex, varied, and immense as Western Civilization? If that precise point in time and place can be found, credit probably belongs to the city-states and kingdoms of the Near East that appeared more than 5,000 years ago. The exact circumstances that gave rise to the earliest Near Eastern civilizations lie hidden in a realm beyond the reach of historical documents. Archeology and anthropology help shed light on these early years, but the historian works primarily with written records to reconstruct the past. From these fragments, a coherent story begins to emerge.

Some of history's earliest surviving records come from a region in modern-day Iraq between the Tigris and Euphrates rivers known as *Mesopotamia* (from two Greek words meaning "between the rivers"). The city-states that flourished in this area as early as 3500 BC invented a type of writing known as *cuneiform* (from the Latin for "wedge-shaped"). Scribes pressed sharpened reeds into soft clay tablets and then baked the tablets, which became as hard and durable as pottery. These tablets, often remarkably small, bore line upon line of hundreds of tiny characters. The intricate symbols at first were not phonetic, like Greek or Latin or modern English, but pictographic, using combinations of wedge impressions to represent "god" or "house" or "warrior." These symbols could be added together to identify more complex things, or even to express abstract ideas. Later, these figures became phonetic and more adaptable. Scribes used cuneiform to keep tax and accounting records, to record wills and deeds, to publish the king's laws, and to pass down myths and legends to future generations. Surviving records remained buried in the ruins of these great civilizations until modern times.

Historians typically call the arc of productive agricultural land stretching counterclockwise from Mesopotamia through modern southern Turkey and down toward the eastern Mediterranean the "fertile crescent." In this region some of man's oldest civilizations rose to power and left their mark on law, commerce, architecture, religion, and literature. A people known as the Sumerians established the earliest urban settlements in Mesopotamia. They built the prominent city-states of Ur, Lagash, Uruk—a constellation of about a dozen in all—just to the northwest of what today is called the Persian Gulf. They often waged war against each other over boundaries and water rights. They developed bronze tools and weapons, farmed the land using sophisticated irrigation systems, traded with distant peoples, and built a complex urban life. Their society was stratified into social classes, ranging from nobles to slaves, each with different legal rights and penalties under the law. At the top, a powerful *lugal* ruled as the gods' appointed king and presided over temple worship as chief priest. The Sumerians placed shrines atop large, terraced temples known as *ziggurats*, the focal point of each city's cult. Here they sought to appease the wrath of their capricious gods who ruled over earth and sky, rivers and storms, and a shadowy afterlife. They preserved their myths of creation and divine judgment and their tales of heroic quests in the stories compiled by the later Babylonians in *The Epic of Gilgamesh*.

In the third millennium BC, the Akkadians from the north under Sargon I (*r.* 1920–1881 BC) conquered the city-states of Sumer and united them under the military and administrative control of the region's first empire, an early example of the drive for universal empire that has appeared so often in Western Civilization. The Akkadians eventually expanded as far as northern Syria. Following turbulent centuries of barbarian invasions and a series of successor kingdoms, the region fell to the Amorites, who established the Babylonian empire. Hammurabi, a great early king of the Amorites, subdued all of the Tigris and Euphrates region under his rule in about 1700 BC. He instituted administrative reforms and issued his landmark law code. The Babylonians developed mathematics, astronomy, and the visual arts to a high degree. Though the name endured, the Babylonian Empire soon fell to the Kassites, to the Assyrians, to the Chaldeans (or New Babylonians), and then to the Persians.

Long before these empires appeared, however, and about as early as the first Sumerians, another great people flourished to the west: the Egyptians. Egypt arose along the rich, black soil of the Nile valley. The Greek historian Herodotus famously called Egypt the "gift of the Nile." And so it was. Annual floods replenished the soil for farmers, and with an elaborate system of canals they controlled the irrigation of their fields. The river served as a highway for commerce deep into Africa, while the surrounding deserts and seas provided natural defenses from hostile neighbors. According to later chroniclers and legends, sometime around 3100 BC a warrior king united Upper and Lower Egypt and established the first ruling dynasty. From this time, the Egyptians built a stable civilization of great sophistication and continuity that endured for over three thousand years.

Most people in the modern West find Egypt's cultural achievements more immediately recognizable than any artifact from ancient Sumer, Babylon, or Persia. The popular imagination easily calls up iconic images of the pharaohs and the Great Pyramids of Giza, of mummies and hieroglyphs. These features of Egyptian civilization did indeed define their culture. The pharaoh (from the Egyptian for "Great House") ruled Egypt as a god on earth and held absolute power. He was a sacred figure, worshiped in life as a child of the gods and in death as one of the high gods. Shrouded in mystery by an elaborate ritual, he combined tremendous political and religious power. All of Egypt belonged to him. He made the law and administered taxes and imperial oversight through a centralized bureaucracy at his command.

The pharaoh's engineers and architects built splendid palaces, temples, and the massive royal tombs known as pyramids. These monumental stone structures required decades and the forced labor of thousands to build, symbolizing for centuries to come either the possibilities of centralized planning or the vanity of earthly ambition. Beneath these tombs, the Egyptians placed the bodies of their mummified kings. Embalmed and wrapped in cloth, the preserved corpses remained intact in airtight chambers, ready to receive the pharaoh's soul whenever it visited earth. At first limited to royalty, the practice of mummification later became widespread, as did the hope in a blessed afterlife.

The Egyptians excelled at practical arithmetic, geometry, astronomy, and the fine arts. They maintained a fairly accurate calendar of 365 days. Artists decorated temples, palaces, and burial chambers with colorful, realistic scenes from myths, the afterlife, daily life in the royal court, or simply animals at play. Surviving examples of Egyptian painting and sculpture embody haunting serenity and poise. Their consistency of style over centuries suggests the conservative temperament of Egyptian civilization. The distinctive system of writing, known as *hieroglyphs* (from two Greek words meaning "sacred carvings"), developed over hundreds of years from pictographic to phonetic. The traditional hieroglyphic script was often reserved for sacred texts and monuments. Modern scholars could not translate hieroglyphics until 1798. In that year, Napoleon's army discovered the Rosetta Stone, which bore an inscription in Greek, demotic (an everyday form of Egyptian writing), and hieroglyphics.

Egyptian religion reflected a view of nature as an orderly whole. The divine and human, the living and the dead, the present world and the afterlife, combined into a meaningful, though often mysterious, tapestry. The earliest Egyptians told stories about the origin of the gods, the creation of man and the world, divine justice, and the afterlife. Their gods, as depicted in stone and paintings, seem utterly calm and self-possessed. They represented the sun, storms, earth, heaven, fertility, and even abstractions. Some gods took human form and some combined an animal head with a human body, while others were entirely animals—sacred bulls and cows, cats and jackals, crocodiles, hawks, and ibises. Over time, Egyptian polytheism became increasingly complex as myths and rituals accumulated from one generation to the next. After a failed attempt by the Pharaoh Akhenaten (r. 1351–1334 BC) to unite all religion under the single worship of the sun disk, Egypt returned to its traditional pantheon of gods.

By most measures of greatness, the Hebrew people achieved nothing on the scale of the Babylonians, the Egyptians, the Greeks, or the Romans. Even at the height of their earthly wealth and power, the Hebrews did not stand among the kingdoms of the world as a great empire. After the reign of only three kings, Israel plunged into ruinous civil war and was swallowed up by neighboring empires. No tourist visits Israel today to see the equivalent of the Pyramids in Egypt, the Acropolis in Athens, or the Coliseum in Rome. Few political theorists would trace democracy or constitutional republicanism directly to Jerusalem. The Hebrews' legacy lies elsewhere than in imperial splendor, monumental architecture, or systems of government. It lies in their treasure of sacred literature.

The first five books of the Hebrew Scriptures, known as the Pentateuch, rooted the ancient Jews in their history and identity as a people. Though these books provide a sweeping narrative of events covering generations, they never attempt a comprehensive or general history of the times. Instead, these books tell a narrowly focused sacred story—a single narrative thread that directs the reader's attention one step at a time to carefully chosen episodes of God's dealings with man. The book of Genesis, after explaining the world's creation, man's disobedience, and God's judgment of the world through a cataclysmic flood, turns quickly to the story of Abraham, the patriarch of the Jews. Abraham came from the city-state of Ur, at that time a coastal town in southeastern Mesopotamia. God called him to leave his home there among the Sumerians and journey to the land east of the Mediterranean and west of the Jordan known as Canaan (called "Palestine" by Herodotus). God announced His covenant to Abraham, promising to give him the land he stood on and to bless him with descendents too numerous to count. From these beginnings, Genesis tells the story of Abraham's family, tracing the covenantal line through Isaac, Jacob, and Jacob's twelve sons. These sons established the twelve "tribes" of Israel, and Genesis ends with their settlement in Egypt as refugees from a bitter famine in Canaan.

The Hebrews remained in the land of Goshen along the eastern delta of the Nile for four hundred years. From one extended family, their numbers grew to a million or more. Fearing their power, one pharaoh enslaved them, forcing them to build public works and to cultivate his fields. The book of Exodus, the second book of the Pentateuch, recounts the dramatic story of the Hebrews' deliverance from bondage in Egypt. For the next forty years, they were led by their great lawgiver Moses, a man reared and educated in the Egyptian royal household. He told them that Yahweh (or Jehovah) had sent him. "Yahweh" means "I am who I am." This God was unlike any god worshipped by the Egyptians or Sumerians or Canaanites. He was the one, universal, and transcendent God, the maker and sustainer of all things. Moses reaffirmed Yahweh's covenant promises to His people, gave them His moral and ceremonial law, and led them through the wilderness toward a Promised Land "flowing with milk and honey." In his final words to his fellow Israelites, Moses reminded them of the terms of God's covenant with them as His chosen people:

> I call heaven and earth to witness against you today, that I have set before you life and death, the blessing and the curse. So choose life in order that you may live, you and your descendents, by loving the Lord [Yahweh] your God, by obeying His voice, and by holding fast to Him; for this is your life and the length of your days, that you may live in the land which the Lord [Yahweh] swore to your fathers, to Abraham, Isaac, and Jacob, to give them. (Deuteronomy 30:19–20)

Israel's dual covenantal identity as a chosen people and a chosen land shaped much of its subsequent history. Under Moses' successor, Joshua, the Hebrews conquered the tribes of Canaan and carved out a nation for themselves. Defeating some peoples utterly, they faced recurrent warfare with other small nations such as the Philistines and the Amalakites. The Hebrew tribes dispersed throughout the region: two settled to the east of the Jordan River and the rest to the north and south between the Jordan and the Mediterranean. For centuries, they lived without a central government and without a king, ruled instead by a long series of judges. Facing constant threats from the Philistine army, the Israelites united under their first king, Saul (r. 1047–1007 BC). Saul achieved decisive early victories against the Philistines, but his reign ended in humiliating defeat at their hands—his decapitated body nailed to a wall and his weapons displayed as trophies in an enemy temple. His son Jonathan also died in battle, ending Saul's ambition to build a royal dynasty.

Israel reached the pinnacle of its political and military might just after 1000 BC under King David (r. 1007–970 BC) and his son Solomon (r. 970–c. 938 BC). David ruled for forty years, united the Israelites, secured the kingdom's borders, and made Jerusalem a great capital city, calling it the "city of David." His poetry, comprising a large part of the Book of Psalms, ranged from beautiful songs of praise, to calls for divine retribution against Israel's enemies, to heart-rending confessions of sin. Despite his disobedience to God's law and the profound disorder and political treason within his family, David became the model of kingship by which the chroniclers of Israel's history judged all subsequent rulers. David's son and chosen heir, Solomon, celebrated for his wealth and wisdom, presided over a golden age of prosperity, security, extensive foreign trade, and the building of the temple in Jerusalem.

Immediately upon Solomon's death, civil war destroyed his kingdom. The kingdom of Israel to the north survived another two hundred years until conquered in 722 BC by the Assyrians, who eventually sent all of Israel's remaining inhabitants into exile. The kingdom of Judah to the south endured until 586 BC, when the Chaldean Empire under Nebuchadnezzar II (r. 605–562 BC) destroyed Jerusalem, taking many captives back to Babylon and dispersing others to distant lands. After the Persians conquered the Chaldean Empire, they allowed the Jews to return to Jerusalem and rebuild the city's walls and temple. This battered region next fell to Alexander the Great (r. 336–323 BC) in the fourth century BC, then passed to the Ptolemies of Egypt after the breakup of Alexander's empire, and then to the Seleucids. The Jews achieved independence from the Seleucids during the revolt in 168 BC led by Judas Maccabeus and his brothers, but Rome intervened in 63 BC and Palestine became part of Rome's expanding empire in the Near East. Though dispersed throughout the Roman Empire, the Jews maintained their religion, their culture, and their ethnic identity for centuries to come.

# CODE OF HAMMURABI

*According to its preface, the law code of Hammurabi (c. 1792–1750 BC)*
*was given him by the gods "to destroy the wicked and the evil, so that the*
*strong may not oppress the weak." It was one of the tools Hammurabi used*
*to solidify his control over an extensive Babylonian (Amorite) empire, which*
*stretched from the Persian Gulf to the Mediterranean.*

c. 1760 BC

When the lofty Anu, King of the Anunnaki, and Bel, Lord of Heaven and Earth,
he who determines the destiny of the land, committed the rule of all mankind to
Marduk, the chief son of Ea; when they made him great among the Igigi; when
they pronounced the lofty name of Babylon; when they made it famous among
the quarters of the world and in its midst established an everlasting kingdom     5
whose foundations were firm as heaven and earth—at that time, Anu and Bel
called me, Hammurabi, the exalted prince, the worshiper of the gods, to cause
justice to prevail in the land, to destroy the wicked and the evil, to prevent the
strong from oppressing the weak, to go forth like the Sun over the Black Head
Race, to enlighten the land and to further the welfare of the people.              10

Hammurabi, the prince, called of Bel, am I, who brought about plenty
and abundance; who made everything for Nippur and Durilu complete; the
exalted supporter of E-kur; the wise king, who restored Eridu to its place; who
purified the sanctuary of E-apsu; who stormed the four quarters of the world;
who made the fame of Babylon great; who rejoiced the heart of Marduk, his      15
lord; who daily served in Esagila; of the seed royal, which Sin begat; who filled
the city of Ur with plenty; the pious and suppliant one, who brought abundance
to E-gis-sir-gal; the diplomatic king, obedient to the mighty Shamash; who
re-founded Sippar; who clothed with green the shrines of Malkat; who decorated E-babbara, which is like a heavenly dwelling; the warrior, the protector    20
of Larsa; who rebuilt E-babbara for Shamash, his helper; the lord, who gave
life to the city of Uruk; who supplied water in abundance to its inhabitants;
who raised the turrets of Eanna; who brought riches to Anu and Nana; the
divine protector of the land; who collected the scattered people of Nisin; who
supplied E-gal-mah with luxurious abundance; the monarch, the city king, the   25

Robert Francis Harper, *The Code of Hammurabi, King of Babylon* (Chicago: University of Chicago Press, 1904), 3–109.

brother of Za-ma-ma; who laid the foundations of the settlement of Kish; who surrounded E-te-me-ur-sag with splendor; who constructed the great shrines of Nana; the patron of the temple of Har-sag-kalama, the grave of the enemy; whose help brings victory; who extended the limits of Cutha; who enlarged
5 Shid-lam in every way; the mighty bull who gores the enemy; the beloved of Tu-tu; who made the city of Borsippa beautiful; the exalted one who was untiring for the welfare of Ezida; the divine king of the city, wise and intelligent, who extended the settlements of Dilbat; who stored up grain for the mighty Urash; the lord adorned with scepter and crown, whom the wise god Ma-ma
10 has clothed with complete power; who defined the confines of Kish; who made sumptuous the splendid banquets in honor of Nin-tu; the wise and perfect one, who determined the pasture and watering places for Lagash and Girsu; who provided large sacrifices for the Temple of Fifty; who seizes the enemy; the favorite of the exalted god; who put into execution the laws of Aleppo; who
15 makes joyful the heart of Anunit; the illustrious prince, the lifting up of whose hands Adad recognizes; who pacifies the heart of Adad, the warrior, in Karkar; who re-established the appointments in E-ud-gal-gal; the king who gave life to Ud-nun-ki; the benefactor of the temple E-mah; the lordly city king; the soldier who has no equal; who presented life to the city of Mashkan-shabri;
20 who poured out abundance over Shid-lam; the wise governor, who captured the bandit caves, who provided a hiding place for the people of Malka in their misfortune; who founded dwelling-places for them in plenty; who determined for all time the splendid sacrifices for Ea and Dam-gal-nunna, who had extended his dominion; the princely king of the city, who subdued the settlements along
25 the Euphrates; the warrior of Dagan, his creator; who protected the people of Mera and Tutul; the exalted prince, who makes the face of Nana to shine; who established splendid banquets for Nin-a-zu; who helps his people in time of need; who establishes in security their property in Babylon; the governor of the people, the servant, whose deeds are pleasing to Anunit; who installed Anunit
30 in E-ul-mash in Agane broadway; who made justice prevail and who ruled the race with right; who returned to Ashur its gracious protecting deity; who made the rising sun to shine brilliantly; the king who made the name of Nana glorious in E-mish-mish in Nineveh; the exalted one, who makes supplication to the great gods; the descendant of Sumulailu, the powerful son of Sinmuballit,
35 the ancient seed of royalty, the powerful king, the Sun of Babylon, who caused light to go forth over the lands of Sumer and Akkad; the king, who caused the four quarters of the world to render obedience; beloved of Nana, am I.

When Marduk sent me to rule the people and to bring help to the country, I established law and justice in the land and promoted the welfare of the
40 people.

1. If a man bring an accusation against a man, and charge him with a capital crime, but cannot prove it, the accuser, shall be put to death.

2. If a man charge a man with sorcery, and cannot prove it, he who is charged with sorcery shall go to the river, into the river he shall throw himself and if the river overcome him, his accuser shall take to himself his estate. If the river show that man to be innocent and he come forth un-harmed, he who charged him with sorcery shall be put to death. He who threw himself into the river shall take to himself the estate of his accuser....

8. If a man steal ox or sheep, ass or pig, or boat—if it be from a temple or a palace, he shall restore thirtyfold; if it be from a freeman, he shall render ten-fold. If the thief have nothing wherewith to pay, he shall be put to death....

14. If a man steal a man's son who is a minor, he shall be put to death.

15. If a man aid a male or female slave of the palace, or a male or female slave of a freeman, to escape from the city gate, he shall be put to death....

21. If a man make a breach in a house, they shall put him to death in front of that breach and they shall thrust him therein.

22. If a man practice brigandage and be captured, that man shall be put to death.

23. If the brigand be not captured, the man who has been robbed shall, in the presence of god, make an itemized statement of his loss, and the city and the governor in whose province and jurisdiction the robbery was committed shall compensate him for whatever was lost.

24. If a life is lost, the city and governor shall pay one mina of silver to his heirs....

27. If an officer or a constable who is in a garrison of the king be captured, and afterward they give his field and garden to another and he conduct his business—if the former return and arrive in his city, they shall restore to him his field and garden and he himself shall conduct his business....

48. If a man owe a debt and Adad inundate his field and carry away the produce, or, through lack of water, grain have not grown in the field, in that year he shall not make any return of grain to the creditor, he shall alter his contract-tablet and he shall not pay the interest for that year....

53. If a man neglect to strengthen his dike and do not strengthen it, and a break be made in his dike and the water carry away the farm-land, the man in whose dike the break has been made shall restore the grain which he has damaged....

104. If a merchant give to an agent grain, wool, oil, or goods of any kind with which to trade, the agent shall write down the value and return the money to the merchant. The agent shall take a sealed receipt for the money which he gives to the merchant....

109. If outlaws collect in the house of a wine-seller and she does not arrest these outlaws and bring them to the palace, that wine-seller shall be put to death.

110. If a priestess who is not living in a convent opens a wine-shop or enters a wine-shop for a drink, they shall burn that woman....

117. If a man be in debt and sell his wife, son, or daughter, or bind them over to service, for three years they shall work in the house of their purchaser or master; in the fourth year they shall be given their freedom....

118. If a man takes a wife and does not arrange with her the proper contracts, that woman is not a legal wife.

129. If the wife of a man be taken in lying with another man, they shall bind them and throw them into the water. If the husband of the woman would save his wife, or if the king would save his male servant, he may....

131. If a man accuse his wife and she had not been taken in lying with another man, she shall take an oath in the name of god and she shall return to her house.

132. If the finger have been pointed at the wife of a man because of another man, and she have not been taken in lying with another man, for her husband's sake she shall throw herself into the river.

133. If a man be captured and there be maintenance in his house and his wife go out of her house, she shall protect her body and she shall not enter into another house. If that woman do not protect her body and enter into another house, they shall call that woman to account and they shall throw her into the water.

134. If a man be captured and there be no maintenance in his house and his wife enter into another house, that woman has no blame....

137. If a man set his face to put away a concubine who has borne him children or a wife who has presented him with children, he shall return to that woman her dowry and shall give to her the income of field, garden, and goods and she shall bring up her children; from the time that her children are grown up, from whatever is given to her children they shall give to her a portion corresponding to that of a son and the man of her choice may marry her.

138. If a man would put away his wife who has not borne him children, he shall give her money to the amount of her marriage settlement and he shall make good to her the dowry which she brought from her father's house and then he may put her away....

141. If the wife of a man who is living in his house sets her face to go out and play the part of a fool, neglect her house, or belittle her husband, they shall call her to account; if her husband says, "I have put her away," he shall let

her go. On her departure nothing shall be given to her for her divorce. If her husband says, "I have not put her away," her husband may take another woman. The first woman shall dwell in the house of her husband as a maid servant.

142. If a woman hates her husband and says, "You shall not have me," they shall inquire into her antecedents for her defects; and if she have been a careful mistress and be without reproach and her husband has been going and greatly belittling her, that woman has no blame. She shall receive her dowry and shall go to her father's house.

143. If she has not been a careful mistress, has gadded about, has neglected her house, and has belittled her husband, they shall throw that woman into the water....

153. If a woman brings about the death of her husband for the sake of another man, they shall impale her.

154. If a man has known his daughter, they shall expel that man from the city....

157. If a man lies in the bosom of his mother after the death of his father, they shall burn both of them....

195. If a son strikes his father, they shall cut off his fingers.

196. If a man destroys the eye of another man, they shall destroy his eye....

200. If a man knocks out a tooth of a man of his own rank, they shall knock out his tooth.

201. If one knocks out a tooth of a freeman, he shall pay one-third mina of silver.

202. If a man strikes his superior, he shall receive sixty strokes with an ox-tail whip in public.

203. If a gentleman strikes a gentleman of his own rank, he shall pay one mina of silver....

209. If a gentleman strikes a gentleman's daughter and bring about a miscarriage, he shall pay ten shekels of silver for her miscarriage.

210. If that woman die, they shall put his daughter to death.

211. If, through a stroke, he brings about a miscarriage to the daughter of a freeman, he shall pay five shekels of silver.

212. If that woman dies, he shall pay one-half mina of silver.

213. If he strikes the female slave of a gentleman and bring about a miscarriage, he shall pay two shekels of silver.

214. If that female slave dies, he shall pay one-third mina of silver.

215. If a physician operates on a gentleman for a severe wound with a bronze lancet and saves the man's life; or if he opens an abscess in the eye of a gentleman with a bronze lancet and saves that man's eye, he shall receive ten shekels of silver....

218. If a physician operates on a gentleman for a severe wound with a bronze lancet and causes the man's death; or opens an abscess in the eye of a gentleman with a bronze lancet and destroys the man's eye, they shall cut off his fingers....

229. If a builder builds a house and did not make its construction firm, and the house which he has built collapses and causes the death of the owner of the house, that builder shall be put to death.

230. If it causes the death of a son of the owner of the house, they shall put to death a son of that builder....

250. If a bull, when passing through the street, gore a man and bring about his death, this case has no remedy.

251. If a man's bull has been wont to gore and they have made known to him his habit of goring, and he has not protected his barns or has not tied him up, and that bull gore the son of a man and bring about his death, he shall pay one-half mina of silver....

The righteous laws, which Hammurabi, the wise king, established and by which he gave the land stable support and pure government. Hammurabi, the perfect king, am I. I was not careless, nor was I neglectful of the Black Head people, whose rule Bel presented and Marduk delivered to me. I provided them with a peaceful country. I opened up difficult barriers and lent them support. With the powerful weapon which Za-má-má and Nana entrusted to me, with the breadth of vision which Ea allotted me, with the might which Marduk gave me, I expelled the enemy to the North and South; I made an end of their raids; I brought health to the land; I made the populace to rest in security; I permitted no one to molest them.

The great gods proclaimed me and I am the guardian governor, whose scepter is righteous and whose beneficent protection is spread over my city. In my bosom I carried the people of the land of Sumer and Akkad; under my protection I brought their brethren into security; in my wisdom I hid them; that the strong might not oppose the weak, and that they should give justice to the orphan and the widow, in Babylon, the city whose turrets Anu and Bel raised; in Esagila, the temple whose foundations are firm as heaven and earth, for the pronouncing of judgments in the land, for the rendering of decisions for the land, and for the righting of wrong, my weighty words I have written upon my monument, and in the presence of my image as king of righteousness have I established.

The king, who is pre-eminent among city kings, am I. My words are precious, my wisdom is unrivaled. By the command of Shamash, the great judge of heaven and earth, may I make righteousness to shine forth on the land. By the order of Marduk, my lord, may no one efface my statues, may my name be

remembered with favor in Esagila forever. Let any oppressed man who has a
cause come before my image as king of righteousness! Let him read the inscription on my monument! Let him give heed to my weighty words! And may my
monument enlighten him as to his cause and may he understand his case! May
he set his heart at ease! And he will exclaim, "Hammurabi indeed is a ruler    5
who is like a real father to his people; he has given reverence to the words of
Marduk, his lord; he has obtained victory for Marduk in North and South; he
has made glad the heart of Marduk, his lord; he has established prosperity for
the people for all time and given a pure government to the land." Let him read
the code and pray with a full heart before Marduk, my lord, and Zarpanit, my    10
lady, and may the protecting deities, the gods who enter Esagila, daily in the
midst of Esagila look with favor on his plans in the presence of Marduk, my
lord, and Zarpanit, my lady!

In the days that are yet to come, for all future time, may the king who
is in the land observe the words of righteousness which I have written upon    15
my monument! May he not alter the judgments of the land which I have pronounced, or the decisions of the country which I have rendered! May he not
efface my statues! If that man have wisdom, if he wish to give his land good
government, let him give attention to the words which I have written upon
my monument! And may this monument enlighten him as to procedure and    20
administration, the judgments which I have pronounced, and the decisions
which I have rendered for the land! And let him rightly rule his Black-Head
people; let him pronounce judgments for them and render for them decisions!
Let him root out the wicked and evildoer from his land! Let him promote the
welfare of his people!    25

Hammurabi, the king of righteousness, whom Shamash has endowed with
justice, am I. My words are weighty; my deeds are unrivaled....

If a future ruler pays attention to my words which I have written upon
my monument, does not efface my judgments, does not overrule my words,
and does not alter my statues, then will Shamash prolong that man's reign, as    30
he has mine, who am king of righteousness, that he may rule his people in
righteousness.

If that man does not pay attention to my words which I have written upon
my monument; if he forgets my curse and does not fear the curse of god; if he
abolishes the judgments which I have formulated, over-rules my words, alters my    35
statues, effaces my name written thereon and writes his own name; on account
of these curses, commission another to do so—as for that man, be he king or
lord or priest-king or commoner, whoever he may be, may the great god, the
father of the gods, who has ordained my reign, take from him the glory of his
sovereignty, may be break his scepter, and curse his fate!    40

May Bel, the lord, who determines destinies, whose command cannot be altered, who has enlarged my dominion, drive him out from his dwelling through a revolt which his hand cannot control and a curse destructive to him. May he determine as his fate a reign of sighs, days few in number, years of famine, darkness without light, death staring him in the face! The destruction of his city, the dispersion of his people, the wresting away of his dominion, the blotting out of his name and memory from the land, may Bel order with his potent command!

May Belit, the august mother, whose command is potent in E-kur,[1] who looks with gracious favor upon my plans, in the place of judgment and decisions pervert his words in the presence of Bel! May she put into the mouth of Bel, the king, the ruin of his land, the destruction of his people and the pouring out of his life like water!

May Ea, the great prince, whose decrees take precedence, the leader of the gods, who knows everything, who prolongs the days of my life, deprive him of knowledge and wisdom! May he bring him to oblivion, and dam up his rivers at their sources! May be not permit corn, which is the life of the people, to grow in his land!

May Shamash, the great judge of heaven and earth, who rules all living creatures, the lord inspiring confidence, overthrow his dominion; may he not grant him his rights! May he make him to err in his path, may he destroy the mass of his troops! May he bring to his view an evil omen of the uprooting of the foundation of his sovereignty, and the ruin of his land.

May the blighting curse of Shamash come upon him quickly! May he cut off his life upon the earth! Below, within the earth, may he deprive his spirit of water!

May Sin, the lord of heaven, my divine creator, whose scimitar shines among the gods, take away from him the crown and throne of sovereignty! May he lay upon him heavy guilt and great sin, which will not depart from him! May be bring to an end the days, months, and years of his reign with sighing and tears! May he multiply the burdens of his sovereignty! May he determine as his fate a life like unto death!

May Adad, the lord of abundance, the regent of heaven and earth, my help-er, deprive him of the rain from heaven and the water-floods from the springs! May he bring his land to destruction through want and hunger! May he break loose furiously over his city and turn his land into a heap by a whirlwind!

May Za-má-má, the great warrior, the chief son of E-kur, who goes at my right hand, shatter his weapons on the field of battle! May he turn day into night for him, and place his enemy over him!

---

[1]The Babylonian equivalent of Olympus

May Ishtar, goddess of battle and conflict, who makes ready my weapons, the gracious protecting deity, who loves my reign, curse his dominion with great fury in her wrathful heart, and turn good into evil from him! May she shatter his weapons on the field of battle and conflict! May she create confusion and revolt for him! May she strike down his warriors, may their blood water the   5 earth! May she cast the bodies of his warriors upon the field in heaps! May she not grant his warriors burial! May she deliver him into the hands of his enemies, and may they carry him away bound into a hostile land!

May Nergal, the mighty among the gods, the warrior without an equal, who grants me victory, in his great power, burn his people like a raging fire of   10 swamp-reed. With his powerful weapon, may be cut him off and may be break his members like an earthen image!

May Nin-tu, the exalted mistress of the lands, the mother who bore me, deny him a son! May she not let him hold a name among his people, nor beget an heir!                                                                                              15

May Nin-kar-ra-ak, the daughter of Anu, who commands favors for me in E-kur, cause to come upon his members until it overcomes his life, a grievous malady, an evil disease, a dangerous sore, which cannot be cured, which the physician cannot diagnose, which he cannot allay with bandages, and which, like the bite of death, cannot be removed! May he lament the loss of his vigor!   20 May the great gods of heaven and earth, the Anunnaki in their assembly, curse with blighting curses the wall of the temple, the construction of this E-babbara, his seed, his land, his army, his people, and his troops!

May Bel with his command which cannot be altered curse him with a powerful curse and may it come upon him speedily!                                      25

# THE HEBREWS:
## CREATION

*The first three chapters of Genesis contain the Hebrew account of God's creation of the world and the fall of man. In these texts God is revealed to be all-powerful, eternally sovereign, and outside the natural world He created, unlike the deities of other ancient Near Eastern peoples.*

### Genesis

1 [1]In the beginning God created the heavens and the earth. [2]The earth was without form and void, and darkness was upon the face of the deep; and the Spirit of God was moving over the face of the waters.

[3]And God said, "Let there be light"; and there was light. [4]And God saw that the light was good; and God separated the light from the darkness. [5]God called the light Day, and the darkness he called Night. And there was evening and there was morning, one day.

[6]And God said, "Let there be a firmament in the midst of the waters, and let it separate the waters from the waters." [7]And God made the firmament and separated the waters which were under the firmament from the waters which were above the firmament. And it was so. [8]And God called the firmament Heaven. And there was evening and there was morning, a second day.

[9]And God said, "Let the waters under the heavens be gathered together into one place, and let the dry land appear." And it was so. [10]God called the dry land Earth, and the waters that were gathered together he called Seas. And God saw that it was good. [11]And God said, "Let the earth put forth vegetation, plants yielding seed, and fruit trees bearing fruit in which is their seed, each according to its kind, upon the earth." And it was so. [12]The earth brought forth vegetation, plants yielding seed according to their own kinds, and trees bearing fruit in which is their seed, each according to its kind. And God saw that it was good. [13]And there was evening and there was morning, a third day.

[14]And God said, "Let there be lights in the firmament of the heavens to separate the day from the night; and let them be for signs and for seasons and for days and years, [15]and let them be lights in the firmament of the heavens to give light upon the earth." And it was so. [16]And God made the two great lights,

the greater light to rule the day, and the lesser light to rule the night; he made the stars also. **17**And God set them in the firmament of the heavens to give light upon the earth, **18**to rule over the day and over the night, and to separate the light from the darkness. And God saw that it was good. **19**And there was evening and there was morning, a fourth day.

**20**And God said, "Let the waters bring forth swarms of living creatures, and let birds fly above the earth across the firmament of the heavens." **21**So God created the great sea monsters and every living creature that moves, with which the waters swarm, according to their kinds, and every winged bird according to its kind. And God saw that it was good. **22**And God blessed them, saying, "Be fruitful and multiply and fill the waters in the seas, and let birds multiply on the earth." **23**And there was evening and there was morning, a fifth day.

**24**And God said, "Let the earth bring forth living creatures according to their kinds: cattle and creeping things and beasts of the earth according to their kinds." And it was so. **25**And God made the beasts of the earth according to their kinds and the cattle according to their kinds, and everything that creeps upon the ground according to its kind. And God saw that it was good. **26**Then God said, "Let us make man in our image, after our likeness; and let them have dominion over the fish of the sea, and over the birds of the air, and over the cattle, and over all the earth, and over every creeping thing that creeps upon the earth." **27**So God created man in his own image, in the image of God he created him; male and female he created them. **28**And God blessed them, and God said to them, "Be fruitful and multiply, and fill the earth and subdue it; and have dominion over the fish of the sea and over the birds of the air and over every living thing that moves upon the earth." **29**And God said, "Behold, I have given you every plant yielding seed which is upon the face of all the earth, and every tree with seed in its fruit; you shall have them for food. **30**And to every beast of the earth, and to every bird of the air, and to everything that creeps on the earth, everything that has the breath of life, I have given every green plant for food." And it was so. **31**And God saw everything that he had made, and behold, it was very good. And there was evening and there was morning, a sixth day.

2 **1**Thus the heavens and the earth were finished, and all the host of them. **2**And on the seventh day God finished his work which he had done, and he rested on the seventh day from all his work which he had done. **3**So God blessed the seventh day and hallowed it, because on it God rested from all his work which he had done in creation.

**4**These are the generations of the heavens and the earth when they were created. In the day that the LORD God made the earth and the heavens, **5**when no plant of the field was yet in the earth and no herb of the field had yet sprung up—for the LORD God had not caused it to rain upon the earth, and there was no man to till the ground; **6**but a mist went up from the earth and watered the whole face of the ground—**7**then the LORD God formed man of dust from the ground, and breathed into his nostrils the breath of life; and man became a living being. **8**And the LORD God planted a garden in Eden, in the east; and there he put the man whom he had formed. **9**And out of the ground the LORD God made to grow every tree that is pleasant to the sight and good for food, the tree of life also in the midst of the garden, and the tree of the knowledge of good and evil....

**15**The LORD God took the man and put him in the garden of Eden to till it and keep it. **16**And the LORD God commanded the man, saying, "You may freely eat of every tree of the garden; **17**but of the tree of the knowledge of good and evil you shall not eat, for in the day that you eat of it you shall die." **18**Then the LORD God said, "It is not good that the man should be alone; I will make him a helper fit for him." **19**So out of the ground the LORD God formed every beast of the field and every bird of the air, and brought them to the man to see what he would call them; and whatever the man called every living creature, that was its name. **20**The man gave names to all cattle, and to the birds of the air, and to every beast of the field; but for the man there was not found a helper fit for him. **21**So the LORD God caused a deep sleep to fall upon the man, and while he slept took one of his ribs and closed up its place with flesh; **22**and the rib which the LORD God had taken from the man he made into a woman and brought her to the man. **23**Then the man said, "This at last is bone of my bones and flesh of my flesh; she shall be called Woman, because she was taken out of Man." **24**Therefore a man leaves his father and his mother and cleaves to his wife, and they become one flesh. **25**And the man and his wife were both naked, and were not ashamed.

3 **1**Now the serpent was more subtle than any other wild creature that the LORD God had made. He said to the woman, "Did God say, 'You shall not eat of any tree of the garden'?" **2**And the woman said to the serpent, "We may eat of the fruit of the trees of the garden; **3**but God said, 'You shall not eat of the fruit of the tree which is in the midst of the garden, neither shall you touch it, lest you die.'" **4**But the serpent said to the woman, "You will not die. **5**For God knows that when you eat of it your eyes will be opened, and you will be like God, knowing good and evil." **6**So when the woman saw that the tree was good for food, and that it was a delight to the eyes, and that the tree was to be desired to make one wise, she took of its fruit and ate; and she also gave some to her husband, and he ate. **7**Then the eyes of both were opened, and they knew

that they were naked; and they sewed fig leaves together and made themselves aprons. **8**And they heard the sound of the LORD God walking in the garden in the cool of the day, and the man and his wife hid themselves from the presence of the LORD God among the trees of the garden. **9**But the LORD God called to

5   the man, and said to him, "Where are you?" **10**And he said, "I heard the sound of thee in the garden, and I was afraid, because I was naked; and I hid myself." **11**He said, "Who told you that you were naked? Have you eaten of the tree of which I commanded you not to eat?" **12**The man said, "The woman whom thou gavest to be with me, she gave me fruit of the tree, and I ate." **13**Then the

10   LORD God said to the woman, "What is this that you have done?" The woman said, "The serpent beguiled me, and I ate."

  **14**The LORD God said to the serpent, "Because you have done this, cursed are you above all cattle, and above all wild animals; upon your belly you shall go, and dust you shall eat all the days of your life. **15**I will put enmity between

15   you and the woman, and between your seed and her seed; he shall bruise your head, and you shall bruise his heel."

  **16**To the woman he said, "I will greatly multiply your pain in childbearing; in pain you shall bring forth children, yet your desire shall be for your husband, and he shall rule over you."

20   **17**And to Adam he said, "Because you have listened to the voice of your wife, and have eaten of the tree of which I commanded you, 'You shall not eat of it,' cursed is the ground because of you; in toil you shall eat of it all the days of your life; **18**thorns and thistles it shall bring forth to you; and you shall eat the plants of the field. **19**In the sweat of your face you shall eat bread till you

25   return to the ground, for out of it you were taken; you are dust, and to dust you shall return."

  **20**The man called his wife's name Eve, because she was the mother of all living. **21**And the LORD God made for Adam and for his wife garments of skins, and clothed them. **22**Then the LORD God said, "Behold, the man has become

30   like one of us, knowing good and evil; and now, lest he put forth his hand and take also of the tree of life, and eat, and live forever"—**23**therefore the LORD God sent him forth from the garden of Eden to till the ground from which he was taken. **24**He drove out the man; and at the east of the garden of Eden he placed the cherubim, and a flaming sword which turned every way, to guard

35   the way to the tree of life.

# THE HEBREWS: COVENANT AND LAW

*Membership in a community bound by a covenant with God to observe His law was the hallmark of Hebrew identity.*

## Genesis

17 ¹When Abram was ninety-nine years old the LORD appeared to Abram, and said to him, "I am God Almighty; walk before me, and be blameless. ²And I will make my covenant between me and you, and will multiply you exceedingly." ³Then Abram fell on his face; and God said to him, ⁴"Behold, my covenant is with you, and you shall be the father of a multitude of nations. ⁵No longer shall your name be Abram, but your name shall be Abraham; for I have made you the father of a multitude of nations. ⁶I will make you exceedingly fruitful; and I will make nations of you, and kings shall come forth from you. ⁷And I will establish my covenant between me and you and your descendants after you throughout their generations for an everlasting covenant, to be God to you and to your descendants after you. ⁸And I will give to you, and to your descendants after you, the land of your sojournings, all the land of Canaan, for an everlasting possession; and I will be their God."

⁹And God said to Abraham, "As for you, you shall keep my covenant, you and your descendants after you throughout their generations. ¹⁰This is my covenant, which you shall keep, between me and you and your descendants after you: Every male among you shall be circumcised. ¹¹You shall be circumcised in the flesh of your foreskins, and it shall be a sign of the covenant between me and you. ¹²He that is eight days old among you shall be circumcised; every male throughout your generations, whether born in your house, or bought with your money from any foreigner who is not of your offspring, ¹³both he that is born in your house and he that is bought with your money, shall be circumcised. So shall my covenant be in your flesh an everlasting covenant. ¹⁴Any uncircumcised male who is not circumcised in the flesh of his foreskin shall be cut off from his people; he has broken my covenant."

¹⁵And God said to Abraham, "As for Sarai your wife, you shall not call her name Sarai, but Sarah shall be her name. ¹⁶I will bless her, and moreover I will

give you a son by her; I will bless her, and she shall be a mother of nations; kings of peoples shall come from her." **17**Then Abraham fell on his face and laughed, and said to himself, "Shall a child be born to a man who is a hundred years old? Shall Sarah, who is ninety years old, bear a child?" **18**And Abraham said
5   to God, "O that Ishmael might live in thy sight!" **19**God said, "No, but Sarah your wife shall bear you a son, and you shall call his name Isaac. I will establish my covenant with him as an everlasting covenant for his descendants after him. **20**As for Ishmael, I have heard you; behold, I will bless him and make him fruitful and multiply him exceedingly; he shall be the father of twelve princes, and
10  I will make him a great nation. **21**But I will establish my covenant with Isaac, whom Sarah shall bear to you at this season next year."
     **22**When he had finished talking with him, God went up from Abraham.... **26**That very day Abraham and his son Ishmael were circumcised; **27**and all the men of his house, those born in the house and those bought with money from
15  a foreigner, were circumcised with him.

> *The exodus of the Hebrew people from bondage in Egypt came to be seen as the central moment in their history, the moment when God sent plagues to force Pharaoh to let His people go, and the Angel of Death passed over the families of the Hebrews to slay the firstborn of the Egyptians. In this selection from Exodus 3, God reveals Himself to Moses in the burning bush on Mount Horeb and commissions Moses to approach Pharaoh to demand their deliverance.*

### Exodus

3   **1**Now Moses was keeping the flock of his father-in-law, Jethro, the priest of Midian; and he led his flock to the west side of the wilderness, and came to Horeb, the mountain of God. **2**And the angel of the LORD appeared to him in a flame of fire out of the midst of a bush; and he looked, and lo, the bush was
20  burning, yet it was not consumed. **3**And Moses said, "I will turn aside and see this great sight, why the bush is not burnt." **4**When the LORD saw that he turned aside to see, God called to him out of the bush, "Moses, Moses!" And he said, "Here am I." **5**Then he said, "Do not come near; put off your shoes from your feet, for the place on which you are standing is holy ground." **6**And he said, "I
25  am the God of your father, the God of Abraham, the God of Isaac, and the God of Jacob." And Moses hid his face, for he was afraid to look at God.
     **7**Then the LORD said, "I have seen the affliction of my people who are in Egypt, and have heard their cry because of their taskmasters; I know their sufferings, **8**and I have come down to deliver them out of the hand of the
30  Egyptians, and to bring them up out of that land to a good and broad land, a

land flowing with milk and honey, to the place of the Canaanites, the Hittites, the Amorites, the Perizzites, the Hivites, and the Jebusites. **9**And now, behold, the cry of the people of Israel has come to me, and I have seen the oppression with which the Egyptians oppress them. **10**Come, I will send you to Pharaoh that you may bring forth my people, the sons of Israel, out of Egypt." **11**But  5
Moses said to God, "Who am I that I should go to Pharaoh, and bring the sons of Israel out of Egypt?" **12**He said, "But I will be with you; and this shall be the sign for you, that I have sent you: when you have brought forth the people out of Egypt, you shall serve God upon this mountain."

**13**Then Moses said to God, "If I come to the people of Israel and say to them,  10
'The God of your fathers has sent me to you,' and they ask me, 'What is his name?' what shall I say to them?" **14**God said to Moses, "I AM WHO I AM." And he said, "Say this to the people of Israel, 'I AM has sent me to you.'" **15**God also said to Moses, "Say this to the people of Israel, 'The LORD, the God of your fathers, the God of Abraham, the God of Isaac, and the God of Jacob, has sent me to you': this is my  15
name for ever, and thus I am to be remembered throughout all generations."

*At Mount Sinai, God made a new covenant binding the entire Hebrew people into a single community, and gave the law governing that community to Moses. From this point on, fidelity to the covenant meant observance of God's law, the central tenets of which were found in the Decalogue, or the Ten Commandments.*

**20** **1**And God spoke all these words, saying, **2**"I am the LORD your God, who brought you out of the land of Egypt, out of the house of bondage. **3**"You shall have no other gods before me. **4**"You shall not make for yourself a graven image, or any likeness of anything that is in heaven above, or that is in  20
the earth beneath, or that is in the water under the earth; **5**you shall not bow down to them or serve them; for I the LORD your God am a jealous God, visiting the iniquity of the fathers upon the children to the third and the fourth generation of those who hate me, **6**but showing steadfast love to thousands of those who love me and keep my commandments.  30

**7**"You shall not take the name of the LORD your God in vain; for the LORD will not hold him guiltless who takes his name in vain.

**8**"Remember the sabbath day, to keep it holy. **9**Six days you shall labor, and do all your work; **10**but the seventh day is a sabbath to the LORD your God; in it you shall not do any work, you, or your son, or your daughter, your manser-  35
vant, or your maidservant, or your cattle, or the sojourner who is within your gates; **11**for in six days the LORD made heaven and earth, the sea, and all that is in them, and rested the seventh day; therefore the LORD blessed the sabbath day and hallowed it.

**12**"Honor your father and your mother, that your days may be long in the land which the LORD your God gives you.

**13**"You shall not kill.

**14**"You shall not commit adultery.

**15**"You shall not steal.

**16**"You shall not bear false witness against your neighbor.

**17**"You shall not covet your neighbor's house; you shall not covet your neighbor's wife, or his manservant, or his maidservant, or his ox, or his ass, or anything that is your neighbor's."

## Deuteronomy

6 **4**"Hear, O Israel: The LORD our God is one LORD; **5**and you shall love the LORD your God with all your heart, and with all your soul, and with all your might. **6**And these words which I command you this day shall be upon your heart; **7**and you shall teach them diligently to your children, and shall talk of them when you sit in your house, and when you walk by the way, and when you lie down, and when you rise.

> *The nature of the covenant, and the consequences of observing or failing to observe it, become clear in the following passage, in which Moses is speaking to the Hebrews before they cross the Jordan River.*

28 **1**"And if you obey the voice of the LORD your God, being careful to do all his commandments which I command you this day, the LORD your God will set you high above all the nations of the earth. **2**And all these blessings shall come upon you and overtake you, if you obey the voice of the LORD your God. **3**Blessed shall you be in the city, and blessed shall you be in the field. **4**Blessed shall be the fruit of your body, and the fruit of your ground, and the fruit of your beasts, the increase of your cattle, and the young of your flock. **5**Blessed shall be your basket and your kneading-trough. **6**Blessed shall you be when you come in, and blessed shall you be when you go out.

**7**"The LORD will cause your enemies who rise against you to be defeated before you; they shall come out against you one way, and flee before you seven ways. **8**The LORD will command the blessing upon you in your barns, and in all that you undertake; and he will bless you in the land which the LORD your God gives you. **9**The LORD will establish you as a people holy to himself, as he has sworn to you, if you keep the commandments of the LORD your God, and walk in his ways. **10**And all the peoples of the earth shall see that you are called by the name of the LORD; and they shall be afraid of you. **11**And the LORD will make you abound in prosperity, in the fruit of your body, and in the fruit of your cattle, and in the fruit of your ground, within the land which the LORD swore to your fathers to give you. [12]The LORD will open to you his good treasury the heavens, to give the rain of your land in its season and to bless all the work of your hands; and you shall lend to many nations, but you shall not borrow. [13]And the LORD will make you the head, and not the tail; and you shall tend upward only, and not downward; if you obey the commandments of the LORD your God, which I command you this day, being careful to do them, [14]and if you do not turn aside from any of the words which I command you this day, to the right hand or to the left, to go after other gods to serve them.

[15]"But if you will not obey the voice of the LORD your God or be careful to do all his commandments and his statutes which I command you this day, then all these curses shall come upon you and overtake you. [16]Cursed shall you be in the city, and cursed shall you be in the field. [17]Cursed shall be your basket and your kneading-trough. [18]Cursed shall be the fruit of your body, and the fruit of your ground, the increase of your cattle, and the young of your flock. [19]Cursed shall you be when you come in, and cursed shall you be when you go out.

[20]"The LORD will send upon you curses, confusion, and frustration, in all that you undertake to do, until you are destroyed and perish quickly, on account of the evil of your doings, because you have forsaken me. [21]The LORD will make the pestilence cleave to you until he has consumed you off the land which you are entering to take possession of it.…

[25]"The LORD will cause you to be defeated before your enemies; you shall go out one way against them, and flee seven ways before them; and you shall be a horror to all the kingdoms of the earth.… [28]The LORD will smite you with madness and blindness and confusion of mind; [29]and you shall grope at noonday, as the blind grope in darkness, and you shall not prosper in your ways; and you shall be only oppressed and robbed continually, and there shall be no one to help you. [30]You shall betroth a wife, and another man shall lie with her; you shall build a house, and you shall not dwell in it; you shall plant a vineyard, and you shall not use the fruit of it.… [32]Your sons and your daughters shall be given to another people, while your eyes look on and fail with longing for them all the day; and it shall not be in the power of your hand to prevent it. [33]A nation which you have not known shall eat up the fruit of your ground and of all your labors; and you shall be only oppressed and crushed continually.…

[36]"The LORD will bring you, and your king whom you set over you, to a nation that neither you nor your fathers have known; and there you shall serve other gods, of wood and stone. [37]And you shall become a horror, a proverb, and a byword among all the peoples where the LORD will lead you away.… [45]All these curses shall come upon you and pursue you and overtake you, till you are destroyed, because you did not obey the voice of the LORD your God, to keep his commandments and his statutes which he commanded you.

**46**They shall be upon you as a sign and a wonder, and upon your descendants forever.

**47**"Because you did not serve the LORD your God with joyfulness and gladness of heart, by reason of the abundance of all things, **48**therefore you shall serve your enemies whom the LORD will send against you, in hunger and thirst, in nakedness, and in want of all things; and he will put a yoke of iron upon your neck, until he has destroyed you....

**58**"If you are not careful to do all the words of this law which are written in this book, that you may fear this glorious and awful name, the LORD your God, **59**then the LORD will bring on you and your offspring extraordinary afflictions, afflictions severe and lasting, and sicknesses grievous and lasting.... **62**Whereas you were as the stars of heaven for multitude, you shall be left few in number; because you did not obey the voice of the LORD your God. **63**And as the LORD took delight in doing you good and multiplying you, so the LORD will take delight in bringing ruin upon you and destroying you; and you shall be plucked off the land which you are entering to take possession of it. **64**And the LORD will scatter you among all peoples, from one end of the earth to the other; and there you shall serve other gods, of wood and stone, which neither you nor your fathers have known.

# THE HEBREWS: KINGSHIP

*The two books of Samuel relate the history of the kingdom of Israel under its first two monarchs, Saul and David, and in so doing describe a model of kingship from which Christian kings and clergy in the West drew inspiration for centuries.*

## I Samuel

8 ¹When Samuel became old, he made his sons judges over Israel.... ³Yet his sons did not walk in his ways, but turned aside after gain; they took bribes and perverted justice. ⁴Then all the elders of Israel gathered together and came to Samuel at Ramah ⁵and said to him, "Behold, you are old and your sons do not walk in your ways; now appoint for us a king to govern us like all the nations." ⁶But the thing displeased Samuel when they said, "Give us a king to govern us." And Samuel prayed to the LORD.

⁷And the LORD said to Samuel, "Hearken to the voice of the people in all that they say to you; for they have not rejected you, but they have rejected me from being king over them.... ⁹Now then, hearken to their voice; only, you shall solemnly warn them, and show them the ways of the king who shall reign over them."

¹⁰So Samuel told all the words of the LORD to the people who were asking a king from him. ¹¹He said, "These will be the ways of the king who will reign over you: he will take your sons and appoint them to his chariots and to be his horsemen, and to run before his chariots; ¹²and he will appoint for himself commanders of thousands and commanders of fifties, and some to plow his ground and to reap his harvest, and to make his implements of war and the equipment of his chariots.... ¹⁴He will take the best of your fields and vineyards and olive orchards and give them to his servants.... ¹⁷He will take the tenth of your flocks, and you shall be his slaves. ¹⁸And in that day you will cry out because of your king, whom you have chosen for yourselves; but the LORD will not answer you in that day."

¹⁹But the people refused to listen to the voice of Samuel; and they said, "No! But we will have a king over us, ²⁰that we also may be like all the nations,

and that our king may govern us and go out before us and fight our battles°."
**21**And when Samuel had heard all the words of the people, he repeated them in the ears of the LORD. **22**And the LORD said to Samuel, "Hearken to their voice, and make them a king." Samuel then said to the men of Israel, "Go every
5    man to his city."

9 **1**There was a man of Benjamin whose name was Kish, the son of Abiel, son of Zeror, son of Becorath, son of Aphiah, a Benjaminite, a man of wealth; **2**and he had a son whose name was Saul, a handsome young man. There was not a man among the people of Israel more handsome than he; from his
10   shoulders upward he was taller than any of the people.

> *Kish sent Saul, with a servant, to seek some asses that had been lost. The two went a considerable distance without finding any trace of them, so when they came to the land of Zuph, where Samuel lived, they resolved to ask him for advice as to which direction they should take.*

**15**Now the day before Saul came, the LORD had revealed to Samuel: **16**"Tomorrow about this time I will send to you a man from the land of Benjamin, and you shall anoint him to be prince over my people Israel. He shall save my people from the hand of the Philistines; for I have seen the
15   affliction of my people, because their cry has come to me." **17**When Samuel saw Saul, the LORD told him, "Here is the man of whom I spoke to you! He it is who shall rule over my people." **18**Then Saul approached Samuel in the gate, and said, "Tell me where is the house of the seer?" **19**Samuel answered Saul, "I am the seer; go up before me to the high place, for today you shall eat with
20   me, and in the morning I will let you go and will tell you all that is on your mind. **20**As for your asses that were lost three days ago, do not set your mind on them, for they have been found. And for whom is all that is desirable in Israel? Is it not for you and for all your father's house?" **21**Saul answered, "Am I not a Benjaminite, from the least of the tribes of Israel? And is not my family
25   the humblest of all the families of the tribe of Benjamin? Why then have you spoken to me in this way?"

Saul dined with Samuel that night, taking the place of honor among some thirty guests. Samuel conversed with Saul that evening and early the following morning before escorting Saul and his servant to their road home.
30   **27**As they were going down to the outskirts of the city, Samuel said to Saul, "Tell the servant to pass on before us, and when he has passed on stop here yourself for a while, that I may make known to you the word of God."

10 **1**Then Samuel took a vial of oil and poured it on his head, and kissed him and said, "Has not the LORD anointed you to be prince over his people

Israel? And you shall reign over the people of °the LORD and you will save them
from the hand of their enemies round about. And this shall be the sign to you
that the LORD has anointed you to be prince over his heritage. **2**When you
depart from me today you will meet two men by Rachel's tomb in the territory
of Benjamin at Zelzah, and they will say to you, 'The asses which you went to     5
seek are found, and now your father has ceased to care about the asses and is
anxious about you, saying, "What shall I do about my son?"' **3**Then you shall
go on from there further and come to the oak of Tabor; three men going up
to God at Bethel will meet you there, one carrying three kids, another carrying three loaves of bread, and another carrying a skin of wine. **4**And they will    10
greet you and give you two loaves of bread, which you shall accept from their
hand. **5**After that you shall come to Gibeath-elohim, where there is a garrison
of the Philistines; and there, as you come to the city, you will meet a band of
prophets coming down from the high place with harp, tambourine, flute, and
lyre before them, prophesying. **6**Then the spirit of the LORD will come mightily    15
upon you, and you shall prophesy with them and be turned into another man.
**7**Now when these signs meet you, do whatever your hand finds to do, for God
is with you. **8**And you shall go down before me to Gilgal; and behold, I am
coming to you to offer burnt offerings and to sacrifice peace offerings. Seven
days you shall wait, until I come to you and show you what you shall do."         20
**9**When he turned his back to leave Samuel, God gave him another heart; and
all these signs came to pass that day....

   **17**Now Samuel called the people together to the LORD at Mizpah; **18**and he
said to the people of Israel, "Thus says the LORD, the God of Israel, 'I brought
up Israel out of Egypt, and I delivered you from the hand of the Egyptians and    25
from the hand of all the kingdoms that were oppressing you.' **19**But you have
this day rejected your God, who saves you from all your calamities and your
distresses; and you have said, 'No! But set a king over us.' Now therefore present
yourselves before the LORD by your tribes and by your thousands."

   **20**Then Samuel brought all the tribes of Israel near, and the tribe of Benjamin    30
was taken by lot. **21**He brought the tribe of Benjamin near by its families, and
the family of Matri was taken by lot; finally he brought the family of Matri near
man by man, and Saul, the son of Kish, was taken by lot. But when they sought
him, he could not be found. **22**So they inquired again of the LORD, "Did the
man come hither?" and the LORD said, "Behold, he has hidden himself among    35
the baggage." **23**Then they ran and fetched him from there; and when he stood
among the people, he was taller than any of the people from his shoulders upward. **24**And Samuel said to all the people, "Do you see him whom the LORD
has chosen? There is none like him among all the people." And all the people
shouted, "Long live the king!"                                                   40

<sup>25</sup>Then Samuel told the people the rights and duties of the kingship; and he wrote them in a book and laid it up before the Lord. Then Samuel sent all the people away, each one to his home. <sup>26</sup>Saul also went to his home at Gibeah, and with him went men of valor whose hearts God had touched. <sup>27</sup>But some
5   worthless fellows said, "How can this man save us?" And they despised him, and brought him no present. But he held his peace....

> *The men of Jabesh offered to make a treaty with the Ammonites, who were besieging them, but the Ammonite commander replied that he would make a treaty with them only on condition that he gouge out all their right eyes, in order to disgrace Israel.*

11 <sup>6</sup>And the spirit of God came mightily upon Saul when he heard these words, and his anger was greatly kindled.... <sup>11</sup>And on the morrow Saul put the people in three companies; and they came into the midst of the camp
10  in the morning watch, and cut down the Ammonites until the heat of the day; and those who survived were scattered, so that no two of them were left together. <sup>12</sup>Then the people said to Samuel, "Who is it that said, 'Shall Saul reign over us?' Bring the men, that we may put them to death." <sup>13</sup>But Saul said, "Not a man shall be put to death this day, for today the Lord has wrought deliverance in
15  Israel." <sup>14</sup>Then Samuel said to the people, "Come, let us go to Gilgal and there renew the kingdom." <sup>15</sup>So all the people went to Gilgal, and there they made Saul king before the Lord in Gilgal. There they sacrificed peace offerings before the Lord, and there Saul and all the men of Israel rejoiced greatly.

12 <sup>1</sup>And Samuel said to all Israel, "Behold, I have hearkened to your voice in
20  all that you have said to me, and have made a king over you. <sup>2</sup>And now, behold, the king walks before you; and I am old and gray, and behold, my sons are with you; and I have walked before you from my youth until this day. <sup>3</sup>Here I am; testify against me before the Lord and before his anointed. Whose ox have I taken? Or whose ass have I taken? Or whom have I defrauded? Whom
25  have I oppressed? Or from whose hand have I taken a bribe to blind my eyes with it? Testify against me and I will restore it to you." <sup>4</sup>They said, "You have not defrauded us or oppressed us or taken anything from any man's hand." <sup>5</sup>And he said to them, "The Lord is witness against you, and his anointed is witness this day, that you have not found anything in my hand." And they said,
30  "He is witness." <sup>6</sup>And Samuel said to the people, "The Lord is witness, who appointed Moses and Aaron and brought your fathers up out of the land of Egypt. <sup>7</sup>Now therefore stand still, that I may plead with you before the Lord concerning all the saving deeds of the Lord which he performed for you and for your fathers. <sup>8</sup>When Jacob went into Egypt and the Egyptians oppressed

them, then your fathers cried to the LORD and the LORD sent Moses and Aaron, who brought forth your fathers out of Egypt, and made them dwell in this place. **9**But they forgot the LORD their God; and he sold them into the hand of Sisera, commander of the army of Jabin, King of Hazor, and into the hand of the Philistines, and into the hand of the King of Moab; and they fought against them. **10**And they cried to the LORD, and said, 'We have sinned, because we have forsaken the LORD, and have served the Baals and the Ashtaroth; but now deliver us out of the hand of our enemies, and we will serve thee.' **11**And the LORD sent Jerubbaal and Barak, and Jephthah, and Samuel, and delivered you out of the hand of your enemies on every side; and you dwelt in safety. **12**And when you saw that Nahash, the King of the Ammonites, came against you, you said to me, 'No, but a king shall reign over us,' when the LORD your God was your king. **13**And now behold the king whom you have chosen, for whom you have asked; behold, the LORD has set a king over you. **14**If you will fear the LORD and serve him and hearken to his voice and not rebel against the commandment of the LORD, and if both you and the king who reigns over you will follow the LORD your God, it will be well; **15**but if you will not hearken to the voice of the LORD, but rebel against the commandment of the LORD, then the hand of the LORD will be against you and your king. **16**Now therefore stand still and see this great thing, which the LORD will do before your eyes. **17**Is it not wheat harvest today? I will call upon the LORD, that he may send thunder and rain; and you shall know and see that your wickedness is great, which you have done in the sight of the LORD, in asking for yourselves a king." **18**So Samuel called upon the LORD, and the LORD sent thunder and rain that day; and all the people greatly feared the LORD and Samuel.

**19**And all the people said to Samuel, "Pray for your servants to the LORD your God, that we may not die; for we have added to all our sins this evil, to ask for ourselves a king." **20**And Samuel said to the people, "Fear not; you have done all this evil, yet do not turn aside from following the LORD, but serve the LORD with all your heart; **21**and do not turn aside after vain things which cannot profit or save, for they are vain. **22**For the LORD will not cast away his people, for his great name's sake, because it has pleased the LORD to make you a people for himself. **23**Moreover as for me, far be it from me that I should sin against the LORD by ceasing to pray for you; and I will instruct you in the good and the right way. **24**Only fear the LORD, and serve him faithfully with all your heart; for consider what great things he has done for you. **25**But if you still do wickedly, you shall be swept away, both you and your king."...

14 **47**When Saul had taken the kingship over Israel, he fought against all his enemies on every side, against Moab, against the Ammonites, against

Edom, against the kings of Zobah, and against the Philistines; wherever he turned he put them to the worse. **⁴⁸**And he did valiantly, and smote the Amalekites, and delivered Israel out of the hands of those who plundered them…. **⁵²**There was hard fighting against the Philistines all the days of Saul; and when Saul saw any strong man, or any valiant man, he attached him to himself.

**15** **¹**And Samuel said to Saul, "The LORD sent me to anoint you king over his people Israel; now therefore hearken to the words of the LORD. **²**Thus says the LORD of hosts, 'I will punish what Amalek did to Israel in opposing them on the way, when they came up out of Egypt. **³**Now go and smite Amalek, and utterly destroy all that they have; do not spare them, but kill both man and woman, infant and suckling, ox and sheep, camel and ass.'"

**⁴**So Saul summoned the people, and numbered them in Telaim, two hundred thousand men on foot, and ten thousand men of Judah. **⁵**And Saul came to the city of Amalek, and lay in wait in the valley. **⁶**And Saul said to the Kenites, "Go, depart, go down from among the Amalekites, lest I destroy you with them; for you showed kindness to all the people of Israel when they came up out of Egypt." So the Kenites departed from among the Amalekites. **⁷**And Saul defeated the Amalekites, from Havilah as far as Shur, which is east of Egypt. **⁸**And he took Agag the king of the Amalekites alive, and utterly destroyed all the people with the edge of the sword. **⁹**But Saul and the people spared Agag, and the best of the sheep and of the oxen and of the fatlings, and the lambs, and all that was good, and would not utterly destroy them; all that was despised and worthless they utterly destroyed.

**¹⁰**The word of the LORD came to Samuel, **¹¹**"I repent that I have made Saul king; for he has turned back from following me, and has not performed my commandments." And Samuel was angry; and he cried to the LORD all night. **¹²**And Samuel rose early to meet Saul in the morning; and it was told Samuel, "Saul came to Carmel, and behold, he set up a monument for himself and turned, and passed on, and went down to Gilgal." **¹³**And Samuel came to Saul, and Saul said to him, "Blessed be you to the LORD; I have performed the commandment of the LORD." **¹⁴**And Samuel said, "What then is this bleating of the sheep in my ears, and the lowing of the oxen which I hear?" **¹⁵**Saul said, "They have brought them from the Amalekites; for the people spared the best of the sheep and of the oxen, to sacrifice to the LORD your God; and the rest we have utterly destroyed." **¹⁶**Then Samuel said to Saul, "Stop! I will tell you what the LORD said to me this night." And he said to him, "Say on."

**¹⁷**And Samuel said, "Though you are little in your own eyes, are you not the head of the tribes of Israel? The LORD anointed you king over Israel. **¹⁸**And the LORD sent you on a mission, and said, 'Go, utterly destroy the sinners, the

Amalekites, and fight against them until they are consumed.' **19**Why then did you not obey the voice of the LORD? Why did you swoop on the spoil, and do what was evil in the sight of the LORD?" **20**And Saul said to Samuel, "I have obeyed the voice of the LORD, I have gone on the mission on which the LORD sent me, I have brought Agag the king of Amalek, and I have utterly destroyed the Amalekites. **21**But the people took of the spoil, sheep and oxen, the best of the things devoted to destruction, to sacrifice to the LORD your God in Gilgal."

**22**And Samuel said, "Has the LORD as great delight in burnt offerings and sacrifices as in obeying the voice of the LORD? Behold, to obey is better than sacrifice, and to hearken than the fat of rams. **23**For rebellion is as the sin of divination, and stubbornness is as iniquity and idolatry. Because you have rejected the word of the LORD, he has also rejected you from being king." **24**And Saul said to Samuel, "I have sinned; for I have transgressed the commandment of the LORD and your words, because I feared the people and obeyed their voice. **25**Now therefore, I pray, pardon my sin, and return with me, that I may worship the LORD." **26**And Samuel said to Saul, "I will not return with you; for you have rejected the word of the LORD, and the LORD has rejected you from being king over Israel." **27**As Samuel turned to go away, Saul laid hold upon the skirt of his robe, and it tore. **28**And Samuel said to him, "The LORD has torn the kingdom of Israel from you this day, and has given it to a neighbor of yours, who is better than you. **29**And also the Glory of Israel will not lie or repent; for he is not a man, that he should repent." **30**Then he said, "I have sinned; yet honor me now before the elders of my people and before Israel, and return with me, that I may worship the LORD your God." **31**So Samuel turned back after Saul; and Saul worshiped the LORD.

**32**Then Samuel said, "Bring here to me Agag the king of the Amalekites." And Agag came to him cheerfully. Agag said, "Surely the bitterness of death is past." **33**And Samuel said, "As your sword has made women childless, so shall your mother be childless among women." And Samuel hewed Agag in pieces before the LORD in Gilgal. **34**Then Samuel went to Ramah; and Saul went up to his house in Gibeah of Saul. **35**And Samuel did not see Saul again until the day of his death, but Samuel grieved over Saul. And the LORD repented that he had made Saul king over Israel.

# 16

**1**The LORD said to Samuel, "How long will you grieve over Saul, seeing I have rejected him from being king over Israel? Fill your horn with oil, and go; I will send you to Jesse the Bethlehemite, for I have provided for myself a king among his sons." **2**And Samuel said, "How can I go? If Saul hears it, he will kill me." And the LORD said, "Take a heifer with you, and say, 'I have come to sacrifice to the LORD.' **3**And invite Jesse to the sacrifice, and I will show you what you shall do; and you shall anoint for me him whom I name to you." <sup>4</sup>Samuel did what the LORD commanded, and came to Bethlehem. The elders of the city came to meet him trembling, and said, "Do you come peaceably?" <sup>5</sup>And he said, "Peaceably; I have come to sacrifice to the LORD; consecrate

5  yourselves, and come with me to the sacrifice." And he consecrated Jesse and his sons, and invited them to the sacrifice.

<sup>6</sup>When they came, he looked on Eliab and thought, "Surely the LORD's anointed is before him." <sup>7</sup>But the LORD said to Samuel, "Do not look on his appearance or on the height of his stature, because I have rejected him; for the

10  LORD sees not as man sees; man looks on the outward appearance, but the LORD looks on the heart." <sup>8</sup>Then Jesse called Abinadab, and made him pass before Samuel. And he said, "Neither has the LORD chosen this one." <sup>9</sup>Then Jesse made Shammah pass by. And he said, "Neither has the LORD chosen this one." <sup>10</sup>And Jesse made seven of his sons pass before Samuel. And Samuel said to Jesse, "The

15  LORD has not chosen these." <sup>11</sup>And Samuel said to Jesse, "Are all your sons here?" And he said, "There remains yet the youngest, but behold, he is keeping the sheep." And Samuel said to Jesse, "Send and fetch him; for we will not sit down till he comes here." <sup>12</sup>And he sent, and brought him in. Now he was ruddy, and had beautiful eyes, and was handsome. And the LORD said, "Arise, anoint

20  him; for this is he." <sup>13</sup>Then Samuel took the horn of oil, and anointed him in the midst of his brothers; and the Spirit of the LORD came mightily upon David from that day forward. And Samuel rose up, and went to Ramah.

<sup>14</sup>Now the Spirit of the LORD departed from Saul, and an evil spirit from the LORD tormented him....

*Saul's servants advised him to seek out a talented harpist to soothe him during the periods he was troubled by the evil spirit. One servant recommended David, so Saul summoned him. David found favor with Saul and became his armor-bearer.*

*Battle with the Philistines drew near. The Philistine giant Goliath challenged a champion of Israel to single combat to decide the issue between the Philistines and the Israelites. Lacking a suitable candidate, the Israelites ignored the challenge and joined battle with the Philistines. Jesse sent David to the army with supplies and orders to bring word of how his older brothers fared. When David heard of Goliath's challenge, he was taken aback that "this uncircumcised Philistine... should defy the armies of the living God," and volunteered to fight. Saul initially refused, owing to David's youth, but David assured the king that he had successfully battled wild animals in defense of his flock, and that God, who had delivered him from the lion and the bear, would also defend him against Goliath. Saul reluctantly agreed and had David outfitted with armor and sword; however, since David was unused to armor and unpracticed in the use of the sword, he chose to fight Goliath with a sling and five stones.*

**17** [41]And the Philistine came on and drew near to David, with his shield-bearer in front of him. [42]And when the Philistine looked, and saw David, he disdained him; for he was but a youth, ruddy and comely in appearance. [43]And the Philistine said to David, "Am I a dog, that you come to me with sticks?" And the Philistine cursed David by his gods. [44]The Philistine said to David, "Come to me, and I will give your flesh to the birds of the air and to the beasts of the field." [45]Then David said to the Philistine, "You come to me with a sword and with a spear and with a javelin; but I come to you in the name of the LORD of hosts, the God of the armies of Israel, whom you have defied. [46]This day the LORD will deliver you into my hand, and I will strike you down, and cut off your head; and I will give the dead bodies of the host of the Philistines this day to the birds of the air and to the wild beasts of the earth; that all the earth may know that there is a God in Israel, [47]and that all this assembly may know that the LORD saves not with sword and spear; for the battle is the LORD's and he will give you into our hand."

[48]When the Philistine arose and came and drew near to meet David, David ran quickly toward the battle line to meet the Philistine. [49]And David put his hand in his bag and took out a stone, and slung it, and struck the Philistine on his forehead; the stone sank into his forehead, and he fell on his face to the ground.

[50]So David prevailed over the Philistine with a sling and with a stone, and struck the Philistine, and killed him; there was no sword in the hand of David. [51]Then David ran and stood over the Philistine, and took his sword and drew it out of its sheath, and killed him, and cut off his head with it. When the Philistines saw that their champion was dead, they fled....

*Saul soon became jealous of the esteem in which David was held, and banished him from the court by giving him a military command. David's success in this post increased his reputation among the Israelites. Saul's daughter Michal loved David, so Saul set a trap for David, hoping to have him killed. Saul promised him Michal's hand in marriage without the customary payment if David should bring him evidence of having slaughtered a hundred Philistines. David successfully fought the Philistines and returned with double the required evidence, so Saul allowed him to marry Michal. However, Saul's fear of David continued to grow, as did David's honor among the Israelites.*

*Saul let it be known among his family and servants that he wanted David killed. Jonathan, Saul's son, interceded for David with his father, with the result that Saul for a time restored David to his favor. But during a period of madness, Saul attacked David, and David fled, aided by Michal and Jonathan.*

*At the shrine of Nob, the priest Ahimelech fed David with holy bread and gave him Goliath's sword. David then began to move through Israel and the surrounding areas, gaining followers. Saul's discovery of Ahimelech's aid to David led to the massacre of eighty-five priests and the inhabitants of Nob.*

*David's small army went to the aid of the inhabitants of Keilah, who were under attack from the Philistines, and defeated the attackers. Saul heard that David was at Keilah and sought to capture him, so after consulting God regarding the intentions of Saul and the men of Keilah, David and his men fled. Saul pursued David for a time, but David was able to escape when Saul was forced to deal with a Philistine invasion.*

**24** ¹When Saul returned from following the Philistines, he was told, "Behold, David is in the wilderness of Engedi." ²Then Saul took three thousand chosen men out of all Israel, and went to seek David and his men in front of the Wildgoats' Rocks. ³And he came to the sheepfolds by the way, where there was a cave; and Saul went in to relieve himself. Now David and his men were sitting in the innermost parts of the cave. ⁴And the men of David said to him, "Here is the day of which the LORD said to you, 'Behold, I will give your enemy into your hand, and you shall do to him as it shall seem good to you.'" Then David arose and stealthily cut off the skirt of Saul's robe. ⁵And afterward David's heart smote him, because he had cut off Saul's skirt. ⁶He said to his men, "The LORD forbid that I should do this thing to my lord, the LORD's anointed, to put forth my hand against him, seeing he is the LORD's anointed." ⁷So David persuaded his men with these words, and did not permit them to attack Saul. And Saul rose up and left the cave, and went upon his way.

⁸Afterward David also arose, and went out of the cave, and called after Saul, "My lord the king!" And when Saul looked behind him, David bowed with his face to the earth, and did obeisance. ⁹And David said to Saul, "Why do you listen to the words of men who say, 'Behold, David seeks your hurt'? ¹⁰Lo, this day your eyes have seen how the LORD gave you today into my hand in the cave; and some bade me kill you, but I spared you. I said, 'I will not put forth my hand against my lord; for he is the LORD's anointed.' ¹¹See, my father, see the skirt of your robe in my hand; for by the fact that I cut off the skirt of your robe, and did not kill you, you may know and see that there is no

wrong or treason in my hands. I have not sinned against you, though you hunt my life to take it. **12**May the LORD judge between me and you, may the LORD avenge me upon you; but my hand shall not be against you. **13**As the proverb of the ancients says, 'Out of the wicked comes forth wickedness'; but my hand shall not be against you. **14**After whom has the king of Israel come out? After     5
whom do you pursue? After a dead dog! After a flea! **15**May the LORD therefore be judge, and give sentence between me and you, and see to it, and plead my cause, and deliver me from your hand."

**16**When David had finished speaking these words to Saul, Saul said, "Is this your voice, my son David?" And Saul lifted up his voice and wept. **17**He     10
said to David, "You are more righteous than I; for you have repaid me good, whereas I have repaid you evil. **18**And you have declared this day how you have dealt well with me, in that you did not kill me when the LORD put me into your hands. **19**For if a man finds his enemy, will he let him go away safe? So may the LORD reward you with good for what you have done to me this day.     15
**20**And now, behold, I know that you shall surely be king, and that the kingdom of Israel shall be established in your hand. **21**Swear to me therefore by the LORD that you will not cut off my descendants after me, and that you will not destroy my name out of my father's house." **22**And David swore this to Saul. Then Saul went home; but David and his men went up to the stronghold....     20

*Despite their apparent reconciliation, David remained in exile, and Saul's army continued to seek him out. Having heard that David was in the wilderness of Ziph, Saul pursued him and set up camp at the hill of Halchilah. That night, David and a companion entered the camp.*

**26** **7**So David and Abishai went to the army by night; and there lay Saul sleeping within the encampment, with his spear stuck in the ground at his head; and Abner and the army lay around him. **8**Then said Abishai to David, "God has given your enemy into your hand this day; now therefore let me pin him to the earth with one stroke of the spear, and I will not strike him twice."     25
**9**But David said to Abishai, "Do not destroy him; for who can put forth his hand against the LORD's anointed and be guiltless?" **10**And David said, "As the LORD lives, the LORD will smite him; or his day shall come to die; or he shall go down into battle and perish. **11**The LORD forbid that I should put forth my hand against the LORD's anointed; but take now the spear that is at his head, and the jar of     30
water, and let us go." **12**So David took the spear and the jar of water from Saul's head; and they went away. No man saw it, or knew it, nor did any awake; for they were all asleep, because a deep sleep from the LORD had fallen upon them.

**13**Then David went over to the other side, and stood afar off on the top of the mountain, with a great space between them; **14**and David called to the     35 army, and to Abner the son of Ner, saying, "Will you not answer, Abner?" Then Abner answered, "Who are you that calls to the king?" **15**And David said to Abner, "Are you not a man? Who is like you in Israel? Why then have you not kept watch over your lord the king? For one of the people came in to destroy

5  the king your lord. **16**This thing that you have done is not good. As the LORD lives, you deserve to die, because you have not kept watch over your lord, the LORD's anointed. And now see where the king's spear is, and the jar of water that was at his head."

**17**Saul recognized David's voice, and said, "Is this your voice, my son Da-

10  vid?" And David said, "It is my voice, my lord, O king." **18**And he said, "Why does my lord pursue after his servant? For what have I done? What guilt is on my hands? **19**Now therefore let my lord the king hear the words of his servant. If it is the LORD who has stirred you up against me, may he accept an offering; but if it is men, may they be cursed before the LORD, for they have driven me

15  out this day that I should have no share in the heritage of the LORD, saying, 'Go, serve other gods.' **20**Now therefore, let not my blood fall to the earth away from the presence of the LORD; for the king of Israel has come out to seek my life, like one who hunts a partridge in the mountains."

**21**Then Saul said, "I have done wrong; return, my son David, for I will no

20  more do you harm, because my life was precious in your eyes this day; behold, I have played the fool, and have erred exceedingly." **22**And David made answer, "Here is the spear, O king! Let one of the young men come over and fetch it. **23**The LORD rewards every man for his righteousness and his faithfulness; for the LORD gave you into my hand today, and I would not put forth my hand

25  against the LORD's anointed. **24**Behold, as your life was precious this day in my sight, so may my life be precious in the sight of the LORD, and may he deliver me out of all tribulation." **25**Then Saul said to David, "Blessed be you, my son David! You will do many things and will succeed in them." So David went his way, and Saul returned to his place....

> *David offered his services to the Philistine King of Gath, and fought for him for some time. When the Philistines were mustering to attack Israel, the king sent David and his men away because his nobles feared that they would change sides during the battle.*

30  **31** **1**Now the Philistines fought against Israel; and the men of Israel fled before the Philistines, and fell slain on Mount Gilboa. **2**And the Philistines overtook Saul and his sons; and the Philistines slew Jonathan and Abinadab and Malchishua, the sons of Saul. **3**The battle pressed hard upon Saul, and the archers found him; and he was badly wounded by the archers. **4**Then Saul said

35  to his armor-bearer, "Draw your sword, and thrust me through with it, lest

these uncircumcised come and thrust me through, and make sport of me." But his armor-bearer would not; for he feared greatly. Therefore Saul took his own sword, and fell upon it. ⁵And when his armor-bearer saw that Saul was dead, he also fell upon his sword, and died with him. ⁶Thus Saul died, and his three sons, and his armor-bearer, and all his men, on the same day together. ⁷And when the men of Israel who were on the other side of the valley and those beyond the Jordan saw that the men of Israel had fled and that Saul and his sons were dead, they forsook their cities and fled; and the Philistines came and dwelt in them.

⁸On the morrow, when the Philistines came to strip the slain, they found Saul and his three sons fallen on Mount Gilboa. ⁹And they cut off his head, and stripped off his armor, and sent messengers throughout the land of the Philistines, to carry the good news to their idols and to the people. ¹⁰They put his armor in the temple of Ashtaroth; and they fastened his body to the wall of Bethshan. ¹¹But when the inhabitants of Jabesh Gilead heard what the Philistines had done to Saul, ¹²all the valiant men arose, and went all night, and took the body of Saul and the bodies of his sons from the wall of Bethshan; and they came to Jabesh and burnt them there. ¹³And they took their bones and buried them under the tamarisk tree in Jabesh, and fasted seven days.

## II Samuel

1 ¹After the death of Saul, when David had returned from the slaughter of the Amalekites, David remained two days in Ziklag; ²and on the third day, behold, a man came from Saul's camp, with his clothes rent and earth upon his head. And when he came to David, he fell to the ground and did obeisance. ³David said to him, "Where do you come from?" And he said to him, "I have escaped from the camp of Israel." ⁴And David said to him, "How did it go? Tell me." And he answered, "The people have fled from the battle, and many of the people also have fallen and are dead; and Saul and his son Jonathan are also dead." ⁵Then David said to the young man who told him, "How do you know that Saul and his son Jonathan are dead?" ⁶And the young man who told him said, "By chance I happened to be on Mount Gilboa; and there was Saul leaning upon his spear; and lo, the chariots and the horsemen were close upon him. ⁷And when he looked behind him, he saw me, and called to me. And I answered, 'Here I am.' ⁸And he said to me, 'Who are you?' I answered him, 'I am an Amalekite.' ⁹And he said to me, 'Stand beside me and slay me; for anguish has seized me, and yet my life still lingers.' ¹⁰So I stood beside him, and slew him, because I was sure that he could not live after he had fallen; and I took the crown which was on his head and the armlet which was on his arm, and I have brought them here to my lord." ¹¹Then David took hold of his clothes, and rent them; and so did all the men who were with him; ¹²and

they mourned and wept and fasted until evening for Saul and for Jonathan his son and for the people of the Lord and for the house of Israel, because they had fallen by the sword. **13**And David said to the young man who told him, "Where do you come from?" And he answered, "I am the son of a sojourner, an Amalekite." **14**David said to him, "How is it you were not afraid to put forth your hand to destroy the Lord's anointed?" **15**Then David called one of the young men and said, "Go, fall upon him." And he smote him so that he died. **16**And David said to him, "Your blood be upon your head; for your own mouth has testified against you, saying, 'I have slain the Lord's anointed.'"

**17**And David lamented with this lamentation over Saul and Jonathan his son, **18**and he said it should be taught to the people of Judah; behold, it is written in the Book of Jashar. He said:

**19**"Thy glory, O Israel, is slain upon thy high places!
　　How are the mighty fallen!
**20**Tell it not in Gath,
　　　publish it not in the streets of Ashkelon;
　　　lest the daughters of the Philistines rejoice,
　　　lest the daughters of the uncircumcised exult.
**21**"Ye mountains of Gilbo'a,
　　　let there be no dew or rain upon you,
　　　　nor upsurging of the deep!
For there the shield of the mighty was defiled,
　　　the shield of Saul, not anointed with oil.
**22**"From the blood of the slain,
　　　from the fat of the mighty,
　　　the bow of Jonathan turned not back,
　　　and the sword of Saul returned not empty.
**23**"Saul and Jonathan, beloved and lovely!
　　　In life and in death they were not divided;
　　　they were swifter than eagles,
　　　they were stronger than lions.
**24**"Ye daughters of Israel, weep over Saul,
　　　who clothed you daintily in scarlet,
　　　who put ornaments of gold upon your apparel.
**25**"How are the mighty fallen
　　　in the midst of the battle!
"Jonathan lies slain upon thy high places.
　　　**26**I am distressed for you, my brother Jonathan;
　　　very pleasant have you been to me;

your love to me was wonderful,
passing the love of women.
27"How are the mighty fallen,
and the weapons of war perished!"

5 ¹Then all the tribes of Israel came to David at Hebron, and said, "Behold, 5
we are your bone and flesh. ²In times past, when Saul was king over us,
it was you that led out and brought in Israel; and the LORD said to you, 'You
shall be shepherd of my people Israel, and you shall be prince over Israel.'"
³So all the elders of Israel came to the king at Hebron; and King David made a
covenant with them at Hebron before the LORD, and they anointed David king 10
over Israel. ⁴David was thirty years old when he began to reign, and he reigned
forty years. ⁵At Hebron he reigned over Judah seven years and six months; and
at Jerusalem he reigned over all Israel and Judah thirty-three years. ⁶And the
king and his men went to Jerusalem against the Jebusites, the inhabitants of
the land, who said to David, "You will not come in here, but the blind and the 15
lame will ward you off"—thinking, "David cannot come in here." ⁷Nevertheless
David took the stronghold of Zion, that is, the city of David. ⁸And David said
on that day, "Whoever would smite the Jebusites, let him get up the water shaft
to attack the lame and the blind, who are hated by David's soul." Therefore it
is said, "The blind and the lame shall not come into the house." ⁹And David 20
dwelt in the stronghold, and called it the city of David. And David built the
city round about from the Millo inward.

¹⁰And David became greater and greater, for the LORD, the God of hosts, was
with him. ¹¹And Hiram king of Tyre sent messengers to David, and cedar trees,
also carpenters and masons who built David a house. ¹²And David perceived 25
that the LORD had established him king over Israel, and that he had exalted his
kingdom for the sake of his people Israel....

¹⁷When the Philistines heard that David had been anointed king over
Israel, all the Philistines went up in search of David; but David heard of it and
went down to the stronghold. ¹⁸Now the Philistines had come and spread out 30
in the valley of Rephaim. ¹⁹And David inquired of the LORD, "Shall I go up
against the Philistines? Wilt thou give them into my hand?" And the LORD
said to David, "Go up; for I will certainly give the Philistines into your hand."
²⁰And David came to Baal Perazim, and David defeated them there; and he
said, "The LORD has broken through my enemies before me, like a bursting 35
flood." Therefore the name of that place is called Baal Perazim. ²¹And the
Philistines left their idols there, and David and his men carried them away.
²²And the Philistines came up yet again, and spread out in the valley of Rephaim.
²³And when David inquired of the LORD, he said, "You shall not go up; go

around to their rear, and come upon them opposite the balsam trees. **24**And when you hear the sound of marching in the tops of the balsam trees, then bestir yourself; for then the Lord has gone out before you to smite the army of the Philistines." **25**And David did as the Lord commanded him, and smote
5  the Philistines from Geba to Gezer.

6 **1**David again gathered all the chosen men of Israel, thirty thousand. **2**And David arose and went with all the people who were with him from Baale Judah, to bring up from there the ark of God, which is called by the name of the Lord of hosts who sits enthroned on the cherubim.... **9**And David was
10  afraid of the Lord that day; and he said, "How can the ark of the Lord come to me?" **10**So David was not willing to take the ark of the Lord into the city of David; but David took it aside to the house of Obed-Edom the Gittite. **11**And the ark of the Lord remained in the house of Obed-Edom the Gittite three months; and the Lord blessed Obed-Edom and all his household. **12**And it
15  was told King David, "The Lord has blessed the household of Obed-Edom and all that belongs to him, because of the ark of God." So David went and brought up the ark of God from the house of Obed-Edom to the city of David with rejoicing; **13**and when those who bore the ark of the Lord had gone six paces, he sacrificed an ox and a fatling. **14**And David danced before the Lord
20  with all his might; and David was girded with a linen ephod. **15**So David and all the house of Israel brought up the ark of the Lord with shouting, and with the sound of the horn. **16**As the ark of the Lord came into the city of David, Michal, the daughter of Saul, looked out of the window, and saw King David leaping and dancing before the Lord; and she despised him in her heart.
25  **17**And they brought in the ark of the Lord, and set it in its place, inside the tent which David had pitched for it; and David offered burnt offerings and peace offerings before the Lord. **18**And when David had finished offering the burnt offerings and the peace offerings, he blessed the people in the name of the Lord of hosts, **19**and distributed among all the people, the whole multitude of
30  Israel, both men and women, to each a cake of bread, a portion of meat, and a cake of raisins. Then all the people departed, each to his house.

**20**And David returned to bless his household. But Michal, the daughter of Saul, came out to meet David and said, "How the king of Israel honored himself today, uncovering himself today before the eyes of his servants' maids,
35  as one of the vulgar fellows shamelessly uncovers himself!" **21**And David said to Michal, "It was before the Lord, who chose me above your father, and above all his house, to appoint me as prince over Israel, the people of the Lord—and I will make merry before the Lord. **22**I will make myself yet more contemptible than this, and I will be abased in your eyes; but by the maids of whom you

have spoken, by them I shall be held in honor." **23**And Michal, the daughter of Saul, had no child to the day of her death.

7 **1**Now when the king dwelt in his house, and the Lord had given him rest from all his enemies round about, **2**the king said to Nathan the prophet, "See now, I dwell in a house of cedar, but the ark of God dwells in a tent." **3**And Nathan said to the king, "Go, do all that is in your heart; for the Lord is with you." **4**But that same night the word of the Lord came to Nathan, **5**"Go and tell my servant David, 'Thus says the Lord: Would you build me a house to dwell in? **6**I have not dwelt in a house since the day I brought up the people of Israel from Egypt to this day, but I have been moving about in a tent for my dwelling. **7**In all places where I have moved with all the people of Israel, did I speak a word with any of the judges of Israel, whom I commanded to shepherd my people Israel, saying, "Why have you not built me a house of cedar?"' **8**Now, therefore, thus you shall say to my servant David, 'Thus says the Lord of hosts, I took you from the pasture, from following the sheep, that you should be prince over my people Israel; **9**and I have been with you wherever you went, and have cut off all your enemies from before you; and I will make for you a great name, like the name of the great ones of the earth. **10**And I will appoint a place for my people Israel, and will plant them, that they may dwell in their own place, and be disturbed no more; and violent men shall afflict them no more, as formerly, **11**from the time that I appointed judges over my people Israel; and I will give you rest from all your enemies. Moreover, the Lord declares to you that the Lord will make you a house. **12**When your days are fulfilled and you lie down with your fathers, I will raise up your offspring after you, who shall come forth from your body, and I will establish his kingdom. **13**He shall build a house for my name, and I will establish the throne of his kingdom forever. **14**I will be his father, and he shall be my son. When he commits iniquity, I will chasten him with the rod of men, with the stripes of the sons of men; **15**but I will not take my steadfast love from him, as I took it from Saul, whom I put away from before you. **16**And your house and your kingdom shall be made sure forever before me; your throne shall be established forever.'"

**17**In accordance with all these words, and in accordance with all this vision, Nathan spoke to David. **18**Then King David went in and sat before the Lord, and said, "Who am I, O Lord God, and what is my house, that thou hast brought me thus far? **19**And yet this was a small thing in thy eyes, O Lord God; thou hast spoken also of thy servant's house for a great while to come, and hast shown me future generations, O Lord God! **20**And what more can David say to thee? For thou knowest thy servant, O Lord God! **21**Because of thy promise, and according to thy own heart, thou hast wrought all this greatness, to make thy servant know it. <sup>22</sup>Therefore thou art great, O Lᴏʀᴅ God; for there is none like thee, and there is no God besides thee, according to all that we have heard with our ears. <sup>23</sup>What other nation on earth is like thy people Israel, whom God went to redeem to be his people, making himself a name, and doing for them great and terrible things, by driving out before his people a nation and its gods? <sup>24</sup>And thou didst establish for thyself thy people Israel to be thy people forever; and thou, O Lᴏʀᴅ, didst become their God. <sup>25</sup>And now, O Lᴏʀᴅ God, confirm forever the word which thou hast spoken concerning thy servant and concerning his house, and do as thou hast spoken; <sup>26</sup>and thy name will be magnified forever, saying, 'The Lᴏʀᴅ of hosts is God over Israel,' and the house of thy servant David will be established before thee. <sup>27</sup>For thou, O Lᴏʀᴅ of hosts, the God of Israel, hast made this revelation to thy servant, saying, 'I will build you a house'; therefore thy servant has found courage to pray this prayer to thee. <sup>28</sup>And now, O Lord Gᴏᴅ, thou art God, and thy words are true, and thou hast promised this good thing to thy servant; <sup>29</sup>now therefore may it please thee to bless the house of thy servant, that it may continue forever before thee; for thou, O Lord Gᴏᴅ, hast spoken, and with thy blessing shall the house of thy servant be blessed forever."…

**11** <sup>1</sup>In the spring of the year, the time when kings go forth to battle, David sent Joab, and his servants with him, and all Israel; and they ravaged the Ammonites, and besieged Rabbah. But David remained at Jerusalem. <sup>2</sup>It happened, late one afternoon, when David arose from his couch and was walking upon the roof of the king's house, that he saw from the roof a woman bathing; and the woman was very beautiful. <sup>3</sup>And David sent and inquired about the woman. And one said, "Is not this Bathsheba, the daughter of Eliam, the wife of Uriah the Hittite?" <sup>4</sup>So David sent messengers, and took her; and she came to him, and he lay with her. (Now she was purifying herself from her uncleanness.) Then she returned to her house. <sup>5</sup>And the woman conceived; and she sent and told David, "I am with child." <sup>6</sup>So David sent word to Joab, "Send me Uriah the Hittite." And Joab sent Uriah to David. <sup>7</sup>When Uriah came to him, David asked how Joab was doing, and how the people fared, and how the war prospered. <sup>8</sup>Then David said to Uriah, "Go down to your house, and wash your feet." And Uriah went out of the king's house, and there followed him a present from the king. <sup>9</sup>But Uriah slept at the door of the king's house with all the servants of his lord, and did not go down to his house. <sup>10</sup>When they told David, "Uriah did not go down to his house," David said to Uriah, "Have you not come from a journey? Why did you not go down to your house?" <sup>11</sup>Uriah said to David, "The ark and Israel and Judah dwell in booths; and my lord Joab and the servants of my lord are camping in the open field; shall I then go to my house, to eat and to drink, and to lie with my wife? As you live, and as your soul lives, I will not do this thing." **12**Then David said to Uriah, "Remain here today also, and tomorrow I will let you depart." So Uriah remained in Jerusalem that day, and the next. **13**And David invited him, and he ate in his presence and drank, so that he made him drunk; and in the evening he went out to lie on his couch with the servants of his lord, but he did not go down to his house.

**14**In the morning David wrote a letter to Joab, and sent it by the hand of Uriah. **15**In the letter he wrote, "Set Uriah in the forefront of the hardest fighting, and then draw back from him, that he may be struck down, and die." **16**And as Joab was besieging the city, he assigned Uriah to the place where he knew there were valiant men. **17**And the men of the city came out and fought with Joab; and some of the servants of David among the people fell. Uriah the Hittite was slain also. **18**Then Joab sent and told David all the news about the fighting; **19**and he instructed the messenger, "When you have finished telling all the news about the fighting to the king, **20**then, if the king's anger rises, and if he says to you, 'Why did you go so near the city to fight? Did you not know that they would shoot from the wall? **21**Who killed Abimelech the son of Jerub-Besheth? Did not a woman cast an upper millstone upon him from the wall, so that he died at Thebez? Why did you go so near the wall?' then you shall say, 'Your servant Uriah the Hittite is dead also.'" **22**So the messenger went, and came and told David all that Joab had sent him to tell. **23**The messenger said to David, "The men gained an advantage over us, and came out against us in the field; but we drove them back to the entrance of the gate. **24**Then the archers shot at your servants from the wall; some of the king's servants are dead; and your servant Uriah the Hittite is dead also." **25**David said to the messenger, "Thus shall you say to Joab, 'Do not let this matter trouble you, for the sword devours now one and now another; strengthen your attack upon the city, and overthrow it.' And encourage him." **26**When the wife of Uriah heard that Uriah her husband was dead, she made lamentation for her husband. **27**And when the mourning was over, David sent and brought her to his house, and she became his wife, and bore him a son. But the thing that David had done displeased the LORD.

**12** **1**And the LORD sent Nathan to David. He came to him, and said to him, "There were two men in a certain city, the one rich and the other poor. **2**The rich man had very many flocks and herds; **3**but the poor man had nothing but one little ewe lamb, which he had bought. And he brought it up, and it grew up with him and with his children; it used to eat of his morsel, and drink from his cup, and lie in his bosom, and it was like a daughter to him.

**4**Now there came a traveler to the rich man, and he was unwilling to take one of his own flock or herd to prepare for the wayfarer who had come to him, but he took the poor man's lamb, and prepared it for the man who had come to him." **5**Then David's anger was greatly kindled against the man; and he said to Nathan, "As the Lord lives, the man who has done this deserves to die; **6**and he shall restore the lamb fourfold, because he did this thing, and because he had no pity."

**7**Nathan said to David, "You are the man. Thus says the Lord, the God of Israel, 'I anointed you king over Israel, and I delivered you out of the hand of Saul; **8**and I gave you your master's house, and your master's wives into your bosom, and gave you the house of Israel and of Judah; and if this were too little, I would add to you as much more. **9**Why have you despised the word of the Lord, to do what is evil in his sight? You have smitten Uriah the Hittite with the sword, and have taken his wife to be your wife, and have slain him with the sword of the Ammonites. **10**Now therefore the sword shall never depart from your house, because you have despised me, and have taken the wife of Uriah the Hittite to be your wife.' **11**Thus says the Lord, 'Behold, I will raise up evil against you out of your own house; and I will take your wives before your eyes, and give them to your neighbor, and he shall lie with your wives in the sight of this sun. **12**For you did it secretly; but I will do this thing before all Israel, and before the sun.'" **13**David said to Nathan, "I have sinned against the Lord." And Nathan said to David, "The Lord also has put away your sin; you shall not die. **14**Nevertheless, because by this deed you have utterly scorned the Lord, the child that is born to you shall die." **15**Then Nathan went to his house.

And the Lord struck the child that Uriah's wife bore to David, and it became sick. **16**David therefore besought God for the child; and David fasted, and went in and lay all night upon the ground. **17**And the elders of his house stood beside him, to raise him from the ground; but he would not, nor did he eat food with them. **18**On the seventh day the child died. And the servants of David feared to tell him that the child was dead; for they said, "Behold, while the child was yet alive, we spoke to him, and he did not listen to us; how then can we say to him the child is dead? He may do himself some harm." **19**But when David saw that his servants were whispering together, David perceived that the child was dead; and David said to his servants, "Is the child dead?" They said, "He is dead." **20**Then David arose from the earth, and washed, and anointed himself, and changed his clothes; and he went into the house of the Lord, and worshiped; he then went to his own house; and when he asked, they set food before him, and he ate. **21**Then his servants said to him, "What is this thing that you have done? You fasted and wept for the child while it was alive; but when the child died, you arose and ate food." **22**He said, "While the child was still alive, I fasted and wept; for I said, 'Who knows whether the LORD will be gracious to me, that the child may live?' **23**But now he is dead; why should I fast? Can I bring him back again? I shall go to him, but he will not return to me." **24**Then David comforted his wife, Bathsheba, and went in to her, and lay with her; and she bore a son, and he called his name Solomon. And the LORD 5 loved him, **25**and sent a message by Nathan the prophet; so he called his name Jedidiah, because of the LORD....

# 13

**1**Now Absalom, David's son, had a beautiful sister, whose name was Tamar; and after a time Amnon, David's son, loved her. **2**And Amnon was so tormented that he made himself ill because of his sister Tamar; for she 10 was a virgin, and it seemed impossible to Amnon to do anything to her. **3**But Amnon had a friend, whose name was Jonadab, the son of Shimeah, David's brother; and Jonadab was a very crafty man. **4**And he said to him, "O son of the king, why are you so haggard morning after morning? Will you not tell me?" Amnon said to him, "I love Tamar, my brother Absalom's sister." 15 **5**Jonadab said to him, "Lie down on your bed, and pretend to be ill; and when your father comes to see you, say to him, 'Let my sister Tamar come and give me bread to eat, and prepare the food in my sight, that I may see it, and eat it from her hand.'"

**6**So Amnon lay down, and pretended to be ill; and when the king came 20 to see him, Amnon said to the king, "Pray let my sister Tamar come and make a couple of cakes in my sight, that I may eat from her hand." **7**Then David sent home to Tamar, saying, "Go to your brother Amnon's house, and prepare food for him." **8**So Tamar went to her brother Amnon's house, where he was lying down. And she took dough, and kneaded it, and made cakes in his sight, 25 and baked the cakes. **9**And she took the pan and emptied it out before him, but he refused to eat. And Amnon said, "Send out everyone from me." So everyone went out from him. **10**Then Amnon said to Tamar, "Bring the food into the chamber, that I may eat from your hand." And Tamar took the cakes she had made, and brought them into the chamber to Amnon her brother. 30 **11**But when she brought them near him to eat, he took hold of her, and said to her, "Come, lie with me, my sister." **12**She answered him, "No, my brother, do not force me; for such a thing is not done in Israel; do not do this wanton folly. **13**As for me, where could I carry my shame? And as for you, you would be as one of the wanton fools in Israel. Now therefore, I pray you, speak to the 35 king; for he will not withhold me from you." **14**But he would not listen to her; and being stronger than she, he forced her, and lay with her.

**15**Then Amnon hated her with very great hatred; so that the hatred with which he hated her was greater than the love with which he had loved her. And

Amnon said to her, "Arise, be gone." [16]But she said to him, "No, my brother; for this wrong in sending me away is greater than the other which you did to me." But he would not listen to her. [17]He called the young man who served him and said, "Put this woman out of my presence, and bolt the door after her." [18]Now she was wearing a long robe with sleeves; for thus were the virgin daughters of the king clad of old. So his servant put her out, and bolted the door after her. [19]And Tamar put ashes on her head, and rent the long robe which she wore; and she laid her hand on her head, and went away, crying aloud as she went. [20]And her brother Absalom said to her, "Has Amnon your brother been with you? Now hold your peace, my sister; he is your brother; do not take this to heart." So Tamar dwelt, a desolate woman, in her brother Absalom's house.

[21]When King David heard of all these things, he was very angry. [22]But Absalom spoke to Amnon, neither good nor bad; for Absalom hated Amnon because he had forced his sister Tamar. [23]After two full years Absalom had sheepshearers at Baal Hazor, which is near Ephraim, and Absalom invited all the king's sons. [24]And Absalom came to the king, and said, "Behold, your servant has sheepshearers; pray let the king and his servants go with your servant." [25]But the king said to Absalom, "No, my son, let us not all go, lest we be burdensome to you." He pressed him, but he would not go but gave him his blessing. [26]Then Absalom said, "If not, pray let my brother Amnon go with us." And the king said to him, "Why should he go with you?" [27]But Absalom pressed him until he let Amnon and all the king's sons go with him. [28]Then Absalom commanded his servants, "Mark when Amnon's heart is merry with wine, and when I say to you, 'Strike Amnon,' then kill him. Fear not; have I not commanded you? Be courageous and be valiant." [29]So the servants of Absalom did to Amnon as Absalom had commanded. Then all the king's sons arose, and each mounted his mule and fled.

[30]While they were on the way, tidings came to David, "Absalom has slain all the king's sons, and not one of them is left." [31]Then the king arose, and rent his garments, and lay on the earth; and all his servants who were standing by rent their garments. [32]But Jonadab, the son of Shimeah, David's brother, said, "Let not my lord suppose that they have killed all the young men the king's sons, for Amnon alone is dead, for by the command of Absalom this has been determined from the day he forced his sister Tamar. [33]Now therefore let not my lord the king so take it to heart as to suppose that all the king's sons are dead; for Amnon alone is dead.".... [35]And Jonadab said to the king, "Behold, the king's sons have come; as your servant said, so it has come about." [36]And as soon as he had finished speaking, behold, the king's sons came, and lifted up their voice and wept; and the king also and all his servants wept very bitterly....

[38]So Absalom fled, and went to Geshur, and was there three years. [39]And the

spirit of the king longed to go forth to Absalom; for he was comforted about Amnon, seeing he was dead.

14 <sup>1</sup>Now Joab the son of Zeruiah perceived that the King's heart went out to Absalom....

*Joab sent a wise woman to David to convince him, by seeking a pardon for one of her sons who had allegedly killed his brother, to recall Absalom to Jerusalem.*

<sup>19</sup>The king said, "Is the hand of Joab with you in all this?" The woman answered     5
and said, "As surely as you live, my lord the king, one cannot turn to the right hand or to the left from anything that my lord the king has said. It was your servant Joab who bade me; it was he who put all these words in the mouth of your handmaid. <sup>20</sup>In order to change the course of affairs your servant Joab did this. But my lord has wisdom like the wisdom of the angel of God to know     10
all things that are on the earth." <sup>21</sup>Then the king said to Joab, "Behold now, I grant this; go, bring back the young man Absalom." <sup>22</sup>And Joab fell on his face to the ground, and did obeisance, and blessed the king; and Joab said, "Today your servant knows that I have found favor in your sight, my lord the king, in that the king has granted the request of his servant." <sup>23</sup>So Joab arose and went     15
to Geshur, and brought Absalom to Jerusalem. <sup>24</sup>And the king said, "Let him dwell apart in his own house; he is not to come into my presence." So Absalom dwelt apart in his own house, and did not come into the king's presence.

<sup>25</sup>Now in all Israel there was no one so much to be praised for his beauty as Absalom; from the sole of his foot to the crown of his head there was no     20
blemish in him. <sup>26</sup>And when he cut the hair of his head (for at the end of every year he used to cut it; when it was heavy on him, he cut it), he weighed the hair of his head, two hundred shekels by the king's weight. <sup>27</sup>There were born to Absalom three sons, and one daughter, whose name was Tamar; she was a beautiful woman. <sup>28</sup>So Absalom dwelt two full years in Jerusalem, without     25
coming into the king's presence. <sup>29</sup>Then Absalom sent for Joab, to send him to the king; but Joab would not come to him. And he sent a second time, but Joab would not come. <sup>30</sup>Then he said to his servants, "See, Joab's field is next to mine, and he has barley there; go and set it on fire." So Absalom's servants set the field on fire. <sup>31</sup>Then Joab arose and went to Absalom at his house, and     30
said to him, "Why have your servants set my field on fire?" <sup>32</sup>Absalom answered Joab, "Behold, I sent word to you, 'Come here, that I may send you to the king, to ask, "Why have I come from Geshur? It would be better for me to be there still."' Now therefore let me go into the presence of the king; and if there is guilt in me, let him kill me.'" <sup>33</sup>Then Joab went to the king, and told him; and he     35

summoned Absalom. So he came to the king, and bowed himself on his face to the ground before the king; and the king kissed Absalom.

15 ¹After this Absalom got himself a chariot and horses, and fifty men to run before him. ²And Absalom used to rise early and stand beside the way of the gate; and when any man had a suit to come before the king for judgment, Absalom would call to him, and say, "From what city are you?" And when he said, "Your servant is of such and such a tribe in Israel," ³Absalom would say to him, "See, your claims are good and right; but there is no man deputed by the king to hear you." ⁴Absalom said moreover, "Oh that I were judge in the land! Then every man with a suit or cause might come to me, and I would give him justice." ⁵And whenever a man came near to do obeisance to him, he would put out his hand, and take hold of him, and kiss him. ⁶Thus Absalom did to all of Israel who came to the king for judgment; so Absalom stole the hearts of the men of Israel.

⁷And at the end of four years Absalom said to the king, "Pray let me go and pay my vow, which I have vowed to the LORD, in Hebron. ⁸For your servant vowed a vow while I dwelt at Geshur in Aram, saying, 'If the LORD will indeed bring me back to Jerusalem, then I will offer worship to the LORD.'" ⁹The king said to him, "Go in peace." So he arose, and went to Hebron. ¹⁰But Absalom sent secret messengers throughout all the tribes of Israel, saying, "As soon as you hear the sound of the trumpet, then say, 'Absalom is king at Hebron!'"¹¹With Absalom went two hundred men from Jerusalem who were invited guests, and they went in their simplicity, and knew nothing. ¹²And while Absalom was offering the sacrifices, he sent for Ahithophel the Gilonite, David's counselor, from his city Giloh. And the conspiracy grew strong, and the people with Absalom kept increasing.

¹³And a messenger came to David, saying, "The hearts of the men of Israel have gone after Absalom."¹⁴Then David said to all his servants who were with him at Jerusalem, "Arise, and let us flee; or else there will be no escape for us from Absalom; go in haste, lest he overtake us quickly, and bring down evil upon us, and smite the city with the edge of the sword." ¹⁵And the king's servants said to the king, "Behold, your servants are ready to do whatever my lord the king decides." ¹⁶So the king went forth, and all his household after him. And the king left ten concubines to keep the house. ¹⁷And the king went forth, and all the people after him; and they halted at the last house.… ²³And all the country wept aloud as all the people passed by, and the king crossed the brook Kidron, and all the people passed on toward the wilderness. ²⁴And Abiathar came up, and lo, Zadok came also, with all the Levites, bearing the ark of the covenant of God; and they set down the ark of God, until the people had all passed out

of the city. **25**Then the king said to Zadok, "Carry the ark of God back into the city. If I find favor in the eyes of the LORD, he will bring me back and let me see both it and his habitation; **26**but if he says, 'I have no pleasure in you,' behold, here I am, let him do to me what seems good to him."... **29**So Zadok and Abiathar carried the ark of God back to Jerusalem; and they remained      5 there. **30**But David went up the ascent of the Mount of Olives, weeping as he went, barefoot and with his head covered; and all the people who were with him covered their heads, and they went up, weeping as they went. **31**And it was told David, "Ahithophel is among the conspirators with Absalom." And David said, "O LORD, I pray thee, turn the counsel of Ahithophel into foolishness."      10 **32**When David came to the summit, where God was worshiped, behold, Hushai the Archite came to meet him with his coat rent and earth upon his head. **33**David said to him, "If you go on with me, you will be a burden to me. **34**But if you return to the city, and say to Absalom, 'I will be your servant, O king; as I have been your father's servant in time past, so now I will be your      15 servant,' then you will defeat for me the counsel of Ahithophel. **35**Are not Zadok and Abiathar the priests with you there? So whatever you hear from the king's house, tell it to Zadok and Abiathar the priests. **36**Behold, their two sons are with them there, Ahimaaz, Zadok's son, and Jonathan, Abiathar's son; and by them you shall send to me everything you hear." **37**So Hushai, David's friend,      20 came into the city, just as Absalom was entering Jerusalem....

*As he fled from Jerusalem, David discovered that Saul's grandson, to whom he had restored Saul's lands and possessions, had joined the revolt. He then came across a supporter of Saul who cursed David as a man of blood, saying that Absalom's revolt was God's punishment for usurping Saul's throne. When his men wanted to kill that man, David prevented them, saying that either the cursing was from God, or God would repay David for having been cursed.*

16 **15**Now Absalom and all the people, the men of Israel, came to Jerusalem, and Ahithophel with him. **16**And when Hushai the Archite, David's friend, came to Absalom, Hushai said to Absalom, "Long live the king! Long live the king!" **17**And Absalom said to Hushai, "Is this your loyalty to your      25 friend? Why did you not go with your friend?" **18**And Hushai said to Absalom, "No; for whom the LORD and this people and all the men of Israel have chosen, his I will be, and with him I will remain. **19**And again, whom should I serve? Should it not be his son? As I have served your father, so I will serve you." **20**Then Absalom said to Ahithophel, "Give your counsel; what shall we do?"      30 **21**Ahithophel said to Absalom, "Go in to your father's concubines, whom he has left to keep the house; and all Israel will hear that you have made yourself odi-

ous to your father, and the hands of all who are with you will be strengthened."
$^{22}$So they pitched a tent for Absalom upon the roof; and Absalom went in to
his father's concubines in the sight of all Israel. $^{23}$Now in those days the counsel
which Ahithophel gave was as if one consulted the oracle of God; so was all the
5    counsel of Ahithophel esteemed, both by David and by Absalom.

17 $^{1}$Moreover Ahithophel said to Absalom, "Let me choose twelve thousand
men, and I will set out and pursue David tonight. $^{2}$I will come upon
him while he is weary and discouraged, and throw him into a panic; and all
the people who are with him will flee. I will strike down the king only, $^{3}$and
10   I will bring all the people back to you as a bride comes home to her husband.
You seek the life of only one man, and all the people will be at peace." $^{4}$And
the advice pleased Absalom and all the elders of Israel. $^{5}$Then Absalom said,
"Call Hushai the Archite also, and let us hear what he has to say." $^{6}$And when
Hushai came to Absalom, Absalom said to him, "Thus has Ahithophel spoken;
15   shall we do as he advises? If not, you speak." $^{7}$Then Hushai said to Absalom,
"This time the counsel which Ahithophel has given is not good." $^{8}$Hushai
said, moreover, "You know that your father and his men are mighty men, and
that they are enraged, like a bear robbed of her cubs in the field. Besides, your
father is expert in war; he will not spend the night with the people. $^{9}$Behold,
20   even now he has hidden himself in one of the pits, or in some other place. And
when some of the people fall at the first attack, whoever hears it will say, 'There
has been a slaughter among the people who follow Absalom.' $^{10}$Then even the
valiant man, whose heart is like the heart of a lion, will utterly melt with fear;
for all Israel knows that your father is a mighty man, and that those who are
25   with him are valiant men. $^{11}$But my counsel is that all Israel be gathered to
you, from Dan to Beersheba, as the sand by the sea for multitude, and that
you go to battle in person. $^{12}$So we shall come upon him in some place where
he is to be found, and we shall light upon him as the dew falls on the ground;
and of him and all the men with him not one will be left. $^{13}$If he withdraws
30   into a city, then all Israel will bring ropes to that city, and we shall drag it into
the valley, until not even a pebble is to be found there." $^{14}$And Absalom and
all the men of Israel said, "The counsel of Hushai the Archite is better than the
counsel of Ahithophel." For the LORD had ordained to defeat the good counsel
of Ahithophel, so that the LORD might bring evil upon Absalom. $^{15}$Then Hushai
35   said to Zadok and Abiathar the priests, "Thus and so did Ahithophel counsel
Absalom and the elders of Israel; and thus and so have I counseled. $^{16}$Now,
therefore, send quickly and tell David, 'Do not lodge tonight at the fords of
the wilderness, but by all means pass over; lest the king and all the people who
are with him be swallowed up.'"... $^{22}$Then David arose, and all the people who

were with him, and they crossed the Jordan; by daybreak not one was left who had not crossed the Jordan. ²³When Ahithophel saw that his counsel was not followed, he saddled his ass, and went off home to his own city. And he set his house in order, and hanged himself; and he died, and was buried in the tomb of his father. ²⁴Then David came to Mahanaim. And Absalom crossed the Jordan with all the men of Israel....

18 ¹Then David mustered the men who were with him, and set over them commanders of thousands and commanders of hundreds. ²And David sent forth the army, one third under the command of Joab, one third under the command of Abishai, the son of Zeruiah, Joab's brother, and one third under the command of Ittai the Gittite. And the king said to the men, "I myself will also go out with you." ³But the men said, "You shall not go out. For if we flee, they will not care about us. If half of us die, they will not care about us. But you are worth ten thousand of us; therefore it is better that you send us help from the city." ⁴The king said to them, "Whatever seems best to you I will do." So the king stood at the side of the gate, while all the army marched out by hundreds and by thousands. ⁵And the king ordered Joab and Abishai and Ittai, "Deal gently for my sake with the young man Absalom." And all the people heard when the king gave orders to all the commanders about Absalom.

⁶So the army went out into the field against Israel; and the battle was fought in the forest of Ephraim. ⁷And the men of Israel were defeated there by the servants of David, and the slaughter there was great on that day, twenty thousand men. ⁸The battle spread over the face of all the country; and the forest devoured more people that day than the sword. ⁹And Absalom chanced to meet the servants of David. Absalom was riding upon his mule, and the mule went under the thick branches of a great oak, and his head caught fast in the oak, and he was left hanging between heaven and earth, while the mule that was under him went on. ¹⁰And a certain man saw it and told Joab, "Behold, I saw Absalom hanging in an oak." ¹¹Joab said to the man who told him, "What, you saw him! Why then did you not strike him there to the ground? I would have been glad to give you ten pieces of silver and a girdle." ¹²But the man said to Joab, "Even if I felt in my hand the weight of a thousand pieces of silver, I would not put forth my hand against the king's son; for in our hearing the king commanded you and Abishai and Ittai, 'For my sake protect the young man Absalom.' ¹³On the other hand, if I had dealt treacherously against his life (and there is nothing hidden from the king), then you yourself would have stood aloof."

¹⁴Jo'ab said, "I will not waste time like this with you." And he took three darts in his hand, and thrust them into the heart of Absalom, while he was

still alive in the oak. <sup>15</sup>And ten young men, Joab's armor-bearers, surrounded Absalom and struck him, and killed him. <sup>16</sup>Then Joab blew the trumpet, and the troops came back from pursuing Israel; for Joab restrained them. <sup>17</sup>And they took Absalom, and threw him into a great pit in the forest, and raised over him a very great heap of stones; and all Israel fled, everyone to his own home. <sup>18</sup>Now Absalom in his lifetime had taken and set up for himself the pillar which is in the King's Valley, for he said, "I have no son to keep my name in remembrance"; he called the pillar after his own name, and it is called Absalom's monument to this day. <sup>19</sup>Then said Ahimaaz, the son of Zadok, "Let me run, and carry tidings to the king that the Lord has delivered him from the power of his enemies." <sup>20</sup>And Joab said to him, "You are not to carry tidings today; you may carry tidings another day, but today you shall carry no tidings, because the king's son is dead." <sup>21</sup>Then Joab said to the Cushite, "Go, tell the king what you have seen." The Cushite bowed before Joab, and ran. <sup>22</sup>Then Ahimaaz, the son of Zadok, said again to Joab, "Come what may, let me also run after the Cushite." And Joab said, "Why will you run, my son, seeing that you will have no reward for the tidings?" <sup>23</sup>"Come what may," he said, "I will run." So he said to him, "Run." Then Ahimaaz ran by the way of the plain, and out-ran the Cushite.

<sup>24</sup>Now David was sitting between the two gates; and the watchman went up to the roof of the gate by the wall, and when he lifted up his eyes and looked, he saw a man running alone. <sup>25</sup>And the watchman called out and told the king. And the king said, "If he is alone, there are tidings in his mouth." And he came apace, and drew near. <sup>26</sup>And the watchman saw another man running; and the watchman called to the gate and said, "See, another man running alone!" The king said, "He also brings tidings." <sup>27</sup>And the watchman said, "I think the running of the foremost is like the running of Ahimaaz, the son of Zadok." And the king said, "He is a good man, and comes with good tidings." <sup>28</sup>Then Ahimaaz cried out to the king, "All is well." And he bowed before the king with his face to the earth, and said, "Blessed be the Lord your God, who has delivered up the men who raised their hand against my lord the king." <sup>29</sup>And the king said, "Is it well with the young man Absalom?" Ahimaaz answered, "When Joab sent your servant, I saw a great tumult, but I do not know what it was." <sup>30</sup>And the king said, "Turn aside, and stand here." So he turned aside, and stood still.

<sup>31</sup>And behold, the Cushite came; and the Cushite said, "Good tidings for my lord the king! For the Lord has delivered you this day from the power of all who rose up against you." <sup>32</sup>The king said to the Cushite, "Is it well with the young man Absalom?" And the Cushite answered, "May the enemies of my lord the king, and all who rise up against you for evil, be like that young man." <sup>33</sup>And the king was deeply moved, and went up to the chamber over the gate, and

wept; and as he went, he said, "O my son Absalom, my son, my son Absalom! Would I had died instead of you, O Absalom, my son, my son!"

**19** ¹It was told Joab, "Behold, the king is weeping and mourning for Absalom." ²So the victory that day was turned into mourning for all the people; for the people heard that day, "The king is grieving for his son." ³And the people stole into the city that day as people steal in who are ashamed when they flee in battle. ⁴The king covered his face, and the king cried with a loud voice, "O my son Absalom, O Absalom, my son, my son!" ⁵Then Joab came into the house to the king, and said, "You have today covered with shame the faces of all your servants, who have this day saved your life, and the lives of your sons and your daughters, and the lives of your wives and your concubines, ⁶because you love those who hate you and hate those who love you. For you have made it clear today that commanders and servants are nothing to you; for today I perceive that if Absalom were alive and all of us were dead today, then you would be pleased. ⁷Now therefore arise, go out and speak kindly to your servants; for I swear by the LORD, if you do not go, not a man will stay with you this night; and this will be worse for you than all the evil that has come upon you from your youth until now." ⁸Then the king arose, and took his seat in the gate. And the people were all told, "Behold, the king is sitting in the gate"; and all the people came before the king....

5
10
15
20

# II
# ANCIENT HELLAS

Western civilization is built on the conviction—or, at least, a sneaking suspicion—that things somehow make sense, that our world is ordered, that the universe is a cosmos and not a chaos. As such, it has two distinguishable sources: Hebrew monotheism and Hellenic rationalism; the belief that everything stems from a single, consistent, coherent creative divine will, and the suspicion that there is an eternal natural order. Both visions found full articulation in the sixth century BC—when, from exile in Babylonia, the prophet Isaiah asserted without equivocation that there was no god but Yahweh and that the Jews were called upon to be a light unto the nations; and when, in Miletus on the coast of Asia Minor, Thales (*c.* 624–*c.* 546 BC), Anaximander (*c.* 610–*c.* 546 BC), and Anaximenes (*c.* 585–*c.* 525 BC) each attempted in various ways to give a rational account (*logos*) of the disparate, complex phenomena about them on the basis of a single set of physical principles.

For at least six centuries, Athens and Jerusalem remained at a distance from one another. Thales is said to have been born in the Aramaic-speaking corner of the eastern Mediterranean whence came the Jews, and the Hebrew tradition may have exercised on him a decisive influence, for Aristotle tells us that he and his successors asserted the unity of the divine. But the god embraced by the philosophers was not the God of Abraham, Isaac, and Joseph, for belief in an eternal natural order is incompatible with the doctrine of the creation. In time, however, with the appearance of Christianity and the Gospel of John's assertion that Jesus Christ is the *logos* (rational speech) made flesh, reason and revelation, Hellenism and Hebraism, became inextricably intertwined. The attempt to make sense of the two in relation to one another has been the motor driving the West ever since.

We cannot be certain when the Hellenes—the people whom the Romans were the first to call Greeks—initially made their way to the lower reaches of the Balkan peninsula. We can only say that they were undoubtedly there when civilization made its first inroads into that region, and we can assert without fear of contradiction that the great kingdoms based at Mycenae, Sparta, Pylos, and Thebes, which are depicted in the epics of Homer, were Greek, for ample physical remains have been found at all of the pertinent sites, and the tablets in Linear B script discovered there have been deciphered as Greek. Moreover, the findings of the most recent excavations conducted at Troy and the diplomatic correspondence between the Hittite empire and these early Hellenes now deciphered are perfectly consistent with the later Greek conviction that, in about 1200 BC, there really was a Trojan War, pitting the kingdoms of the Greek mainland against an alien Troy.

These early Greeks were not, however, monotheists. Nor were the Greeks of Homer's and Hesiod's day. The first clear-cut evidence that we have for monotheism is to be found in the fragments of the pre-Socratic philosopher Xenophanes of Colophon (c. 570–c. 480 BC), who lived in Ionia at the time of the Persian conquest; and, like the Milesian philosophers whose intellectual heir he was, he was in no way representative. "Mortal men," he wrote,

> imagine that the gods are begotten and that they have human dress and speech and shape. If oxen or horses or lions had hands to draw with and to make works of art, as men do, then horses would draw the forms of gods like horses and oxen, like oxen, and they would make their gods' shapes similar to the bodily shape that they themselves each had. The Ethiopians say their gods are snub-nosed and black skinned, the Thracians that they are blue-eyed and red-headed. Homer and Hesiod have attributed to the gods everything which brings shame and reproach among men: theft, adultery, and fraud.

Xenophanes denied that "the one god" is in any way "like mortal creatures, either in bodily form or in the thought of his mind." He insisted that "the whole of him sees, the whole of him thinks, the whole of him hears" and that "he always stays motionless in the same place," since "it is not fitting that he should move about now this way, now that." Without effort, he observed, this god "wields all things by the thought of his mind."

In the six centuries that had passed between the Trojan War and the emergence of Greek philosophy, the Hellenic world had evidently changed a great deal. As we now know, the great kingdoms had collapsed in the face of invasions; in Hellas, civilization had disappeared and great migrations took place; and when political order re-emerged, as it did some four centuries later, it took a new and unprecedented form conducive to the emergence of rationalism.

In most regards, this new civilization was less impressive than the old. It was simpler and less grand, it was far less pretentious. But, in one regard, it was truly remarkable—for it conferred authority not on kings claiming divine descent and exercising suzerainty over mandarin bureaucrats trained in the intricacies of syllabic writing and charged with the management of the realm's economy, but on ordinary farmers (all capable of learning to read, thanks to the alphabet) who took responsibility for their own livelihood and defense, and who met at regular intervals in assembly to deliberate in common concerning the advantageous, the just, and the good. These farmers formed what they called a *polis*, using a term meaning citadel or high place, and they took pride in their self-reliance and regarded their participation in politics ("the things of the *polis*") as the central feature of their lives.

Thus, when Alcaeus of Lesbos (*c.* 620–*c.* 580 BC) lamented his fate as an exile, he made it clear that political rivalry was the one thing he really missed. "What a wretch I am," he wrote,

> Condemned by fate to live the life of a country boor.
> I yearn, Agesilaidas, to hear the herald summon the assembly and
>       the council.
> These things which my father and my father's father
> Grew old possessing among the citizens (who do each other
>       harm)—
> From these I am cast out: an exile on the frontiers.
> Like Onomacles, I have made my home in solitude here, and
>       I [plot] war as one
> In whose veins flows the blood of the wolf.

Theognis of Megara would later respond to the prospect of poverty in much the same fashion. To flee it, he wrote, "a man must hurl himself from the high rocks / Into the vastness of the sea. / For poverty will subdue any man / And he will be unable to say or do anything of note: / For his tongue will be tied." And when Euripides pondered the meaning of liberty, he put the following words in the mouth of the leader of Athens: "Being free is this: Whoever wishes to bring useful advice before the public may do so. In this way, whoever longs for eminence can shine—while the man lacking this desire remains silent. What could be more equitable in a city than this?" A quarter of a millennium before Aristotle came on the scene, the Hellenes had come to believe that man is a political animal and that those deprived of participation in public deliberation live subhuman lives.

Behind Greek practice and belief lay an unspoken premise. Those who competed in council and assembly and took such pride in doing so rarely, if ever, stopped to consider the full import of what they were doing. But, in later times, when Xenophon (*c.* 430–354 BC) and Aristotle explained to them the underlying logic of their conduct, they grasped the point immediately. "All creatures," observed the former, "seem in a similar fashion to take pleasure in food, drink, sleep, and sex. But the love of honor does not grow up in animals lacking speech (*alogois*)." Aristotle reiterated the point: What made man a political animal was his possession of *logos*. Other animals could make noise (*phone*), but only human beings reasoned in speech; and in doing so, he implied, they took it for granted that reason is somehow adequate to reality—that the exercise of *logos* in public deliberation is well-suited to successful policymaking. In such an environment, where human beings vied for primacy in applying reason to the management of civic life and did so consistently and customarily as a matter of course, where the *polis* was regarded as a *kosmos* or ordered whole and politics was thought amenable to rational analysis, it was not difficult for men, such as Thales, Anaximander, Anaximenes, and Xenophanes to take the next logical step and consider whether the universe as a whole was not also a *kosmos* of sorts—ordered by a divine principle, if not by a divine personage, and open to inquiry on the part of man.

It would be a mistake to think of the Greeks as rationalists. By and large, they were, in fact, a superstitious lot. But, whether witting or not, they ordered their lives as citizens in accord with what Gottfried Wilhelm Leibniz (1646–1716) on the eve of the Enlightenment would call "the principle of reason's sufficiency," and there were those within their midst who followed through in the most radical fashion on the logic underlying their conduct. If today, we read Herodotus, Thucydides, Plato, Xenophon, and Aristotle, if we study the tragedies of Aeschylus, Sophocles, and Euripides, if we grapple with the comedies of Aristophanes, it is to one degree or another because they reflect this culture of intense political involvement and exemplify the profound ruminations concerning human nature and man's place in the scheme of things that it inspired.

Every one of these figures wrote in or not long after the fifth century BC. All but Herodotus and Aristotle were Athenians, and these two foreigners were more closely associated with Athens than with their city of birth. None of these writers would have been in a position to do what they did had the Greeks in general, and the Athenians in particular, not flourished in this period. That the Hellenes were fated to flourish was not, however, a foregone conclusion. The *polis* emerged at a time when the Greeks were relatively isolated. They were aware of the Assyrian empire, but it was distant, and the Kingdom of Lydia, based at Sardis in Asia Minor, was a threat only to the Greeks living in cities on the Asia Minor coast. Achaemenid Persia, which appeared on the scene in 546 BC when it defeated Lydia, was another matter. It conquered the Ionian coast of Asia Minor soon after seizing Sardis, and in due course it extended its writ to the islands just off the coast. If the Athenians sent aid to the Ionian Greeks when they staged a revolt in 499 BC, it was not entirely an act of generosity. They feared, and rightly so, that the Persian juggernaut would someday come their way; and when that revolt collapsed, it did.

The Achaemenid threat was formidable. Darius I of Persia (*r.* 522–486 BC) ruled a vast empire that extended from Macedonia and Egypt in the west to the Indus Valley in the east, and he had never known defeat. The resources at his command were vast, and he was not inclined to brook resistance. It came, then, as a great shock when he learned that a small city with a population of 30,000 adult men had defeated his armada and slaughtered his men on the plains at Marathon. The Athenians were able to achieve this in part because they were fighting on their own ground in defense of their farms while the Great King of Persia was attempting to project power more than a thousand miles from the center of his realm. They were also able to do so because the military technology of these apparently backward Hellenes was superior to that of the Persians. The latter depended upon artillery, in the form of archers, to break up whatever enemy formation they encountered and then upon cavalry to rout the confused multitude that survived the artillery barrage. They had rarely, if ever, encountered a disciplined phalanx of infantrymen sporting armor capable of deflecting their arrows, and at Marathon they discovered, to their dismay, that horses will not force their way through a wall of shields and that, on uneven ground, where it is impossible to outflank a well-placed infantry line, cavalry is useless against a hoplite phalanx fielded by Greeks.

Athens' victory in 490 BC was an event of world-historical importance. "The battle of Marathon," wrote John Stuart Mill (1806–1873), "even as an event in English history, is more important than the battle of Hastings. If the issue of that day had been different, the Britons and the Saxons might still have been wandering in the woods." Athens' victory left the Greeks free, and the verdict handed down that day was reaffirmed a decade thereafter when Darius's heir Xerxes I (r. 486–465 BC) led a great army and navy into Greece; the Hellenic navy defeated his armada in battle at Salamis; and the Greek infantry overwhelmed the Persians once again at the battle of Plataea. It was their accomplishment in these and subsequent battles that gave the Athenians the supreme sense of confidence that underpins the tragedies of Aeschylus, Sophocles, and Euripides, the comedies of Aristophanes, the histories of Thucydides and Xenophon, and the philosophical activity of Socrates and Plato. It is not fortuitous that the only thing mentioned on Aeschylus's tombstone was his participation in the battle of Marathon. When asked why he had no intention of listing his tragedies, he is said to have replied, "Scraps from the banquet of Homer!"

Of course, the Athenians did not have an unbroken record of success. Within twenty years of their victory at Salamis, they found themselves embroiled in war with Sparta, and that fratricidal struggle lasted, off and on, for nearly sixty years, to the end of the fifth century, when they lost the position of preeminence in Greece that they had secured for themselves in the wake of the Persian Wars. Nor did their defeat pave the way for a Spartan hegemony. Lacedaemon had the requisite ambition, but it was not up to the task, and in the second half of the fourth century BC. Philip II of Macedon (r. 359–336 BC) and his son Alexander the Great (r. 336–323 BC) successfully exploited the divisions in Greece in such a fashion as to establish a lasting Macedonian dominion.

At least initially, however, failure did little harm in Greece to the life of the mind. If anything, the travails of the Hellenes intensified rumination. Herodotus's account of the Persian Wars and of the difficulties encountered by Darius and Xerxes is, at least in part, inspired by reflections on overreaching by Athens. Thucydides' history of the Peloponnesian War is an extended meditation on the Athenian and Spartan regimes caught up in that great contest, and the issues that he raised were never far from the minds of Plato and Aristotle, as even a cursory glance at the regime typology elaborated in *The Republic* and *The Politics* will reveal. If victory, especially when unexpected, inspires great confidence, unanticipated defeat can occasion reflection, and in this case that is precisely what it did.

In Greek, the word *historia* means inquiry, and it was this word, in the plural, that Herodotus deployed to describe his account of the Persian Wars. If we still read the Greeks today, it is because they were the first to engage in *historia* in the natural and in what we call the social sciences, and it is from them that we, their heirs, still learn to frame the inquiries in which we ourselves engage. Wonder is, as Plato's Socrates observes, a very philosophical passion, and wonder is the gift that the Greeks gave us.

# THE HISTORY

## HERODOTUS (*c. 484–425* BC)

*Herodotus, the "Father of History," a Greek from the Ionian coast of Asia Minor, based his history of the Persian Wars on extensive research, including travels in Persia. He believed the conflict could be understood as a clash of cultures, and that the Greeks' victory illustrated the superiority of a free people. He explained that he wrote* The History *"in the hope of thereby preserving from decay the remembrance of what men have done, and of preventing the great and wonderful actions of the Greeks and the Barbarians from losing their due meed of glory; and withal to put on record what were the grounds of their feud." In this selection from Book III, Herodotus depicted a group of prominent Persians discussing the relative merits of monarchy, aristocracy, and democracy. As was customary in ancient historical writing, their speeches are set pieces of Herodotus's composition, and should not be taken as transcripts of actual speeches.*

III§80 And now when five days were gone, and the hubbub had settled down, the conspirators met together to consult about the situation of affairs. At this meeting speeches were made, to which many of the Greeks give no credence, but they were made nevertheless. Otanes recommended that the management of public affairs should be entrusted to the whole nation. "To me," he said, 5 "it seems advisable that we should no longer have a single man to rule over us—the rule of one is neither good nor pleasant. You cannot have forgotten to what lengths Cambyses went in his haughty tyranny, and the haughtiness of the Magi you have yourselves experienced. How indeed is it possible that monarchy should be a well-adjusted thing when it allows a man to do as he likes 10 without being answerable? Such license is enough to stir strange and unwonted thoughts in the heart of the worthiest of men. Give a person this power, and straightway his manifold good things puff him up with pride, while envy is so natural to human kind that it cannot but arise in him. But pride and envy

*The History of Herodotus*, translated by George Rawlinson (New York: Appleton & Company, 1866), 393–95.

together include all wickedness; both leading on to deeds of savage violence. True it is that kings, possessing as they do all that heart can desire, ought to be void of envy, but the contrary is seen in their conduct towards the citizens. They are jealous of the most virtuous among their subjects, and wish their death;

5    while they take delight in the meanest and basest, being ever ready to listen to the tales of slanderers. A king, besides, is beyond all other men inconsistent with himself. Pay him court in moderation, and he is angry because you do not show him more profound respect—show him profound respect, and he is offended again, because (as he says) you fawn on him. But the worst of all

10    is, that he sets aside the laws of the land, puts men to death without trial, and subjects women to violence. The rule of the many, on the other hand, has, in the first place, the fairest of names, to wit, *isonomy*; and further it is free from all those outrages which a king is wont to commit. There, places are given by lot, the magistrate is answerable for what he does, and measures rest with the

15    commonalty. I vote, therefore, that we do away with monarchy, and raise the people to power. For the people are all in all."

III§81 Such were the sentiments of Otanes. Megabyzus spoke next, and advised the setting up of an oligarchy. "In all that Otanes has said to persuade you to put down monarchy," he observed, "I fully concur; but his recommendation

20    that we should call the people to power seems to me not the best advice. For there is nothing so void of understanding, nothing so full of wantonness as the unwieldy rabble. It were folly not to be borne for men, while seeking to escape the wantonness of a tyrant, to give themselves up to the wantonness of a rude unbridled mob. The tyrant, in all his doings, at least knows what he is

25    about, but a mob is altogether devoid of knowledge; for how should there be any knowledge in a rabble, untaught, and with no natural sense of what is right and fit? It rushes wildly into state affairs with all the fury of a stream swollen in the winter, and confuses everything. Let the enemies of the Persians be ruled by democracies; but let us choose out from the citizens a certain number of the

30    worthiest, and put the government into their hands. For thus both we ourselves shall be among the governors, and power being entrusted to the best men, it is likely that the best counsels will prevail in the state."

III§82 This was the advice which Megabyzus gave, and after him Darius came forward, and spoke as follows. "All that Megabyzus said against democracy was

35    well said, I think; but about oligarchy he did not speak advisedly; for take these three forms of government, democracy, oligarchy, and monarchy, and let them each be at their best, I maintain that monarchy far surpasses the other two. What government can possibly be better than that of the very best man in the

whole state? The counsels of such a man are like himself, and so he governs the mass of the people to their heart's content; while at the same time his measures against evil-doers are kept more secret than in other states. Contrariwise, in oligarchies, where men vie with each other in the service of the commonwealth, fierce enmities are apt to arise between man and man, each wishing to be leader, and to carry his own measures; whence violent quarrels come, which lead to open strife, often ending in bloodshed. Then monarchy is sure to follow; and this too shows how far that rule surpasses all others. Again, in a democracy, it is impossible but that there will be malpractices: these malpractices, however, do not lead to enmities, but to close friendships, which are formed among those engaged in them, who must hold well together to carry on their villainies. And so things go on until a man stands forth as champion of the commonalty, and puts down the evil-doers. Straightway the author of so great a service is admired by all, and from being admired soon comes to be appointed king; so that here too it is plain that monarchy is the best government. Lastly, to sum up all in a word, whence, I ask, was it that we got the freedom which we enjoy? Did democracy give it us, or oligarchy, or a monarch? As a single man recovered our freedom for us, my sentence is that we keep to the rule of one. Even apart from this, we ought not to change the laws of our forefathers when they work fairly; for to do so, is not well."

III§83Such were the three opinions brought forward at this meeting; the four other Persians voted in favor of the last. Otanes, who wished to give his countrymen a democracy, when he found the decision against him, arose a second time, and spoke thus before the assembly, "Brother conspirators, it is plain that the king who is to be chosen will be one of ourselves, whether we make the choice by casting lots for the prize, or by letting the people decide which of us they will have to rule over them, or in any other way. Now, as I have neither a mind to rule nor to be ruled, I shall not enter the lists with you in this matter. I withdraw, however, on one condition—none of you shall claim to exercise rule over me or my seed forever." The six agreed to these terms, and Otanes withdrew and stood aloof from the contest. And still to this day the family of Otanes continues to be the only free family in Persia; those who belong to it submit to the rule of the king only so far as they themselves choose; they are bound, however, to observe the laws of the land like the other Persians.

# PERICLES' FUNERAL ORATION
## THUCYDIDES (*c.* 470–*c.* 400 BC)

*During a twenty-year exile from Athens which he incurred as the leader
of a failed military campaign in 423, Thucydides spent his time writing a
history of the Peloponnesian War. In the first book of his* History, *he tells
us about his method and purpose:*

Of the events of the war I have not ventured to speak from any
chance information, nor according to any notion of my own; I have
described nothing but what I either saw myself, or learned from
others of whom I made the most careful and particular inquiry.
The task was a laborious one, because eye-witnesses of the same
occurrences gave different accounts of them, as they remembered
or were interested in the actions of one side or the other. And very
likely the strictly historical character of my narrative may be disap-
pointing to the ear. But if he who desires to have before his eyes
a true picture of the events which have happened, and of the like
events which may be expected to happen hereafter in the order of
human things, shall pronounce what I have written to be useful,
then I shall be satisfied. My history is an everlasting possession, not
a prize composition which is heard and forgotten.

*Thucydides looked for rational causes for events because he believed, as he tells
us in the paragraph just quoted, that similar events would occur in the future
if the same causes were present. He used speeches inserted in his narrative as
vehicles for conveying his analysis, as we see in* Pericles' Funeral Oration,
*in which Thucydides had Pericles compare Athens and Sparta. However,
as he wrote in Book I, "I have...put into the mouth of each speaker the
sentiments proper to the occasion, expressed as I thought he would be likely
to express them, while at the same time I endeavored, as nearly as I could,
to give the general purport of what was actually said." The ideals Pericles
points to were clearly those of mid-fifth century Athenians.*

Thucydides, *The History of the Peloponnesian War*, translated by Rex Warner, with an introduction
and notes by M. I. Finley (Penguin Classics, 1954, Revised edition, 1972), 143–51. Translation
copyright © Rex Warner, 1954. Introduction and Appendices copyright © M. I. Finley, 1972.
Reprinted with permission.

In the same winter the Athenians, following their annual custom, gave a public funeral for those who had been the first to die in the war. These funerals are held in the following way: two days before the ceremony the bones of the fallen are brought and put in a tent which has been erected, and people make whatever
5    offerings they wish to their own dead. Then there is a funeral procession in which coffins of cypress wood are carried on wagons. There is one coffin for each tribe, which contains the bones of members of that tribe. One empty bier is decorated and carried in the procession: this is for the missing, whose bodies could not be recovered. Everyone who wishes to, both citizens and foreign-
10   ers, can join in the procession, and the women who are related to the dead are there to make their laments at the tomb. The bones are laid in the public burial place, which is in the most beautiful quarter outside the city walls. Here the Athenians always bury those who have fallen in war. The only exception is those who died at Marathon, who, because their achievement was considered
15   absolutely outstanding, were buried on the battlefield itself.

When the bones have been laid in the earth, a man chosen by the city for his intellectual gifts and for his general reputation makes an appropriate speech in praise of the dead, and after the speech all depart. This is the procedure at these burials, and all through the war, when the time came to do so, the Athe-
20   nians followed this ancient custom. Now, at the burial of those who were the first to fall in the war Pericles,[1] the son of Xanthippus, was chosen to make the speech. When the moment arrived, he came forward from the tomb and, standing on a high platform, so that he might be heard by as many people as possible in the crowd, he spoke as follows:

25   Many of those who have spoken here in the past have praised the institu-tion of this speech at the close of our ceremony. It seemed to them a mark of honor to our soldiers who have fallen in war that a speech should be made over them. I do not agree. These men have shown themselves valiant in action, and it would be enough, I think, for their glories to be proclaimed in action, as you
30   have just seen it done at this funeral organized by the state. Our belief in the courage and manliness of so many should not be hazarded on the goodness or badness of one man's speech. Then it is not easy to speak with a proper sense of balance, when a man's listeners find it difficult to believe in the truth of what one is saying. The man who knows the facts and loves the dead may well think
35   that an oration tells less than what he knows and what he would like to hear: others who do not know so much may feel envy for the dead, and think the

---

[1]Pericles was the leading statesman in Athens from the late 460s until his death in 429 BC. He presided over the transformation of the Delian League into an Athenian empire, using the trib-ute exacted from the Delian poleis to introduce payment for public service, to support writers and artists, and to rebuild Athenian temples destroyed during the Persian Wars.

orator over-praises them, when he speaks of exploits that are beyond their own capacities. Praise of other people is tolerable only up to a certain point, the point where one still believes that one could do oneself some of the things one is hearing about. Once you get beyond this point, you will find people becoming jealous and incredulous. However, the fact is that this institution was set up and     5 approved by our forefathers, and it is my duty to follow the tradition and do my best to meet the wishes and the expectations of every one of you.

I shall begin by speaking about our ancestors, since it is only right and proper on such an occasion to pay them the honor of recalling what they did. In this land of ours there have always been the same people living from generation to    10 generation up till now, and they, by their courage and their virtues, have handed it on to us a free country. They certainly deserve our praise. Even more so do our fathers deserve it. For to the inheritance they had received they added all the empire we have now, and it was not without blood and toil that they handed it down to us of the present generation. And then we ourselves, assembled here    15 today, who are mostly in the prime of life, have, in most directions, added to the power of our empire and have organized our state in such a way that it is perfectly well able to look after itself both in peace and in war.

I have no wish to make a long speech on subjects familiar to you all, so I shall say nothing about the war-like deeds by which we acquired our power or    20 the battles in which we or our fathers gallantly resisted our enemies, Greek or foreign. What I want to do is, in the first place, to discuss the spirit in which we faced our trials and also our constitution and the way of life which has made us great. After that I shall speak in praise of the dead, believing that this kind of speech is not inappropriate to the present occasion, and that this whole as-    25 sembly, of citizens and foreigners, may listen to it with advantage.

Let me say that our system of government does not copy the institutions of our neighbors. It is more the case of our being a model to others than of our imitating anyone else. Our constitution is called a democracy because power is in the hands not of a minority but of the whole people. When it is a question of    30 settling private disputes, everyone is equal before the law; when it is a question of putting one person before another in positions of public responsibility, what counts is not membership of a particular class, but the actual ability which the man possesses. No one, so long as he has it in him to be of service to the state, is kept in political obscurity because of poverty. And, just as our political life is free    35 and open, so is our day-to-day life in our relations with each other. We do not get into a state with our next-door neighbor if he enjoys himself in his own way, nor do we give him the kind of black looks which, though they do no real harm, still do hurt people's feelings. We are free and tolerant in our private lives; but in public affairs we keep to the law. This is because it commands our deep respect.    40

We give our obedience to those whom we put in positions of authority, and we obey the laws themselves, especially those which are for the protection of the oppressed, and those unwritten laws which it is an acknowledged shame to break.

5   And here is another point. When our work is over, we are in a position to enjoy all kinds of recreation for our spirits. There are various kinds of contests and sacrifices regularly throughout the year; in our own homes we find a beauty and a good taste which delight us every day and which drive away our cares. Then the greatness of our city brings it about that all the good things from all over the world flow in to us, so that to us it seems just as natural to enjoy foreign

10  goods as our own local products.

Then there is a great difference between us and our opponents in our attitude towards military security. Here are some examples: Our city is open to the world, and we have no periodical deportations in order to prevent people observing or finding out secrets which might be of military advantage to the

15  enemy. This is because we rely, not on secret weapons, but on our own real courage and loyalty. There is a difference, too, in our educational systems. The Spartans, from their earliest boyhood, are submitted to the most laborious training in courage; we pass our lives without all these restrictions, and yet are just as ready to face the same dangers as they are. Here is a proof of this: When

20  the Spartans invade our land, they do not come by themselves, but bring all their allies with them; whereas we, when we launch an attack abroad, do the job by ourselves and, though fighting on foreign soil, do not often fail to defeat opponents who are fighting for their own hearths and homes. As a matter of fact, none of our enemies has ever yet been confronted with our total strength,

25  because we have to divide our attention between our navy and the many missions on which our troops are sent on land. Yet, if our enemies engage a detachment of our forces and defeat it, they give themselves credit for having thrown back our entire army; or, if they lose, they claim that they were beaten by us in full strength. There are certain advantages, I think, in our way of meeting danger

30  voluntarily, with an easy mind, instead of with a laborious training, with natural rather than with state-induced courage. We do not have to spend our time practicing to meet sufferings which are still in the future; and when they are actually upon us we show ourselves just as brave as these others who are always in strict training. This is one point in which, I think, our city deserves to be

35  admired. There are also others:

Our love of what is beautiful does not lead to extravagance; our love of the things of the mind does not make us soft. We regard wealth as something to be properly used, rather than as something to boast about. As for poverty, no one need be ashamed to admit it: the real shame is in not taking practical measures

40  to escape from it. Here each individual is interested not only in his own affairs

but in the affairs of the state as well: even those who are mostly occupied with their own business are extremely well-informed on general politics—this is a peculiarity of ours: we do not say that a man who takes no interest in politics is a man who minds his own business; we say that he has no business here at all. We Athenians, in our own persons, take our decisions on policy or submit them to proper discussions: for we do not think that there is an incompatibility between words and deeds; the worst thing is to rush into action before the consequences have been properly debated. And this is another point where we differ from other people. We are capable at the same time of taking risks and of estimating them beforehand. Others are brave out of ignorance; and, when they stop to think, they begin to fear. But the man who can most truly be accounted brave is he who best knows the meaning of what is sweet in life and of what is terrible, and then goes out undeterred to meet what is to come.

Again, in questions of general good feeling there is a great contrast between us and most other people. We make friends by doing good to others, not by receiving good from them. This makes our friendship all the more reliable, since we want to keep alive the gratitude of those who are in our debt by showing continued goodwill to them: whereas the feelings of one who owes us something lack the same enthusiasm, since he knows that, when he repays our kindness, it will be more like paying back a debt than giving something spontaneously. We are unique in this. When we do kindnesses to others, we do not do them out of any calculations of profit or loss: we do them without afterthought, relying on our free liberality. Taking everything together then, I declare that our city is an education to Greece, and I declare that in my opinion each single one of our citizens, in all the manifold aspects of life, is able to show himself the rightful lord and owner of his own person, and do this, moreover, with exceptional grace and exceptional versatility. And to show that this is no empty boasting for the present occasion, but real tangible fact, you have only to consider the power which our city possesses and which has been won by those very qualities which I have mentioned. Athens, alone of the states we know, comes to her testing time in a greatness that surpasses what was imagined of her. In her case, and in her case alone, no invading enemy is ashamed at being defeated, and no subject can complain of being governed by people unfit for their responsibilities. Mighty indeed are the marks and monuments of our empire which we have left. Future ages will wonder at us, as the present age wonders at us now. We do not need the praises of a Homer, or of anyone else whose words may delight us for the moment, but whose estimation of facts will fall short of what is really true. For our adventurous spirit has forced an entry into every sea and into every land; and everywhere we have left behind us everlasting memorials of good done to our friends or suffering inflicted on our enemies.

This, then, is the kind of city for which these men, who could not bear the thought of losing her, nobly fought and nobly died. It is only natural that every one of us who survive them should be willing to undergo hardships in her service. And it was for this reason that I have spoken at such length about

5   our city, because I wanted to make it clear that for us there is more at stake than there is for others who lack our advantages; also I wanted my words of praise for the dead to be set in the bright light of evidence. And now the most important of these words has been spoken. I have sung the praises of our city; but it was the courage and gallantry of these men, and of people like them, which made

10  her splendid. Nor would you find it true in the case of many of the Greeks, as it is true of them, that no words can do more than justice to their deeds.

To me it seems that the consummation which has overtaken these men shows us the meaning of manliness in its first revelation and in its final proof. Some of them, no doubt, had their faults; but what we ought to remember first

15  is their gallant conduct against the enemy in defense of their native land. They have blotted out evil with good, and done more service to the commonwealth than they ever did harm in their private lives. No one of these men weakened because he wanted to go on enjoying his wealth: no one put off the awful day in the hope that he might live to escape his poverty and grow rich. More to

20  be desired than such things, they chose to check the enemy's pride. This, to them, was a risk most glorious, and they accepted it, willing to strike down the enemy and relinquish everything else. As for success or failure, they left that in the doubtful hands of Hope, and when the reality of battle was before their faces, they put their trust in their own selves. In the fighting, they thought it

25  more honorable to stand their ground and suffer death than to give in and save their lives. So they fled from the reproaches of men, abiding with life and limb the brunt of battle; and, in a small moment of time, the climax of their lives, a culmination of glory, not of fear, were swept away from us.

So and such they were these men—worthy of their city. We who remain

30  behind may hope to be spared their fate, but must resolve to keep the same daring spirit against the foe. It is not simply a question of estimating the advantages in theory. I could tell you a long story (and you know it as well as I do) about what is to be gained by beating the enemy back. What I would prefer is that you should fix your eyes every day on the greatness of Athens as

35  she really is, and should fall in love with her. When you realize her greatness, then reflect that what made her great was men with a spirit of adventure, men who knew their duty, men who were ashamed to fall below a certain standard. If they ever failed in an enterprise, they made up their minds that at any rate the city should not find their courage lacking to her, and they gave to her the

40  best contribution that they could. They gave her their lives, to her and to all

of us, and for their own selves they won praises that never grow old, the most splendid of sepulchers—not the sepulcher in which their bodies are laid, but where their glory remains eternal in men's minds, always there on the right occasion to stir others to speech or to action. For famous men have the whole earth as their memorial. It is not only the inscriptions on their graves in their own country that mark them out; no, in foreign lands also, not in any visible form but in people's hearts, their memory abides and grows. It is for you to try to be like them. Make up your minds that happiness depends on being free, and freedom depends on being courageous. Let there be no relaxation in fact of the perils of the war. The people who have most excuse for despising death are not the wretched and unfortunate, who have no hope of doing well for themselves, but those who run the risk of a complete reversal in their lives, and who would feel the difference most intensely if things went wrong for them. Any intelligent man would find a humiliation caused by his own slackness more painful to bear than death, when death comes to him unperceived, in battle, and in the confidence of his patriotism.

For these reasons I shall not commiserate with those parents of the dead, who are present here. Instead I shall try to comfort them. They are well aware that they have grown up in a world where there are many changes and chances. But this is good fortune—for men to end their lives with honor, as these have done, and for you honorably to lament them: their life was set to a measure where death and happiness went hand in hand. I know that it is difficult to convince you of this. When you see other people happy you will often be reminded of what used to make you happy too. One does not feel sad at not having some good thing which is outside one's experience: real grief is felt at the loss of something which one is used to. All the same, those of you who are of the right age must bear up and take comfort in the thought of having more children. In your own homes these new children will prevent you from brooding over those who are no more, and they will be a help to the city, too, both in filling the empty places, and in assuring her security. For it is impossible for a man to put forward fair and honest views about our affairs if he has not, like everyone else, children whose lives may be at stake. As for those of you who are now too old to have children, I would ask you to count as gain the greater part of your life, in which you have been happy, and remember that what remains is not long, and let your hearts be lifted up at the thought of the fair fame of the dead. One's sense of honor is the only thing that does not grow old, and the last pleasure when one is worn out with age, is not, as the poet said, making money, but having the respect of one's fellow men.

As for those of you here who are sons or brothers of the dead, I can see a hard struggle in front of you. Everyone always speaks well of the dead, and, even if you rise to the greatest heights of heroism, it will be a hard thing for you to get the reputation of having come near, let alone equaled, their standard. When one is alive, one is always liable to the jealousy of one's competitors, but when one is out of the way, the honor one receives is sincere and unchallenged.

5    Perhaps I should say a word or two on the duties of women to those among you who are now widowed. I can say all I have to say in a short word of advice. Your great glory is not to be inferior to what God has made you, and the greatest glory of a woman is to be least talked about by men, whether they are praising you or criticizing you. I have now, as the law demanded, said what I

10   had to say. For the time being our offerings to the dead have been made, and for the future their children will be supported at the public expense by the city, until they come of age. This is the crown and prize which she offers, both to the dead and to their children, for the ordeals which they have faced. Where the rewards of valor are the greatest, there you will find also the best and brav-

15   est spirits among the people. And now, when you have mourned for your dear ones, you must depart.'

# CRITO
## PLATO (427–347 BC)

*Virtually everything we know about Socrates (c. 469–399 BC) comes from the work of his devoted pupil Plato. Although Socrates features in many of Plato's dialogues, we come closest to the man himself in the group which tells the story of his death.*

*In 399 BC, the Athenian poet Meletus and others haled Socrates before an Athenian court on charges of having corrupted the youth of Athens and having attempted to undermine the city's religion. In* The Apology, *Plato recorded Socrates' defense at his trial. In an attempt to prove wrong the Delphic oracle, which had said that there was no man wiser than he, Socrates went to a series of men who had reputations for wisdom. When he questioned them, he discovered that in fact they were not wise at all:*

The effect of these investigations of mine, gentlemen, has been to arouse against me a great deal of hostility, and hostility of a particularly bitter and persistent kind, which has resulted in various malicious suggestions, including the description of me as a professor of wisdom. This is due to the fact that whenever I succeed in disproving another person's claim to wisdom in a given subject, the bystanders assume that I know everything about that subject myself. But the truth of the matter, gentlemen, is pretty certainly this: that real wisdom is the property of God, and this oracle is his way of telling us that human wisdom has little or no value. It seems to me that he is not referring literally to Socrates, but has merely taken my name as an example, as if he would say to us "The wisest of you men is he who has realized, like Socrates, that in respect of wisdom he is really worthless."

That is why I still go about seeking and searching in obedience to the divine command, if I think that anyone is wise, whether citizen

Plato, *The Last Days of Socrates*, translated with an introduction by Hugh Tredennick (Penguin Classics, 1954, Third edition, 1969), 52, 61–62, 79–96. Copyright © Hugh Tredennick, 1954, 1959, 1969. Reprinted with permission.

or stranger; and when I think that any person is not wise, I try to help the cause of God by proving that he is not....

*Socrates then told the court what his response would be if they offered to acquit him on the condition that he give up philosophy:*

Gentlemen, I am your very grateful and devoted servant, but I owe a greater obedience to God than to you; and so long as I draw breath and have my faculties, I shall never stop practising philosophy and exhorting you and elucidating the truth for everyone that I meet.... I shall do this to everyone that I meet, young or old, foreigner or fellow-citizen; but especially to you my fellow-citizens, inasmuch as you are closer to me in kinship. This, I do assure you, is what my God commands; and it is my belief that no greater good has ever befallen you in this city than my service to my God; for I spend all my time going about trying to persuade you, young and old, to make your first and chief concern not for your bodies nor for your possessions, but for the highest welfare of your souls, proclaiming as I go 'Wealth does not bring goodness, but goodness brings wealth and every other blessing, both to the individual and to the state.' Now if I corrupt the young by this message, the message would seem to be harmful; but if anyone says that my message is different from this, he is talking nonsense. And so, gentlemen, I would say, 'You can please yourselves whether you listen to Anytus or not, and whether you acquit me or not; you know that I am not going to alter my conduct, not even if I have to die a hundred deaths.'

*Likening himself to a gadfly attacking a sluggish horse, Socrates urged the Athenians to accept his exhortations and reproaches as a gift from God and spare his life for their own sakes. However, the court convicted him and sentenced him to death.*

*In* Crito, *the scene shifts to Socrates' prison cell nearly a month later. Socrates' friends had spent the time since his trial attempting to arrange his escape. They had reckoned without Socrates' own refusal to be rescued.*

**Socrates:** Here already, Crito? Surely it is still early?
**Crito:** Indeed it is.
**Socrates:** About what time?
**Crito:** Just before dawn.
5    **Socrates:** I wonder that the warder paid any attention to you.
**Crito:** He is used to me now, Socrates, because I come here so often; besides, he is under some small obligation to me.
**Socrates:** Have you only just come, or have you been here for long?

Crito: Fairly long.

Socrates: Then why didn't you wake me at once, instead of sitting by my bed so quietly?

Crito: I wouldn't dream of such a thing, Socrates. I only wish I were not so sleepless and depressed myself. I have been wondering at you, because I saw how comfortably you were sleeping; and I deliberately didn't wake you because I wanted you to go on being as comfortable as you could. I have often felt before in the course of my life how fortunate you are in your disposition, but I feel it more than ever now in your present misfortune when I see how easily and placidly you put up with it.

Socrates: Well, really, Crito, it would be hardly suitable for a man of my age to resent having to die.

Crito: Other people just as old as you are get involved in these misfortunes, Socrates, but their age doesn't keep them from resenting it when they find themselves in your position.

Socrates: Quite true. But tell me, why have you come so early?

Crito: Because I bring bad news, Socrates; not so bad from your point of view, I suppose, but it will be very hard to bear for me and your other friends, and I think that I shall find it hardest of all.

Socrates: Why, what is this news? Has the boat come in from Delos—the boat which ends my reprieve when it arrives?

Crito: It hasn't actually come in yet, but I expect that it will be here to-day, judging from the report of some people who have just arrived from Sunium and left it there. It's quite clear from their account that it will be here to-day; and so by to-morrow, Socrates, you will have to—to end your life.

Socrates: Well, Crito, I hope that it may be for the best; if the gods will it so, so be it. All the same, I don't think it will arrive today.

Crito: What makes you think that?

Socrates: I will try to explain. I think I am right in saying that I have to die on the day after the boat arrives?

Crito: That's what the authorities say, at any rate.

Socrates: Then I don't think it will arrive on this day that is just beginning, but on the day after. I am going by a dream that I had in the night, only a little while ago. It looks as though you were right not to wake me up.

Crito: Why, what was the dream about?

Socrates: I thought I saw a gloriously beautiful woman dressed in white robes, who came up to me and addressed me in these words: 'Socrates, To the pleasant land of Phthia on the third day you shall come.'

Crito: Your dream makes no sense, Socrates.

Socrates: To my mind, Crito, it is perfectly clear.

Crito: Too clear, apparently. But look here, Socrates, it is still not too late to take my advice and escape. Your death means a double calamity for me. I shall not only lose a friend whom I can never possibly replace, but besides a great many people who don't know you and me very well will be sure to think
5  that I let you down, because I could have saved you if I had been willing to spend the money; and what could be more contemptible than to get a name for thinking more of money than of your friends? Most people will never believe that it was you who refused to leave this place although we tried our hardest to persuade you.

10  Socrates: But my dear Crito, why should we pay so much attention to what 'most people' think? The really reasonable people, who have more claim to be considered, will believe that the facts are exactly as they are.

Crito: You can see for yourself, Socrates, that one has to think of popular opinion as well. Your present position is quite enough to show that the capacity of
15  ordinary people for causing trouble is not confined to petty annoyances, but has hardly any limits if you once get a bad name with them.

Socrates: I only wish that ordinary people *had* an unlimited capacity for doing harm; then they might have an unlimited power for doing good; which would be a splendid thing, if it were so. Actually they have neither. They cannot
20  make a man wise or stupid; they simply act at random.

Crito: Have it that way if you like; but tell me this, Socrates. I hope that you aren't worrying about the possible effects on me and the rest of your friends, and thinking that if you escape we shall have trouble with informers for having helped you to get away, and have to forfeit all our property or pay
25  an enormous fine, or even incur some further punishment? If any idea like that is troubling you, you can dismiss it altogether. We are quite entitled to run that risk in saving you, and even worse, if necessary. Take my advice, and be reasonable.

Socrates: All that you say is very much in my mind, Crito, and a great deal
30  more besides.

Crito: Very well, then, don't let it distress you. I know some people who are willing to rescue you from here and get you out of the country for quite a moderate sum. And then surely you realize how cheap thee informers are to buy off; we shan't need much money to settle them; and I think you've got
35  enough of my money for yourself already. And then even supposing that in your anxiety for my safety you feel that you oughtn't to spend my money, there are these foreign gentlemen staying in Athens who are quite willing to spend theirs. One of them, Simmias of Thebes, has actually brought the money with him for this very purpose; and Cebes and a number of others
40  are quite ready to do the same. So as I say, you mustn't let any fears on these

grounds make you slacken your efforts to escape; and you mustn't feel any misgivings about what you said at your trial, that you wouldn't know what to do with yourself if you left this country. Wherever you go, there are plenty of places where you will find a welcome; and if you choose to go to Thessaly, I have friends there who will make much of you and give you complete protection, so that no one in Thessaly can interfere with you.

Besides, Socrates, I don't even feel that it is right for you to try to do what you are doing, throwing away your life when you might save it. You are doing your best to treat yourself in exactly the same way as your enemies would, or rather did, when they wanted to ruin you. What is more, it seems to me that you are letting your sons down, too. You have it in your power to finish their bringing up and education, and instead of that you are proposing to go off and desert them, and so far as you are concerned they will have to take their chance. And what sort of chance are they likely to get? The sort of thing that usually happens to orphans when they lose their parents. Either one ought not to have children at all, or one ought to see their upbringing and education through to the end. It strikes me that you are taking the line of least resistance, whereas you ought to make the choice of a good man and a brave one, considering that you profess to have made goodness your object all through life. Really, I am ashamed, both on your account and on ours your friends'; it will look as though we had played something like a coward's part all through this affair of yours. First there was the way you came into court when it was quite unnecessary—that was the first act; then there was the conduct of the defense—that was the second; which makes it appear that we have let you slip out of our hands through some lack of courage and enterprise on our part, because we didn't save you, and you didn't save yourself, when it would have been quite possible and practicable, if we had been any use at all.

There, Socrates; if you aren't careful, besides the suffering there will be all this disgrace for you and us to bear. Come, make up your mind. Really it's too late for that now; you ought to have it made up already. There is no alternative; the whole thing must be carried through during this coming night. If we lose any more time, it can't be done, it will be too late. I appeal to you, Socrates, on every ground; take my advice and please don't be unreasonable!

Socrates: My dear Crito, I appreciate your warm feelings very much—that is, assuming that they have some justification; if not, the stronger they are, the harder they will be to deal with. Very well, then; we must consider whether we ought to follow your advice or not. You know that this is not a new idea of mine; it has always been my nature never to accept advice from any of my friends unless reflection shows that it is the best course that reason offers. I cannot abandon the principles which I used to hold in the past simply because this accident has happened to me; they seem to me to be much as they were, and I respect and regard the same principles now as before. So

5 unless we can find better principles on this occasion, you can be quite sure that I shall not agree with you; not even if the power of the people conjures up fresh hordes of bogies to terrify our childish minds, by subjecting us to chains and executions and confiscations of our property.

Well, then, how can we consider the question most reasonably? Sup-
10 pose that we begin by reverting to this view which you hold about people's opinions. Was it always right to argue that some opinions should be taken seriously but not others? Or was it always wrong? Perhaps it was right before the question of my death arose, but now we can see clearly that it was a mistaken persistence in a point of view which was really irresponsible nonsense.
15 I should like very much to inquire into this problem, Crito, with your help, and to see whether the argument will appear in any different light to me now that I am in this position, or whether it will remain the same; and whether we shall dismiss it or accept it.

Serious thinkers, I believe, have always held some such view as the one
20 which I mentioned just now: that some of the opinions which people entertain should be respected, and others should not. Now I ask you, Crito, don't you think that this is a sound principle?—You are safe from the prospect of dying tomorrow, in all human probability; and you are not likely to have your judgment upset by this impending calamity. Consider, then; don't you
25 think that this is a sound enough principle, that one should not regard all the opinions that people hold, but only some and not others? What do you say? Isn't that a fair statement?

Crito: Yes, it is.

Socrates: In other words, one should regard the good ones and not the bad?
30 Crito: Yes.

Socrates: The opinions of the wise being good, and the opinions of the foolish bad?

Crito: Naturally.

Socrates: To pass on, then: what do you think of the sort of illustration that I
35 used to employ? When a man is in training, and taking it seriously, does he pay attention to all praise and criticism and opinion indiscriminately, or only when it comes from the one qualified person, the actual doctor or trainer?

Crito: Only when it comes from the one qualified person.

Socrates: Then he should be afraid of the criticism and welcome the praise of
40 the one qualified person, but not those of the general public.

Crito: Obviously.

Socrates: So he ought to regulate his actions and exercises and eating and drinking by the judgment of his instructor, who has expert knowledge, rather than by the opinions of the rest of the public.

Crito: Yes, that is so. 5

Socrates: Very well. Now if he disobeys the one man and disregards his opinion and commendations, and pays attention to the advice of the many who have no expert knowledge, surely he will suffer some bad effect?

Crito: Certainly.

Socrates: And what is this bad effect? Where is it produced?—I mean, in what 10 part of the disobedient person?

Crito: His body, obviously; that is what suffers.

Socrates: Very good. Well now, tell me, Crito—we don't want to go through all the examples one by one—does this apply as a general rule, and above all to the sort of actions which we are trying to decide about: just and unjust, 15 honourable and dishonourable, good and bad? Ought we to be guided and intimidated by the opinion of the many or by that of the one—assuming that there is someone with expert knowledge? Is it true that we ought to respect and fear this person more than all the rest put together; and that if we do not follow his guidance we shall spoil and mutilate that part of us which, as 20 we used to say, is improved by right conduct and destroyed by wrong? Or is this all nonsense?

Crito: No, I think it is true, Socrates.

Socrates: Then consider the next step. There is a part of us which is improved by healthy actions and ruined by unhealthy ones. If we spoil it by taking the 25 advice of non-experts, will life be worth living when this part is once ruined? The part I mean is the body; do you accept this?

Crito: Yes.

Socrates: Well, is life worth living with a body which is worn out and ruined in health? 30

Crito: Certainly not.

Socrates: What about the part of us which is mutilated by wrong actions and benefitted by right ones? Is life worth living with this part ruined? Or do we believe that this part of us, whatever it may be, in which right and wrong operate, is of less importance than the body? 35

Crito: Certainly not.

Socrates: Is it really more precious?

Crito: Much more.

Socrates: In that case, my dear fellow, what we ought to consider is not so much what people in general will say about us but how we stand with the expert 40 in right and wrong, the one authority, who represents the actual truth. So in the first place your proposition is not correct when you say that we should consider popular opinion in questions of what is right and honorable and good, or the opposite. Of course one might object 'All the same, the people

5    have the power to put us to death.'

**Crito:** No doubt about that! Quite true, Socrates; it is a possible objection.

**Socrates:** But so far as I can see, my dear fellow, the argument which we have just been through is quite unaffected by it. At the same time I should like you to consider whether we are still satisfied on this point: that the really

10    important thing is not to live, but to live well.

**Crito:** Why, yes.

**Socrates:** And that to live well means the same thing as to live honourably or rightly?

**Crito:** Yes.

15  **Socrates:** Then in the light of this agreement we must consider whether or not it is right for me to try to get away without an official discharge. If it turns out to be right, we must make the attempt; if not, we must let it drop. As for the considerations you raise about expense and reputation and bringing up children, I am afraid, Crito, that they represent the reflections of the

20    ordinary public, who put people to death, and would bring them back to life if they could, with equal indifference to reason. Our real duty, I fancy, since the argument leads that way, is to consider one question only, the one which we raised just now: Shall we be acting rightly in paying money and showing gratitude to these people who are going to rescue me, and in escap-

25    ing or arranging the escape ourselves, or shall we really be acting wrongly in doing all this? If it becomes clear that such conduct is wrong, I cannot help thinking that the question whether we are sure to die, or to suffer any other ill effect for that matter, if we stand our ground and take no action, ought not to weigh with us at all in comparison with the risk of doing what

30    is wrong.

**Crito:** I agree with what you say, Socrates; but I wish you would consider what we ought to *do*.

**Socrates:** Let us look at it together, my dear fellow; and if you can challenge any of my arguments, do so and I will listen to you; but if you can't, be a good

35    fellow and stop telling me over and over again that I ought to leave this place without official permission. I am very anxious to obtain your approval before I adopt the course which I have in mind; I don't want to act against your convictions. Now give your attention to the starting point of this inquiry—I hope that you will be satisfied with my way of stating it—and try to answer

40    my questions to the best of your judgment.

**Crito:** Well, I will try.

**Socrates:** Do we say that one must never willingly do wrong, or does it depend upon circumstances? Is it true, as we have often agreed before, that there is no sense in which wrongdoing is good or honourable? Or have we jettisoned all our former convictions in these last few days? Can you and I at our age, 5 Crito, have spent all these years in serious discussions without realizing that we were not better than a pair of children? Surely the truth is just what we have always said. Whatever the popular view is, and whether the alternative is pleasanter than the present one or even harder to bear, the fact remains that to do wrong is in every sense bad and dishonourable for the person who 10 does it. Is that our view, or not?

**Crito:** Yes, it is.

**Socrates:** Then in no circumstances must one do wrong.

**Crito:** No.

**Socrates:** In that case one must not even do wrong when one is wronged, which 15 most people regard as the natural course.

**Crito:** Apparently not.

**Socrates:** Tell me another thing, Crito: ought one to do injuries or not?

**Crito:** Surely not, Socrates.

**Socrates:** And tell me: is it right to do an injury in retaliation, as most people 20 believe, or not?

**Crito:** No, never.

**Socrates:** Because, I suppose, there is no difference between injuring people and wronging them.

**Crito:** Exactly. 25

**Socrates:** So one ought not to return a wrong or an injury to any person, whatever the provocation is. Now be careful, Crito, that in making these single admissions you do not end by admitting something contrary to your real beliefs. I know that there are and always will be few people who think like this; and consequently between those who do think so and those 30 who do not there can be no agreement on principle; they must always feel contempt when they observe one another's decisions. I want even you to consider very carefully whether you share my views and agree with me, and whether we can proceed with our discussion from the established hypothesis that it is never right to do a wrong or return a wrong or defend one's self 35 against injury by retaliation; or whether you dissociate yourself from any share in this view as a basis for discussion. I have held it for a long time, and still hold it; but if you have formed any other opinion, say so and tell me what it is. If, on the other hand, you stand by what we have said, listen to my next point. 40

**Crito:** Yes, I stand by it and agree with you. Go on.

**Socrates:** Well, here is my next point, or rather question. Ought one to fulfill all one's agreements, provided that they are right, or break them?

**Crito:** One ought to fulfill them.

5 **Socrates:** Then consider the logical consequence. If we leave this place without first persuading the State to let us go, are we or are we not doing an injury, and doing it in a quarter where it is least justifiable? Are we or are we not abiding by our first agreements?

**Crito:** I can't answer your question, Socrates; I am not clear in my mind.

10 **Socrates:** Look at it in this way. Suppose that while we were preparing to run away from here (or however one should describe it) the Laws and Constitution of Athens were to come and confront us and ask this question: 'Now, Socrates, what are you proposing to do? Can you deny that by this act which you are contemplating you intend, so far as you have the power, to destroy us, the

15 laws, and the whole state as well? Do you imagine that a city can continue to exist and not be turned upside down, if the legal judgments which are pronounced in it have no force but are nullified and destroyed by private persons?'—how shall we answer this question, Crito, and others of the same kind? There is much that could be said, especially by a professional advocate,

20 to protest against the invalidation of this law which enacts that judgments once pronounced shall be binding. Shall we say 'Yes, I do intend to destroy the laws, because the state wronged me by passing a faulty judgment at my trial'? Is this to be our answer, or what?

**Crito:** What you have just said, by all means, Socrates.

25 **Socrates:** Then what supposing the Laws say 'Was there provision for this in the agreement between you and us, Socrates? Or did you undertake to abide by whatever judgments the state pronounced?' If we expressed surprise at such language, they would probably say: 'Never mind our language, Socrates, but answer our questions; after all, you are accustomed to the method of question

30 and answer. Come now, what charge to you bring against us and the State, that you are trying to destroy us? Did we not give you life in the first place? Was it not through us that your father married your mother and begot you? Tell us, have you any complaint against those of us Laws that deal with marriage?' 'No, none,' I should say. 'Well, have you any against the laws which

35 deal with children's upbringing and education, such as you had yourself? Are you not grateful to those of us Laws which were instituted for this end, for requiring your father to give you a cultural and physical education?' 'Yes,' I should say. 'Very good. Then since you have been born and brought up and educated, can you deny, in the first place, that you were our child and

40 servant, both you and your ancestors? And if this is so, do you imagine that

what is right for us is equally right for you, and that whatever we try to do
to you, you are justified in retaliating? You did not have equality of rights
with your father, or your employer (supposing that you had had one), to
enable you to retaliate; you were not allowed to answer back when you were
scolded or to hit back when you were beaten, or to do a great many other     5
things of the same kind. Do you expect to have such licence against your
country and its laws that if we try to put you to death in the belief that it is
right to do so, you on your part will try your hardest to destroy your country
and us its Laws in return? And will you, the true devotee of goodness, claim
that you are justified in doing so? Are you so wise as to have forgotten that   10
compared with your mother and father and all the rest of your ancestors
your country is something far more precious, more venerable, more sacred,
and held in greater honour both among gods and among all reasonable men?
Do you not realize that you are even more bound to respect and placate the
anger of your country than your father's anger? that if you cannot persuade   15
your country you must do whatever it orders, and patiently submit to any
punishment that it imposes, whether it be flogging or imprisonment? And
if it leads you out to war, to be wounded or killed, you must comply, and it
is right that you should do so; you must not give way or retreat or abandon
your position. Both in war and in the law-courts and everywhere else you   20
must do whatever your city and your country commands, or else persuade
it in accordance with universal justice; but violence is a sin even against your
parents, and it is a far greater sin against your country.' What shall we say to
this, Crito?—That what the Laws say is true, or not?

**Crito:** Yes, I think so.   25

**Socrates:** 'Consider, then, Socrates,' the Laws would probably continue, 'whether
it is also true for us to say that what you are now trying to do to us is not right.
Although we have brought you into the world and reared you and educated
you, and given you and all your fellow-citizens a share in all the good things
at our disposal, nevertheless by the very fact of granting our permission we   30
openly proclaim this principle: that any Athenian, on attaining to manhood
and seeing for himself the political organization of the state and us its Laws,
is permitted, if he is not satisfied with us, to take his property and go away
wherever he likes. If any of you chooses to go to one of our colonies, supposing that he should not be satisfied with us and the state, or to emigrate to any   35
other country, not one of us laws hinders or prevents him from going away
wherever he likes, without any loss of property. On the other hand, if any
one of you stands his ground when he can see how we administer justice and
the rest of our public organization, we hold that by so doing he has in fact
undertaken to do anything that we tell him; and we maintain that anyone   40

who disobeys is guilty of doing wrong on three separate counts: first because we are his parents, and secondly because we are his guardians; and thirdly because, after promising obedience, he is neither obeying us nor persuading us to change our decision if we are at fault in any way; and although all our orders are in the form of proposals, not of savage commands, and we give him the choice of either persuading us or doing what we say, he is actually doing neither. These are the charges, Socrates, to which we say that you will be liable if you do what you are contemplating; and you will not be the least culpable of your fellow-countrymen, but one of the most guilty.' If I said 'Why do you say that?' they would no doubt pounce upon me with perfect justice and point out that there are very few people in Athens who have entered into this agreement with them as explicitly as I have. They would say 'Socrates, we have substantial evidence that you are satisfied with us and with the State. You would not have been so exceptionally reluctant to cross the borders of your country if you had not been exceptionally attached to it. You have never left the city to attend a festival or for any other purpose, except on some military expedition; you have never traveled abroad as other people do, and you have never felt the impulse to acquaint yourself with another country or constitution; you have been content with us and with our city. You have definitely chosen us, and undertaken to observe us in all your activities as a citizen; and as the crowning proof that you are satisfied with our city, you have begotten children in it. Furthermore, even at the time of your trial you could have proposed the penalty of banishment, if you had chosen to do so; that is, you could have done then with the sanction of the state what you are now trying to do without it. But whereas at that time you made a noble show of indifference if you had to die, and in fact preferred death, as you said, to banishment, now you show no respect for your earlier professions, and no regard for us, the Laws, whom you are trying to destroy; you are behaving like the lowest type of menial, trying to run away in spite of the contracts and undertakings by which you agreed to live as a member of our state. Now first answer this question: Are we or are we not speaking the truth when we say that you have undertaken, in deed if not in word, to live your life as a citizen in obedience to us?'

What are we to say to that, Crito? Are we not bound to admit it?

**Crito:** We cannot help it, Socrates.

**Socrates:** 'It is a fact, then,' they would say, 'that you are breaking covenants and undertakings made with us, although you made them under no compulsion or misunderstanding, and were not compelled to decide in a limited time; you had seventy years in which you could have left the country, if you were not satisfied with us or felt that the agreements were unfair. You did not

choose Sparta or Crete—your favourite models of good government—or
any other Greek or foreign state; you could not have absented yourself from
the city less if you had been lame or blind or decrepit in some other way.
It is quite obvious that you stand by yourself above all other Athenians in
your affection for this city and for us, its Laws—who would care for a city          5
without laws? And now, after all this, are you not going to stand by your
agreement? Yes, you are, Socrates, if you will take our advice; and then you
will at least escape being laughed at for leaving the city.'

'We invite you to consider what good you will do to yourself or your friends
if you commit this breach of faith and stain your conscience. It is fairly obvi-          10
ous that the risk of being banished and either losing their citizenship or having
their property confiscated will extend to your friends as well. As for yourself,
if you go to one of the neighbouring states, such as Thebes or Megara, which
are both well governed, you will enter them as an enemy to their constitution, and all good patriots will eye you with suspicion as a destroyer of law          15
and order. Incidentally you will confirm the opinion of the jurors who tried
you that they gave a correct verdict; a destroyer of laws might very well be
supposed to have a destructive influence upon young and foolish human
beings. Do you intend, then, to avoid well governed states and the higher
forms of human society? and if you do, will life be worth living? Or will you          20
approach these people and have the impudence to converse with them? What
arguments will you use, Socrates? The same which you used here, that goodness and integrity, institutions and laws, are the most precious possessions
of mankind? Do you not think that Socrates and everything about him will
appear in a disreputable light? You certainly ought to think so. But perhaps          25
you will retire from this part of the world and go to Crito's friends in Thessaly?
That is the home of indiscipline and laxity, and no doubt they would enjoy
hearing the amusing story of how you managed to run away from prison by
arraying yourself in some costume or putting on a shepherd's smock or some
other conventional runaway's disguise, and altering your personal appearance.          30
And will no one comment on the fact that an old man of your age, probably
with only a short time left to live, should dare to cling so greedily to life,
at the price of violating the most stringent laws? Perhaps not, if you avoid
irritating anyone. Otherwise, Socrates, you will hear a good many humiliating
comments. So you will live as the toady and slave of all the populace, liter-          35
ally "roystering in Thessaly," as though you had left this country for Thessaly
to attend a banquet there; and where will your discussions about goodness
and uprightness be then, we should like to know? But of course you want
to live for your children's sake, so that you may be able to bring them up
and educate them. Indeed! by first taking them off to Thessaly and making          40

foreigners of them, so that they may have that additional enjoyment? Or if that is not your intention, supposing that they are brought up here with you still alive, will they be better cared for and educated without you, because of course your friends will look after them? Will they look after your children if you go away to Thessaly, and not if you go away to the next world? Surely if those who profess to be your friends are worth anything, you must believe that they would care for them.

'No, Socrates; be advised by us your guardians, and do not think more of your children or of your life or of anything else than you think of what is right; so that when you enter the next world you may have all this to plead in your defense before the authorities there. It seems clear that if you do this thing, neither you nor any of your friends will be the better for it or be more upright or have a cleaner conscience here in this world, nor will it be better for you when you reach the next. As it is, you will leave this place, when you do, as the victim of a wrong done not by us, the Laws, but by your fellowmen. But if you leave in that dishonourable way, returning wrong for wrong and evil for evil, breaking your agreements and covenants with us, and injuring those whom you least ought to injure—yourself, your friends, your country, and us—then you will have to face our anger in your lifetime, and in that place beyond when the laws of the other world know that you have tried, so far as you could, to destroy even us their brothers, they will not receive you with a kindly welcome. Do not take Crito's advice, but follow ours.'

That, my dear friend Crito, I do assure you, is what I seem to hear them saying, just as a mystic seems to hear the strains of music; and the sound of their arguments rings so loudly in my head that I cannot hear the other side. I warn you that, as my opinion stands at present, it will be useless to urge a different view. However, if you think that you will do any good by it, say what you like.

**Crito:** No, Socrates, I have nothing to say.

**Socrates:** Then give it up, Crito, and let us follow this course, since God points out the way.

# THE REPUBLIC
## PLATO (427–347 BC)

*In these sections from Books VIII and IX of* The Republic, *Socrates and his students discover the connection between order in the city and order in the soul, between the constitution of government and the constitution of individual character. Earlier, in Book VII, Socrates used an allegory of human bondage and liberation to ponder how the soul turns and rises from ignorance and illusion to reason and truth.*

**Socrates:** Democracy, I suppose, should come next. A study of its rise and character should help us to recognize the democratic type of man and set him beside the others for judgment.

**Glaucon:** Certainly that course would fit in with our plan.

**Socrates:** If the aim of life in an oligarchy is to become as rich as possible, that 5 insatiable craving would bring about the transition to democracy. In this way: since the power of the ruling class is due to its wealth, they will not want to have laws restraining prodigal young men from ruining themselves by extravagance. They will hope to lend these spendthrifts money on their property and buy it up, so as to become richer and more influential than 10 ever. We can see at once that a society cannot hold wealth in honor and at the same time establish a proper self-control in its citizens. One or the other must be sacrificed.

**Glaucon:** Yes, that is fairly obvious.

**Socrates:** In an oligarchy, then, this neglect to curb riotous living sometimes 15 reduces to poverty men of a not ungenerous nature. They settle down in idleness, some of them burdened with debt, some disfranchised, some both at once; and these drones are armed and can sting. Hating the men who have acquired their property and conspiring against them and the rest of society, they long for a revolution. Meanwhile the usurers, intent upon their own 20 business, seem unaware of their existence; they are too busy planting their

*Republic of Plato*, translated by Francis MacDonald Cornford (Oxford: Clarendon Press, 1941), 222–29, 274–92. By permission of Oxford University Press.

own stings into any fresh victim who offers them an opening to inject the poison of their money; and while they multiply their capital by usury, they are also multiplying the drones and the paupers. When the danger threatens to break out, they will do nothing to quench the flames, either in the way we mentioned, by forbidding a man to do what he likes with his own, or by the next best remedy, which would be a law enforcing a respect for right conduct. If it were enacted that, in general, voluntary contracts for a loan should be made at the lender's risk, there would be less of this shameless pursuit of wealth and a scantier crop of those evils I have just described.

**Glaucon:** Quite true.

**Socrates:** But, as things are, this is the plight to which the rulers of an oligarchy, for all these reasons, reduce their subjects. As for themselves, luxurious indolence of body and mind makes their young men too lazy and effeminate to resist pleasure or to endure pain; and the fathers, neglecting everything but money, have no higher ideals in life than the poor. Such being the condition of rulers and subjects, what will happen when they are thrown together, perhaps as fellow-travelers by sea or land to some festival or on a campaign, and can observe one another's demeanor in a moment of danger? The rich will have no chance to feel superior to the poor. On the contrary, the poor man, lean and sunburnt, may find himself posted in battle beside one who, thanks to his wealth and indoor life, is panting under his burden of fat and showing every mark of distres. 'Such men', he will think, 'are rich because we are cowards'; and when he and his friends meet in private, the word will go round: 'These men are no good: they are at our mercy.'

**Glaucon:** Yes, that is sure to happen.

**Socrates:** This state, then, is in the same precarious condition as a person so unhealthy that the least shock from outside will upset the balance or, even without that, internal disorder will break out. It falls sick and is at war with itself on the slightest occasion, as soon as one party or the other calls in allies from a neighboring oligarchy or democracy; and sometimes civil war begins with no help from without.

**Glaucon:** Quite true.

**Socrates:** And when the poor win, the result is a democracy. They kill some of the opposite party, banish others, and grant the rest an equal share in civil rights and government, officials being usually appointed by lot.

**Glaucon:** Yes, that is how a democracy comes to be established, whether by force of arms or because the other party is terrorized into giving way.

**Socrates:** Now what is the character of this new régime? Obviously the way they govern themselves will throw light on the democratic type of man.

**Glaucon:** No doubt.

**Socrates:** First of all, they are free. Liberty and free speech are rife everywhere; anyone is allowed to do what he likes.

**Glaucon:** Yes, so we are told.

**Socrates:** That being so, every man will arrange his own manner of life to suit his pleasure. The result will be a greater variety of individuals than under 5 any other constitution. So it may be the finest of all, with its variegated pattern of all sorts of characters. Many people may think it the best, just as women and children might admire a mixture of colors of every shade in the pattern of a dress. At any rate if we are in search of a constitution, here is a good place to look for one. A democracy is so free that it contains a sample 10 of every kind; and perhaps anyone who intends to found a state, as we have been doing, ought first to visit this emporium of constitutions and choose the model he likes best.

**Glaucon:** He will find plenty to choose from.

**Socrates:** Here, too, you are not obliged to be in authority, however competent 15 you may be, or to submit to authority, if you do not like it; you need not fight when your fellow citizens are at war, nor remain at peace when they do, unless you want peace; and though you may have no legal right to hold office or sit on juries, you will do so all the same if the fancy takes you. A wonderfully pleasant life, surely, for the moment. 20

**Glaucon:** For the moment, no doubt.

**Socrates:** There is a charm, too, in the forgiving spirit shown by some who have been sentenced by the courts. In a democracy you must have seen how men condemned to death or exile stay on and go about in public, and no one takes any more notice than he would of a spirit that walked invisible. There 25 is so much tolerance and superiority to petty considerations; such a contempt for all those fine principles we laid down in founding our commonwealth, as when we said that only a very exceptional nature could turn out a good man, if he had not played as a child among things of beauty and given himself only to creditable pursuits. A democracy tramples all such notions 30 under foot; with a magnificent indifference to the sort of life a man has led before he enters politics, it will promote to honor anyone who merely calls himself the people's friend.

**Glaucon:** Magnificent indeed.

**Socrates:** These then, and such as these, are the features of a democracy, an agree- 35 able form of anarchy with plenty of variety and an equality of a peculiar kind for equals and unequals alike.

**Glaucon:** All that is notoriously true.

**Socrates:** Now consider the corresponding individual character. Or shall we take his origin first, as we did in the case of the constitution? 40

**Glaucon:** Yes.

**Socrates:** I imagine him as the son of our miserly oligarch, brought up under his father's eye and in his father's ways. So he too will enforce a firm control over all such pleasures as lead to expense rather than profit—unnecessary pleasures, as they have been called. But, before going farther, shall we draw the distinction between necessary and unnecessary appetites, so as not to argue in the dark?

**Glaucon:** Please do so.

**Socrates:** There are appetites which cannot be got rid of, and there are all those which it does us good to fulfill. Our nature cannot help seeking to satisfy both these kinds; so they may fairly be described as necessary. On the other hand, 'unnecessary' would be the right name for all appetites which can be got rid of by early training and which do us no good and in some cases do harm. Let us take an example of each kind, so as to form a general idea of them. The desire to eat enough plain food—just bread and meat—to keep in health and good condition may be called necessary. In the case of bread the necessity is twofold, since it not only does us good but is indispensable to life; whereas meat is only necessary in so far as it helps to keep us in good condition. Beyond these simple needs the desire for a whole variety of luxuries is unnecessary. Most people can get rid of it by early discipline and education; and it is as prejudicial to intelligence and self-control as it is to bodily health. Further, these unnecessary appetites might be called expensive, whereas the necessary ones are rather profitable, as helping a man to do his work. The same distinctions could be drawn in the case of sexual appetite and all the rest.

**Glaucon:** Yes.

**Socrates:** Now, when we were speaking just now of drones, we meant the sort of man who is under the sway of a host of unnecessary pleasures and appetites, in contrast with our miserly oligarch, over whom the necessary desires are in control. Accordingly, we can now go back to describe how the democratic type develops from the oligarchical. I imagine it usually happens in this way. When a young man, bred, as we were saying, in a stingy and uncultivated home, has once tasted the honey of the drones and keeps company with those dangerous and cunning creatures, who know how to purvey pleasures in all their multitudinous variety, then the oligarchical constitution of his soul begins to turn into a democracy. The corresponding revolution was effected in the state by one of the two factions calling in the help of partisans from outside. In the same way one of the conflicting sets of desires in the soul of this youth will be reinforced from without by a group of kindred passions; and if the resistance of the oligarchical faction in him is strengthened by remonstrances and reproaches coming from his father, perhaps, or his friends, the opposing parties will soon be battling within him. In some cases the democratic interest yields to the oligarchical: a sense of shame gains a footing in the young man's soul, and some appetites are crushed, others banished, until order is restored. 5

Glaucon: Yes, that happens sometimes.

Socrates: But then again, perhaps, owing to the father's having no idea how to bring up his son, another brood of desires, akin to those which were banished, are secretly nursed up until they become numerous and strong. These draw the young man back into clandestine commerce with his old associates, 10 and between them they breed a whole multitude. In the end, they seize the citadel of the young man's soul, finding it unguarded by the trusty sentinels which keep watch over the minds of men favored by heaven. Knowledge, right principles, true thoughts, are not at their post; and the place lies open to the assault of false and presumptuous notions. So he turns again to those 15 lotus-eaters and now throws in his lot with them openly. If his family send reinforcements to the support of his thrifty instincts, the impostors who have seized the royal fortress shut the gates upon them, and will not even come to parley with the fatherly counsels of individual friends. In the internal conflict they gain the day; modesty and self-control, dishonored and 20 insulted as the weaknesses of an unmanly fool, are thrust out into exile; and the whole crew of unprofitable desires take a hand in banishing moderation and frugality, which, as they will have it, are nothing but churlish meanness. So they take possession of the soul which they have swept clean, as if purified for initiation into higher mysteries; and nothing remains but 25 to marshal the great procession bringing home Insolence, Anarchy, Waste, and Impudence, those resplendent divinities crowned with garlands, whose praises they sing under flattering names: Insolence they call good breeding, Anarchy freedom, Waste magnificence, and Impudence a manly spirit. Is not that a fair account of the revolution which gives free rein to unnecessary 30 and harmful pleasures in a young man brought up in the satisfaction only of the necessary desires?

Glaucon: Yes, it is a vivid description.

Socrates: In his life thenceforward he spends as much time and pains and money on his superfluous pleasures as on the necessary ones. If he is lucky enough 35 not to be carried beyond all bounds, the tumult may begin to subside as he grows older. Then perhaps he may recall some of the banished virtues and cease to give himself up entirely to the passions which ousted them; and now he will set all his pleasures on a footing of equality, denying to none its equal rights and maintenance, and allowing each in turn, as it presents 40 itself, to succeed, as if by the chance of the lot, to the government of his soul until it is satisfied. When he is told that some pleasures should be sought and valued as arising from desires of a higher order, others chastised and enslaved because the desires are base, he will shut the gates of the citadel against the

5    messengers of truth, shaking his head and declaring that one appetite is as good as another and all must have their equal rights. So he spends his days indulging the pleasure of the moment, now intoxicated with wine and music, and then taking to a spare diet and drinking nothing but water; one day in hard training, the next doing nothing at all, the third apparently immersed

10   in study. Every now and then he takes a part in politics, leaping to his feet to say or do whatever comes into his head. Or he will set out to rival someone he admires, a soldier it may be, or, if the fancy takes him, a man of business. His life is subject to no order or restraint, and he has no wish to change an existence which he calls pleasant, free, and happy.

15   **Glaucon:** That well describes the life of one whose motto is liberty and equality.

**Socrates:** Yes, and his character contains the same fine variety of pattern that we found in the democratic state; it is as multifarious as that epitome of all types of constitution. Many a man, and many a woman too, will find in it something to envy. So we may see in him the counterpart of democracy, and

20   call him the democratic man.

**Glaucon:** We may.

**Socrates:** Now there remains only the most admired of all constitutions and characters—despotism and the despot. How does despotism arise? That it comes out of democracy is fairly clear. Does the change take place in the

25   same sort of way as the change from oligarchy to democracy? Oligarchy was established by men with a certain aim in life: the good they sought was wealth, and it was the insatiable appetite for money-making to the neglect of everything else that proved its undoing. Is democracy likewise ruined by greed for what it conceives to be the supreme good?

30   **Glaucon:** What good do you mean?

**Socrates:** Liberty. In a democratic country you will be told that liberty is its noblest possession, which makes it the only fit place for a free spirit to live in.

**Glaucon:** True; that is often said.

**Socrates:** Well then, as I was saying, perhaps the insatiable desire for this good

35   to the neglect of everything else may transform a democracy and lead to a demand for despotism. A democratic state may fall under the influence of unprincipled leaders, ready to minister to its thirst for liberty with too deep draughts of this heady wine; and then, if its rulers are not complaisant enough to give it unstinted freedom, they will be arraigned as accursed oligarchs

40   and punished. Law-abiding citizens will be insulted as nonentities who hug

their chains; and all praise and honor will be bestowed, both publicly and in private, on rulers who behave like subjects and subjects who behave like rulers. In such a state the spirit of liberty is bound to go to all lengths.

Glaucon: Inevitably.

Socrates: It will make its way into the home, until at last the very animals  5
catch the infection of anarchy. The parent falls into the habit of behaving like the child, and the child like the parent: the father is afraid of his sons, and they show no fear or respect for their parents, in order to assert their freedom. Citizens, resident aliens, and strangers from abroad are all on an equal footing. To descend to smaller matters, the schoolmaster timidly flat-  10
ters his pupils, and the pupils make light of their masters as well as of their attendants. Generally speaking, the young copy their elders, argue with them, and will not do as they are told; while the old, anxious not to be thought disagreeable tyrants, imitate the young and condescend to enter into their jokes and amusements. The full measure of popular liberty is reached when  15
the slaves of both sexes are quite as free as the owners who paid for them; and I had almost forgotten to mention the spirit of freedom and equality in the mutual relations of men and women.

Glaucon: Well, to quote Aeschylus, we may as well speak 'the word that rises to our lips'.  20

Socrates: Certainly; so I will. No one who had not seen it would believe how much more freedom the domestic animals enjoy in a democracy than elsewhere. The very dogs behave as if the proverb 'like mistress, like maid' applied to them; and the horses and donkeys catch the habit of walking down the street with all the dignity of freemen, running into anyone they  25
meet who does not get out of their way. The whole place is simply bursting with the spirit of liberty.

Glaucon: No need to tell me that. I have often suffered from it on my way out of the town.

Socrates: Putting all these items together, you can see the result: the citizens  30
become so sensitive that they resent the slightest application of control as intolerable tyranny, and in their resolve to have no master they end by dis-regarding even the law, written or unwritten.

Glaucon: Yes, I know that only too well.

Socrates: Such then, I should say, is the seed, so full of fair promise, from which  35
springs despotism.

Glaucon: Promising indeed. But what is the next stage?

Socrates: The same disease that destroyed oligarchy breaks out again here, with all the more force because of the prevailing license, and enslaves democ-racy. The truth is that, in the constitution of society, quite as much as in  40

the weather or in plants and animals, any excess brings about an equally violent reaction. So the only outcome of too much freedom is likely to be excessive subjection, in the state or in the individual; which means that the culmination of liberty in democracy is precisely what prepares the way for
5    the cruelest extreme of servitude under a despot. But I think you were asking rather about the nature of that disease which afflicts democracy in common with oligarchy and reduces it to slavery.

**Glaucon:** Yes, I was.

**Socrates:** What I had in mind was that set of idle spendthrifts, among whom the
10    bolder spirits take the lead. We compared these leaders, if you remember, to drones armed with stings, the stingless drones being their less enterprising followers. In any society where these two groups appear they create disorder, as phlegm and bile do in the body. Hence the lawgiver, as a good physician of the body politic, should take measures in advance, no less than the prudent
15    bee-keeper who tries to forestall the appearance of drones, or, failing that, cuts them out, cells and all, as quickly as he can.

**Glaucon:** Quite true.

**Socrates:** Then, to gain a clearer view of our problem, let us suppose the demo-cratic commonwealth to be divided into three parts, as in fact it is. One
20    consists of the drones we have just described. Bred by the spirit of licence, in a democracy this class is no less numerous and much more energetic than in an oligarchy, where it is despised and kept out of office and so remains weak for lack of exercise. But in a democracy it furnishes all the leaders, with a few exceptions; its keenest members make the speeches and transact
25    the business, while the other drones settle on the benches round, humming applause to drown any opposition. Thus nearly the whole management of the commonwealth is in its hands.

**Glaucon:** Quite true.

**Socrates:** Meanwhile, a second group is constantly emerging from the mass.
30    Where everyone is bent upon making money, the steadiest characters tend to amass the greatest wealth. Here is a very convenient source from which the drones can draw an abundance of honey.

**Glaucon:** No doubt; they cannot squeeze any out of men of small means.

**Socrates:** 'The rich,' I believe, is what they call this class which provides prov-
35    ender for the drones.

**Glaucon:** Yes.

**Socrates:** The third class will be the 'people', comprising all the peasantry who work their own farms, with few possessions and no interest in politics. In a democracy this is the largest class and, when once assembled, its power
40    is supreme.

**Glaucon:** Yes, but it will not often meet, unless it gets some share of the honey.

**Socrates:** Well, it always does get its share, when the leaders are distributing to the people what they have taken from the well-to-do, always provided they can keep the lion's share for themselves. The plundered rich are driven to     5
defend themselves in debate before the Assembly and by any measures they can compass; and then, even if they have no revolutionary designs, the other party accuse them of plotting against the people and of being reactionary oligarchs. At last, when they see the people unwittingly misled by such denunciation into attempts to treat them unjustly, then, whether they wish     10
it or not, they become reactionaries in good earnest. There is no help for it; the poison is injected by the sting of those drones we spoke of. Then follow impeachments and trials, in which each party arraigns the other.

**Glaucon:** Quite so.

**Socrates:** And the people always put forward a single champion of their interests,     15
whom they nurse to greatness. Here, plainly enough, is the root from which despotism invariably springs.

**Glaucon:** Yes.

**Socrates:** How does the transformation of the people's champion into a despot begin? You have heard the legend they tell of the shrine of Lycaean Zeus in     20
Arcadia: how one who tastes a single piece of human flesh mixed in with the flesh of the sacrificial victims is fated to be changed into a wolf. In the same way the people's champion, finding himself in full control of the mob, may not scruple to shed a brother's blood; dragging him before a tribunal with the usual unjust charges, he may foully murder him, blotting out a man's life     25
and tasting kindred blood with unhallowed tongue and lips; he may send men to death or exile with hinted promises of debts to be cancelled and estates to be redistributed. Is it not thenceforth his inevitable fate either to be destroyed by his enemies or to seize absolute power and be transformed from a human being into a wolf?     30

**Glaucon:** It is.

**Socrates:** Here, then, we have the party-leader in the civil war against property. If he is banished, and then returns from exile in despite of his enemies, he will come back a finished despot. If they cannot procure his banishment or death by denouncing him to the state, they will conspire to assassinate him.     35
Then comes the notorious device of all who have reached this stage in the despot's career, the request for a body guard to keep the people's champion safe for them. The request is granted, because the people, in their alarm on his account, have no fear for themselves.

**Glaucon:** Quite true.     40

**Socrates:** This is a terrifying sight for the man of property, who is charged with being not merely rich but the people's enemy. He will follow the oracle's advice to Croesus,

> To flee by Hermus' pebbly shore,
> Dreading the coward's shame no more.

**Glaucon:** Well, he would have little chance to dread it a second time.

**Socrates:** True; if he is caught, no doubt he will be done to death; whereas our champion himself does not, like Hector's charioteer, 'measure his towering length in dust,' but on the contrary, overthrows a host of rivals and stands erect in the chariot of the state, no longer protector of the people, but its absolute master.

**Glaucon:** Yes, it must come to that.

**Socrates:** And now shall we describe the happy condition of the man and of the country which harbors a creature of this stamp?

**Glaucon:** By all means.

**Socrates:** In the early days he has a smile and a greeting for everyone he meets; disclaims any absolute power; makes large promises to his friends and to the public; sets about the relief of debtors and the distribution of land to the people and to his supporters; and assumes a mild and gracious air towards everybody. But as soon as he has disembarrassed himself of his exiled enemies by coming to terms with some and destroying others, he begins stirring up one war after another, in order that the people may feel their need of a leader, and also be so impoverished by taxation that they will be forced to think of nothing but winning their daily bread, instead of plotting against him. Moreover, if he suspects some of cherishing thoughts of freedom and not submitting to his rule, he will find a pretext for putting them at the enemy's mercy and so making away with them. For all these reasons a despot must be constantly provoking wars.

**Glaucon:** He must.

**Socrates:** This course will led to his being hated by his countrymen more and more. Also, the bolder spirits among those who have helped him to power and now hold positions of influence will begin to speak their mind to him and among themselves and to criticize his policy. If the despot is to maintain his rule, he must gradually make away with all these malcontents, until he has not a friend or an enemy left who is of any account. He will need to keep a sharp eye open for anyone who is courageous or high-minded or intelligent or rich; it is his happy fate to be at war with all such, whether he likes it or not, and to lay his plans against them until he has purged the commonwealth.

**Glaucon:** A fine sort of purgation!

**Socrates:** Yes, the exact opposite of the medical procedure, which removes the worst elements in the bodily condition and leaves the best.

**Glaucon:** There seems to be no choice, if he is to hold his power.

**Socrates:** No; he is confined to the happy alternatives of living with people most of whom are good for nothing and who hate him into the bargain, 5 or not living at all. And the greater the loathing these actions inspire in his countrymen, the more he will need trustworthy recruits to strengthen his bodyguard. Where will he turn to find men on whom he can rely?

**Glaucon:** They will come flocking of their own accord, if he offers enough pay. 10

**Socrates:** Foreigners of all sorts, you mean—yet another swarm of drones. But why not draw upon the home supply? He could rob the citizens of their slaves, emancipate them, and enroll them in his bodyguard.

**Glaucon:** No doubt they would be the most faithful adherents he could find.

**Socrates:** What an enviable condition for the despot, to put his trust in such 15 friends as these, when he has made away with his earlier supporters! He will, of course, be the admiration of all this band of new-made citizens, whose company he will enjoy when every decent person shuns him with loathing. It is not for nothing that the tragic drama is thought to be a storehouse of wisdom, and above all Euripides, whose profundity of thought appears in 20 the remark that 'despots grow wise by converse with the wise', meaning no doubt by the wise these associates we have described.

**Glaucon:** Yes, and Euripides praises absolute power as godlike, with much more to the same effect. So do the other poets.

**Socrates:** That being so, the tragedians will give a further proof of their wisdom 25 if they will excuse us and all states whose constitution resembles ours, when we deny them admittance on the ground that they sing the praises of despotism. At the same time, I expect they will go the round of other states, where they will hire actors with fine sonorous voices to sway the inclination of the assembled crowd towards a despotic or a democratic constitution. Naturally 30 they are honored and well paid for these services, by despots chiefly, and in a less degree by democracies. But the higher they mount up the scale of commonwealths, the more their reputation flags, like a climber who gives in for lack of breath. However, we are wandering from our subject. Let us go back to the despot's army. How is he to maintain this fine, ever-shifting 35 array of nondescripts?

**Glaucon:** No doubt he will spend any treasure there may be in the temples, so long as it will last, as well as the property of his victims, thus lightening the war-taxes imposed on the people.

**Socrates:** And when the source fails? 40

**Glaucon:** Clearly he will support himself, with his boon-companions, minions, and mistresses, from his parent's estate.

**Socrates:** I understand: the despot and his comrades will be maintained by the common people which gave him birth.

5 **Glaucon:** Inevitably.

**Socrates:** But how if the people resent this and say it is not right for the father to support his grown-up son—it ought to be the other way about; they did not bring him into being and set him up in order that, when he had grown great, they should be the slaves of their own slaves and support them together

10 with their master and the rest of his rabble; he was to be the champion to set them free from the rich and the so-called upper class. Suppose they now order him and his partisans to leave the country, as a father might drive his son out of the house along with his riotous friends?

**Glaucon:** Then, to be sure, the people will learn what sort of a creature it has

15 bred and nursed to greatness in its bosom, until now the child is too strong for the parent to drive out.

**Socrates:** Do you mean that the despot will dare to lay violent hands on this father of his and beat him if he resists?

**Glaucon:** Yes, when once he has disarmed him.

20 **Socrates:** So the despot is a parricide, with no pity for the weakness of age. Here, it seems, is absolutism openly avowed. The people, as they say, have escaped the smoke only to fall into the fire, exchanging service to free men for the tyranny of slaves. That freedom which knew no bounds must now put on the livery of the most harsh and bitter servitude, where the slave has

25 become the master.

**Glaucon:** Yes, that is what happens.

**Socrates:** May we say, then, that we have now sufficiently described the transition from democracy to despotism, and what despotism is like when once established?

30 **Glaucon:** Yes, quite sufficiently.

**Socrates:** Last comes the man of despotic character. It remains to ask how he develops from the democratic type, what he is like, and whether his life is one of happiness or of misery.

**Glaucon:** Yes.

35 **Socrates:** Here I feel the need to define, more fully than we have so far done, the number and nature of the appetites. Otherwise it will not be so easy to see our way to a conclusion.

**Glaucon:** Well, it is not too late.

**Socrates:** Quite so. Now, about the appetites, here is the point I want to make

40 plain. Among the unnecessary pleasures and desires, some, I should say, are

unlawful. Probably they are innate in every one; but when they are disciplined by law and by the higher desires with the aid of reason, they can in some people be got rid of entirely, or at least left few and feeble, although in others they will be comparatively strong and numerous.

**Glaucon:** What kind of desires do you mean? 5

**Socrates:** Those which bestir themselves in dreams, when the gentler part of the soul slumbers and the control of reason is withdrawn; then the wild beast in us, full-fed with meat or drink, becomes rampant and shakes off sleep to go in quest of what will gratify its own instincts. As you know, it will cast away all shame and prudence at such moments and stick at nothing. In fantasy it 10 will not shrink from intercourse with a mother or anyone else, man, god, or brute, or from forbidden food or any deed of blood. In a word, it will go to any length of shamelessness and folly.

**Glaucon:** Quite true.

**Socrates:** It is otherwise with a man sound in body and mind, who, before he 15 goes to sleep, awakens the reason within him to feed on high thoughts and questionings in collected meditation. If he has neither starved nor surfeited his appetites, so that, lulled to rest, no delights or griefs of theirs may trouble that better part, but leave it free to reach out, in pure and independent thought, after some new knowledge of things past, present, or to come; if, 20 likewise, he has soothed his passions so as not to fall asleep with his anger roused against any man; if, in fact, he does not take his rest until he has quieted two of the three elements in his soul and awakened the third wherein wisdom dwells, then he is in a fair way to grasp the truth of things, and the visions of his dreams will not be unlawful. However, we have been carried 25 away from our point, which is that in every one of us, even those who seem most respectable, there exist desires, terrible in their untamed lawlessness, which reveal themselves in dreams. Do you agree?

**Glaucon:** I do.

**Socrates:** Remember, then, our account of the democratic man, how his character 30 was shaped by his early training under a parsimonious father, who respected only the businesslike desires, dismissing the unnecessary ones as concerned with frivolous embellishments. Then, associating with more sophisticated people who were a prey to those lawless appetites we have just described, he fell into their ways, and hatred of his father's miserliness drove him into 35 every sort of extravagance. But, having a better disposition than his corrupters, he came to a compromise between the two conflicting ways of life, making the best of both with what he called moderation and avoiding alike the meanness of the one and the license of the other. So the oligarchical man was transformed into the democratic type. 40

**Glaucon:** Yes, I hold by that description.

**Socrates:** Now imagine him grown old in his turn, with a young son bred in his ways, who is exposed to the same influences, drawn towards the utter lawlessness which his seducers call perfect freedom, while on the other side
5    his father and friends lend their support to the compromise. When those terrible wizards who would conjure up an absolute ruler in the young man's soul begin to doubt the power of their spells, in the last resort they contrive to engender in him a master passion, to champion the mob of idle appetites which are for dividing among themselves all available plunder—a passion
10   that can only be compared to a great winged drone. Like a swarm buzzing round this creature, the other desires come laden with incense and perfumes, garlands and wine, feeding its growth to the full on the pleasures of a dissolute life, until they have implanted the sting of a longing that cannot be satisfied. Then at last this passion, as leader of the soul, takes madness for
15   the captain of its guard and breaks out in frenzy; if it can lay hold upon any thoughts or desires that are of good report and still capable of shame, it kills them or drives them forth, until it has purged the soul of all sobriety and called in the partisans of madness to fill the vacant place.

**Glaucon:** That is a complete picture of how the despotic character develops.
20   **Socrates:** Is not this the reason why lust has long since been called a tyrant? A drunken man, too, has something of this tyrannical spirit; and so has the lunatic who dreams that he can lord it over all mankind and heaven besides. Thus, when nature or habit or both have combined the traits of drunkenness, lust, and lunacy, then you have the perfect specimen of the despotic man.
25   **Glaucon:** Quite true....

## The Allegory of the Cave

**Socrates:** Next, said I, here is a parable to illustrate the degrees in which our nature may be enlightened or unenlightened. Imagine the condition of men living in a sort of cavernous chamber underground, with an entrance open to the light and a long passage all down the cave. Here they have been from
30   childhood, chained by the leg and also by the neck, so that they cannot move and can see only what is in front of them, because the chains will not let them turn their heads. At some distance higher up is the light of a fire burning behind them; and between the prisoners and the fire is a track with a parapet built along it, like the screen at a puppet-show, which hides the
35   performers while they show their puppets over the top.

**Glaucon:** I see, said he.

**Socrates:** Now behind this parapet imagine persons carrying along various artificial objects, including figures of men and animals in wood or stone or other materials, which project above the parapet. Naturally, some of these persons will be talking, others silent.

**Glaucon:** It is a strange picture, he said, and a strange sort of prisoners.                                    5

**Socrates:** Like ourselves, I replied; for in the first place prisoners so confined would have seen nothing of themselves or of one another, except the shadows thrown by the fire-light on the wall of the Cave facing them, would they?

**Glaucon:** Not if all their lives they had been prevented from moving their heads.                                    10

**Socrates:** And they would have seen a little of the objects carried past.

**Glaucon:** Of course.

**Socrates:** Now, if they could talk to one another, would they not suppose that their words referred only to those passing shadows which they saw?

**Glaucon:** Necessarily.                                    15

**Socrates:** And suppose their prison had an echo from the wall facing them? When one of the people crossing behind them spoke, they could only suppose that the sound came from the shadow passing before their eyes.

**Glaucon:** No doubt.

**Socrates:** In every way, then, such prisoners would recognize as reality nothing    20 but the shadows of those artificial objects.

**Glaucon:** Inevitably.

**Socrates:** Now consider what would happen if their release from the chains and the healing of their unwisdom should come about in this way. Suppose one of them set free and forced suddenly to stand up, turn his head, and walk with    25 eyes lifted to the light; all these movements would be painful, and he would be too dazzled to make out the objects whose shadows he had been used to see. What do you think he would say, if someone old him that what he had formerly seen was meaningless illusion, but now, being somewhat nearer to reality and turned towards more real objects, he was getting a truer view?    30 Suppose further that he were shown the various objects being carried by and were made to say, in reply to questions, what each of them was. Would he not be perplexed and believe the objects now shown him to be not so real as what he formerly saw?

**Glaucon:** Yes, not nearly so real.                                    35

**Socrates:** And if he were forced to look at the fire-light itself, would not his eyes ache, so that he would try to escape and turn back to the things which he could see distinctly, convinced that they really were clearer than these other objects now being shown to him?

**Glaucon:** Yes.

**Socrates:** And suppose someone were to drag him away forcibly up the steep and rugged ascent and not let him go until he had hauled him out into the sunlight, would he not suffer pain and vexation at such treatment, and, when
5        he had come out into the light, find his eyes so full of its radiance that he could not see a single one of the things that he was now told were real?

**Glaucon:** Certainly he would not see them all at once.

**Socrates:** He would need, then, to grow accustomed before he could see things in that upper world. At first it would be easiest to make out shadows, and
10       then the images of men and things reflected in water, and later on the things themselves. After that, it would be easier to watch the heavenly bodies and the sky itself by night, looking at the light of the moon and stars rather than the Sun and the Sun's light in the day-time.

**Glaucon:** Yes, surely.

15   **Socrates:** Last of all, he would be able to look at the Sun and contemplate its nature, not as it appears when reflected in water or any alien medium, but as it is in itself in its own domain.

**Glaucon:** No doubt.

**Socrates:** And now he would begin to draw the conclusion that it is the Sun that
20       produces the seasons and the course of the year and controls everything in the visible world, and moreover is in a way the cause of all that he and his companions used to see.

**Glaucon:** Clearly he would come at last to the conclusion.

**Socrates:** Then if he called to mind his fellow prisoners and what passed for
25       wisdom in his former dwelling-place, he would surely think himself happy in the change and be sorry for them. They may have had a practice of honoring and commending one another, with prizes for the man who had the keenest eye for the passing shadows and the best memory for the order in which they followed or accompanied one another, so that he could make a good guess
30       as to which was going to come next. Would our released prisoner be likely to covet those prizes or to envy the men exalted to honor and power in the Cave? Would he not feel like Homer's Achilles, that he would far sooner 'be on earth as a hired servant in the house of a landless man or endure anything rather than go back to his old beliefs and live in the old way?

35   **Glaucon:** Yes, he would prefer any fate to such a life.

**Socrates:** Now imagine what would happen if he went down again to take his former seat in the Cave. Coming suddenly out of the sunlight, his eyes would be filled with darkness. He might be required once more to deliver his opinion on those shadows, in competition with the prisoners who had
40       never been released, while his eyesight was still dim and unsteady; and it

might take some time to become used to the darkness. They would laugh at him and say that he had gone up only to come back with his sight ruined; it was worth no one's while even to attempt the ascent. If they could lay hands on the man who was trying to set them free and lead them up, they would kill him.                                                                                          5

Glaucon: Yes, they would.

Socrates: Every feature in this parable, my dear Glaucon, is meant to fit our earlier analysis. The prison dwelling corresponds to the region revealed to us through the sense of sight, and the firelight within it to the power of the Sun. The ascent to see the things in the upper world you may take as standing   10 for the upward journey of the soul into the region of the intelligible; then you will be in possession of what I surmise, since that is what you wish to be told. Heaven knows whether it is true; but this, at any rate, is how it appears to me. In the world of knowledge, the last thing to be perceived and only with great difficulty is the essential Form of Goodness. Once it is perceived,   15 the conclusion must follow that, for all things, this is the cause of whatever is right and good; in the visible world it gives birth to light and to the lord of light, while it is itself sovereign in the intelligible world and the parent of intelligence and truth. Without having had a vision of this Form no one can act with wisdom, either in his own life or in matters of state.                        20

Glaucon: So far as I can understand, I share your belief.

Socrates: Then you may also agree that it is no wonder if those who have reached this height are reluctant to manage the affairs of men. Their souls long to spend all their time in that upper world—naturally enough, if here once more our parable holds true. Nor, again, is it at all strange that one who   25 comes from the contemplation of divine things to the miseries of human life should appear awkward and ridiculous when, with eyes still dazed and not yet accustomed to the darkness, he is compelled, in a law-court or elsewhere, to dispute about the shadows of justice or the images that cast those shadows, and to wrangle over the notions of what is right in the minds of men who   30 have never beheld Justice itself.

Glaucon: It is not at all strange.

Socrates: No; a sensible man will remember that the eyes may be confused in two ways—by a change from light to darkness or from darkness to light; and he will recognize that the same thing happens to the soul. When he   35 sees it troubled and unable to discern anything clearly, instead of laughing thoughtlessly, he will ask whether, coming from a brighter existence, its un-accustomed vision is obscured by the darkness, in which case he will think its condition enviable and its life a happy one; or whether, emerging from the depths of ignorance, it is dazzled by excess of light. if so, he will rather   40 feel sorry for it; or, if he were inclined to laugh, that would be less ridiculous than to laugh at the soul which has come down from the light.

**Glaucon:** That is a fair statement.

**Socrates:** If this is true, then, we must conclude that education is not what it is said to be by some, who profess to put knowledge into a soul which does not possess it, as if they could put sight into blind eyes. On the contrary, our own account signifies that the soul of every man does possess the power of learning the truth and the organ to see it with; and that, just as one might have to turn the whole body round in order that the eye should see light instead of darkness, so the entire soul must be turned away from this changing world, until its eye can bear to contemplate reality and that supreme splendor which we have called the Good. Hence there may well be an art whose aim would be to effect this very thing, the conversion of the soul, in the readiest way; not to put the power of sight into the soul's eye, which already has it, but to ensure that, instead of looking in the wrong direction, it is turned the way it ought to be.

**Glaucon:** Yes it may well be so.

**Socrates:** It looks, then, as though wisdom were different from those ordinary virtues, as they are called, which are not far removed from bodily qualities, in that they can be produced by habituation and exercise in a soul which has not possessed them from the first. Wisdom, it seems, is certainly the virtue of some diviner faculty, which never loses its power, though its use for good or harm depends on the direction towards which it is turned. You must have noticed in dishonest men with a reputation for sagacity the shrewd glance of a narrow intelligence piercing the objects to which it is directed. There is nothing wrong with their power of vision, but it has been forced into the service of evil, so that the keener its sight, the ore harm it works.

**Glaucon:** Quite true.

**Socrates:** And yet if the growth of a nature like this had been pruned from earliest childhood, cleared of those clinging overgrowths which come of gluttony and all luxurious pleasure and, like leaden weights charged with affinity to this mortal world, hang upon the soul, bending its vision downwards; if, freed from these, the soul were turned round towards true reality, then this same power in these very men would see the truth as keenly as the objects it is turned to now....

# THE POLITICS
## ARISTOTLE (384–322 BC)

*Unlike Plato, who believed that reality existed in a separate world of Forms and was therefore to be sought through introspection, Aristotle thought that one might discern reality through observation of existing phenomena. Thus, whereas Plato constructed a purely imaginary republic in keeping with his views of the just state, Aristotle examined the actual workings of more than a 150 different Greek poleis to determine the kind of political system most likely to promote the good life. His starting point is his assumption that "man is by nature an animal intended to live in a polis."*

*Aristotle categorized nearly all of the knowledge of his day in any number of subjects: philosophy, political philosophy, music, literature, poetry, theology, and zoology. As world historian William McNeill has argued, "one seems to confront not a man so much as a thinking machine" when meeting this Macedonian philosopher and student of Plato's. This proved true in ethics as well. In Aristotle's thinking, man is a being of action. Consequently, he should act with moderation, prudence, and self-respect. No longer could the polis provide all answers as it had in the youth of Socrates. Man, by Aristotle's time, through reason and observation, must find his own answers in nature and in himself.*

All associations aim at some good; and the particular association which is the most sovereign of all, and includes all the rest, will pursue this aim most, and will thus be directed to the most sovereign of all goods. This most sovereign and inclusive association is the polis, as it is called, or the political association....

First of all, there must necessarily be a union or pairing of those who cannot 5
exist without one another. Male and female must unite for the reproduction of the species—not from deliberate intention, but from the natural impulse, which exists in animals generally as it also exists in plants, to leave behind them

From Michael Curtis, *The Great Political Theories,* Volume I (New York: Avon Books, 1961), 59–94. Copyright © 1961 by Avon Books. Copyright © 1981 by Michael Curtis. Reprinted by permission of HarperCollins Publishers.

something of the same nature as themselves. Next, there must necessarily be a union of the naturally ruling element with the element which is naturally ruled, for the preservation of both. The element which is able, by virtue of its intelligence, to exercise forethought, is naturally a ruling and master element;

5   the element which is able, by virtue of its bodily power, to do what the other element plans, is a ruled element, which is naturally in a state of slavery; and master and slave have accordingly a common interest....

The first result of these two elementary associations [of male and female, and of master and slave] is the household or family, ... naturally instituted for the

10  satisfaction of daily recurrent needs. The next form of association—which is also the *first* to be formed from more households than one, and for the satisfaction of something more than daily recurrent needs—is the village. The most natural form of the village appears to be that of a colony or offshoot from a family.... This is the reason why each Greek polis was originally ruled—as the peoples

15  of the barbarian world still are—by kings. They were formed of persons who were already monarchically governed.

The fact that men generally were governed by kings in ancient times, and that some still continue to be governed in that way, is the reason that leads us all to assert that the gods are also governed by a king. We make the lives of the

20  gods in the likeness of our own—as we also make their shapes....

The final and perfect association, formed from a number of villages, is the polis—an association which may be said to have reached the height of full self-sufficiency; or rather we may say that while it *grows* for the sake or mere life, it *exists* for the sake of a good life.

25  Because it is the completion of associations existing by nature, every polis exists by nature, having itself the same quality as the earlier associations from which it grew. It is the end or consummation to which those associations move, and the "nature" of things consists in their end or consummation; for what each thing is when its growth is completed we call the nature of that thing, whether

30  it be a man or a horse or a family...the end, or final cause, is the best. Now self-sufficiency is the end, and so the best.

From these considerations it is evident that the polis belongs to the class of things that exist by nature, and that man is by nature an animal intended to live in a polis. He who is without a polis, by reason of his own nature and not of

35  some accident, is either a poor sort of being, or a being higher than man: he is like the man of whom Homer wrote in denunciation: "Clanless and lawless and heartless is he." The man who is such by nature at once plunges into a passion for war; he is in the position of a solitary advanced piece in a game of draughts.

The reason why man is a being meant for political association, in a higher

40  degree than bees or other gregarious animals can ever associate, is evident.

Nature, according to our theory, makes nothing in vain; and man alone of the animals is furnished with the faculty of language. The mere making of sounds serves to indicate pleasure and pain, and is thus a faculty that belongs to animals in general: their nature enables them to attain the point at which they have perceptions of pleasure and pain, and can signify those perceptions    5
to one another. But language serves to declare what is advantageous and what is the reverse, and it therefore serves to declare what is just and what is unjust. It is the peculiarity of man, in comparison with the rest of the animal world, that he alone possesses a perception of good and evil, of the just and the unjust, and of other similar qualities; and it is association in these things which makes    10
a family and a polis....

The polis is prior in the order of nature to the family and the individual, since the whole is necessarily prior to the part. If the whole body be destroyed, there will not be a foot or a hand....

We thus see that the polis exists by nature and that it is prior to the indi-    15
vidual. Not being self-sufficient when they are isolated, all individuals are so many parts all equally depending on the whole. The man who is isolated—who is unable to share in the benefits of political association, or has no need to share because he is already self-sufficient—is no part of the polis, and must therefore be either a beast or a god.    20

There is therefore an immanent impulse in all men towards an association of this order. But the man who first *constructed* such an association was none the less the greatest of benefactors. Man, when perfected, is the best of animals; but if he be isolated from law and justice he is the worst of all. If man be without virtue, he is a most unholy and savage being, and worse than all others in the indulgence of lust and gluttony. Justice belongs to the polis; for justice, which    25
is the determination of what is just, is an ordering of the political association.


...Every state is composed of households. The parts of household management will correspond to the parts of which the household itself is constituted. A complete household consists of slaves and freemen. But every subject of inquiry should first be examined in its simplest elements; and the primary and simplest    30
elements of the household are the connection of master and slave, that of the husband and wife, and that of parents and children. The factors to be examined are therefore three—first, the association of master and slave; next, the marital association; and lastly, what may be called the parental association. But besides the three factors which thus present themselves for examination there    35
is also a fourth, which some regard as identical with the whole of household management, and others as its principal part. This is the element called "the art of acquisition."

We may first speak of master and slave. There are some who hold that the exercise of authority over slaves is a form of science. They believe that the management of a household, the control of slaves, the authority of the statesman, and the rule of the monarchs, are all the same. There are others, however, who
5 regard the control of slaves by a master as contrary to nature. In their view the distinction of master and slave is due to law or convention; there is no natural difference between them; the relation of master and slave is based on force, and being so based has no warrant in justice.…

We may make the assumption that property is part of the household, and that
10 the art of acquiring property is a part of household management; and we may do so because it is impossible to live well, or indeed to live at all, unless the necessary conditions are present. We may further assume that, just as each art which has a definite sphere must necessarily be furnished with the appropriate instruments if its function is to be discharged, so the same holds good in the
15 sphere of household management. Finally, we may also assume that instruments are partly inanimate and partly animate: the pilot, for instance, has an inanimate instrument in the rudder, and an animate instrument in the look-out man. On the basis of these assumptions we may conclude that each article of property is an instrument for the purpose of life; that property in general is
20 the sum of such instruments; that the slave is an animate article of property; and that subordinates, or servants, in general may be described as animate instruments which are prior to other inanimate instruments. There are instruments of *production*; but articles of household property [such as the slave or other chattels] are instruments of *action*. Life is action and not production; and therefore the slave [being an instrument for the purpose of life] is a servant in
25 the sphere of action.…

An "article of property" is a term that is used in the same sense in which the term "part" is also used. Now a part is not only a part of something other than itself: it also belongs entirely to that other thing. It is the same with an article of property as it is with a part. Accordingly, while the master is merely
30 the master of the slave, and does not belong to him, the slave is not only the slave of his master; he also belongs entirely to him.

From these considerations we can see clearly what is the nature of the slave and what is his capacity. We attain these definitions—first, that "anybody who by his nature is not his own man, but another's, is by his nature a slave"; sec-
35 ondly, that "anybody who, being a man, is an article of property, is another's man"; and thirdly, that "an article of property is an instrument intended for the purpose of action and separable from its possession."

Ruling and being ruled not only belongs to the category of things necessary, but also to that of things expedient; and there are species in which a distinction is already marked, immediately at birth, between those of its members who are intended for being ruled and those who are intended to rule.... There are also many kinds both of ruling and ruled elements. This being the case, the rule which is exercised over the better sort of ruled elements is a better sort of rule—as, for example, rule exercised over a man is better than rule over an animal. The reason is that a function is a higher and better function when the elements which go to its discharge are higher and better elements; and where one element rules and another is ruled, we may speak of those elements as going together to discharge a function.... In *all* cases where there is a compound, constituted of more than one part but forming one common entity—whether the parts be continuous or discrete—a ruling element and a ruled can always be traced. This characteristic is present in animate beings by virtue of the whole constitution of nature, inanimate as well as animate; for even in things which are inanimate there is a sort of ruling principle, such as is to be found, for example, in a musical harmony.

Whatever may be said of inanimate things, it is certainly possible, as we have said, to observe in animate beings—and to observe there first—the presence of a ruling authority, both of the sort exercised by a master over slaves and of the sort exercised by a statesman over fellow citizens. The soul rules the body with the sort of authority of a statesman or a monarch.... It is clearly natural and beneficial to the body that it should be ruled by the soul, and again it is natural and beneficial to the affective part of the soul that it should be ruled by the mind and the rational part; whereas the equality of the two elements, or their reverse relation, is always detrimental. What holds good in man's inner life also holds good outside it; and the same principle is true of the relation of man to animals as is true of the relation of his soul to his body. Tame animals have a better nature than wild, and it is better for all such animals that they should be ruled by man because they then get the benefit of preservation. Again, the relation of male to female is naturally that of the superior to the inferior—of the ruling to the ruled. This general principle must similarly hold good of all human beings generally.

We may thus conclude that all men who differ from others as much as the body differs from the soul, or an animal from a man—all such are by nature slaves, and it is better for them, on the very same principle as in the other cases just mentioned, to be ruled by a master. A man is thus by nature a slave if he is capable of becoming the property of another, and if he participates in reason to the extent of apprehending it in another, though destitute of it himself. Herein he differs from animals, which do not apprehend reason, but simply obey their instincts. But the use which is made of the slave diverges but little from the use made of tame animals; both he and they supply their owner with bodily help in meeting his daily requirements....

5     It is nature's intention also to erect a physical difference between the body of the freeman and that of the slave, giving the latter strength for the menial duties of life, but making the former upright in carriage and useful for the various purposes of civic life—a life which tends, as it develops, to be divided into military service and the occupations of peace.

10     ...It is thus clear that, just as some are by nature free, so others are by nature slaves, and for these latter the condition of slavery is both beneficial and just.

But it is easy to see that those who hold an opposite view are also in a way correct. There is also a kind of slave, and of slavery, which exists by law or convention. The law in virtue of which those vanquished in war are held to

15 belong to the victor is in effect a sort of convention. That slavery can be justified by such a convention is a principle against which a number of jurists bring what may be called an "indictment of illegality." They regard it as a detestable notion that anyone who is subjugated by superior power should become the slave and subject of the person who has the power to subjugate him, and who

20 is his superior in power. Some, however, support it.... The cause of this divergence of view is to be found in the following consideration. There is a sense in which goodness, when it is furnished with material resources, has the greatest power to subjugate; and a victor is always preeminent in respect of *some* sort of good. This connection of power with goodness or some sort of good leads to

25 the idea that "power goes with goodness"...the dispute between the two sides thus comes to turn exclusively on the point of justice. On this point, one side holds that justice is a relation of mutual goodwill..., the other side holds that the rule of a superior is in itself, and by itself, justice.... If the divergent views are pitted separately against one another..., neither view has any cogency, or

30 even plausibility, against the view that the superior *in goodness* ought to rule over, and be the master of, his inferiors....

     There are some who, clinging, as they think, to a sort of justice, assume that slavery in war is always and everywhere just. Simultaneously, however, they contradict that assumption; for in the first place it is possible that the original

35 cause of a war may not be just, and in the second place no one would ever say that a person who does not deserve to be in a condition of slavery is really a slave. If such a view were accepted, the result would be that men reputed to be of the highest rank would be turned into slaves or the children of slaves, if it happened to them or their parents to be captured and sold into slavery. This

is the reason why Greeks do not like to call such persons slaves, but prefer to confine the term to barbarians. They are driven, in effect, to admit that there are some who are everywhere and inherently slaves, and others who are everywhere and inherently free. The same line of thought is followed in regard to nobility, as well as slavery. Greeks regard themselves as noble not only in their own    5
country, but absolutely and in all places; but they regard barbarians as noble only in their own country—thus assuming that there is one sort of nobility and freedom which is absolute, and another which is only relative.

...It is thus clear that there is some reason for the divergence of view which has been discussed, and that not all those who are actually slaves, or actually    10
freemen, are natural slaves or natural freemen. It is also clear that there are cases where such a distinction exists, and that here it is beneficial and just that the former should actually be a slave and the latter a master—the one being ruled, and the other exercising the kind of rule for which he is naturally intended and therefore acting as master. But a wrong exercise of his rule by a master is a thing    15
which is disadvantageous for both master and slave. The part and the whole, like the body and the soul, have an identical interest; and the slave is a part of the master, in the sense of being a living but separate part of his body. There is thus a community of interest, and a relation of friendship, between master and slave, when both of them naturally merit the position in which they stand. But    20
the reverse is true when matters are otherwise and slavery rests merely on legal sanction and superior *power*.

The authority of the master and that of the statesman are different from one another, and it is *not* the case that all kinds of authority are, as some thinkers hold, identical. The authority of the statesman is exercised over men who are    25
naturally free; that of the master over men who are slaves; and again the authority generally exercised over a household by its head is that of a monarch, while the authority of the statesman is an authority over freemen and equals. But there *may be* a science [of ruling] which belongs to masters, and another [of serving] which belongs to slaves....                                              30

...The head of the household rules over both wife and children, and rules over both as free members of the household, he exercises a different sort of rule in either case. His rule over his wife is like that of a statesman over fellow citizens; his rule over his children is like that of a monarch over subjects. The male is naturally fitter to command than the female, except where there is some    35
departure from nature; and age and maturity are similarly fitter to command than youth and immaturity. In most cases where rule of the statesman's sort is exercised there is an interchange of ruling and being ruled: the members of

a political association aim by their very nature at being equal and differing in nothing. Even so, and in spite of this aim, it is none the less true that when one body of citizens is ruling, and the other is being ruled, the former desires to establish a difference—in outward forms, in modes of address, and in titles of
5    respect. The relation of the male to the female is permanently that in which the statesman stands to his fellow-citizens. Paternal rule over children, on the other hand, is like that of a king over his subjects. The male parent is in a position of authority both in virtue of the affection to which he is entitled and by right of his seniority; and his position is thus in the nature of royal authority. Homer,
10   therefore, was right and proper in using the invocation *Father of Gods and of men* to address Zeus, who is king of them all. A king ought to be naturally superior to his subjects, and yet of the same stock as they are; and this is the case with the relation of age to youth, and of parent to child.

…Is the goodness of those who naturally rule the same as the goodness of those
15   who are naturally ruled, or does it differ? If we say that both of them ought to share in the nobility of goodness, why should one of them permanently rule, and the other be permanently ruled? The difference between them cannot be simply a difference of degree…the difference between ruler and ruled is one of kind. If, on the other hand, we say that one of them ought, and the other ought
20   not, to share, we commit ourselves to a strange view. How can the ruler rule properly, or the subject be properly ruled, unless they are both temperate and just? Anyone who is licentious or cowardly will utterly fail to do his duty. The conclusion which clearly emerges is that both classes must share in goodness, but that there must be different kinds of goodness for them—just as there are
25   also different kinds of goodness among different classes of the ruled.
     The soul has naturally two elements, a ruling and a ruled; and each has its different goodness, one belonging to the rational and ruling element, and the other to the irrational and ruled…. [I]t is a general law that there should be naturally ruling elements and elements naturally ruled…. The rule of the
30   freeman over the slave is one kind of rule; that of the male over the female another; that of the grown man over the child another still. It is true that all these persons possess in common the different parts of the soul; but they possess them in different ways…. [T]hey must all share in moral goodness but not in the same way—each sharing only to the extent required for the discharge
35   of his or her function. The ruler, accordingly, must possess moral goodness in its full and perfect form because his function, regarded absolutely and in its full nature, demands a master-artificer, and reason is such a master-artificer; but all other persons need only possess moral goodness to the extent required of them.

A polis or state belongs to the order of "compounds," in the same way as all other things which form a single "whole," but a "whole" composed, none the less, of a number of different parts.... A state is a compound made up of citizens; and this compels us to consider who should properly be called a citizen and what a citizen really is. The nature of citizenship, like that of the state, is a question   5 which is often disputed: there is no general agreement on a single definition: the man who is a citizen in a democracy is often not one in an oligarchy.... A citizen is not one by virtue of residence in a given place: resident aliens and slaves share with them a common place of residence. Nor can the name of citizen be given to those who share in civic rights only to the extent of being entitled to   10 sue and be sued in the courts. This is a right which belongs also to aliens who share its enjoyment by virtue of a treaty.... Also we may also dismiss children who are still too young to be entered on the roll of citizens, or men who are old enough to have been excused from civic duties. There is a sense in which the young and the old may both be called citizens, but it is not altogether an   15 unqualified sense: we must add the reservation that the young are undeveloped, and the old superannuated citizens.

What we have to define is the citizen in the strict and unqualified sense, who has no defect that has to be made good before he can bear the name—no defect such as youth or age, or such as those attaching to disfranchised or exiled   20 citizens. The citizen in this strict sense is best defined by the one criterion, "a man who shares in the administration of justice and in the holding of office."

...[C]onstitutions obviously differ from one another in kind, and some of them are obviously inferior and some superior in quality; for constitutions which are defective and perverted...are necessarily inferior to those which are   25 free from defects. It follows that...the citizen under each different kind of constitution must also necessarily be different. We may thus conclude that the citizen of our definition is particularly and especially the citizen of a democracy. Citizens living under other kinds of constitution *may* possibly, but do not necessarily, correspond to the definition. There are some states, for example, in   30 which there is no popular element: such states have no regular meetings of the assembly, but only meetings specially summoned; and [so far as membership of the courts is concerned] they remit the decision of cases to special bodies. In Sparta, for example, the Ephors take cases of contracts (not as a body, but each sitting separately); the Council of Elders take cases of homicide; and some other   35 authority may take other cases. Much the same is also true of Carthage, where a number of bodies of magistrates have each the right to decide all cases.

But...in constitutions other than the democratic, members of the assembly and the courts do not hold that office for an indeterminate period. They hold it for a limited term; and it is to persons with such a tenure that the citizen's   40 function of deliberating and judging is assigned in these constitutions. The nature of citizenship in general emerges clearly from these considerations; and our final definitions will accordingly be: (1) "he who enjoys the right of sharing in deliberative or judicial office attains thereby the status of a citizen of his state," and (2) "a state, in its simplest terms, is a body of such persons adequate in number for achieving a self-sufficient existence."

**III§2**For practical purposes, it is usual to define a citizen as "one born of citizen parents on both sides," and not on the father's or mother's side only; but sometimes this requirement is carried still farther back, to the length of two, three, or more stages of ancestry. This popular and facile definition has induced some thinkers to raise the question, "How did the citizen of the third of fourth stage of ancestry himself come to be a citizen?".... The matter is really simple. If, in their day, they enjoyed constitutional rights in the sense of our own definition…they were certainly citizens. It is obviously impossible to apply the requirement of descent from a citizen father or a citizen mother to those who were the first inhabitants or original founders of a state.

A more serious difficulty is perhaps raised by the case of those who have acquired constitutional rights as the result of a revolutionary change in the constitution…. The question raised by such an addition to the civic body is not the question of fact, "Who is actually a citizen?" It is the question of justice, "Are men rightly or wrongly such?" It must be admitted, however, that the further question may well be raised, "Can a man who is not justly a citizen be really a citizen, and is not the unjust the same thing as the unreal?" Obviously there are holders of office who have no just title to their office; but we none the less call them office-holders, though we do not say they are justly such. Citizens too, are defined by the fact of holding a sort of office; and it follows, therefore that those who have received this sort of office after a change in the constitution must, in practice, be called citizens.

The question whether, in justice, they are citizens or not is a different matter…. The problem raised by this larger question is that of deciding when a given act can, and when it cannot, be considered to be the act of the state. We may take as an example the case of an oligarchy or tyranny which changes into a democracy. In such a case there are some who are reluctant to fulfil public contracts—arguing that such contracts were made by the governing tyrant, and not by the state—and unwilling to meet other obligations of a similar nature. But the question here raised would seem to be closely allied to a question which takes us still further—"On what principles ought we to say that a state has retained its identity, or, conversely, that it has lost its identity and become a different state?"

The most obvious mode of dealing with this question is to consider simply territory and population. On this basis we may note that the territory and population of a state may be divided into two (or more) sections, with some of the population residing in one block of territory, and some of it in another. This difficulty need not be regarded as serious. The identity of a polis is not   5
constituted by its walls.

...Still assuming a single population inhabiting a single territory, shall we say that the state retains its identity as long as the stock of its inhabitants continues to be the same...and shall we thus apply to the state the analogy of rivers and fountains, to which we ascribe a constant identity in spite of the fact that part   10
of their water is always flowing in and part always flowing out? Or must we take a different view, and say that while the population remains the same, for the reason already mentioned the *state* may none the less change?

...If a polis is a form of association, and if this form of association is an association of citizens in a polity or constitution, it would seem to follow in-   15
evitably that when the constitution suffers a change in kind, and becomes a different constitution, the polis also will cease to be the same polis, and will also change its identity. We may cite an analogy from the drama. We say that a chorus which appears at one time as a comic and at another as a tragic chorus is not continuously the same, but alters its identity—and this in spite of the   20
fact that the members often remain the same.... The criterion to which we must chiefly look in determining the identity of the state is the criterion of the constitution....

Is the excellence of a good man and that of a good citizen identical or different?... Citizens differ in capacity but the end which they all serve is safety in the   25
working of their association; and this association consists in the constitution. The conclusion to which we are thus led is that the excellence of the citizen must be an excellence relative to the constitution. It follows on this that if there are several different kinds of constitution...there cannot be a single absolute excellence of the good citizen. But the good man is a man so called in virtue of   30
a single absolute excellence.

It is thus clear that it is possible to be a good citizen without possessing the excellence which is the quality of the good man.... In the best state the excellence of being a good citizen must belong to all citizens indifferently, because that is the condition necessary for the state being the best state; but the excellence   35
of being a good man cannot possibly belong to all—unless, indeed, we hold that every citizen of a good state must also be a good man.... There is a further point to be made. Just as a living being is composed of soul and body, or the soul of the different elements of reason and appetite, or the household of man

and wife, or property of master and slave, so the polis too is composed of different and unlike elements…. [T]he polis is composed that there cannot be a
single excellence common to all the citizens, any more than there can be a single
excellence common to the leader of a dramatic chorus and his assistant.

5      It is clear from these considerations that the excellence of the good citizen
and that of the good man are not in *all* cases identical. But the question may
still be raised whether there are not *some* cases in which there is identity. We
call a good ruler a "good" and "prudent" man, and we say of the statesman that
he ought to be "prudent." We may thus assume that, in the case of the ruler,
10    the excellence of the good citizen is identical with that of the good man. But
we have to remember that subjects too are citizens. It therefore follows that the
excellence of the good citizen cannot be identical with that of the good man in
all cases, though it may be when he is a ruler.

        Men hold in esteem the double capacity which consists in knowing both
15    how to rule and how to obey, and they regard the excellence of a worthy citizen
as consisting in a good exercise of this double capacity. Now if the excellence
of the good man is in the one order of ruling, while that of the good citizen is
in both orders of ruling and obeying, these two excellences cannot be held in
the same esteem. The position thus being that we find men holding (1) that
20    ruler and ruled should have different sorts of knowledge, and not one identical
sort, and (2) that the citizen should have both sorts of knowledge, and share
in both.

        There is rule of the sort which is exercised by a master; and by this we mean
the sort of rule connected with menial duties. Here it is not necessary for the
25    ruler to know how to do, but only to know how to use the ruled: indeed the
former kind of knowledge (by which we mean an ability to do menial services
personally) has a servile character. In some states the working classes were once
upon a time excluded from office, in the days before the institution of the
extreme form of democracy. The occupations pursued by men who are subject
30    to rule of the sort just mentioned need never be studied by the good man, or
by the statesman, or by the good citizen—except occasionally and in order to
satisfy some personal need…. But there is also rule of the sort which is exercised
over persons who are similar in birth to the ruler, and are similarly free. Rule of
this sort is what we call political rule; and this is the sort of rule which the ruler
35    must begin to learn by being ruled and by obeying—just as one learns to be a
commander of cavalry by serving under another commander, or to be a general
of infantry by serving under another general and by acting first as colonel and,
even before that, as captain. This is why it is a good saying that "you cannot be
a ruler unless you have first been ruled." Ruler and ruled [under this system of
40    political rule] have indeed different excellences; but the fact remains that the

good citizen must possess the knowledge and the capacity requisite for ruling as well as for being ruled, and the excellence of a citizen may be defined as consisting in "a knowledge of rule over free men from both points of view."

A good man, like a good citizen, will need knowledge from both points of view. Accordingly, on the assumption that the temperance and justice required   5
for ruling have a special quality, and equally that the temperance and justice required for being a subject in a free state have *their* special quality, the excellence of the good man (*e.g.*, his justice) will not be one sort of excellence. It will include different sorts—one sort which fits him to act as a ruler, and one which fits him to act as a subject....                                              10

"Prudence" is the only form of goodness which is peculiar to the ruler. The other forms must, it would seem, belong equally to rulers and subjects....The form of goodness peculiar to subjects cannot be "prudence," and may be defined as "right opinion." The ruled may be compared to flute-makers: rulers are like flute-players who use what the flute-makers make.                                15

III§5Is citizenship in the true sense to be limited to those who have the right of sharing in office, or must mechanics be also included in the ranks of citizens? If we hold that mechanics, who have no share in the offices of the state, are also to be included, we shall have some citizens who can never achieve the excellence of the good citizen since they have no experience of ruling. If, on   20
the other hand, mechanics should not be called citizens, in what class are they to be placed? They are not resident aliens, neither are they foreigners: what is their class? The best form of state will not make the mechanic a citizen. In states where mechanics *are* admitted to citizenship we shall have to say that the citizen excellence of which we have spoken cannot be attained by every citizen,   25
or by all who are simply free men, but can only be achieved by those who are free from menial duties.

Constitutions are various: there must thus be various kinds of citizens; more especially, there must be various kinds of citizens who are subjects. In one variety of constitution it will be necessary that mechanics and labourers should   30
be citizens: in other varieties it will be impossible. It will be impossible, for example, where there is a constitution of the type termed "aristocratic," with offices distributed on the basis of worth and excellence; for a man who lives the life of a mechanic or labourer cannot pursue the things which belong to excellence. The case is different in oligarchies. Even there, it is true, a labourer cannot be a   35
citizen (participation in office depending on a high property qualification); but a mechanic may, for the simple reason that craftsmen often become rich men.

These considerations prove two things—that there are several different kinds of citizens, and that the name of citizen is particularly applicable to those who

share in the offices and honours of the state. Homer accordingly speaks in the *Iliad* of a man being treated "like an alien man, *without honour*," and it is true that those who do not share in the offices and honours of the state are just like resident aliens. Two conclusions also emerge from our discussion of the ques-
5    tion, "Is the excellence of the good man identical with that of the good citizen, or different from it?" The first is that there are some states in which the good man and the good citizen are identical, and some in which they are different. The second is that, in states of the former type, it is not all good citizens who are also good men, but only those among them who hold the position of states-
10   men—in other words those who direct or are capable of directing, either alone or in conjunction with others, the conduct of public affairs.

…A constitution (or polity) may be defined as "the organization of a polis, in respect of its offices generally, but especially in respect of that particular office which is sovereign in all issues." The civic body…is everywhere the sovereign of
15   the state; in fact the civic body is the polity (or constitution) itself. In democratic states, for example, the people is sovereign: in oligarchies, on the other hand, the few have that position; and this difference of the sovereign bodies is the reason why we say that the two types of constitution differ—as we may equally apply the same reasoning to other types besides these.…
20        What is the nature of the end for which the state exists, and what are the various kinds of authority to which men and their associations are subject?… [M]an is an animal impelled by his nature to live in a polis. A *natural impulse* is thus one reason why men desire to live a social life even when they stand in no need of mutual succour; but they are also drawn together by a *common interest*,
25   in proportion as each attains a share in good life. The good life is the chief end, both for the community as a whole and for each of us individually. But men also come together, and form and maintain political association, merely for the sake of life; for perhaps there is some element of the good even in the simple act of living, so long as the evils of existence do not preponderate too heavily.
30   It is an evident fact that most men cling hard enough to life to be willing to endure a good deal of suffering, which implies that life has in it a sort of healthy happiness and a natural quality of pleasure.…
It is easy enough to distinguish the various kinds of rule or authority of which men commonly speak.… The rule of a master is one kind; and here,
35   though there is really a common interest which unites the natural master and the natural slave, the fact remains that the rule is primarily exercised with a view to the master's interest, and only incidentally with a view to that of the slave, who must be preserved in existence if the rule itself is to remain. Rule over wife and children, and over the household generally, is a second kind of rule, which

we have called by the name of household management. Here the rule is either exercised in the interest of the ruled or for the attainment of some advantage common to both ruler and ruled. Essentially it is exercised in the interest of the ruled, as is also plainly the case with other arts besides that of ruling, such as medicine and gymnastics—though an art may incidentally be exercised for the   5 benefit of its practitioner, and there is nothing to prevent a trainer from becoming occasionally a member of the class he instructs, in the same sort of way as a steersman is always one of the crew. Thus a trainer or steersman primarily considers the good of those who are subject to his authority; but when he becomes one of them personally, he incidentally shares in the benefit of that good—the   10 steersman thus being also a member of the crew, and the trainer (though still a trainer) becoming also a member of the class which he instructs.

This principle also applies to a third kind of rule—that exercised by the holders of political office. When the constitution of a state is constructed on the principle that its members are equals and peers, the citizens think it proper   15 that they should hold office by turns. At any rate this is the natural system, and the system which used to be followed in the days when men believed that they ought to serve by turns, and each assumed that others would take over the duty of considering his benefit, just as he had himself, during his term of office, considered the interest of others. To-day the case is altered. Moved by   20 the profits to be derived from office and the handling of public property, men want to hold office continuously. The conclusion which follows is clear. Those constitutions which consider the common interest are *right* constitutions, judged by the standard of absolute justice. Those constitutions which consider only the personal interest of the rulers are all *wrong* constitutions, or *perversions* of   25 the right forms. Such perverted forms are despotic...whereas the polis is an association of freemen...the term "constitution" signifies the same thing as the term "civic body." The civic body in every polis is the sovereign; and the sovereign must necessarily be either One, or Few, or Many. On this basis we may say that when the One, or the Few, or the Many rule with a view to the   30 common interest, the constitutions under which they do so must necessarily be right constitutions. On the other hand the constitutions directed to the personal interest of the One, or the Few, or the Masses must necessarily be perversions.... Among forms of government by a single person Kingship denotes the species which looks to the common interest. Among forms of government by a few   35 persons Aristocracy is of a similar species either because the best are the rulers, or because its object is what is best for the state and its members. Finally, when the masses govern the state with a view to the common interest, the name used for this species is the generic name common to all constitutions—the name of

"Polity." There is a good reason for the usage.... It is possible for one man, or a few, to be of outstanding excellence; but when it comes to a large number, we can hardly expect a fine edge of all the varieties of excellence. What we can expect particularly is the military kind of excellence, which is the kind that shows itself in a mass. This is the reason why the defense forces are the most sovereign body under this constitution, and those who possess arms are the persons who enjoy constitutional rights....

Three perversions correspond to these three right constitutions. Tyranny is the perversion of Kingship; Oligarchy of Aristocracy; and Democracy of Polity. Tyranny is a government by a single person directed to the interest of that person; Oligarchy is directed to the interest of the well-to-do; Democracy is directed to the interest of the poorer classes. None of the three is directed to the advantage of the whole body of citizens.

Tyranny, as has just been said, is single-person government of the political association on the lines of despotism: oligarchy exists where those who have property are the sovereign authority of the constitution; and conversely democracy exists where the sovereign authority is composed of the poorer classes, and not of the owners of property. We have defined democracy as the sovereignty of numbers; but we can conceive a case in which the majority who hold the sovereignty in a state are the well-to-do. Similarly oligarchy is generally stated to be the sovereignty of a small number; but it might conceivably happen that the poorer classes were fewer in number than the well-to-do, and yet—in virtue of superior vigour—were the sovereign authority of the constitution. In neither case could the definition previously given of these constitutions be regarded as true. We might attempt to overcome the difficulty by combining both of the factors—wealth with paucity of numbers, and poverty with mass. On this basis oligarchy might be defined as the constitution under which the rich, being also few in number, hold the offices of the state; and similarly democracy might be defined as the constitution under which the poor, being also many in number, are in control. But this involves us in another difficulty. If our new definition is exhaustive, and there are no forms of oligarchy and democracy other than those enumerated in that definition, what names are we to give to the constitutions just suggested as conceivable—those where the wealthy form a majority and the poor a minority, and where the wealthy majority in the one case, and the poor minority in the other, are the sovereign authority of the constitution? The course of the argument thus appears to show that the factor of number—the small number of the sovereign body in oligarchies, or the large number in democracies—is an accidental attribute, due to the simple fact that the wealthy are generally few and the poor are generally numerous.

Therefore the…real ground of the difference between oligarchy and democracy is poverty and riches, not numbers. It is inevitable that any constitution should be an oligarchy if the rulers under it are rulers in virtue of riches, whether they are few or many; and it is equally inevitable that a constitution under which the poor rule should be a democracy.                                                              5

It happens, however, that the rich are few and the poor are numerous…. It is only a few who have riches, but all alike share in free status.…

Both oligarchs and democrats have a hold on a sort of conception of justice; but they both fail to carry it far enough, and neither of them expresses the true conception of justice in the whole of its range. In democracies, for example,    10 justice is considered to mean equality. It does mean equality—but equality for those who are equal, and not for all. In oligarchies, again, inequality in the distribution of office is considered to be just; and indeed it is—but only for those who are unequal, and not for all. The advocates of oligarchy and democracy both refuse to consider this factor—who are the persons to whom    15 their principles properly apply—and they both make erroneous judgments. The reason is that they are judging *in their own case*; and most men, as a rule, are bad judges where their own interests are involved. Justice is relative to persons; and a just distribution is one in which the relative values of the things given correspond to those of the persons receiving…. But the advocates of oligarchy    20 and democracy, while they agree about what constitutes equality in the *thing*, disagree about what constitutes it in *persons*. The main reason for this is the reason just stated—they are judging, and judging erroneously, in their own case; but there is also another reason—they are misled by the fact that they are professing a sort of conception of justice, and professing it up to a point, into    25 thinking that they profess one which is absolute and complete. The oligarchs think that superiority on one point—in their case wealth—means superiority on all: the democrats believe that equality in one respect—for instance, that of free birth—means equality all round.

Both sides, however, fail to mention the really cardinal factor. If property    30 were the end for which men came together and formed an association, men's share of the state would be proportionate to their share of property; and in that case the argument of the oligarchical side—that it is not just for a man who has contributed one pound to share equally in a sum of a hundred pounds with the man who has contributed all the rest—would appear to be a strong argument.    35 But the end of the state is not mere life; it is, rather, a good quality of life.… [I]t is the cardinal issue of goodness or badness in the life of the polis which always engages the attention of any state that concerns itself to secure a system of good laws well obeyed. The conclusion which clearly follows is that any polis

which is truly so called, and is not merely one in name, must devote itself to the end of encouraging goodness. Otherwise, a political association sinks into a mere alliance, which only differs in space from other forms of alliance where the members live at a distance from one another. Otherwise, too, law becomes
5  a mere covenant—or (in the phrase of the Sophist Lycophron) "a guarantor of men's rights against one another"—instead of being, as it should be, a rule of life such as will make the members of a polis good and just.

...It is clear, therefore, that a polis is not an association for residence on a common site, or for the sake of preventing mutual injustice and easing exchange.
10  These are indeed conditions which must be present before a polis can exist; but the presence of all these conditions is not enough, in itself, to constitute a polis. What constitutes a polis is an association of households and clans in a good life, for the sake of attaining a perfect and self-sufficing existence. This consummation, however, will not be reached unless the members inhabit one and the
15  self-same place and practise intermarriage. Therefore the various institutions of a common social life—marriage-connexions, kin-groups, religious gatherings, and social pastimes generally—arose in cities. But these institutions are the business of friendship. It is friendship which consists in the pursuit of a common social life. The end and purpose of a polis is the good life, and the institutions of social
20  life are means to that end. A polis is constituted by the association of families and villages in a perfect and self-sufficing existence; and such an existence, on our definition, consists in a life of true felicity and goodness.

It is therefore for the sake of good actions, and not for the sake of social life, that political associations must be considered to exist.... Those who contribute
25  most to an association of this character have a greater share in the polis...than those who are equal to them (or even greater) in free birth and descent, but unequal in civic excellence, or than those who surpass them in wealth but are surpassed by them in excellence. From what has been said it is plain that both sides to the dispute about constitutions...profess only a partial conception of justice.

30  There are several alternatives: the people at large; the wealthy; the better sort of men; the one man who is best of all; the tyrant. But all these alternatives appear to involve unpleasant results: indeed, how can it be otherwise?... What if the poor, on the ground of their being a majority, proceed to divide among themselves the possessions of the wealthy—will not this be unjust? "No, by
35  heaven" (a democrat may reply); "it has been justly decreed so by the sovereign." "But if this is not the extreme of injustice" (we may reply in turn), "what *is*?" Whenever a majority of any sort, irrespective of wealth or poverty, divides

---

[1]Where are your claws?

among its members the possessions of a minority, that majority is obviously ruining the state.... A tyrant uses coercion by virtue of superior power in just the same sort of way as the people coerce the wealthy. Is it just that a minority composed of the wealthy should rule? If they too behave like the others—if they plunder and confiscate the property of the people—can their action be called     5
just? If it can, the action of the people, in the converse case, must equally be termed just. It is clear that all these acts of oppression...are mean and unjust. Should the better sort of men have authority and be sovereign in all matters? In that case, the rest of the citizens will necessarily be debarred from honors, since they will not enjoy the honor of holding civic office. We speak of offices     10
as honors; and when a single set of persons hold office permanently, the rest of the community must necessarily be debarred from all honors. It is better than any of the other alternatives that the one best man should rule? This is still more oligarchical...because the number of those debarred from honors is even greater. It may perhaps be urged that there is still another alternative;     15
that it is a poor sort of policy to vest sovereignty in any person...subject as persons are to the passions that beset men's souls; and that it is better to vest it in law.... But the law itself may incline either towards oligarchy or towards democracy; and what difference will the sovereignty of law then make in the problems which have just been raised? The consequences already stated will     20
follow just the same.

There is this to be said for the Many. Each of them by himself may not be of a good quality; but when they all come together it is possible that they may surpass—collectively and as a body, although not individually—the quality of the few best. Feasts to which many contribute may excel those provided at one     25
man's expense. In the same way, when there are many, each can bring his share of goodness and moral prudence; and when all meet together the people may thus become something in the nature of a single person, who—as he has many feet, many hands, and many senses—may also have many qualities of charac-ter and intelligence. This is the reason why the Many are also better judges of     30
music and the writings of poets: some appreciate one part, some another, and all together appreciate all.

    ...It is not clear, however, that this combination of qualities, which we have made the ground of distinction between the many and the few best, is true of all popular bodies and all large masses of men. Perhaps it may be said,     35
"By heaven, it is clear that there are some bodies of which it cannot possibly be true; for if you include them, you would, by the same token, be bound to include a herd of beasts. That would be absurd; and yet what difference is there between these bodies and a herd of beasts?" All the same, and in spite of this

objection, there is nothing to prevent the view we have stated from being true of *some* popular bodies....

What are the *matters* over which freemen, or the general body of citizens—men of the sort who neither have wealth nor can make any claim on the ground of goodness—should properly exercise sovereignty? It may be argued, from one point of view, that it is dangerous for men of this sort to share in the highest offices, as injustice may lead them into wrongdoing, and thoughtlessness into error. But it may also be argued, from another point of view, that there is serious risk in not letting them have *some* share in the enjoyment of power; for a state with a body of disfranchised citizens who are numerous and poor must necessarily be a state which is full of enemies. The alternative left is to let them share in the deliberative and judicial functions; and we thus find Solon, and some of the other legislators, giving the people the two general functions of electing the magistrates to office and of calling them to account at the end of their tenure of office, but *not* the right of holding office themselves in their individual capacity.... When they all meet together, the people display a good enough gift of perception, and combined with the better class they are of service to the state (just as impure food, when it is mixed with pure, makes the whole concoction more nutritious than a small amount of the pure would be); but each of them is imperfect in the judgments he forms by himself.

But this arrangement of the constitution presents some difficulties. The first difficulty is that...experts may be better at both judging and choosing... It would thus appear that the people should not be made sovereign, either in the matter of the election of magistrates or in that of their examination. But in the first place we have to remember our own previous argument of the combination of qualities which is to be found in the people—provided, that is to say, that they are not debased in character. Each individual may indeed, be a worse judge than the experts; but all, when they meet together, are either better than experts or at any rate no worse. In the second place, there are a number of arts in which the creative artist is not the only, or even the best, judge. These are the arts whose products can be understood and judged even by those who do not possess any skill in the art. A house, for instance, is something which can be understood by others besides the builder: indeed the user of a house—or in other words the householder—will judge it even better than he does. In the same way a pilot will judge a rudder better than a shipwright does; and the diner—not the cook—will be the best judge of a feast....

There is a second difficulty still to be faced, which is connected with the first. It would seem to be absurd that persons of a poor quality should be sovereign on issues which are more important than those assigned to the better sort of citizens. The election of magistrates, and their examination at the end of their tenure, are the most important of issues; and yet there are constitutions, as we have seen, under which these issues are assigned to popular bodies, and where a popular body is sovereign in all such matters. To add to the difficulty, membership of the assembly, which carries deliberative and judicial functions, is vested in persons of little property and of any age; but a high property qualification 5 is demanded from those who serve as treasurers or generals, or hold any of the highest offices. This difficulty too may, however, be met in the same way as the first; and the practice followed in these constitutions is perhaps, after all, correct. It is not the individual member of the judicial court, or the council, or the assembly, who is vested with office: it is the court as a whole, the council as 10 a whole, the popular assembly as a whole, which is vested; and each individual member—whether of the council, the assembly, or the court—is simply a part of the whole. It is therefore just and proper that the people, from which the assembly, the council, and the court are constituted, should be sovereign on issues more important than those assigned to the better sort of citizens. It 15 may be added that the collective property of the members of all these bodies is greater than that of the persons who either as individuals or as members of small bodies hold the highest offices....

Above all rightly constituted laws should be the final sovereign; and personal rule, whether it be exercised by a single person or a body of persons, should be 20 sovereign only in those matters on which law is unable, owing to the difficulty of framing general rules, for all contingencies, to make an exact pronouncement. But what rightly constituted laws ought to be is a matter that is not yet clear; and here we are still confronted by the difficulty...that law itself may have a bias in favor of one class or another. Equally with the constitutions to which 25 they belong...laws must be good or bad, just or unjust. The one clear fact is that laws must be constituted in accordance with constitutions; and if this is the case, it follows that laws which are in accordance with right constitutions must necessarily be just, and laws which are in accordance with wrong or perverted constitutions must be unjust.                                                      30

In all arts and sciences the end in view is some good. In the most sovereign of all the arts and sciences—and this is the art and science of politics—the end in view is the greatest good and the good which is most pursued. The good in the sphere of politics is justice; and justice consists in what tends to promote the common interest. General opinion makes it consist in some sort of equal- 35 ity.... Justice involves two factors—things, and the persons to whom things are assigned—and it considers that persons who are equal should have assigned to them equal things. But here there arises a question which must not be overlooked. Equals and unequals—yes; but equals and unequals *in what*? This is a question which raises difficulties, and involves us in philosophical speculation on politics. It is possible to argue that offices and honors ought to be distributed unequally on the basis of superiority *in any respect whatsoever*—even though there were similarity, and no shadow of any difference, in every other respect;

5  and it may be urged, in favour of this argument, that where people differ from one another there must be a difference in what is just and proportionate to their merits. If this argument were accepted, the mere fact of a better complexion, or greater height, or any other such advantage, would establish a claim for a greater share of political rights to be given to its possessor. But is not the

10  argument obviously wrong? To be clear that it is, we have only to study the analogy of the other arts and sciences. If you were dealing with a number of flute-players who were equal in their art, you would not assign them flutes on the principle that the better born should have a greater amount. Nobody will play the better for being better born; and it is to those who are better at the

15  job that the better supply of tools should be given. Let us suppose a man who is superior to others in flute-playing, but far inferior in birth and beauty. Birth and beauty may be greater goods than ability to play the flute, and those who possess them may, upon balance, surpass the flute-player more in these qualities than he surpasses them in his flute-playing; but the fact remains that he

20  is the man who ought to get the better supply of flutes.... In matters political there is no good reason for basing a claim to the exercise of authority on any and every kind of superiority. Some may be swift and others slow; but it is in athletic contests that the superiority of the swift received its reward. Claims to political rights must be based on the ground of contribution to the elements

25  which constitute the being of the state. There is thus good ground for the claims to honor and office which are made by persons of good descent, free birth, or wealth. Those who hold office must necessarily be free men and taxpayers: a state could not be composed entirely of men without means, any more than it could be composed entirely of slaves. But we must add that if wealth and

30  free birth are necessary elements, the temper of justice and a martial habit are also necessary. These too are elements which must be present if men are to live together in a state. The one difference is that the first two elements are necessary to the simple existence of a state, and the last two for its good life.

If we are thinking in terms of contribution to the state's existence, all of the

35  elements mentioned, or at any rate several of them, may properly claim to be recognized in the award of honours and office; but if we are thinking in terms of contribution to its good life, then culture and goodness may be regarded as having the justest claim. On the other hand—and following our principle that it is not right for men who are equal in one respect, and only in one, to

have an equal share of all things, or for men who are superior in one respect to have a superior share of everything—we are bound to consider all constitutions which recognize such claims as perverted forms. There is a certain sense in which all the contributors of the different elements are justified in the claims they advance, though none of them is absolutely justified. (a) The rich are so far justified that they have a larger share of the land, which is a matter of public interest: they are also, as a rule, more reliable in matters of contract. (b) The free and the nobly born may claim recognition together as being closely connected. The better-born are citizens to a greater extent than the low-born; and good birth has always honour in its own country. Also good birth means goodness of the whole stock. (c) Similarly we may also allow that goodness of character has a just claim; for in our view the virtue of justice, which is necessarily accompanied by all the other virtues is a virtue which acts in social relations. (d) But there is a further claim that may also be urged. The many may urge their claims against the few: taken together and compared with the few they are stronger, richer, and better.

Who is to govern when the claims of different groups are simultaneously present? Suppose, for example, that the good are exceedingly few in number: how are we to settle their claim? Must we only have regard to the fact that they are few for the function they have to discharge; and must we therefore inquire whether they will be able to manage a state, or numerous enough to compose one? Here there arises a difficulty which applies not only to the good, but to all the different claimants for political office and honor. It may equally be held that there is no justice in the claim of a few to rule on the ground of their greater wealth, or on that of their better birth; and there is an obvious reason for holding this view. If there is any *one* man who in turn is richer than all the rest, this one man must rule over all on the very same ground of justice; and similarly any one man who is pre-eminent in point of good birth must carry the day over those who claim on the ground of birth. The same logic may be applied in the matter of merit or goodness. If some one man be a better man than all the other good men who belong to the civic body, this one man should be sovereign on the very same ground of justice.... Similarly, where one man is stronger than all the rest—or a group of more than one, but fewer than the Many, is stronger—that one man or group must be sovereign instead of the Many....

...If there is one person (or several persons, but yet not enough to form the full measure of a state) so pre-eminently superior in goodness that there can be no comparison between the goodness and political capacity which he shows (or several show, when there is more than one) and what is shown by the rest, such a person, or such persons, can no longer be treated as part of a state. Being so greatly superior to others in goodness and political capacity,

they will suffer injustice if they are treated as worthy only of an equal share; for a person of this order may very well be like a god among men. They are a law in themselves. It would be a folly to attempt to legislate for them. Reasons of this nature will serve to explain why democratic states institute the rule of
5   ostracism. Such states are held to aim at equality above anything else; and with that aim in view they used to pass a sentence of ostracism on those whom they regarded as having too much influence owing to their wealth or the number of their connections or any other form of political strength.

If wrong or perverted forms adopt this policy of leveling with a view to their
10  own particular interest, something the same is also true of forms which look to the common good. This rule of proportion may also be observed in the arts and sciences generally. A painter would not permit a foot which exceeded the bounds of symmetry, however beautiful it might be, to appear in a figure on his canvas. A shipwright would not tolerate a stern, or any other part of a ship, which was
15  out of proportion. A choirmaster would not admit to a choir a singer with a greater compass and a finer voice than any of the other members. In view of this general rule, a policy of leveling need not prevent a monarch who practices it from being in harmony with his state—provided that his government is otherwise beneficial; and thus the argument in favor of ostracism possesses a kind of
20  political justice in relation to any of the recognized forms of pre-eminence.... The real question is rather, "What is to be done when we meet with a man of outstanding eminence in goodness?" Nobody, we may assume, would say that such a man ought to be banished and sent into exile. But neither would any man say that he ought to be subject to others.... The only alternative left—and
25  this would also appear to be the natural course—is for all others to pay a willing obedience to the man of outstanding goodness. Such men will accordingly be the permanent kings in their states.

...Is it more expedient to be ruled by the one best man, or by the best laws? Those who hold that kingship is expedient argue that law can only lay down
30  general rules; it cannot issue commands to deal with various different conjunctures; and the rule of the letter of law is therefore a folly in any and every art. It is clear that a constitution based on the letter and rules of law is not the best constitution.... But that from which the element of passion is wholly absent is better than that to which such an element clings. Law contains no element
35  of passion; but such an element must always be present in the human mind. The rejoinder may, however, be made that the individual mind, if it loses in this way, gains something in return: it can deliberate better, and decide better, on particular issues. These considerations lead us to conclude that the one best man must be a law-giver, and there must be a body of laws, but these laws must

not be sovereign where they fail to hit the mark—though they must be so in all other cases. There is, however, a whole class of matters which cannot be decided at all, or cannot be decided properly, by rules of law.

…Justice for equals means their being ruled as well as their ruling, and therefore involves rotation of office. But when we come to that, we already come to law.    5
The rule of law is therefore preferable to that of a single citizen…. If there are a number of cases which law seems unable to determine, it is also true that a person would be equally unable to find an answer to these cases. Law trains the holders of office expressly in its own spirit, and then sets them to decide and settle those residuary issues which it cannot regulate, "as justly as in them lies."    10
It also allows them to introduce any improvements which may seem to them, as the result of experience, to be better than the existing laws. He who commands that law should rule may thus be regarded as commanding that God and reason alone should rule; he who commands that a man should rule adds the character of the beast. Appetite has that character; and high spirit, too, perverts the holders    15
of office, even when they are the best of men. Law [as the pure voice of God and reason] may thus be defined as "Reason free from all passion."

To seek for justice is to seek for a neutral authority; and law is a neutral authority. But laws resting on unwritten custom are even more sovereign, and concerned with issues of still more sovereign importance, than written laws;    20
and this suggests that, even if the rule of a man be safer than the rule of written law, it need not therefore be safer than the rule of unwritten law.

…No one disputes the fact that law will be the best ruler and judge on the issues on which it is competent. It is because law cannot cover the whole of the ground, and there are subjects which cannot be included in its scope, that    25
difficulties arise and the question comes to be debated, "Is the rule of the best law preferable to that of the best man?" Matters of detail, which belong to the sphere of deliberation, are obviously matters on which it is not possible to lay down a law. The advocates of the rule of law do not deny that such matters ought to be judged by men; they only claim that they ought to be judged by    30
many men rather than one. *All* persons in office who have been trained by the law will have a good judgment; and it may well be regarded as an absurdity that a single man should do better in seeing with two eyes, judging with two ears, or acting with two hands and feet, than many could do with many. Indeed, it is actually the practice of monarchs to take to themselves, as it were, many eyes    35
and ears and hands and feet, and to use as colleagues those who are friends of their rule and their person. The colleagues of a monarch must be his friends: otherwise they will not act in accordance with his policy. But if they are friends of his person and rule, they will also be—as a man's friends always are—his

equals and peers; and in believing that his friends should have office he is also committed to the belief that his equals and peers should have office....

The study of politics first, has to consider which is the best constitution, and what qualities a constitution must have to come closest to the ideal when there
5   are no external factors...to hinder its doing so. Secondly, politics has to consider which sort of constitution suits which sort of civic body. The attainment of the best constitution is likely to be impossible for the general run of states; and the good law-giver and the true statesman must therefore have their eyes open not only to what is the absolute best, but also to what is the best in relation to
10  actual conditions. Thirdly, politics has also to consider the sort of constitution where the student of politics must be able to study a *given* constitution, just as it stands and simply with a view to explaining how it may have arisen and how it may be made to enjoy the longest possible life. The sort of case which we have in mind is where a state has neither the ideally best constitution (or even the
15  elementary conditions needed for it) nor the best constitution possible under the actual conditions, but has only a constitution of an inferior type. Fourthly, and in addition to all these functions, politics has also to provide a knowledge of the type of constitution which is best suited to states in general. Most of the writers who treat of politics—good as they may be in other respects—fail
20  when they come to deal with matters of practical *utility*. We have not only to study the ideally best constitution. We have also to study the type of constitution which is practicable—and with it, and equally, the type which is easiest to work and most suitable to states generally.... The sort of constitutional system which ought to be proposed is one which men can be easily induced, and will
25  be readily able, to graft onto the system they already have. It is as difficult a matter to reform an old constitution as it is to construct a new one; as hard to unlearn a lesson as it was to learn it initially. The true statesman...must be able to help *any* existing constitution. He cannot do so unless he knows how many different kinds of constitutions there are.
30       ...The student of politics should also learn to distinguish the laws which are absolutely best from those which are appropriate to each constitution.... A constitution may be defined as "an organization of offices in a state, by which the method of their distribution is fixed, the sovereign authority is determined, and the nature of the end to be pursued by the association and all its members
35  is prescribed." Laws, as distinct from the frame of the constitution, are the rules by which the magistrates should exercise their powers, and should watch and check transgressors. The same laws cannot possibly be equally beneficial to *all* oligarchies or to *all* democracies.

If we adopt as true the statements made in the *Ethics*—(1) that a truly happy life is a life of goodness lived in freedom from impediments, and (2) that goodness consists in a mean—it follows that the best way of life is one which consists in a mean, and a mean of the kind attainable by every individual. Further, the same criteria which determine whether the citizen-body have a good or bad way 5 of life must also apply to the constitution; for a constitution is the way of life of a citizen-body. In all states there may be distinguished three parts, or classes, of the citizen-body—the very rich; the very poor; and the middle class which forms the mean. Now it is admitted, as a general principle, that moderation and the mean are always best. We may therefore conclude that in the ownership 10 of all gifts of fortune a middle condition will be the best. Men who are in this condition are the most ready to listen to reason. Those who belong to either extreme—the over-handsome, the over-strong, the over-noble, the over-wealthy; or at the opposite end the over-poor, the over-weak, the utterly ignoble—find it hard to follow the lead of reason. Men in the first class tend more to violence and 15 serious crime: men in the second tend too much to roguery and petty offences; and most wrongdoing arises either from violence or roguery. It is a further merit of the middle class that its members suffer least from ambition, which both in the military and the civil sphere is dangerous to states. It must also be added that those who enjoy too many advantages—strength, wealth, connections, 20 and so forth—are both unwilling to obey and ignorant how to obey. This is a defect which appears in them from the first, during childhood and in home-life: nurtured in luxury, they never acquire a habit of discipline, even in the matter of lessons. But there are also defects in those who suffer from the opposite extreme of a lack of advantages: they are far too mean and poor-spirited. We have thus, 25 on the one hand, people who are ignorant how to rule and only know how to obey, as if they were so many slaves, and, on the other hand, people who are ignorant how to obey any sort of authority and only know how to rule as if they were masters of slaves. The result is a state, not of freemen, but only of slaves and masters: a state of envy on the one side and on the other contempt. 30 Nothing could be further removed from the spirit of friendship or the temper of a political community. Community depends on friendship; and when there is enmity instead of friendship, men will not even share the same path. A state aims at being, as far as it can be, a society composed of equals and peers and the middle class, more than any other, has this sort of composition. It follows that 35 a state which is based on the middle class is bound to be the best constituted in respect of the elements of which, on our view, a state is naturally composed. The middle classes…enjoy a greater security themselves than any other class. They do not, like the poor, covet the goods of others; nor do others covet their possessions, as the poor covet those of the rich. Neither plotting against others, not plotted against themselves, they live in freedom from danger; and we may well approve the prayer of Phocylides

*Many things are best for the middling;*
5        *Fain would I be of the state's middle class.*

...It is clear from our argument, first, that the best form of political society is one where power is vested in the middle class, and, secondly, that good government is attainable in those states where there is a large middle class—large enough, if possible, to be stronger than both of the other classes, but at any
10    rate large enough to be stronger than either of them singly; for in that case its addition to either will suffice to turn the scale, and will prevent either of the opposing extremes from becoming dominant. It is therefore the greatest of blessings for a state that its members should possess a moderate and adequate property. Where some have great possessions, and others have nothing at all, the
15    result is either an extreme democracy or an unmixed oligarchy; or it may even be—indirectly, and as a reaction against both of thee extremes—a tyranny.
      ...It is clear that the middle type of constitution is best. It is the one type free from faction; where the middle class is large, there is least likelihood of faction and dissension among the citizens. Large states are generally more free
20    from faction just because they have a large middle class. In small states, on the other hand, it is easy for the whole population to be divided into only two classes; nothing is left in the middle, and all—or almost all—are either poor or rich. The reason why democracies are generally more secure and more permanent than oligarchies is the character of their middle class, which is more numerous,
25    and is allowed a larger share in the government, than it is in oligarchies. Where democracies have no middle class, and the poor are greatly superior in number, trouble ensues, and they are speedily ruined. It must also be considered a proof of its value that the best legislators have come from the middle class. Solon was one, as his own poems prove: Lycurgus was another (and not, as is sometimes
30    said, a member of the royal family); and the same is true of Charondas and most of the other legislators.
      ...Most constitutions are either democratic or oligarchical. In the first place, the middle class is in most states generally small; and the result is that as soon as one or other of the two main classes—the owners of property and the
35    masses—gains the advantage, it oversteps the mean, and drawing the constitution in its own direction it institutes, as the case may be, either a democracy or an oligarchy. In the second place, factious disputes and struggles readily arise between the masses and the rich; and no matter which side may win the day, it refuses to establish a constitution based on the common interest and the prin-

ciple of equality, but, preferring to exact as the prize of victory a greater share of constitutional rights, it institutes, according to its principles, a democracy or an oligarchy. Thirdly, the policy of the two states which have held the ascendancy in Greece, Athens and Sparta, has also been to blame. Each has paid an exclusive regard to its own type of constitution; the one has instituted democracies in the    5
states under its control, and the other has set up oligarchies: each has looked to its own advantage, and neither to that of the states it controlled. These three reasons explain why a middle or mixed type of constitution has never been established—or, at the most, has only been established on a few occasions and in a few states.                                                                               10

There are three elements, or "powers," in each constitution. The first of the three is the deliberative element concerned with common affairs, and its proper constitution: the second is the element of the magistracies: the third is the judicial element, and the proper constitution of that element.

The deliberative element is sovereign (1) on the issues of war and peace, and    15
the making and breaking of alliances; (2) in the enacting of laws; (3) in cases where the penalty of death, exile, and confiscation is involved; and (4) in the appointment of magistrates and the calling of them to account on the expiration of their office. Three different arrangements of this element are possible: first, to give the decision on *all* the issues it covers to *all* the citizens; secondly, to give    20
the decision on *all* the issues to *some* of the citizens (either by referring them all to one magistracy or combination of magistracies, or by referring different issues to different magistracies); and thirdly, to give the decision on *some issues to all* the citizens, and on *other issues to some* of them.

The first of these arrangements, which assigns all the issues of deliberation    25
to all the citizens, is characteristic of democracies: the equality which it implies is exactly what the people desire. But there are a number of different ways in which it may be effected. First, all the citizens may meet to deliberate in relays, and not in a single body.... They assemble only for the purpose of enacting laws, for dealing with constitutional matters, and for hearing the announce-    30
ments of the magistrates. A second way is that all the citizens should meet to deliberate in a single body, but only for the three purposes of appointing and examining the magistrates, enacting laws, and dealing with issues of war and peace. The other matters will then be left for the deliberation of the magistracies assigned to deal with each branch; but appointment to such magistracies    35
will be open—whether it is made by election or by lot—to all the citizens. A third way is that the citizens should meet for the two purposes of appointing and examining the magistrates, and deliberating on issues of war and foreign policy, but other matters...should be left to the control of boards of magistrates

which, as far as possible, are kept elective—boards to which men of experience and knowledge ought to be appointed. A fourth way is that all should meet to deliberate on all issues, and boards of magistrates should have no power of giving a decision on any issue, but only that of making preliminary investigations.

5   This is the way in which extreme democracy—a form of democracy analogous, as we have suggested, to the dynastic form of oligarchy and the tyrannical form of monarchy—is nowadays conducted.

All these ways of arranging the distribution of deliberative power are democratic. A second system of arrangement, which may also be carried into effect

10   in a number of different ways, is that *some* of the citizens should deliberate on *all* matters. This is characteristic of oligarchy. One way of carrying this second system into effect is that the members of the deliberative body should be eligible on the basis of a moderate property qualification, and should therefore be fairly numerous.… A second way of giving effect to this system is that membership

15   of the deliberative body should belong only to selected persons—and not to all persons—but that these persons should act, as before, in obedience to the rules of law. Another way of carrying this system into effect is that those who possess the power of deliberation should recruit themselves by co-optation, or should simply succeed by heredity, and should have the power of overruling the laws.…

20   A third system of arrangement is that *some* of the citizens should deliberate on *some* matters—but not on all. For instance, all the citizens may exercise the deliberative power in regard to war and peace and the examination of magistrates; but the magistrates only may exercise that power on issues other than these, and these magistrates may be appointed by election. When this is the

25   case, the constitution is an aristocracy. Another alternative is that some issues of deliberation should go to persons appointed by election, and others to persons appointed by lot (with the chance of the lot either open to all or open only to candidates selected in advance), or, again, that all issues should go to a mixed body of elected persons and persons appointed by lot, deliberating together.

30   Such ways of arrangement are partly characteristic of a "polity" verging on aristocracy, and partly of a pure "polity."

A democracy will do well to apply a plan of compulsory attendance to the deliberative assembly. The results of deliberation are better when all deliberate together; when the populace is mixed with the notables and they, in their

35   turn, with the populace. It is also in the interest of a democracy that the parts of the state should be represented in the deliberative body by an equal number of members, either elected for the purpose or appointed by the use of the lot. It is also in its interest, when the members of the populace largely exceed the notables who have political experience, that payment for attendance at the

40   assembly should not be given to all the citizens, but only to so many as will

balance the number of the notables or, alternatively, that the lot should be used to eliminate the excess of ordinary citizens over the notables.

The policy which is in the interest of oligarchies is to co-opt to the deliberative body some members drawn from the populace; or, alternatively, to erect an institution of the type which exists in some states, under the name of "preliminary council" or "council of legal supervision," and then to allow the citizen-body to deal with any issues which have already been considered, in advance, by the members of this institution.... Another line of policy which is in the interest of oligarchies is that the people should only be free to vote for measures which are identical, or at any rate in agreement, with those submitted by the government; or, alternatively, that the people as a whole should have a consultative voice, but the deliberative organ should be the body of magistrates. If the latter alternative is adopted, it should be applied in a way which is the opposite of the practice followed in "politics." The people should be sovereign for the purpose of rejecting proposals, but not for the purpose of passing them; and any proposals which they pass should be referred back to the magistrates.... These are our conclusions in regard to the deliberative or sovereign element in the constitution.

The executive element...like the deliberative, admits of a number of different arrangements. These differences arise on a variety of points: (1) the number of the magistracies; (2) the subjects with which they deal; and (3) the length of the tenure of each.... In some states the tenure is six months; in some it is a less period; in others it is a year; and in others, again, it is a longer period. We have not only to compare these periods; we have also to inquire generally whether magistracies should be held for life, or for a long term of years, or neither for life nor for a long term but only for shorter periods, and whether, in that case, the same person should hold office more than once, or each should be eligible only for a single term.... There is also (4) a further point to be considered—the method of appointment; and this raises three questions—who should be eligible; who should have the right of election; and how should the election be conducted? We have first to distinguish the various methods which it is possible to apply to each of these questions, and then, on that basis, we have to determine the particular form of magistracies which will suit a particular form of constitution.... The title of magistracy should, on the whole, be reserved for those which are charged with the duty, in some given field, of deliberating, deciding, and giving instructions—and more especially with the duty of giving instructions, which is the special mark of the magistrate.... In large states it is both possible and proper that a separate magistracy should be allotted to each separate function. The number of the citizens makes it convenient for a

number of persons to enter an office: it permits some of the offices to be held only once in a lifetime, and others (though held more than once) to be held again only after a long interval; and, apart from convenience, each function gets better attention when it is the only one undertaken, and not one among
5   a number of others.

In small states, on the other hand, a large number of functions have to be accumulated in the hands of but a few persons. The small number of the citizens makes it difficult for many persons to be in office together; and if there were, who would be their successors? It is true that small states sometimes need the same
10   magistracies, and the same laws about their tenure and duties, as large states. But it is also true that large states need their magistracies almost continuously, and small states only need theirs at long intervals....

Which matters need the attention of different local magistracies acting in different places, and which ought to be controlled by one central magistracy
15   acting for the whole area? The maintenance of order is an example. It raises the question whether we should have one person to keep order in the market-place and another in another place, or whether we should have a single person to keep order in every place. We have also to consider whether to allocate duties on the basis of the subject to be handled, or on that of the class of persons concerned:
20   e.g., should we have one officer for the whole subject of the maintenance of order, or a separate officer for the class of children and another for that of women? We have also to take into account the difference of constitutions.... Shall we say that the magistracies too, as well as the magistrates, differ in some respects from one constitution to another; and shall we then add, as a qualification,
25   that in some cases the same magistracies are suitable, but in other cases they are bound to differ?

Here the three points on which differences arise are (1) the membership of the courts; (2) their competence; and (3) the machinery for appointing the members. Membership raises the question whether the courts are to be constituted from
30   all the citizens or from a section; competence raises the question how many kinds of courts there are; the machinery of appointment raises the question whether appointment should be by vote or by lot.

... We must have one or other of the following systems. (1) All the citizens should be eligible to judge on all the matters we have distinguished, and should
35   be chosen for the purpose either (a) by vote or (b) by lot. (2) All the citizens should be eligible to judge on all these matters; but for some of them the courts should be recruited by vote, and for others by lot. (3) All the citizens should be eligible to judge, but only on part of these matters; and the courts concerned with that part should all be similarly recruited, partly by vote and partly by

lot.… There will be an equal number of systems if a sectional method be followed—*i.e.*, if it is only a section of the citizens, and not all, who are eligible
to sit in the courts. In that case we may have (1) judges drawn from a section
by vote to judge on all matters; or (2) judges drawn from a section by lot to
judge on all matters; or (3) judges drawn from a section by vote for some mat-     5
ters and by lot for others [but, together, judging on *all* matters]; or (4) judges
sitting in a limited number of courts, which are similarly recruited partly by
vote and partly by lot. It will be seen that these last four systems, as has just
been said, correspond exactly to the previous four. In addition, we may have
a conjunction of both sorts of systems; for example we may have some courts     10
with members drawn from the whole civic body, others with members drawn
from a section of civic body, and others, again, with a mixed membership (the
same court being, in that case, composed of members drawn from the whole
and of members drawn from a section); and again we may have the members
appointed either by vote, or by lot, or by a mixture of both.                    15

    This gives us a complete list of all the possible systems on which courts can
be constituted. The first sort of system, in which the membership of the courts is
drawn from all, and the courts decide on all matters, is democratic. The second
sort, in which the membership is drawn from a section, and the courts decide
on all matters, is oligarchical. The third sort, in which the membership of some   20
courts is drawn from all, and that of others from a section, is characteristic of
aristocracies and "polities."

# THE NICOMACHEAN ETHICS
## ARISTOTLE (384–322 BC)

I§1Every art and every inquiry, and similarly every action and pursuit, is thought to aim at some good; and for this reason the good has rightly been declared to be that at which all things aim. But a certain difference is found among ends; some are activities, others are products apart from the activities that produce them. Where there are ends apart from the actions, it is the nature of the prod- 5 ucts to be better than the activities. Now, as there are many actions, arts, and sciences, their ends also are many; the end of the medical art is health, that of shipbuilding a vessel, that of strategy victory, that of economics wealth. But where such arts fall under a single capacity—as bridle-making and the other arts concerned with the equipment of horses fall under the art of riding, and 10 this and every military action under strategy, in the same way other arts fall under yet others—in all of these the ends of the master arts are to be preferred to all the subordinate ends; for it is for the sake of the former that the latter are pursued. It makes no difference whether the activities themselves are the ends of the actions, or something else apart from the activities, as in the case of the 15 sciences just mentioned....

X§7If happiness is activity in accordance with virtue, it is reasonable that it should be in accordance with the highest virtue; and this will be that of the best thing in us. Whether it be reason or something else that is this element which is thought to be our natural ruler and guide and to take thought of things noble 20 and divine, whether it be itself also divine or only the most divine element in us, the activity of this in accordance with its proper virtue will be perfect happiness. That this activity is contemplative we have already said.

Now this would seem to be in agreement both with what we said before and with the truth. For, firstly, this activity is the best (since not only is reason 25 the best thing in us, but the objects of reason are the best of knowable objects); and, secondly, it is the most continuous, since we can contemplate truth more

*The Nicomachean Ethics of Aristotle*, translated by Sir David Ross (London: Oxford University Press, 1954): 1, 263–66. By permission of Oxford University Press.

continuously than we can *do* anything. And we think happiness ought to have
pleasure mingled with it, but the activity of philosophic wisdom is admittedly
the pleasantest of virtuous activities; at all events the pursuit of it is thought
to offer pleasures marvelous for their purity and their enduringness, and it is
to be expected that those who know will pass their time more pleasantly than
those who inquire.

And the self-sufficiency that is spoken of must belong most to the contemplative activity. For while a philosopher, as well as a just man or one possessing
any other virtue, needs the necessaries of life, when they are sufficiently equipped
with things of that sort the just man needs people towards whom and with
whom he shall act justly, and the temperate man, the brave man, and each of
the others is in the same case, but the philosopher, even when by himself, can
contemplate truth, and the better the wiser he is he can perhaps do so better if
he has fellow workers, but still he is the most self-sufficient. And this activity
alone would seem to be loved for its own sake; for nothing arises from it apart
from the contemplating, while from practical activities we gain more or less
apart from the action.

And happiness is thought to depend on leisure; for we are busy that we
may have leisure, and make war that we may live in peace. Now the activity of
the practical virtues is exhibited in political or military affairs, but the actions
concerned with these seem to be un-leisurely. Warlike actions are completely
so (for no one chooses to be at war, or provokes war, for the sake of being at
war; anyone would seem absolutely murderous if he were to make enemies of
his friends in order to bring about battle and slaughter); but the action of the
statesman also is un-leisurely, and aims—beyond the political action itself—at
despotic power and honors, or at all events happiness, for him and his fellow
citizens—a happiness different from political action, and evidently sought as
being different. So if among virtuous actions political and military actions are
distinguished by nobility and greatness, and these are un-leisurely and aim at an
end and are not desirable for their own sake, but the activity of reason, which
is contemplative, seems both to be superior in serious worth and to aim at no
end beyond itself, and to have its pleasure proper to itself (and this augments
the activity), and the self-sufficiency, leisureliness, un-weariedness (so far as
this is possible for man), and all the other attributes ascribed to the supremely
happy man are evidently those connected with this activity, it follows that this
will be the complete happiness of man, if it be allowed a complete term of lie
(for none of the attributes of happiness is *in*complete).

But such a life would be too high for man; for it is not in so far as he is man
that he will live so, but in so far as something divine is present in him; and by
so much as this is superior to our composite nature is its activity superior to

that which is the exercise of the other kind of virtue. If reason is divine, then, in comparison with man, the life according to it is divine in comparison with human life. But we must not follow those who advise us, being men, to think of human things, and, being mortal, of mortal things, but must, so far as we can, make ourselves immortal, and strain every nerve to live in accordance with 5 the best thing in us; for even if it be small in bulk, much more does it in power and worth surpass everything. This would seem, too, to be each man himself, since it is the authoritative and better part of him. It would be strange, then, if he were to choose not the life of his self but that of something else. And what we said before will apply now: that which is proper to each thing is by nature 10 best and most pleasant for each thing; for man, therefore, the life according to reason is best and pleasantest, since reason more than anything else *is* man. This life therefore is also the happiest....

# III
# THE HELLENISTIC WORLD

One dates the Hellenistic period from roughly 323 BC, the death of
Alexander the Great, to 30 BC, the death of Cleopatra, the last Hellenistic queen in Egypt. These dates, of course, are somewhat flexible,
the constructs of scholars and historians attempting to make rough things
delicate. Some historians begin the period earlier, others later. Even though
historians disagree on exact dates, they willingly agree that in the period following the decline of classical Greece and the polis, Greek ideas spread throughout
the known civilized world, east to west, thanks to Alexander the Great. But,
because these ideas represented watered-down versions of Hellenic thought,
scholars refer to the period and the ideas as "Hellenistic."

Regardless of what one determines in hindsight, the greatness of classical
Greece passed quickly. Several things contributed to this decline. Tragically,
especially given the sacrifices at such noble and symbolic anti-Oriental battles
of Marathon and Thermopylae, the Greeks never overcame their own jealousies
and suspicions of one another, resulting in brutal and vicious civil wars, only
half a century after the Occidental successes in the Persian Wars. "The free cities
were torn asunder by mutual hatred and by class wars," historian Christopher
Dawson explained in *Progress and Religion*. "They found no place for the greatest
minds of the age—perhaps the greatest minds of any age—who were forced
to take service with tyrants and kings." Dawson, of course, was referring to
Socrates, Plato, and Aristotle, the founders of Western philosophy. Each of the
great philosophers described and defended the best of what had come before
them, fully realizing that the glory days of Greece had long passed. Each served,
vitally, as an anamnesis—a reminder of right reason and first principles. Though
their spirit failed to reawaken Hellenic patriotism, it did preserve it for the
inspiration of later generations and cultures.

Taking advantage of this chaos and the tumult of the Greek city-states, the
loss of Occidental patriotism, and the rise of cultural decadence, Philip II of
Macedon (r. 359–336 BC) and his son, Alexander (r. 336–323 BC), conquered
the former and remaining Greek city-states, and spread Hellenism through
most of the known world, creating, as Dawson noted, a "real world-wide
civilization which influenced the culture of all the peoples of Asia as far east
as North-West India and Turkestan." The expansion of Greek ideals into the

outer world diluted the ideas at home and abroad. "Hellenic civilization collapsed not by a failure of nerve," Dawson concluded, "but by a failure of life." Its traditional philosophies and theologies no longer maintained a hold on its peoples. And, as twentieth century scholars such as Dawson, Russell Kirk, Eric Voegelin, and T. S. Eliot argued, when the root of any culture fails, the culture must die quickly thereafter. The farmer "citizen-soldier" had once stood at the very heart of Hellenic culture at the momentous battles of Thermopylae and Marathon, Dawson argued. Before and during the classical period, the average Greek preserved patriotism, a love of local community and family, seeing his land and his religion as "inseparable from the family tombs and the shrine of the local hero." The culturally decadent—the businessman seeking only profit or the unmanly men who played games all day in an urban setting—replaced the citizen soldier in the Hellenistic period, Dawson lamented.

Philip and Alexander of Macedonia remain two of history's most interesting personalities. At the time of the death of Socrates, their native land had been home to a tribal and rural people with a number of competing monarchs. A question had long existed in the minds of the Greeks and the Macedonians as to just how Greek the Macedonians were. Many Greeks considered their northern neighbors to be little better than the other barbarians of the non-civilized world. Like the Romans, many Macedonians simultaneously desired the fruits of Greek culture while rejecting the Greek citizenry as lacking in manly virtue. A brilliantly ruthless politician and military tactician who considered himself very Greek, Philip centralized the Macedonian government and army under his control. He also improved the massive and traditional Macedonian cavalry and infantry, innovating with the use of the pike. Fighting for the glory of Greece and manipulatively employing patriotic Greek symbols, Philip conquered and centralized many of the former Greek city-states by 338 BC. Once he had achieved Greek unification, Philip hoped to conquer Persia to the east and the rising commercial republic of Carthage in the west. Two years after his victories in Macedonia and Greece, Philip was assassinated, an assassination most likely orchestrated by his wife.

A ruthless man of action, Alexander quickly re-established control of Macedonia and Greece after the assassination of his father, quashing emergent and latent Greek independence movements. The great world historian J. M. Roberts claimed Alexander's counterrevolution against the Greeks "was the real end of four centuries of Greek history," thus officially beginning the Hellenistic period. In 334 BC, at the age of 22, Alexander, who had once been tutored by Aristotle, began to implement his father's larger plans of conquering the east and the west. Inspired by the Homeric Achilles and probably considering himself divine, Alexander led nearly 46,000 men and conquered the Persians at Issus, the Syrians, and the Egyptians as far west as Siwah in North Africa. Turning east again, Alexander and his men entered the Near East through Damascus. Following the Tigris River through Persia, Alexander burned the capital of the ancient Oriental empire, and conquered all the way to the Indus and Ganges rivers. Stopped at the Ganges, supposedly because his men feared the mounted elephant troops of the Indians, Alexander headed west.

On his imperial outings, Alexander brought scholars and scientists with him. He often gave power to locals he conquered (as he had done after the Greek independence movements of 324), as long as they pledged allegiance to him. Importantly, he and his men married local women to solidify relationships, politically, culturally, and biologically. In one famous (or infamous!) wedding, Alexander presided over the marriage of 18,000 persons. Indeed, one cannot easily exaggerate the importance of Alexander's march and influence. Through his martial treks, he carried Greek culture and language to the Persians, to the Egyptians, and to the various Semitic peoples. This would become essential in laying the foundation for what Saint Paul described to the peoples of Galatia, when considering the coming of the Incarnate Word, as the "fullness of times."

When Alexander died of a fever at the age of 33 in 323 BC in Babylon, his empire, the largest the world had yet seen, fractured into many parts. The three most important remnants were the Macedonian kingdom, the Seleucid monarchy (much of former Persia), and Ptolemaic Egypt (of which Cleopatra would be the last queen), each founded by the *diadochi*, former leaders of Alexander's armies. In addition to a number of resulting city-states and smaller kingdoms, these three empires spread Greek ideas throughout the Mediterranean and near-Eastern worlds. Greek, or a form of it, became the language of commerce, and Greek ideas, though watered down from the classical period, penetrated the upper levels of local cultures. Equally important, through the encouragement of the various post-Alexandrian empires, Greeks from the original Greek islands emigrated to various parts of the new empires. One could find typical Greek institutions, such as temples and gymnasiums, throughout the Hellenistic world. Hellenistic Greece prospered economically and urbanized quickly; literacy, literature, science, medicine, and technology flourished as well in this period. The writings of Judas Maccabeus (the first and second Book of Maccabees of the Old Testament/Apocrypha) offer some of our best descriptions of the infiltration and penetration of Greek culture into the local cultures. Judas rejected the Hellenistic influences of the Seleucid monarchy, taking up arms, rebelling, and forming alliances with foreign powers in his struggles for Hebraic independence and orthodoxy.

Much of what developed in the Hellenistic period, especially in terms of the intellectual life, remains a vibrant force throughout the course and history of Western civilization. The philosophies of the Hellenistic period—in particular, Cynicism, Epicureanism, and Stoicism—have greatly shaped Western civilization. This is not to suggest the life of the mind prevailed during the Hellenistic period. Indeed, the mystery cults flourished during this time. But, for those reaching beyond mere superstition, the three philosophies mentioned above offered a post-polis view of the world. Indeed, with the loss of the traditional polis, Greeks had to look elsewhere for meaning. Politics, in particular, no longer satisfied intellectual needs. And, with science taking on a serious life of its own during the Hellenistic period, philosophy became a study of ethics. Cynicism, as founded by Diogenes (*c.* 412–323 BC), claimed that one should reject the norms and complications of life as mere artificial constructions. Instead, one should choose to satisfy the simplest and most basic of human needs, thumbing one's nose at society. Consequently, he advocated impoverishment and the abolition of marriage. Hellenistic society, in return, considered Diogenes and his followers as mere dogs (hence, the term Cynics—to be doglike!), though they also respected Diogenes for his independence. So respected and feared was Diogenes that even his personal insult to Alexander the Great went unpunished.

A second Hellenstic philosopher, Epicurus of Samos (342/1–270 BC), argued that nothing existed beyond matter and the absence of matter. "So death, the most terrifying of ills, is nothing to us, since so long as we exist, death is not with us; but when death comes, then we do not exist," he wrote in his "Letter to Menoeceus." Even the gods, he claimed, merely represented matter that had reached a higher stage than humans. One lived virtuously (that is, through prudence, justice, temperance, fortitude) to match the order of the ever-existing and continuing universe. One chose such a life through free will. As with the Cynics, Epicurus and his followers advocated the rejection of a conventional life in politics, the pursuit of wealth, and the traditional norms of love. Despite their own beliefs about divinity, the Epicureans considered Epicurus somewhat supernatural, and they maintained a rigid orthodoxy of thought after his death.

The final philosophy, Stoicism, developed by a former Cynic, Zeno of Citium (336/5–264/3 BC), and his student, Cleanthes of Assos (*c.* 330–230 BC), argued that one must accept one's fate in the order of the universe. Indeed, one must conform to the dictates of the natural law, itself an emanation of the first principle of order, life, and reason, the artistic fire, the *Logos*. As a school of thought, it borrowed heavily from the teachings and writings of Heraclitus, Plato, and Aristotle. Indeed, in some ways, it merely made an ethical religion out of a synthesis (and, at times, significant revision) of the teachings of these three. The Logos itself, the first principle, was God, synonymous with Providence and Fate. God allowed Himself to be divided into many parts and aspects, but He would, in His own time, bring all things back to right order and unity. No wrong or evil can come from God, as He is the source of all good through the Logos. Evil, therefore, springs from the individual human will violating and countering the Natural Law.

The term Stoicism comes from the name of the area in which Zeno lectured—an outdoor porch, the *Stoa poikile*. In the classical and early Christian world, Stoicism went through three phases or schools. The "early Stoa" of Zeno and Cleanthes; the "middle Stoa" of Virgil (70–19 BC), Cicero (106–43 BC) (to a certain extent, though he called himself a New Academician), and Seneca; and the "late Stoa" of Marcus Aurelius (121–180). The latter two schools, interestingly enough, anticipated some form of incarnate Logos. One can find the most important and telling expression of this in the second school in Virgil's fourth Eclogue.

> The last great age the Sybil told has come; The new order of centuries is born; The Virgin now returns, and the reign of Saturn; The new generation now comes down from heaven…. The Age of Iron gives way to the Golden Age…. Commencement of the glory, freedom from Earth's bondage to its perpetual fear. Our crimes are going to be erased at last. This child will share in the life of the gods and he will see and be seen in the company of heroes, And he will be ruler of the world.

By the time of Marcus Aurelius, the Stoic philosopher and Emperor believed the Roman Empire itself to be an incarnation of the Logos.

Stoicism, in its various forms, has remained the most important Hellenistic influence on Western civilization. From Saints John and Paul, through Saint Augustine, through Petrarch, John Calvin, Sir Thomas More, Stoicism has readily mixed with Christianity. Or, from the Christian perspective, Christianity has sanctified what it found in Stoicism. Saint John began his stunning prologue to his Gospel with the revelation that Christ was the Incarnate Logos. Saint Paul offered a blatantly Stoic philosophy of history in Chapter One of his letter to the Colossians—"He is the first born of creation…." At Mars Hill, Saint Paul quoted the Stoics: "In Him, we move and live and have our being." The original Stoic hymn read, "In Zeus, we move and live and have our being." Even in the late twentieth and early twenty-first century, Stoicism remains a potent force. One can find it directly in the minds of such diverse figures as cultural critic Russell Kirk, Vietnam torture survivor James Stockdale, and Canadian drummer and writer Neil Peart. Still, as the great philosopher Josef Pieper has noted, one should not again separate Stoicism from its Christian ally. An "un-Christian stoicism," he wrote, "is secretly allied with presumption and despair and confronts in defiant invulnerability—without fear, but also without hope—the evils of existence, which it sees with admirable clarity."

# I MACCABEES

*From the time Alexander the Great's empire was split among the Diadochi until 198 BC, Palestine was under the control of the Ptolemaic kings of Egypt, who were noted for their willingness to tolerate religious diversity. During this period, many Jews came to respect Hellenistic culture, though others protested the inherent incompatibility of Judaism and Hellenism. In 198 BC, however, the Seleucid King Antiochus III (r. 222–187 BC) defeated Ptolemy V (r. 204–181 BC) in battle and acquired control of Palestine. The new Seleucid monarch, Antiochus IV Epiphanes (r. 175–164 BC), began to meddle in Jewish affairs, taking advantage of the difference of opinion in the Jewish community regarding cooperation with the Greeks; in an attempt to force the Jews to adopt Greek ways, he built an altar to Zeus in the courtyard of the Temple in Jerusalem. The two books of Maccabees tell the story of the revolt of the Jews against the attempt of Antiochus to destroy their identity by forcing them to violate the covenant. Additionally, Hellenistic acceptance of sensuality, promiscuity, and homosexuality offended orthodox Jews such as Judas and his family. To defeat Seleucid rule, the Maccabees formed an alliance with republican Rome. This agreement, which resulted in the defeat of the Greeks and the cleansing of the Jewish Temple in 165 BC, as celebrated in Hanukkah, also brought a Roman presence to the Holy Land. This laid the foundations for what Paul noted in his letter to the Galatians: Jesus came in "the fullness of times," a Jewish religion, Greek culture, and Roman polity. The Jewish feast of Hanukkah celebrates the victory of Judas Maccabeus and the cleansing of the Temple in 165 BC.*

1 ¹And it happened after that Alexander, son of Philip, the Macedonian, who came out of the land of Chettim, had smitten Darius, King of the Persians and Medes, that he reigned in his stead, the first over Greece, ²and made many wars, and won many strongholds, and slew the kings of the earth,

*The Translation of the Greek Old Testament Scriptures, Including the Apocrypha*, translated by Lancelot C. L. Brenton (London: Samuel Bagster, 1896).

[3]and went through to the ends of the earth, and took spoils of many nations, insomuch that the earth was quiet before him; whereupon he was exalted and his heart was lifted up. [4]And he gathered a mighty strong host and ruled over countries, nations, and kings, who became tributaries unto him.

[5]And after these things he fell sick, and perceived that he should die. [6]Wherefore he called his servants such as were honorable, and had been brought up with him from his youth, and parted his kingdom among them while he was yet alive. [7]So Alexander reigned twelve years, and then died. [8]And his servants ruled every one in his place. [9]And after his death they all put crowns upon themselves; so did their sons after them many years. And evils were multiplied in the earth.

[10]And there came out of them a wicked root Antiochus, surnamed Epiphanes, son of Antiochus the king, who had been an hostage at Rome, and he reigned in the hundred and thirty and seventh year of the kingdom of the Greeks.

[11]In those days went there out of Israel wicked men who persuaded many, saying, "Let us go and make a covenant with the heathen that are round about us. For since we departed from them we have had much sorrow." [12]So this device pleased them well. [13]Then certain of the people were so forward herein that they went to the King, who gave them license to do after the ordinances of the heathen. [14]Whereupon they built a place of exercise at Jerusalem according to the customs of the heathen, [15]and made themselves uncircumcised, and forsook the holy covenant, and joined themselves to the heathen, and were sold to do mischief.

[16]Now when the kingdom was established before Antiochus, he thought to reign over Egypt that he might have the dominion of two realms. [17]Wherefore he entered into Egypt with a great multitude, with chariots, and elephants, and horsemen, and a great navy, [18]and made war against Ptolemy, King of Egypt. But Ptolemy was afraid of him and fled, and many were wounded to death. [19]Thus they got the strong cities in the land of Egypt and he took the spoils thereof.

[20]And after Antiochus had smitten Egypt, he returned again in the hundred forty and third year, and went up against Israel and Jerusalem with a great multitude, [21]and entered proudly into the sanctuary, and took away the golden altar, the candlestick of light, and all the vessels thereof, [22]and the table of the shewbread, the pouring vessels, the vials, the censers of gold, the veil, the crown, and the golden ornaments that were before the temple, all which he pulled off. [23]He took also the silver and the gold, and the precious vessels; also he took the hidden treasures, which he found.

[24]And when he had taken all away, he went into his own land, having made a great massacre, and spoken very proudly. [25]Therefore there was a great mourning in Israel, in every place where they were; [26]so that the princes and

elders mourned, the virgins and young men were made feeble, and the beauty of women was changed. <sup>27</sup>Every bridegroom took up lamentation, and she that sat in the marriage chamber was in heaviness. <sup>28</sup>The land also was moved for the inhabitants thereof, and all the house of Jacob was covered with confusion.

<sup>29</sup>And after two years fully expired, the King sent his chief collector of tribute unto the cities of Judea, who came unto Jerusalem with a great multitude <sup>30</sup>and spoke peaceable words unto them; but all was deceit, for when they had given him credence, he fell suddenly upon the city, and smote it very sore, and destroyed much people of Israel. <sup>31</sup>And when he had taken the spoils of the city, he set it on fire, and pulled down the houses and walls thereof on every side. <sup>32</sup>But the women and children took they captive, and possessed the cattle.

<sup>33</sup>Then they built the City of David with a great and strong wall, and with mighty towers, and made it a stronghold for them. <sup>34</sup>And they put therein a sinful nation, wicked men, and fortified themselves therein. <sup>35</sup>They stored it also with armor and victuals, and when they had gathered together the spoils of Jerusalem, they laid them up there, and so they became a sore snare, <sup>36</sup>for it was a place to lie in wait against the sanctuary, and an evil adversary to Israel.

<sup>37</sup>Thus they shed innocent blood on every side of the sanctuary, and defiled it. <sup>38</sup>Insomuch that the inhabitants of Jerusalem fled because of them. Whereupon the city was made an habitation of strangers, and became strange to those that were born in her; and her own children left her. <sup>39</sup>Her sanctuary was laid waste like a wilderness, her feasts were turned into mourning, her sabbaths into reproach, her honor into contempt. <sup>40</sup>As had been her glory, so was her dishonor increased, and her excellency was turned into mourning.

<sup>41</sup>Moreover, King Antiochus wrote to his whole kingdom that all should be one people <sup>42</sup>and everyone should leave his laws. So all the heathen agreed according to the commandment of the King. <sup>43</sup>Yea, many also of the Israelites consented to his religion, and sacrificed unto idols, and profaned the sabbath.

<sup>44</sup>For the King had sent letters by messengers unto Jerusalem and the cities of Judea that they should follow the strange laws of the land, <sup>45</sup>and forbid burnt offerings, sacrifice, and drink offerings in the Temple; and that they should profane the sabbaths and festival days <sup>46</sup>and pollute the sanctuary and holy people; <sup>47</sup>set up altars, groves, and chapels of idols, and sacrifice swine's flesh and unclean beasts. <sup>48</sup>That they should also leave their children uncircumcised, and make their souls abominable with all manner of uncleanness and profanation, <sup>49</sup>to the end they might forget the law, and change all the ordinances.

<sup>50</sup>And whosoever would not do according to the commandment of the King, he said, he should die. <sup>51</sup>In the self-same manner wrote he to his whole kingdom, and appointed overseers over all the people, commanding the cities of Judea to sacrifice, city by city. <sup>52</sup>Then many of the people were gathered

unto them; to wit, everyone that forsook the law; and so they committed evils in the land; [53]and drove the Israelites into secret places, even wheresoever they could flee for succor.

[54]Now the fifteenth day of the month Kislev, in the hundred forty and
5    fifth year,[1] they set up the abomination of desolation upon the altar, and built idol altars throughout the cities of Judea on every side; [55]and burnt incense at the doors of their houses, and in the streets.

[56]And when they had rent in pieces the books of the law which they found, they burnt them with fire. [57]And whosoever was found with any the book of
10    the testament, or if any committed to the law, the King's commandment was that they should put him to death. [58]Thus did they by their authority unto the Israelites every month, to as many as were found in the cities. [59]Now the five and twentieth day of the month they did sacrifice upon the idol altar, which was upon the altar of God.

15        [60]At which time, according to the commandment, they put to death certain women that had caused their children to be circumcised. [61]And they hanged the infants about their necks, and rifled their houses, and slew them that had circumcised them. [62]Howbeit many in Israel were fully resolved and confirmed in themselves not to eat any unclean thing. [63]Wherefore the rather to die that
20    they might not be defiled with meats, and that they might not profane the holy covenant, so then they died. [64]And there was very great wrath upon Israel.

2   [1]In those days arose Mattathias the son of John, the son of Simeon, a priest of the sons of Joarib, from Jerusalem, and dwelt in Modin. [2]And he had five sons—John, called Caddis; [3]Simon, called Thassi; [4]Judas, who was
25    called Maccabeus; [5]Eleazar, called Avaran; and Jonathan, whose surname was Apphus.

[6]And when he saw the blasphemies that were committed in Judea and Jerusalem [7]he said, "Woe is me! Wherefore was I born to see this misery of my people, and of the holy city, and to dwell there when it was delivered into the
30    hand of the enemy, and the sanctuary into the hand of strangers? [8]Her temple is become as a man without glory. [9]Her glorious vessels are carried away into captivity, her infants are slain in the streets, her young men with the sword of the enemy. [10]What nation has not had a part in her kingdom and gotten of her spoils? [11]All her ornaments are taken away; of a free woman she is become
35    a bond-slave. [12]And, behold, our sanctuary, even our beauty and our glory, is laid waste, and the Gentiles have profaned it. [13]To what end therefore shall we live any longer?"

---

[1]3 December 168 BC

**14**Then Mattathias and his sons rent their clothes, and put on sackcloth, and mourned very sore.

**15**In the meanwhile, the King's officers, such as compelled the people to revolt, came into the city Modin to make them sacrifice. **16**And when many of Israel came unto them, Mattathias also and his sons came together.

**17**Then answered the King's officers and said to Mattathias on this wise, "You are a ruler, and an honorable and great man in this city, and strengthened with sons and brethren. **18**Now, therefore, come first and fulfill the King's commandment, like as all the heathen have done. Yea, and the men of Judea also, and such as remain at Jerusalem. So shall you and your house be in the number of the King's friends, and you and your children shall be honored with silver and gold, and many rewards."

**19**Then Mattathias answered and spoke with a loud voice, "Though all the nations that are under the King's dominion obey him, and fall away everyone from the religion of their fathers, and give consent to his commandments, **20** yet will I and my sons and my brethren walk in the covenant of our fathers. **21**God forbid we should forsake the law and the ordinances. **22**We will not hearken to the King's words to go from our religion, either on the right hand or the left."

**23**Now when he had finished speaking these words, there came one of the Jews in the sight of all to sacrifice on the altar which was at Modin, according to the King's commandment. **24**Which thing, when Mattathias saw, he was inflamed with zeal and his reins trembled, neither could he forbear to show his anger according to judgment; wherefore he ran and slew him upon the altar. **25**Also the King's commissioner, who compelled men to sacrifice, he killed at that time, and the altar he pulled down. **26**Thus dealt he zealously for the law of God like as Phineas did unto Zambri, the son of Salom.

**27**And Mattathias cried throughout the city with a loud voice, saying, "Whosoever is zealous of the law, and maintains the covenant, let him follow me." **28**So he and his sons fled into the mountains, and left all that ever they had in the city. **29**Then many that sought after justice and judgment went down into the wilderness to dwell there. **30**Both they, and their children, and their wives; and their cattle; because afflictions increased sore upon them.

**31**Now when it was told the King's servants, and the host that was at Jerusalem, in the City of David, that certain men, who had broken the king's commandment, were gone down into the secret places in the wilderness, **32**they pursued after them a great number and, having overtaken them, they camped against them, and made war against them on the sabbath day. **33**And they said unto them, "Let that which you have done hitherto suffice; come forth, and do according to the commandment of the King, and you shall live."

[34]But they said, "We will not come forth, neither will we do the King's commandment to profane the sabbath day." [35]So then they gave them the battle with all speed. [36]Howbeit they answered them not, neither cast they a stone at them, nor stopped the places where they lay hid, [37]but said, "Let us die all in our innocency. Heaven and earth will testify for us that you put us to death wrongfully." [38]So they rose up against them in battle on the sabbath and slew them, with their wives and children and their cattle, to the number of a thousand people.

[39]Now when Mattathias and his friends understood hereof, they mourned for them right sore. [40]And one of them said to another, "If we all do as our brethren have done, and fight not for our lives and laws against the heathen, they will now quickly root us out of the earth." [41]At that time therefore they decreed, saying, "Whosoever shall come to make battle with us on the sabbath day, we will fight against him; neither will we die all, as our brethren that were murdered in the secret places."

[42]Then came there unto him a company of Assideans who were mighty men of Israel, even all such as were voluntarily devoted unto the law. [43]Also all they that fled for persecution joined themselves unto them, and were a stay unto them. [44]So they joined their forces, and smote sinful men in their anger, and wicked men in their wrath; but the rest fled to the heathen for succor.

[45]Then Mattathias and his friends went round about and pulled down the altars. [46]And what children soever they found within the coast of Israel un-circumcised, those they circumcised valiantly. [47]They pursued also after the proud men, and the work prospered in their hand. [48]So they recovered the law out of the hand of the Gentiles, and out of the hand of kings, neither suffered they the sinner to triumph....

8 [1]Now Judas had heard of the fame of the Romans, that they were mighty and valiant men, and such as would lovingly accept all that joined themselves unto them, and make a league of amity with all that came unto them; [2]and that they were men of great valor. It was told him also of their wars and noble acts which they had done among the Galatians, and how they had conquered them and brought them under tribute; [3]and what they had done in the country of Spain for the winning of the mines of the silver and gold which is there; [4]and that by their policy and patience they had conquered all the place, though it were very far from them; and the kings also that came against them from the uttermost part of the earth, till they had discomfited them, and given them a great overthrow, so that the rest did give them tribute every year.

[5]Beside this, how they had discomfited in battle Philip and Perseus, King of the Citims, with others that lifted up themselves against them, and had overcome

them. **6**How also Antiochus, the great King of Asia that came against them in battle, having an hundred and twenty elephants, with horsemen, chariots, and a very great army, was discomfited by them; **7**and how they took him alive, and covenanted that he and such as reigned after him should pay a great tribute and give hostages, and that which was agreed upon, **8**and the country of India, and Media and Lydia, and of the goodliest countries, which they took of him and gave to King Eumenes.[2]

**9**Moreover how the Grecians had determined to come and destroy them; **10**and that they, having knowledge thereof, sent against them a certain captain, and fighting with them slew many of them, and carried away captives their wives and their children, and spoiled them, and took possession of their lands, and pulled down their strongholds, and brought them to be their servants unto this day.

**11**It was told him besides how they destroyed and brought under their dominion all other kingdoms and isles that at any time resisted them. **12**But with their friends and such as relied upon them, they kept amity. And that they had conquered kingdoms both far and nigh, insomuch as all that heard of their name were afraid of them. **13**Also that, whom they would help to a kingdom, those reign; and whom again they would, they displace. Finally, that they were greatly exalted. **14**Yet for all this, none of them wore a crown or was clothed in purple, to be magnified thereby. **15**Moreover, how they had made for themselves a senate house, wherein three hundred and twenty men sat in council daily, consulting always for the people, to the end they might be well ordered. **16**And that they committed their government to one man every year, who ruled over all their country, and that all were obedient to that one, and that there was neither envy nor emulation among them.

**17**In consideration of these things, Judas chose Eupolemus, the son of John, the son of Accos, and Jason, the son of Eleazar, and sent them to Rome to make a league of amity and confederacy with them, **18**and to entreat them that they would take the yoke from them; for they saw that the kingdom of the Grecians did oppress Israel with servitude.

**19**They went therefore to Rome, which was a very great journey, and came into the Senate, where they spoke and said. **20**"Judas Maccabeus with his brethren, and the people of the Jews, have sent us unto you to make a confederacy and peace with you, and that we might be registered your confederates and friends." **21**So that matter pleased the Romans well.

**22**And this is the copy of the epistle which the Senate wrote back again in tables of brass, and sent to Jerusalem, that there they might have by them a memorial of peace and confederacy:

---

[2]Eumenes II, King of Pergamon (197–159 BC)

<sup>23</sup>Good success be to the Romans, and to the people of the Jews, by sea and by land for ever. The sword also and enemy be far from them.

<sup>24</sup>If there come first any war upon the Romans or any of their confederates throughout all their dominion, <sup>25</sup>the people of the Jews shall help them, as the time shall be appointed, with all their heart. <sup>26</sup>Neither shall they give anything unto them that make war upon them, or aid them with victuals, weapons, money, or ships, as it has seemed good unto the Romans; but they shall keep their covenants without taking anything therefore. <sup>27</sup>In the same manner also, if war come first upon the nation of the Jews, the Romans shall help them with all their heart, according as the time shall be appointed them. <sup>28</sup>Neither shall victuals be given to them that take part against them, or weapons, or money, or ships, as it has seemed good to the Romans; but they shall keep their covenants, and that without deceit.

<sup>29</sup>According to these articles did the Romans make a covenant with the people of the Jews. <sup>30</sup>Howbeit if hereafter the one party or the other shall think to meet to add or diminish anything, they may do it at their pleasures, and whatsoever they shall add or take away shall be ratified.

<sup>31</sup>And as touching the evils that Demetrius does to the Jews, we have written unto him, saying, "Wherefore have you made your yoke heavy upon our friends and confederates the Jews? <sup>32</sup>If therefore they complain any more against you, we will do them justice, and fight with thee by sea and by land…."

12 <sup>1</sup>Now when Jonathan saw that time served him, he chose certain men and sent them to Rome for to confirm and renew the friendship that they had with them. <sup>2</sup>He sent letters also to the Lacedaemonians, and to other places, for the same purpose. <sup>3</sup>So they went unto Rome, and entered into the Senate and said, "Jonathan the high priest, and the people of the Jews, sent us unto you, to the end you should renew the friendship which you had with them, and league, as in former time. <sup>4</sup>Upon this the Romans gave them letters unto the governors of every place that they should bring them into the land of Judea peaceably. <sup>5</sup>And this is the copy of the letters which Jonathan wrote to the Lacedaemonians:

<sup>6</sup>Jonathan the high priest, and the elders of the nation, and the priests, and the other of the Jews, unto the Lacedaemonians their brethren send greeting.

<sup>7</sup>There were letters sent in times past unto Onias, the High Priest, from Darius, who reigned then among you, to signify that you are our brethren, as the copy here underwritten specifies. <sup>8</sup>At which time Onias entreated the ambassador that was sent honourably, and received the letters, wherein declaration was made of the league and friendship.

⁹Therefore we also, albeit we need none of these things, that we have the holy books of scripture in our hands to comfort us, ¹⁰have nevertheless attempted to send unto you for the renewing of brotherhood and friendship, lest we should become strangers unto you altogether; for there is a long time passed since you sent unto us.

¹¹We therefore at all times without ceasing, both in our feasts, and other convenient days, do remember you in the sacrifices which we offer, and in our prayers, as reason is, and as it becomes us to think upon our brethren. ¹²And we are right glad of your honor.

¹³As for ourselves, we have had great troubles and wars on every side, forsomuch as the kings that are round about us have fought against us. ¹⁴Howbeit we would not be troublesome unto you, nor to others of our confederates and friends, in these wars, ¹⁵for we have help from heaven that succors us, so as we are delivered from our enemies, and our enemies are brought under foot. ¹⁶For this cause we chose Numenius, the son of Antiochus, and Antipater, the son of Jason, and sent them unto the Romans to renew the amity that we had with them, and the former league. ¹⁷We commanded them also to go unto you, and to salute and to deliver you our letters concerning the renewing of our brotherhood. ¹⁸Wherefore now you shall do well to give us an answer thereto.

¹⁹And this is the copy of the letters which Oniares sent:

²⁰Areus, King of the Lacedaemonians, to Onias, the High Priest, greeting.

²¹It is found in writing, that the Lacedaemonians and Jews are brethren, and that they are of the stock of Abraham. ²²Now therefore, since this is come to our knowledge, you shall do well to write unto us of your prosperity. ²³We do write back again to you that your cattle and goods are ours, and ours are yours. We do command therefore our ambassadors to make report unto you on this wise....

# LETTER TO MENOECEUS
## EPICURUS (*c.* 341–270 BC)

*Epicurus founded one of the chief philosophical schools of the Hellenistic
period. His fundamental teaching was the importance of seeking rational
pleasure and avoiding those things that would give one pain; in consequence, he advocated withdrawing from active life together with a small,
select group of friends. Epicurus believed that human beings, like the rest
of the universe, were composed of atoms that simply broke apart at death;
hence, there was no point in troubling oneself about the gods, since they
could have no serious influence on one's fate, nor in worrying about death,
since it was merely "the cessation of life."*

Let no one be slow to seek wisdom when he is young nor weary in the search
of it when he has grown old. For no age is too early or too late for the health
of the soul. And to say that the season for studying philosophy has not yet
come, or that it is past and gone, is like saying that the season for happiness is
not yet or that it is now no more. Therefore, both old and young alike ought     5
to seek wisdom, the former in order that, as age comes over him, he may be
young in good things because of the grace of what has been, and the latter in
order that, while he is young, he may at the same time be old, because he has
no fear of the things which are to come. So we must exercise ourselves in the
things which bring happiness, since, if that be present, we have everything,     10
and, if that be absent, all our actions are directed towards attaining it. Those
things which without ceasing I have declared unto you, do them, and exercise
yourself in them, holding them to be the elements of right life. First believe
that God is a living being immortal and blessed, according to the notion of a
god indicated by the common sense of mankind; and so believing, you shall not     15
affirm of him anything that is foreign to his immortality or that is repugnant
to his blessedness. Believe about him whatever may uphold both his blessedness and his immortality. For there are gods, and the knowledge of them is

*Epochs of Philosophy: Stoic and Epicurean*, edited by Robert Drew Hicks (New York: Scribner's
Sons, 1910), 167–73.

manifest; but they are not such as the multitude believe, seeing that men do not steadfastly maintain the notions they form respecting them. Not the man who denies the gods worshipped by the multitude, but he who affirms of the gods what the multitude believes about them is truly impious. For the utter-

5   ances of the multitude about the gods are not true preconceptions but false assumptions; hence it is that the greatest evils happen to the wicked and the greatest blessings happen to the good from the hand of the gods, seeing that they are always favorable to their own good qualities and take pleasure in men like themselves, but reject as alien whatever is not of their kind.

10   Accustom yourself to believing that death is nothing to us, for good and evil imply the capacity for sensation, and death is the privation of all sentience; therefore a correct understanding that death is nothing to us makes the mortality of life enjoyable, not by adding to life a limitless time, but by taking away the yearning after immortality. For life has no terrors for him who has thoroughly

15   understood that there are no terrors for him in ceasing to live. Foolish, therefore, is the man who says that he fears death, not because it will pain when it comes, but because it pains in the prospect. Whatever causes no annoyance when it is present, causes only a groundless pain in the expectation. Death, therefore, the most awful of evils, is nothing to us, seeing that, when we are, death is not

20   come, and, when death is come, we are not. It is nothing, then, either to the living or to the dead, for with the living it is not and the dead exist no longer. But in the world, at one time men shun death as the greatest of all evils, and at another time choose it as a respite from the evils in life. The wise man does not deprecate life nor does he fear the cessation of life. The thought of life is no

25   offense to him, nor is the cessation of life regarded as an evil. And even as men choose of food not merely and simply the larger portion, but the more pleasant, so the wise seek to enjoy the time which is most pleasant and not merely that which is longest. And he who admonishes the young to live well and the old to make a good end speaks foolishly, not merely because of the desirability of

30   life, but because the same exercise at once teaches to live well and to die well. Much worse is he who says that it were good not to be born, but when once one is born to pass quickly through the gates of Hades. For if he truly believes this, why does he not depart from life? It would be easy for him to do so once he were firmly convinced. If he speaks only in jest, his words are foolishness as

35   those who hear him do not believe.

We must remember that the future is neither wholly ours nor wholly not ours, so that neither must we count upon it as quite certain to come nor despair of it as quite certain not to come.

We must also reflect that of desires some are natural, others are groundless;

40   and that of the natural some are necessary as well as natural, and some natural

only. And of the necessary desires some are necessary if we are to be happy, some
if the body is to be rid of uneasiness, some if we are even to live. He who has a
clear and certain understanding of these things will direct every preference and
aversion toward securing health of body and tranquility of mind, seeing that
this is the sum and end of a blessed life. For the end of all our actions is to be        5
free from pain and fear, and, when once we have attained all this, the tempest
of the soul is laid; seeing that the living creature has no need to go in search
of something that is lacking, nor to look for anything else by which the good
of the soul and of the body will be fulfilled. When we are pained because of
the absence of pleasure, then, and then only, do we feel the need of pleasure.       10
Wherefore we call pleasure the alpha and omega of a blessed life. Pleasure is
our first and kindred good. It is the starting-point of every choice and of every
aversion, and to it we come back, inasmuch as we make feeling the rule by
which to judge of every good thing.

And since pleasure is our first and native good, for that reason we do not        15
choose every pleasure whatsoever, but will often pass over many pleasures when
a greater annoyance ensues from them. And often we consider pains superior
to pleasures when submission to the pains for a long time brings us as a consequence a greater pleasure. While therefore all pleasure because it is naturally
akin to us is good, not all pleasure is worthy of choice, just as all pain is an evil        20
and yet not all pain is to be shunned. It is, however, by measuring one against
another, and by looking at the conveniences and inconveniences, that all these
matters must be judged. Sometimes we treat the good as an evil, and the evil,
on the contrary, as a good. Again, we regard independence of outward things
as a great good, not so as in all cases to use little, but so as to be contented        25
with little if we have not much, being honestly persuaded that they have the
sweetest enjoyment of luxury who stand least in need of it, and that whatever
is natural is easily procured and only the vain and worthless hard to win. Plain
fare gives as much pleasure as a costly diet, when once the pain of want has
been removed, while bread and water confer the highest possible pleasure when        30
they are brought to hungry lips. To habituate one's self, therefore, to simple
and inexpensive diet supplies all that is needful for health, and enables a man
to meet the necessary requirements of life without shrinking, and it places us
in a better condition when we approach at intervals a costly fare and renders
us fearless of fortune.        35

When we say, then, that pleasure is the end and aim, we do not mean the
pleasures of the prodigal or the pleasures of sensuality, as we are understood
to do by some through ignorance, prejudice, or willful misrepresentation. By
pleasure we mean the absence of pain in the body and of trouble in the soul.
It is not an unbroken succession of drinking-bouts and of revelry, not sexual        40

lust, not the enjoyment of the fish and other delicacies of a luxurious table, which produce a pleasant life; it is sober reasoning, searching out the grounds of every choice and avoidance, and banishing those beliefs through which the greatest tumults take possession of the soul. Of all this the beginning and the
5    greatest good is wisdom. Therefore wisdom is a more precious thing even than philosophy; from it spring all the other virtues, for it teaches that we cannot live pleasantly without living wisely, honorably, and justly; nor live wisely, honorably, and justly without living pleasantly. For the virtues have grown into one with a pleasant life, and a pleasant life is inseparable from them.

10    Who, then, is superior in your judgment to such a man? He holds a holy belief concerning the gods, and is altogether free from the fear of death. He has diligently considered the end fixed by nature, and understands how easily the limit of good things can be reached and attained, and how either the duration or the intensity of evils is but slight. Fate, which some introduce as sovereign
15    over all things, he scorns, affirming rather that some things happen of necessity, others by chance, others through our own agency. For he sees that necessity destroys responsibility and that chance is inconstant; whereas our own actions are autonomous, and it is to them that praise and blame naturally attach. It were better, indeed, to accept the legends of the gods than to bow beneath that
20    yoke of destiny which the natural philosophers have imposed.

The one holds out some faint hope that we may escape if we honor the gods, while the necessity of the naturalists is deaf to all entreaties. Nor does he hold chance to be a god, as the world in general does, for in the acts of a god there is no disorder; nor to be a cause, though an uncertain one, for he believes that no good or evil is dispensed by chance to men so as to make life blessed,
25    though it supplies the starting-point of great good and great evil. He believes that the misfortune of the wise is better than the prosperity of the fool. It is better, in short, that what is well judged in action should not owe its successful issue to the aid of chance.

Exercise yourself in these and related precepts day and night, both by
30    yourself and with one who is likeminded; then never, either in waking or in dream, will you be disturbed, but will live as a god among men. For man loses all semblance of mortality by living in the midst of immortal blessings.

# THE DISCOURSES
## EPICTETUS (*c.* 50–138 BC)

*Epictetus was a freedman (i.e., a manumitted slave) from Phrygia in the
Roman province of Asia. He became a noted teacher of Stoicism, the most
important of the Hellenistic philosophies. The Stoic philosophy originated in
Athens with Zeno (336–264 BC), who taught that all things were connected
by an inner spark of the divine; everything that happened did so as part of
a providential ordering of the universe. Epictetus himself stressed the common humanity of man; he also emphasized the Stoic view that one should
cultivate apathy toward external conditions and realize that true virtue lay
within oneself. His teachings were recorded by his disciple Arrian.*

I must die: if instantly, I will die instantly; if in a short time, I will dine first;
and when the hour comes, then I will die. How? As becomes one who restores
what is not his own.                                                    *Discourses I, 1*

---

From every event that happens in the world it is easy to celebrate Providence,
if a person has but these two qualities in himself: a faculty of considering what   5
happens to each individual and a grateful temper. Without the first, he will
not perceive the usefulness of things which happen, and without the other, he
will not be thankful for them. If God had made colors, and had not made the
faculty of seeing them, what would have been their use? None. On the other
hand, if he had made the faculty of observation, without objects to observe,   10
what would have been the use of that? None. Again, if he had formed both the
faculty and the objects, but had not made light? Neither in that case would
they have been of any use.

Who is it then that has fitted each of these to the other? Who is it that has
fitted the sword to the scabbard, and the scabbard to the sword? Is there no   15
such Being? From the very construction of a complete work, we are used to
declare positively that it must be the operation of some artificer, and not the

*The Works of Epictetus*, translated by Thomas Wentworth Higginson (Boston: Little, Brown, and
Company, 1865), 18–20, 28–31, 50, 114–15, 205–6, 379, 393, 427.

effect of mere chance. Does every such work, then, demonstrate an artificer;
and do not visible objects, and the sense of seeing, and light, demonstrate one?
Do not the difference of the sexes, and their inclination to each other, and the
use of their several powers; do not these things demonstrate an artificer? Most
5   certainly they do....

    God has introduced man as a spectator of himself and his works; and not
only as a spectator, but an interpreter of them.                    *Discourses I, 6*

---

If what philosophers say of the kinship between God and men be true, what
has anyone to do but, like Socrates, when he is asked what countryman he is,
10  never to say that he is a citizen of Athens, or of Corinth, but of the universe?...
[Men] alone are qualified to partake of a communication with the Deity, being
connected with him by reason; why may not such a one call himself a citizen of
the universe? Why not a son of God?                                *Discourses I, 9*

---

Why should any one person envy another? Why should he be impressed with
15  awe by those who have great possessions, or are placed in high rank? Especially if
they are powerful and passionate? For what will they do to us? The things which
they can do, we do not regard; the things about which we are concerned, they
cannot reach. Who then, after all, shall hold sway over a person thus disposed?
                                                                    *Discourses I, 9*

---

What else can I do, a lame old man, but sing hymns to God? Were I a night-
20  ingale, I would act the part of a nightingale; were I a swan, the part of a swan.
But since I am a reasonable creature, it is my duty to praise God. This is my
business; I do it. Nor will I ever desert this post, so long as it is permitted me;
and I call on you to join in the same song.                        *Discourses I, 16*

---

You are a primary existence. You are a distinct portion of the essence of God,
25  and contain a certain part of him in yourself. Why then are you ignorant of your
noble birth? Why do not you consider whence you came?... You carry a God
about with you, poor wretch, and know nothing of it. Do you suppose I mean
some god without you of gold or silver? It is within yourself that you carry him;
and you do not observe that you profane him by impure thoughts and unclean
30  actions. If the mere external image of God were present, you would not dare to
act as you do; and when God himself is within you, and hears and sees all, are
not you ashamed to think and act thus, insensible of your own nature, and at
enmity with God?                                                   *Discourses II, 8*

---

Do not you know that both sickness and death must overtake us? At what employment? The husbandman at his plough, the sailor on his voyage. For, indeed, at what employment ought you be taken? For my own part, I would be found engaged in nothing but in the regulation of my own will; how to render it undisturbed, unrestrained, uncompelled, free. I would be found studying this,  5
that I may be able to say to God, "Have I transgressed your commands? Have I perverted the powers, the senses, the instincts, which you have given me? Have I ever accused you, or censured your dispensations? I have been sick, because it was your pleasure, like others; but I willingly. I have been poor, it being your will; but with joy. I have not been in power, because it was not your will, and  10
power I have never desired. Have you ever seen me saddened because of this? Have I not always approached you with a cheerful countenance, prepared to execute your commands and the indications of your will? Is it your pleasure that I should depart from this assembly? I depart. I give you all thanks that you have thought me worthy to have a share in it with you, to behold your works, and  15
to join with you in comprehending your administration." Let death overtake me while I am thinking, while I am writing, while I am reading such things as these.                                                        *Discourses III, 5*

_____

Sickness is an impediment to the body, but not to the will, unless itself pleases. Lameness is an impediment to the leg, but not to the will; and say this to yourself  20
with regard to everything that happens. For you will find it to be an impediment to something else, but not truly to yourself.                    *Enchiridion, §9*

_____

Women from fourteen years old are flattered by men with the title of mistresses. Therefore, perceiving that they are regarded only as qualified to give men pleasure, they begin to adorn themselves, and in that to place all their hopes. It is  25
worthwhile, therefore, to take care that they may perceive themselves honored only so far as they appear beautiful in their demeanor, and modestly virtuous.
                                                        *Enchiridion, §40*

_____

All things serve and obey the laws of the universe—the earth, the sea, the sun, the stars, and the plants and animals of the earth. Our body likewise obeys the same laws, in being sick and well, young and old, and passing through the other  30
changes they decree. It is therefore reasonable that what depends on ourselves, that is, our own understanding, should not be the only rebel against natural law. For the universe is powerful and superior, and consults the best for us by governing in conjunction with the whole. And further, opposition, besides that it is unreasonable, and produces nothing except a vain struggle, throws us into pain  35
and sorrows.                                                *Fragment 131*

# IV
# THE ROMAN REPUBLIC

According to tradition, in 753 BC the city of Rome humbly began along the banks of the Tiber, the largest river on the western coast of Italy. Consisting at this point of scattered villages taking advantage of the famous seven hills of Rome, the city grew from a small polis to a great administrative center that controlled the entire Mediterranean by giving it a political and cultural unity. During the Principate of Octavian Augustus (r. 27 BC–AD 14), which marked the final transformation of the Republic, Vergil's *Aeneid*, the national epic of the Augustan Age, memorialized the mission of the Roman people in the following words:

> Let others better mold the running mass
> Of metals, and inform the breathing brass,
> And soften into flesh a marble face;
> Plead better at the bar; describe the skies,
> And when the stars descend, and when they rise.
> But, Rome, 'tis thine alone, with awful sway,
> To rule mankind, and make the world obey,
> Disposing peace and war by thy own majestic way;
> To tame the proud, the fetter'd slave to free:
> These are imperial arts, and worthy thee.

The Republic honed these "imperial arts" by cultivating a culture based on *virtus* (martial courage) and thus brought the ancient world to its final stage.

Although modern historians are often frustrated by the Romans' willingness to allow the establishment of their priesthoods, festivals, and distinctive rituals to remain in the obscure founding era described by the historian Livy (59 BC–AD 17), the Romans were, first and foremost, a religious people. Their religion emphasized the successful repetition of rituals with a deep respect for the past and for the tradition from which the ritual emerged. Most importantly, Roman religion worked: The practice of rites and ceremonies led their armies to victory, their progeny to increase, and Roman power to grow.

The Roman people overthrew their last king, Tarquinius Superbus, in 509 BC, thus beginning the long evolution of the Roman Republic. From this date until 287 BC, the two social orders of Patricians and Plebeians struggled for political power. Intertwined periods of social unrest and constant military activity, whether expansionistic or in response to threats, mark this era as well. During this time, the Romans developed the major offices, institutions, and assemblies of their experiment in power sharing, culminating in a largely democratic regime.

Since the Romans during the Republic viewed action in the public sphere as the highest activity of man, they competed for the magistracies (offices) with great energy and commitment. Beginning the *cursus honorum* with requisite military service as a military tribune, aspiring Romans could serve as Aediles, Quaestor, or Tribunes before reaching the level of the magistrates with *imperium* (military power over life and death) like the Praetor or the Consul, the highest goal for most of the elite Romans. Having attained the consulship, and a subsequent provincial command later in the Republic, a Roman might reach the final magistracy and serve as censor. By the late Republic, all citizens were eligible for office and all voted.

The people of Rome participated in politics by serving in the army and in the assemblies. For most of the Republican period, political rights and military service were closely intertwined. The most select assembly, the Senate, consisted of the leading men of the best families of Rome. The *Comitia Centuriata*, consisting of 192 Centuries, essentially voted for the major magistrates, while the *Comitia Tributa*, consisting of 33 Tribes, voted for the tribunes. Although the Senate may seem an advisory body, its decrees (*Senatus consulta*) carried much weight.

While reading Polybius (*c.* 203–120 BC) will help flesh out the various roles of the different elements of the Roman Constitution, his shrewd observations only partly explain the workings of the system. Like most pre-modern people, the Romans had a profound regard for antiquity and developed a deeply conservative system. They relied on a sense of *Auctoritas* combined with *Mos maiorum* (the customs of their ancestors). Members of the Senate all had served the Roman state for many years. Although the Republic did foster a senatorial aristocracy, its members generally operated cautiously with regard for the interests of the state. Even though the Roman system operated on ideas of hierarchy and deference, the senatorial aristocracy remained closely connected with other elements of society through webs of patron and client relationships.

Under this republican constitution, the Romans conquered Italy, then Carthage, the major western power, and then each of the Hellenistic kingdoms. These conquests and the development of a territorial empire placed severe strains of the previous system and eventually destroyed it. "New Men" rose outside the traditional avenue of power. The haphazard development of a Mediterranean empire provided scope for opportunities and ambition not previously available. Finally, politicians realized that much could be gained working outside the bounds of old system (ignoring the *cursus honorum* and balance of power created by competition within the bounds of the constitutional system).

In comparing the Romans to the Greek culture they conquered (and which in turn, conquered them), the Roman historian Sallust (86–34 BC) in his work *Catilina* (Book 8:3–5) explained:

> But because writers of great talent flourished there, the actions of the Athenians are celebrated over the world as the most splendid achievements. Thus, the merit of those who have acted is estimated at the highest point to which illustrious intellects could exalt it in their writings. But among the Romans there was never any such abundance of writers; for, with them, the most able men were the most actively employed. No one exercised the mind independently of the body: every man of ability chose to act rather than narrate, and was more desirous that his own merits should be celebrated by others than that he himself should record theirs.

Although the Roman Republic lacked a Herodotus or Thucydides to chronicle their success, the Romans were able to develop men of action because of their regard for the customs and values passed down from generation to generation.

Romans aspired to the simple ideal of the farmer, soldier, and politician. They expected that these values be taught at home through the foundational institution of the family. Through the *History of Titus Livius* (Livy) with his vivid portrayals of heroic deeds, and the great poem of Publius Vergilius Maro (70 BC–AD 19), the *Aeneid*, the Romans inculcated in childhood virtues such as *pietas* (duty), *gravitas* (sense of seriousness), *constantia* (evenness), and *magnitudo animi* (greatness of spirit). These virtues represent the best of the Republic and were sorely missing at its end.

Perhaps curiously, the second great development of the Roman Republic, considering the constitution as the first, was the rise of the Roman Empire, Rome's gradually developed hegemony over the entire Mediterranean World. Following the Punic Wars (264–146 BC), from 200–31 BC the Romans conquered the Hellenistic kingdoms of the eastern Mediterranean. These wars resulted in several consequences which placed unendurable pressure on the Roman state. First, the state of almost permanent war from 509–31 BC could not help but put a deep strain on the Roman constitution, especially considering the intensity of the first century wars. Second, war provided scope for ambition, wealth, and prestige outside the bounds of the traditional Roman system. Third, while warfare originally complemented the Roman political system, increasingly the professional military establishment produced stresses on this system. Fourth, the growth of the Roman Empire beyond Italy, the fruit of the second Punic War, required a provincial administration that opened the system to more new men. Finally, the institutionalization of extra-constitutional avenues to power led to the willingness of many men to operate outside the traditional system to gain what they wanted: power and office. The careers of the Gracchi, Marius, Sulla, Pompey, Crassus, and Caesar testify to this willingness and the catastrophic century (133–31 BC) in which they destroyed the Republic.

Looking back from his first century vantage point, Cicero (106–43 BC) poignantly lamented:

> Long before our time, the customs of our ancestors molded admirable men, and in turn those eminent men upheld the ways and institutions of their forebears. Our age, however, inherited the Republic as if it were some beautiful painting of bygone ages, its colors already fading through great antiquity; and not only has our time neglected to freshen the colors of the picture, but we have failed to preserve its form and outlines.

This statement reflects both the Roman Republican appreciation of tradition and the paucity of men during Cicero's lifetime who might, by committing themselves to public good over private gain, recover the devotion to the Senate and people of Rome (SPQR) and its constitution that characterized the Republican Period. Ultimately, the Roman Republic's success in conquering and incorporating its conquests served as the instrument of its demise into the fiction of the Principate.

# THE HISTORIES
## POLYBIUS (*c.* 200–118 BC)

*Polybius, a Greek from the Peloponnesus, was a leader of the Achaean League. Between 167 and 151 BC, he lived as a hostage in Rome, where he had the opportunity to study the Roman constitution and to write a history of Rome's rise to mastery of the Mediterranean.*

**VI§1**I am aware that some will be at a loss to account for my interrupting the course of my narrative for the sake of entering upon the following disquisition on the Roman constitution. But I think that I have already in many passages made it fully evident that this particular branch of my work was one of the necessities imposed on me by the nature of my original design; and I pointed    5
this out with special clearness in the preface which explained the scope of my history. I there stated that the feature of my work which was at once the best in itself, and the most instructive to the students of it, was that it would enable them to know and fully realize in what manner, and under what kind of constitution, it came about that nearly the whole world fell under the power    10
of Rome in somewhat less than fifty-three years—an event certainly without precedent. This being my settled purpose, I could see no more fitting period than the present for making a pause, and examining the truth of the remarks about to be made on this constitution. In private life if you wish to satisfy yourself as to the badness or goodness of particular persons, you would not, if you wish    15
to get a genuine test, examine their conduct at a time of uneventful repose, but in the hour of brilliant success or conspicuous reverse. For the true test of a perfect man is the power of bearing with spirit and dignity violent changes of fortune. An examination of a constitution should be conducted in the same way; and therefore being unable to find in our day a more rapid or more signal    20
change than that which has happened to Rome, I reserved my disquisition on its constitution for this place....

*The Histories of Polybius*, translated by Evelyn S. Shuckburgh (London: MacMillan and Company, 1889), I: 458–59, 468–74, 501–6.

**VI§2**…What is really educational and beneficial to students of history is the clear view of the causes of events, and the consequent power of choosing the better policy in a particular case. Now in every practical undertaking by a state we must regard as the most powerful agent for success or failure the form of its
5    constitution; for from this as from a fountain-head all conceptions and plans of action not only proceed, but attain their consummation….

**VI§11**I have given an account of the constitution of Lycurgus, I will now endeavor to describe that of Rome at the period of their disastrous defeat at Cannae…. As for the Roman constitution, it had three elements, each of them possessing
10   sovereign powers; and their respective share of power in the whole state had been regulated with such a scrupulous regard to equality and equilibrium, that no one could say for certain, not even a native, whether the constitution as a whole were an aristocracy or democracy or despotism. And no wonder; for if we confine our observation to the power of the consuls we should be inclined
15   to regard it as despotic; if on that of the Senate, as aristocratic; and if finally one looks at the power possessed by the people it would seem a clear case of a democracy. What the exact powers of these several parts were, and still, with slight modifications, are, I will now state.

**VI§12**The Consuls, before leading out the legions, remain in Rome and are su-
20   preme masters of the administration. All other magistrates, except the Tribunes, are under them and take their orders. They introduce foreign ambassadors to the Senate; bring matters requiring deliberation before it; and see to the execution of its decrees. If, again, there are any matters of state which require the authorization of the people, it is their business to see to them, to summon
25   the popular meetings, to bring the proposals before them, and to carry out the decrees of the majority. In the preparations for war also, and in a word in the entire administration of a campaign, they have all but absolute power. It is competent to them to impose on the allies such levies as they think good, to appoint the Military Tribunes, to make up the roll for soldiers and select those
30   that are suitable. Besides they have absolute power of inflicting punishment on all who are under their command while on active service; and they have author-ity to expend as much of the public money as they choose, being accompanied by a quaestor who is entirely at their orders. A survey of these powers would in fact justify our describing the constitution as despotic—a clear case of royal
35   government. Nor will it affect the truth of my description if any of the institu-tions I have described are changed in our time, or in that of our posterity; and the same remarks apply to what follows.

**VI§13**The Senate has first of all the control of the treasury, and regulates the receipts and disbursements alike. For the Quaestors cannot issue any public money for the various departments of the state without a decree of the Senate, except for the service of the Consuls. The Senate controls also what is by far the largest and most important expenditure, that, namely, which is made by the censors every *lustrum*[1] for the repair or construction of public buildings; this money cannot be obtained by the censors except by the grant of the Senate. Similarly all crimes committed in Italy requiring a public investigation, such as treason, conspiracy, poisoning, or willful murder, are in the hands of the Senate. Besides, if any individual or state among the Italian allies requires a controversy to be settled, a penalty to be assessed, help or protection to be afforded—all this is the province of the Senate. Or again, outside Italy, if it is necessary to send an embassy to reconcile warring communities, or to remind them of their duty, or sometimes to impose requisitions upon them, or to receive their submission, or finally to proclaim war against them—this too is the business of the Senate. In like manner the reception to be given to foreign ambassadors in Rome, and the answers to be returned to them, are decided by the Senate. With such business the people have nothing to do. Consequently, if one were staying at Rome when the Consuls were not in town, one would imagine the constitution to be a complete aristocracy; and this has been the idea entertained by many Greeks, and by many kings as well, from the fact that nearly all the business they had with Rome was settled by the Senate.

**VI§14**After this one would naturally be inclined to ask what part is left for the people in the constitution, when the Senate has these various functions, especially the control of the receipts and expenditure of the exchequer;[2] and when the Consuls, again, have absolute power over the details of military preparation, and an absolute authority in the field? There is, however, a part left the people, and it is a most important one. For the people is the sole fountain of honor and of punishment; and it is by these two things and these alone that dynasties and constitutions and, in a word, human society are held together; for where the distinction between them is not sharply drawn both in theory and practice, there no undertaking can be properly administered—as indeed we might expect when good and bad are held in exactly the same honor. The people then are the only court to decide matters of life and death; and even in cases where the penalty is money, if the sum to be assessed is sufficiently serious, and especially when the accused have held the higher magistracies. And in regard to this

---

[1]*Lustrum*—a five-year period
[2]*Exchequer*—an institution responsible for the collection and management of state revenues

arrangement there is one point deserving especial commendation and record. Men who are on trial for their lives at Rome, while sentence is in process of being voted—if even only one of the tribes whose votes are needed to ratify the sentence has not voted—have the privilege at Rome of openly departing
5 and condemning themselves to a voluntary exile. Such men are safe at Naples or Praeneste or at Tibur, and at other towns with which this arrangement has been duly ratified on oath.

Again, it is the people who bestow offices on the deserving, which are the most honorable rewards of virtue. It has also the absolute power of passing or
10 repealing laws; and, most important of all, it is the people who deliberate on the question of peace or war. And when provisional terms are made for alliance, suspension of hostilities, or treaties, it is the people who ratify them or the reverse.

These considerations again would lead one to say that the chief power in
15 the state was the people's, and that the constitution was a democracy.

**VI§15**Such, then, is the distribution of power between the several parts of the state. I must now show how each of these several parts can, when they choose, oppose or support each other.

The Consul, then, when he has started on an expedition with the powers I
20 have described, is to all appearance absolute in the administration of the business in hand; still he has need of the support both of people and Senate, and, without them, is quite unable to bring the matter to a successful conclusion. For it is plain that he must have supplies sent to his legions from time to time; but without a decree of the Senate they can be supplied neither with corn, nor
25 clothes, nor pay, so that all the plans of a commander must be futile, if the Senate is resolved either to shrink from danger or hamper his plans. And again, whether a Consul shall bring any undertaking to a conclusion or no depends entirely upon the Senate; for it has absolute authority at the end of a year to send another Consul to supersede him, or to continue the existing one in his
30 command. Again, even to the successes of the generals the Senate has the power to add distinction and glory, and on the other hand to obscure their merits and lower their credit. For these high achievements are brought in tangible form before the eyes of the citizens by what are called "triumphs." But these triumphs the commanders cannot celebrate with proper pomp, or in some cases celebrate
35 at all, unless the Senate concurs and grants the necessary money. As for the people, the Consuls are pre-eminently obliged to court their favor, however distant from home may be the field of their operations; for it is the people, as I have said before, that ratifies, or refuses to ratify, terms of peace and treaties; but most of all because when laying down their office they have to give an account

of their administration before it. Therefore in no case is it safe for the Consuls to neglect either the Senate or the good-will of the people.

**VI§16**As for the Senate, which possesses the immense power I have described, in the first place it is obliged in public affairs to take the multitude into account, and respect the wishes of the people; and it cannot put into execution the penalty   5 for offences against the republic, which are punishable with death, unless the people first ratify its decrees. Similarly even in matters which directly affect the senators—for instance, in the case of a law diminishing the Senate's traditional authority, or depriving senators of certain dignities and offices, or even actually cutting down their property—even in such cases the people have the sole power   10 of passing or rejecting the law. But most important of all is the fact that, if the Tribunes interpose their veto, the Senate not only are unable to pass a decree, but cannot even hold a meeting at all, whether formal or informal. Now, the Tribunes are always bound to carry out the decree of the people, and above all things to have regard to their wishes; therefore, for all these reasons the Senate   15 stands in awe of the multitude, and cannot neglect the feelings of the people.

**VI§17**In like manner the people on its part is far from being independent of the Senate, and is bound to take its wishes into account both collectively and individually. For contracts, too numerous to count, are given out by the censors in all parts of Italy for the repairs or construction of public buildings; there is also   20 the collection of revenue from many rivers, harbors, gardens, mines, and land— everything, in a word, that comes under the control of the Roman government; and in all these the people at large are engaged; so that there is scarcely a man, so to speak, who is not interested either as a contractor or as being employed in the works. For some purchase the contracts from the censors for themselves; and   25 others go partners with them; while others again go security for these contractors, or actually pledge their property to the treasury for them. Now over all these transactions the Senate has absolute control. It can grant an extension of time; and in case of unforeseen accident can relieve them from it altogether, if they are absolutely unable to fulfill it. And there are many details in which the Senate   30 can inflict great hardships, or, on the other hand, grant great indulgences to the contractors; for in every case the appeal is to it. But the most important point of all is that the judges are taken from its members in the majority of trials, whether public or private, in which the charges are heavy. Consequently, all citizens are much at its mercy; and being alarmed at the uncertainty as to when they may   35 need its aid, are cautious about resisting or actively opposing its will. And for a similar reason men do not rashly resist the wishes of the Consuls, because one and all may become subject to their absolute authority on a campaign.

**VI§18**The result of this power of the several estates for mutual help or harm is a union sufficiently firm for all emergencies, and a constitution than which it is impossible to find a better. For whenever any danger from without compels them to unite and work together, the strength which is developed by the State is so extraordinary, that everything required is unfailingly carried out by the
5 eager rivalry shown by all classes to devote their whole minds to the need of the hour, and to secure that any determination come to should not fail for want of promptitude; while each individual works, privately and publicly alike, for the accomplishment of the business in hand. Accordingly, the peculiar constitution of the State makes it irresistible, and certain of obtaining whatever it determines
10 to attempt. Nay, even when these external alarms are past, and the people are enjoying their good fortune and the fruits of their victories, and, as usually happens, growing corrupted by flattery and idleness, show a tendency to violence and arrogance—it is in these circumstances, more than ever, that the constitution is seen to possess within itself the power of correcting abuses. For when
15 any one of the three classes becomes puffed up, and manifests an inclination to be contentious and unduly encroaching, the mutual interdependency of all the three, and the possibility of the pretensions of any one being checked and thwarted by the others, must plainly check this tendency; and so the proper equilibrium is maintained by the impulsiveness of the one part being checked
20 by its fear of the other....

**VI§51**Now the Carthaginian constitution seems to me originally to have been well contrived in these most distinctively important particulars. For they had kings, and the Gerusia[3] had the powers of an aristocracy, and the multitude were supreme in such things as affected them; and on the whole the adjustment of
25 its several parts was very like that of Rome and Sparta. But about the period of its entering on the Hannibalian war the political state of Carthage was on the decline, that of Rome improving. For whereas there is in every body, or polity, or business a natural stage of growth, zenith, and decay; and whereas everything in them is at its best at the zenith; we may thereby judge of the difference between
30 these two constitutions as they existed at that period. For exactly so far as the strength and prosperity of Carthage preceded that of Rome in point of time, by so much was Carthage then past its prime, while Rome was exactly at its zenith, as far as its political constitution was concerned. In Carthage therefore the influence of the people in the policy of the state had already risen to be
35 supreme, while at Rome the Senate was at the height of its power; and so, as in the one measures were deliberated upon by the many, in the other by the best

---

[3]*Gerusia*—Council of Elders

men, the policy of the Romans in all public undertakings proved the stronger; on which account, though they met with capital disasters, by force of prudent counsels they finally conquered the Carthaginians in the war.

**VI§52**If we look however at separate details, for instance at the provisions for carrying on a war, we shall find that whereas for a naval expedition the    5
Carthaginians are the better trained and prepared—as it is only natural with a people with whom it has been hereditary for many generations to practice this craft, and to follow the seaman's trade above all nations in the world—yet, in regard to military service on land, the Romans train themselves to a much higher pitch than the Carthaginians. The former bestow their whole atten-   10
tion upon this department; whereas the Carthaginians wholly neglect their infantry, though they do take some slight interest in the cavalry. The reason of this is that they employ foreign mercenaries, the Romans native and citizen levies. It is in this point that the latter polity is preferable to the former. They have their hopes of freedom ever resting on the courage of mercenary troops;   15
the Romans on the valor of their own citizens and the aid of their allies. The result is that even if the Romans have suffered a defeat at first, they renew the war with undiminished forces, which the Carthaginians cannot do. For, as the Romans are fighting for country and children, it is impossible for them to relax the fury of their struggle; but they persist with obstinate resolution until they   20
have overcome their enemies. What has happened in regard to their navy is an instance in point. In skill the Romans are much behind the Carthaginians, as I have already said; yet the upshot of the whole naval war has been a decided triumph for the Romans, owing to the valor of their men. For although nautical science contributes largely to success in sea-fights, still it is the courage of the   25
marines that turns the scale most decisively in favor of victory. The fact is that Italians as a nation are by nature superior to Phoenicians and Libyans both in physical strength and courage; but still their habits also do much to inspire the youth with enthusiasm for such exploits. One example will be sufficient of the pains taken by the Roman state to turn out men ready to endure anything to   30
win a reputation in their country for valor.

**VI§53**Whenever one of their illustrious men dies, in the course of his funeral, the body with all its paraphernalia is carried into the forum to the Rostra, as a raised platform there is called, and sometimes is propped upright upon it so as to be conspicuous, or, more rarely, is laid upon it. Then with all the people   35
standing round, his son, if he has left one of full age and he is there, or, failing him, one of his relations, mounts the Rostra and delivers a speech concerning the virtues of the deceased, and the successful exploits performed by him in

his lifetime. By these means the people are reminded of what has been done, and made to see it with their own eyes—not only such as were engaged in the actual transactions but those also who were not;--and their sympathies are so deeply moved, that the loss appears not to be confined to the actual mourners, but to be a public one affecting the whole people. After the burial and all the usual ceremonies have been performed, they place the likeness of the deceased in the most conspicuous spot in his house, surmounted by a wooden canopy or shrine. This likeness consists of a mask made to represent the deceased with extraordinary fidelity both in shape and color. These likenesses they display at public sacrifices adorned with much care. And when any illustrious member of the family dies, they carry these masks to the funeral, putting them on men whom they thought as like the originals as possible in height and other personal peculiarities. And these substitutes assume clothes according to the rank of the person represented; if he was a consul or praetor, a toga with purple stripes; if a censor, whole purple; if he had also celebrated a triumph or performed any exploit of that kind, a toga embroidered with gold. These representatives also ride themselves in chariots, while the fasces and axes, and all the other customary insignia of the particular offices, lead the way, according to the dignity of the rank in the state enjoyed by the deceased in his lifetime; and on arriving at the Rostra they all take their seats on ivory chairs in their order. There could not easily be a more inspiring spectacle than this for a young man of noble ambitions and virtuous aspirations. For can we conceive any one to be unmoved at the sight of all the likenesses collected together of the men who have earned glory, all as it were living and breathing? Or what could be a more glorious spectacle?

VI§54Besides the speaker over the body about to be buried, after having finished the panegyric of this particular person, starts upon the others whose representatives are present, beginning with the most ancient, and recounts the successes and achievements of each. By this means the glorious memory of brave men is continually renewed; the fame of those who have performed any noble deed is never allowed to die; and the renown of those who have done good service to their country becomes a matter of common knowledge to the multitude, and part of the heritage of posterity. But the chief benefit of the ceremony is that it inspires young men to shrink from no exertion for the general welfare, in the hope of obtaining the glory which awaits the brave. And what I say is confirmed by this fact. Many Romans have volunteered to decide a whole battle by single combat; not a few have deliberately accepted certain death, some in time of war to secure the safety of the rest, some in time of peace to preserve the safety of the commonwealth. There have also been instances of men in office putting their own sons to death, in defiance of every custom and law, because they rated the interests of their country higher than those of natural ties even with their nearest and dearest. There are many stories of this kind, related of many men in Roman history; but one will be enough for our present purpose; and I will give the name as an instance to prove the truth of my words.

**VI§55**The story goes that Horatius Cocles, while fighting with two enemies at 5 the head of the bridge over the Tiber, which is the entrance to the city on the north, seeing a large body of men advancing to support his enemies, and fearing that they would force their way into the city, turned round, and shouted to those behind him to hasten back to the other side and break down the bridge. They obeyed him; and whilst they were breaking the bridge, he remained at 10 his post receiving numerous wounds, and checked the progress of the enemy; his opponents being panic stricken, not so much by his strength as by the audacity with which he held his ground. When the bridge had been broken down, the attack of the enemy was stopped; and Cocles then threw himself into the river with his armor on and deliberately sacrificed his life, because he 15 valued the safety of his country and his own future reputation more highly than his present life, and the years of existence that remained to him. Such is the enthusiasm and emulation for noble deeds that are engendered among the Romans by their customs.

**VI§56**Again the Roman customs and principles regarding money transactions 20 are better than those of the Carthaginians. In the view of the latter nothing is disgraceful that makes for gain; with the former nothing is more disgraceful than to receive bribes and to make profit by improper means. For they regard wealth obtained from unlawful transactions to be as much a subject of reproach, as a fair profit from the most unquestioned source is of commendation. A proof of 25 the fact is this. The Carthaginians obtain office by open bribery, but among the Romans the penalty for it is death. With such a radical difference, therefore, between the rewards offered to virtue among the two peoples, it is natural that the ways adopted for obtaining them should be different also.

But the most important difference for the better which the Roman com- 30 monwealth appears to me to display is in their religious beliefs. For I conceive that what in other nations is looked upon as a reproach, I mean a scrupulous fear of the gods, is the very thing which keeps the Roman commonwealth together. To such an extraordinary height is this carried among them, both in private and public business, that nothing could exceed it. Many people might 35 think this unaccountable; but in my opinion their object is to use it as a check upon the common people. If it were possible to form a state wholly of philosophers, such a custom would perhaps be unnecessary. But seeing that every

multitude is fickle, and full of lawless desires, unreasoning anger, and violent passion, the only resource is to keep them in check by mysterious terrors and scenic effects of this sort. Wherefore, to my mind, the ancients were not acting without purpose or at random, when they brought in among the vulgar those
5    opinions about the gods, and the belief in the punishments in Hades; much rather do I think that men nowadays are acting rashly and foolishly in rejecting them. This is the reason why, apart from anything else, Greek statesmen, if entrusted with a single talent, though protected by ten checking-clerks, as many seals, and twice as many witnesses, yet cannot be induced to keep faith;
10   whereas among the Romans, in their magistracies and embassies, men have the handling of a great amount of money, and yet from pure respect to their oath keep their faith intact. And, again, in other nations it is a rare thing to find a man who keeps his hands out of the public purse, and is entirely pure in such matters; but among the Romans it is a rare thing to detect a man in the act of
15   committing such a crime....

# Marcus Cato
## Plutarch (*c.* 46–120)

*In his* Parallel Lives, *a series of biographies in which he paired the life of
a prominent Greek with that of a prominent Roman, the Greek moralist
Plutarch paired Marcus Cato (234–149 BC), also known as Cato the Elder
or Cato the Censor, with Aristides the Just (520–468 BC), an Athenian
statesman and general during the Persian Wars and a noted example of
integrity in public life. Since Plutarch's interest lay in the moral lessons
to be drawn from such character studies, his portrayal of Marcus Cato
provides an excellent description of the qualities the Romans prized during
the Republican period.*

Marcus Cato, we are told, was born at Tusculum, though (till he betook himself to civil and military affairs) he lived and was bred up in the country of the
Sabines, where his father's estate lay. His ancestors seeming almost entirely
unknown, he himself praises his father Marcus, as a worthy man and a brave
soldier, and Cato, his great-grandfather, too, as one who had often obtained   5
military prizes, and who, having lost five horses under him, received, on the
account of his valor, the worth of them out of the public exchequer. Now it
being the custom among the Romans to call those who, having no repute by
birth, made themselves eminent by their own exertions, new men or upstarts,
they called even Cato himself so, and so he confessed himself to be as to any   10
public distinction or employment, but yet asserted that in the exploits and
virtues of his ancestors he was very ancient. His third name originally was not
Cato, but Priscus, though afterwards he had the surname of Cato, by reason
of his abilities; for the Romans call a skilful or experienced man Catus. He was
of a ruddy complexion and grey-eyed; as the writer, who, with no good-will,   15
made the following epigram upon him lets us see:

*Plutarch's Lives of Illustrious Men*, translated by John Dryden, edited by Arthur Hugh Clough
(Boston: Little, Brown, and Company, 1888), 242–54.

*Porcius, who snarls at all in every place,*
*With his grey eyes, and with his fiery face,*
*Even after death will scarce admitted be*
*Into the infernal realms by Hecate.*

5    He gained, in early life, a good habit of body by working with his own hands, and living temperately, and serving in war; and seemed to have an equal proportion both of health and strength. And he exerted and practiced his eloquence through all the neighborhood and little villages; thinking it as requisite as a second body, and an all but necessary organ to one who looks forward to
10    something above a mere humble and inactive life. He would never refuse to be counsel for those who needed him, and was, indeed, early reckoned a good lawyer, and, ere long, a capable orator.

Hence his solidity and depth of character showed itself gradually more and more to those with whom he was concerned, and claimed, as it were, employ-
15    ment in great affairs and places of public command. Nor did he merely abstain from taking fees for his counsel and pleading, but did not even seem to put any high price on the honour which proceeded from such kind of combats, seeming much more desirous to signalize himself in the camp and in real fights; and while yet but a youth, had his breast covered with scars he had received from
20    the enemy: being (as he himself says) but seventeen years old when he made his first campaign; in the time when Hannibal, in the height of his success, was burning and pillaging all Italy. In engagements he would strike boldly, without flinching, stand firm to his ground, fix a bold countenance upon his enemies, and with a harsh threatening voice accost them, justly thinking himself and telling
25    others that such a rugged kind of behavior sometimes terrifies the enemy more than the sword itself. In his marches he bore his own arms on foot, whilst one servant only followed, to carry the provision for his table, with whom he is said never to have been angry or hasty whilst he made ready his dinner or supper, but would, for the most part, when he was free from military duty, assist and
30    help him himself to dress it. When he was with the army, he used to drink only water; unless, perhaps, when extremely thirsty, he might mingle it with a little vinegar, or if he found his strength fail him, take a little wine.

The little country house of Manius Curius, who had been thrice carried in triumph, happened to be near his farm; so that often going thither, and
35    contemplating the small compass of the place, and plainness of the dwelling, he formed an idea of the mind of the person, who being one of the greatest of the Romans, and having subdued the most warlike nations, nay, had driven Pyrrhus out of Italy, now, after three triumphs, was contented to dig in so small a piece of ground, and live in such a cottage. Here it was that the ambassadors

of the Samnites, finding him boiling turnips in the chimney corner, offered him a present of gold; but he sent them away with this saying; that he, who was content with such a supper, had no need of gold; and that he thought it more honorable to conquer those who possessed the gold, than to possess the gold itself. Cato, after reflecting upon these things, used to return and, reviewing 5 his own farm, his servants, and housekeeping, increase his labor and retrench all superfluous expenses.

When Fabius Maximus took Tarentum, Cato, being then but a youth, was a soldier under him; and being lodged with one Nearchus, a Pythagorean, desired to understand some of his doctrine, and hearing from him the language, 10 which Plato also uses, that pleasure is evil's chief bait; the body the principal calamity of the soul; and that those thoughts which most separate and take it off from the affections of the body most enfranchise and purify it; he fell in love the more with frugality and temperance. With this exception, he is said not to have studied Greek until when he was pretty old; and in rhetoric to have 15 then profited a little by Thucydides, but more by Demosthenes; his writings, however, are considerably embellished with Greek sayings and stories; nay, many of these, translated word for word, are placed with his own apophthegms and sentences.

There was a man of the highest rank, and very influential among the 20 Romans, called Valerius Flaccus, who was singularly skillful in discerning excellence yet in the bud, and also much disposed to nourish and advance it. He, it seems, had lands bordering upon Cato's; nor could he but admire when he understood from his servants the manner of his living, how he labored with his own hands, went on foot betimes in the morning to the courts to assist those 25 who wanted his counsel: how, returning home again, when it was winter, he would throw a loose frock over his shoulders, and in the summer time would work without anything on among his domestics, sit down with them, eat of the same bread, and drink of the same wine. When they spoke, also, of other good qualities, his fair dealing and moderation, mentioning also some of his 30 wise sayings, he ordered that he should be invited to supper; and thus becoming personally assured of his fine temper and his superior character, which, like a plant, seemed only to require culture and a better situation, he urged and persuaded him to apply himself to state affairs at Rome. Thither, therefore, he went, and by his pleading soon gained many friends and admirers; but, Valerius 35 chiefly assisting his promotion, he first of all got appointed tribune in the army, and afterwards was made quaestor, or treasurer. And now becoming eminent and noted, he passed, with Valerius himself, through the greatest commands, being first his colleague as consul, and then censor. But among all the ancient senators, he most attached himself to Fabius Maximus; not so much for the honour of 40 his person, and the greatness of his power, as that he might have before him his habit and manner of life, as the best examples to follow; and so he did not hesitate to oppose Scipio the Great, who, being then but a young man, seemed to set himself against the power of Fabius, and to be envied by him. For being

5   sent together with him as treasurer, when he saw him, according to his natural custom, make great expenses, and distribute among the soldiers without sparing, he freely told him that the expense in itself was not the greatest thing to be considered, but that he was corrupting the frugality of the soldiers, by giving them the means to abandon themselves to unnecessary pleasures and luxuries.

10  Scipio answered, that he had no need for so accurate a treasurer (bearing on as he was, so to say, full sail to the war), and that he owed the people an account of his actions, and not of the money he spent. Hereupon Cato returned from Sicily and, together with Fabius, made loud complaints in the open senate of Scipio's lavishing unspeakable sums, and childishly loitering away his time in

15  wrestling matches and comedies, as if he were not to make war, but holiday; and thus succeeded in getting some of the tribunes of the people sent to call him back to Rome, in case the accusations should prove true. But Scipio demonstrating, as it were, to them, by his preparations, the coming victory, and, being found merely to be living pleasantly with his friends, when there was

20  nothing else to do, but in no respect because of that easiness and liberality at all the more negligent in things of consequence and moment, without impediment, set sail toward the war.

Cato grew more and more powerful by his eloquence, so that he was commonly called the Roman Demosthenes; but his manner of life was yet more

25  famous and talked of. For oratorical skill was, as an accomplishment, commonly studied and sought after by all young men; but he was very rare who would cultivate the old habits of bodily labor, or prefer a light supper, and a breakfast which never saw the fire, or be in love with poor clothes and a homely lodging, or could set his ambition rather on doing without luxuries than on possessing

30  them. For now the state, unable to keep its purity by reason of its greatness, and having so many affairs, and people from all parts under its government, was fain to admit many mixed customs and new examples of living. With reason, therefore, everybody admired Cato, when they saw others sink under labors and grow effeminate by pleasures; and yet beheld him unconquered by

35  either, and that not only when he was young and desirous of honor, but also when old and grey-headed, after a consulship and triumph; like some famous victor in the games, persevering in his exercise and maintaining his character to the very last. He himself says that he never wore a suit of clothes which cost more than a hundred drachmas; and that, when he was general and consul, he

40  drank the same wine which his workmen did; and that the meat or fish which

was bought in the meat-market for his dinner did not cost above thirty asses. All which was for the sake of the commonwealth, that so his body might be the hardier for the war. Having a piece of embroidered Babylonian tapestry left him, he sold it; because none of his farmhouses were so much as plastered. Nor did he ever buy a slave for above fifteen hundred drachmas; as he did not seek    5 for effeminate and handsome ones, but able sturdy workmen, horse-keepers and cow-herds: and these he thought ought to be sold again, when they grew old, and no useless servants fed in the house. In short, he reckoned nothing a good bargain which was superfluous; but whatever it was, though sold for a farthing, he would think it a great price, if you had no need of it; and was for    10 the purchase of lands for sowing and feeding, rather than grounds for sweeping and watering.

Some imputed these things to petty avarice, but others approved of him, as if he had only the more strictly denied himself for the rectifying and amending of others. Yet certainly, in my judgment, it marks an over-rigid temper for a    15 man to take the work out of his servants as out of brute beasts, turning them off and selling them in their old age, and thinking there ought to be no further commerce between man and man than whilst there arises some profit by it. We see that kindness or humanity has a larger field than bare justice to exercise itself in; law and justice we cannot, in the nature of things, employ on others than    20 men; but we may extend our goodness and charity even to irrational creatures; and such acts flow from a gentle nature, as water from an abundant spring. It is doubtless the part of a kind-natured man to keep even worn-out horses and dogs, and not only take care of them when they are foals and whelps, but also when they are grown old. The Athenians, when they built their Hecatompedon,    25 turned those mules loose to feed freely which they had observed to have done the hardest labor. One of these (they say) came once of itself to offer its service, and ran along with, nay, and went before, the teams which drew the wagons up to the acropolis, as if it would incite and encourage them to draw more stoutly; upon which there passed a vote that the creature should be kept at the public    30 charge even till it died. The graves of Cimon's horses, which thrice won the Olympian races, are yet to be seen close by his own monument. Old Xanthippus, too (amongst many others who buried the dogs they had bred up), entombed his which swam after his galley to Salamis, when the people fled from Athens, on the top of a cliff, which they call the Dog's Tomb to this day. Nor are we to    35 use living creatures like old shoes or dishes and throw them away when they are worn out or broken with service; but if it were for nothing else, but by way of study and practice in humanity, a man ought always to pre-habituate himself in these things to be of a kind and sweet disposition. As to myself, I would not so much as sell my draught ox on the account of his age, much less for a small    40 piece of money sell a poor old man, and so chase him, as it were, from his own country, by turning him not only out of the place where he has lived a long while, but also out of the manner of living he has been accustomed to, and that more especially when he would be as useless to the buyer as to the seller.

5   Yet Cato for all this glories that he left that very horse in Spain which he used in the wars when he was consul, only because he would not put the public to the charge of his freight. Whether these acts are to be ascribed to the greatness or pettiness of his spirit, let everyone argue as they please.

For his general temperance, however, and self-control he really deserves

10  the highest admiration. For when he commanded the army, he never took for himself, and those that belonged to him, above three bushels of wheat for a month, and somewhat less than a bushel and a half a day of barley for his baggage-cattle. And when he entered upon the government of Sardinia, where his predecessors had been used to require tents, bedding and clothes upon the

15  public account, and to charge the state heavily with the cost of provisions and entertainments for a great train of servants and friends, the difference he showed in his economy was something incredible. There was nothing of any sort for which he put the public to expense; he would walk without a carriage to visit the cities, with one only of the common town officers, who carried his dress,

20  and a cup to offer libation with. Yet though he seemed thus easy and sparing to all who were under his power, he, on the other hand, showed most inflexible severity and strictness in what related to public justice, and was rigorous and precise in what concerned the ordinances of the commonwealth; so that the Roman government never seemed more terrible, nor yet more mild than

25  under his administration.

His very manner of speaking seemed to have such a kind of idea with it; for it was courteous, and yet forcible; pleasant, yet overwhelming; facetious, yet austere; sententious, and yet vehement; like Socrates, in the description of Plato, who seemed outwardly to those about him to be but a simple, talkative,

30  blunt fellow; whilst at the bottom he was full of such gravity and matter, as would even move tears and touch the very hearts of his auditors. And, therefore, I know not what has persuaded some to say that Cato's style was chiefly like that of Lysias. However, let us leave those to judge of these things who profess most to distinguish between the several kinds of oratorical style in Latin; whilst

35  we write down some of his memorable sayings; being of the opinion that a man's character appears much more by his words than, as some think it does, by his looks.

Being once desirous to dissuade the common people of Rome from their unseasonable and impetuous clamor for largesses and distributions of corn, he

40  began thus to harangue them: "It is a difficult task, O citizens, to make speeches

to the belly, which has no ears." Reproving, also, their sumptuous habits, he said it was hard to preserve a city where a fish sold for more than an ox. He had a saying, also, that the Roman people were like sheep; for they, when single, do not obey, but when altogether in a flock, they follow their leaders: "So you," said he, "when you have got together in a body, let yourselves be guided by those          5 whom singly you would never think of being advised by." Discoursing of the power of women: "Men," said he, "usually command women; but we command all men, and the women command us." But this, indeed, is borrowed from the sayings of Themistocles, who, when his son was making many demands of him by means of the mother, said, "O woman, the Athenians govern the Greeks;          10 I govern the Athenians, but you govern me, and your son governs you; so let him use his power sparingly, since, simple as he is, he can do more than all the Greeks together." Another saying of Cato's was, that the Roman people did not only fix the value of such and such purple dyes, but also of such and such habits of life: "For," said he, "as dyers most of all dye such colors as they see to be most          15 agreeable, so the young men learn, and zealously affect, what is most popular with you." He also exhorted them that, if they were grown great by their virtue and temperance, they should not change for the worse; but if intemperance and vice had made them great, they should change for the better; for by that means they were grown indeed quite great enough. He would say, likewise, of          20 men who wanted to be continually in office, that apparently they did not know their road; since they could not do without beadles to guide them on it. He also reproved the citizens for choosing still the same men as their magistrates: "For you will seem," said he, "either not to esteem government worth much, or to think few worthy to hold it." Speaking, too, of a certain enemy of his, who          25 lived a very base and discreditable life: "It is considered," he said, "rather as a curse than a blessing on him, that this fellow's mother prays that she may leave him behind her." Pointing at one who had sold the land which his father had left him, and which lay near the seaside, he pretended to express his wonder at his being stronger even than the sea itself; for what it washed away with a          30 great deal of labor, he with a great deal of ease drank away. When the senate, with a great deal of splendor, received King Eumenes on his visit to Rome, and the chief citizens strove who should be most about him, Cato appeared to regard him with suspicion and apprehension; and when one that stood by, too, took occasion to say that he was a very good prince and a great lover of          35 the Romans: "It may be so," said Cato; "but by nature this same animal of a king is a kind of man-eater;" nor, indeed, were there ever kings who deserved to be compared with Epaminondas, Pericles, Themistocles, Manius Curius, or Hamilcar, surnamed Barcas. He used to say, too, that his enemies envied him because he had to get up every day before light and neglect his own business to          40 follow that of the public. He would also tell you that he had rather be deprived of the reward for doing well than not to suffer the punishment for doing ill; and that he could pardon all offenders but himself.

5 The Romans having sent three ambassadors to Bithynia, of whom one was gouty, another had his skull trepanned, and the other seemed little better than a fool, Cato, laughing, gave out that the Romans had sent an embassy which had neither feet, head, nor heart. His interest being entreated by Scipio, on account of Polybius, for the Achaean exiles, and there happening to be a great discussion in the senate about it, some being for, and some against their return, 10 Cato, standing up, thus delivered himself: "Here do we sit all day long, as if we had nothing to do but beat our brains whether these old Greeks should be carried to their graves by the bearers here or by those in Achaea." The senate voting their return, it seems that a few days after Polybius's friends further wished that it should be further moved in the senate that the said banished 15 persons should receive again the honors which they first had in Achaea; and to this purpose they sounded Cato for his opinion; but he, smiling, answered, that Polybius, Ulysses like, having escaped out of the Cyclops' den, wanted, it would seem, to go back again because he had left his cap and belt behind him. He used to assert, also, that wise men profited more by fools, than fools 20 by wise men for that wise men avoided the faults of fools, but that fools would not imitate the good examples of wise men. He would profess, too, that he was more taken with young men that blushed than with those who looked pale; and that he never desired to have a soldier that moved his hands too much in marching, and his feet too much in fighting; or snored louder than he shouted. 25 Ridiculing a fat, overgrown man: "What use," said he, "can the state turn a man's body to, when all between the throat and groin is taken up by the belly?" When one who was much given to pleasures desired his acquaintance, begging his pardon, he said he could not live with a man whose palate was of a quicker sense than his heart. He would likewise say that the soul of a lover lived in the 30 body of another: and that in his whole life he most repented of three things; one was, that he had trusted a secret to a woman; another that he went by water when he might have gone by land; the third, that he had remained one whole day without doing any business of moment. Applying himself to an old man who was committing some vice: "Friend," said he, "old age has of itself 35 blemishes enough; do not you add to it the deformity of vice." Speaking to a tribune, who was reputed a poisoner, and was very violent for the bringing in of a bill, in order to make a certain law: "Young man," cried he, "I know not which would be better, to drink what you mix, or confirm what you would put up for a law." Being reviled by a fellow who lived a profligate and wicked 40 life: "A contest," replied he, "is unequal between you and me: for you can hear

ill words easily, and can as easily give them: but it is unpleasant to me to give such, and unusual to hear them." Such was his manner of expressing himself in his memorable sayings.

Being chosen consul, with his friend and familiar Valerius Flaccus, the government of that part of Spain which the Romans called the Hither Spain fell to his lot. Here, as he was engaged in reducing some of the tribes by force, and bringing over others by good words, a large army of barbarians fell upon him, so that there was danger of being disgracefully forced out again. He therefore called upon his neighbors, the Celtiberians, for help; and on their demanding two hundred talents for their assistance, everybody else thought it intolerable that even the Romans should promise barbarians a reward for their aid; but Cato said there was no discredit or harm in it; for, if they overcame, they would pay them out of the enemy's purse, and not out of their own; but if they were overcome, there would be nobody left either to demand the reward or to pay it. However, he won that battle completely, and, after that, all his other affairs succeeded splendidly. Polybius says that, by his command, the walls of all the cities on this side of the river Baetis were in one day's time demolished, and yet there were a great many of them full of brave and warlike men. Cato himself says that he took more cities than he stayed days in Spain. Neither is this a mere rhodomontade, if it be true that the number was four hundred. And though the soldiers themselves had got much in the fights, yet he distributed a pound of silver to every man of them, saying, it was better that many of the Romans should return home with silver, rather than a few with gold. For himself, he affirms, that of all the things that were taken, nothing came to him beyond what he ate and drank. "Neither do I find fault," continued he, "with those that seek to profit by these spoils, but I had rather compete in valor with the best, than in wealth with the richest, or with the most covetous in love of money." Nor did he merely keep himself clear from taking anything, but even all those who more immediately belonged to him. He had five servants with him in the army; one of whom, called Paccus, bought three boys out of those who were taken captive; which Cato coming to understand, the man, rather than venture into his presence, hanged himself. Cato sold the boys, and carried the price he got for them into the public exchequer.

Scipio the Great, being his enemy, and desiring, whilst he was carrying all things so successfully, to obstruct him, and take the affairs of Spain into his own hands, succeeded in getting himself appointed his successor in the government, and, making all possible haste, put a term to Cato's authority. But he, taking with him a convoy of five cohorts of foot and five hundred horse to attend him home, overthrew by the way the Lacetanians, and taking from them six hundred deserters, caused them all to be beheaded; upon which Scipio seemed to be in indignation, but Cato, in mock disparagement of himself, said, "Rome would become great indeed, if the most honorable and great men would not yield up the first place of valor to those who were more obscure, and when they who were of the commonalty (as he himself was) would contend in valor with

5    those who were most eminent in birth and honor." The senate having voted to change nothing of what had been established by Cato, the government passed away under Scipio to no manner of purpose, in idleness and doing nothing; and so diminished his credit much more than Cato's. Nor did Cato, who now received a triumph, remit after this and slacken the reins of virtue, as many do,

10   who strive not so much for virtue's sake, as for vainglory, and having attained the highest honors, as the consulship and triumphs, pass the rest of their life in pleasure and idleness, and quit all public affairs. But he, like those who are just entered upon public life for the first time, and thirst after gaining honor and glory in some new office, strained himself, as if he were but just setting out;

15   and offering still publicly his service to his friends and citizens, would give up neither his pleadings nor his soldiery.

      He accompanied and assisted Tiberius Sempronius, as his lieutenant, when he went into Thrace and to the Danube; and, in the quality of tribune, went with Manius Acilius into Greece, against Antiochus the Great, who, after Hannibal,

20   more than any one struck terror into the Romans. For having reduced once more under a single command almost the whole of Asia, all, namely, that Seleucus Nicator had possessed, and having brought into obedience many warlike nations of the barbarians, he longed to fall upon the Romans, as if they only were now worthy to fight with him. So across he came with his forces, pretending,

25   as a specious cause of the war, that it was to free the Greeks, who had indeed no need of it, they having been but newly delivered from the power of King Philip and the Macedonians, and made independent, with the free use of their own laws, by the goodness of the Romans themselves: so that all Greece was in commotion and excitement, having been corrupted by the hopes of royal aid

30   which the popular leaders in their cities put them into. Manius, therefore, sent ambassadors to the different cities; and Titus Flaminius (as is written in the account of him) suppressed and quieted most of the attempts of the innovators, without any trouble. Cato brought over the Corinthians, those of Patrae and Aegium, and spent a good deal of time at Athens. There is also an oration of his

35   said to be extant which he spoke in Greek to the people; in which he expressed his admiration of the virtue of the ancient Athenians, and signified that he came with a great deal of pleasure to be a spectator of the beauty and greatness of their city. But this is a fiction; for he spoke to the Athenians by an interpreter, though he was able to have spoken himself; but he wished to observe the usage

40   of his own country, and laughed at those who admired nothing but what was

in Greek. Jesting upon Postumius Albinus, who had written an historical work in Greek, and requested that allowances might be made for his attempt, he said that allowance indeed might be made if he had done it under the express compulsion of an Amphictyonic decree. The Athenians, he says, admired the quickness and vehemence of his speech; for an interpreter would be very long in repeating what he expressed with a great deal of brevity; but on the whole he professed to believe that the words of the Greeks came only from their lips, whilst those of the Romans came from their hearts.

Now Antiochus, having occupied with his army the narrow passages about Thermopylae, and added palisades and walls to the natural fortifications of the place, sat down there, thinking he had done enough to divert the war; and the Romans, indeed, seemed wholly to despair of forcing the passage; but Cato, calling to mind the compass and circuit which the Persians had formerly made to come at this place, went forth in the night, taking along with him part of the army. Whilst they were climbing up, the guide, who was a prisoner, missed the way, and wandering up and down by impracticable and precipitous paths, filled the soldiers with fear and despondency. Cato, perceiving the danger, commanded all the rest to halt, and stay where they were, whilst he himself, taking along with him one Lucius Manlius, a most expert man at climbing mountains, went forward with a great deal of labor and danger, in the dark night, and without the least moonshine, among the wild olive-trees and steep craggy rocks, there being nothing but precipices and darkness before their eyes, till they struck into a little pass which they thought might lead down into the enemy's camp. There they put up marks upon some conspicuous peaks which surmount the hill called Callidromon, and, returning again, they led the army along with them to the said marks, till they got into their little path again, and there once made a halt; but when they began to go further, the path deserted them at a precipice, where they were in another strait and fear; nor did they perceive that they were all this while near the enemy. And now the day began to give some light, when they seemed to hear a noise, and presently after to see the Greek trenches and the guard at the foot of the rock. Here, therefore, Cato halted his forces, and commanded the troops from Firmum only, without the rest, to stick by him, as he had always found them faithful and ready. And when they came up and formed around him in close order, he thus spoke to them: "I desire," he said, "to take one of the enemy alive, that so I may understand what men these are who guard the passage; their number; and with what discipline, order, and preparation they expect us; but this feat," continued he, "must be an act of a great deal of quickness and boldness, such as that of lions, when they dart upon some timorous animal." Cato had no sooner thus expressed himself, but the Firmans forthwith rushed down the mountain, just as they were, upon

the guard, and, falling unexpectedly upon them, affrighted and dispersed them all. One armed man they took, and brought to Cato, who quickly learned from him that the rest of the forces lay in the narrow passage about the king; that those who kept the tops of the rocks were six hundred choice Aetolians. Cato,
5   therefore, despising the smallness of their number and carelessness, forthwith drawing his sword, fell upon them with a great noise of trumpets and shouting. The enemy, perceiving them thus tumbling, as it were, upon them from the precipices, flew to the main body, and put all things into disorder there.

In the meantime, whilst Manius was forcing the works below, and pouring
10  the thickest of his forces into the narrow passages, Antiochus was hit in the mouth with a stone, so that his teeth being beaten out by it, he felt such excessive pain, that he was fain to turn away with his horse; nor did any part of his army stand the shock of the Romans. Yet, though there seemed no reasonable hope of flight, where all paths were so difficult, and where there were deep
15  marshes and steep rocks, which looked as if they were ready to receive those who should stumble, the fugitives, nevertheless, crowding and pressing together in the narrow passages, destroyed even one another in their terror of the swords and blows of the enemy. Cato (as it plainly appears) was never over-sparing of his own praises, and seldom shunned boasting of any exploit; which quality,
20  indeed, he seems to have thought the natural accompaniment of great actions; and with these particular exploits he was highly puffed up; he says that those who saw him that day pursuing and slaying the enemies were ready to assert that Cato owed not so much to the public as the public did to Cato; nay, he adds, that Manius the consul, coming hot from the fight, embraced him for a great
25  while, when both were all in a sweat; and then cried out with joy that neither he himself, no, nor all the people together, could make him a recompense equal to his actions. After the fight he was sent to Rome, that he himself might be the messenger of it: and so, with a favorable wind, he sailed to Brundusium, and in one day got from thence to Tarentum; and having travelled four days more,
30  upon the fifth, counting from the time of his landing, he arrived at Rome, and so brought the first news of the victory himself; and filled the whole city with joy and sacrifices, and the people with the belief that they were able to conquer every sea and every land.

These are pretty nearly all the eminent actions of Cato relating to military
35  affairs: in civil policy, he was of opinion that one chief duty consisted in accusing and indicting criminals. He himself prosecuted many, and he would also assist others who prosecuted them, nay, would even procure such, as he did the Petilii against Scipio; but not being able to destroy him, by reason of the nobleness of his family, and the real greatness of his mind, which enabled him to trample all
40  calumnies under foot, Cato at last would meddle no more with him; yet joining

with the accusers against Scipio's brother Lucius, he succeeded in obtaining a sentence against him, which condemned him to the payment of a large sum of money to the state; and being insolvent, and in danger of being thrown into jail, he was, by the interposition of the tribunes of the people, with much ado dismissed. It is also said of Cato, that when he met a certain youth, who had effected the disgrace of one of his father's enemies, walking in the market-place, he shook him by the hand, telling him, that this was what we ought to sacrifice to our dead parents—not lambs and goats, but the tears and condemnations of their adversaries. But neither did he himself escape with impunity in his management of affairs; for if he gave his enemies but the least hold, he was still in danger, and exposed to be brought to justice. He is reported to have escaped at least fifty indictments; and one above the rest, which was the last, when he was eighty-six years old, about which time he uttered the well-known saying, that it was hard for him who had lived with one generation of men, to plead now before another. Neither did he make this the least of his lawsuits; for, four years after, when he was fourscore and ten, he accused Servilius Galba: so that his life and actions extended, we may say, as Nestor's did, over three ordinary ages of man. For, having had many contests, as we have related, with Scipio the Great, about affairs of state, he continued them down to Scipio the younger, who was the adopted grandson of the former, and the son of that Paulus who overthrew Perseus and the Macedonians.

Ten years after his consulship, Cato stood for the office of censor, which was indeed the summit of all honor, and in a manner the highest step in civil affairs; for besides all other power, it had also that of an inquisition into every one's life and manners. For the Romans thought that no marriage, or rearing of children, nay, no feast or drinking-bout, ought to be permitted according to every one's appetite or fancy, without being examined and inquired into; being indeed of opinion that a man's character was much sooner perceived in things of this sort than in what is done publicly and in open day. They chose, therefore, two persons, one out of the patricians, the other out of the commons, who were to watch, correct, and punish, if any one ran too much into voluptuousness, or transgressed the usual manner of life of his country; and these they called Censors. They had power to take away a horse, or expel out of the senate anyone who lived intemperately and out of order. It was also their business to take an estimate of what everyone was worth, and to put down in registers everybody's birth and quality; besides many other prerogatives. And therefore the chief nobility opposed his pretensions to it. Jealousy prompted the patricians, who thought that it would be a stain to everybody's nobility, if men of no original honor should rise to the highest dignity and power; while others, conscious of their own evil practices, and of the violation of the laws and customs of their country, were afraid of the austerity of the man; which, in an office of such great power, was likely to prove most uncompromising and severe. And so, consulting among themselves, they brought forward seven candidates in opposition to him, who sedulously set themselves to court the people's favor by fair promises,

5 as though what they wished for was indulgent and easy government. Cato, on the contrary, promising no such mildness, but plainly threatening evil livers, from the very hustings openly declared himself, and exclaiming that the city needed a great and thorough purgation, called upon the people, if they were wise, not to choose the gentlest, but the roughest of physicians; such a one, he

10 said, he was, and Valerius Flaccus, one of the patricians, another; together with him, he doubted not but he should do something worth the while, and that by cutting to pieces and burning like a hydra all luxury and voluptuousness. He added, too, that he saw all the rest endeavoring after the office with ill intent, because they were afraid of those who would exercise it justly, as they ought.

15 And so truly great and so worthy of great men to be its leaders was, it would seem, the Roman people, that they did not fear the severity and grim countenance of Cato, but rejecting those smooth promisers who were ready to do all things to ingratiate themselves, they took him, together with Flaccus; obeying his recommendations not as though he were a candidate, but as if he had had

20 the actual power of commanding and governing already.

Cato named, as chief of the senate, his friend and colleague Lucius Valerius Flaccus, and expelled, among many others, Lucius Quintius, who had been consul seven years before, and (which was greater honor to him than the consulship) brother to that Titus Flaminius who overthrew King Philip. The reason

25 he had for his expulsion was this. Lucius, it seems, took along with him in all his commands a youth whom he had kept as his companion from the flower of his age, and to whom he gave as much power and respect as to the chiefest of his friends and relations.

Now it happened that Lucius being consular governor of one of the prov-

30 inces, the youth setting himself down by him, as he used to do, among other flatteries with which he played upon him, when he was in his cups, told him he loved him so dearly that, "though there was a show of gladiators to be seen at Rome, and I," he said, "had never beheld one in my life; and though I, as it were, longed to see a man killed, yet I made all possible haste to come to you."

35 Upon this Lucius, returning his fondness, replied, "Do not be melancholy on that account; I can remedy that." Ordering therefore, forthwith, one of those condemned to die to be brought to the feast, together with the headsman and axe, he asked the youth if he wished to see him executed. The boy answering that he did, Lucius commanded the executioner to cut off his neck; and this

40 several historians mention; and Cicero, indeed, in his dialogue *De Senectute*,

introduces Cato relating it himself. But Livy says that he that was killed was
a Gaulish deserter, and that Lucius did not execute him by the stroke of the
executioner, but with his own hand; and that it is so stated in Cato's speech.

Lucius being thus expelled out of the senate by Cato, his brother took it very
ill, and appealing to the people, desired that Cato should declare his reasons;                5
and when he began to relate this transaction of the feast, Lucius endeavored
to deny it; but Cato challenging him to a formal investigation, he fell off and
refused it, so that he was then acknowledged to suffer deservedly. Afterwards,
however, when there was some show at the theatre, he passed by the seats where
those who had been consuls used to be placed, and taking his seat a great way        10
off, excited the compassion of the common people, who presently with a great
noise made him go forward, and as much as they could tried to set right and
salve over what had happened. Manilius, also, who, according to the public
expectation, would have been next consul, he threw out of the senate, because,
in the presence of his daughter, and in open day, he had kissed his wife. He said      15
that, as for himself, his wife never came into his arms except when there was
great thunder; so that it was for jest with him, that it was a pleasure for him,
when Jupiter thundered.

His treatment of Lucius, likewise the brother of Scipio, and one who had
been honored with a triumph, occasioned some odium against Cato; for he             20
took his horse from him, and was thought to do it with a design of putting an
affront on Scipio Africanus, now dead. But he gave most general annoyance by
retrenching people's luxury; for though (most of the youth being thereby already
corrupted) it seemed almost impossible to take it away with an open hand and
directly, yet going, as it were, obliquely around, he caused all dress, carriages,       25
women's ornaments, household furniture, whose price exceeded one thousand
five hundred drachmas, to be rated at ten times as much as they were worth;
intending by thus making the assessments greater, to increase the taxes paid
upon them. He also ordained that upon every thousand asses of property of this
kind, three should be paid, so that people, burdened with these extra charges,       30
and seeing others of as good estates, but more frugal and sparing, paying less
into the public exchequer, might be tried out of their prodigality. And thus, on
the one side, not only those were disgusted at Cato who bore the taxes for the
sake of their luxury, but those, too, who on the other side laid by their luxury
for fear of the taxes. For people in general reckon that an order not to display      35
their riches is equivalent to the taking away of their riches, because riches are
seen much more in superfluous than in necessary things. Indeed this was what
excited the wonder of Ariston the philosopher; that we account those who possess
superfluous things more happy than those who abound with what is necessary
and useful. But when one of his friends asked Scopas, the rich Thessalian, to       40

give him some article of no great utility, saying that it was not a thing that he had any great need or use for himself, "In truth," replied he, "it is just these useless and unnecessary things that make my wealth and happiness." Thus the desire of riches does not proceed from a natural passion within us, but arises
5 rather from vulgar out-of-doors opinion of other people.

Cato, notwithstanding, being little solicitous as to those who exclaimed against him, increased his austerity. He caused the pipes, through which some persons brought the public water into their houses and gardens, to be cut, and threw down all buildings which jutted out into the common streets. He beat
10 down also the price in contracts for public works to the lowest, and raised it in contracts for farming the taxes to the highest sum; by which proceedings he drew a great deal of hatred upon himself. Those who were of Titus Flaminius's party cancelled in the senate all the bargains and contracts made by him for the repairing and carrying on of the sacred and public buildings as un-advan-
15 tageous to the commonwealth. They incited also the boldest of the tribunes of the people to accuse him and to fine him two talents. They likewise much opposed him in building the court or basilica, which he caused to be erected at the common charge, just by the senate-house, in the market-place, and called by his own name, the Porcian. However, the people, it seems, liked his censorship
20 wondrously well; for, setting up a statue for him in the temple of the goddess of Health, they put an inscription under it, not recording his commands in war or his triumph, but to the effect that this was Cato the Censor, who, by his good discipline and wise and temperate ordinances, reclaimed the Roman commonwealth when it was declining and sinking down into vice. Before this
25 honor was done to himself, he used to laugh at those who loved such kind of things, saying, that they did not see that they were taking pride in the work-manship of brass-founders and painters; whereas the citizens bore about his best likeness in their breasts. And when any seemed to wonder that he should have never a statue, while many ordinary persons had one, "I would," said he,
30 "much rather be asked, why I have not one, than why I have one." In short, he would not have any honest citizen endure to be praised, except it might prove advantageous to the commonwealth. Yet still he had passed the highest com-mendation on himself; for he tells us that those who did anything wrong, and were found fault with, used to say it was not worthwhile to blame them, for
35 they were not Catos. He also adds, that they who awkwardly mimicked some of his actions were called left-handed Catos; and that the senate in perilous times would cast their eyes on him, as upon a pilot in a ship, and that often when he was not present they put off affairs of greatest consequence. These things are indeed also testified of him by others; for he had a great authority in the city,
40 alike for his life, his eloquence, and his age.

He was also a good father, an excellent husband to his wife, and an extraordinary economist; and as he did not manage his affairs of this kind carelessly, and as things of little moment, I think I ought to record a little further whatever was commendable in him in these points. He married a wife more noble than rich; being of opinion that the rich and the high-born are equally     5
haughty and proud; but that those of noble blood would be more ashamed of base things, and consequently more obedient to their husbands in all that was fit and right. A man who beat his wife or child laid violent hands, he said, on what was most sacred; and a good husband he reckoned worthy of more praise than a great senator; and he admired the ancient Socrates for nothing so much     10
as for having lived a temperate and contented life with a wife who was a scold, and children who were half-witted.

As soon as he had a son born, though he had never such urgent business upon his hands, unless it were some public matter, he would be by when his wife washed it and dressed it in its swaddling clothes. For she herself suckled it, nay,     15
she often too gave her breast to her servants' children, to produce, by suckling the same milk, a kind of natural love in them to her son. When he began to come to years of discretion, Cato himself would teach him to read, although he had a servant, a very good grammarian, called Chilo, who taught many others; but he thought not fit, as he himself said, to have his son reprimanded     20
by a slave, or pulled, it may be, by the ears when found tardy in his lesson: nor would he have him owe to a servant the obligation of so great a thing as his learning; he himself, therefore (as we were saying), taught him his grammar, law, and his gymnastic exercises. Nor did he only show him, too, how to throw a dart, to fight in armor, and to ride, but to box also and to endure both heat     25
and cold, and to swim over the most rapid and rough rivers. He says, likewise, that he wrote histories, in large characters, with his own hand, that so his son, without stirring out of the house, might learn to know about his countrymen and forefathers; nor did he less abstain from speaking anything obscene before his son, than if it had been in the presence of the sacred virgins, called vestals.     30
Nor would he ever go into the bath with him; which seems indeed to have been the common custom of the Romans. Sons-in-law used to avoid bathing with fathers-in-law, disliking to see one another naked; but having, in time, learned of the Greeks to strip before men, they have since taught the Greeks to do it even with the women themselves.                                                      35

Thus, like an excellent work, Cato formed and fashioned his son to virtue; nor had he any occasion to find fault with his readiness and docility; but as he proved to be of too weak a constitution for hardships, he did not insist on requiring of him any very austere way of living. However, though delicate in health, he proved a stout man in the field, and behaved himself valiantly when     40

Paulus Aemilius fought against Perseus; where when his sword was struck from him by a blow, or rather slipped out of his hand by reason of its moistness, he so keenly resented it, that he turned to some of his friends about him, and taking them along with him again fell upon the enemy; and having by a long fight and much force cleared the place, at length found it among great heaps of arms, and the dead bodies of friends as well as enemies piled one upon another. Upon which Paulus, his general, much commended the youth; and there is a letter of Cato's to his son, which highly praised his honorable eagerness for the recovery of his sword. Afterwards he married Tertia, Aemilius Paulus's daughter, and sister to Scipio; nor was he admitted into this family less for his own worth than his father's. So that Cato's care in his son's education came to a very fitting result.

He purchased a great many slaves out of the captives taken in war, but chiefly brought up the young ones, who were capable to be, as it were, broken and taught like whelps and colts. None of these ever entered another man's house, except sent either by Cato himself or his wife. If any one of them were asked what Cato did, they answered merely that they did not know. When a servant was at home, he was obliged either to do some work or sleep, for indeed Cato loved those most who used to lie down often to sleep, accounting them more docile than those who were wakeful, and more fit for anything when they were refreshed with a little slumber. Being also of opinion that the great cause of the laziness and misbehavior of slaves was their running after their pleasures, he fixed a certain price for them to pay for permission amongst themselves, but would suffer no connections out of the house. At first, when he was but a poor soldier, he would not be difficult in anything which related to his eating, but looked upon it as a pitiful thing to quarrel with a servant for the belly's sake; but afterwards, when he grew richer, and made any feasts for his friends and colleagues in office, as soon as supper was over he used to go with a leather thong and scourge those who had waited or dressed the meat carelessly. He always contrived, too, that his servants should have some difference one among another, always suspecting and fearing a good understanding between them. Those who had committed anything worthy of death, he punished if they were found guilty by the verdict of their fellow-servants. But being after all much given to the desire of gain, he looked upon agriculture rather as a pleasure than profit; resolving, therefore, to lay out his money in safe and solid things, he purchased ponds, hot baths, grounds full of fuller's earth, remunerative lands, pastures, and woods; from all which he drew large returns, nor could Jupiter himself, he used to say, do him much damage. He was also given to the form of usury, which is considered most odious, in traffic by sea; and that thus: he desired that those whom he put out his money to should have many partners;

when the number of them and their ships came to be fifty, he himself took
one share through Quintio his freedman, who therefore was to sail with the
adventurers, and take a part in all their proceedings, so that thus there was no
danger of losing his whole stock, but only a little part, and that with a prospect
of great profit. He likewise lent money to those of his slaves who wished to        5
borrow, with which they bought also other young ones, whom, when they had
taught and bred up at his charges, they would sell again at the year's end; but
some of them Cato would keep for himself, giving just as much for them as
another had offered. To incline his son to be of his kind or temper, he used to
tell him that it was not like a man, but rather like a widow woman, to lessen     10
an estate. But the strongest indication of Cato's avaricious humor was when he
took the boldness to affirm that he was a most wonderful, nay, a godlike man,
who left more behind him than he had received.

He was now grown old, when Carneades the Academic, and Diogenes the
Stoic, came as deputies from Athens to Rome, praying for release from a penalty   15
of five hundred talents laid on the Athenians, in a suit, to which they did not
appear, in which the Oropians were plaintiffs and Sicyonians judges. All the
most studious youth immediately waited on these philosophers, and frequently,
with admiration, heard them speak. But the gracefulness of Carneades's oratory, whose ability was really greatest, and his reputation equal to it, gathered   20
large and favorable audiences, and ere long filled, like a wind, all the city with
the sound of it. So that it soon began to be told that a Greek, famous even to
admiration, winning and carrying all before him, had impressed so strange a
love upon the young men, that quitting all their pleasures and pastimes, they
ran mad, as it were, after philosophy; which indeed much pleased the Romans   25
in general; nor could they but with much pleasure see the youth receive so
welcomely the Greek literature, and frequent the company of learned men. But
Cato, on the other side, seeing the passion for words flowing into the city, from
the beginning took it ill, fearing lest the youth should be diverted that way,
and so should prefer the glory of speaking well before that of arms and doing    30
well. And when the fame of the philosophers increased in the city, and Caius
Acilius, a person of distinction, at his own request, became their interpreter to
the senate at their first audience, Cato resolved, under some specious pretence,
to have all philosophers cleared out of the city; and, coming into the senate,
blamed the magistrates for letting these deputies stay so long a time without   35
being dispatched, though they were persons that could easily persuade the
people to what they pleased; that therefore in all haste something should be
determined about their petition, that so they might go home again to their own
schools, and declaim to the Greek children, and leave the Roman youth to be
obedient, as hitherto, to their own laws and governors.                          40

Yet he did this not out of any anger, as some think, to Carneades; but because he wholly despised philosophy, and out of a kind of pride scoffed at the Greek studies and literature; as, for example, he would say, that Socrates was a prating, seditious fellow, who did his best to tyrannize over his country,
5    to undermine the ancient customs, and to entice and withdraw the citizens to opinions contrary to the laws. Ridiculing the school of Isocrates, he would add, that his scholars grew old men before they had done learning with him, as if they were to use their art and plead causes in the court of Minos in the next world. And to frighten his son from anything that was Greek, in a more
10   vehement tone than became one of his age, he pronounced, as it were, with the voice of an oracle, that the Romans would certainly be destroyed when they began once to be infected with Greek literature; though time indeed has shown the vanity of this his prophecy; as, in truth, the city of Rome has risen to its highest fortune while entertaining Grecian learning. Nor had he an aver-
15   sion only against the Greek philosophers, but the physicians also; for having, it seems, heard how Hippocrates, when the king of Persia sent for him, with offers of a fee of several talents, said, that he would never assist barbarians who were enemies to the Greeks; he affirmed, that this was now become a common oath taken by all physicians, and enjoined his son to have a care and avoid them;
20   for that he himself had written a little book of prescriptions for curing those who were sick in his family; he never enjoined fasting to anyone, but ordered them either vegetables, or the meat of a duck, pigeon, or leveret; such kind of diet being of light digestion and fit for sick folks, only it made those who ate it dream a little too much; and by the use of this kind of physic, he said, he not
25   only made himself and those about him well, but kept them so.

However, for this his presumption he seemed not to have escaped unpun-ished; for he lost both his wife and his son; though he himself, being of a strong, robust constitution, held out longer; so that he would often, even in his old days, address himself to women, and when he was past a lover's age, married a young
30   woman, upon the following pretence: Having lost his own wife, he married his son to the daughter of Paulus Aemilius, who was sister to Scipio; so that being now a widower himself, he had a young girl who came privately to visit him, but the house being very small, and a daughter-in-law also in it, this practice was quickly discovered; for the young woman seeming once to pass through it
35   a little too boldly, the youth, his son, though he said nothing, seemed to look somewhat indignantly upon her. The old man perceiving and understanding that what he did was disliked, without finding any fault or saying a word, went away, as his custom was, with his usual companions to the market: and among the rest, he called aloud to one Salonius, who had been a clerk under him, and
40   asked him whether he had married his daughter? He answered no, nor would

he, till he had consulted him. Said Cato, "Then I have found out a fit son-in-law
for you, if he should not displease by reason of his age; for in all other points
there is no fault to be found in him; but he is indeed, as I said, extremely old."
However, Salonius desired him to undertake the business, and to give the young
girl to whom he pleased, she being a humble servant of his, who stood in need          5
of his care and patronage. Upon this Cato, without any more ado, told him he
desired to have the damsel himself. These words, as may well be imagined, at
first astonished the man, conceiving that Cato was as far off from marrying, as
he from a likelihood of being allied to the family of one who had been consul
and had triumphed; but perceiving him in earnest, he consented willingly; and          10
going onwards to the forum, they quickly completed the bargain.

Whilst the marriage was in hand, Cato's son, taking some of his friends
along with him, went and asked his father if it were for any offence he brought
in a stepmother upon him? But Cato cried out, "Far from it, my son, I have no
fault to find with you or anything of yours; only I desire to have many children,      15
and to leave the commonwealth more such citizens as you are." Pisistratus, the
tyrant of Athens, made, they say, this answer to his sons, when they were grown
men, when he married his second wife, Timonassa of Argos, by whom he had,
it is said, Iophon and Thessalus. Cato had a son by this second wife, to whom,
from his mother, he gave the surname of Salonius. In the meantime, his eldest          20
died in his praetorship; of whom Cato often makes mention in his books, as
having been a good man. He is said, however, to have borne the loss moderately and like a philosopher, and was nothing the more remiss in attending to
affairs of state; so that he did not, as Lucius Lucullus and Metellus Pius did,
grow languid in his old age, as though public business were a duty once to be          25
discharged, and then quitted; nor did he, like Scipio Africanus, because envy
had struck at his glory, turn from the public, and change and pass away the
rest of his life without doing anything; but as one persuaded Dionysius, that
the most honorable tomb he could have would be to die in the exercise of his
dominion; so Cato thought that old age to be the most honorable which was          30
busied in public affairs; though he would, now and then, when he had leisure,
recreate himself with husbandry and writing.

And, indeed, he composed various books and histories; and in his youth
he addicted himself to agriculture for profit's sake; for he used to say he had
but two ways of getting—agriculture and parsimony; and now, in his old age,          35
the first of these gave him both occupation and a subject of study. He wrote
one book on country matters, in which he treated particularly even of making
cakes and preserving fruit; it being his ambition to be curious and singular in
all things. His suppers, at his country house, used also to be plentiful; he daily
invited his friends and neighbors about him, and passed the time merrily with          40

them; so that his company was not only agreeable to those of the same age, but even to younger men; for he had had experience in many things, and had been concerned in much, both by word and deed, that was worth the hearing. He looked upon a good table as the best place for making friends; where the
5    commendations of brave and good citizens were usually introduced, and little said of base and unworthy ones; as Cato would not give leave in his company to have anything, either good or ill, said about them.

Some will have the overthrow of Carthage to have been one of his last acts of state; when, indeed, Scipio the younger did by his valor give it the last blow,
10   but the war, chiefly by the counsel and advice of Cato, was undertaken on the following occasion. Cato was sent to the Carthaginians and Masinissa, King of Numidia, who were at war with one another, to know the cause of their differ-ence. He, it seems, had been a friend of the Romans from the beginning; and they, too, since they were conquered by Scipio, were of the Roman confederacy,
15   having been shorn of their power by loss of territory and a heavy tax. Finding Carthage, not (as the Romans thought) low and in an ill condition, but well manned, full of riches and all sorts of arms and ammunition, and perceiving the Carthaginians carry it high, he conceived that it was not a time for the Romans to adjust affairs between them and Masinissa; but rather that they themselves
20   would fall into danger, unless they should find means to check this rapid new growth of Rome's ancient irreconcilable enemy. Therefore, returning quickly to Rome, he acquainted the senate that the former defeats and blows given to the Carthaginians had not so much diminished their strength, as it had abated their imprudence and folly; that they were not become weaker, but more experienced
25   in war, and did only skirmish with the Numidians to exercise themselves the better to cope with the Romans: that the peace and league they had made was but a kind of suspension of war which awaited a fairer opportunity to break out again.

Moreover, they say that, shaking his gown, he took occasion to let drop
30   some African figs before the senate. And on their admiring the size and beauty of them, he presently added, that the place that bore them was but three days' sail from Rome. Nay, he never after this gave his opinion, but at the end he would be sure to come out with this sentence, *Also, Carthage, methinks, ought utterly to be destroyed.* But Publius Scipio Nasica would always declare his opinion to
35   the contrary, in these words, "It seems requisite to me that Carthage should still stand." For seeing his countrymen to be grown wanton and insolent, and the people made, by their prosperity, obstinate and disobedient to the senate, and drawing the whole city, whither they would, after them, he would have had the fear of Carthage to serve as a bit to hold the contumacy of the multitude; and
40   he looked upon the Carthaginians as too weak to overcome the Romans, and

too great to be despised by them. On the other side, it seemed a perilous thing
to Cato that a city which had been always great, and was now grown sober and
wise, by reason of its former calamities, should still lie, as it were, in wait for
the follies and dangerous excesses of the over-powerful Roman people; so that
he thought it the wisest course to have all outward dangers removed, when they      5
had so many inward ones among themselves.

Thus Cato, they say, stirred up the third and last war against the Carthaginians: but no sooner was the said war begun, than he died, prophesying of
the person that should put an end to it who was then only a young man; but,
being tribune in the army, he in several fights gave proof of his courage and      10
conduct. The news of which being brought to Cato's ears at Rome, he thus
expressed himself:

> *The only wise man of them all is he,*
> *The others e'en as shadows flit and flee.*

This prophecy Scipio soon confirmed by his actions.                                15

Cato left no posterity, except one son by his second wife, who was named,
as we said, Cato Salonius; and a grandson by his eldest son, who died. Cato
Salonius died when he was praetor, but his son Marcus was afterwards consul,
and he was grandfather of Cato the philosopher, who for virtue and renown
was one of the most eminent personages of his time.                                20

# ON DUTIES
## MARCUS TULLIUS CICERO (*c.* 103–43 BC)

*So identified was Marcus Tullius Cicero with the republic that historian
Russell Kirk wrote, "With Cicero fell the Republic." Marc Antony's men had
hunted Cicero down at his villa, cutting off his head and hands, and placing them on the rostrum of the Roman Senate to show Antony's ascendency
over the old Republic. Cicero himself had given many famous speeches at
that very spot, and scholars have often regarded him as one of the greatest
orators ever. Cicero knew the Republic had fallen long before his own age,
its spirit being forgotten. Still, he argued for a reclamation of beauty and
decorum in civilized society, as ordered by the Natural Law. "True law
is right reason in agreement with Nature," Cicero argued. "The Natural
Law is of universal application, unchanging and everlasting; it summons
to duty by its commands, and averts from wrongdoing by its prohibitions.
And it does not lay its commands or prohibitions upon good men in vain,
although neither have any effect upon the wicked. Any attempt to alter
this law is sinful, nor it is allowable to try to repeal a part of it, and it is
impossible to abolish it entirely. We cannot be freed from its obligations by
Senate or People, and we need not look outside ourselves for an expounder
or interpreter of it. And there will not be different laws at Rome and at
Athens, or different laws now and in the future, but one eternal and unchangeable law will be valid for all nations and for all times, and there
will be one master and one rule, that is, God, over us all, for He is the
author of this law, its promulgator, and its enforcing judge."*

*Cicero's immense influence on Western civilization could never be
properly measured. Not only might one rightly regard him as the single
most influential Roman on many of the church fathers, as such as Saints
Ambrose, Jerome, and Augustine, but one must also recognize his influence
on the American founding as well. John Adams once admitted in his diary
that he loved reciting Cicero's orations as much as anything: "The sweetness*

---

*Cicero, On Duties*, translated by Harry C. Edinger (Indianapolis: Bobbs-Merrill, 1974):
3, 5–6, 8,–10, 12–14, 22–23, 27–29, 32–35, 40–45. 51–54, 84–85, 128–33, 135–27,
139–41. 

*and grandeur of his sounds, and the harmony of his numbers give pleasure*
*enough to reward the reading if one understood none of his meaning. Besides,*
*I find it a noble exercise. It exercises my lungs, raises my spirits, opens my*
*pores, quickens the circulation, and so contributes to [my] health."* [1]

 *Though he considered himself a "New Academician," Cicero presented*
*a very Stoic understanding of the virtues and of the cosmos in his* On
Duties, *a letter written to his son, in hopes it might present an anamnesis*
*of the republic spirit to Rome or to whatever civilization might follow in its*
*wake. Though very practical at one level,* On Duties *also attempts to stir*
*the imagination of its reader at much deeper levels. As Cicero had written*
*through the voice of Quintus in* Of the Laws *"[The oak] survives, Atticus,*
*and it will always survive: its roots are in the imagination. No farmer's*
*cultivation can preserve a tree as long as one sown in a poet's verse." One*
*only has to remember the tree for it to take root again.*

44 BC

**I§1**By now you should have a good supply of philosophical rules and theories,
Marcus my son, since you have spent a year in Athens itself as a student of
Cratippus. The reputation of both the teacher and the city is extremely high.
Cratippus can provide you with knowledge, Athens with inspiration. Yet in spite
5 of such advantages, I think you might follow my practice. I have always found
it profitable to combine Latin and Greek studies, and I have done this not only
in philosophy, but also in the practice of speaking. You, too, will eventually have
equal command over both languages if you combine their study. In this respect
I believe I have been very useful to the Romans, so that beginners in Greek as
10 well as educated people believe themselves far more at ease both in speaking and
in judging the languages....

**I§4**Since I have decided to write down something to send you on this occasion
(there will be more later), I especially want to begin with what is most suitable
to your age and my position. Although in philosophy many profound and useful
15 ideas have been the subject of subtle and eloquent debates among philosophers,
the most widely relevant one seems to be their lessons and teachings about responsibility, whether your business is that of a public official or an ordinary citizen,
in the law courts or at home, whether you are acting alone or are entering into
an agreement with someone else: all good actions in life come from maintaining
20 your responsibilities; when you neglect them the result is discredit.

**I§5**The inquiry into duty is common to all philosophers: is there anyone who
would dare to call himself a philosopher without having handed on instructions

---

[1]Quoted in Carl J. Richard, *Twelve Greeks and Romans Who Changed the World*, 187.

about duty? There are, of course, some schools of philosophy that completely distort duty when they define the greatest good and the worst evil. Take, for example, the man who has established the kind of highest good that has nothing in common with virtue, that is measured by the individual's convenience, not by his morality. If that man is consistent and is not in the meantime overcome    5 by natural goodness, he cannot cultivate friendship, or justice, or openness of character. In fact, a man of courage who considers pain the greatest evil, or a temperate man who declares indulgence to be the greatest good, is surely an impossible contradiction....

[§11]To begin with, nature has bestowed on every species of living things the    10 instinct to protect its own life and limb, to avoid what it believes will be harmful, and to hunt and provide everything necessary to maintain life, such as nourishment, shelter and other similar requirements. Other instincts common to all living things are the desire for intercourse for the sake of procreation and some degree of affection toward the offspring thus brought forth. The great-    15 est difference between man and beast, however, is this: that the beast adapts itself to what is at hand and what is present only to the extent that a physical reaction impels it; it perceives the past and the future only slightly. But man is endowed with reason, by which he perceives inferences and sees the causes of facts, that is, he is fully aware of what we might call their antecedents or their    20 origins; he compares resemblances and connects with or weaves into present circumstances those in the future; he easily sees the entire course of life and prepares beforehand the things necessary to its conduct.

[§12]By the power of reason nature also associates one man with another to form a society of common culture and life; to begin with, it implants in the parents    25 a certain individual love toward those children born from them; then it drives a man to desire the existence of groups and gatherings of people and to participate in them. For these reasons he is then anxious to acquire the necessary accompaniments of civilization and comfort, not for himself alone, but for his wife, his children, and others he holds dear and ought to defend. This concern    30 also stimulates men's characters and makes them superior in accomplishment.

[§13]Inquiry into and searching for truth are primary characteristics of mankind. So when we are free from business obligations and other preoccupations, we become eager to see something new, to hear and learn something; we begin to think that knowledge about the mysteries and wonders of the world is neces-    35 sary to a happy life. This eagerness leads to the recognition that what is true, simple, and straightforward is most congenial to human nature. A striving for

independence accompanies this eagerness to contemplate the truth, so that a
man whose character is well-formed by nature does not wish to obey anyone
except an adviser or teacher, or someone who holds power lawfully and correctly
for the common good. This striving creates breadth of character and indiffer-
5    ence to external conditions.

[§14]The power of natural understanding is not negligible, because by it man,
alone among living things, experiences the essence of order, the essence of
*decorum*, and develops a true knowledge of moderation in action and speech.
This is also particularly true of whatever objects the eyes perceive: no other
10   animal grasps their beauty, their attractiveness, or the symmetry of their parts.
The natural understanding, transferring an image of this perception from the
eyes to the mind, begins to think that it should respect beauty, symmetry, and
order a great deal more in planning and action. This understanding begins to
see to it that none of its actions are unseemly or unmanly; eventually in every
15   thought and deed it is careful neither to do or to think of anything dishonorable. The particular good that we are seeking is gathered and constructed from
these attitudes, and even if men do not commonly admire it, it is still good.
What we say about the good is correct: even if no one praises it, it is by nature
praiseworthy....

20    [§20]The principle that applies most broadly to the three remaining virtues is
the one that holds together the society of humans among themselves or what
might be called the "community of life." It has two parts: justice, in which
virtue's splendor is unsurpassed and from which good men derive their reputation; and, related to justice, generosity, which may also be called kindliness or
25   beneficence.
     The first function of justice is to see that no man shall harm another unless
he has been wounded by wrongdoing. The second is to see that each man uses
public property for public benefit and his private property for himself.

[§21]In nature nothing is private property. Property becomes private by longstand-
30   ing occupation, that is, people once settled on vacant land; or by conquest, that
is, someone gained control in a war; or by a law, by a contract, a stipulation
or by casting of lots. It is on this principle that the Arpinates own the land of
Arpinum and Tusculum belongs to the Tusculans. The definition of individual
private possessions is analogous. It follows that each man should remain in pos-
35   session of what he obtains for himself, since what had once naturally been shared
becomes each man's own. It follows from this that whoever craves another's
possessions violates a basic condition of human society.

I§22Plato wrote brilliantly on this point: "We have not been born for ourselves alone; our native land claims a portion of our origin, our friends claim a portion."[2] The Stoics like to repeat that everything that comes into being in the world is created for the benefit of man, that even men themselves are born for mankind's sake, that people can be helpful among themselves, one to another. The Stoics say that we should follow nature's lead in this and that we should contribute to the public benefit by the mutual interchange of obligations, by both giving and receiving. By our skills, by our efforts, by our capacities we should thus link men together into a human society.

I§23Trust is basic to justice. By trust I mean stability and truth in promises and in agreements.... There are two classifications of injustice. One part includes those who act unjustly. The other part includes men who, even if they have the power to do so, fail to protect from abuse those people against whom other men commit violence. The man who unjustly does harm to someone else, either in anger or because some other passion arouses him, acts as if he were striking a companion. But the man who does not avert an act of violence, or offer resistance if he has the power, is just as much at fault as if he betrayed his parents, or friends, or his fatherland.

I§24Those crimes that men commit deliberately to cause harm often arise from fear. I mean that a man who makes up his mind to harm someone else fears that he might suffer some injury himself unless he commits the crime. On the whole, however, men resort to criminal activity to get possession of what they crave. Greed is the clearest motive of crime....

I§41....Now wrongdoing originates in one of two ways: either by force or by deception; deception is like a little fox, force like the lion. Both are most uncharacteristic of man, but deception should arouse greater contempt. Taking all forms of injustice into account, none is more deadly than that practiced by people who act as if they are good men when they are being most treacherous....

I§53Now there are several levels in human society. Apart from mankind as a whole, which we shall now leave out of the discussion, there is the more restricted level of belonging to the same race, the same tribe, and the same language: these join men together very closely. An even closer relationship is to belong to the same city; for fellow citizens hold many things in common: the forum, temples, colonnades, roads, laws, statutes, courtroom, voting rights, and most important,

---

[2]Plato, *Epistle IX*, (to Archytas)

customs and observances and the arrangements and agreements that thousands have entered into with thousands of others. Even closer are the ties among a group of relatives. From the all-embracing society of mankind as a whole, you see, the discussion narrows down to something small and circumscribed.

5 **I§54**We may assume that it is naturally common to living things to have the desire to procreate. The first stage of society, then, is in the basic man-wife relationship; a second stage is in the children of that union; and a third state is in the single household where the members share everything. The household is the foundation of the city, what we might call the "seed-bed" of the state. There 10 follow the relationships "brother" and "sister" and then those of "cousin" and "second cousin." When a single house cannot shelter all of them, they migrate to other houses as if they were going out to colonies. Marriages and alliances of families deriving from those marriages follow, and they result in even more relatives. These propagations and off-shoots are the beginnings of states. So 15 blood relationship links men together in good will and affection; **I§55**for it is worth a great deal to have common ancestral monuments, to employ the same religious rites, and to possess common burial places.

Yet of all associations none takes higher rank, none is more secure, than when good men who are alike in character have joined in fellowship. The moral 20 goodness that I have mentioned so often stirs us even when we perceive it in a stranger; it makes us friends with a man in whom it is obviously present. **I§56**I grant that any virtue attracts us and causes us to love those in whom it appears to be present. Justice and generosity, however, have this effect beyond all other virtues. Also, nothing is more conducive to friendship and intimacy than the 25 similarity of character among good men. Men who have the same interests and the same outlook take satisfaction each in the other as much as in himself. The Pythagorean ideal of friendship takes on reality; one replaces the many. Furthermore, the sharing that the reciprocal giving and receiving of kindnesses creates is great; as long as the exchange is mutual and acceptable, it binds those 30 between whom it takes place by an unbreakable relationship.

**I§57**When you examine everything with your mind and spirit, no relationship is more important, none is more attractive than the relationship each one of us has with our country. Our parents are dear, our children are dear, our relatives, our friends; but the fatherland alone embraces all of our deep feelings. What 35 good man would hesitate to meet death for its sake, if he could be of any use to it? That is why I find so detestable the viciousness of those men who have torn their fatherland to pieces with every kind of crime, who have been and still are working for its complete destruction.

I§58If there should arise any need to estimate or choose by comparison those who are entitled to receive your highest duty, the fatherland and the parents should come first: our debt to their kindness is the largest. The children and the household in general come next: they depend on us alone and cannot look to any other refuge. The last place goes to the deserving friends: your destiny is                     5 often intertwined with theirs. For this reason, one owes the basic protections in life especially to those groups of people I have just enumerated; but it is especially in one's friendships that one finds the real strength of a shared life and households, advice, conversations, encouragements, consolations, and even occasional arguments. A friendship that a similarity of character has cemented            10 together is the most pleasant of all.

I§59In carrying out all these obligations, you have to be cautious about what each person most needs, and what each person can accomplish or not, even without us. When you take this into consideration, the degrees of relationship are not going to be identical to those of circumstances. There are duties that            15 one owes more to some people than to others....

I§65I conclude that we should consider strong and courageous not those men who inflict injury but those who protect others from injury. Moreover, a genu-ine, wise nobility of character decides that the moral excellence that nature requires above all consists of accomplishments, not of reputation; a man of such        20 character prefers to be a true leader, not an apparent one. You cannot count among great men those who depend on the instability of an inexperienced mob. Also, insofar as a man has an ambitious character, his lust after a reputation easily drives him on to criminal acts. Reputation, of course, is a sensitive topic, because you can find hardly anyone who, once he has taken on hardships and          25 broached dangers, does not desire a bit of fame as if that were the payment for his accomplishments.

I§66Two distinctive traits especially identify beyond doubt a strong and domi-nant character. One trait is contempt for external circumstances, when one is convinced that men ought to respect, to desire, and to pursue only what is moral        30 and right; that men should be subject to nothing, not to another man, not to some disturbing passion, not to Fortune. The second trait, when your character has the disposition I outlined just now, is to perform the kind of services that are significant and most beneficial; but they should also be services that are a severe challenge, that are filled with ordeals, and that endanger not only your        35 life but also the many comforts that make life attractive.

**I§67**Of these two traits, all the glory, magnificence, and the advantage, too, let us not forget, are in the second, while the drive and the discipline that make men great are in the former. A certain quality exists there that breeds individuals of outstanding vigor who are not affected by ordinary concerns. Two signs help us to recognize this particular quality: if you decide that only what is moral is good, and if you are free from any mental turbulence. You must believe that it is characteristic of a strong and heroic mind to consider trivial what most people think glorious and attractive, and to despise those things with unshakable, inflexible discipline. To endure reverses that seem bitter, the many varying events that happen during men's life and fortune, to endure them so that you depart not one inch from your basic nature, not a jot from a wise man's self-respect: that is the mark of a strong spirit and of great consistency.

**I§68**However, it is inconsistent for a man who is impervious to fear to succumb to physical desire, or for a man who has shown that hard work cannot destroy him to yield to pleasure. So you must beware of desire and pleasure. You must also shun the greed for money; nothing is as good an index of a narrow and trivial spirit as the love of wealth; nothing is more upstanding and glorious than the contempt for wealth if you are not wealthy, or if you have wealth, to apply it to benefits and generosity. Infatuation with a glorious reputation should be avoided, as I said above; for that takes away freedom, and men of great spirit ought to pursue independence by every means. Of course you should not grasp military commands; you should even try to evade them occasionally and sometimes submit your resignation.

**I§69**You must also be free from any disturbance of the spirit, both from lust and fear, as well as from anxiety or sensuality or anger, so that you possess both mental tranquility and calm; with them goes self-control as well as self-esteem. There exist and have existed many men who, in pursuit of the tranquility I speak of, have withdrawn from public affairs and taken refuge in retirement. Among them are the most distinguished philosophers, the leading teachers, and certain serious and thoughtful men. They could not endure the habits of the people or of the rulers, and a great many have lived in the country, taking pleasure in their own private estates.

**I§70**These men had the same object as kings: to be in want of nothing whatsoever, to be in no one else's service, to enjoy freedom, whose definition is to live in just the way you want. Those who desire power pursue this goal just like the retiring people I mentioned. The one group, however, think they can attain their aim if they possess great wealth; the others if they are content with their small private property. In this matter you can condemn neither group's convictions, of course, but the life of those who withdraw is both easier and safer and less harsh or harmful to others. On the other hand, the life of men who have devoted themselves to government and to the administration of great enterprises is more beneficial to the human race and more advantageous to their 5 own fame and magnificence....

I§72Nature blesses some men with the talents for governing. They should cast aside any hesitation, take public office and help operate the government. There is no alternative way to rule the state, or to reveal a man's greatness of spirit. Men who govern a state, no less than philosophers and probably even more 10 than philosophers, should possess both greatness and the contempt for merely human affairs that I constantly mention, the tranquil spirit and the independence. These are the conditions of freedom from fear and they are necessary to a life of seriousness and self-control.

I§73These attitudes are easier for philosophers to achieve insofar as their way of 15 life is less exposed to the blows of fortune and insofar as philosophers do not feel the need of numerous possessions, and because they cannot fall very disastrously if anything evil happens to them. It is not without reason that men who govern the state are prone to stronger disturbances of the spirit and greater ambition for accomplishment than men who retire. Therefore statesmen require more 20 greatness of spirit and freedom from annoyances. The man who undertakes the task of governing should also beware that he does not consider only the moral correctness of an action; he should also consider whether he has the ability to carry it through. At the same time he should remember not to despair uselessly through cowardice and not to be excessively confident through eagerness. In any 25 transaction, he must apply hardheaded forethought before he begins....

I§85Those who are going to be in charge of the government should most certainly remember two teachings of Plato. The first instructs them to watch over the interests of the citizens in such a way as to refer to it in everything they do and to forget completely about their own interests. The second tells them to 30 minister to the entire body of the state so as not to neglect the majority while they are vigilant for a particular sector. We may compare Plato's advice to legal guardianship: one should administer the estate for the advantage of the legal wards, not for the profit of the guardians. Men who take care of one group of citizens but neglect another group introduce into the state an extremely 35 destructive circumstance, treason and discord. The result is that some appear to be leaders of the people while others appear to support the aristocrats, but there are few who lead the whole populace.

I§86This situation caused great strife among the Athenians, and in Rome the result was not merely conspiracies but destructive civil wars as well. A self-controlled and courageous citizen, who conceivably could hold the highest rank in the state, will shun these things, will hate them, will devote himself entirely
5    to government, will not pursue wealth or power, and will be guardian over the whole state so that he might work to everyone's advantage. Of course he will not involve anyone in hatred and blame by false criminal charges and, in general, will so cling to justice and morality that, as long as he upholds them, he would rather suffer any misfortune, however severe, and go to meet death rather than
10   abandon the qualities I mentioned.

I§87Campaigning for public office and fighting for election are on the whole quite degrading. Again, Plato speaks brilliantly about this: "those who argue with each other about who should rule the state act like sailors who fight over who should steer the boat." He also teaches that, "we shall regard as enemies
15   only those who bear arms against us, not those who might wish to govern the state out of private conviction."…

I§88Of course you should not listen to men who think you must be bitterly angry with your foes and who imagine this is the sign of a great and strong man. Nothing is more praiseworthy, nothing more worthy of a great and outstanding man
20   than a reasonable and forgiving attitude. Among free peoples, where everyone enjoys equal rights, you must practice courtesy and what we might call detachment. Those qualities will prevent us from lapsing into profitless and repulsive bad temper if we become annoyed when people barge in at inconvenient times or pester us with irritating questions. Yet gentleness and mercy deserve approval
25   only as long as strictness continues to be effective on behalf of the state: without such severity no one can run the government. Also, all criticism and correction ought to be free from insult and should be used for the benefit of the state, not the profit of the person who punishes or verbally corrects another.

I§89One should also be careful that the punishment does not surpass the
30   crime and that some people receive beatings while others do not even receive a reprimand, both for the same crime. In administering punishment, the most important thing to avoid is anger; for the man who attempts to mete out punishments in a state of anger will not maintain the balance between "too much" and "too little." The "mean" appeals to the Peripatetics, and so it should, if only
35   they did not praise hot temper and say that it is a profitable gift of nature. You should restrain your temper at all times, of course; one should hope that the men who head the state resemble the law, for the law does not punish because it is angry but because it is just.

I§90Let us shun haughtiness, arrogance, and especially overbearing pride, even when things go well for us, rolling along just as we wish. For it is only the changeable man who reacts violently to bad luck or to good luck. An even temper in every phase of life, always the same expression, the same face: that is admirable, a quality we learn from Socrates and Gaius Laelius as well. I note 5 that even Philip, King of Macedonia, although his son outdistanced him in military exploits and renown, was never surpassed in adaptability and human feeling. Philip was unfailingly great, Alexander was frequently scandalous. So those who teach that the higher we rise, the more humbly we should conduct ourselves are clearly giving correct advice.... Men who have become unbridled 10 and excessively self-confident through prosperity ought to be led, as it were, into the ring of reason and philosophy, so they can see the fragility of men's circumstances and the changeability of luck.

I§91Even when you are most prosperous, you should make the greatest possible use of your friends' advice, and you should allow their influence to be even 15 greater than before. In those same circumstances we must beware of lending an open ear to flatterers and of allowing them to praise us excessively. It is easy to be trapped by flattery. We begin to think we are the type of person that men should really praise. That is the beginning of innumerable crimes, since men who overrate themselves because of other men's flattery expose themselves to 20 shameless ridicule and get involved in the extremes of misjudgment. That is surely enough on these matters.

I§92The following conclusion is inevitable: those who rule states perform the most significant and boldest actions because nothing extends more widely or affects more people than an entire government. However, there are also many 25 courageous individuals, past and present, who, although they live in retirement, carry out certain great inquiries or enterprises but content themselves within the boundaries of their own business. They fall half-way between philosophers and those who conduct public affairs, and they take pleasure in their own private estate, not expanding it by every possible means, not excluding their relatives 30 from its benefits, but rather sharing it with both friends and the state if there is need. The first obligation is to acquire such an estate honestly, not by some shameful or despicable transaction. Second, its expansion should be the result of planning, industry, and thrift. Lastly, it should prove itself beneficial to as many as possible, as long as they deserve it; it should not serve lust and dis- 35 sipation in preference to generosity and usefulness. By observing these rules a man can live richly, impressively, independently and yet also plainly, honestly, and as a true friend of man.

[§93]It follows that I must speak about the one remaining category of morality, the one where we find the sense of shame and the qualities that we may say give shape to a life: restraint, self-control, a complete conquest of anxieties, and moderation in all things. This area deals with what Latin calls *decorum* and what
5   Greek calls *prepon*. It has the property of being inseparable from morality.

[§94]What is moral is "becoming," and what is "becoming" is moral. It is easier to understand the nature of the difference between *decorum* and what is moral than to explain it. Whatever is "fitting" appears only when moral correctness has preceded it. So *decorum* appears not only in the category of moral correct-
10  ness that I must talk about here but also in the three preceding categories. (1) To think and to speak wisely and to carry out your actions prudently, and to see the truth in every situation and to support it: these are signs of *decorum*. On the opposite side, to be tricked, to be mistaken, to hesitate, to go astray are as "indecorous" as insanity or being simpleminded. (2) Also, everything just is
15  becoming, while unjust actions, since they are degrading, are unbecoming. (3) The relationship with courage is similar. An action of manliness and great spirit seems worthy of a man and becoming; an opposite action is as unbecoming as it is degrading.

[§95]That is why this quality that I call *decorum* surely pertains to every category
20  of morality. The relation between them is such that *decorum* requires no tortu-ous reasoning process to grasp; on the contrary, it is as plain as day. *Decorum* is a distinct quality that can be traced in every kind of virtue. It is possible to detach it from virtue, but more in speculative theory than in fact. Just as it is impossible to separate loveliness and physical beauty from health so this *decorum*
25  that I am discussing is thoroughly blended with virtue, and yet it is possible to separate them in the mind and in thought.

[§96]It can, moreover, be divided into two groups: we understand a certain general *decorum*, which is connected with all types of moral correctness, and another subsidiary *decorum*, which relates to separate classifications of moral correctness.
30  General *decorum* is usually defined in this way: *decorum* is a quality consistent with the superiority of man insofar as his nature surpasses that of other living things. The subsidiary part to the whole is defined like this: *decorum* is the achieve-ment of a harmony with nature that reveals a man's moderation and self-control, together with that certain outlook that characterizes a free man....

35  [§110]However, on the whole, each man should retain his particular qualities, though not the harmful ones; that will make it easier for him to preserve the

*decorum* that we are seeking. We have the obligation to act in such a way that we do not put ourselves in opposition to nature in general, and yet we must follow our particular nature without violating the general one. Even if other pursuits are more important and attractive, we should nevertheless measure our own ambitions against the yardstick of our own nature. It is not profitable to     5
fight against nature or to pursue something that you cannot attain....

I§114...If we have a choice, we shall work faithfully at those things that are most suitable to us. If from time to time necessity pushes us into affairs that are alien to our character, complete care, forethought, and application must be brought to bear. In such circumstances we should act with as much fitness     10
as possible, since complete *decorum* cannot be expected. One must strive not so much to accomplish good results that may not be granted to us as to avoid bad faults....

II§21Now whatever men bestow upon another man to enrich and promote him, they bestow either because of good will when they like someone for whatever     15
reason; or because of the man's achievement if they respect his character and think that he deserves the greatest good fortune; or because they put their trust in someone and think that he takes a great interest in their affairs; or because they fear someone's wealth or, conversely, expect something from someone, as when kings or demagogues make various lavish gifts; or finally because they     20
are enticed by bribes or rewards. This last is undoubtedly the most sordid motive and the most unfair one, both to those who are ensnared in it as well as to those who try to use it.

II§22It is an evil business when one tries to do something with money that should be done by virtue. But because such subventions are frequently unavoidable, I     25
shall discuss how a man should use them, once I have discussed topics that are more relevant to virtue. Men go so far as to subject themselves to the rule and power of another man for a variety of reasons. They are influenced by good will, or by the extent of benefits received, or by the glamour of the other man's prestige, or by the hope that submission will be advantageous to themselves, or     30
by fear that they might be compelled to obey force; or they are enticed by the hope of largesse and by promises, or finally, as we often witness in our government, seduced by a bribe.

II§23However, among all qualities there is no more appropriate way to preserve and defend one's resources than to be well-liked, nothing less appropriate than     35
to be feared. Ennius has an excellent verse,

*They hate the man they fear; and when one man hates*
*Another, he hopes to see him dead.*

Recently men realized, if they did not know it before, that no power can
resist the hate of the multitude. The death of a recent notorious tyrant is not
5   the only one that makes clear how relentlessly the hatred men feel works toward destruction; the citizens oppressed by weapons endured this tyrant.... But
comparable assassinations of other tyrants also make this clear, and hardly one
of them avoided such an end. To arouse fear in others is a bad guarantee of
longevity, while on the other hand good will is faithful into eternity.

10  **II§24**Men who dominate and command other men, whom they have subjugated
by force, have to apply some harshness, just as the owner uses harshness toward
his slaves if he cannot control them any other way. But it is completely senseless
for men in a free city to act in such a way that it causes others to live in fear:
no one could be more insane. Although an individual's wealth and power may
15  circumvent the laws, although he may threaten liberty, nevertheless laws and
liberty eventually rise to the surface again, either by anonymous expressions of
opposition or by secret arrangements to secure election to important offices.
But the wounds caused by the suspension of freedom hurt worse than those
caused by maintaining it. So let us embrace a rule that applies widely and that
20  is extremely effective not only in maintaining safety but also in acquiring wealth
and power, namely, that there should be no fear, that one should hold affection
dear. This is the easiest way for us to attain what we want both in private affairs
and in the government....

**III§18**Those who measure everything by rewards and profits and who do not
25  assign more importance to right conduct than to profit constantly weigh right
conduct against what they consider profitable when they are making a decision.
Good men never do this.... It is extremely shameful not only to value what
seems profitable more highly than what is right conduct, but also to compare
these with each other and to debate inwardly about them.

30  The question is, then, why do situations constantly arise that cause discussion
and that make us hesitate about our course of conduct? They arise whenever there
is hesitation about the essential nature of the action under consideration.

**III§19**It often happens in particular circumstances that what people usually
consider a shameful act turns out to be not shameful at all. For the sake of
35  example, let me mention a single case that has applications beyond itself. What
crime could possibly be greater than the slaying of a man, or, worse, of a man
who is your close friend? But has anyone who has killed a tyrant, no matter

how close he was to him, stained himself with a crime? It does not seem so, of course, to the Roman people, who think that this is the most attractive of all remarkable deeds. In this case does benefit outweigh right conduct? Far from it: benefit resulted from right conduct.

Therefore, we must set up a rule; then we will not make any mistake if     5
it ever happens that something we consider profitable seems to be in conflict with what we know is right conduct. If we follow this rule when we compare actions, we shall never desert our moral duty.

**III§20**As far as possible, this rule will be consistent with the thought and learning of the Stoics.... The Stoics believe that right conduct is identical with expedi-   10
ent conduct and that no action whatsoever is expedient that is not also right conduct. This Stoic position is more attractive than the one taken by those who say that right conduct is inexpedient and that expedient actions are not right conduct.... But let me return to the rule.

**III§21**To deprive another man of something, to increase your own comfort by   15
making another man miserable, is more against nature than death, poverty, pain, and any other misfortune that can happen to one's body or one's possessions. In the first place, such an act does away with human society and social co-operation. If we are so demoralized that a man will rob or injure another man to achieve a private advantage, it necessarily follows that what is pre-eminently "according   20
to nature," the social structure of the human race, will disintegrate.

**III§22**For example, if each separate limb of the body had the ability to think and believed that it would be able to strengthen itself by drawing out the strength of a near-by limb, it necessarily follows that the whole body would grow weak and perish. In the same way, if every one of us should seize the possessions of   25
others, should drag off what he could for his private advantage, it follows neces-sarily that society and co-operation among men would be destroyed. One can grant that as individuals men prefer to acquire the things that make life enjoy-able for themselves, rather than for strangers. That is completely natural. But nature does not allow us to increase our own resources, property, and wealth   30
by plundering other peoples'.

**III§23**It is forbidden to harm another person for one's own private benefit. This idea is established not only by nature, that is, by the law of nations, but also similarly by the laws of peoples, the laws that support the government in various individual states. Laws look to this end, they have this purpose: that   35
the society of citizens remain undisturbed; whoever disrupts this society is

punished with exile and death, with fines and prison. The very plan of nature itself demonstrates this much more effectively. That plan is law for both gods and men; whoever wishes to obey that law (and everyone obeys who wants to live according to nature) will never go so far as to attack another man and to
5   appropriate for himself what he has seized from someone else.

**III§24**Greatness of soul and high courage and courtesy, a sense of justice and generosity are far more in accord with nature than sensuality, existence itself, or wealth. In fact, it is the mark of a great and exalted spirit to weigh these things against the common benefit and then reject them and count them as nothing.
10  To rob another man for one's private advantage is more against nature than death, pain, and similar things.

**III§25**By the same argument, it is more "according to nature" to take upon yourself enormous work and trouble in order to preserve and aid all the nations, if that is possible, and to imitate the renowned Hercules: his fame among men
15  kept alive the memory of his good deeds and earned him a place in the council of the heavenly gods. These actions are preferable to living for yourself, not merely apart from every trouble, but also in the midst of all kind of delicacies, amid the most refined pleasures, surpassing all others in beauty and strength. For this reason, every person of the greatest and most brilliant talent infinitely
20  prefers a life of action to the alternative. A result is that the man who obeys nature is quite unable to harm another man.

**III§26**Next consider the man who injures another man in order to secure some advantage of himself. He either believes that he is not doing anything against nature or he thinks that to harm another human being is not worse than death,
25  poverty, pain, or even the loss of children, relatives, or friends. What kind of discussion can you hold with him if he believes that wronging another man is not an action against nature? His concept of "man" simply does not include what is essentially human. If he thinks doing harm should in fact be avoided but believes those other things like death, poverty, and pain are much worse, he
30  is wrong. He falsely assumes that any injury to the body or any loss of property is more serious than injuries of the soul. So there ought to be one single rule for everyone: that what benefits each individual and what benefits all mankind should be identical. If any individual seizes an advantage for himself, the whole of human society will break apart.

35  **III§27**Furthermore, if nature demands that a man be willing to help another man, whoever he might be, for the simple reason that he is a human being, it

necessarily follows that, according to the same nature, the advantage of all men is shared. If this assumption is correct, one and the same law of nature binds all of us. If this last assertion is also correct, we are certainly restrained by a law of nature from harming another human being.

III§28 The first assertion is true and so, therefore, is the last. The contention 5 that some people advance is absurd, of course: they argue that they would not deprive a parent or brother of anything for their own advantage but that there is another standard applicable to all other citizens. These people do not submit themselves to any law or to any obligation to co-operate with fellow citizens for the common benefit. Their attitude destroys any co-operation within the city. 10 In the same way, those who say that one standard should be applied to fellow citizens but another to foreigners, destroy the common society of the human race. When that disappears, good deeds, generosity, kindness, and justice are also removed root and branch.

We must draw the conclusion that people who do away with these qualities 15 are disrespectful even against the immortal gods. They destroy the co-operation among men which the gods instituted. The strongest bond in this co-operation is the thought that it is more against nature if one man deprives another for his own advantage than if that man himself suffers destruction of any kind, either to his property, or to his person, or even to the spirit itself…that are not 20 characterized by justice, because this one virtue is the mistress and queen of all the others.

III§29 Perhaps someone might say, "But consider a wise man who is dying of hunger. Will he not take food from another man, a man who is quite useless for anything?" [Not true at all. For my life is not more useful to me than that par- 25 ticular disposition of mind that prevents me from harming anyone for my own advantage.] "Second: suppose a good man could steal clothing from Phalaris, that cruel and monstrous tyrant, to keep himself from dying of cold. Should he not do it?" These hypothetical cases are extremely easy to decide.

III§30 If you take something for your private use away from another man who is 30 useless to anyone, you act inhumanly and against the law of nature. However, if you are the kind of person who can bestow a great benefit on the state and human society by remaining alive, then there is no blame if you deprive another man of something to sustain your life. Yet if this is not the situation, each man should endure his own suffering rather than reduce the benefits of another person. In 35 summary, neither disease nor dire want, nothing of that kind is more contrary to nature than coveting and stealing another man's belongings. Disregard of the common benefit is against nature because it is unjust.

**III§31**The same law of nature preserves and defines the benefits common to all men. It will ultimately decree that commodities necessary to life may be transferred from a slothful and useless man to a man who is wise, good, and strong, one who would greatly reduce the common good if he should die. However, the law should act in such a way that the good man does not use this as an excuse for doing wrong because he has a good opinion of himself and loves himself. Thus he will always perform his duty while considering the benefit of men and, as I always repeat, that of the human society....

**III§35**Now when some apparent advantage offers itself, we are inevitably attracted to it. But when we examine it closely, when we see that immorality is involved in the circumstances that present an appearance of expediency, then we are not forced to relinquish the advantage; we merely have to realize that expediency cannot exist in the same place as immorality. If nothing is as contrary to nature as immorality, since nature desires the right, the appropriate, the consistent, and shuns their opposites; and if nothing is so much according to nature as expediency, then surely expediency and immorality cannot exist in the very same set of circumstances. However, Zeno thought that we have been born for right conduct and that it alone should be sought out. On the other hand, Aristotle thought that men should consider right conduct more important in any calculation than anything else. From both opinions it necessarily follows that what is right conduct is either the only good or the greatest good. What is good is doubtlessly expedient, and so whatever is right conduct is expedient.

**III§36**The false reasoning of unscrupulous men, once it has seized on something apparently expedient, immediately distinguishes between that and right conduct. That is the origin of assassins' daggers, of poisonings, of forged wills, of thefts and embezzlements, of plunderings and lootings of allies and fellow citizens. That is the source of desire for excessive wealth, for intolerable power, ultimately even the desire to act like a king in states that have self-rule. Nothing more shocking, nothing more repulsive than such desires can be imagined. Men draw the wrong conclusions and envisage rewards for these actions, they do not see the penalties. I do not mean punishment by the law, which men often evade, but the punishment of degradation itself, which is extremely harsh.

**III§37**This group of vacillators should be whipped out of society; they are completely criminal and ungodly. They debate with themselves whether they should follow what they see to be right conduct, or whether, with full knowledge, they should corrupt themselves with crime. There is crime in the mere act of deliberation, even if they do not decide on a criminal action. For this reason,

since it is wicked merely to think about certain courses of action, they should simply have no place in your deliberations. Furthermore, no deliberation should ever be based on the expectation or assumption that you are going to conceal or cover up your actions. If we have made any progress at all in philosophy, we should be sufficiently convinced that, even if we could hide our actions from     5
all mankind and from all the gods, we should never do anything greedy, unjust, lustful, or intemperate.

III§38 To illustrate this truth Plato introduces the well-known Gyges. Once when the ground had split apart after some violent rainstorms, Gyges climbed down into the cleft, as the story goes, and discovered a bronze horse. There were     10
doors in the flanks of the horse, and when they were opened he saw the body of a dead human of unusual size. There was a god ring on one of his fingers. Gyges removed the ring, put it on his own finger and then went back to the gathering of shepherds (he was one of the King's shepherds). There he discovered that, when he had turned the bezel of the ring toward his palm, he was     15
invisible to everyone. But he was still able to see everything and became visible again when he had turned his ring back to its proper position. So, making use of the advantage offered by this ring, he seduced the queen, and with her as a helper brought about the death of his master, the King. He removed all those who he believed were standing in his way, and he was completely invisible as     20
he performed these crimes. Thus, with the help of the ring he swiftly rose to be king of Lydia. The point is if a wise man had this same ring, he would not think he was any freer to do wrong than if he did not have it. Good men seek right conduct, not conduct that has to remain concealed....

III§41 ...However, we must not relinquish our own personal advantages and     25
surrender them to other people when we need them ourselves. Each man must protect his own advantage insofar as it can be realized without harm to another person....

III§43 Friendships are especially liable to throw moral duties into confusion. It is a violation of your moral duty to fail to perform what you can properly do on     30
behalf of a friend. But to do something unjust on his behalf is also a violation. The rule covering this whole area is short and easily grasped. You must never subordinate your friendships to ambitions that appear to you to be advantageous, election to office, for example, making money, sexual gratification, or other apparently advantageous objectives. Yet a good man will never act against     35
the state or against his oath and trust for the sake of a friend, not even if he is actually the judge in a friend's trial....

**III§45**I am, you understand, speaking about everyday friendships. No concessions of that sort are possible among wise and perfect men. They say that Damon and Phintias, the Pythagoreans, were devoted to each other in a remarkable way. When Dionysius the tyrant set the day of execution for one of them, the one
5    condemned to death requested a few days delay to arrange for the maintenance of his relatives. The other friend went bail for his appearance in court; he had to die if his friend did not return. When the condemned man returned on the set day, the tyrant was amazed at their mutual trust and asked that they accept him as the third partner in their friendship.

10   **III§46**Even in friendships, therefore, when you compare what seems advantageous with right action, the mere appearance of advantage should yield, and right action should prevail. Moreover, when friends ask you to do things that are not right, the scruple of conscience and trustworthiness should take precedence over friendship. In this way we will select the correct duty, and it is a principle
15   of selection that we are seeking....

# THE CONSPIRACY OF CATILINE
## SALLUST (86–*c.* 34 BC)

*Sallust, a partisan of Julius Caesar, was active in Roman politics dur-
ing the years of Caesar's dictatorship. The following passage, from the
prologue to* The Conspiracy of Catiline, *vividly describes what Sallust
saw as the decay of Roman civic virtue in the years after the Punic Wars.
He contrasts the morals of his own day with those that prevailed during
the early Republic.*

§5...The subject itself seems to exhort me, since this part of my history has put
me in mind of the morals of the state, to go back and to detail in a few words the
institutions of our ancestors at home and in war; how they managed the republic,
and how great they left it; and how, being changed by degrees, from being the
most glorious and the best, it became the worst and most flagitious.    5

§6The city Rome, as I have understood, the Trojans at first founded and inhabited;
who, under the guidance of Æneas, flying from their country, wandered about in
uncertain settlements; and with them were the Aborigines, a wild race of men,
without laws and government, free and unrestrained. When, however, they collected into one city, although of different race and dissimilar language, and each    10
living in a different manner, it is incredible to be told how easily they became
one people. But after their state, being improved in number of people, manners,
and territory, appeared sufficiently prosperous and sufficiently powerful, as most
mortal things are treated, envy arose out of their prosperity. Therefore kings of
the neighboring nations began to harass them in war, while few of their friends    15
were allies. For the rest, struck with fear, stood aloof from their dangers. But the
Romans, busy at home and in war, used all expedition, made preparations; each
exhorted his neighbor, marched out to meet the enemy, and protected their liberty,
their country, and their parents by their arms. Afterwards, when they had repelled
the dangers by their valor, they carried aid to their allies and friends, and rather    20
by giving than by receiving kindnesses they gained friendships.

*The Catiline and Jugurthine Wars of Sallust* (Oxford: Henry Slatter, 1841), 4–10.

They had a lawful government, and the name of their government was royal. Chosen men, whose body, through years, was infirm, but whose mind was strong in wisdom, consulted for the state. These, either through their age or the similarity of their charge, were called *fathers*. But when kingly government,
5   which at first proved a means of preserving their liberty and advancing the public interest, degenerated into haughtiness and tyranny, the custom being changed, they chose for themselves, as annual officers, two magistrates. By this means they thought that the human mind would least of all become overbearing.

§7But at that time everyone began more and more to exert himself, and to have
10  his ability in readiness. For by kings good men are more suspected than the bad, and to them the virtue of others is always formidable. But it is incredible to be told how much in a short time the state increased, its liberty being obtained; so great a desire of glory had now come on. Now the youth, as soon as capable of bearing arms, learnt the art of war by labor with experience in the camp; and
15  rather in beautiful arms and war-horses than in harlots and banquets, placed their pleasure. To such men as these therefore, labor was not unaccustomed; no place was too rugged or difficult, no enemy in arms was formidable. Their valor had subdued everything. But in glory there was the highest emulation amongst them. Everyone was zealous to strike the enemy, to scale the wall, and
20  to be beheld while he was performing such an exploit. These they esteemed riches—this noble glory and real nobility. They were greedy of praise, lavish of their money. They longed for boundless glory, moderate riches. I could relate in what places the Roman people with a small band defeated the greatest forces of the enemy, and what cities fortified by nature they took by fighting, did not
25  such a relation draw me off too far from my purpose.

§8But in truth Fortune rules in everything. It celebrates or obscures everything at its pleasure, rather than according to truth. The actions of the Athenians, in my opinion, were great and glorious enough, but, however, a little less than they are represented by fame.
30       But because the great genius of writers flourished there, the exploits of the Athenians are celebrated for the greatest throughout the world. Therefore their valor who have done these things is accounted as great as the finest genius could extol them by language. But the Roman people never had that advantage, because each man who was the wisest was most engaged in the service of the
35  state. No one cultivated the mind without the body. Each one who was the best preferred to act than to speak, that his own good deeds should be praised by others than himself to write those of others.

§9Good manners were therefore practiced at home and abroad. Their unanimity was very great, their covetousness very small. Justice and equity flourished among them, not more by the laws than by nature. Their strifes, their discords, and their grudges they carried on with their enemies. Citizens contended with citizens concerning virtue. In the worship of the gods they were magnificent, at home frugal, 5 and faithful to their friends. By these two arts, boldness in war and by equity when peace had followed, they managed themselves and the republic. Of which things I have these as the greatest proofs, that in war punishment was more often inflicted on those who had fought against the enemy contrary to orders, and who when recalled had been too slow in retreating, than on those who had ventured 10 to desert their standards, or when beaten to quit their posts. In peace however, by kindness rather than by fear they managed the government, and when they had received an injury, they chose rather to forgive than to revenge it.

§10But when by labor and justice the state increased, great kings were conquered in war, fierce nations and mighty people were subdued by arms, Carthage the 15 rival of the Roman empire, had utterly perished, all seas and lands were open, fortune began to be enraged, and confound everything. They who had easily endured dangers, doubtful and difficult trials, to them ease and riches, desirable by the rest of mankind, became a burden and a calamity. Therefore at first the love of money, then that of power increased. These things became, as it were, 20 the foundation of all evils. For avarice overthrew faith, honesty, and all the other good acts; and instead of them it taught men pride, cruelty, to neglect the gods, and to consider everything venal. Ambition forced many men to become false, to have one thing hidden in their hearts, another ready on their tongue, to value friendships and enmities, not according to reality, but interest, and rather to 25 have a good appearance than a good disposition. These things at first began to increase by degrees, sometimes to be punished. Afterwards when the infection swept on like a pestilence, the state was changed, the government, from the most just and best, became cruel and intolerable.

§11But at first ambition more than avarice influenced the minds of the Romans. 30 Which vice, however, was the nearer to virtue. For glory, honor, command, the good and slothful equally wish for themselves. But the former strives by the right course; to the latter, because good qualities are wanting, he works by tricks and deceits. Avarice has a longing after money, which no wise man ever desired. This passion, as if it were imbued with deadly poisons, enervates the 35 body and mind of man. It is always boundless, insatiable, is neither diminished by plenty nor want. But after Lucius Sulla, the republic being seized by force of laws, from a good beginning turned out ill—all men began to plunder and

spoil—one man coveted a house, another lands, nor had the victors any modesty or moderation, but committed foul and cruel actions against the citizens. To this was added that Lucius Sulla, contrary to the custom of the ancients, had treated luxuriously and too liberally the army which he had commanded
5 in Asia, in order to make it faithful to himself. These pleasant and voluptuous countries had easily in time of peace softened the fierce minds of the soldiery. There first of all, the army of the Roman people became accustomed to love, to drink, to admire statues, paintings, and carved vessels, to plunder them in public and private, to rob the temples, and pollute all things both sacred and
10 profane. Therefore these soldiers, after they had gained the victory, left nothing to the conquered; for success tries the minds of wise men, much less could they, when their morals were corrupted, use their victory with moderation.

§12After that riches began to be an honor and glory, and command and power followed them, virtue began to languish, poverty to be accounted matter of
15 reproach, and innocence to be considered as malignity. Therefore from riches, luxury and avarice with pride came in upon our youth. They ravaged and wasted everything, their own property they valued at a trifle, that of other persons they coveted, and had not the least care for, or moderation in, shame, modesty, sacred or profane things, which were all the same to them. It is worthwhile, when you
20 shall have taken a view of their houses and villas built up after the manner of cities, to visit the temples of the gods, which our fathers, the most religious of men, built; but they used to adorn the shrines of their gods with their piety, their own houses with glory, nor took anything from the conquered except the liberty of doing mischief; but the others, on the contrary, the most cowardly of
25 men, by means of the greatest wickedness, took away from our allies all those things which the bravest men, when victors, had left to the enemies, just as if the doing of injury was forsooth the use of power.

§13For why should I relate those things which are credible to no one except to those who have seen them—that mountains have been leveled, seas built over
30 by many private persons, whose riches appear to me to have been a jest, since those which they might have used honorably, they hastened to abuse disgracefully? But no less a desire of wantoning, gluttony, and other fashion had come on, women exhibited their shame in the open air, for the sake of feasting they ransacked every place by sea and land, and slept before there was any desire of
35 sleep, they waited not for hunger nor thirst, nor cold nor fatigue, but anticipated all these things through their luxury. These things inflamed the youth, when their property had failed, to crimes; the mind when stained by evil practices was not easily free from lusts, and so was the more entirely given up in every way to getting and spending.

# V
# THE ROMAN EMPIRE

Assigning specific dates to the second, or "imperial," phase of Roman history is a difficult task. Historians generally agree that the "Roman Empire" emerged from the century-long revolution that finally destroyed the Roman Republic toward the end of the first century BC. But Octavian (63 BC–AD 14), the first Roman "emperor" and universally known by his imperial title "Caesar Augustus," completed the dismantling of the Republic so cleverly that it is not possible to say exactly when the first phase of Rome's history ended and the second began. As a further complication, Rome actually acquired the largest portion of its "empire" during the republican phase of its history. But, there is no denying that by the beginning of the new millennium, Roman government had come under the domination of its "emperors" and would remain so in the West until the fifth century AD. Even after the last Western Emperor was toppled in 476, however, the Eastern Roman Empire based on Constantinople (Byzantium) endured for almost another thousand years until conquered by the Ottoman Turks in 1453.

Across the five centuries commonly regarded as the lifespan of the Roman Empire, citizens of this vast world state knew two centuries of *Pax Romana* ("Roman Peace"), a century of almost unrelenting crisis, and two final centuries of "twilight" during which an effort at recovery and rebuilding was undertaken by famously strong and visionary leaders, but ultimately could not be sustained. The mere fact that Romans found the capacity to reconstitute their state after the bloodshed and tumult of the multiple civil wars that brought the Republic to collapse is ample testimony to their genius for government. The strength and longevity of imperial Rome rested on political, military, economic, and spiritual foundations and can be explained primarily by the institutions that kept it orderly, defended its frontiers, generated its wealth, and fostered patriotic citizens. For many generations, the Empire held together and prospered even when unimaginably incompetent and murderously corrupt men held the imperial title. Although some, like the historian Tacitus (*c.* 56–*c.* 117), would denounce Octavian for finishing off the Republic, the Roman Empire stands as one of the most illustrious chapters in the history of the West. As the eighteenth-century historian Edward Gibbon (1737–1794) wrote in *The Decline and Fall of the Roman Empire:* "If a man were called to fix the period in the history of the world during which the condition of the human race was most happy and prosperous, he would, without hesitation, name that which elapsed from the death of Domitian [AD 96] to the accession of Commodus [AD 180]." While even the best periods of imperial Roman history were not without blemish, and decades of bad times came with the good, "the grandeur that was Rome" amounts to one of the richest sources of the Western Heritage.

Historians refer to the first phase of the Roman Empire as the "Principate." *Princeps,* or "first citizen," was a title Octavian took from the Senate after he defeated Mark Antony in 31 BC and put an end to the civil war that had broken out in the wake of Julius Caesar's assassination thirteen years earlier. In 27 BC, the Senate granted Octavian the title *Augustus,* or "revered one," symbolizing the supremacy of his authority over the Roman state. Octavian was also known as "Caesar," which reminded people that he was the late leader's adoptive heir. Still another title, *imperator,* literally the one who possessed *imperium,* or power to command, was bestowed upon Octavian, and this would come to us easily enough as "emperor." By such accumulation of honorific titles and public trading on his family connection with the man who, had he lived, might well have been Rome's first monarch in five hundred years, Octavian absorbed power over the Roman state in the manner of an emperor without at one stroke destroying the traditional republican offices. While the popular assemblies of the Republic withered away, Octavian retained the Senate as a sounding board and advisory body, as did future emperors. But the freedom of this once powerful deliberative body to stand against Rome's "first citizen" was virtually nonexistent. Still, Augustus's failure to make clearer the power relationship between ruler and Senate would be the source of much trouble across the centuries to come. Another of Augustus's shortcomings, which became a persistent flaw in the imperial system, was the failure to prescribe a method for the imperial succession. Lethal violence often attended transitions from one emperor to another.

This chapter's first selection recounts, in Augustus's own words, how he incorporated republican offices into a new imperial structure and also explains how his strong rule contributed to peace and prosperity in a society that was hungry for them. Indeed, the reign of Augustus ushered in a period of nearly two centuries of "Roman Peace," perhaps the longest period of general tranquility in recorded history. The boundaries of the Empire at that time stretched from Scotland to the Sahara Desert, and from the Iberian peninsula to the frontiers of Persia. Only the Germanic and Celtic tribes of northern and eastern Europe, the peoples of central and southern Africa, and the largely unknown nations of the Asian heartland were beyond the reach or control of the Caesars. The Mediterranean Sea was a Roman lake as well as a spacious commercial highway, and Roman vessels were equally at home on the Black Sea and the Atlantic

Ocean. The Empire itself was knit together by well-constructed roads and bridges, watered by elaborate systems of aqueducts, patrolled and protected by the greatest army in the world, administered by another smaller army of civil servants, and further sustained by remarkably flexible and enlightened laws. Emperors, of course, held court at Rome and, after Constantine's reign (*r.* 306–337), at a second capital he established in the East. But, while beneficent rulers could exert positive sway over the imperial apparatus, the notoriously bad emperors of the *Pax Romana*—men like Caligula (*r.* 37–41) and Nero (*r.* 54–68), for example—were powerless to wreck or even do significant harm to the far-flung and seemingly indestructible pillars of the state.

One such pillar was Roman law. It has been said that law was "the greatest and most enduring achievement of the [Roman] Empire." Roman law, writes another source, was "logical, practical, orderly, and—within the limits of a society of slaves and masters—relatively fair." Romans understood there to be three kinds of law. "Civil law" *(ius civile)* governed Roman citizens and was enacted by the legislative authorities of the state. During the Empire, civil law was typically decreed by the emperor. As the Romans increasingly mixed with and conquered foreign peoples, they noticed that certain principles commonly informed the legal systems of many states. They called this body of law *ius gentium,* "the law of nations," and although it remained largely a body of principles, its provisions could take on the force of law if a magistrate embodied them in an edict. Thus, the *ius gentium* played its part in establishing the broad foundations of Roman law on which the Western world would continue to build. Finally, there was "natural law" *(ius naturale)*, a concept that comported well with the idea of Rome as a world state and owed much to the Stoic principle that rational laws explained the operations of nature and could be discerned by men who shared a capacity for reason with the divine creator. It would not be wrong to resort to the words of the republican statesman Cicero (106–43 BC) to describe the understanding of law that prevailed throughout the Empire: "True law is right reason conformable to nature; universal, unchangeable, eternal." That Justinian's great *Corpus Juris Civile*, a sixth-century AD project, would become "the cornerstone for the structure of medieval, and much of modern, law" affirms the brilliance and timelessness of Roman jurisprudence.

The Empire was similarly sustained by an extensive network of roads and unusually effective provincial administration. The Roman highway system expanded significantly during the time of "Roman Peace," and it extended to the borders of the Empire, and sometimes beyond. Roads were extremely well-constructed and maintained. Their decay, in fact, coincided with the breakdown of the Empire itself. Commerce could thrive because travel throughout the Empire was relatively easy, inexpensive, and safe. Imperial Romans generally took an enlightened approach to governing the dozens of provinces as well. At the head of the administration of each province was a governor who issued orders in the name of the emperor and was assisted by a staff of civil servants, who, by the second century AD, were recruited largely on the basis of merit. While governors were sometimes corrupt, they were seldom tyrants and typically respected the rights and customs of those whom they governed. Indeed, another key buttress of the remarkable stability of the Empire was the grant of citizenship rights to those peoples brought under Roman dominion, a practice that had begun more selectively during the Republic as a reward for the good behavior of conquered peoples.

The army also played a vitally important role in securing and sustaining the Roman Empire. The vaunted legions were the core of the army, while provincial auxiliary units increasingly undertook the duties of local policing and defense. Not only did the army defend the vast frontiers, but it served as an essential vehicle of social mobility and acculturation. Numerous emperors would come from the ranks of the military, and service in the army educated countless new imperial inhabitants in the deeply rooted traditions of the Roman state and society. Many of Europe's greatest cities today—Paris, Vienna, Cologne, for example—originated as army camps or veterans' colonies.

The remaining supports of the Empire, as Russell Kirk emphasized, were spiritual. They focused on three words: *labor, pietas,* and *fatum.* "Whatever was good in imperial Rome," wrote Kirk, "lies in those words." Each had found expression in the poetry of Virgil (70–19 BC). By *labor*, the poet meant the dignity of labor and the ethic of honest toil, which were especially the virtues of the small farmer, long the backbone of Roman society. *Pietas* spoke to a pervasive reverence for and sense of duty to the gods, which also expressed themselves in a profound love of country. *Fatum*, lastly, meant a sense of "Rome's duty, imposed by unknowable powers, to bring peace to the world, to maintain the cause of order and justice and freedom, and to withstand barbarism." Stoicism provided an additional source of spiritual cohesion to the Empire. The influence of this religious philosophy is especially visible in the *Meditations* of Marcus Aurelius (*r.* 161–180), the last of Rome's "five good emperors" whose death began the breakdown of "Roman Peace" and the onset of a century of crisis that presaged the Empire's eventual collapse.

The decline of the Roman Empire spanned three centuries and resulted from numerous factors. Pressure on the frontier from barbarian tribes, repeated outbreaks of plague, frequent and bloody turnover of emperors, rampant brigandage and the resulting deterioration of the economy assaulted the security and prosperity of the world state. The third century AD was one of protracted crisis, reaching its most intense phase between 235 and 284 AD, during which time twenty different men, many of them generals, ascended the throne. The need to defend against numerous invasion threats bloated the soldiers' ranks with more and more non-Romans and changed the culture and ethos of the army, at the same time the costs of defense eroded the solvency of the government. Frequent assassinations and civil wars shook the stability of the political order and brought a spate of corrupt and incompetent leaders to power, with often reckless economic policies following in their wake. The proliferation of new religious beliefs, many of which seemed to offer Romans an escape from the increasingly threatening and uncertain realities of the present, weakened the traditional spiritual foundations of the society. It was as if every one of the "pillars" of the Empire discussed earlier was weakening in its turn.

Diocletian (*r.* 284–305) and Constantine (*r.* 305–337) rescued the Empire from the third-century crisis and put in place reforms that bought the Roman state decades more of renewed stability. But, pressure from beyond the frontiers re-intensified and, in AD 410, Visigoths sacked Rome—the first time in eight hundred years the imperial city had been overrun by hostile forces from abroad. Sixty years of complicated dealings with a collection of the Germanic tribes who were, by then, both inside and outside the old imperial frontiers, followed the trauma of 410, and in 476 the Germanic general Odoacer (435–493) deposed the Emperor Romulus Augustulus and declared to the authorities in Constantinople that the West no longer needed an emperor. Whether this moment deserves to be regarded as the "fall" of the Roman Empire, or merely one more step in the transformation of it, the reality of the world state had unmistakably come to an end in the fifth century. Such Roman universalism that lived on resided principally in the domain of ideas, or in the spiritual realm with the concept of Rome as the seat of authority of the new universal faith.

# Res Gest ae Divi Augusti
## Augustus (63 BC–AD 14)
### Roman Emperor (27 BC–AD 14)

*This text is a kind of resumé in which Augustus enumerated his own accomplishments.*

Below is a copy of the deeds of the divine Augustus, by which he subjected the whole world to the dominion of the Roman people, and of the amounts which he expended upon the Republic and the Roman people, as engraved upon two brazen columns which are set up at Rome.

1. In my twentieth year, acting upon my own judgment and at my own expense, I raised an army by means of which I restored to liberty the Republic, which had been oppressed by the tyranny of a faction. On account of this the Senate, by laudatory decrees, admitted me to its order in the consulship of Gaius Pansa and Aulus Hirtius, and at the same time gave me consular rank in the expression of opinion, and gave me the *imperium*. It also voted that I, as *pro-praetor*, together with the consuls, should see to it that the Republic suffered no harm. In the same year, moreover, when both consuls had perished in war, the people made me consul, and triumvir for organizing the Republic.

2. Those who killed my father[1] I drove into exile by lawful judgments, avenging their crime, and afterwards, when they waged war against the Republic, I twice defeated them in battle.[2]

3. I undertook civil and foreign wars by land and sea throughout the whole world, and as victor I showed mercy to all surviving citizens. Foreign peoples who could be pardoned with safety, I preferred to preserve rather than to destroy. About five hundred thousand Roman citizens took the military

---

[1]Julius Caesar. Octavian was actually his great-nephew, but Julius Caesar had adopted him as his son.

[2]At Philippi (42 BC)

---

*Translations and Reprints from the Original Source of European History: Monumentum Ancyranum. The Deeds of Augustus*, Vol. I, edited by William Farley (Philadelphia: University of Pennsylvania, Department of History, 1898), 12–80.

oath of allegiance to me. Of these I have settled in colonies or sent back to their *municipia*, upon the expiration of their terms of service, somewhat over three hundred thousand, and to all these I have given lands purchased by me, or money for farms, out of my own means. I have captured six hundred ships, besides those which were smaller than triremes.

4. Twice I have triumphed in the ovation, and three times in the curule triumph, and I have been twenty-one times saluted as *imperator*.[3] After that, when the Senate decreed me many triumphs, I declined them. Likewise, I often deposited the laurels in the Capitol in fulfillment of vows which I had also made in battle. On account of enterprises brought to a successful issue on land and sea by me, or by my lieutenants under my auspices, the Senate fifty-five times decreed that there should be a thanksgiving to the immortal gods. The number of days, moreover, on which thanksgiving was rendered in accordance with the decree of the Senate was eight hundred ninety. In my triumphs there have been led before my chariot nine kings or children of kings. When I wrote these words, I had been thirteen times consul and was in the thirty-seventh year of the tribunician power.

5. The dictatorship which was offered to me by the people and the Senate, both when I was absent and when I was present, in the consulship of Marcus Marcellus and Lucius Arruntius, I did not accept. At a time of the greatest dearth of grain I did not refuse the charge of the food supply, which I so administered that in a few days, at my own expense, I freed the whole people from the anxiety and danger in which they then were. The annual and perpetual consulship offered to me at that time I did not accept.

6. During the consulship of Marcus Vinucius and Quintus Lucretius, and afterwards in that of Publius and Gnaeus Lentulus, and a third time in that of Paullus Fabius Maximus and Quintus Tubero, by the consent of the Senate and the Roman people I was voted the sole charge of the laws and of morals, with the fullest power; but I accepted the proffer of no office which was contrary to the customs of Rome. The measures of which the Senate at that time wished me to take charge, I accomplished in virtue of my possession of the tribunician power. In this office I five times associated with myself a colleague, with the consent of the Senate.

7. For ten years in succession I was one of the triumvirs for organizing the Republic. Up to that day on which I write these words I have been *princeps* of the Senate through forty years. I have been *pontifex maximus*, augur, a

---

[3]The title of *imperator* traditionally recognized important military victories; it was not used as the official title of the princeps until the reign of Vespasian (AD 69–79).

member of the quindecemviral college of the sacred rites, of the septemviral college of the banquets, an Arval Brother, a member of the Titian sodality, and a fetial.[4]

8. In my fifth consulship, by order of the people and the Senate, I increased the number of the patricians. Three times I have revised the list of the      5 Senate. In my sixth consulship, with Marcus Agrippa as colleague, I made a census of the people. I performed the lustration after forty-one years. In this lustration the number of Roman citizens was four million, sixty-three thousand. Again assuming the consular power in the consulship of Gaius Censorinus and Gaius Asinius, I alone performed the lustration. At this      10 census the number of Roman citizens was four million, two hundred thirty thousand. A third time, assuming the consular power in the consulship of Sextus Pompeius and Sextus Appuleius, with Tiberius Caesar as colleague, I performed the lustration. At this lustration the number of Roman citizens was four million, nine hundred thirty-seven thousand. By new legislation I      15 have restored many customs of our ancestors which had now begun to fall into disuse, and I have myself also committed to posterity many examples worthy of imitation.

9. The Senate decreed that every fifth year vows for my good health should be performed by the consuls and the priests. In accordance with these      20 vows games have been often celebrated during my lifetime, sometimes by the four chief colleges, sometimes by the consuls. In private, also, and as municipalities, the whole body of citizens have constantly sacrificed at every shrine for my good health.

10. By a decree of the Senate my name has been included in the Salian hymn,      25 and it has been enacted by law that I should be sacrosanct, and that as long as I live I should be invested with the tribunician power. I refused to be made *pontifex maximus* in the place of a colleague still living, when the people tendered me that priesthood which my father held. I accepted that office after several years, when he was dead who had seized it during      30 a time of civil disturbance; and at the comitia for my election, during the consulship of Publius Sulpicius and Gaius Valgius, so great a multitude assembled as, it is said, had never before been in Rome.

11. Close to the temples of Honor and Virtue, near the Capena gate, the Senate consecrated, in honor of my return, an altar to Fortune the Restorer, and      35 upon this altar it ordered that the *pontifices* and the Vestal virgins should offer sacrifice yearly on the anniversary of the day on which I returned into

---

[4]All of these refer to various priestly offices under the Republic.

the city from Syria in the consulship of Quintus Lucretius and Marcus Vinucius, and it called the day the Augustalia, from our cognomen.

12. By a decree of the Senate at the same time a part of the prætors and tribunes of the people with the consul Quintus Lucretius and leading citizens were sent into Campania to meet me, an honor which up to this time has been decreed to no one but me. When I returned from Spain and Gaul after successfully arranging the affairs of those provinces, in the consulship of Tiberius Nero and Publius Quintilius, the Senate voted that in honor of my return an altar of the Augustan Peace should be consecrated in the Campus Martius, and upon this altar it ordered the magistrates and priests and vestal virgins to offer sacrifices on each anniversary.

13. Janus Quirinus, which it was the purpose of our fathers to close when there was peace won by victory throughout the whole empire of the Roman people on land and sea, and which, before I was born, from the foundation of the city, was reported to have been closed twice in all, the Senate three times ordered to be closed while I was *princeps*.

14. My sons,[5] the Caesars Gaius and Lucius, whom Fortune snatched from me in their youth, the Senate and Roman people, in order to do me honor, designated as consuls in the fifteenth year of each, with the intention that they should enter upon that magistracy after five years. And the Senate decreed that from the day in which they were introduced into the forum they should share in the public counsels. Moreover the whole body of the Roman knights gave them the title, *principes* of the youth, and gave to each a silver buckler and spear.

15. To each man of the Roman *plebs* I paid three hundred sesterces in accordance with the last will of my father; and in my own name, when consul for the fifth time, I gave four hundred sesterces from the spoils of the wars; again, moreover, in my tenth consulship I gave from my own estate four hundred sesterces to each man by way of *congiarium*; and in my eleventh consulship I twelve times made distributions of food, buying grain at my own expense; and in the twelfth year of my tribunician power I three times gave four hundred sesterces to each man. These my donations have never been made to less than two hundred fifty thousand men. In my twelfth consulship and the eighteenth year of my tribunician power I gave to three hundred twenty thousand of the city *plebs* sixty *denarii* apiece. In the colonies of my soldiers, when consul for the fifth time, I gave to each man a thousand sesterces from the spoils; about a hundred and twenty thousand

---

[5]Actually Augustus's grandsons, the sons of his daughter Julia and her husband, Marcus Agrippa

men in the colonies received that triumphal donation. When consul for
the thirteenth time I gave sixty *denarii* to the *plebs* who were at that time
receiving public grain; these men were a little more than two hundred
thousand in number.

16. For the lands which in my fourth consulship, and afterwards in the consulship     5
of Marcus Crassus and Cnaeus Lentulus, the augur, I assigned to soldiers,
I paid money to the *municipia*. The sum which I paid for Italian farms was
about six hundred million sesterces, and that for lands in the provinces was
about two hundred sixty millions. Of all those who have established colonies
of soldiers in Italy or in the provinces I am the first and only one within the     10
memory of my age to do this. And afterward in the consulship of Tiberius
Nero and Cnaeus Piso, and also in that of Gaius Antistius and Decimus
Laelius, and in that of Gaius Calvisius and Lucius Pasienus, and in that of
Lucius Lentulus and Marcus Messala, and in that of Lucius Caninius and
Quintus Fabricius, I gave gratuities in money to the soldiers whom I sent     15
back to their *municipia* at the expiration of their terms of service, and for
this purpose I freely spent four hundred million sesterces.

17. Four times I have aided the public treasury from my own means, to such
extent that I have furnished to those in charge of the treasury one hundred
fifty million sesterces. And in the consulship of Marcus Lepidus and Lucius     20
Arruntius I paid into the military treasury which was established by my
advice that from it gratuities might be given to soldiers who had served a
term of twenty or more years, one hundred and seventy million sesterces
from my own estate.

18. Beginning with that year in which Gnaeus and Publius Lentulus were     25
consuls, when the imposts failed, I furnished aid sometimes to a hundred
thousand men, and sometimes to more, by supplying grain or money for
the tribute from my own land and property.

19. I constructed the Curia, and the Chalcidicum adjacent thereto, the temple
of Apollo on the Palatine, with its porticoes, the temple of the divine Julius,     30
the Lupercal, the portico to the Circus of Flaminius, which I allowed to
bear the name, Portico Octavia, from his name who constructed the earlier
one in the same place; the Pulvinar at the Circus Maximus, the temples
of Jupiter the Vanquisher and Jupiter the Thunderer, on the Capitol, the
temple of Quirinus, the temples of Minerva and Juno Regina and of Jupiter     35
Libertas, on the Aventine, the temple of the Lares on the highest point of
the Via Sacra, the temple of the divine Penates on the Velian hill, the temple
of Youth, and the temple of the Great Mother on the Palatine.

20. The Capitol and the Pompeian theatre have been restored by me at enormous expense for each work, without any inscription of my name. Aqueducts which were crumbling in many places by reason of age I have restored, and I have doubled the water which bears the name Marcian by turning a new spring into its course. The Forum Julium and the basilica which was between the temple of Castor and the temple of Saturn, works begun and almost completed by my father, I have finished; and when that same basilica was consumed by fire, I began its reconstruction on an enlarged site, inscribing it with the names of my sons; and if I do not live to complete it, I have given orders that it be completed by my heirs. In accordance with a decree of the Senate, while consul for the sixth time, I have restored eighty-two temples of the gods, passing over none which was at that time in need of repair. In my seventh consulship I constructed the Flaminian way from the city to Ariminum, and all the bridges except the Mulvian and Minucian.

21. Upon private ground I have built with the spoils of war the temple of Mars the Avenger, and the Augustan Forum. Beside the temple of Apollo, I built upon ground, bought for the most part at my own expense, a theatre, to bear the name of Marcellus, my son-in-law. From the spoils of war I have consecrated gifts in the Capitol, and in the temple of the divine Julius, and in the temple of Apollo, and in the temple of Vesta, and in the temple of Mars the Avenger; these gifts have cost me about a hundred million sesterces. In my fifth consulship I remitted to the *municipia* and Italian colonies the thirty-five thousand pounds given me as coronary gold on the occasion of my triumphs, and thereafter, as often as I was proclaimed imperator, I did not accept the coronary gold which the *municipia* and colonies voted to me as kindly as before.

22. Three times in my own name, and five times in that of my sons or grandsons, I have given gladiatorial exhibitions; in these exhibitions about ten thousand men have fought. Twice in my own name, and three times in that of my grandson, I have offered the people the spectacle of athletes gathered from all quarters. I have celebrated games four times in my own name, and twenty-three times in the turns of other magistrates. In behalf of the college of quindecemvirs, I, as master of the college, with my colleague Agrippa, celebrated the Secular Games in the consulship of Gaius Furnius and Gaius Silanus. When consul for the thirteenth time, I first celebrated the Martial games, which since that time the consuls have given in successive years. Twenty-six times in my own name, or in that of my sons and grandsons, I have given hunts of African wild beasts in the circus, the forum, the amphitheatres, and about thirty-five hundred beasts have been killed.

23. I gave the people the spectacle of a naval battle beyond the Tiber, where now is the grove of the Caesars. For this purpose an excavation was made eighteen hundred feet long and twelve hundred wide. In this contest thirty beaked ships, triremes or biremes, were engaged, besides more of smaller size. About three thousand men fought in these vessels in addition to the rowers.

24. In the temples of all the cities of the province of Asia, I, as victor, replaced the ornaments of which he with whom I was at war had taken private possession when he despoiled the temples. Silver statues of me, on foot, on horseback and in quadrigas, which stood in the city to the number of about eighty, I removed, and out of their money value I placed golden gifts in the temple of Apollo in my own name, and in the names of those who had offered me the honor of the statues.

25. I have freed the sea from pirates. In that war with the slaves delivered to their masters for punishment about thirty thousand slaves who had fled from their masters and taken up arms against the state. The whole of Italy voluntarily took the oath of allegiance to me, and demanded me as leader in that war in which I conquered at Actium. The provinces of Gaul, Spain, Africa, Sicily, and Sardinia swore the same allegiance to me. There were more than seven hundred senators who at that time fought under my standards, and among these, up to the day on which these words are written, eighty-three have either before or since been made consuls, and about one hundred and seventy have been made priests.

26. I have extended the boundaries of all the provinces of the Roman people which were bordered by nations not yet subjected to our sway. I have reduced to a state of peace the Gallic and Spanish provinces, and Germany, the lands enclosed by the ocean from Gades to the mouth of the Elbe. The Alps from the region nearest the Adriatic as far as the Tuscan Sea I have brought into a state of peace, without waging an unjust war upon any people. My fleet has navigated the ocean from the mouth of the Rhine as far as the boundaries of the Cimbri, where before that time no Roman had ever penetrated by land or sea; and the Cimbri and Charydes and Semnones and other German peoples of that section, by means of legates, sought my friendship and that of the Roman people. By my command and under my auspices two armies at almost the same time have been led into Ethiopia and into Arabia, which is called "the Happy," and very many of the enemy of both peoples have fallen in battle, and many towns have been captured. Into Ethiopia the advance was as far as Nabata, which is next to Meroe. In Arabia the army penetrated as far as the confines of the Sabaei, to the town Mariba.

27. I have added Egypt to the empire of the Roman people. Of greater Armenia, when its King Artaxes was killed I could have made a province, but I preferred, after the example of our fathers, to deliver that kingdom to Tigranes, the son of King Artavasdes, and grandson of King Tigranes; and this I did through Tiberius Nero, who was then my son-in-law. And afterwards, when the same people became turbulent and rebellious, they were subdued by Gaius, my son, and I gave the sovereignty over them to King Ariobarzanes, the son of Artabazes, King of the Medes, and after his death to his son Artavasdes. When he was killed I sent into that kingdom Tigranes, who was sprung from the royal house of the Armenians. I recovered all the provinces across the Adriatic Sea, which extend toward the east, and Cyrenaica, at that time for the most part in the possession of kings, together with Sicily and Sardinia, which had been engaged in a servile war.

28. I have established colonies of soldiers in Africa, Sicily, Macedonia, the two Spains, Achaia, Asia, Syria, Gallia Narbonensis, and Pisidia. Italy also has twenty-eight colonies established under my auspices, which within my lifetime have become very famous and populous....

31. Embassies have been many times sent to me from the kings of India, a thing never before seen in the case of any ruler of the Romans. Our friendship has been sought by means of ambassadors by the Bastarnae and the Scythians, and by the kings of the Sarmatae, who are on either side of the Tanais, and by the kings of the Albani, the Hiberi, and the Medes....

34. In my sixth and seventh consulships, when I had put an end to the civil wars, after having obtained complete control of affairs by universal consent, I transferred the Republic from my own dominion to the authority of the Senate and Roman people. In return for this favor on my part I received by decree of the Senate the title Augustus, the door-posts of my house were publicly decked with laurels, a civic crown was fixed above my door, and in the Julian Curia was placed a golden shield which, by its inscription, bore witness that it was given to me by the Senate and Roman people on account of my valor, clemency, justice, and piety. After that time I excelled all others in dignity, but of power I held no more than those also held who were my colleagues in any magistracy.

35. While I was consul for the thirteenth time the Senate and the equestrian order and the entire Roman people gave me the title of father of the fatherland, and decreed that it should be inscribed upon the vestibule of my house and in the Curia, and in the Augustan Forum beneath the quadriga which had been, by decree of the Senate, set up in my honor. When I wrote these words I was in my seventy-sixth year.

# THE ANNALS
## PUBLIUS CORNELIUS TACITUS (*c.* 56–*c.* 117)

*The Roman historian Tacitus, a provincial of Republican leanings and a master of irony, saw little to admire in the ruling class of the first century.*

§1Rome at the beginning was ruled by kings. Freedom and the consulship were established by Lucius Brutus. Dictatorships were held for a temporary crisis. The power of the *decemvirs* did not last beyond two years, nor was the consular jurisdiction of the military tribunes of long duration. The despotisms of Cinna and Sulla were brief, the rule of Pompeius and of Crassus soon yielded 5 before Caesar, the arms of Lepidus and Antonius before Augustus, who, when the world was wearied by civil strife, subjected it to empire under the title of "Princeps."

But the successes and reverses of the old Roman people have been recorded by famous historians; and fine intellects were not wanting to describe the times 10 of Augustus, till growing sycophancy scared them away. The histories of Tiberius, Caius, Claudius, and Nero, while they were in power, were falsified through terror, and after their death were written under the irritation of a recent hatred. Hence my purpose is to relate a few facts about Augustus—more particularly his last acts, then the reign of Tiberius, and all which follows, without either 15 bitterness or partiality, from any motives to which I am far removed.

§2When after the destruction of Brutus and Cassius there was no longer any army of the commonwealth, when Pompeius was crushed in Sicily, and when, with Lepidus pushed aside and Antonius slain, even the Julian faction had only Caesar left to lead it, then, dropping the title of triumvir, and giving out that he 20 was a consul, and was satisfied with a tribune's authority for the protection of the people, Augustus won over the soldiers with gifts, the populace with cheap corn, and all men with the sweets of repose, and so grew greater by degrees,

*The Annals of Tacitus*, translated by Alfred John Church and William Jackson Brodribb (London: MacMillan and Company, 1906), 1–3.

while he concentrated in himself the functions of the Senate, the magistrates, and the laws.

He was wholly unopposed, for the boldest spirits had fallen in battle, or in the proscription, while the remaining nobles, the readier they were to be
5   slaves, were raised the higher by wealth and promotion, so that, aggrandized by revolution, they preferred the safety of the present to the dangerous past. Nor did the provinces dislike that condition of affairs, for they distrusted the government of the Senate and the people, because of the rivalries between the leading men and the rapacity of the officials, while the protection of the laws
10  was unavailing, as they were continually deranged by violence, intrigue, and finally by corruption.

§3 Augustus meanwhile, as supports to his despotism, raised to the pontificate and curule aedileship Claudius Marcellus, his sister's son, while a mere stripling, and Marcus Agrippa, of humble birth, a good soldier, and one who had shared his
15  victory, to two consecutive consulships, and as Marcellus soon afterwards died, he also accepted him as his son-in-law. Tiberius Nero and Claudius Drusus, his step-sons, he honored with imperial titles, although his own family was as yet undiminished. For he had admitted the children of Agrippa, Caius and Lucius, into the house of the Caesars; and before they had yet laid aside the dress of
20  boyhood he had most fervently desired, with an outward show of reluctance, that they should be entitled "princes of the youth" and be consuls-elect.

When Agrippa died, and Lucius Caesar, as he was on his way to our armies in Spain, and Caius while returning from Armenia, still suffering from a wound, were prematurely cut off by destiny, or by their step-mother Livia's treachery,
25  Drusus too having long been dead, Nero remained alone of the step-sons, and in him everything tended to centre. He was adopted as a son, as a colleague in empire and a partner in the tribunician power, and paraded through all the armies, no longer through his mother's secret intrigues, but at her open sugges- tion. For she had gained such a hold on the aged Augustus that he drove out
30  as an exile into the island of Planasia his only grand-son, Agrippa Postumus, who, though devoid of worthy qualities, and having only the brute courage of physical strength, had not been convicted of any gross offence. And yet Augus- tus had appointed Germanicus, Drusus' offspring, to the command of eight legions on the Rhine, and required Tiberius to adopt him, although Tiberius
35  had a son, now a young man, in his house; but he did it that he might have several safeguards to rest on.

He had no war at the time on his hands except against the Germans, which was rather to wipe out the disgrace of the loss of Quintilius Varus and his army than out of an ambition to extend the empire, or for any adequate recompense.

At home all was tranquil, and there were magistrates with the same titles; there was a younger generation, sprung up since the victory of Actium, and even many of the older men had been born during the civil wars. How few were left who had seen the republic!

§4 Thus the state had been revolutionized, and there was not a vestige left of the 5 old sound morality. Stripped of equality, all looked up to the commands of a sovereign without the least apprehension for the present, while Augustus in the vigor of life could maintain his own position, that of his house, and the general tranquility. When in advanced old age, he was worn out by a sickly frame, and the end was near and new prospects opened, a few spoke in vain of the blessings 10 of freedom, but most people dreaded and some longed for war. The popular gossip of the large majority fastened itself variously on their future masters. "Agrippa was savage, and had been exasperated by insult, and neither from age nor experience in affairs was equal to so great a burden. Tiberius Nero was of mature years, and had established his fame in war, but he had the old arrogance 15 inbred in the Claudian family, and many symptoms of a cruel temper, though they were repressed, now and then broke out. He had also from earliest infancy been reared in an imperial house; consulships and triumphs had been heaped on him in his younger days; even in the years which, on the pretext of seclusion he spent in exile at Rhodes, he had had no thoughts but of wrath, hypocrisy, 20 and secret sensuality. There was his mother too with a woman's caprice. They must, it seemed, be subject to a female and to two striplings besides, who for a while would burden, and some day rend asunder the state."

§5 While these and like topics were discussed, the infirmities of Augustus increased, and some suspected guilt on his wife's part. For a rumor had gone 25 abroad that a few months before he had sailed to Planasia on a visit to Agrippa, with the knowledge of some chosen friends, and with one companion, Fabius Maximus; that many tears were shed on both sides, with expressions of affection, and that thus there was a hope of the young man being restored to the home of his grand-father. This, it was said, Maximus had divulged to his wife 30 Marcia, she again to Livia. All was known to Caesar, and when Maximus soon afterwards died, by a death some thought to be self-inflicted, there were heard at his funeral wailings from Marcia, in which she reproached herself for having been the cause of her husband's destruction.

Whatever the fact was, Tiberius as he was just entering Illyria was summoned 35 home by an urgent letter from his mother, and it has not been thoroughly ascertained whether at the city of Nola he found Augustus still breathing or quite lifeless. For Livia had surrounded the house and its approaches with a strict watch, and favorable bulletins were published from time to time, till, provision having been made for the demands of the crisis, one and the same report told men that Augustus was dead and that Tiberius Nero was master of the state….

# NERO
## SUETONIUS (*c.* 69–140)

*Suetonius, for a brief time private secretary to the Emperor Hadrian (117–138), wrote a lively, at times gossipy, series of biographies of the rulers from Julius Caesar to Domitian titled* On the Lives of the Caesars. *His life of Nero (37–68) illustrates his inclination to include scandals as well as details of public life, and it must be said that Nero certainly provided a wealth of material for such a biography.*

§9He began his reign with an ostentation of dutiful regard to the memory of Claudius, whom he buried with the utmost pomp and magnificence, pronouncing the funeral oration himself, and then had him enrolled amongst the gods. He paid likewise the highest honors to the memory of his father, Domitius. He left the management of affairs, both public and private, to his mother. The   5
word which he gave the first day of his reign to the tribune on guard was "the best of mothers," and afterwards he frequently appeared with her in the streets of Rome in her litter. He settled a colony at Antium, in which he placed the veteran soldiers belonging to the guards; and obliged several of the richest centurions of the first rank to transfer their residence to that place, where he   10
likewise made a noble harbor at a prodigious expense.

§10To establish still further his character, he declared that he designed to govern according to the model of Augustus; and omitted no opportunity of showing his generosity, clemency, and complaisance. The more burdensome taxes he either entirely took off, or diminished. The rewards appointed for informers   15
by the Papian law, he reduced to a fourth part, and distributed to the people four hundred sesterces a man. To the noblest of the senators who were much reduced in their circumstances, he granted annual allowances, in some cases as much as five hundred thousand sesterces; and to the pretorian cohorts a monthly allowance of corn *gratis*. When called upon to subscribe the sentence,   20

Suetonius, *The Lives of the Twelve Caesars*, translated by Alexander Thompson (London: George Bell and Sons, 1893), 342–43, 356–57, 361–64, 366–67, 370–71, 377–79.

according to custom, of a criminal condemned to die, "I wish," said he, "I had never learnt to read and write." He continually saluted people of the several orders by name, without a prompter.

When the senate returned him their thanks for his good government, he replied to them, "It will be time enough to do so when I shall have deserved it." He admitted the common people to see him perform his exercises in the Campus Martius. He frequently declaimed in public, and recited verses of his own composing, not only at home, but in the theatre; so much to the joy of all the people that public prayers were appointed to be put up to the gods upon that account; and the verses which had been publicly read were, after being written in gold letters, consecrated to Jupiter Capitolinus....

§26Petulancy, lewdness, luxury, avarice, and cruelty he practiced at first with reserve and in private, as if prompted to them only by the folly of youth; but, even then, the world was of opinion that they were the faults of his nature, and not of his age. After it was dark, he used to enter the taverns disguised in a cap or a wig, and ramble about the streets in sport, which was not void of mischief. He used to beat those he met coming home from supper; and, if they made any resistance, would wound them, and throw them into the common-sewer. He broke open and robbed shops, establishing an auction at home for selling his booty. In the scuffles which took place on those occasions, he often ran the hazard of losing his eyes, and even his life, being beaten almost to death by a senator for handling his wife indecently. After this adventure, he never again ventured abroad at that time of night without some tribunes following him at a little distance. In the day-time he would be carried to the theatre incognito in a litter, placing himself upon the upper part of the proscenium, where he not only witnessed the quarrels which arose on account of the performances, but also encouraged them. When they came to blows, and stones and pieces of broken benches began to fly about, he threw them plentifully amongst the people, and once even broke a praetor's head.

§27His vices gaining strength by degrees, he laid aside his jocular amusements, and all disguise, breaking out into enormous crimes without the least attempt to conceal them. His revels were prolonged from mid-day to midnight, while he was frequently refreshed by warm baths and, in the summer time, by such as were cooled with snow. He often supped in public, in the Naumachia, with the sluices shut, or in the Campus Martius, or the Circus Maximus, being waited upon at table by common prostitutes of the town, and Syrian strumpets and glee-girls. As often as he went down the Tiber to Ostia, or coasted through the gulf of Baiae, booths furnished as brothels and eating-houses were erected along the shore and river banks, before which stood matrons who, like bawds and hostesses, allured him to land. It was also his custom to invite himself to supper with his friends; at one of which was expended no less than four millions of sesterces in chaplets, and at another something more in roses.

§28 Besides the abuse of free-born lads, and the debauch of married women,      5
he committed a rape upon Rubria, a Vestal Virgin. He was upon the point of marrying Acte, his freedwoman, having suborned some men of consular rank to swear that she was of royal descent. He gelded the boy Sporus, and endeavored to transform him into a woman. He even went so far as to marry him, with all the usual formalities of a marriage settlement, the rose-colored nuptial veil, and   10
a numerous company at the wedding. When the ceremony was over, he had him conducted like a bride to his own house, and treated him as his wife. It was jocularly observed by some person "that it would have been well for mankind had such a wife fallen to the lot of his father Domitius." This Sporus he carried about with him in a litter round the solemn assemblies and fairs of Greece, and   15
afterwards at Rome through the Sigillaria, dressed in the rich attire of an empress, kissing him from time to time as they rode together. That he entertained an incestuous passion for his mother, but was deterred by her enemies, for fear that this haughty and overbearing woman should, by her compliance, get him entirely into her power, and govern in everything, was universally believed,    20
especially after he had introduced amongst his concubines a strumpet who was reported to have a strong resemblance to Agrippina....

§33 He began the practice of parricide and murder with Claudius himself; for although he was not the contriver of his death, he was privy to the plot. Nor did he make any secret of it, but used afterwards to commend, in a Greek proverb,    25
mushrooms as food fit for the gods, because Claudius had been poisoned with them. He traduced his memory both by word and deed in the grossest manner; one while charging him with folly, another while with cruelty. For he used to say by way of jest that he had ceased *morari*[1] amongst men, pronouncing the first syllable long, and treated as null many of his decrees and ordinances, as   30
made by a doting old blockhead. He enclosed the place where his body was burnt with only a low wall of rough masonry.

He attempted to poison Britannicus, as much out of envy because he had a sweeter voice as from apprehension of what might ensue from the respect which the people entertained for his father's memory. He employed for this purpose   35

---

[1] A play upon the Greek word μωρος, signifying a fool, while the Latin *morari*, from *moror*, means "to dwell" or "continue."

a woman named Locusta, who had been a witness against some persons guilty of like practices. But the poison she gave him, working more slowly than he expected and only causing a purge, he sent for the woman, and beat her with his own hand, charging her with administering an antidote instead of poison;
5 and upon her alleging in excuse that she had given Britannicus but a gentle mixture in order to prevent suspicion, "Think you," said he, "that I am afraid of the Julian law," and obliged her to prepare, in his own chamber and before his eyes, as quick and strong a dose as possible. This he tried upon a kid; but the animal lingering for five hours before it expired, he ordered her to go to
10 work again. And when she had done, he gave the poison to a pig, which dying immediately, he commanded the potion to be brought into the eating-room and given to Britannicus, while he was at supper with him. The prince had no sooner tasted it than he sunk on the floor, Nero meanwhile, pretending to the guests that it was only a fit of the falling sickness, to which, he said, he was
15 subject. He buried him the following day, in a mean and hurried way, during violent storms of rain. He gave Locusta a pardon, and rewarded her with a great estate in land, placing some disciples with her, to be instructed in her trade.

§34His mother being used to make strict inquiry into what he said or did, and to reprimand him with the freedom of a parent, he was so much offended that
20 he endeavored to expose her to public resentment by frequently pretending a resolution to quit the government and retire to Rhodes. Soon afterwards, he deprived her of all honor and power, took from her the guard of Roman and German soldiers, banished her from the palace and from his society, and persecuted her in every way he could contrive, employing persons to harass her
25 when at Rome with law-suits, and to disturb her in her retirement from town with the most scurrilous and abusive language, following her about by land and sea. But being terrified with her menaces and violent spirit, he resolved upon her destruction, and thrice attempted it by poison. Finding, however, that she had previously secured herself by antidotes, he contrived machinery by which
30 the floor over her bed-chamber might be made to fall upon her while she was asleep in the night.

This design miscarrying likewise, through the little caution used by those who were in the secret, his next stratagem was to construct a ship which could be easily shivered, in hopes of destroying her either by drowning, or by the deck
35 above her cabin crushing her in its fall. Accordingly, under color of a pretended reconciliation, he wrote her an extremely affectionate letter, inviting her to Baiae to celebrate with him the festival of Minerva. He had given private orders to the captains of the galleys which were to attend her to shatter to pieces the ship in which she had come by falling foul of it, but in such manner that it might

appear to be done accidentally. He prolonged the entertainment, for the more convenient opportunity of executing the plot in the night; and at her return for Bauli, instead of the old ship which had conveyed her to Baiae, he offered that which he had contrived for her destruction. He attended her to the vessel in a very cheerful mood, and, at parting with her, kissed her breasts; after which he  5
sat up very late in the night, waiting with great anxiety to learn the issue of his project. But receiving information that everything had fallen out contrary to his wish, and that she had saved herself by swimming.

Not knowing what course to take, upon her freedman, Lucius Agerinus, bringing word, with great joy, that she was safe and well, he privately dropped  10
a poniard by him. He then commanded the freedman to be seized and put in chains, under pretence of his having been employed by his mother to assassinate him; at the same time ordering her to be put to death, and giving out that, to avoid punishment for her intended crime, she had laid violent hands upon herself.  15

Other circumstances, still more horrible, are related on good authority; as that he went to view her corpse, and handling her limbs, pointed out some blemishes, and commended other points; and that, growing thirsty during the survey, he called for drink. Yet he was never afterwards able to tear the stings of his own conscience for this atrocious act, although encouraged by the  20
congratulatory addresses of the army, the Senate, and people. He frequently affirmed that he was haunted by his mother's ghost, and persecuted with the whips and burning torches of the Furies. Nay, he attempted by magical rites to bring up her ghost from below, and soften her rage against him. When he was in Greece, he durst not attend the celebration of the Eleusinian mysteries, at  25
the initiation of which impious and wicked persons are warned by the voice of the herald from approaching the rites.

Besides the murder of his mother, he had been guilty of that of his aunt; for, being obliged to keep her bed in consequence of a complaint in her bowels, he paid her a visit, and she, being then advanced in years, stroking his downy  30
chin, in the tenderness of affection, said to him, "May I but live to see the day when this is shaved for the first time, and I shall then die contented." He turned, however, to those about him, made a jest of it, saying that he would have his beard immediately taken off, and ordered the physicians to give her more violent purgatives. He seized upon her estate before she had expired, suppressing her  35
will that he might enjoy the whole himself....

$37From this period he butchered, without distinction or quarter, all whom his caprice suggested as objects for his cruelty, and upon the most frivolous pretences. To mention only a few: Salvidienus Orfitus was accused of letting

out three taverns attached to his house in the forum to some cities for the use of their deputies at Rome. The charge against Cassius Longinus, a lawyer who had lost his sight, was that he kept amongst the busts of his ancestors that of Caius Cassius, who was concerned in the death of Julius Caesar. The only charge
5   objected against Paetus Thrasea was that he had a melancholy cast of features, and looked like a schoolmaster.

He allowed but one hour to those whom he obliged to kill themselves; and, to prevent delay, he sent them physicians "to cure them immediately, if they lingered beyond that time;" for so he called bleeding them to death. There was at
10   that time an Egyptian of a most voracious appetite, who would digest raw flesh, or anything else that was given him. It was credibly reported that the Emperor was extremely desirous of furnishing him with living men to tear and devour. Being elated with his great success in the perpetration of crimes, he declared that no prince before himself ever knew the extent of his power. He threw out
15   strong intimations that he would not even spare the senators who survived, but would entirely extirpate that order, and put the provinces and armies into the hands of the Roman knights and his own freedmen. It is certain that he never gave or vouchsafed to allow anyone the customary kiss, either on entering or departing, or even returned a salute. And at the inauguration of a work, the cut
20   through the Isthmus, he, with a loud voice amidst the assembled multitude, uttered a prayer that the undertaking might prove fortunate for himself and the Roman people, without taking the smallest notice of the Senate....

§40 The world, after tolerating such an emperor for little less than fourteen years, at length forsook him; the Gauls, headed by Julius Vindex, who at that time
25   governed the province as pro-praetor, being the first to revolt. Nero had been formerly told by astrologers that it would be his fortune to be at last deserted by all the world; and this occasioned that celebrated saying of his, "An artist can live in any country," by which he meant to offer as an excuse for his practice of music that it was not only his amusement as a prince, but might be his sup-
30   port when reduced to a private station. Yet some of the astrologers promised him, in his forlorn state, the rule of the East, and some in express words the kingdom of Jerusalem. But the greater part of them flattered him with assurances of his being restored to his former fortune. And being most inclined to believe the latter prediction, upon losing Britain and Armenia, he imagined
35   he had run through all the misfortunes which the fates had decreed him. But when, upon consulting the oracle of Apollo at Delphi, he was advised to beware of the seventy-third year, as if he were not to die till then, never thinking of Galba's age, he conceived such hopes, not only of living to advanced years, but of constant and singular good fortune, that having lost some things of great

value by shipwreck, he scrupled not to say amongst his friends that the fishes would bring them back to him.

At Naples he heard of the insurrection in Gaul, on the anniversary of the day on which he killed his mother, and bore it with so much unconcern as to excite a suspicion that he was really glad of it, since he had now a fair opportunity  5
of plundering those wealthy provinces by the right of war. Immediately going to the gymnasium, he witnessed the exercise of the wrestlers with the greatest delight. Being interrupted at supper with letters which brought yet worse news, he expressed no greater resentment than only to threaten the rebels. For eight days together, he never attempted to answer any letters, nor give any orders,  10
but buried the whole affair in profound silence.

§49 All who surrounded him now pressing him to save himself from the indignities which were ready to befall him, he ordered a pit to be sunk before his eyes, of the size of his body, and the bottom to be covered with pieces of marble put together, if any could be found about the house; and water and wood to be got  15
ready for immediate use about his corpse; weeping at everything that was done, and frequently saving, "What an artist is now about to perish!" Meanwhile, letters being brought in by a servant belonging to Phaon, he snatched them out of his hand, and there read that he had been declared an enemy by the Senate, and that search was making for him, that he might be punished according to  20
the ancient custom of the Romans. He then inquired what kind of punishment that was; and being told that the practice was to strip the criminal naked, and scourge him to death while his neck was fastened within a forked stake, he was so terrified that he took up two daggers which he had brought with him, and after feeling the points of both, put them up again, saying, "The fatal hour is  25
not yet come."

One while, he begged of Sporus to begin to wail and lament; another while, he entreated that one of them would set him an example by killing himself; and then again, he condemned his own want of resolution in these words, "I yet live, to my shame and disgrace. This is not becoming for Nero; it is not  30
becoming. You ought in such circumstances to have a good heart. Come, then; courage, man!" The horsemen who had received orders to bring him away alive were now approaching the house. As soon as he heard them coming, he uttered with a trembling voice the following verse, "The noise of swift-heeled steeds assails my ears."  35

He drove a dagger into his throat, being assisted in the act by Epaphroditus, his secretary. A centurion bursting in just as he was half-dead, and applying his cloak to the wound, pretending that he was come to his assistance, he made no other reply but this, "Tis too late;" and "Is this your loyalty?" Immediately after

pronouncing these words, he expired, with his eyes fixed and starting out of his head, to the terror of all who beheld him. He had requested of his attendants, as the most essential favor, that they would let no one have his head, but that by all means his body might be burnt entire. And this, Icelus, Galba's freedman,
5    granted. He had but a little before been discharged from the prison into which he had been thrown, when the disturbances first broke out.

§50The expenses of his funeral amounted to two hundred thousand sesterces; the bed upon which his body was carried to the pile and burnt, being covered with the white robes, interwoven with gold, which he had worn upon the
10   calends of January preceding. His nurses, Ecloge and Alexandra, with his con- cubine Acte, deposited his remains in the tomb belonging to the family of the Domitii, which stands upon the top of the Hill of the Gardens, and is to be seen from the Campua Martius. In that monument, a coffin of porphyry, with an altar of marble of Luna over it, is enclosed by a wall built of stone brought
15   from Thasos.

# MEDITATIONS
## MARCUS AURELIUS ANTONINUS (121–180)
### EMPEROR OF ROME (161–180)

*Marcus Aurelius, last of the Five Good Emperors and a Stoic, kept a journal in which he conscientiously made notes as ideas—especially ideas for self-improvement—occurred to him.*

c. 170–180

§1From my grandfather Verus[1] I learned good morals and the government of my temper.

§2From the reputation and remembrance of my father, modesty and a manly character.

§3From my mother, piety and beneficence, and abstinence, not only from evil     5
deeds, but even from evil thoughts; and further simplicity in my way of living, far removed from the habits of the rich.

§4From my great-grandfather, not to have frequented public schools, and to have had good teachers at home, and to know that on such things a man should spend liberally.     10

§5From my governor, to be neither of the green nor of the blue party at the games in the Circus, nor a partisan either of the Parmularius or the Scutarius[2] at the gladiators' fights; from him too I learned endurance of labor, and to want little, and to work with my own hands, and not to meddle with other people's affairs, and not to be ready to listen to slander.     15

§6From Diognetus, not to busy myself about trifling things, and not to give credit to what was said by miracle-workers and jugglers about incantations and

---

[1]Marcus Annius Verus, who raised Marcus Aurelius, whose father died when he was three
[2]The *Parmularis* carried a small round shield, and the *Scutoris* bore a large oblong shield.

---

*The Apology, Phaedo, and Crito of Plato: The Golden Sayings of Epictetus; The Meditations of Marcus Aurelius*, edited by Charles W. Eliot (New York: Collier and Sons, 1909), 193–99.

the driving away of dæmons and such things; and not to breed quails [for fight-ing], nor to give myself up passionately to such things; and to endure freedom of speech; and to have become intimate with philosophy; and to have been a hearer, first of Bacchius, then of Tandasis and Marcianus; and to have written
5    dialogues in my youth; and to have desired a plank bed and skin, and whatever else of the kind belongs to the Grecian discipline.

§7From Rusticus[3] I received the impression that my character required im-provement and discipline; and from him I learned not to be led astray to sophistic emulation, nor to writing on speculative matters, nor to delivering
10   little hortatory orations, nor to showing myself off as a man who practices much discipline, or does benevolent acts in order to make a display; and to abstain from rhetoric, and poetry, and fine writing; and not to walk about in the house in my outdoor dress, nor to do other things of the kind; and to write my letters with simplicity, like the letter which Rusticus wrote from Sinuessa
15   to my mother; and with respect to those who have offended me by words, or done me wrong, to be easily disposed to be pacified and reconciled, as soon as they have shown a readiness to be reconciled; and to read carefully, and not to be satisfied with a superficial understanding of a book; nor hastily to give my assent to those who talk overmuch; and I am indebted to him for being
20   acquainted with the discourses of Epictetus, which he communicated to me out of his own collection.

§8From Apollonius I learned freedom of will and undeviating steadiness of purpose; and to look to nothing else, not even for a moment, except to reason; and to be always the same, in sharp pains, on the occasion of the loss of a child,
25   and in long illness; and to see clearly in a living example that the same man can be both most resolute and yielding, and not peevish in giving his instruction; and to have had before my eyes a man who clearly considered his experience and his skill in expounding philosophical principles as the smallest of his merits; and from him I learned how to receive from friends what are esteemed favors,
30   without being either humbled by them or letting them pass unnoticed.

§9From Sextus,[4] a benevolent disposition, and the example of a family governed in a fatherly manner, and the idea of living conformably to nature; and gravity without affectation, and to look carefully after the interests of friends, and to tolerate ignorant persons, and those who form opinions without consideration:

---

[3]Quintus Junius Rusticus (c. 100–c. 170), Stoic philosopher and twice consul of Rome
[4]Sextus of Chaeronea, a grandson of Plutarch

he had the power of readily accommodating himself to all, so that intercourse with him was more agreeable than any flattery; and at the same time he was most highly venerated by those who associated with him; and he had the faculty both of discovering and ordering, in an intelligent and methodical way, the principles necessary for life; and he never showed anger or any other passion,    5 but was entirely free from passion, and also most affectionate; and he could express approbation without noisy display, and he possessed much knowledge without ostentation.

§10From Alexander, the grammarian, to refrain from fault-finding, and not in a reproachful way to chide those who uttered any barbarous or solecistic or   10 strange-sounding expression; but dexterously to introduce the very expression which ought to have been used, and in the way of answer or giving confirmation, or joining in an inquiry about the thing itself, not about the word, or by some other fit suggestion.

§11From Fronto[5] I learned to observe what envy and duplicity and hypocrisy   15 are in a tyrant, and that generally those among us who are called Patricians are rather deficient in paternal affection.

§12From Alexander the Platonic, not frequently nor without necessity to say to any one, or to write in a letter, that I have no leisure; nor continually to excuse the neglect of duties required by our relation to those with whom we live, by   20 alleging urgent occupations.

§13From Catulus, not to be indifferent when a friend finds fault, even if he should find fault without reason, but to try to restore him to his usual disposition; and to be ready to speak well of teachers, as it is reported of Domitius and Athenodotus; and to love my children truly.                                         25

§14From my brother Severus, to love my kin, and to love truth, and to love justice; and through him I learned to know Thrasea, Helvidius, Cato, Dion, Brutus; and from him I received the idea of a polity in which there is the same law for all, a polity administered with regard to equal rights and equal freedom of speech, and the idea of a kingly government which respects most of all the   30 freedom of the governed; I learned from him also consistency and undeviating steadiness in my regard for philosophy, and a disposition to do good, and to give

---

[5]Marcus Cornelius Fronto (*c.* 100–170), grammarian, rhetorician, and consul who emigrated to Rome from Numidia

to others readily, and to cherish good hopes, and to believe that I am loved by my friends; and in him I observed no concealment of his opinions with respect to those whom he condemned, and that his friends had no need to conjecture what he wished or did not wish, but it was quite plain.

5  **§15**From Maximus I learned self-government, and not to be led aside by anything; and cheerfulness in all circumstances, as well as in illness; and a just admixture in the moral character of sweetness and dignity, and to do what was set before me without complaining. I observed that everybody believed that he thought as he spoke, and that in all that he did he never had any bad intention;
10  and he never showed amazement and surprise, and was never in a hurry, and never put off doing a thing, nor was perplexed nor dejected, nor did he ever laugh to disguise his vexation, nor, on the other hand, was he ever passionate or suspicious. He was accustomed to do acts of beneficence and was ready to forgive, and was free from all falsehood; and he presented the appearance of a
15  man who could not be diverted from right rather than of a man who had been improved. I observed, too, that no man could ever think that he was despised by Maximus, or ever venture to think himself a better man. He had also the art of being humorous in an agreeable way.

   **§16**In my father[6] I observed mildness of temper, and unchangeable resolution
20  in the things which he had determined after due deliberation; and no vainglory in those things which men call honors; and a love of labor and perseverance; and a readiness to listen to those who had anything to propose for the common weal; and undeviating firmness in giving to every man according to his deserts; and a knowledge derived from experience of the occasions for vigorous action
25  and for remission.

   And I observed that he had overcome all passion for joys; and he considered himself no more than any other citizen, and he released his friends from all obligation to sup with him or to attend him of a necessity when he went abroad, and those who failed to accompany him by reason of any urgent circumstances,
30  always found him the same.

   I observed, too, his habit of careful inquiry in all matters of deliberation, and his persistency, and that he never stopped his investigation through being satisfied with appearances which first present themselves; and that his disposition was to keep his friends, and not to be soon tired of them, nor yet to be
35  extravagant in his affection; and to be satisfied on all occasions, and cheerful; and to foresee things a long way off, and to provide for the smallest without

---

[6]Antoninus Pius, Emperor of Rome (138–161) and foster father of Marcus Aurelius

display; and to check immediately popular applause and flattery, and to be ever watchful over the things which were necessary for the administration of the empire, and to be a good manager of the expenditure, and patiently to endure the blame which he got for such conduct; and he was neither superstitious with respect to the gods, nor did he court men by gifts or by trying to please them, 5 or by flattering the populace; but he showed sobriety in all things and firmness, and never any mean thoughts or action, nor love of novelty.

And the things which conduce in any way to the commodity of life, and of which fortune gives an abundant supply, he used without arrogance and without excusing himself; so that when he had them, he enjoyed them without 10 affectation, and when he had them not he did not want them. No one could ever say of him that he was either a sophist or a flippant slave or a pedant; but everyone acknowledged him to be a man ripe, perfect, above flattery, able to manage his own and other men's affairs.

Besides this, he honored those who were true philosophers, and he did not 15 reproach those who pretended to be philosophers, nor yet was he easily led by them. He was also easy in conversation, and he made himself agreeable without any offensive affectation. He took a reasonable care of his body's health, not as one who was greatly attached to life, nor out of regard to personal appearance, nor yet in a careless way, but so that, through his own attention, he very seldom 20 stood in need of the physician's art or of medicine or external applications.

He was most ready to give way without envy to those who possessed any particular faculty, such as that of eloquence or knowledge of the law or of morals, or of anything else; and he gave them his help, that each might enjoy reputation according to his deserts; and he always acted conformably to the institutions of 25 his country, without showing any affectation of doing so.

Further, he was not fond of change, nor unsteady, but he loved to stay in the same places, and to employ himself about the same things; and after his paroxysms of headache he came immediately fresh and vigorous to his usual occupations. His secrets were not many, but very few and very rare, and these 30 only about public matters; and he showed prudence and economy in the exhibition of the public spectacles and the construction of public buildings, his donations to the people, and in such things, for he was a man who looked to what ought to be done, not to the reputation which is got by a man's acts.

He did not take the bath at unseasonable hours; he was not fond of build- 35 ing houses, nor curious about what he ate, nor about the texture and color of his clothes, nor about the beauty of his slaves. His dress came from Lorium, his villa on the coast, and from Lanuvium generally. We know how he behaved to the toll-collector at Tusculum who asked his pardon; and such was all his behavior. 40

There was in him nothing harsh, nor implacable, nor violent, nor, as one may say, anything carried to the sweating point; but he examined all things severally as if he had abundance of time, and without confusion, in an orderly way, vigorously and consistently. And that might be applied to him which is
5   recorded of Socrates, that he was able both to abstain from, and to enjoy, those things which many are too weak to abstain from, and to enjoy, those things which many are too weak to abstain from, and cannot enjoy without excess. But to be strong enough both to bear the one and to be sober in the other is the mark of a man who has a perfect and invincible soul, such as he showed in
10  the illness of Maximus.

§17To the gods I am indebted for having good grandfathers, good parents, a good sister, good teachers, good associates, good kinsmen and friends, nearly everything good. Further, I owe it to the gods that I was not hurried into any offence against any of them, though I had a disposition which, if opportunity
15  had offered, might have led me to do something of this kind; but, through their favor, there never was such a concurrence of circumstances as put me to the trial.

Further, I am thankful to the gods that I was not longer brought up with my grandfather's concubine, and that I preserved the flower of my youth, and that
20  I did not make proof of my virility before the proper season, but even deferred the time; that I was subjected to a ruler and a father who was able to take away all pride from me, and to bring me to the knowledge that it is possible for a man to live in a palace without wanting either guards or embroidered dresses, or torches and statues, and suchlike show; but it is in such a man's power to
25  bring himself very near to the fashion of a private person, without being for this reason either meaner in thought, or more remiss in action, with respect to the things which must be done for the public interest in a manner that befits a ruler.

I thank the gods for giving me such a brother, who was able by his moral
30  character to rouse me to vigilance over myself, and who, at the same time, pleased me by his respect and affection; that my children have not been stupid nor deformed in body; that I did not make more proficiency in rhetoric, poetry, and the other studies, in which I should perhaps have been completely engaged, if I had seen that I was making progress in them; that I made haste to place
35  those who brought me up in the station of honor which they seemed to desire without putting them off with hope of my doing it sometime after, because they were then still young; that I knew Apollonius, Rusticus, Maximus.

That I received clear and frequent impressions about living according to nature, and what kind of a life that is, so that, so far as depended on the gods, and their gifts and help, and inspirations, nothing hindered me from forthwith living according to nature, though I still fall short of it through my own fault, and though not observing the admonitions of the gods, and, I may almost say, their direct instructions.

That my body has held out so long in such a kind of life; that I never touched 5 either Benedicta or Theodotus, and that, after having fallen into amatory passions, I was cured; and, though I was often out of humor with Rusticus, I never did anything of which I had occasion to repent; that, though it was my mother's fate to die young, she spent the last years of her life with me.

That, whenever I wished to help any man in his need, or on any other 10 occasion, I was never told that I had not the means of doing it; and that to myself the same necessity never happened, to receive anything from another; that I have such a wife so obedient, so affectionate, and so simple; that I had abundance of good masters for my children; and that remedies have been shown to me by dreams, both others, and against blood-spitting and giddiness; ... and 15 that, when I had an inclination to philosophy, I did not fall into the hands of any sophist, and that I did not waste my time on writing, or in the resolution of syllogisms, or occupy myself about the investigation of appearances in the heavens; for all these things require the help of the gods and fortune.

# THE INSTITUTES
## JUSTINIAN I (482–565)
### EASTERN ROMAN EMPEROR (527–565)

*The history of the written law of the Roman Empire began in 450 BC with the Law of the Twelve Tables. Not surprisingly, legislation, magisterial pronouncements, judicial precedents, and imperial edicts accumulated over the course of the succeeding centuries until it became very difficult to find the law that applied to any particular case. Jurists from the second century on began to clarify the principles on which Roman law was based, and in 438 Theodosius II (r. 401–450) issued a compilation of imperial constitutions that became the West's version of Roman law until the beginning of the twelfth century.*

*The authoritative codification of Roman law, the* Corpus Juris Civilis, *was the work of legal scholars at the court of Justinian in Constantinople. After the study of this work began in the West about 1100, it came to have a powerful impact on the way medieval kings viewed their authority. Further, the principles and methods of Roman law were incorporated into the legal systems of most continental European monarchies from the thirteenth century on.*

533

IN THE NAME OF OUR LORD JESUS CHRIST.

THE EMPEROR CAESAR FLAVIUS JUSTINIANUS, VANQUISHER OF THE ALAMANI, GOTHS, FRANCS, GERMANS, ANTES, ALANI, VANDALS, AFRICANS, PIOUS, HAPPY, GLORIOUS, TRIUMPHANT CONQUEROR, EVER-AUGUST, TO THE YOUTH DESIROUS OF STUDYING THE LAW, GREETING.     5

The Imperial Majesty should be not only made glorious by arms, but also strengthened by laws that, alike in time of peace and in time of war, the state may be well governed, and that the Emperor may not only be victorious in the field of battle, but also may by every legal means repel the iniquities of men who abuse the laws, and may at once religiously uphold justice and triumph     10
over his conquered enemies.

*The Institutes of Justinian,* edited by Thomas Collett Sandars (London: Longmans, Green, and Company, 1917), 1–3, 5–10, 12–15, 26–30.

1. By our incessant labors and great care, with the blessing of God, we have attained this double end. The barbarian nations reduced under our yoke know our efforts in war; to which also Africa and very many other provinces bear witness, which, after so long an interval, have been restored to the dominion of Rome and our empire, by our victories gained through the favor of heaven. All nations moreover are governed by laws which we have already either promulgated or compiled.

2. When we had arranged and brought into perfect harmony the hitherto confused mass of imperial constitutions, we then extended our care to the vast volumes of ancient law; and, sailing as it were across the mid-ocean, have now completed, through the favor of heaven, a work that once seemed beyond hope.

3. When by the blessing of God this task was accomplished, we summoned the most eminent Tribonian, master and ex-quaestor of our palace, together with the illustrious Theophilus and Dorotheus, professors of law, all of whom have on many occasions proved to us their ability, legal knowledge, and obedience to our orders; and we have specially charged them to compose, under our authority and advice, *Institutes*, so that you may no more learn the first elements of law from old and erroneous sources, but apprehend them by the clear light of imperial wisdom; and that your minds and ears may receive nothing that is useless or misplaced, but only what obtains in actual practice. So that, whereas, formerly, the junior students could scarcely, after three years' study, read the imperial constitutions, you may now commence your studies by reading them, you who have been thought worthy of an honor and a happiness so great as that the first and last lessons in the knowledge of the law should issue for you from the mouth of the emperor.

4. When, therefore, by the assistance of the same eminent person Tribonian and that of other illustrious and learned men, we had compiled the fifty books, called *Digests* or *Pandects*, in which is collected the whole ancient law, we directed that these *Institutes* should be divided into four books, which might serve as the first elements of the whole science of law.

5. In these books a brief exposition is given of the ancient laws, and of those also which, overshadowed by dis-use, have been again brought to light by our imperial authority.

6. These four books of *Institutes* thus compiled from all the *Institutes* left us by the ancients, and chiefly from the commentaries of our Gaius, both in

his *Institutes* and in his work on daily affairs, and also from many other commentaries, we presented to us by the three learned men we have above named. We have read and examined them and have accorded to them all the force of our constitutions.

7. Receive, therefore, with eagerness, and study with cheerful diligence, these 5 our laws, and show yourselves persons of such learning that you may conceive the flattering hope of yourselves being able, when your course of legal study is completed, to govern our empire in the different portions that may be entrusted to your care.

Given at Constantinople on the eleventh day of the calends of December, in 10 the third consulate of the Emperor Justinian, ever August.

### Book I, Title 1—*De Justitia et Jure*

Justice is the constant and perpetual wish to render everyone his due.

1. Jurisprudence is the knowledge of things divine and human; the science of the just and the unjust.

2. Having explained these general terms, we think we shall commence our 15 exposition of the law of the Roman people most advantageously if our explanation is at first plain and easy, and is then carried on into details with the utmost care and exactness. For, if at the outset we overload the mind of the student while yet new to the subject and unable to bear much, with a multitude and variety of topics, one of two things will happen—we shall 20 either cause him wholly to abandon his studies or, after great toil, and often after great distrust of himself (the most frequent stumbling-block in the way of youth), we shall at last conduct him to the point to which, if he had been led by a smoother road, he might, without great labor and without any distrust of his own powers, have been sooner conducted. 25

3. The maxims of law are these: to live honestly, to hurt no one, to give everyone his due.

4. The study of law is divided into two branches; that of public and that of private law. Public law is that which regards the government of the Roman Empire; private law, that which concerns the interests of individuals. We 30 are now to treat of the latter, which is composed of three elements, and consists of precepts belonging to natural law, to the law of nations, and to the civil law.

### Book I, Title 2—*De Jure Naturali, Gentium, et Civili*

The law of nature is that law which nature teaches to all animals. For this law does not belong exclusively to the human race, but belongs to all animals, whether of the air, the earth, or the sea. Hence comes that yoking together of male and female, which we term matrimony; hence the procreation and bringing up of children. We see, indeed, that all the other animals besides man are considered as having knowledge of this law.

1. Civil law is thus distinguished from the law of nations. Every community governed by laws and customs uses partly its own law, partly laws common to all mankind. The law which a people makes for its own government belongs exclusively to that state, and is called the civil law, as being the law of the particular state. But the law which natural reason appoints for all mankind obtains equally among all nations, and is called the law of nations, because all nations make use of it. The people of Rome, then, are governed partly by their own laws, and partly by the laws which are common to all mankind. What is the nature of these two component parts of our law we will set forth in the proper place.

2. Civil law takes its name from the state which it governs, as, for instance, from Athens; for it would be very proper to speak of the laws of Solon or Draco as the civil law of Athens. And thus the law which the Roman people make use of is called the civil law of the Romans, or that of the Quirites, as being used by the Quirites; for the Romans are called Quirites from Quirinus. But whenever we speak of civil law, without adding of what state we are speaking, we mean our own law: just as when "the poet" is spoken of without any name being expressed, the Greeks mean the great Homer, and we Romans mean Virgil. The law of nations is common to all mankind, for nations have established certain laws, as occasion and the necessities of human life required. Wars arose, and in their train followed captivity and then slavery, which is contrary to the law of nature; for by that law all men are originally born free. Further, from this law of nations almost all contracts were at first introduced, as, for instance, buying and selling, letting and hiring, partnership, deposits, loans returnable in kind, and very many others.

3. Our law is written and unwritten, just as among the Greeks some of their laws were written and others not written. The written part consists of laws, *plebiscita, senatus-consulta*, enactments of emperors, edicts of magistrates, and answers of jurisprudents....

6. That which seems good to the Emperor has also the force of law; for the people, by the *lex regia*, which is passed to confer on him his power, make

over to him their whole power and authority. Therefore whatever the Emperor ordains by rescript, or decides in adjudging a cause, or lays down by edict, is unquestionably law; and it is these enactments of the Emperor that are called constitutions. Of these, some are personal, and are not to be drawn into precedent, such not being the intention of the Emperor. 5 Supposing the Emperor has granted a favor to any man on account of his merits, or inflicted some punishment, or granted some extraordinary relief, the application of these acts does not extend beyond the particular individual. But the other constitutions, being general, are undoubtedly binding on all.... 10

9. The unwritten law is that which usage has established; for ancient customs, being sanctioned by the consent of those who adopt them, are like laws.

10. The civil law is not improperly divided into two kinds, for the division seems to have had its origin in the customs of the two states Athens and Lacedae- mon. For in these states it used to be the case, that the Lacedaemonians 15 rather committed to memory what they were to observe as law, while the Athenians rather kept safely what they had found written in their laws.

11. The laws of nature, which all nations observe alike, being established by a divine providence, remain ever fixed and immutable. But the laws which every state has enacted, undergo frequent changes, either by the tacit consent 20 of the people, or by a new law being subsequently passed.

12. All our law relates either to persons, or to things, or to actions. Let us first speak of persons; as it is of little purpose to know the law, if we do not know the persons for whom the law was made.

### Book I, Title 3—*De Jure Personarum*

The chief division in the rights of persons is this: men are all either free or 25 slaves.

1. Freedom, from which is derived the term free as applied to men, is the natural power of doing each what we please, unless prevented either by force or by law.

2. Slavery is an institution of the law of nations, by which one man is made 30 the property of another, contrary to natural right.

3. Slaves are denominated *servi* because generals order their captives to be sold, and thus preserve them, and do not put them to death. Slaves are also called *mancipia*, because they are taken from the enemy by the strong hand.

4. Slaves either are born or become so. They are born so when their mother is a slave; they become so either by the law of nations, that is, by captivity or by the civil law, as when a free person, above the age of twenty, suffers himself to be sold, that he may share the price given for him.

5. In the condition of slaves there is no distinction; but there are many distinctions among free persons; for they are either born free, or have been set free....

### Book I, Title 8—*De His, Qui Sui Vel Alieni Juris Sunt*

We now come to another division relative to the rights of persons; for some persons are *sui juris*, some are subject to the power of others. Of those, again, who are subject to others, some are in the power of ascendants, others in that of masters. Let us, then, treat of those who are subject to others; for, when we have ascertained who these are, we shall at the same time discover who are *sui juris*. And first let us consider those who are in the power of masters.

1. Slaves are in the power of masters, a power derived from the law of nations: for among all nations it may be remarked that masters have the power of life and death over their slaves, and that everything acquired by the slave is acquired for the master.

2. But at the present day no persons under our rule may use violence towards their slaves, without a reason recognized by the law, or ever to an extreme extent. For, by a constitution of the Emperor Antoninus Pius, he who without any reason kills his own slave is to be punished equally with one who has killed the slave of another. The excessive severity of masters is also restrained by another constitution of the same Emperor. For, when consulted by certain governors of provinces on the subject of slaves, who fled for refuge either to temples or the statues of the Emperors, he decided that if the severity of masters should appear excessive, they might be compelled to make sale of their slaves upon equitable terms, so that the masters might receive the value; and this was a very wise decision, as it concerns the public good that no one should mis-use his own property. The following are the terms of this rescript of Antoninus, which was sent to Aelius Marcianus: "The power of masters over their slaves ought to be preserved un-impaired, nor ought any man to be deprived of his right. But it is for the interest of all masters themselves that relief prayed on good grounds against cruelty, the denial of sustenance, or any other intolerable injury should not be refused. Examine, therefore, into the complaints of the slaves who have fled from the house of Julius Sabinus, and taken refuge at the statue of the Emperor; and,

if you find that they have been too harshly treated or wantonly disgraced, order them to be sold, so that they may not fall again under the power of their master; and, if Sabinus attempt to evade my constitution, I would have him know, that I shall severely punish his disobedience."

## Book I, Title 9—*De Patria Potestate*

Our children, begotten in lawful marriage, are in our power                5

1. Marriage, or matrimony, is a joining together of a man and woman, carrying with it a mode of life in which they are inseparable.

2. The power which we have over our children is peculiar to the citizens of Rome; for no other people have a power over their children, such as we have over ours.                                                                      10

3. The child born to you and your wife is in your power. And so is the child born to your son of his wife, that is, your grand-son or grand-daughter; so are your great-grandchildren, and all your other descendants. But a child born of your daughter is not in your power, but in the power of its own father....                                                                          15

# VI
# EARLY CHRISTIANITY

The Roman Empire has bequeathed to us many permanent gifts, including law, the republican principles of our constitution, and architecture. Although the Romans certainly did not intend to do so, they also cultivated a Mediterranean-wide world ripe for the gradual conquest of a new form of monotheism, Christianity. As such, Christianity, and the culture it gave rise to, is a remarkable product of the period of Roman history known as the *Pax Romana*, and more poignantly, the final and greatest development of antiquity.

A study of early Christianity must remain sensitive to its rise within three contexts: Roman, Hellenistic Greek, and Jewish. Each context affected the growth and shape of the religion. Ultimately though, Christianity, the unsophisticated late arrival on the stage of antiquity, was the transforming element in its interaction with all three contexts, but particularly the Greek and the Roman. As the early Christian theologian and apologist Tertullian (*c.* AD 160–post 220) exclaimed, "We are but of yesterday, yet we fill your cities, islands, forts, towns, councils, even camps, tribes, decuries, the palace, the senate, the forum; we have left you the temples alone."

Christianity arose as a tiny sect in a small, backward province in the Roman Empire. It represented a new development in an old cultural world where paganism was a way of life. From a historical point of view, the sources for its early history are late and limited primarily to the Pauline epistles and Gospels of Matthew, Mark, Luke, and John. These sources reveal the first attempts at systematic presentation and early evidence of controversy and crises. Scholars do agree that these writings saw three stages, moving from authentic material of eye-witnesses to oral traditions, and culminating in authorial versions.

The four Gospels present the life and teaching of Jesus of Nazareth. Born in obscurity around 4 BC (the year Herod died), Jesus' life peaked in the years of his public career after the rise of John the Baptist, who began preaching in the 15$^{th}$ year of Tiberius. During this three-year period (*c.* AD 30–33) he taught of the coming kingdom of God, calling for repentance and a constant subversion of the ways of the world.

Jesus' disciples firmly believed in the fact of his resurrection. Their faith blossomed into the church at Pentecost, and Christianity quickly grew, primarily through the efforts of the apostle Paul, beyond its Jewish roots into the wider Mediterranean world. Christianity appealed to the classical world for a variety of reasons, ranging from the nature of its teachings, to its universal and exclusive appeal, and its distinct mode of life. When faced with persecution first from Jewish and then Roman authorities, Christians did not hesitate to model the heroism of their founder and die as martyrs. The success and spread of Christianity, however, depended on the resolution of three issues: its relations with the Roman state; its development of an organization; and its attainment of intellectual and social respectability.

Christianity began with bloody individual encounters with the Roman state, which grew to persecution, followed by a period of tolerance leading to official status. Jesus was condemned under Pontius Pilate, a Roman procurator. In imitation of their teacher, both Peter and Paul were executed by the Roman state. At first, as Pliny the Younger's correspondence with the Roman Emperor Trajan (r. 98–117) confirms, the Roman state did not seek actively to persecute Christians. During the reigns of Domitian (r. 81–96), who styled himself Master and God, Decius (r. 249–251), and Diocletian (r. 285–305) persecution was more widespread and severe. Although heavily criticized by Christian apologists such as Lactantius (c. 230–320), Diocletian's persecution sought to preserve unity and harmony with the pagan gods. With the conversion of the Emperor Constantine in AD 312 followed by the Edict of Milan in AD 313, Christianity's fortunes with regards to the Roman state changed quickly from persecution to tolerance and eventual favor. The Emperor Theodosius I (379–395) gave Christianity official status in AD 380 and subsequently forbade pagan practice in AD 391. The conversion of Roman emperors raised issues ranging from imperial benevolence and imperial interference (see Pope Gelasius, 492–496) to Christian triumphalism (see Eusebius).

During its struggle and eventual accommodation by the Roman state, Christianity grew from its apostolic origins into a Roman Catholic Church, which, because of the strength of its institutions, dominated the Roman Empire in a way no pagan cult ever had. Texts like the Didache (c. AD 100) give witness to the earliest officials: bishops (*episkopoi*), priests (*presbyteroi*), deacons (*diakonoi*). By the mid-second century, a "monarchical" episcopate unified the Christian communities in the different urban centers throughout the Empire. The Church furthered the office of the episcopate by applying "apostolic succession" to the administrative geography of the Empire. By the fourth century, every urban center in the Empire had its own Christian bishop, the recognized head of each Christian community.

Much like the Roman cultural world, its predecessor in claims of universality, the Church, following the Petrine idea contained in Matthew 16:16–18, centered on the city of Rome. The importance of this city as a religious center was based on Peter's position of leadership and the fact that both Peter and Paul had suffered martyrdom there. Although Rome's importance as a political center began to diminish in the late second century, it retained its antiquity and significant name, although by the third century it lacked the imperial court. The Emperor Theodosius insisted that all believe as the Bishop of Rome does. Later figures, such as Pope Leo I (440–461), would greatly advance the theory of papal primacy. The success of early church councils, in which the bishop of Rome played roles that greatly varied in significance, ensured that a powerful tension would continue between monarchical and collegial views of the church.

To attain intellectual and social respectability, the Church had to address the issues of the development of a canon and a creed, as well as to decide how to deal with Greco-Roman culture. Early in the history of Christianity, the fathers of the Church recognized the need to establish a definitive body of revelation. Although not formally addressed by an ecumenical council until Trent, the development of a canon of scripture grew from Irenaeus in the second century, through the most authoritative statement by Athanasius in the fourth century, to a final statement (for antiquity) at the local Council of Carthage in 455. Of course, the most influential version was the Vulgate of Jerome.

In a similar vein, the church required a definitive statement of Christian teachings. For the fathers, authority rested equally in scripture and tradition. In 434, Vincent of Lérins expressed that the Church "take great care that we hold that which has been believed everywhere, always, and by all," thus establishing criteria of universality, antiquity, and consensus. For the most part, the Church fathers expected the gathering of the successors of the apostles (bishops) at councils to be the seats of authority. Apart from problems with Gnosticism, which enabled the articulation of the canon of Scripture, the early church faced two great problems, Trinitarian and Christological, which gave rise respectively to the heresies of Arianism and Monophysitism. The four ecumenical councils Nicaea (325), Constantinople (381), Ephesus (431), and Chalcedon (451) sought to address these problems.

In its confrontation with classical culture, the church reacted in two ways. Following the ascetic Epicurean impulse of withdrawal from the world, some early Christians chose monasticism. Others followed a more Stoic model of activity within the world and embraced and eventually transformed Greco-Roman culture. As Jerome (c. 347–420) relates in beautiful Latin prose his famous dream in which Christ accuses him of being a Ciceronian rather than a Christian, Church fathers felt the tension between the two extremes deeply.

Christian monasticism arose in the early fourth century in Egypt from both classical ascetic ideals and Jewish antecedents. The father of monasticism,

Anthony (*c.* 251–356), stressed the eremitic ideal of withdrawal to the desert (*heremos*), while Pachomius (*c.* 292–348) taught the cenobitic (common life). Much like earlier stories of Christian martyrs, the tales of these "white martyrs," particularly the *Life of Anthony* by Athanasius (*c.* 293–373) and the writings of Jerome, spread throughout the Empire. Initially both the eastern and western parts of the Roman Empire felt the pull of eremitic life. Eventually, the cenobitic (communal) model, institutionalized in the *Rule* of Benedict of Nursia (480–545), came to dominate the West. Both forms represent a conscious and comprehensive abandonment of the ancient civic ideal.

Beginning with the Christian apologists of the second century, the church fathers who embraced and transformed classical culture created a third great age of Latin literature as they struggled with questions about Christianity and Judaism, Christianity and pagan philosophy, and Christians living in a pagan world. During the Patristic Age (300–600), a richly varied bouquet of intellects forged a culture both classical and Christian. The twentieth-century theologian Hans Urs von Balthasar described the men of this age as follows:

> Greatness, depth, boldness, flexibility, certainty and a flaming love— the virtues of youth, are the marks of patristic theology. Perhaps the Church will never again see the likes of such an array of larger-than-life figures that mark the period from Irenaeus to Athanasius, Basil, Cyril, Chrysostom, Ambrose, and Augustine—not to mention the army of the lesser fathers. Life and doctrine are immediately one. Of them all it is true what Kierkegaard said of Chrysostom: "He gesticulated with his whole existence."

The four Latin fathers, in particular, embodied the transformation of the Roman world into the Christian world that would evolve into the medieval world. Ambrose (339–397), the Bishop of Milan, not only made Greek thought accessible to the Latin West, but he also, in his relationship with the Emperor Theodosius, demonstrated that a Christian bishop could act much like an Old Testament prophet. Jerome (342–420), secretary to Pope Damasus (*r.* 366–384), translated the Bible into the Latin form that would reign in the West until the Reformation. Among the many writings of Augustine of Hippo (354–430), three in particular stand out. His *Confessions* represent the first true work of introspection and chronicle the transformation of a man through the major currents of thought at the end of antiquity. His *City of God* provides the first theology of history and changed the way Christians would view the world in which they lived forever. His *On Christian Doctrine* marked the first systematic exposition of how Christian learning related to the well-developed *Paideia* of Greco-Roman antiquity. Finally, Gregory the Great (*c.* 540–604), pope from 590–604, marked the transition to the medieval world and ensured that Christianity would continue to grow as a cultural force.

By the sixth century, Christianity had thoroughly permeated the former Roman world and become the bearer of ancient culture and languages. Christian bishops dominated the spiritual, intellectual, and political landscapes. Their churches began to mark deeply the topography of ancient urban centers. While in sites often not sought out by their Roman ancestors, Christian monks sought to preserve the learning of antiquity and the Christian faith, now several centuries old. In so doing they nurtured a transformed culture that would endure until the sixteenth century.

# THE GOSPEL ACCORDING TO MATTHEW

*In the Sermon on the Mount, Jesus challenged his hearers to spiritual and moral transformation in preparation for the Kingdom of Heaven.*

5 ¹Seeing the crowds, he went up on the mountain, and when he sat down his disciples came to him. ²And he opened his mouth and taught them, saying:

³"Blessed are the poor in spirit, for theirs is the kingdom of heaven."

⁴"Blessed are those who mourn, for they shall be comforted." 5

⁵"Blessed are the meek, for they shall inherit the earth."

⁶"Blessed are those who hunger and thirst for righteousness, for they shall be satisfied."

⁷"Blessed are the merciful, for they shall obtain mercy."

⁸"Blessed are the pure in heart, for they shall see God." 10

⁹"Blessed are the peacemakers, for they shall be called sons of God."

¹⁰"Blessed are those who are persecuted for righteousness' sake, for theirs is the kingdom of heaven."

¹¹"Blessed are you when men revile you and persecute you and utter all kinds of evil against you falsely on my account. ¹²Rejoice and be glad, for your 15 reward is great in heaven, for so men persecuted the prophets who were before you."

¹³"You are the salt of the earth; but if salt has lost its taste, how shall its saltiness be restored? It is no longer good for anything except to be thrown out and trodden under foot by men. ¹⁴You are the light of the world. A city set 20 on a hill cannot be hid. ¹⁵Nor do men light a lamp and put it under a bushel, but on a stand, and it gives light to all in the house. ¹⁶Let your light so shine before men that they may see your good works and give glory to your Father who is in heaven."

¹⁷"Think not that I have come to abolish the law and the prophets; I have 25 come not to abolish them but to fulfill them. ¹⁸For truly, I say to you, till heaven and earth pass away, not an iota, not a dot, will pass from the law until all is accomplished. ¹⁹Whoever then relaxes one of the least of these command-

ments and teaches men so, shall be called least in the kingdom of heaven; but he who does them and teaches them shall be called great in the kingdom of heaven. **20**For I tell you, unless your righteousness exceeds that of the scribes and Pharisees, you will never enter the kingdom of heaven."

5      **21**"You have heard that it was said to the men of old, 'You shall not kill; and whoever kills shall be liable to judgment.' **22**But I say to you that everyone who is angry with his brother shall be liable to judgment; whoever insults his brother shall be liable to the council, and whoever says, 'You fool!' shall be liable to the hell of fire. **23**So if you are offering your gift at the altar, and there

10     remember that your brother has something against you, **24**leave your gift there before the altar and go; first be reconciled to your brother, and then come and offer your gift. **25**Make friends quickly with your accuser, while you are going with him to court, lest your accuser hand you over to the judge, and the judge to the guard, and you be put in prison; **26**truly, I say to you, you will never get

15     out till you have paid the last penny."

       **27**"You have heard that it was said, 'You shall not commit adultery.' **28**But I say to you that everyone who looks at a woman lustfully has already committed adultery with her in his heart. **29**If your right eye causes you to sin, pluck it out and throw it away; it is better that you lose one of your members than that

20     your whole body be thrown into hell. **30**And if your right hand causes you to sin, cut it off and throw it away; it is better that you lose one of your members than that your whole body go into hell."

       **31**"It was also said, 'Whoever divorces his wife, let him give her a certificate of divorce.' **32**But I say to you that everyone who divorces his wife, except on

25     the ground of un-chastity, makes her an adulteress; and whoever marries a divorced woman commits adultery."

       **33**"Again you have heard that it was said to the men of old, 'You shall not swear falsely, but shall perform to the Lord what you have sworn.' **34**But I say to you, Do not swear at all, either by heaven, for it is the throne of God, **35**or by the earth, for

30     it is his footstool, or by Jerusalem, for it is the city of the great King. **36**And do not swear by your head, for you cannot make one hair white or black. **37**Let what you say be simply 'Yes' or 'No'; anything more than this comes from evil."

       **38**"You have heard that it was said, 'An eye for an eye and a tooth for a tooth.' **39**But I say to you, Do not resist one who is evil. But if any one strikes

35     you on the right cheek, turn to him the other also; **40**and if anyone would sue you and take your coat, let him have your cloak as well; **41**and if anyone forces you to go one mile, go with him two miles.**42**Give to him who begs from you, and do not refuse him who would borrow from you."

       **43**"You have heard that it was said, 'You shall love your neighbor and hate

40     your enemy.' **44**But I say to you, Love your enemies and pray for those who

persecute you, **45**so that you may be sons of your Father who is in heaven; for he makes his sun rise on the evil and on the good, and sends rain on the just and on the unjust. **46**For if you love those who love you, what reward have you? Do not even the tax collectors do the same? **47**And if you salute only your brethren, what more are you doing than others? Do not even the Gentiles do the same? **48**You, therefore, must be perfect, as your heavenly Father is perfect."

6 **1**"Beware of practicing your piety before men in order to be seen by them; for then you will have no reward from your Father who is in heaven. **2**Thus, when you give alms, sound no trumpet before you, as the hypocrites do in the synagogues and in the streets, that they may be praised by men. Truly, I say to you, they have received their reward. **3**But when you give alms, do not let your left hand know what your right hand is doing, **4**so that your alms may be in secret; and your Father who sees in secret will reward you."

**5**"And when you pray, you must not be like the hypocrites; for they love to stand and pray in the synagogues and at the street corners, that they may be seen by men. Truly, I say to you, they have received their reward. **6**But when you pray, go into your room and shut the door and pray to your Father who is in secret; and your Father who sees in secret will reward you."

**7**"And in praying do not heap up empty phrases as the Gentiles do; for they think that they will be heard for their many words. **8**Do not be like them, for your Father knows what you need before you ask him. **9**Pray then like this: Our Father who art in heaven, Hallowed be thy name. **10**Thy kingdom come. Thy will be done on earth as it is in heaven. **11**Give us this day our daily bread; **12**and forgive us our debts, as we also have forgiven our debtors. **13**And lead us not into temptation, but deliver us from evil. **14**For if you forgive men their trespasses, your heavenly Father also will forgive you; **15**but if you do not forgive men their trespasses, neither will your Father forgive your trespasses."

**16**"And when you fast, do not look dismal, like the hypocrites, for they disfigure their faces that their fasting may be seen by men. Truly, I say to you, they have received their reward. **17**But when you fast, anoint your head and wash your face, **18**that your fasting may not be seen by men but by your Father who is in secret; and your Father who sees in secret will reward you."

**19**"Do not lay up for yourselves treasures on earth, where moth and rust consume and where thieves break in and steal, **20**but lay up for yourselves treasures in heaven, where neither moth nor rust consumes and where thieves do not break in and steal. **21**For where your treasure is, there will your heart be also."

**22**"The eye is the lamp of the body. So, if your eye is sound, your whole body will be full of light; **23**but if your eye is not sound, your whole body will be full of darkness. If then the light in you is darkness, how great is the darkness!

**24**"No one can serve two masters; for either he will hate the one and love the other, or he will be devoted to the one and despise the other. You cannot serve God and mammon."

**25**"Therefore I tell you, do not be anxious about your life, what you shall eat or what you shall drink, nor about your body, what you shall put on. Is not life more than food, and the body more than clothing? **26**Look at the birds of the air: they neither sow nor reap nor gather into barns, and yet your heavenly Father feeds them. Are you not of more value than they? **27**And which of you by being anxious can add one cubit to his span of life? **28**And why are you anxious about clothing? Consider the lilies of the field, how they grow; they neither toil nor spin; **29**yet I tell you, even Solomon in all his glory was not arrayed like one of these. **30**But if God so clothes the grass of the field, which today is alive and tomorrow is thrown into the oven, will he not much more clothe you, O men of little faith? **31**Therefore do not be anxious, saying, 'What shall we eat?' or 'What shall we drink?' or 'What shall we wear?' **32**For the Gentiles seek all these things; and your heavenly Father knows that you need them all. **33**But seek first his kingdom and his righteousness, and all these things shall be yours as well. **34**Therefore do not be anxious about tomorrow, for tomorrow will be anxious for itself. Let the day's own trouble be sufficient for the day."

7 **1**"Judge not, that you be not judged. **2**For with the judgment you pronounce you will be judged, and the measure you give will be the measure you get. **3**Why do you see the speck that is in your brother's eye, but do not notice the log that is in your own eye? **4**Or how can you say to your brother, 'Let me take the speck out of your eye,' when there is the log in your own eye? **5**You hypocrite, first take the log out of your own eye, and then you will see clearly to take the speck out of your brother's eye."

**6**"Do not give dogs what is holy; and do not throw your pearls before swine, lest they trample them under foot and turn to attack you."

**7**"Ask, and it will be given you; seek, and you will find; knock, and it will be opened to you. **8**For everyone who asks receives, and he who seeks finds, and to him who knocks it will be opened. **9**Or what man of you, if his son asks him for bread, will give him a stone? **10**Or if he asks for a fish, will give him a serpent? **11**If you then, who are evil, know how to give good gifts to your children, how much more will your Father who is in heaven give good things to those who ask him! **12**So whatever you wish that men would do to you, do so to them; for this is the law and the prophets."

**13**"Enter by the narrow gate; for the gate is wide and the way is easy, that leads to destruction, and those who enter by it are many. **14**For the gate is narrow and the way is hard, that leads to life, and those who find it are few."

[15]"Beware of false prophets, who come to you in sheep's clothing but inwardly are ravenous wolves. [16]You will know them by their fruits. Are grapes gathered from thorns, or figs from thistles? [17]So, every sound tree bears good fruit, but the bad tree bears evil fruit. [18]A sound tree cannot bear evil fruit, nor can a bad tree bear good fruit. [19]Every tree that does not bear good fruit is cut    5
down and thrown into the fire. [20]Thus you will know them by their fruits."

[21]"Not everyone who says to me, 'Lord, Lord,' shall enter the kingdom of heaven, but he who does the will of my Father who is in heaven. [22]On that day many will say to me, 'Lord, Lord, did we not prophesy in your name, and cast out demons in your name, and do many mighty works in your name?' [23]And then    10
will I declare to them, 'I never knew you; depart from me, you evildoers.'"

[24]"Everyone then who hears these words of mine and does them will be like a wise man who built his house upon the rock; [25]and the rain fell, and the floods came, and the winds blew and beat upon that house, but it did not fall, because it had been founded on the rock. [26]And everyone who hears these    15
words of mine and does not do them will be like a foolish man who built his house upon the sand; [27]and the rain fell, and the floods came, and the winds blew and beat against that house, and it fell; and great was the fall of it."

[28]And when Jesus finished these sayings, the crowds were astonished at his teaching, [29]for he taught them as one who had authority, and not as their scribes....    20

**16** [13]Now when Jesus came into the district of Caesarea Philippi, he asked his disciples, "Who do men say that the Son of man is?" [14]And they said, "Some say John the Baptist, others say Elijah, and others Jeremiah or one of the prophets."

[15]He said to them, "But who do you say that I am?"    25

[16]Simon Peter replied, "You are the Christ, the Son of the living God."

[17]And Jesus answered him, "Blessed are you, Simon Bar-Jona! For flesh and blood has not revealed this to you, but my Father who is in heaven. [18]And I tell you, you are Peter, and on this rock I will build my church, and the powers of death shall not prevail against it. [19]I will give you the keys of the kingdom of    30
heaven, and whatever you bind on earth shall be bound in heaven, and whatever you loose on earth shall be loosed in heaven." [20]Then he strictly charged the disciples to tell no one that he was the Christ.

[21]From that time Jesus began to show his disciples that he must go to Jerusalem and suffer many things from the elders and chief priests and scribes,    35
and be killed, and on the third day be raised. [22]And Peter took him and began to rebuke him, saying, "God forbid, Lord! This shall never happen to you." [23]But he turned and said to Peter, "Get behind me, Satan! You are a hindrance to me; for you are not on the side of God, but of men."

<sup>24</sup>Then Jesus told his disciples, "If any man would come after me, let him deny himself and take up his cross and follow me. <sup>25</sup>For whoever would save his life will lose it, and whoever loses his life for my sake will find it. <sup>26</sup>For what will it profit a man if he gains the whole world and forfeits his life? Or what shall a man give in return for his life? <sup>27</sup>For the Son of man is to come with his angels in the glory of his Father, and then he will repay every man for what he has done. <sup>28</sup>Truly, I say to you, there are some standing here who will not taste death before they see the Son of man coming in his kingdom."…

22 <sup>1</sup>And again Jesus spoke to them in parables, saying, <sup>2</sup>"The kingdom of heaven may be compared to a king who gave a marriage feast for his son, <sup>3</sup>and sent his servants to call those who were invited to the marriage feast; but they would not come. <sup>4</sup>Again he sent other servants, saying, 'Tell those who are invited, Behold, I have made ready my dinner, my oxen and my fat calves are killed, and everything is ready; come to the marriage feast.' <sup>5</sup>But they made light of it and went off, one to his farm, another to his business, <sup>6</sup>while the rest seized his servants, treated them shamefully, and killed them. <sup>7</sup>The king was angry, and he sent his troops and destroyed those murderers and burned their city. <sup>8</sup>Then he said to his servants, 'The wedding is ready, but those invited were not worthy. <sup>9</sup>Go therefore to the thoroughfares, and invite to the marriage feast as many as you find.' <sup>10</sup>And those servants went out into the streets and gathered all whom they found, both bad and good; so the wedding hall was filled with guests."

<sup>11</sup>"But when the king came in to look at the guests, he saw there a man who had no wedding garment; <sup>12</sup>and he said to him, 'Friend, how did you get in here without a wedding garment?' And he was speechless. <sup>13</sup>Then the king said to the attendants, 'Bind him hand and foot, and cast him into the outer darkness; there men will weep and gnash their teeth.' <sup>14</sup>For many are called, but few are chosen."

<sup>15</sup>Then the Pharisees went and took counsel how to entangle him in his talk. <sup>16</sup>And they sent their disciples to him, along with the Herodians, saying, "Teacher, we know that you are true, and teach the way of God truthfully, and care for no man; for you do not regard the position of men. <sup>17</sup>Tell us, then, what you think. Is it lawful to pay taxes to Caesar, or not?"

<sup>18</sup>But Jesus, aware of their malice, said, "Why put me to the test, you hypocrites? <sup>19</sup>Show me the money for the tax." And they brought him a coin. <sup>20</sup>And Jesus said to them, "Whose likeness and inscription is this?" <sup>21</sup>They said, "Caesar's." Then he said to them, "Render therefore to Caesar the things that are Caesar's, and to God the things that are God's." <sup>22</sup>When they heard it, they marveled; and they left him and went away.

²³The same day Sadducees came to him, who say that there is no resurrection; and they asked him a question, ²⁴saying, "Teacher, Moses said, 'If a man dies, having no children, his brother must marry the widow, and raise up children for his brother.' ²⁵Now there were seven brothers among us; the first married, and died, and having no children left his wife to his brother. ²⁶So, too, the second and third, down to the seventh. ²⁷After them all, the woman died. ²⁸In the resurrection, therefore, to which of the seven will she be wife? For they all had her."

²⁹But Jesus answered them, "You are wrong, because you know neither the scriptures nor the power of God. ³⁰For in the resurrection they neither marry nor are given in marriage, but are like angels in heaven. ³¹And as for the resurrection of the dead, have you not read what was said to you by God, ³²'I am the God of Abraham, and the God of Isaac, and the God of Jacob'? He is not God of the dead, but of the living." ³³And when the crowd heard it, they were astonished at his teaching.

³⁴But when the Pharisees heard that he had silenced the Sadducees, they came together. ³⁵And one of them, a lawyer, asked him a question, to test him. ³⁶"Teacher, which is the great commandment in the law?" ³⁷And he said to him, "You shall love the Lord your God with all your heart, and with all your soul, and with all your mind. ³⁸This is the great and first commandment. ³⁹And a second is like it, You shall love your neighbor as yourself. ⁴⁰On these two commandments depend all the law and the prophets."…

**28** ¹⁶Now the eleven disciples went to Galilee, to the mountain to which Jesus had directed them. ¹⁷And when they saw him they worshiped him; but some doubted. ¹⁸And Jesus came and said to them, "All authority in heaven and on earth has been given to me. ¹⁹Go therefore and make disciples of all nations, baptizing them in the name of the Father and of the Son and of the Holy Spirit, ²⁰teaching them to observe all that I have commanded you; and lo, I am with you always, to the close of the age."

# The Gospel According to John

*In language that would especially have struck a chord with a Greek audience, the opening of John's Gospel proclaims the central mystery of the Christian faith: the Incarnation of the eternal Word in the person of Jesus Christ.*

**1** [1]In the beginning was the Word,[1] and the Word was with God, and the Word was God. [2]He was in the beginning with God; [3]all things were made through him, and without him was not anything made that was made. [4]In him was life, and the life was the light of men. [5]The light shines in the darkness, and the darkness has not overcome it. [6]There was a man sent from God, whose name was John. [7]He came for testimony, to bear witness to the light, that all might believe through him. [8]He was not the light, but came to bear witness to the light. [9]The true light that enlightens every man was coming into the world. [10]He was in the world, and the world was made through him, yet the world knew him not. [11]He came to his own home, and his own people received him not. [12]But to all who received him, who believed in his name, he gave power to become children of God; [13]who were born, not of blood nor of the will of the flesh nor of the will of man, but of God. [14]And the Word became flesh and dwelt among us, full of grace and truth; we have beheld his glory, glory as of the only Son from the Father.... 5

10

15

*In the following passage, the end of the final chapter, the Evangelist addressed the expectation, common among the first generation of Christians, that Christ's return was imminent and would occur before he himself died.*

**21** [15]When they had finished breakfast, Jesus said to Simon Peter, "Simon, son of John, do you love me more than these?" He said to him, "Yes, Lord; you know that I love you." He said to him, "Feed my lambs." [16]A second time he said to him, "Simon, son of John, do you love me?" He said to

---

[1]Word (*logos*) was a term replete with meaning both for Jews influenced by Greek thought, who used it to refer to the God's agent in creation of and communication with the world, and for Stoics, for whom the *logos* was the principle of inter-connectedness of the world.

him, "Yes, Lord; you know that I love you." He said to him, "Tend my sheep."
[17]He said to him the third time, "Simon, son of John, do you love me?" Peter
was grieved because he said to him the third time, "Do you love me?" And he
said to him, "Lord, you know everything; you know that I love you." Jesus said
to him, "Feed my sheep. [18]Truly, truly, I say to you, when you were young, you
girded yourself and walked where you would; but when you are old, you will
stretch out your hands, and another will gird you and carry you where you do
not wish to go." [19](This he said to show by what death he was to glorify God.)
And after this he said to him, "Follow me."

[20]Peter turned and saw following them the disciple whom Jesus loved,
who had lain close to his breast at the supper and had said, "Lord, who is it
that is going to betray you?" [21]When Peter saw him, he said to Jesus, "Lord,
what about this man?" [22]Jesus said to him, "If it is my will that he remain until
I come, what is that to you? Follow me!" [23]The saying spread abroad among
the brethren that this disciple was not to die; yet Jesus did not say to him that
he was not to die, but, "If it is my will that he remain until I come, what is
that to you?" [24]This is the disciple who is bearing witness to these things, and
who has written these things; and we know that his testimony is true. [25]But
there are also many other things which Jesus did; were every one of them to
be written, I suppose that the world itself could not contain the books that
would be written.

# ACTS OF THE APOSTLES

*The Acts of the Apostles records the history of the early Church from the Ascension and the descent of the Holy Spirit at Pentecost through Paul's missionary journeys and his first imprisonment in Rome.*

1 <sup></sup>¹In the first book, O Theophilus, I have dealt with all that Jesus began to do and teach, ²until the day when he was taken up, after he had given commandment through the Holy Spirit to the apostles whom he had chosen. ³To them he presented himself alive after his passion by many proofs, appearing to them during forty days, and speaking of the kingdom of God. ⁴And while staying with them he charged them not to depart from Jerusalem, but to wait for the promise of the Father, which, he said, "you heard from me, ⁵for John baptized with water, but before many days you shall be baptized with the Holy Spirit."

⁶So when they had come together, they asked him, "Lord, will you at this time restore the kingdom to Israel?" ⁷He said to them, "It is not for you to know times or seasons which the Father has fixed by his own authority. ⁸But you shall receive power when the Holy Spirit has come upon you; and you shall be my witnesses in Jerusalem and in all Judea and Samaria and to the end of the earth." ⁹And when he had said this, as they were looking on, he was lifted up, and a cloud took him out of their sight. ¹⁰And while they were gazing into heaven as he went, behold, two men stood by them in white robes, ¹¹and said, "Men of Galilee, why do you stand looking into heaven? This Jesus, who was taken up from you into heaven, will come in the same way as you saw him go into heaven."

¹²Then they returned to Jerusalem from the mount called Olivet, which is near Jerusalem, a sabbath day's journey away; ¹³and when they had entered, they went up to the upper room, where they were staying, Peter and John and James and Andrew, Philip and Thomas, Bartholomew and Matthew, James the son of Alphaeus and Simon the Zealot and Judas the son of James. ¹⁴All these with one accord devoted themselves to prayer, together with the women and Mary the mother of Jesus, and with his brothers.

**15**In those days Peter stood up among the brethren (the company of persons was in all about a hundred and twenty), and said, **16**"Brethren, the scripture had to be fulfilled, which the Holy Spirit spoke beforehand by the mouth of David, concerning Judas who was guide to those who arrested Jesus. **17**For he was numbered among us, and was allotted his share in this ministry. **18**(Now this man bought a field with the reward of his wickedness; and falling headlong, he burst open in the middle and all his bowels gushed out. **19**And it became known to all the inhabitants of Jerusalem, so that the field was called in their language Akeldama, that is, Field of Blood.) **20**For it is written in the book of Psalms, 'Let his habitation become desolate, and let there be no one to live in it'; and 'His office let another take.' **21**So one of the men who have accompanied us during all the time that the Lord Jesus went in and out among us, **22**beginning from the baptism of John until the day when he was taken up from us—one of these men must become with us a witness to his resurrection." **23**And they put forward two, Joseph called Barsabbas, who was surnamed Justus, and Matthias. **24**And they prayed and said, "Lord, who knowest the hearts of all men, show which one of these two Thou hast chosen **25**to take the place in this ministry and apostleship from which Judas turned aside, to go to his own place." **26**And they cast lots for them, and the lot fell on Matthias; and he was enrolled with the eleven apostles.

**2** **1**When the day of Pentecost had come, they were all together in one place. **2**And suddenly a sound came from heaven like the rush of a mighty wind, and it filled all the house where they were sitting. **3**And there appeared to them tongues as of fire, distributed and resting on each one of them. **4**And they were all filled with the Holy Spirit and began to speak in other tongues, as the Spirit gave them utterance.

**5**Now there were dwelling in Jerusalem Jews, devout men from every nation under heaven. **6**And at this sound the multitude came together, and they were bewildered, because each one heard them speaking in his own language. **7**And they were amazed and wondered, saying, "Are not all these who are speaking Galileans? **8**And how is it that we hear, each of us in his own native language? **9**Parthians and Medes and Elamites and residents of Mesopotamia, Judea and Cappadocia, Pontus and Asia, **10**Phrygia and Pamphylia, Egypt and the parts of Libya belonging to Cyrene, and visitors from Rome, both Jews and proselytes, **11**Cretans and Arabians, we hear them telling in our own tongues the mighty works of God." **12**And all were amazed and perplexed, saying to one another, "What does this mean?" **13**But others mocking said, "They are filled with new wine."

$^{14}$But Peter, standing with the eleven, lifted up his voice and addressed them, "Men of Judea and all who dwell in Jerusalem, let this be known to you, and give ear to my words. $^{15}$For these men are not drunk, as you suppose, since it is only the third hour of the day; $^{16}$but this is what was spoken by the prophet Joel: $^{17}$'And in the last days it shall be, God declares, that I will pour out my   5
Spirit upon all flesh, and your sons and your daughters shall prophesy, and your young men shall see visions, and your old men shall dream dreams; $^{18}$yea, and on my menservants and my maidservants in those days I will pour out my Spirit; and they shall prophesy. $^{19}$And I will show wonders in the heaven above and signs on the earth beneath, blood, and fire, and vapor of smoke; $^{20}$the sun   10
shall be turned into darkness and the moon into blood, before the day of the Lord comes, the great and manifest day. $^{21}$And it shall be that whoever calls on the name of the Lord shall be saved.' $^{22}$Men of Israel, hear these words: Jesus of Nazareth, a man attested to you by God with mighty works and wonders and signs which God did through him in your midst, as you yourselves know—$^{23}$this   15
Jesus, delivered up according to the definite plan and foreknowledge of God, you crucified and killed by the hands of lawless men. $^{24}$But God raised him up, having loosed the pangs of death, because it was not possible for him to be held by it. $^{25}$For David says concerning him, 'I saw the Lord always before me, for he is at my right hand that I may not be shaken; $^{26}$therefore my heart   20
was glad, and my tongue rejoiced; moreover my flesh will dwell in hope. $^{27}$For Thou wilt not abandon my soul to Hades, nor let Thy Holy One see corruption. $^{28}$Thou hast made known to me the ways of life; Thou wilt make me full of gladness with Thy presence.' $^{29}$Brethren, I may say to you confidently of the patriarch David that he both died and was buried, and his tomb is with us to   25
this day. $^{30}$Being therefore a prophet, and knowing that God had sworn with an oath to him that he would set one of his descendants upon his throne, $^{31}$he foresaw and spoke of the resurrection of the Christ, that he was not abandoned to Hades, nor did his flesh see corruption. $^{32}$This Jesus God raised up, and of that we all are witnesses. $^{33}$Being therefore exalted at the right hand of God, and   30
having received from the Father the promise of the Holy Spirit, he has poured out this which you see and hear. $^{34}$For David did not ascend into the heavens; but he himself says, 'The Lord said to my Lord, Sit at my right hand, $^{35}$till I make thy enemies a stool for thy feet.' $^{36}$Let all the house of Israel therefore know assuredly that God has made him both Lord and Christ, this Jesus whom   35
you crucified."

$^{37}$Now when they heard this they were cut to the heart, and said to Peter and the rest of the apostles, "Brethren, what shall we do?" $^{38}$And Peter said to them, "Repent, and be baptized every one of you in the name of Jesus Christ for the forgiveness of your sins; and you shall receive the gift of the Holy Spirit.   40

³⁹For the promise is to you and to your children and to all that are far off, every one whom the Lord our God calls to him." ⁴⁰And he testified with many other words and exhorted them, saying, "Save yourselves from this crooked generation." ⁴¹So those who received his word were baptized, and there were added that day about three thousand souls.

⁴²And they devoted themselves to the apostles' teaching and fellowship, to the breaking of bread and the prayers. ⁴³And fear came upon every soul; and many wonders and signs were done through the apostles. ⁴⁴And all who believed were together and had all things in common; ⁴⁵and they sold their possessions and goods and distributed them to all, as any had need. ⁴⁶And day by day, attending the temple together and breaking bread in their homes, they partook of food with glad and generous hearts, ⁴⁷praising God and having favor with all the people. And the Lord added to their number day by day those who were being saved....

9 ¹But Saul, still breathing threats and murder against the disciples of the Lord, went to the high priest ²and asked him for letters to the synagogues at Damascus, so that if he found any belonging to the Way, men or women, he might bring them bound to Jerusalem.

³Now as he journeyed he approached Damascus, and suddenly a light from heaven flashed about him. ⁴And he fell to the ground and heard a voice saying to him, "Saul, Saul, why do you persecute me?" ⁵And he said, "Who are you, Lord?" And he said, "I am Jesus, whom you are persecuting; ⁶but rise and enter the city, and you will be told what you are to do." ⁷The men who were traveling with him stood speechless, hearing the voice but seeing no one. ⁸Saul arose from the ground; and when his eyes were opened, he could see nothing; so they led him by the hand and brought him into Damascus. ⁹And for three days he was without sight, and neither ate nor drank.

¹⁰Now there was a disciple at Damascus named Ananias. The Lord said to him in a vision, "Ananias." And he said, "Here I am, Lord." ¹¹And the Lord said to him, "Rise and go to the street called Straight, and inquire in the house of Judas for a man of Tarsus named Saul; for behold, he is praying, ¹²and he has seen a man named Ananias come in and lay his hands on him so that he might regain his sight." ¹³But Ananias answered, "Lord, I have heard from many about this man, how much evil he has done to Thy saints at Jerusalem; ¹⁴and here he has authority from the chief priests to bind all who call upon Thy name."

¹⁵But the Lord said to him, "Go, for he is a chosen instrument of mine to carry my name before the Gentiles and kings and the sons of Israel; ¹⁶for I will show him how much he must suffer for the sake of my name." ¹⁷So Ananias departed and entered the house. And laying his hands on him he

said, "Brother Saul, the Lord Jesus who appeared to you on the road by which you came, has sent me that you may regain your sight and be filled with the Holy Spirit." [18]And immediately something like scales fell from his eyes and he regained his sight. Then he rose and was baptized, [19]and took food and was strengthened. For several days he was with the disciples at Damascus. [20]And in the synagogues immediately he proclaimed Jesus, saying, "He is the Son of God." [21]And all who heard him were amazed, and said, "Is not this the man who made havoc in Jerusalem of those who called on this name? And he has come here for this purpose, to bring them bound before the chief priests." [22]But Saul increased all the more in strength, and confounded the Jews who lived in Damascus by proving that Jesus was the Christ.

[23]When many days had passed, the Jews plotted to kill him, [24]but their plot became known to Saul. They were watching the gates day and night, to kill him; [25]but his disciples took him by night and let him down over the wall, lowering him in a basket. [26]And when he had come to Jerusalem he attempted to join the disciples; and they were all afraid of him, for they did not believe that he was a disciple. [27]But Barnabas took him, and brought him to the apostles, and declared to them how on the road he had seen the Lord, who spoke to him, and how at Damascus he had preached boldly in the name of Jesus.

[28]So he went in and out among them at Jerusalem, [29]preaching boldly in the name of the Lord. And he spoke and disputed against the Hellenists; but they were seeking to kill him. [30]And when the brethren knew it, they brought him down to Caesarea, and sent him off to Tarsus. [31]So the church throughout all Judea and Galilee and Samaria had peace and was built up; and walking in the fear of the Lord and in the comfort of the Holy Spirit it was multiplied.

[32]Now as Peter went here and there among them all, he came down also to the saints that lived at Lydda. [33]There he found a man named Aeneas, who had been bedridden for eight years and was paralyzed. [34]And Peter said to him, "Aeneas, Jesus Christ heals you; rise and make your bed." And immediately he rose. [35]And all the residents of Lydda and Sharon saw him, and they turned to the Lord.

[36]Now there was at Joppa a disciple named Tabitha, which means Dorcas. She was full of good works and acts of charity. [37]In those days she fell sick and died; and when they had washed her, they laid her in an upper room. [38]Since Lydda was near Joppa, the disciples, hearing that Peter was there, sent two men to him entreating him, "Please come to us without delay." [39]So Peter rose and went with them. And when he had come, they took him to the upper room. All the widows stood beside him weeping, and showing tunics and other garments which Dorcas made while she was with them. [40]But Peter put them all outside and knelt down and prayed; then turning to the body he said, "Tabitha, rise."

And she opened her eyes, and when she saw Peter she sat up. [41]And he gave her his hand and lifted her up. Then calling the saints and widows he presented her alive. [42]And it became known throughout all Joppa, and many believed in the Lord. [43]And he stayed in Joppa for many days with one Simon, a tanner....

5      1 1 [1]Now the apostles and the brethren who were in Judea heard that the Gentiles also had received the word of God. [2]So when Peter went up to Jerusalem, the circumcision party criticized him, [3]saying, "Why did you go to uncircumcised men and eat with them?" [4]But Peter began and explained to them in order, [5]"I was in the city of Joppa praying; and in a trance I saw a 10 vision, something descending, like a great sheet, let down from heaven by four corners; and it came down to me. [6]Looking at it closely I observed animals and beasts of prey and reptiles and birds of the air. [7]And I heard a voice saying to me, 'Rise, Peter; kill and eat.' [8]But I said, 'No, Lord; for nothing common or unclean has ever entered my mouth.' [9]But the voice answered a second time 15 from heaven, 'What God has cleansed you must not call common.' [10]This happened three times, and all was drawn up again into heaven.

[11]At that very moment three men arrived at the house in which we were, sent to me from Caesarea. [12]And the Spirit told me to go with them, making no distinction. These six brethren also accompanied me, and we entered the 20 man's house. [13]And he told us how he had seen the angel standing in his house and saying, 'Send to Joppa and bring Simon called Peter; [14]he will declare to you a message by which you will be saved, you and all your household.' [15]As I began to speak, the Holy Spirit fell on them just as on us at the beginning. [16]And I remembered the word of the Lord, how he said, 'John baptized with 25 water, but you shall be baptized with the Holy Spirit.' [17]If then God gave the same gift to them as he gave to us when we believed in the Lord Jesus Christ, who was I that I could withstand God?" [18]When they heard this they were silenced. And they glorified God, saying, "Then to the Gentiles also God has granted repentance unto life."

30           [19]Now those who were scattered because of the persecution that arose over Stephen traveled as far as Phoenicia and Cyprus and Antioch, speaking the word to none except Jews. [20]But there were some of them, men of Cyprus and Cyrene, who on coming to Antioch spoke to the Greeks also, preaching the Lord Jesus. [21]And the hand of the Lord was with them, and a great 35 number that believed turned to the Lord. [22]News of this came to the ears of the church in Jerusalem, and they sent Barnabas to Antioch. [23]When he came and saw the grace of God, he was glad; and he exhorted them all to remain faithful to the Lord with steadfast purpose; [24]for he was a good man, full of the Holy Spirit and of faith. And a large company was added to the Lord.

$^{25}$So Barnabas went to Tarsus to look for Saul; $^{26}$and when he had found him, he brought him to Antioch. For a whole year they met with the church, and taught a large company of people; and in Antioch the disciples were for the first time called Christians.

$^{27}$Now in these days prophets came down from Jerusalem to Antioch. 5 $^{28}$And one of them named Agabus stood up and foretold by the Spirit that there would be a great famine over all the world; and this took place in the days of Claudius. $^{29}$And the disciples determined, every one according to his ability, to send relief to the brethren who lived in Judea; $^{30}$and they did so, sending it to the elders by the hand of Barnabas and Saul.... 10

13 $^{1}$Now in the church at Antioch there were prophets and teachers, Barnabas, Simeon who was called Niger, Lucius of Cyrene, Manaen, a member of the court of Herod the tetrarch, and Saul. $^{2}$While they were worshiping the Lord and fasting, the Holy Spirit said, "Set apart for me Barnabas and Saul for the work to which I have called them." $^{3}$Then after fasting and praying they 15 laid their hands on them and sent them off.

$^{4}$So, being sent out by the Holy Spirit, they went down to Seleucia; and from there they sailed to Cyprus. $^{5}$When they arrived at Salamis, they proclaimed the word of God in the synagogues of the Jews. And they had John to assist them. $^{6}$When they had gone through the whole island as far as 20 Paphos, they came upon a certain magician, a Jewish false prophet, named Bar-Jesus. $^{7}$He was with the proconsul, Sergius Paulus, a man of intelligence, who summoned Barnabas and Saul and sought to hear the word of God. $^{8}$But Elymas the magician (for that is the meaning of his name) withstood them, seeking to turn away the proconsul from the faith. $^{9}$But Saul, who is also called 25 Paul, filled with the Holy Spirit, looked intently at him $^{10}$and said, "You son of the devil, you enemy of all righteousness, full of all deceit and villainy, will you not stop making crooked the straight paths of the Lord? $^{11}$And now, behold, the hand of the Lord is upon you, and you shall be blind and unable to see the sun for a time." Immediately mist and darkness fell upon him and he went about 30 seeking people to lead him by the hand. $^{12}$Then the proconsul believed, when he saw what had occurred, for he was astonished at the teaching of the Lord.

$^{13}$Now Paul and his company set sail from Paphos, and came to Perga in Pamphylia. And John left them and returned to Jerusalem; $^{14}$but they passed on from Perga and came to Antioch of Pisidia. And on the sabbath day they 35 went into the synagogue and sat down. $^{15}$After the reading of the law and the prophets, the rulers of the synagogue sent to them, saying, "Brethren, if you have any word of exhortation for the people, say it." $^{16}$So Paul stood up, and motioning with his hand said: "Men of Israel, and you that fear God, listen.

[17]The God of this people Israel chose our fathers and made the people great during their stay in the land of Egypt, and with uplifted arm he led them out of it. [18]And for about forty years he bore with them in the wilderness. [19]And when he had destroyed seven nations in the land of Canaan, he gave them their

5   land as an inheritance, for about four hundred and fifty years. [20]And after that he gave them judges until Samuel the prophet. [21]Then they asked for a king; and God gave them Saul the son of Kish, a man of the tribe of Benjamin, for forty years. [22]And when he had removed him, he raised up David to be their king; of whom he testified and said, 'I have found in David the son of Jesse a

10  man after my heart, who will do all my will.'"

[23]"Of this man's posterity God has brought to Israel a Savior, Jesus, as he promised. [24]Before his coming John had preached a baptism of repentance to all the people of Israel. [25]And as John was finishing his course, he said, 'What do you suppose that I am? I am not he. No, but after me one is com-

15  ing, the sandals of whose feet I am not worthy to untie.' [26]Brethren, sons of the family of Abraham, and those among you that fear God, to us has been sent the message of this salvation. [27]For those who live in Jerusalem and their rulers, because they did not recognize him nor understand the utterances of the prophets which are read every sabbath, fulfilled these by condemning him.

20  [28]Though they could charge him with nothing deserving death, yet they asked Pilate to have him killed. [29]And when they had fulfilled all that was written of him, they took him down from the tree, and laid him in a tomb. [30]But God raised him from the dead; [31]and for many days he appeared to those who came up with him from Galilee to Jerusalem, who are now his witnesses to the

25  people. [32]And we bring you the good news that what God promised to the fathers, [33]this he has fulfilled to us their children by raising Jesus; as also it is written in the second psalm, 'Thou art my Son, today I have begotten thee.' [34]And as for the fact that he raised him from the dead, no more to return to corruption, he spoke in this way, 'I will give you the holy and sure bless-

30  ings of David.' [35]Therefore he says also in another psalm, 'Thou wilt not let Thy Holy One see corruption.' [36]For David, after he had served the counsel of God in his own generation, fell asleep, and was laid with his fathers, and saw corruption; [37]but he whom God raised up saw no corruption. [38]Let it be known to you therefore, brethren, that through this man forgiveness of

35  sins is proclaimed to you, [39]and by him every one that believes is freed from everything from which you could not be freed by the law of Moses. [40]Beware, therefore, lest there come upon you what is said in the prophets: [41]'Behold, you scoffers, and wonder, and perish; for I do a deed in your days, a deed you will never believe, if one declares it to you.'"

⁴²As they went out, the people begged that these things might be told them the next sabbath. ⁴³And when the meeting of the synagogue broke up, many Jews and devout converts to Judaism followed Paul and Barnabas, who spoke to them and urged them to continue in the grace of God. ⁴⁴The next sabbath almost the whole city gathered together to hear the word of God. ⁴⁵But when the Jews saw the multitudes, they were filled with jealousy, and contradicted what was spoken by Paul, and reviled him. ⁴⁶And Paul and Barnabas spoke out boldly, saying, "It was necessary that the word of God should be spoken first to you. Since you thrust it from you, and judge yourselves unworthy of eternal life, behold, we turn to the Gentiles. ⁴⁷For so the Lord has commanded us, saying, 'I have set you to be a light for the Gentiles, that you may bring salvation to the uttermost parts of the earth.'"

⁴⁸And when the Gentiles heard this, they were glad and glorified the word of God; and as many as were ordained to eternal life believed. ⁴⁹And the word of the Lord spread throughout all the region. ⁵⁰But the Jews incited the devout women of high standing and the leading men of the city, and stirred up persecution against Paul and Barnabas, and drove them out of their district. ⁵¹But they shook off the dust from their feet against them, and went to Iconium. ⁵²And the disciples were filled with joy and with the Holy Spirit....

15 ¹But some men came down from Judea and were teaching the brethren, "Unless you are circumcised according to the custom of Moses, you cannot be saved." ²And when Paul and Barnabas had no small dissension and debate with them, Paul and Barnabas and some of the others were appointed to go up to Jerusalem to the apostles and the elders about this question. ³So, being sent on their way by the church, they passed through both Phoenicia and Samaria, reporting the conversion of the Gentiles, and they gave great joy to all the brethren. ⁴When they came to Jerusalem, they were welcomed by the church and the apostles and the elders, and they declared all that God had done with them. ⁵But some believers who belonged to the party of the Pharisees rose up, and said, "It is necessary to circumcise them, and to charge them to keep the law of Moses."

⁶The apostles and the elders were gathered together to consider this matter. ⁷And after there had been much debate, Peter rose and said to them, "Brethren, you know that in the early days God made choice among you, that by my mouth the Gentiles should hear the word of the gospel and believe. ⁸And God who knows the heart bore witness to them, giving them the Holy Spirit just as he did to us; ⁹and he made no distinction between us and them, but cleansed their hearts by faith. ¹⁰Now therefore why do you make trial of God by putting a yoke upon the neck of the disciples which neither our fathers nor we have been

able to bear? [11]But we believe that we shall be saved through the grace of the Lord Jesus, just as they will." [12]And all the assembly kept silence; and they listened to Barnabas and Paul as they related what signs and wonders God had done through them among the Gentiles.

[13]After they finished speaking, James replied, "Brethren, listen to me. [14]Simeon has related how God first visited the Gentiles, to take out of them a people for his name. [15]And with this the words of the prophets agree, as it is written, [16]'After this I will return, and I will rebuild the dwelling of David, which has fallen; I will rebuild its ruins, and I will set it up, [17]that the rest of men may seek the Lord, and all the Gentiles who are called by my name, [18]says the Lord, who has made these things known from of old.' [19]Therefore my judgment is that we should not trouble those of the Gentiles who turn to God, [20]but should write to them to abstain from the pollutions of idols and from un-chastity and from what is strangled and from blood. [21]For from early generations Moses has had in every city those who preach him, for he is read every sabbath in the synagogues."

[22]Then it seemed good to the apostles and the elders, with the whole church, to choose men from among them and send them to Antioch with Paul and Barnabas. They sent Judas called Barsabbas, and Silas, leading men among the brethren, [23]with the following letter: "The brethren, both the apostles and the elders, to the brethren who are of the Gentiles in Antioch and Syria and Cilicia, greeting. [24]Since we have heard that some persons from us have troubled you with words, unsettling your minds, although we gave them no instructions, [25]it has seemed good to us, having come to one accord, to choose men and send them to you with our beloved Barnabas and Paul, [26]men who have risked their lives for the sake of our Lord Jesus Christ. [27]We have therefore sent Judas and Silas, who themselves will tell you the same things by word of mouth. [28]For it has seemed good to the Holy Spirit and to us to lay upon you no greater burden than these necessary things: [29]that you abstain from what has been sacrificed to idols and from blood and from what is strangled and from un-chastity. If you keep yourselves from these, you will do well. Farewell."

[30]So when they were sent off, they went down to Antioch; and having gathered the congregation together, they delivered the letter. [31]And when they read it, they rejoiced at the exhortation. [32]And Judas and Silas, who were themselves prophets, exhorted the brethren with many words and strengthened them. [33]And after they had spent some time, they were sent off in peace by the brethren to those who had sent them.[35]But Paul and Barnabas remained in Antioch, teaching and preaching the word of the Lord, with many others also.

[36]And after some days Paul said to Barnabas, "Come, let us return and visit the brethren in every city where we proclaimed the word of the Lord, and see

how they are." <sup>37</sup>And Barnabas wanted to take with them John called Mark.
<sup>38</sup>But Paul thought best not to take with them one who had withdrawn from
them in Pamphylia, and had not gone with them to the work. <sup>39</sup>And there arose
a sharp contention, so that they separated from each other; Barnabas took Mark
with him and sailed away to Cyprus, <sup>40</sup>but Paul chose Silas and departed, being
commended by the brethren to the grace of the Lord. <sup>41</sup>And he went through
Syria and Cilicia, strengthening the churches....

17 <sup>1</sup>Now when they had passed through Amphipolis and Apollonia, they
came to Thessalonica, where there was a synagogue of the Jews.
<sup>2</sup>And Paul went in, as was his custom, and for three weeks he argued with
them from the scriptures, <sup>3</sup>explaining and proving that it was necessary for
the Christ to suffer and to rise from the dead, and saying, "This Jesus, whom I
proclaim to you, is the Christ." <sup>4</sup>And some of them were persuaded, and joined
Paul and Silas; as did a great many of the devout Greeks and not a few of the
leading women.

<sup>5</sup>But the Jews were jealous, and taking some wicked fellows of the rabble,
they gathered a crowd, set the city in an uproar, and attacked the house of
Jason, seeking to bring them out to the people. <sup>6</sup>And when they could not find
them, they dragged Jason and some of the brethren before the city authorities,
crying, "These men who have turned the world upside down have come here
also, <sup>7</sup>and Jason has received them; and they are all acting against the decrees of
Caesar, saying that there is another king, Jesus." <sup>8</sup>And the people and the city
authorities were disturbed when they heard this. <sup>9</sup>And when they had taken
security from Jason and the rest, they let them go.

<sup>10</sup>The brethren immediately sent Paul and Silas away by night to Beroea;
and when they arrived they went into the Jewish synagogue. <sup>11</sup>Now these Jews
were more noble than those in Thessalonica, for they received the word with all
eagerness, examining the scriptures daily to see if these things were so. <sup>12</sup>Many
of them therefore believed, with not a few Greek women of high standing as
well as men. <sup>13</sup>But when the Jews of Thessalonica learned that the word of God
was proclaimed by Paul at Beroea also, they came there too, stirring up and
inciting the crowds. <sup>14</sup>Then the brethren immediately sent Paul off on his way
to the sea, but Silas and Timothy remained there. <sup>15</sup>Those who conducted Paul
brought him as far as Athens; and receiving a command for Silas and Timothy
to come to him as soon as possible, they departed.

<sup>16</sup>Now while Paul was waiting for them at Athens, his spirit was provoked
within him as he saw that the city was full of idols. <sup>17</sup>So he argued in the synagogue with the Jews and the devout persons, and in the marketplace every day
with those who chanced to be there. <sup>18</sup>Some also of the Epicurean and Stoic

philosophers met him. And some said, "What would this babbler say?" Others said, "He seems to be a preacher of foreign divinities"—because he preached Jesus and the resurrection. [19]And they took hold of him and brought him to the Areopagus, saying, "May we know what this new teaching is which you present? [20]For you bring some strange things to our ears; we wish to know therefore what these things mean." [21]Now all the Athenians and the foreigners who lived there spent their time in nothing except telling or hearing something new.

[22]So Paul, standing in the middle of the Areopagus, said: "Men of Athens, I perceive that in every way you are very religious. [23]For as I passed along, and observed the objects of your worship, I found also an altar with this inscription, 'To an unknown god.' What therefore you worship as unknown, this I proclaim to you. [24]The God who made the world and everything in it, being Lord of heaven and earth, does not live in shrines made by man, [25]nor is he served by human hands, as though he needed anything, since he himself gives to all men life and breath and everything. [26]And he made from one every nation of men to live on all the face of the earth, having determined allotted periods and the boundaries of their habitation, [27]that they should seek God, in the hope that they might feel after him and find him. Yet he is not far from each one of us, [28]for 'In him we live and move and have our being'; as even some of your poets have said, 'For we are indeed his offspring.' [29]Being then God's offspring, we ought not to think that the Deity is like gold, or silver, or stone, a representation by the art and imagination of man. [30]The times of ignorance God overlooked, but now he commands all men everywhere to repent, [31]because he has fixed a day on which he will judge the world in righteousness by a man whom he has appointed, and of this he has given assurance to all men by raising him from the dead."

[32]Now when they heard of the resurrection of the dead, some mocked; but others said, "We will hear you again about this." [33]So Paul went out from among them. [34]But some men joined him and believed, among them Dionysius the Areopagite and a woman named Damaris and others with them....

**22** [1]"Brethren and fathers, hear the defense which I now make before you." [2]And when they heard that he addressed them in the Hebrew language, they were the more quiet. And he said, [3]"I am a Jew, born at Tarsus in Cilicia, but brought up in this city at the feet of Gamaliel, educated according to the strict manner of the law of our fathers, being zealous for God as you all are this day. [4]I persecuted this Way to the death, binding and delivering to prison both men and women, [5]as the high priest and the whole council of elders bear me witness. From them I received letters to the brethren, and I journeyed to Damascus to take those also who were there and bring them in bonds to Jerusalem to be punished."

⁶"As I made my journey and drew near to Damascus, about noon a great light from heaven suddenly shone about me. ⁷And I fell to the ground and heard a voice saying to me, 'Saul, Saul, why do you persecute me?' ⁸And I answered, 'Who are you, Lord?' And he said to me, 'I am Jesus of Nazareth whom you are persecuting.' ⁹Now those who were with me saw the light but did not hear the voice of the one who was speaking to me. ¹⁰And I said, 'What shall I do, Lord?' And the Lord said to me, 'Rise, and go into Damascus, and there you will be told all that is appointed for you to do.' ¹¹And when I could not see because of the brightness of that light, I was led by the hand by those who were with me, and came into Damascus."

¹²"And one Ananias, a devout man according to the law, well spoken of by all the Jews who lived there, ¹³came to me, and standing by me said to me, 'Brother Saul, receive your sight.' And in that very hour I received my sight and saw him. ¹⁴And he said, 'The God of our fathers appointed you to know his will, to see the Just One and to hear a voice from his mouth; ¹⁵for you will be a witness for him to all men of what you have seen and heard. ¹⁶And now why do you wait? Rise and be baptized, and wash away your sins, calling on his name.'"

¹⁷"When I had returned to Jerusalem and was praying in the temple, I fell into a trance ¹⁸and saw him saying to me, 'Make haste and get quickly out of Jerusalem, because they will not accept your testimony about me.' ¹⁹And I said, 'Lord, they themselves know that in every synagogue I imprisoned and beat those who believed in thee. ²⁰And when the blood of Stephen thy witness was shed, I also was standing by and approving, and keeping the garments of those who killed him.' ²¹And he said to me, 'Depart; for I will send you far away to the Gentiles.'"

²²Up to this word they listened to him; then they lifted up their voices and said, "Away with such a fellow from the earth! For he ought not to live." ²³And as they cried out and waved their garments and threw dust into the air, ²⁴the tribune commanded him to be brought into the barracks, and ordered him to be examined by scourging, to find out why they shouted thus against him. ²⁵But when they had tied him up with the thongs, Paul said to the centurion who was standing by, "Is it lawful for you to scourge a man who is a Roman citizen, and un-condemned?" ²⁶When the centurion heard that, he went to the tribune and said to him, "What are you about to do? For this man is a Roman citizen." ²⁷So the tribune came and said to him, "Tell me, are you a Roman citizen?" And he said, "Yes." ²⁸The tribune answered, "I bought this citizenship

for a large sum." Paul said, "But I was born a citizen." **29**So those who were about to examine him withdrew from him instantly; and the tribune also was afraid, for he realized that Paul was a Roman citizen and that he had bound him. **30**But on the morrow, desiring to know the real reason why the Jews accused

5      him, he unbound him, and commanded the chief priests and all the council to meet, and he brought Paul down and set him before them....

# GALATIANS

*Paul wrote this epistle, probably in AD 54 or 55, out of concern that the
churches of Galatia had come under the influence of Judaizers—those who
would force Gentile converts to undergo circumcision and adhere fully to
the demands of the Mosaic law.*

1 ¹Paul an apostle—not from men nor through man, but through Jesus
Christ and God the Father, who raised him from the dead—²and all the
brethren who are with me, To the churches of Galatia: ³Grace to you and peace
from God the Father and our Lord Jesus Christ, ⁴who gave himself for our sins
to deliver us from the present evil age, according to the will of our God and
Father; ⁵to whom be the glory forever and ever. Amen.

⁶I am astonished that you are so quickly deserting him who called you in
the grace of Christ and turning to a different gospel—⁷not that there is another
gospel, but there are some who trouble you and want to pervert the gospel of
Christ. ⁸But even if we, or an angel from heaven, should preach to you a gospel
contrary to that which we preached to you, let him be accursed. ⁹As we have
said before, so now I say again, If anyone is preaching to you a gospel contrary
to that which you received, let him be accursed.

¹⁰Am I now seeking the favor of men, or of God? Or am I trying to please
men? If I were still pleasing men, I should not be a servant of Christ. ¹¹For I
would have you know, brethren, that the gospel which was preached by me is
not man's gospel. ¹²For I did not receive it from man, nor was I taught it, but it
came through a revelation of Jesus Christ. ¹³For you have heard of my former life
in Judaism, how I persecuted the church of God violently and tried to destroy
it; ¹⁴and I advanced in Judaism beyond many of my own age among my people,
so extremely zealous was I for the traditions of my fathers. ¹⁵But when he who
had set me apart before I was born, and had called me through his grace, ¹⁶was
pleased to reveal his Son to me, in order that I might preach him among the
Gentiles, I did not confer with flesh and blood, ¹⁷nor did I go up to Jerusalem
to those who were apostles before me, but I went away into Arabia; and again
I returned to Damascus. ¹⁸Then after three years I went up to Jerusalem to visit

Cephas, and remained with him fifteen days. **19**But I saw none of the other apostles except James the Lord's brother. **20**(In what I am writing to you, before God, I do not lie!) **21**Then I went into the regions of Syria and Cilicia. **22**And I was still not known by sight to the churches of Christ in Judea; **23**they only heard it said, "He who once persecuted us is now preaching the faith he once tried to destroy." **24**And they glorified God because of me.

2 **1** Then after fourteen years I went up again to Jerusalem with Barnabas, taking Titus along with me. **2**I went up by revelation; and I laid before them (but privately before those who were of repute) the gospel which I preach among the Gentiles, lest somehow I should be running or had run in vain. **3**But even Titus, who was with me, was not compelled to be circumcised, though he was a Greek. **4**But because of false brethren secretly brought in, who slipped in to spy out our freedom which we have in Christ Jesus, that they might bring us into bondage—**5**to them we did not yield submission even for a moment, that the truth of the gospel might be preserved for you. **6**And from those who were reputed to be something (what they were makes no difference to me; God shows no partiality)—those, I say, who were of repute added nothing to me; **7**but on the contrary, when they saw that I had been entrusted with the gospel to the uncircumcised, just as Peter had been entrusted with the gospel to the circumcised **8**(for he who worked through Peter for the mission to the circumcised worked through me also for the Gentiles), **9**and when they perceived the grace that was given to me, James and Cephas and John, who were reputed to be pillars, gave to me and Barnabas the right hand of fellowship, that we should go to the Gentiles and they to the circumcised; **10**only they would have us remember the poor, which very thing I was eager to do.

**11**But when Cephas came to Antioch I opposed him to his face, because he stood condemned. **12**For before certain men came from James, he ate with the Gentiles; but when they came he drew back and separated himself, fearing the circumcision party. **13**And with him the rest of the Jews acted insincerely, so that even Barnabas was carried away by their insincerity. **14**But when I saw that they were not straightforward about the truth of the gospel, I said to Cephas before them all, "If you, though a Jew, live like a Gentile and not like a Jew, how can you compel the Gentiles to live like Jews?" **15**We ourselves, who are Jews by birth and not Gentile sinners, **16**yet who know that a man is not justified by works of the law but through faith in Jesus Christ, even we have believed in Christ Jesus, in order to be justified by faith in Christ, and not by works of the law, because by works of the law shall no one be justified. **17**But if, in our endeavor to be justified in Christ, we ourselves were found to be sinners, is Christ then an agent of sin? Certainly not! **18**But if I build up again those things which I tore down, then I prove myself a transgressor. For I through the law died to the law, that I might live to God. **20**I have been crucified with Christ; it is no longer I who live, but Christ who lives in me; and the life I now live in the flesh I live by faith in the Son of God, who loved me and gave himself for me. **21**I do not nullify the grace of God; for if justification were through the law, then Christ died to no purpose.                                        5

**3** **1**O foolish Galatians! Who has bewitched you, before whose eyes Jesus Christ was publicly portrayed as crucified? **2**Let me ask you only this: Did you receive the Spirit by works of the law, or by hearing with faith? **3**Are you so foolish? Having begun with the Spirit, are you now ending with   10 the flesh? **4**Did you experience so many things in vain?—if it really is in vain. **5**Does he who supplies the Spirit to you and works miracles among you do so by works of the law, or by hearing with faith?

**6**Thus Abraham "believed God, and it was reckoned to him as righteousness." **7**So you see that it is men of faith who are the sons of Abraham. **8**And   15 the scripture, foreseeing that God would justify the Gentiles by faith, preached the gospel beforehand to Abraham, saying, "In you shall all the nations be blessed." **9**So then, those who are men of faith are blessed with Abraham who had faith. **10**For all who rely on works of the law are under a curse; for it is written, "Cursed be everyone who does not abide by all things written in the book   20 of the law, and do them." **11**Now it is evident that no man is justified before God by the law; for "He who through faith is righteous shall live"; **12**but the law does not rest on faith, for "He who does them shall live by them." **13**Christ redeemed us from the curse of the law, having become a curse for us—for it is written, "Cursed be everyone who hangs on a tree"—**14**that in Christ Jesus the   25 blessing of Abraham might come upon the Gentiles, that we might receive the promise of the Spirit through faith. **15**To give a human example, brethren: no one annuls even a man's will, or adds to it, once it has been ratified. **16**Now the promises were made to Abraham and to his offspring. It does not say, "And to offsprings," referring to many; but, referring to one, "And to your offspring,"   30 which is Christ. **17**This is what I mean: the law, which came four hundred and thirty years afterward, does not annul a covenant previously ratified by God, so as to make the promise void. **18**For if the inheritance is by the law, it is no longer by promise; but God gave it to Abraham by a promise.

**19**Why then the law? It was added because of transgressions, till the off-   35 spring should come to whom the promise had been made; and it was ordained by angels through an intermediary. **20**Now an intermediary implies more than one; but God is one. **21**Is the law then against the promises of God? Certainly not; for if a law had been given which could make alive, then righteousness

would indeed be by the law. **²²**But the scripture consigned all things to sin, that what was promised to faith in Jesus Christ might be given to those who believe. **²³**Now before faith came, we were confined under the law, kept under restraint until faith should be revealed. **²⁴**So that the law was our custodian until Christ
5 came, that we might be justified by faith. **²⁵**But now that faith has come, we are no longer under a custodian; **²⁶**for in Christ Jesus you are all sons of God, through faith. **²⁷**For as many of you as were baptized into Christ have put on Christ. **²⁸**There is neither Jew nor Greek, there is neither slave nor free, there is neither male nor female; for you are all one in Christ Jesus. **²⁹**And if you are
10 Christ's, then you are Abraham's offspring, heirs according to promise.

4 **¹**I mean that the heir, as long as he is a child, is no better than a slave, though he is the owner of all the estate; **²**but he is under guardians and trustees until the date set by the father. **³**So with us; when we were children, we were slaves to the elemental spirits of the universe. **⁴**But when the time had
15 fully come, God sent forth his Son, born of woman, born under the law, **⁵**to redeem those who were under the law, so that we might receive adoption as sons. **⁶**And because you are sons, God has sent the Spirit of his Son into our hearts, crying, "Abba! Father!" **⁷**So through God you are no longer a slave but a son, and if a son then an heir.

20 **⁸**Formerly, when you did not know God, you were in bondage to beings that by nature are no gods; **⁹**but now that you have come to know God, or rather to be known by God, how can you turn back again to the weak and beggarly elemental spirits, whose slaves you want to be once more? **¹⁰**You observe days, and months, and seasons, and years! **¹¹**I am afraid I have labored over
25 you in vain.

**¹²**Brethren, I beseech you, become as I am, for I also have become as you are. You did me no wrong; **¹³**you know it was because of a bodily ailment that I preached the gospel to you at first; **¹⁴**and though my condition was a trial to you, you did not scorn or despise me, but received me as an angel of God, as
30 Christ Jesus. **¹⁵**What has become of the satisfaction you felt? For I bear you witness that, if possible, you would have plucked out your eyes and given them to me. **¹⁶**Have I then become your enemy by telling you the truth?

**¹⁷**They make much of you, but for no good purpose; they want to shut you out, that you may make much of them. **¹⁸**For a good purpose it is always good
35 to be made much of, and not only when I am present with you.

**¹⁹**My little children, with whom I am again in travail until Christ be formed in you! **²⁰**I could wish to be present with you now and to change my tone, for I am perplexed about you.

<sup>21</sup>Tell me, you who desire to be under law, do you not hear the law? <sup>22</sup>For it is written that Abraham had two sons, one by a slave and one by a free woman. <sup>23</sup>But the son of the slave was born according to the flesh, the son of the free woman through promise. <sup>24</sup>Now this is an allegory: these women are two covenants. One is from Mount Sinai, bearing children for slavery; she is Hagar. <sup>25</sup>Now Hagar is Mount Sinai in Arabia; she corresponds to the present Jerusalem, for she is in slavery with her children. <sup>26</sup>But the Jerusalem above is free, and she is our mother. <sup>27</sup>For it is written, "Rejoice, O barren one who does not bear; break forth and shout, you who are not in travail; for the children of the desolate one are many more than the children of her that is married." <sup>28</sup>Now we, brethren, like Isaac, are children of promise. <sup>29</sup>But as at that time he who was born according to the flesh persecuted him who was born according to the Spirit, so it is now. <sup>30</sup>But what does the scripture say? "Cast out the slave and her son; for the son of the slave shall not inherit with the son of the free woman." <sup>31</sup>So, brethren, we are not children of the slave but of the free woman.

5 <sup>1</sup>For freedom Christ has set us free; stand fast therefore, and do not submit again to a yoke of slavery. <sup>2</sup>Now I, Paul, say to you that if you receive circumcision, Christ will be of no advantage to you. <sup>3</sup>I testify again to every man who receives circumcision that he is bound to keep the whole law. <sup>4</sup>You are severed from Christ, you who would be justified by the law; you have fallen away from grace. <sup>5</sup>For through the Spirit, by faith, we wait for the hope of righteousness. <sup>6</sup>For in Christ Jesus neither circumcision nor un-circumcision is of any avail, but faith working through love. <sup>7</sup>You were running well; who hindered you from obeying the truth? <sup>8</sup>This persuasion is not from him who calls you. <sup>9</sup>A little leaven leavens the whole lump. <sup>10</sup>I have confidence in the Lord that you will take no other view than mine; and he who is troubling you will bear his judgment, whoever he is. <sup>11</sup>But if I, brethren, still preach circumcision, why am I still persecuted? In that case the stumbling block of the cross has been removed. <sup>12</sup>I wish those who unsettle you would mutilate themselves!

<sup>13</sup>For you were called to freedom, brethren; only do not use your freedom as an opportunity for the flesh, but through love be servants of one another. <sup>14</sup>For the whole law is fulfilled in one word, "You shall love your neighbor as yourself." <sup>15</sup>But if you bite and devour one another take heed that you are not consumed by one another. <sup>16</sup>But I say, walk by the Spirit, and do not gratify the desires of the flesh. <sup>17</sup>For the desires of the flesh are against the Spirit, and the desires of the Spirit are against the flesh; for these are opposed to each other, to prevent you from doing what you would. <sup>18</sup>But if you are led by the Spirit you are not under the law. <sup>19</sup>Now the works of the flesh are plain: fornication,

impurity, licentiousness, [20]idolatry, sorcery, enmity, strife, jealousy, anger, self-ishness, dissension, party spirit, [21]envy, drunkenness, carousing, and the like. I warn you, as I warned you before, that those who do such things shall not inherit the kingdom of God. [22]But the fruit of the Spirit is love, joy, peace, patience, kindness, goodness, faithfulness, [23]gentleness, self-control; against such there is no law. [24]And those who belong to Christ Jesus have crucified the flesh with its passions and desires. [25]If we live by the Spirit, let us also walk by the Spirit. [26]Let us have no self-conceit, no provoking of one another, no envy of one another.

6 [1]Brethren, if a man is overtaken in any trespass, you who are spiritual should restore him in a spirit of gentleness. Look to yourself, lest you too be tempted. [2]Bear one another's burdens, and so fulfill the law of Christ. [3]For if anyone thinks he is something, when he is nothing, he deceives himself. [4]But let each one test his own work, and then his reason to boast will be in himself alone and not in his neighbor. [5]For each man will have to bear his own load. [6]Let him who is taught the word share all good things with him who teaches. [7]Do not be deceived; God is not mocked, for whatever a man sows, that he will also reap. [8]For he who sows to his own flesh will from the flesh reap corruption; but he who sows to the Spirit will from the Spirit reap eternal life. [9]And let us not grow weary in well-doing, for in due season we shall reap, if we do not lose heart. [10]So then, as we have opportunity, let us do good to all men, and especially to those who are of the household of faith.

[11]See with what large letters I am writing to you with my own hand. [12]It is those who want to make a good showing in the flesh that would compel you to be circumcised, and only in order that they may not be persecuted for the cross of Christ. [13]For even those who receive circumcision do not themselves keep the law, but they desire to have you circumcised that they may glory in your flesh. [14]But far be it from me to glory except in the cross of our Lord Jesus Christ, by which the world has been crucified to me, and I to the world. [15]For neither circumcision counts for anything, nor un-circumcision, but a new creation. [16]Peace and mercy be upon all who walk by this rule, upon the Israel of God. [17]Henceforth let no man trouble me; for I bear on my body the marks of Jesus. [18]The grace of our Lord Jesus Christ be with your spirit, brethren. Amen.

# PRESCRIPTION AGAINST HERETICS
## TERTULLIAN (*c.* 160–*c.* 220)

*The early Christians faced a dilemma: Was it permissible, or even desirable, to seek formal education in the schools of the Roman Empire, or should they isolate themselves from the surrounding culture to avoid the dangers to their faith posed by pagan learning? On the one hand, they could more effectively evangelize among the educated classes of the Empire if they could explain the faith in terms familiar to those steeped in Greek philosophy or Latin literature. On the other, however, philosophy promoted argumentation rather than faith; much Greek and Latin literature teemed with immorality and references to pagan gods.*

*Tertullian, a Carthaginian lawyer, blamed Greek philosophy for the growth of heresy. He saw no need for Christian teaching to be explained rationally; indeed, he argued that he "believed because it was absurd" that God should have redeemed mankind by Christ's Incarnation as a helpless infant and His death on a Cross.*

…These are "the doctrines" of men and "of demons" produced for itching ears of the spirit of this world's wisdom: this the Lord called "foolishness" and "chose the foolish things of the world"[1] to confound even philosophy itself. For (philosophy) it is which is the material of the world's wisdom, the rash interpreter of the nature and the dispensation of God. Indeed heresies are themselves    5
instigated by philosophy. From this source came the Aeons, and I know not what infinite forms, and the trinity of man in the system of Valentinus, who was of Plato's school. From the same source came Marcion's better god, with all his tranquility; he came of the Stoics. Then, again, the opinion that the soul dies is held by the Epicureans; while the denial of the restoration of the body    10
is taken from the aggregate school of all the philosophers; also, when matter is made equal to God, then you have the teaching of Zeno; and when any doctrine is alleged touching a god of fire, then Heraclitus comes in.

---

[1]I Corinthians 1:27

---

*The Ante-Nicene Fathers*, edited by A. Roberts and J. Donaldson (New York: Charles Scribner's Sons, 1903), III: 246.

The same subject-matter is discussed over and over again by the heretics and the philosophers the same arguments are involved. Whence comes evil? Why is it permitted? What is the origin of man? and in what way does he come? Besides the question which Valentinus has very lately proposed—Whence comes
5  God? Which he settles with the answer, From *enthymesis* and *ectroma*. Unhappy Aristotle! who invented for these men dialectics, the art of building up and pulling down an art so evasive in its propositions, so far-fetched in its conjectures, so harsh in its arguments, so productive of contentions—embarrassing even to itself, retracting everything, and really treating of nothing. Whence spring
10  those "fables and endless genealogies"[2] and "unprofitable questions"[3] and "words which spread like a cancer?"[4] From all these, when the apostle would restrain us, he expressly names *philosophy* as that which he would have us be on our guard against. Writing to the Colossians, he says, "See that no one beguile you through philosophy and vain deceit, after the tradition of men, and contrary
15  to the wisdom of the Holy Ghost."[5] He had been at Athens, and had in his interviews (with its philosophers) become acquainted with that human wisdom which pretends to know the truth, whilst it only corrupts it, and is itself divided into its own manifold heresies by the variety of its mutually repugnant sects.

What indeed has Athens to do with Jerusalem? What concord is there be-
20  tween the Academy[6] and the Church; what between heretics and Christians? Our instruction comes from "the porch of Solomon,"[7] who had himself taught that "the Lord should be sought in simplicity of heart." Away with all attempts to produce a mottled Christianity of Stoic, Platonic, and dialectic composition! We want no curious disputation after possessing Christ Jesus, no inquisition
25  after enjoying the gospel! With our faith, we desire no further belief. For this is our palmary faith, that there is nothing which we ought to believe besides....

---

[2] I Timothy 1:4
[3] Titus 3:9
[4] II Timothy 2:17
[5] Colossians 2:8
[6] Plato's school in Athens
[7] The Porch of Solomon referred to a part of the Temple in Jerusalem where the Apostles preached (Acts 3:11).

# ON PHILOSOPHY
## CLEMENT OF ALEXANDRIA (*c.* 150–*c.* 200)

*Clement of Alexandria was probably born in Athens, but he spent most of his life teaching "Christian philosophy" at Alexandria. Clement recognized that many Greek philosophers had taught much that was true—and from whom could they have received these truths except from God, the source of all truth?*

I§2...Those cannot condemn the Greeks who have only a mere hearsay knowledge of their opinions, and have not entered into a minute investigation in each department, in order to [develop an] acquaintance with them.... So philosophy does not ruin life by being the originator of false practices and base deeds, although some have calumniated it, though it be the clear image of truth, a    5
divine gift to the Greeks; nor does it drag us away from the faith, as if we were bewitched by some delusive art, but rather, so to speak, by the use of an ampler circuit, obtains a common exercise demonstrative of the faith....

I§5Accordingly, before the advent of the Lord, philosophy was necessary to the Greeks for righteousness. And now it becomes conducive to piety, being a kind    10
of preparatory training to those who attain to faith through demonstration. "For your foot," it is said, "will not stumble, if you refer what is good, whether belonging to the Greeks or to us, to Providence."[1] For God is the cause of all good things; but of some primarily, as of the Old and the New Testament; and of others by consequence, as philosophy. Perchance, too, philosophy was given    15
to the Greeks directly and primarily, till the Lord should call the Greeks. For this was a schoolmaster to bring "the Hellenic mind", as the law, the Hebrews, to Christ. Philosophy, therefore, was a preparation, paving the way for him who is perfected in Christ.

"Now," says Solomon, "defend wisdom, and it will exalt you, and it will    20
shield you with a crown of pleasure."[2] For when you have strengthened wisdom

---

[1]Proverbs 3:23
[2]Proverbs 4:8–9

---

*The Writings of Clement of Alexandria*, translated by William Wilson (Edinburgh: T. & T. Clark, 1867), 360, 366, 374, 379–80, 404–5 [modernized].

with a cope by philosophy, and with right expenditure, you will preserve it unassailable by sophists. The way of truth is therefore one. But into it, as into a perennial river, streams flow from all sides....

I§7The Greek preparatory culture, therefore, with philosophy itself, is shown
5   to have come down from God to men, not with a definite direction, but in the way in which showers fall down on the good land, and on the dunghill, and on the houses....

I§9Some, who think themselves naturally gifted, do not wish to touch either philosophy or logic; nay, more, they do not wish to learn natural science. They
10   demand bare faith alone, as if they wished, without bestowing any care on the vine, straightway to gather clusters from the first.... I call him truly learned who brings everything to bear on the truth, so that from geometry, music, grammar, and philosophy itself, culling what is useful, he guards the faith against assault.... And he who brings everything to bear on a right life, procuring examples from
15   the Greeks and barbarians, this man is an experienced searcher after truth... And how necessary is it for him who desires to be partaker of the power of God to treat of intellectual subjects by philosophizing!...

I§16...The Hellenic philosophy then, according to some, apprehended the truth accidentally, dimly, partially; as others will have it, was set a-going by the
20   devil. Several suppose that certain powers, descending from heaven, inspired the whole of philosophy. But if the Hellenic philosophy comprehends not the whole extent of the truth, and besides is destitute of strength to perform the commandments of the Lord, yet it prepares the way for the truly royal teaching; training in some way or other, and molding the character, and fitting him who
25   believes in Providence for the reception of the truth.

# ON CHRISTIAN DOCTRINE
## AUGUSTINE (*c.* 354–*c.* 430)
### BISHOP OF HIPPO (396–430)

*Augustine, Bishop of Hippo, unquestionably the greatest and most influential of the Latin Church Fathers, agreed with Clement that Christians should make use of the teachings of the Greek philosophers, especially Plato.*

397

Moreover, if those who are called philosophers, and especially the Platonists, have said aught that is true and in harmony with our faith, we are not only not to shrink from it, but to claim it for our own use from those who have unlawful possession of it. For, as the Egyptians had not only the idols and heavy burdens which the people of Israel hated and fled from, but also vessels and ornaments 5 of gold and silver and garments which the same people when going out of Egypt appropriated to themselves, designing them for a better use, not doing this on their own authority, but by the command of God, the Egyptians themselves, in their ignorance, providing them with things which they themselves were not making a good use of; in the same way all branches of heathen learning have 10 not only false and superstitious fancies and heavy burdens of unnecessary toil, which every one of us, when going out under the leadership of Christ from the fellowship of the heathen, ought to abhor and avoid; but they contain also liberal instruction which is better adapted to the use of the truth and some most excellent precepts of morality; and some truths in regard even to the worship 15 of the One God are found among them. Now these are, so to speak, their gold and silver, which they did not create themselves, but dug out of the mines of God's providence which are everywhere scattered abroad, and are perversely and unlawfully prostituting to the worship of devils. These, therefore, the Christian, when he separates himself in spirit from the miserable fellowship of these men, 20 ought to take away from them, and to devote to their proper use in preaching the gospel. Their garments, also—that is, human institutions such as are adapted to that intercourse with men which is indispensable in this life—we must take and turn to a Christian use....

---

*The Works of Aurelius Augustine, Bishop of Hippo*, edited by Marcus Dods (Edinburgh: T. & T. Clark, 1892), 75–76.

# THE MARTYRDOM OF PERPETUA

*Although Roman authorities were, in general, tolerant of the religions of their subjects, Christianity posed a particular difficulty. The Christians, like the Jews, refused to acknowledge any deity other than God, but whereas the Jewish refusal was rooted in long-standing ancestral tradition, something the Romans could fully appreciate, in Roman eyes the Christians had no such excuse: they worshipped as God a man the Romans themselves had executed as a criminal. Further, they called each other brother and sister, and held love feasts; they also had secret meetings in which they admitted to eating flesh and drinking blood. Ordinary Romans put all this together and came quickly to the conclusion that Christians did not make desirable neighbors; from time to time in the first two centuries of the Christian period, they demanded that the authorities take action against them. Thus, until the Decian persecution of AD 250, Roman persecutions of Christians were localized and occurred largely in response to popular demand.*

*The events described in* The Martyrdom of Perpetua *occurred in Carthage in AD 202. This work is particularly remarkable because it includes the first-person narrative of Perpetua herself, as well as an eye-witness account of the martyrdom. Stories like these helped convert many to Christianity for, as Tertullian (c. 160–c. 220) put it, "the blood of the martyrs is the seed of the Church."*

202

If instances of ancient faith which both testified to the grace of God and edified persons were written expressly for God's honor and humans' encouragement, why shouldn't recent events be similarly recorded for those same purposes? For these events will likewise become part of the past and vital to posterity, in spite of the fact that contemporary esteem for antiquity tends to minimize    5
their value. And those who maintain that there is a single manifestation of the one Holy Spirit throughout the ages ought to consider that since a fullness of grace has been decreed for the last days of the world these recent events should be considered of greater value because of their proximity to those days. For "In

*A Lost Tradition: Women Writers of the Early Church*, edited by Patricia Wilson-Kastner et al. (Lanham, MD: University Press of America, 1981), 19–30. Reprinted with permission of University Press of America, Inc.; permission conveyed through Copyright Clearance Center, Inc.

the last days," says the Lord, "I shall diffuse my spirit over all humanity and their sons and daughters shall prophesy; the young shall see visions, and the old shall dream dreams."[1]

Just as we valued those prophecies, so we acknowledge and reverence the
5   new visions which were promised. And we consider the other powers of the Holy Spirit to be instruments of the Church to which that same Spirit was sent to administer all gifts to all people, just as the Lord allotted. For this reason we deem it necessary to disseminate the written accounts for the glory of God, lest anyone with a weak or despairing faith might think that supernatural grace
10  prevailed solely among the ancients who were honored either by their experience of martyrdom or visions. For God always fulfills what he promises, either as proof to non-believers or as an added grace to believers.

And so, brothers and dear ones, we share with you those things which we have heard and touched with our hands, so that those of you who were eye-
15  witnesses of these deeds may be reminded of the glory of the Lord, and those of you now learning of it through this narration may associate yourselves with the holy martyrs and, through time, with the Lord Jesus Christ to whom there is glory and honor forever. Amen.

Arrested were some young catechumens; Revocatus and Felicitas (both
20  servants), Saturninus, Secundulus, and Vibia Perpetua, a young married woman about twenty years old, of good family and upbringing. She had a father, mother, two brothers (one was a catechumen like herself), and an infant son at the breast. The following account of her martyrdom is her own, a record in her own words of her perceptions of the event.

25  While I was still with the police authorities (she said) my father out of love for me tried to dissuade me from my resolution. "Father," I said, "do you see here, for example, this vase, or pitcher, or whatever it is?" "I see it," he said. "Can it be named anything else than what it really is?" I asked, and he said, "No." "So I also cannot be called anything else than what I am, a Christian."
30  Enraged by my words my father came at me as though to tear out my eyes. He only annoyed me, but he left, overpowered by his diabolical arguments.

For a few days my father stayed away. I thanked the Lord and felt relieved because of my father's absence. At this time we were baptized and the Spirit instructed me not to request anything from the baptismal waters except endur-
35  ance of physical suffering.

A few days later we were imprisoned. I was terrified because never before had I experienced such darkness. What a terrible day! Because of crowded conditions and rough treatment by the soldiers the heat was unbearable. My condition was

---

[1]Acts 2: 17–18

aggravated by my anxiety for my baby. Then Tertius and Pomponius, those kind deacons who were taking care of our needs, paid for us to be moved for a few hours to a better part of the prison where we might refresh ourselves. Leaving the dungeon we all went about our own business. I nursed my child, who was already weak from hunger. In my anxiety for the infant I spoke to my mother about him, tried to console my brother, and asked that they care for my son. I suffered intensely because I sensed their agony on my account. These were the trials I had to endure for many days. Then I was granted the privilege of having my son remain with me in prison. Being relieved of my anxiety and concern for the infant, I immediately regained my strength. Suddenly the prison became my palace, and I loved being there rather than any other place.

Then my brother said to me, "Dear sister, you already have such a great reputation that you could ask for a vision indicating whether you will be condemned or freed." Since I knew that I could speak with the Lord, whose great favors I had already experienced, I confidently promised to do so. I said I would tell my brother about it the next day. Then I made my request and this is what I saw.

There was a bronze ladder of extraordinary height reaching up to heaven, but it was so narrow that only one person could ascend at a time. Every conceivable kind of iron weapon was attached to the sides of the ladder: swords, lances, hooks, and daggers. If anyone climbed up carelessly or without looking upwards, he would be mangled as the flesh adhered to the weapons. Crouching directly beneath the ladder was a monstrous dragon who threatened those climbing up and tried to frighten them from ascent.

Saturus went up first. Because of his concern for us he had given himself up voluntarily after we had been arrested. He had been our source of strength, but was not with us at the time of the arrest. When he reached the top of the ladder he turned to me and said, "Perpetua, I'm waiting for you, but be careful not to be bitten by the dragon." I told him that in the name of Jesus Christ the dragon could not harm me. At this the dragon slowly lowered its head as though afraid of me. Using its head as the first step, I began my ascent.

At the summit I saw an immense garden, in the center of which sat a tall, grey-haired man dressed like a shepherd, milking sheep. Standing around him were several thousand white-robed people. As he raised his head he noticed me and said, "Welcome, my child." Then he beckoned me to approach and gave me a small morsel of the cheese he was making. I accepted it with cupped hands and ate it. When all those surrounding us said "Amen," I awoke, still tasting the sweet cheese. I immediately told my brother about the vision, and we both realized that we were to experience the sufferings of martyrdom. From then on we gave up having any hope in this world.

A few days later there was a rumor that our case was to be heard. My father, completely exhausted from his anxiety, came from the city to see me, with the intention of weakening my faith. "Daughter," he said, "have pity on my grey head. Have pity on your father if I have the honor to be called father by you, if with these hands I have brought you to the prime of your life, and if I have always favored you above your brothers, do not abandon me to the reproach of men. Consider your brothers; consider your mother and your aunt; consider your son who cannot live without you. Give up your stubbornness before you destroy all of us. None of us will be able to speak freely if anything happens to you."

These were the things my father said out of love, kissing my hands and throwing himself at my feet. With tears he called me not daughter, but woman. I was very upset because of my father's condition. He was the only member of my family who would find no reason for joy in my suffering. I tried to comfort him saying, "Whatever God wants at this tribunal will happen, for remember that our power comes not from ourselves but from God." But utterly dejected, my father left me.

One day as we were eating we were suddenly rushed off for a hearing. We arrived at the forum and the news spread quickly throughout the area near the forum, and a huge crowd gathered. We went up to the prisoners' platform. All the others confessed when they were questioned. When my turn came my father appeared with my son. Dragging me from the step, he begged, "Have pity on your son!"

Hilarion, the governor, who assumed power after the death of the proconsul Minucius Timinianus, said, "Have pity on your father's grey head; have pity on your infant son; offer sacrifice for the Emperor's welfare". But I answered, "I will not." Hilarion asked, "Are you a Christian?" And I answered, "I am a Christian." And when my father persisted in his attempts to dissuade me, Hilarion ordered him thrown out, and he was beaten with a rod. My father's injury hurt me as much as if I myself had been beaten, and I grieved because of his pathetic old age. Then the sentence was passed; all of us were condemned to the beasts. We were overjoyed as we went back to the prison cell. Since I was still nursing my child who was ordinarily in the cell with me, I quickly sent the deacon Pomponius to my father's house to ask for the baby, but my father refused to give him up. Then God saw to it that my child no longer needed my nursing, nor were my breasts inflamed. After that I was no longer tortured by anxiety about my child or by pain in my breasts.

A few days later while all of us were praying, in the middle of a prayer I suddenly called out the name "Dinocrates." I was astonished since I hadn't thought about him till then. When I recalled what had happened to him I was very disturbed and decided right then that I had not only the right, but the obligation, to pray for him. So I began to pray repeatedly and to make moaning sounds to the Lord in his behalf. During that same night I had this vision: I saw Dinocrates walking away from one of many very dark places. He seemed very hot and thirsty, his face grimy and colorless. The wound on his face was just as it had been when he died. This Dinocrates was my blood-brother who at the age of seven died very tragically from a cancerous disease which so disfigured his face that his death was repulsive to everyone. It was for him that I now prayed. But neither of us could reach the other because of the great distance between. In the place where Dinocrates stood was a pool filled with water, and the rim of the pool was so high that it extended far above the boy's height. Dinocrates stood on his toes as if to drink the water but in spite of the fact that the pool was full, he could not drink because the rim was so high!

I realized that my brother was in trouble, but I was confident that I could help him with his problem. I prayed for him every day until we were transferred to the arena prison where we were to fight wild animals on the birthday of Geta Caesar.[2] And I prayed day and night for him, moaning and weeping so that my petition would be granted.

On the day that we were kept in chains, I had the following vision: I saw the same place as before, but Dinocrates was clean, well-dressed, looking refreshed. In place of the wound there was a scar, and the fountain which I had seen previously now had its rim lowered to the boy's waist. On the rim, over which water was flowing constantly, there was a golden bowl filled with water. Dinocrates walked up to it and began to drink; the bowl never emptied. And when he was no longer thirsty, he gladly went to play as children do. Then I awoke, knowing that he had been relieved of his suffering.

A few days passed. Pudens, the official in charge of the prison (the official who had gradually come to admire us for our persistence), admitted many prisoners to our cell so that we might mutually encourage each other. As the day of the games drew near, my father, overwhelmed with grief, came again to see me. He began to pluck out his beard and throw it on the ground. Falling on his face before me, he cursed his old age, repeating such things as would move all creation. And I grieved because of his old age.

The day before the battle in the arena, in a vision I saw Pomponius the deacon coming to the prison door and knocking very loudly. I went to open the gate for him. He was dressed in a loosely fitting white robe, wearing richly decorated sandals. He said to me, "Perpetua, come. We're waiting for you!" He took my hand and we began to walk over extremely rocky and winding paths. When we finally arrived short of breath, at the arena, he led me to the center

[2]Publius Septimus Geta, son of Emperor Septimius Severus (r. 193–211)

saying, "Don't be frightened! I'll be here to help you." He left me and I stared out over a huge crowd which watched me with apprehension. Because I knew that I had to fight with the beasts, I wondered why they hadn't yet been turned loose in the arena. Coming towards me was some type of Egyptian, horrible to

5   look at, accompanied by fighters who were to help defeat me. Some handsome young men came forward to help and encourage me. I was stripped of my clothing, and suddenly I was a man. My assistants began to rub me with oil as was the custom before a contest, while the Egyptian was on the opposite side rolling in the sand. Then a certain man appeared, so tall that he towered above

10  the amphitheatre. He wore a loose purple robe with two parallel stripes across the chest; his sandals were richly decorated with gold and silver. He carried a rod like that of an athletic trainer, and a green branch on which were golden apples. He motioned for silence and said, "If this Egyptian wins, he will kill her with the sword; but if she wins, she will receive this branch." Then he withdrew.

15      We both stepped forward and began to fight with our fists. My opponent kept trying to grab my feet but I repeatedly kicked his face with my heels. I felt myself being lifted up into the air and began to strike at him as one who was no longer earth-bound. But when I saw that we were wasting time, I put my two hands together, linked my fingers, and put his head between them. As he

20  fell on his face I stepped on his head. Then the people began to shout and my assistants started singing victory songs. I walked up to the trainer and accepted the branch. He kissed me and said, "Peace be with you, my daughter." And I triumphantly headed towards the Sanavivarian Gate.[3] Then I woke up realizing that I would be contending not with wild animals but with the devil himself.

25  I knew, however, that I would win. I have recorded the events which occurred up to the day before the final contest. Let anyone who wishes to record the events of the contest itself, do so.

        The saintly Saturus also related a vision which he had and it is recorded here in his own hand. Our suffering had ended (he said), and we were being

30  carried towards the east by four angels whose hands never touched us. And we floated upward, not in a supine position, but as though we were climbing a gentle slope. As we left the earth's atmosphere we saw a brilliant light, and I said to Perpetua who was at my side, "This is what the Lord promised us. We have received His promise."

35      And while we were being carried along by those four angels we saw a large open space like a splendid garden landscaped with rose trees and every variety of flower. The trees were as tall as cypresses whose leaves rustled gently and incessantly. And there in that garden-sanctuary were four other angels, more

---

[3]*Sanavivarian Gate*—the Gate of Life, through which victorious gladiators exited the arena

dazzling than the rest. And when they saw us they showed us honor, saying to the other angels in admiration, "Here they are! They have arrived."

And those four angels who were carrying us began trembling in awe and set us down. And we walked through a violet-strewn field where we met Jocundus, Saturninus, and Artaxius, who were burned alive in that same persecution, and Quintus, also a martyr, who had died in prison. We were asking them where they had been, when the other angels said to us, "First, come this way. Go in and greet the Lord."

We went up to a place where the walls seemed constructed of light. At the entrance of the place stood four angels who put white robes on those who entered. We went in and heard a unified voice chanting endlessly, "Holy, holy, holy." We saw a white-haired man sitting there who, in spite of his snowy white hair, had the features of a young man. His feet were not visible. On his right and left were four elderly gentlemen and behind them stood many more. As we entered we stood in amazement before the throne. Four angels supported us as we went up to kiss the aged man, and he gently stroked our faces with his hands. The other elderly men said to us, "Stand up." We rose and gave the kiss of peace. Then they told us to enjoy ourselves. I said to Perpetua, "You have your wish." She answered, "I thank God, for although I was happy on earth, I am much happier here right now."

Then we went out, and before the gates we saw Optatus, the Bishop, on the right and Aspasius the priest and teacher on the left, both looking sad as they stood there separated from each other. They knelt before us saying, "Make peace between us, for you've gone away and left us this way." But we said to them "Aren't you our spiritual father, and our teacher? Why are you kneeling before us?" We were deeply touched and we embraced them. And Perpetua began to speak to them in Greek and we invited them into the garden beneath a rose tree. While we were talking with them, the angels said to them, "Let them refresh themselves, and if you have any dissensions among you, forgive one another." This disturbed both of them and the angels said to Optatus, "Correct your people who flock to you as though returning from the games, fighting about the different teams." It seemed to us that they wanted to close the gates, and there we began to recognize many of our friends, among whom were martyrs. We were all sustained by an indescribable fragrance which completely satisfied us. Then in my joy, I awoke.

The remarkable visions narrated above were those of the blessed martyrs Saturus and Perpetua, just as they put them in writing. As for Secundulus, while he was still in prison God gave him the grace of an earlier exit from this world, so that he could escape combat with the wild beasts. But his body, though not his soul, certainly felt the sword.

As for Felicitas, she too was touched by God's grace in the following manner. She was pregnant when arrested, and was now in her eighth month. As the
day of the contest approached she became very distressed that her martyrdom
might be delayed, since the law forbade the execution of a pregnant woman.
5   Then she would later have to shed her holy and innocent blood among common criminals. Her friends in martyrdom were equally sad at the thought of
abandoning such a good friend to travel alone on the same road to hope.

And so, two days before the contest, united in grief they prayed to the Lord.
Immediately after the prayers her labor pains began. Because of the additional
10  pain natural for an eighth-month delivery, she suffered greatly during the birth,
and one of the prison guards taunted her, "If you're complaining now, what will
you do when you'll be thrown to the wild beasts? You didn't think of them when
you refused to sacrifice." She answered, "Now it is I who suffer, but then another
shall be in me to bear the pain for me, since I am now suffering for Him." And
15  she gave birth to a girl whom one of her sisters reared as her own daughter.

Since the Holy Spirit has permitted, and by permitting has willed, that
the events of the contest be recorded, we have no choice but to carry out the
injunction (rather, the sacred trust) of Perpetua, in spite of the fact that it will
be an inferior addition to the magnificent events already described. We are
20  adding an instance of Perpetua's perseverance and lively spirit. At one time the
prisoners were being treated with unusual severity by the commanding officer
because certain deceitful men had intimated to him that the prisoners might
escape by some magic spells. Perpetua openly challenged him; "Why don't you
at least allow us to freshen up, the most noble of the condemned, since we be-
25  long to Caesar and are about to fight on his birthday? Or isn't it to your credit
that we should appear in good condition on that day?" The officer grimaced
and blushed, then ordered that they be treated more humanely and that her
brothers and others be allowed to visit and dine with them. By this time the
prison warden was himself a believer.

30  On the day before the public games, as they were eating the last meal, commonly called the free meal, they tried as much as possible to make it instead
an *agape*. In the same spirit they were exhorting the people, warning them to
remember the judgment of God, asking them to be witnesses to the prisoners'
joy in suffering, and ridiculing the curiosity of the crowd. Saturus told them,
35  "Won't tomorrow's view be enough for you? Why are you so eager to see something you hate? Friends today, enemies tomorrow! Take a good look so you'll
recognize us on that day." Then they all left the prison amazed, and many of
them began to believe.

The day of their victory dawned, and with joyful countenances they marched
40  from the prison to the arena as though on their way to heaven. If there was any

trembling it was from joy, not fear. Perpetua followed with quick step as a true spouse of Christ, the darling of God, her brightly flashing eyes quelling the gaze of the crowd. Felicitas too, joyful because she had safely survived childbirth and was now able to participate in the contest with the wild animals, passed from one shedding of blood to another; from mid-wife to gladiator, about to 5 be purified after child-birth by a second baptism. As they were led through the gate they were ordered to put on different clothes; the men, those of the priests of Saturn, the women, those of the priestesses of Ceres. But that noble woman stubbornly resisted even to the end. She said, "We've come this far voluntarily in order to protect our rights, and we've pledged our lives not to recapitulate on 10 any such matter as this. We made this agreement with you." Injustice bowed to justice and the guard conceded that they could enter the arena in their ordinary dress. Perpetua was singing victory psalms as if already crushing the head of the Egyptian. Revocatus, Saturninus, and Saturus were warning the spectators, and as they came within sight of Hilarion they informed him by nods and gestures, 15 "You condemn us; God condemns you." This so infuriated the crowds that they demanded the scourging of these men in front of the line of gladiators. But the ones so punished rejoiced in that they had obtained yet another share in the Lord's suffering.

Whoever said, "Ask and you shall receive," granted to these petitioners the 20 particular death that each one chose. For whenever the martyrs were discussing among themselves their choice of death, Saturus used to say that he wished to be thrown in with all the animals so that he might wear a more glorious crown. Accordingly, at the outset of the show he was matched against a leopard but then called back; then he was mauled by a bear on the exhibition platform. Now 25 Saturus detested nothing as much as a bear and he had already decided to die by one bite from the leopard. Consequently, when he was tied to a wild boar, the professional gladiator who had tied the two was pierced instead and died shortly after the games ended, while Saturus was merely dragged about. And when he was tied up on the bridge in front of the bear, the bear refused to come out of 30 his den; and so a second time Saturus was called back unharmed.

For the young women the devil had readied a mad cow, an animal not usually used at these games, but selected so that the women's sex would be matched with that of the animal. After being stripped and enmeshed in nets, the women were led into the arena. How horrified the people were as they saw 35 that one was a young girl and the other, her breasts dripping with milk, had just recently given birth to a child. Consequently both were recalled and dressed in loosely fitting gowns.

Perpetua was tossed first and fell on her back. She sat up, and being more concerned with her sense of modesty than with her pain, covered her thighs 40 with her gown which had been torn down one side. Then finding her hair-clip which had fallen out, she pinned back her loose hair, thinking it not proper for a martyr to suffer with disheveled hair; it might seem that she was mourning in her hour of triumph. Then she stood up. Noticing that Felicitas was badly

5   bruised, she went to her, reached out her hands and helped her to her feet. As they stood there the cruelty of the crowds seemed to be appeased and they were sent to the Sanavivarian Gate. There Perpetua was taken care of by a certain catechumen, Rusticus, who stayed near her. She seemed to be waking from a deep sleep (so completely had she been entranced and imbued with the Spirit).

10  She began to look around her and to everyone's astonishment asked, "When are we going to be led out to that cow, or whatever it is." She would not believe that it had already happened until she saw the various markings of the tossing on her body and clothing. Then calling for her brother she said to him and to the catechumen, "Remain strong in your faith and love one another. Do not

15  let our excruciating sufferings become a stumbling block for you."

Meanwhile, at another gate Saturus was similarly encouraging the soldier, Pudens. "Up to the present," he said, "I've not been harmed by any of the animals, just as I've foretold and predicted. So that you will now believe completely, watch as I go back to die from a single leopard bite." And so that the end of that

20  contest, Saturus was bitten once by the leopard that had been set loose, and bled so profusely from that one wound that as he was coming back the crowd shouted in witness to his second baptism: "Salvation by being cleansed; Salvation by being cleansed;" And that man was truly saved who was cleansed in this way.

Then Saturus said to Pudens the soldier, "Goodby, and remember my faith.

25  Let these happenings be a source of strength for you, rather than a cause for anxiety." Then asking Pudens for a ring from his finger, he dipped it into the wound and returned it to Pudens as a legacy, a pledge and remembrance of his death. And as he collapsed, he was thrown with the rest to that place reserved for the usual throat-slitting. And when the crowd demanded that the prisoners

30  be brought out into the open so that they might feast their eyes on death by the sword, they voluntarily arose and moved where the crowd wanted them. Before doing so they kissed each other so that their martyrdom would be completely perfected by the rite of the kiss of peace.

The others, without making any movement or sound, were killed by the

35  sword. Saturus in particular, since he had been the first to climb the ladder and was to be Perpetua's encouragement, was the first to die. But Perpetua, in order to feel some of the pain, groaning as she was struck between the ribs, took the gladiator's trembling hand guided it to her throat. Perhaps it was that so great a woman, feared as she was by the unclean spirit, could not have been slain

40  had she not herself willed it.

O brave and fortunate martyrs, truly called and chosen to give honor to our Lord Jesus Christ! And anyone who is elaborating upon, or who reverences or worships that honor, should read these more recent examples, along with the ancient, as sources of encouragement for the Christian community. In this way, there will be new examples of courage witnessing to the fact that even in our day the same Holy Spirit is still efficaciously present, along with the all powerful God the Father and Jesus Christ our Lord, to whom there will always be glory and endless power. Amen.

# LIFE OF CONSTANTINE
## EUSEBIUS PAMPHILUS (*c.* 260–*c.* 340)

*Eusebius, who took the name Pamphilus in honor of a highly respected teacher martyred about 309, became Bishop of Caesarea in 314, two years after the victory of the Emperor Constantine (306–337) at the Milvian Bridge that led to the legalization of Christianity. Eusebius's best-known work is his* History of the Church, *but he was a prolific writer, and he did not allow advancing age to slow him down, for he produced both his* Life of Constantine *and the* Oration in Praise of Constantine *while in his late seventies. He wrote these works as a close friend and confidant of the Emperor, so much of what he tells us in them he heard directly from Constantine or witnessed himself.*

*The selections from the* Life of Constantine *that follow tell the story of Constantine's vision on the eve of his battle against Maxentius in 312 and his subsequent legalization of Christianity, his reaction to the Arian controversy, and his role at the Council of Nicaea in 325.*

### Of the Death of Constantine

[I§1]Already have all mankind united in celebrating with joyous festivities the completion of the second and third decennial periods[1] of this great Emperor's reign: already, on the occasion of the first of these periods, have we ourselves received him as a triumphant conqueror in the assembly of God's ministers, and greeted him with the due need of praise: and still more recently we have woven as it were garlands of eulogistic words, wherewith we encircled his sacred head in his own palace on the thirtieth anniversary of his reign.    5

But now, while I much desire to give utterance to some of the sentiments I have been accustomed to entertain, I stand perplexed and doubtful which way to turn, being wholly lost in wonder at the extraordinary spectacle before me.    10
For to whatever quarter I direct my view, whether to the east, or to the west, or over the whole world, or toward heaven itself, I see the blessed Emperor

---

[1]*Decennial period*—decade

Eusebius Pamphilus, *Ecclesiastical History: The Life of the Blessed Emperor Constantine* (London: Samuel Bagster and Sons, 1845), 1–4, 24–30, 32–37, 106–10, 119–21, 122–26, 293–302.

everywhere present. On earth I behold his sons, like some new reflectors of his brightness, diffusing everywhere the luster of their father's character; and I see *him* still living and powerful, and governing the general interests of mankind more completely than ever before, being multiplied as it were by the succession
5   of his children to the Imperial power. They had indeed previously shared the dignity of Caesars; but now, being invested with their father's entire authority, and graced by his accomplishments, for the excellence of their piety they are proclaimed by the titles of Sovereign, Augustus, Worshipful, and Emperor....

## How God Honors Pious Princes, But Destroys Tyrants

I§3And whereas He has given assurance that those who glorify and honor Him
10  will meet with an ample recompense at His hands, while those who set themselves against Him as enemies and adversaries will compass the ruin of their own souls; already has He established the truth of these His own declarations. He has shown that the lives of those tyrants who denied and opposed Him have had a fearful end, and at the same time has made it manifest that even the death
15  of His servant, as well as his life, is worthy of admiration and praise, and justly claims the memorial, not merely of perishable, but of immortal records.

Mankind have indeed devised some consolation for the frail and precarious duration of human life, and have thought by the erection of monuments to secure immortal honors to the memory of their ancestors. Some have employed the vivid
20  delineations and colors of painting; some have carved statues from lifeless blocks of wood; while others, by engraving their inscriptions deep on tablets and monuments of wood and stone, have sought to keep the virtues of those whom they honored in perpetual remembrance. All these indeed are perishable, and consumed by the lapse of time, being representations of the corruptible body, and incapable
25  of expressing the image of the immortal soul. And yet these seemed sufficient to those who had no well-grounded hope of happiness after the termination of this mortal life. But God, that God, I say, who is the Preserver of the universe, has treasured up with Himself, for those who love godliness, greater blessings than human thought has conceived; and, by giving the earnest and first-fruits of
30  future rewards even here, assures, in some sort, immortal hopes to mortal eyes. The ancient oracles of the prophets, delivered to us in the Scripture, declare this; the lives of pious men, who shone in old time with every virtue, attest the same; and our own days prove it to be true, wherein Constantine, who alone of all that ever wielded the Roman power was the friend of God, the Sovereign of all, has
35  appeared to all mankind so bright an example of a godly life.[2]...

---

[2]Eusebius, like many of his contemporaries, was prepared to overlook Constantine's less admirable actions because of the favor he showed to Christianity. Those who had lived through

### He Resolves to Deliver Rome from the Tyranny of Maxentius

I§26While therefore he regarded the entire world as one immense body, and perceived that the head of it all, the royal city of the Roman empire, was bowed down by the weight of a tyrannous oppression; at first he had left the task of liberation to those who governed the other divisions of the empire, as being his superiors in point of age. But when none of these proved able to afford relief,      5 and those who had attempted it had experienced a disastrous termination of their enterprise, he said that life was without enjoyment to him as long as he saw the Imperial City thus afflicted, and prepared himself for the effectual suppression of the tyranny.

### After Reflecting on the Downfall of Those Who had Worshipped Idols, He Made Choice of Christianity

I§27Being convinced, however, that he needed some more powerful aid than his    10 military forces could afford him, on account of the wicked and magical enchantments which were so diligently practiced by the tyrant, he began to seek for Divine assistance; deeming the possession of arms and a numerous soldiery of secondary importance, but trusting that the co-operation of a Deity would be his security against defeat or misfortune. He considered, therefore, on what God he might    15 rely for protection and assistance. While engaged in this inquiry, the thought occurred to him that, of the many Emperors who had preceded him, those who had rested their hopes in a multitude of gods, and served them with sacrifices and offerings, had in the first place been deceived by flattering predictions and oracles which promised them all prosperity, and at last had met with an unhappy end,    20 while not one of their gods had stood by to warn them of the impending wrath of Heaven. On the other hand, he recollected that his father, who had pursued an entirely opposite course, who had condemned their error, and honored the one Supreme God during his whole life, had found Him to be the Savior and Protector of his empire, and the Giver of every good thing. Reflecting on this, and    25 well weighing the fact that they who had trusted in many gods had also fallen by manifold forms of death without leaving behind them either family or offspring, stock, name, or memorial among men: and considering further that those who had already taken arms against the tyrant, and had marched to the battlefield under the protection of a multitude of gods, had met with a dishonorable end    30 (for one of them had shamefully retreated from the contest without a blow, and the other, being slain in the midst of his own troops, had become, as it were, the mere sport of death); reviewing, I say, all these considerations, he judged it to be

the Great Persecution, and then had seen Constantine completely transform imperial policy toward the Church virtually overnight, saw the hand of Providence clearly in these events.

folly indeed to join in the idle worship of those who were no gods, and, after such convincing evidence, to wander from the truth; and therefore felt it incumbent on him to honor no other than the God of his father.

### How, While He was Praying, God Sent Him a Vision of a Cross of Light in the Heavens at Mid-Day, With an Inscription Admonishing Him to Conquer by That

I§28Accordingly he called on Him with earnest prayer and supplications
5   that He would reveal to him who He was, and stretch forth His right hand to help him in his present difficulties. And while he was thus praying with fervent entreaty, a most marvelous sign appeared to him from heaven, the account of which it might have been difficult to receive with credit had it been related by any other person. But since the victorious Emperor himself
10  long afterwards declared it to the writer of his history, when he was honored with his acquaintance and society, and confirmed his statement by an oath, who could hesitate to accredit the relation, especially since the testimony of after-time has established its truth? He said that about mid-day, when the sun was beginning to decline, he saw with his own eyes the trophy of a cross
15  of light in the heavens, above the sun, and bearing the inscription, *Conquer By This*. At this sight, he himself was struck with amazement, and his whole army also, which happened to be following him on some expedition, and witnessed the miracle.

### How the Christ of God Appeared to Him in his Sleep And Commanded Him to Use in his Wars a Standard Made in the Form of a Cross

I§29He said, moreover, that he doubted within himself what the import of this
20  apparition could be. And while he continued to ponder and reason on its meaning, night imperceptibly drew on; and in his sleep the Christ of God appeared to him with the same sign which he had seen in the heavens, and commanded him to procure a standard made in the likeness of that sign, and to use it as a safeguard in all engagements with his enemies.

### The Making of the Standard of the Cross

25  I§30At dawn of day he arose, and communicated the secret to his friends: and then, calling together the workers in gold and precious stones, he sat in the midst of them and described to them the figure of the sign he had seen, bidding them represent it in gold and precious stones. And this representation I myself have had an opportunity of seeing.

## A Description of the Standard of the Cross,
## Which the Romans Now Call the Labarum

I§31Now it was made in the following manner. A long spear, overlaid with gold, formed the figure of the cross by means of a piece transversely laid over it. On the top of the whole was fixed a crown, formed by the inter-texture of gold and precious stones; and on this, two letters indicating the name of Christ, symbolized the Savior's title by means of its first characters, the letter P being    5
intersected by X exactly in its centre: and these letters the Emperor was in the habit of wearing on his helmet at a later period. From the transverse piece which crossed the spear was suspended a kind of streamer of purple cloth, covered with a profuse embroidery of most brilliant precious stones; and which, being also richly inter-laced with gold, presented an indescribable degree of beauty to the   10
beholder. This banner was of a square form, and the upright staff, which in its full extent was of great length, bore a golden half-length portrait of the pious Emperor and his children on its upper part, beneath the trophy of the cross, and immediately above the embroidered streamer. The Emperor constantly made use of this salutary sign as a safeguard against every adverse and hostile   15
power, and commanded that others similar to it should be carried at the head of all his armies.

## Constantine Receives Instruction,
## And Reads the Sacred Scriptures

I§32These things were done shortly afterwards. But at the time above specified, being struck with amazement at the extraordinary vision, and resolving to worship no other God save Him who had appeared to him, he sent for those who   20
were acquainted with the mysteries of His doctrines, and inquired who that God was, and what was intended by the sign of the vision he had seen.

They affirmed that He was God, the only begotten Son of the one and only God: that the sign which had appeared was the symbol of immortality, and the trophy of that victory over death which He had gained in time past   25
when sojourning on earth. They taught him also the causes of His advent, and explained to him the true account of His incarnation. Thus he sought instruction in these matters, but was still impressed with wonder at the divine manifestation which had been presented to his sight. Comparing, therefore, the heavenly vision with the interpretation given, he found his judgment confirmed; and, in   30
the persuasion that the knowledge of these things had been imparted to him by Divine teaching, he determined thenceforth to devote himself to the perusal of the Inspired writings.

Moreover, he made the priests of God his counselors, and deemed it incumbent on him to honor the God who had appeared to him with all devotion.   35

And after this, being fortified by well-grounded hopes in Him, he undertook to quench the fury of the fire of tyranny.…

## Defeat of Maxentius's Armies in Italy

I§37Constantine, however, filled with compassion on account of all these miseries, began to arm himself with all war-like preparation against the tyranny.
5 Assuming therefore the Supreme God as his patron, and invoking His Christ to be his preserver and aid, and setting the victorious trophy, the salutary symbol, in front of his soldiers and body-guard, he marched with his whole forces, eager to re-instate the Romans in the freedom they had inherited from their ancestors.

10    And whereas, Maxentius, trusting more in his magic arts than in the affection of his subjects, dared not even advance outside the city gates, but had guarded every place and district and city subject to his tyranny with large bodies of soldiers and numberless ambuscades; the Emperor, confiding in the help of God, advanced against the first and second and third divisions of the tyrant's
15 forces, defeated them all with ease at the first assault, and made his way into the very interior of Italy.

## Death of Maxentius on the Bridge of the Tiber

I§38And already he was approaching very near Rome itself, when, to save him from the necessity of fighting with all the Romans for the tyrant's sake, God Himself drew the tyrant, as it were by secret cords, a long way outside the gates.

20    And now those miracles recorded in Holy Writ, which God of old wrought against the ungodly (discredited by most as fables, yet believed by the faithful) did He in very deed confirm to all alike, believers and unbelievers, who were eye-witnesses of the wonders I am about to relate. For as once in the days of Moses and the Hebrew nation, who were worshippers of God, He cast Pharaoh's
25 chariots and his host into the waves, and drowned his chosen chariot-captains in the Red Sea—so at this time did Maxentius, and the soldiers and guards with him, sink to the bottom as a stone when, in his flight before the divinely-aided forces of Constantine, he essayed to cross the river which lay in his way, over which he had made a strong bridge of boats, and had framed an engine of
30 destruction, really against himself, but in the hope of ensnaring thereby him who was beloved by God. For his God stood by the one to protect him, while the other, destitute of His aid, proved to be the miserable contriver of these secret devices to his own ruin. So that one might well say, "He made a pit, and digged it, and shall fall into the ditch which he made. His mischief shall return

3Psalm 7: 15–16

upon his own head, and his iniquity shall come down upon his own pate."[3] Thus, in the present instance, under divine direction, the machine erected on the bridge, with the ambuscade concealed therein, giving way unexpectedly before the appointed time, the passage began to sink down, and the boats with the men in them went bodily to the bottom. And first the wretch himself, then his armed attendants and guards, even as the sacred oracles had before described, "sank as lead in the mighty waters." So that they who thus obtained victory from God might well, if not in the same words, yet in fact in the same spirit as the people of His great servant Moses, sing and speak as they did concerning the impious tyrant of old: "Let us sing unto the Lord, for He has been glorified exceedingly: the horse and his rider has He thrown into the sea. He is become my helper and my shield unto salvation."[4] And again, "Who is like You, O Lord, among the gods? Who is like You, glorious in holiness, marvelous in praises, doing wonders?"[5]

## Constantine's Entry into Rome

[1§39]Having then at this time sung these and such-like praises to God, the Ruler of all and the Author of victory, after the example of His great servant Moses, Constantine entered the Imperial City in triumph. And here the whole body of the Senate, and others of rank and distinction in the city, freed as it were from the restraint of a prison, along with the whole Roman populace, their countenances expressive of the gladness of their hearts, received him with acclamations and excess of joy; men, women, and children, with countless multitudes of servants, greeting him as deliverer, preserver, and benefactor with incessant shouts. But he, being possessed of inward piety toward God, was neither rendered arrogant by these plaudits, nor uplifted by the praises he heard. But, being sensible that he had received help from God, he immediately rendered a thanksgiving to Him as the Author of his victory.

## Of the Statue of Constantine Holding a Cross, and its Inscription

[1§40]Moreover, by many writings and monumental inscriptions he made known to all men the salutary symbol, setting up this great trophy of victory over his enemies in the midst of the Imperial City, and expressly causing it to be engraven in indelible characters that the salutary sign was the preservative of the Roman government and of the entire Empire. Accordingly, he immediately ordered a lofty spear in the figure of a cross to be placed beneath the hand of a statue

[4]Exodus 15: 1–2
[5]Exodus 15: 11

representing himself in the most frequented part of Rome, and the following inscription to be engraved on it in the Latin language: *By Virtue of this Salutary Sign, Which is the True Symbol of Valor, I have Preserved and Liberated Your City from the Yoke of Tyranny. I Have also Set at Liberty the Roman Senate and People,*
5      *and Restored them to their Ancient Greatness and Splendor.*

### Rejoicings Throughout the Provinces; and Constantine's Acts of Grace

**I§41**Thus the pious Emperor, glorying in the confession of the victorious cross, proclaimed the Son of God to the Romans with great boldness of testimony. And all the inhabitants of the city with one consent, both Senate and people, reviving, as it were, from the pressure of a bitter and tyrannical domination,
10    seemed to enjoy the rays of a purer light, and to experience the renovating power of a fresh and new existence. All the nations too, as far as the limit of the western ocean, being set free from the calamities which had heretofore distressed them, and gladdened by joyous festivals, ceased not to praise him as the victorious, the pious, the common benefactor; all indeed, with one voice and one mouth,
15    declared that Constantine had appeared through the special favor of God as a general blessing to mankind. The imperial edict also was everywhere published whereby those who had been wrongfully deprived of their estates were permitted again to enjoy their own, while those who had unjustly suffered exile were recalled to their homes. Moreover, he freed from imprisonment and from every
20    kind of danger and fear those who by reason of the tyrant's cruelty had been subject to these sufferings....

### Origin of the Difference Between Alexander and Arius— These Questions are not fit Subjects for Controversy[6]

**II§69**[Constantine said,] "I understand, then, that the occasion of your present controversy is to be traced to the following circumstances; that you, Alexander, demanded of the presbyters what opinion they severally maintained respecting

---

[6]Alexander, Patriarch of Alexandria, had attempted to silence one of his priests, Arius, who maintained Jesus was subordinate to God the Father. Arius's argument went something like this: God is, by definition, eternal. Jesus was born in a stable in Bethlehem, so he had a beginning. And what son is the same age as his father? So since Jesus is younger than God, he is less than God.

The problem, from Alexander's point of view, was not only that what Arius was saying was contrary to what he understood to be apostolic teaching, but also that Arius, who was what Marvin O'Connell has referred to as a "master pamphleteer," had begun to spread his views among the tradesmen and sailors of the city. When Alexander tried to take action against him, Arius left Alexandria, and in some areas the bishops welcomed him. By the time Constantine got involved, most of the Church in the East was in an uproar.

a certain passage in the Divine law, or rather, I should say, that you asked them something connected with an unprofitable question; and then that you, Arius, inconsiderately gave utterance to objections which ought never to have been conceived at all, or if conceived, should have been buried in profound silence. Hence it was that a dissension arose between you; the meeting of the synod was 5 prohibited; and the holy people, rent into diverse parties, no longer preserved the unity of the one body. Now therefore do you both exhibit an equal degree of forbearance, and receive the advice which your fellow-servant feels himself justly entitled to give? What, then, is this advice?"

"It was wrong in the first instance to propose such questions as these, or 10 to reply to them when propounded. For those points of discussion which are enjoined by the authority of no law, but rather suggested by the contentious spirit which is fostered by misused leisure, even though they may be intended merely as an intellectual exercise, ought certainly to be confined to the region of our own thoughts, and neither hastily produced in the public assemblies 15 of the saints, nor unadvisedly entrusted to the general ear. For how very few are there able either accurately to comprehend, or adequately to explain subject so sublime and abstruse in their nature? Or, granting that one were fully competent for this, in how few ordinary minds will he succeed in producing conviction? Or who, again, in dealing with questions of such subtle nicety as 20 these, can secure himself against a dangerous declension from the truth? It is incumbent therefore on us in these cases to be sparing of our words, lest, in case we ourselves are unable, through the feebleness of our natural faculties, to give a clear explanation of the subject before us, or, on the other hand, in case the slowness of our hearers' understandings disables them from arriving at an 25 accurate apprehension of what we say, from one or other of these causes we reduce the people to the alternative either of blasphemy or schism."

### An Exhortation to Unanimity

II§70"Let therefore both the unguarded question and the inconsiderate answer receive your mutual forgiveness. For your difference has not arisen on any leading doctrines or precepts of the Divine law, nor have you introduced any 30 new dogma respecting the worship of God. You are in truth of one and the same judgment: you may therefore well join in that communion which is the symbol of united fellowship."

### There Should be no Contention Because of Expressions in Themselves of Little Moment

II§71"For as long as you continue to contend about these truly insignificant questions, it is not fitting that so large a portion of God's people should be under 35 the direction of your judgment, since you are thus divided between yourselves. I believe it indeed to be not merely unbecoming, but positively evil, that such should be the case. But I will appeal to your good sense by a familiar instance to illustrate my meaning. You know that philosophers, while they all adhere to the general tenets of their respective sects, are frequently at issue on some particular assertion or statement, and yet, though they may differ as to the perfection of a principle, they are recalled to harmony of sentiment by the uniting power of their common doctrines. If this be true, is it not far more reasonable that you, who are the ministers of the Supreme God, should be of one mind respecting the profession of the same religion? But let us still more thoughtfully and with closer attention examine what I have said, and see whether it be right that, on the ground of some trifling and foolish verbal difference between ourselves, brethren should assume towards each other the attitude of enemies, and the august meeting of the synod be rent by profane disunion, because we will wrangle together on points so trivial and altogether unessential? Surely this conduct is unworthy of us, and rather characteristic of childish ignorance than consistent with the wisdom of priests and men of sense. Let us withdraw ourselves with a good will from these temptations of the devil. Our great God and common Savior has granted the same light to us all."

"Permit me, who am His servant, to bring my task to a successful issue, under the direction of His Providence, that I may be enabled through my exhortations, and diligence, and earnest admonition to recall His people to the fellowship of one communion. For since you have, as I said, but one faith, and one sentiment respecting our religion, and since the Divine commandment in all its parts enjoins on us all the duty of maintaining a spirit of concord, let not the circumstance which has led to a slight difference between you, since it affects not the general principles of truth, be allowed to prolong any division or schism among you. And this I say without in any way desiring to force you to entire unity of judgment in regard to this truly idle question, whatever its real nature may be. For the dignity of your synod may be preserved, and the communion of your whole body maintained unbroken, however wide a difference may exist among you as to unimportant matters. For we are not all of us like-minded on every subject, nor is there such a thing as one disposition and judgment common to all alike. As far then as regards the Divine Providence, let there be one faith, and one understanding among you, one united judgment in reference to God. But as to your subtle disputations on questions of little or no significance, though you may be unable to harmonize in sentiment, such differences should be consigned to the secret custody of your own minds and thoughts. And now, let the precious bonds of common affection, let faith in the truth, let the honor due to God and the observance of His law continue immovably established

among you. Resume, then, your mutual feelings of affection and regard: permit
the whole body of the people once more to unite in that embrace which should
be natural to all; and do ye yourselves, having purified your souls, as it were,
from every angry thought, once more return to your former fellowship. For it
often happens that when a reconciliation is effected by the removal of the causes    5
of enmity, friendship becomes even sweeter than it was before."…

## He Orders a Council to Assemble at Nicæa

III§6Resolved, therefore, to bring, as it were, a divine array against this enemy, he
convoked a general council, and invited the speedy attendance of bishops from
all quarters, in letters expressive of the honorable estimation in which he held
them. Nor was this merely the issuing of a bare command, but the Emperor's    10
condescension contributed much to its being carried into effect, for he allowed
some the use of the public means of conveyance, while he afforded to others an
ample supply of horses for their transport. The place, too, selected for the synod,
the city Nicæa in Bithynia (which derived its name from *Victory*) was appropriate to the occasion. As soon then as the imperial injunction was generally made    15
known, all with the utmost celerity hastened to obey it, as though they would
outstrip one another in a race, for they were impelled by the anticipation of a
happy result to the conference, by the hope of enjoying present peace, and the
desire of beholding something new and strange in the person of so admirable
an Emperor. Now when they were all assembled, it appeared evident that the    20
proceeding was the work of God, inasmuch as men who had been most widely
separated, not merely in sentiment, but also personally, and by difference of
country, place, and nation, were here brought together and comprised within
the walls of a single city, forming, as it were, a vast garland of priests, composed
of a variety of the choicest flowers.    25

## Of the General Council, at which Bishops
## from all Nations were Present

III§7In effect, the most distinguished of God's ministers from all the Churches
which abounded in Europe, Africa, and Asia were here assembled. And a single
house of prayer, as though divinely enlarged, sufficed to contain at once Syrians
and Cilicians, Phœnicians and Arabians, delegates from Palestine, and others
from Egypt; Thebans and Libyans, with those who came from the region of    30
Mesopotamia. A Persian bishop, too, was present at this conference, nor was
even a Scythian found wanting to the number. Pontus, Galatia, and Pamphylia,
Cappadocia, Asia, and Phrygia furnished their most distinguished prelates; while
those who dwelt in the remotest districts of Thrace and Macedonia, of Achaia and
Epirus, were notwithstanding in attendance. Even from Spain itself, one whose    35

fame was widely spread took his seat as an individual in the great assembly. The
prelate of the Imperial City was prevented from attending by extreme old age;
but his presbyters were present, and supplied his place. Constantine is the first
prince of any age who bound together such a garland as this with the bond of
5   peace, and presented it to Christ his Savior as a thank-offering for the victories
he had obtained over every foe, thus exhibiting in our own times a similitude
of the apostolic company.

## The Assembly was Composed, as in the Acts of the Apostles, of Individuals from Various Nations

III§8For it is said that in the Apostles' age, devout men were gathered from every
nation under heaven; among whom were Parthians, and Medes, and Elamites,
10  and the dwellers in Mesopotamia, and in Judea and Cappadocia, in Pontus and
Asia, Phrygia and Pamphylia, in Egypt, and the parts of Libya about Cyrene; and
strangers of Rome, Jews and proselytes, Cretes and Arabians. Now the defect of
that assembly was that not all who composed it were ministers of God; but in
the present company, the number of bishops exceeded two hundred and fifty,
15  while that of the presbyters and deacons in their train, and the crowd of acolytes
and other attendants was altogether beyond computation....

## Meeting in the Palace, at which Constantine Appeared, and Took his Seat in the Assembly

III§10Now when the appointed day arrived on which the council met for the
final solution of the questions in dispute, each member attended to deliver his
judgment in the central building of the palace, which appeared to exceed the rest
20  in magnitude. On each side of the interior of this were many seats disposed in
order, which were occupied by those who had been invited to attend, according
to their rank. As soon, then, as the whole assembly had seated themselves with
becoming gravity, a general silence prevailed, in expectation of the emperor's
arrival. And first of all three of his immediate family entered in succession, and
25  others also preceded his approach, not of the soldiers or guards who usually
accompanied him, but only friends who avowed the faith of Christ. And now,
all rising at the signal which indicated the emperor's entrance, at last he himself
proceeded through the midst of the assembly, like some heavenly messenger of
God, clothed in raiment which glittered as it were with rays of light, reflecting
30  the glowing radiance of a purple robe, and adorned with the brilliant splendor
of gold and precious stones. Such was the external appearance of this person;
and with regard to his mind, it was evident that he was distinguished by piety
and godly fear. This was indicated by his downcast eyes, the blush on his coun-

tenance, and the modesty of his gait. For the rest of his personal excellencies, he surpassed all present in height of stature and beauty of form, as well as in majestic dignity of mien, and invincible strength of vigor. All these graces, united to a suavity of manner, and a serenity becoming his imperial station, declared the excellence of his mental qualities to be above all praise. As soon as he had advanced to the upper end of the seats, at first he remained standing, and when a low chair of wrought gold had been set for him, he waited until the bishops had beckoned to him, and then sat down, and after him the whole assembly did the same.

## Silence of the Council after some Words Spoken by the Bishop Eusebius

III§11The bishop who occupied the chief place in the right division of the assembly then rose and, addressing the Emperor, delivered a concise speech, in a strain of praise and thanksgiving to Almighty God on his behalf. When he had resumed his seat, silence ensued, and all regarded the Emperor with fixed attention; on which he looked serenely round on the assembly with a cheerful aspect, and, having collected his thoughts, in a calm and gentle tone gave utterance to the following words.

## Constantine's Address to the Council in Praise of Peace

III§12"It was once my chief desire, dearest friends, to enjoy the spectacle of your united presence; and now that this desire is fulfilled, I feel myself bound to render thanks to God, the universal King, because, in addition to all His other benefits, He has granted me a blessing higher than all the rest in permitting me to see you not only all assembled together, but all united in a common harmony of sentiment. I pray therefore that no malignant adversary may henceforth interfere to mar our happy state; I pray that, now the impious hostility of the tyrants has been forever removed by the power of God our Savior, that spirit who delights in evil may devise no other means for exposing the divine records to blasphemous calumny: for, in my judgment, intestine strife within the Church of God is far more evil and dangerous than any kind of war or conflict; and thus our differences appear to me more grievous than any outward trouble. Accordingly, when, by the will and with the co-operation of God, I had been victorious over my enemies, and thought that nothing more remained but to render thanks to Him, and sympathize in the joy of those whom he had restored to freedom through my instrumentality; as soon as I heard that intelligence which I had least expected to receive, I mean the news of your dissension, I judged it to be of no secondary importance, but with the earnest desire that a remedy for this evil also might be found through my means, I immediately sent

to require your presence. And now I rejoice in beholding your assembly; but I feel that my desires will be most completely fulfilled when I can see you all united in one judgment, and that common spirit of peace and concord prevailing amongst you all, which it becomes you, as consecrated to the service of God, to
5  commend to others. Delay not, then, dear friends: delay not, ministers of God and faithful servants of Him who is our common Lord and Savior. Begin from this moment to discard the causes of that dis-union which has existed among you, and remove the perplexities of controversy by embracing the principles of peace. For by such conduct you will at the same time be acting in a manner
10  most pleasing to the supreme God, and you will confer an exceeding favor on me who am your fellow-servant."

### In What Manner He Led the Dissentient Bishops to Unite in Harmony of Sentiment

III§13As soon as the Emperor had spoken these words in the Latin tongue, which another present rendered into Greek, he gave permission to those who presided in the council to deliver their opinions. On this some began to accuse
15  their neighbors, who defended themselves, and recriminated in their turn. In this manner numberless assertions were put forth by each party, and a violent controversy arose at the very commencement. Notwithstanding this, the Emperor gave patient audience to all alike, and received every proposition with steadfast attention, and by occasionally assisting the argument of each party in
20  turn, he gradually disposed even the most vehement disputants to a reconciliation. At the same time, by the affability of his address to all, and his use of the Greek language (with which he was not altogether unacquainted) he appeared in a truly attractive and amiable light, persuading some, convincing others by his reasonings, praising those who spoke well, and urging all to unity of senti-
25  ment, until at last he succeeded in bringing them to one mind and judgment respecting every disputed questions....

# In Praise of the Emperor Constantine
## Eusebius Pamphilus (*c.* 260–*c.* 340)

*Eusebius's* Oration in Praise of Constantine *is of particular interest for its argument that monarchy was the Christian form of government and its analogy of Heaven to a royal court.*

336

[1]We celebrate this day the solemn festival of our great Emperor, and we, his servants, rejoice therein, feeling the inspiration of our sacred theme. He who presides over our solemnity is the Great Sovereign Himself; He, I mean, who is truly great; of whom I affirm (nor will the sovereign who hears me be offended, but will rather approve of this ascription of praise to God) that He is above and beyond all created things, the Highest, the Greatest, the most Mighty One; whose throne is the arch of heaven, and the earth the footstool of his feet. His being none can worthily comprehend; and the ineffable splendor of the glory which surrounds Him repels the gaze of every eye from His Divine majesty. His ministers are the heavenly hosts; His armies the supernal powers, who own allegiance to Him as their Master, Lord, and King. The countless multitudes of angels, the companies of archangels, the choirs of holy spirits draw from and reflect His radiance as from the fountains of everlasting light. Yea, every light, and specially those divine and incorporeal intelligences whose place is beyond the heavenly sphere, celebrate this august Sovereign with lofty and sacred strains of praise. The vast expanse of heaven, like an azure veil, is interposed between those without, and those who inhabit His royal mansions, while round this expanse the sun and moon, with the rest of the heavenly luminaries (like torch-bearers around the entrance of the imperial palace) perform, in honor of their Sovereign, their appointed courses; holding forth, at the word of His command, an ever-burning light to those whose lot is cast in the darker regions without the pale of heaven.

And surely when I remember that our own victorious Emperor renders praises to this Mighty Sovereign, I do well to follow him, knowing as I do that to Him alone we owe that imperial power under which we live. The pious Caesars, instructed by their father's wisdom, acknowledge Him as the source of every blessing. The soldiery, the entire body of the people, both in the country

and in the cities of the empire, with the governors of the several provinces, assembling together in accordance with the precept of their great Savior and Teacher, worship Him. In short, the whole family of mankind, of every nation, tribe, and tongue, both collectively and severally, however diverse their opinions
5   on other subjects, are unanimous in this one confession; and, in obedience to the reason implanted in them, and the spontaneous and uninstructed impulse of their own minds, unite in calling on the One and only God. Nay, does not the universal frame of earth acknowledge Him her Lord, and declare, by the vegetable and animal life which she produces, her subjection to the will of a
10  superior Power? The rivers, flowing with abundant stream, and the perennial fountains, springing from hidden and exhaustless depths, ascribe to Him the cause of their marvelous source. The mighty waters of the sea, enclosed in chambers of unfathomable depth, and the swelling surges, which lift themselves on high, and menace, as it were, the earth itself, shrink back when they approach
15  the shore, checked by the power of His Divine law. The duly measured fall of winter's rain, the rolling thunder, the lightning's flash, the eddying currents of the winds, and the airy courses of the clouds all reveal His presence to those to whom His Person is invisible. The all-radiant sun, who holds his constant career through the lapse of ages, owns Him Lord alone and, obedient to His
20  will, dares not depart from his appointed path. The inferior splendor of the moon, alternately diminished and increased at stated periods, is subject to His Divine command. The beauteous mechanism of the heavens, glittering with the hosts of stars, moving in harmonious order, and preserving the measure of each several orbit, proclaims Him the giver of all light. Yea, all the heavenly
25  luminaries, maintaining at His will and word a grand and perfect unity of motion, pursue the track of their ethereal career, and complete in the lapse of revolving ages, their distant course.

     The alternate recurrence of day and night, the changing seasons, the order and proportion of the universe all declare the manifold wisdom of His bound-
30  less power. To Him the unseen agencies which hold their course throughout the expanse of space render the due tribute of praise. To Him this terrestrial globe itself, to Him the heavens above, and the choirs beyond the vault of heaven give honor as to their mighty Sovereign. The angelic hosts greet Him with ineffable songs of praise; and the spirits which draw their being from
35  incorporeal light adore Him as their Creator and their God. The everlasting ages which were before this heaven and earth, with other periods beside them, infinite, and antecedent to all visible creation, acknowledge Him the sole and supreme Sovereign and Lord.

     Lastly, He who is in all, before, and after all, His only begotten Son and
40  pre-existent Word, the great High Priest of the mighty God, elder than all time

and every age, devoted to His Father's glory, first and alone makes intercession with Him for the salvation of mankind. Supreme and pre-eminent Ruler of the universe, He shares the glory of His Father's kingdom, for He is that Light which, transcendent above the universe, encircles the Father's Person, interposing and dividing between the eternal and uncreated Essence and all derived existence;      5 that Light which, streaming from on high, proceeds from that Deity who knows not origin or end and illumines the super-celestial regions, and all that heaven itself contains, with the radiance of wisdom bright beyond the splendor of the sun. This is He who holds a supreme and universal dominion over this world, who is over and in all things, and pervades all things visible and invisible;      10 the Word of God. From whom and by whom our divinely-favored Emperor, receiving, as it were, a transcript of the Divine sovereignty directs, in imitation of God Himself, the administration of this world's affairs.

**II** This only begotten Word of God reigns, from ages which had no beginning, to infinite and endless ages, the partner of His Father's kingdom. And our      15 Emperor, ever beloved by Him, who derives the source of imperial authority from above, and is strong in the power of his sacred title, has controlled the empire of the world for a long period of years. Again, that Preserver of the universe orders these heavens and earth, and the celestial kingdom, consistently with His Father's will. Even so our emperor whom He loves, by bringing those whom he      20 rules on earth to the only begotten Word and Savior, renders them fit subjects of His kingdom. And as He who is the common Preserver of mankind, by His invisible and Divine power as the good shepherd, drives far away from His flock, like savage beasts, those apostate spirits which once flew through the airy tracts above this earth and fastened on the souls of men; so this His friend, graced by      25 His heavenly favor with victory over all his foes, subdues and chastens the open adversaries of the truth in accordance with the usages of war.

He who is the pre-existent Word, the Preserver of all things, imparts to His disciples the seeds of true wisdom and salvation, and at once enlightens and gives them understanding in the knowledge of His Father's kingdom. Our      30 Emperor, His friend, acting as interpreter to the Word of God, aims at recalling the human race to the knowledge of God; proclaiming clearly in the ears of all, and declaring with powerful voice the laws of truth and godliness to all who dwell on the earth. Once more, the universal Savior expands the heavenly gates of His Father's kingdom to those whose course is thitherward from this word.      35

Our Emperor, emulous of His divine example, having purged his earthly dominion from every stain of impious error, invites each holy and pious worshipper within his imperial mansions, earnestly desiring to save with all its crew that mighty vessel of which he is the appointed pilot. And he alone of all

who have wielded the imperial power of Rome being honored by the Supreme
Sovereign and a reign of three decennial periods, now celebrates this festival,
not, as his ancestors might have done, in honor of infernal demons, or the
apparitions of seducing spirits, or of the fraud and deceitful arts of impious
5   men; but as an act of thanksgiving to Him by whom he has thus been honored,
and in acknowledgment of the blessings he has received at His hands. He does
not, in imitation of ancient usage, defile his imperial mansions with blood and
gore, nor propitiate the infernal deities with fire, and smoke, and sacrificial
offerings; but dedicates to the universal Sovereign a pleasant and acceptable
10  sacrifice, even his own imperial soul, and a mind truly fitted for the service of
God. For this sacrifice alone is grateful to Him, and this sacrifice our Emperor
has learned, with purified mind and thoughts, to present as an offering without
the intervention of fire and blood, while, his own piety strengthened by the
truthful doctrines with which his soul is stored, he sets forth in magnificent
15  language the praises of God, and imitates His divine philanthropy by his own
imperial acts. Wholly devoted to Him, he dedicates himself as a noble offering,
a first-fruit of that world the government of which is entrusted to his charge.
This first and greatest sacrifice our Emperor first dedicates to God; and then,
as a faithful shepherd, he offers, not "famous hecatombs of firstling lambs,"
20  but the souls of that flock which is the object of his care, those rational beings
whom he leads to the knowledge and pious worship of God.

**III**And gladly does He accept and welcome this sacrifice, and commend the pre-
senter of so august and noble an offering by protracting his reign to a lengthened
period of years, giving larger proofs of His beneficence in proportion to the
25  Emperor's holy services to Himself. Accordingly He permits him to celebrate each
successive festival during great and general prosperity throughout the empire,
advancing one of his sons, at the recurrence of each decennial period, to a share
of his own imperial power. The eldest, who bears his father's name,[1] he received
as his partner in the empire about the close of the first decade of his reign. The
30  second,[2] next in point of age, at the second; and the third[3] in like manner at
the third decennial period, the occasion of this our present festival. And now
that the fourth period has commenced, and the time of his reign is still further
prolonged, he desires to extend his imperial authority by calling still more of his

---

[1]Constantine II (316–340) ruled the western provinces after his father's death until he was
killed in a war against his brother Constans.
[2]Constantius II (317–361) ruled the eastern provinces between 337 and his death; following a
brief civil war in 350, he also ruled the West.
[3]Constans (320–35) ruled Italy and North Africa until the death of Constantine II left him
sole ruler in the West. He was murdered by a rebel.

kindred to partake his power;[4] and, by the appointment of the Caesars, fulfills the predictions of the holy prophets, according to what they uttered ages before: "And the saints of the Most High shall take the kingdom."[5]

And thus the Almighty Sovereign Himself accords an increase both of years and of children to our most pious Emperor, and renders his sway over the nations of the world still fresh and flourishing, as though it were even now springing up in its earliest vigor. He it is who appoints him this present festival, in that He has made him victorious over every enemy that disturbed his peace. He it is who displays him as an example of true godliness to the human race. And thus our Emperor, like the radiant sun, illuminates the most distant subjects of his empire through the presence of the Caesars, as with the far piercing rays of his own brightness. To us who occupy the eastern regions he has given a son worthy of himself; a second and a third respectively to other departments of his empire, to be as it were brilliant reflectors of the light which proceeds from himself. Once more, having harnessed, as it were, under the selfsame yoke the four most noble Caesars as horses in the imperial chariot, he sits on high and directs their course by the reins of holy harmony and concord; and, himself everywhere present and observant of every event, thus traverses every region of the world.

Lastly, invested as he is with a semblance of heavenly sovereignty, he directs his gaze above, and frames his earthly government according to the pattern of that Divine original, feeling strength in its conformity to the monarchy of God. And this conformity is granted by the universal Sovereign to man alone of the creatures of this earth: for He only is the author of sovereign power, who decrees that all should be subject to the rule of one. And surely monarchy far transcends every other constitution and form of government, for that democratic equality of power which is its opposite may rather be described as anarchy and disorder. Hence there is one God, and not two, or three, or more, for to assert a plurality of gods is plainly to deny the being of God at all. There is one Sovereign, and His Word and royal Law is one; a Law not expressed in syllables and words, not written or engraved on tablets, and therefore subject to the ravages of time; but the living and self-subsisting Word, who Himself is God, and who administers His Father's kingdom on behalf of all who are after Him and subject to His power. His attendants are the heavenly hosts; the myriads of God's angelic ministers; the super-terrestrial armies, of unnumbered multitude; and those unseen

---

[4]Constantine wanted to divide the Empire among his three sons and a nephew. The army, however, would not accept this arrangement. At Constantine's death, the soldiers murdered all his male relatives except his three sons and two sons of his half-brother, who were both little boys. One of these children was Julian, known as Julian the Apostate (361–363), the only subsequent Roman Emperor to favor a return to traditional paganism.

[5]Daniel 7:18

spirits within heaven itself, whose agency is employed in regulating the order of this world. Ruler and chief of all these is the royal Word, acting as Regent of the Supreme Sovereign. To Him the names of Captain, and great High Priest, Prophet of the Father, Angel of mighty counsel, Brightness of the Father's light,

5 Only begotten Son, with a thousand other titles, are ascribed in the oracles of the sacred writers. And the Father, having constituted Him the living Word, and Law, and Wisdom, the fullness of all blessing, has presented this best and greatest gift to all who are the subjects of His sovereignty. And He Himself, who pervades all things, and is everywhere present, unfolding His Father's bounties

10 to all with unsparing hand, has accorded a specimen of His sovereign power even to His rational creatures of this earth, in that He has provided the mind of man, who is formed after His own image, with divine faculties, whence it is capable of other virtues also, which flow from the same heavenly source. For He only is wise who is the only God. He only is essentially good. He only is

15 of mighty power, the Parent of justice, the Father of reason and wisdom, the Fountain of light and life, the Dispenser of truth and virtue. In a word, the Author of empire itself, and of all dominion and power.

# THE NICENE CREED

*The Council of Nicaea adopted the following statement as its official position on the Arian heresy.*

325

We believe in one God, the Father Almighty, maker of all things visible and invisible; and in one Lord, Jesus Christ, the Son of God, the only-begotten of his Father, of the substance of the Father, God of God, Light of Light, very God of very God, begotten, not made, being of one substance with the Father. By whom all things were made, both which be in heaven and in earth. Who for us    5
men and for our salvation came down and was incarnate and was made man. He suffered and the third day he rose again, and ascended into heaven. And he shall come again to judge both the quick and the dead. And we believe in the Holy Ghost. And whosoever shall say that there was a time when the Son of God was not, or that before he was begotten he was not, or that he was made    10
of things that were not, or that he is of a different substance or essence from the Father, or that he is a creature, or subject to change or conversion—all that so say, the Catholic and Apostolic Church anathematizes them.

*A Select Library of Nicene and Post-Nicene Fathers of the Christian Church*, Second Series, edited by Philip Schaff and Henry Wace (New York: Charles Scribner's Sons, 1905), XIV:3.

# CITY OF GOD

## AUGUSTINE (*c.* 260–*c.* 430)
### BISHOP OF HIPPO (396–430)

*c.* 410

### Preface, Explaining His Design in Undertaking This Work

[1]The glorious city of God is my theme in this work, which you, my dearest
son Marcellinus, suggested, and which is due to you by my promise. I have
undertaken its defense against those who prefer their own gods to the Founder
of this city—a city surpassingly glorious, whether we view it as it still lives by
faith in this fleeting course of time, and sojourns as a stranger in the midst of     5
the ungodly, or as it shall dwell in the fixed stability of its eternal seat, which
it now with patience waits for, expecting until "righteousness shall return unto
judgment"[1] and it obtain, by virtue of its excellence, final victory and perfect
peace. A great work this, and an arduous; but God is my helper. For I am
aware what ability is requisite to persuade the proud how great is the virtue     10
of humility, which raises us, not by a quite human arrogance, but by a divine
grace, above all earthly dignities that totter on this shifting scene. For the King
and Founder of this city of which we speak, has in Scripture uttered to His
people a dictum of the divine law in these words: "God resists the proud, but
gives grace unto the humble."[2] But this, which is God's prerogative, the inflated     15
ambition of a proud spirit also affects, and dearly loves that this be numbered
among its attributes, to

Show pity to the humbled soul, And crush the sons of pride.[3]

And therefore, as the plan of this work we have undertaken requires, and as
occasion offers, we must speak also of the earthly city, which, though it be     20
mistress of the nations, is itself ruled by its lust of rule....

---

[1]Psalm 94:15
[2]James 4:6, I Peter 5:5
[3]Virgil, *Aenid*, VI:854

---

*The Works of Aurelius Augustine, Bishop of Hippo*, edited by Marcus Dods (Edinburgh: T & T
Clark, 1871), I:1–2, 138–40; II:47–48, 322–28.

### Whether the Great Extent of the Empire, Which has been Acquired Only by Wars, is to be Reckoned Among the Good Things Either of the Wise or the Happy

[§3]Now, therefore, let us see how it is that they dare to ascribe the very great extent and duration of the Roman Empire to those gods whom they contend that they worship honorably, even by the obsequies of vile games and the ministry of vile men. Although I should like first to inquire for a little what reason,
5   what prudence, there is in wishing to glory in the greatness and extent of the Empire when you cannot point out the happiness of men who are always rolling, with dark fear and cruel lust, in warlike slaughters and in blood, which, whether shed in civil or foreign war, is still human blood; so that their joy may be compared to glass in its fragile splendor, of which one is horribly afraid lest
10  it should be suddenly broken in pieces.

That this may be more easily discerned, let us not come to naught by being carried away with empty boasting, or blunt the edge of our attention by loud-sounding names of things when we hear of peoples, kingdoms, provinces. But let us suppose a case of two men; for each individual man, like one letter in a
15  language, is as it were the element of a city or kingdom, however far-spreading in its occupation of the earth. Of these two men let us suppose that one is poor, or rather of middling circumstances; the other very rich. But the rich man is anxious with fears, pining with discontent, burning with covetousness, never secure, always uneasy, panting from the perpetual strife of his enemies, adding
20  to his patrimony indeed by these miseries to an immense degree, and by these additions also heaping up most bitter cares. But that other man of moderate wealth is contented with a small and compact estate, most dear to his own family, enjoying the sweetest peace with his kindred neighbors and friends, in piety religious, benignant in mind, healthy in body, in life frugal, in manners
25  chaste, in conscience secure. I know not whether anyone can be such a fool that he dare hesitate which to prefer.

As, therefore, in the case of these two men, so in two families, in two nations, in two kingdoms, this test of tranquility holds good; and if we apply it vigilantly and without prejudice, we shall quite easily see where the mere show of happi-
30  ness dwells, and where real felicity. Wherefore if the true God is worshipped, and if He is served with genuine rites and true virtue, it is advantageous that good men should long reign both far and wide. Nor is this advantageous so much to themselves as to those over whom they reign. For, so far as concerns themselves, their piety and probity, which are great gifts of God, suffice to give
35  them true felicity, enabling them to live well the life that now is, and afterwards to receive that which is eternal. In this world, therefore, the dominion of good

men is profitable, not so much for themselves as for human affairs. But the dominion of bad men is hurtful chiefly to themselves who rule, for they destroy their own souls by greater license in wickedness; while those who are put under them in service are not hurt except by their own iniquity. For to the just all the evils imposed on them by unjust rulers are not the punishment of crime, but    5
the test of virtue. Therefore the good man, although he is a slave, is free; but the bad man, even if he reigns, is a slave, and that not of one man, but, what is far more grievous, of as many masters as he has vices; of which vices when the divine Scripture treats, it says, "For of whom any man is overcome, to the same he is also the bond-slave."[4]                                                        10

## How Like Kingdoms Without Justice are to Robberies

**IV§4**Justice being taken away, then, what are kingdoms but great robberies? For what are robberies themselves, but little kingdoms? The band itself is made up of men; it is ruled by the authority of a prince, it is knit together by the pact of the confederacy; the booty is divided by the law agreed on. If, by the admittance of abandoned men, this evil increases to such a degree that it holds    15
places, fixes abodes, takes possession of cities, and subdues peoples, it assumes the more plainly the name of a kingdom, because the reality is now manifestly conferred on it, not by the removal of covetousness, but by the addition of impunity. Indeed, that was an apt and true reply which was given to Alexander the Great by a pirate who had been seized. For when that king had asked the    20
man what he meant by keeping hostile possession of the sea, he answered with bold pride, "What you mean by seizing the whole earth; but because I do it with a petty ship, I am called a robber, while you who does it with a great fleet are styled emperor."…

## Of the Nature of the Two Cities, the Earthly and the Heavenly

**IV§28**Accordingly, two cities have been formed by two loves: the earthly by the    25
love of self, even to the contempt of God; the heavenly by the love of God, even to the contempt of self. The former, in a word, glories in itself, the latter in the Lord. For the one seeks glory from men; but the greatest glory of the other is God, the witness of conscience. The one lifts up its head in its own glory; the other says to its God, "You are my glory, and the lifter up of my head."[5] In    30
the one, the princes and the nations it subdues are ruled by the love of ruling;

---

[4]II Peter 2:19
[5]Psalm 3:3

in the other, the princes and the subjects serve one another in love, the latter obeying, while the former take thought for all. The one delights in its own strength, represented in the persons of its rulers; the other says to its God, "I will love You, O Lord, my strength."[6] And therefore the wise men of the one
5    city, living according to man, have sought for profit to their own bodies or souls, or both, and those who have known God "glorified Him not as God, neither were thankful, but became vain in their imaginations, and their foolish heart was darkened; professing themselves to be wise"—that is, glorying in their own wisdom, and being possessed by pride—"they became fools, and changed the
10   glory of the incorruptible God into an image made like to corruptible man, and to birds, and four-footed beasts, and creeping things."[7] For they were either leaders or followers of the people in adoring images, "and worshiped and served the creature more than the Creator, who is blessed forever."[8] But in the other city there is no human wisdom, but only godliness, which offers due worship
15   to the true God, and looks for its reward in the society of the saints, of holy angels as well as holy men, "that God may be all in all."[9]...

### Of the Order and Law which Obtain in Heaven and Earth, Whereby it Comes to Pass that Human Society is Served by Those who Rule It

XIX§14The whole use, then, of things temporal has a reference to this result of earthly peace in the earthly community, while in the city of God it is con-nected with eternal peace. And therefore, if we were irrational animals, we
20   should desire nothing beyond the proper arrangement of the parts of the body and the satisfaction of the appetites—nothing, therefore, but bodily comfort and abundance of pleasures, that the peace of the body might contribute to the peace of the soul. For if bodily peace be wanting, a bar is put to the peace even of the irrational soul, since it cannot obtain the gratification of its appe-
25   tites. And these two together help out the mutual peace of soul and body, the peace of harmonious life and health. For as animals, by shunning pain, show that they love bodily peace and, by pursuing pleasure to gratify their appetites, show that they love peace of soul, so their shrinking from death is a sufficient indication of their intense love of that peace which binds soul and body in close
30   alliance. But, as man has a rational soul, he subordinates all this which he has in common with the beasts to the peace of his rational soul, that his intellect

---

[6]Psalm 18:1
[7]Romans 1:22–23
[8]Romans 1:25
[9]I Corinthians 15:28

may have free play and may regulate his actions, and that he may thus enjoy the well-ordered harmony of knowledge and action which constitutes, as we have said, the peace of the rational soul. And for this purpose he must desire to be neither molested by pain, nor disturbed by desire, nor extinguished by death, that he may arrive at some useful knowledge by which he may regulate   5
his life and manners.

But, owing to the liability of the human mind to fall into mistakes, this very pursuit of knowledge may be a snare to him unless he has a divine Master, whom he may obey without misgiving, and who may at the same time give him such help as to preserve his own freedom. And because, so long as he is in this   10
mortal body, he is a stranger to God, he walks by faith, not by sight; and he therefore refers all peace, bodily or spiritual or both, to that peace which mortal man has with the immortal God, so that he exhibits the well-ordered obedience of faith to eternal law. But as this divine Master inculcates two precepts—the love of God and the love of our neighbor—and as in these precepts a man finds   15
three things he has to love: God, himself, and his neighbor—and that he who loves God loves himself thereby, it follows that he must endeavor to get his neighbor to love God, since he is ordered to love his neighbor as himself. He ought to make this endeavor in behalf of his wife, his children, his household, all within his reach, even as he would wish his neighbor to do the same for him   20
if he needed it; and consequently he will be at peace, or in well-ordered concord, with all men, as far as in him lies. And this is the order of this concord, that a man, in the first place, injure no one, and, in the second, do good to everyone he can reach. Primarily, therefore, his own household are his care, for the law of nature and of society gives him readier access to them and greater opportunity   25
of serving them. And hence the apostle says, "Now, if any provide not for his own, and especially for those of his own house, he has denied the faith, and is worse than an infidel."[10] This is the origin of domestic peace, or the well-ordered concord of those in the family who rule and those who obey. For they who care for the rest rule—the husband the wife, the parents the children, the masters   30
the servants; and they who are cared for obey—the women their husbands, the children their parents, the servants their masters. But in the family of the just man who lives by faith and is as yet a pilgrim journeying on to the celestial city, even those who rule serve those whom they seem to command; for they rule not from a love of power, but from a sense of the duty they owe to others—not   35
because they are proud of authority, but because they love mercy.

---

[10]I Timothy 5:8

### Of the Liberty Proper to Man's Nature, and the Servitude Introduced by Sin—A Servitude in Which the Man Whose Will is Wicked is the Slave of his Own Lust, Though He is Free so Far as Regards Other Men

**XIX§15**This is prescribed by the order of nature: it is thus that God has created man. For "let them," He says, "have dominion over the fish of the sea, and over the fowl of the air, and over every creeping thing which creeps on the earth."[11] He did not intend that His rational creature, who was made in His image, should have dominion over anything but the irrational creation—not man over

5    man, but man over the beasts. And hence the righteous men in primitive times were made shepherds of cattle rather than kings of men, God intending thus to teach us what the relative position of the creatures is, and what the desert of sin; for it is with justice, we believe, that the condition of slavery is the result of sin. And this is why we do not find the word "slave" in any part of Scripture

10   until righteous Noah branded the sin of his son with this name.[12] It is a name, therefore, introduced by sin and not by nature. The origin of the Latin word for slave is supposed to be found in the circumstance that those who by the law of war were liable to be killed were sometimes preserved by their victors, and were hence called servants. And these circumstances could never have arisen

15   save through sin. For even when we wage a just war, our adversaries must be sinning; and every victory, even though gained by wicked men, is a result of the first judgment of God, who humbles the vanquished either for the sake of removing or of punishing their sins. Witness that man of God, Daniel, who, when he was in captivity, confessed to God his own sins and the sins of his

20   people, and declares with pious grief that these were the cause of the captivity.[13] The prime cause, then, of slavery is sin, which brings man under the dominion of his fellow—that which does not happen save by the judgment of God, with whom is no unrighteousness, and who knows how to award fit punishments to every variety of offence. But our Master in heaven says, "Everyone who sins is

25   the servant of sin."[14] And thus there are many wicked masters who have religious men as their slaves, and who are yet themselves in bondage; "for of whom a man is overcome, of the same is he brought in bondage."[15] And beyond question it is a happier thing to be the slave of a man than of lust; for even this very lust of ruling, to mention no others, lays waste men's hearts with the most ruthless

30   dominion. Moreover, when men are subjected to one another in a peaceful order,

---

[11]Genesis 1:26
[12]Genesis 9:25
[13]Daniel 9:4–19
[14]John 8:34
[15]II Peter 2:19

the lowly position does as much good to the servant as the proud position does harm to the master. But by nature, as God first created us, no one is the slave either of man or of sin. This servitude is, however, penal, and is appointed by that law which enjoins the preservation of the natural order and forbids its disturbance; for if nothing had been done in violation of that law, there would      5
have been nothing to restrain by penal servitude. And therefore the apostle admonishes slaves to be subject to their masters, and to serve them heartily and with good-will, so that, if they cannot be freed by their masters, they may themselves make their slavery in some sort free, by serving not in crafty fear, but in faithful love, until all unrighteousness pass away, and all principality and   10
every human power be brought to nothing, and God be all in all.

## Of Equitable Rule

**XIX§16**And therefore, although our righteous fathers had slaves, and administered their domestic affairs so as to distinguish between the condition of slaves and the heirship of sons in regard to the blessings of this life, yet in regard to the worship of God, in Whom we hope for eternal blessings, they took an equally   15
loving oversight of all the members of their household. And this is so much in accordance with the natural order that the head of the household was called *paterfamilias*; and this name has been so generally accepted that even those whose rule is unrighteous are glad to apply it to themselves. But those who are true fathers of their households desire and endeavor that all the members of   20
their household, equally with their own children, should worship and win God, and should come to that heavenly home in which the duty of ruling men is no longer necessary, because the duty of caring for their everlasting happiness has also ceased; but, until they reach that home, masters ought to feel their position of authority a greater burden than servants their service. And if any member of   25
the family interrupts the domestic peace by disobedience, he is corrected either by word or blow, or some kind of just and legitimate punishment, such as society permits, that he may himself be the better for it, and be re-adjusted to the family harmony from which he had dislocated himself. For as it is not benevolent to give a man help at the expense of some greater benefit he might receive, so   30
it is not innocent to spare a man at the risk of his falling into graver sin. To be innocent, we must not only do harm to no man, but also restrain him from sin or punish his sin, so that either the man himself who is punished may profit by his experience, or others be warned by his example. Since, then, the house ought to be the beginning or element of the city, and every beginning bears reference   35
to some end of its own kind, and every element to the integrity of the whole of which it is an element, it follows plainly enough that domestic peace has a rela-

tion to civic peace—in other words, that the well-ordered concord of domestic obedience and domestic rule has a relation to the well-ordered concord of civic obedience and civic rule. And therefore it follows, further, that the father of the family ought to frame his domestic rule in accordance with the law of the city, 5    so that the household may be in harmony with the civic order.

### What Produces Peace, and What Discord, Between the Heavenly and Earthly Cities

**XIX§17** But the families which do not live by faith seek their peace in the earthly advantages of this life; while the families which live by faith look for those eternal blessings which are promised, and use as pilgrims such advantages of time and of earth as do not fascinate and divert them from God, but rather aid them 10    to endure with greater ease, and to keep down the number of those burdens of the corruptible body which weigh upon the soul. Thus the things necessary for this mortal life are used by both kinds of men and families alike, but each has its own peculiar and widely different aim in using them. The earthly city, which does not live by faith, seeks an earthly peace, and the end it proposes, 15    in the well-ordered concord of civic obedience and rule, is the combination of men's wills to attain the things which are helpful to this life. The heavenly city, or rather the part of it which sojourns on earth and lives by faith, makes use of this peace only because it must, until this mortal condition which necessitates it shall pass away. Consequently, so long as it lives like a captive and a stranger 20    in the earthly city, though it has already received the promise of redemption, and the gift of the Spirit as the earnest of it, it makes no scruple to obey the laws of the earthly city, whereby the things necessary for the maintenance of this mortal life are administered; and thus, as this life is common to both cities, so there is a harmony between them in regard to what belongs to it. But, as 25    the earthly city has had some philosophers whose doctrines is condemned by the divine teaching, and who, being deceived either by their own conjectures or by demons, supposed that many gods must be invited to take an interest in human affairs, and assigned to each a separate function and a separate depart-ment—to one the body, to another the soul; and in the body itself, to one the 30    head, to another the neck, and each of the other members to one of the gods; and in like manner, in the soul, to one god the natural capacity was assigned, to another education, to another anger, to another lust; and so the various affairs of life were assigned—cattle to one, corn to another, wine to another, oil to another, the woods to another, money to another, navigation to another, wars 35    and victories to another, marriages to another, births and fecundity to another, and other things to other gods: and as the celestial city, on the other hand, knew that one God only was to be worshipped, and that to Him alone was due that service which the Greeks call λατρεια, and which can be given only to a god, it has come to pass that the two cities could not have common laws of religion, and that the heavenly city has been compelled in this matter to dissent, and to become obnoxious to those who think differently, and to stand the brunt of their anger and hatred and persecutions, except in so far as the minds of their enemies have been alarmed by the multitude of the Christians and quelled by the manifest protection of God accorded to them.

This heavenly city, then, while it sojourns on earth, calls citizens out of all nations, and gathers together a society of pilgrims of all languages, not scrupling about diversities in the manners, laws, and institutions, whereby earthly peace is secured and maintained, but recognizing that, however various these are, they all tend to one and the same end of earthly peace. It therefore is so far from rescinding and abolishing these diversities that it even preserves and adopts them, so long only as no hindrance to the worship of the one supreme and true God is thus introduced. Even the heavenly city, therefore, while in its state of pilgrimage, avails itself of the peace of earth, and, so far as it can without injuring faith and godliness, desires and maintains a common agreement among men regarding the acquisition of the necessaries of life, and makes this earthly peace bear upon the peace of heaven; for this alone can be truly called and esteemed the peace of the reasonable creatures, consisting as it does in the perfectly ordered and harmonious enjoyment of God and of one another in God. When we shall have reached that peace, this mortal life shall give place to one that is eternal, and our body shall be no more this animal body which by its corruption weighs down the soul, but a spiritual body feeling no want, and in all its members subjected to the will. In its pilgrim state the heavenly city possesses this peace by faith; and by this faith it lives righteously when it refers to the attainment of that peace every good action towards God and man; for the life of the city is a social life....

# LETTER TO ANASTASIUS I
## GELASIUS I, POPE (492–496) TO
### ANASTASIUS I (*c.* 430–518), EMPEROR (491–518)

*Debates over the question of the relationship of Christ's humanity to His divinity divided the Church for most of the fourth and fifth centuries. As Eusebius's account of the Council of Nicaea made clear, emperors were from time to time prepared to urge a compromise in these serious theological disputes in the interests of unity, much to the dismay of churchmen, especially those from the West, whose native Latin rendered incomprehensible many of the theological subtleties debated so heatedly in the Greek East. In an attempt to appease a large group of Christians who rejected the theological position adopted by the Council of Chalcedon in 451—a position Western churchmen considered definitive—the Emperor Zeno (r. 474–491) issued a compromise statement in 482 that led to a temporary schism between Rome and Constantinople. During the course of this schism, Pope Gelasius I wrote the following letter to Zeno's successor, Anastasius I. This letter was quoted in Western discussions of the proper relationship between spiritual and temporal authority for nearly a thousand years.*

*c.* 494

... There are two powers, august Emperor, by which this world is chiefly ruled; namely, the sacred authority of the priests and the royal power. Of these, that of the priests is the more weighty, since they have to render an account for even the kings of men in the divine judgment. You are also aware, dear son, that while you are permitted honorably to rule over human kind, yet in things divine you    5
bow your head humbly before the leaders of the clergy and await from their hands the means of your salvation. In the reception and proper disposition of the heavenly mysteries you recognize that you should be subordinate rather than superior to the religious order, and that in these matters you depend on their judgment rather than wish to force them to follow your will.    10

If the ministers of religion, recognizing the supremacy granted you from heaven in matters affecting the public order, obey your laws, lest otherwise they might obstruct the course of secular affairs by irrelevant considerations,

*Readings in European History*, edited by James Harvey Robinson (New York: Ginn and Company, 1904), I:72–73.

with what readiness should you not yield them obedience to whom is assigned the dispensing of the sacred mysteries of religion. Accordingly, just as there is no slight danger in the case of the priests if they refrain from speaking when the service of the divinity requires, so there is no little risk for those who disdain—which God forbid—when they should obey. And if it is fitting that the hearts of the faithful should submit to all priests in general who properly administer divine affairs, how much the more is obedience due to the bishop of that see[1] which the Most High ordained to be above all others, and which is consequently dutifully honored by the devotion of the whole Church....

[1] *See*—diocese, bishopric

# VII
# THE EARLY MIDDLE AGES

Although only a date of significance because it gives some finality to an ongoing process, AD 476 familiarly marks a transition from the Ancient to the Medieval World. Despite the long shadow cast by Roman civilization, the subsequent medieval world offered a sharp contrast with antiquity. While the re-conquests of the Emperor Justinian (*r.* 518–527) would temporarily return the Mediterranean world to its Roman imperial unity, from AD 476 onward, a civilization developed in Western Europe continuing the fusion of classical and Christian elements under the guidance of the Germanic Rulers and the Catholic Church.

The world of late antiquity produced three heirs: the Islamic World, the Byzantine Empire, and the Christian kingdoms of the Germanic West. The Islamic World inherited the ancient core of Mesopotamia, Palestine, Syria, Egypt, Roman Africa, and Spain. The Islamic Caliphates united this world with an uncompromising monotheism and culture based on the teachings of Muhammad as contained in the Koran. The Byzantine, or Eastern Roman, Empire continued the cultural heritage of the Christian Roman Empire, albeit in the Greek language and with developing cultural forms of their own. The Germanic kingdoms carried on the heritage of the Western Roman Empire in culture and the Latin language.

The period from AD 500–750 experienced the transformation of the Germanic West. Slowly, the earlier Germanic kingdoms centered on the Mediterranean collapsed. The Arian Vandals fell to Justinian's general Belisarius in AD 532–534. The Arian Ostrogoths, despite the promising rule of Theodoric (493–526) fell in the devastating war with the Byzantines (535–555). The Visigoths, who remained Arian until 589, managed to hold out against the Byzantine Empire, only to fall to the Muslims (711–716). The Lombards, Arians who entered Italy in 568 and warred with both popes and Byzantines (755, 756), fell to the Franks (773–774). The power of endurance in the West resided in one institution, the Catholic Church, and in two Germanic peoples, the Anglo-Saxons and the Franks.

Even during the decline of the Roman Empire in the West, the status of the popes had begun to rise. In the late fourth century, the pagan urban prefect of Rome, Praetextatus, illustrated the importance of the Bishop of Rome in his statement to Pope Damasus (*r.* 366–384), "make me the Bishop of Rome, and I will be a Christian tomorrow." By the pontificate of Gregory the Great (590–604), the papacy had completely assumed the role of the once-powerful urban prefect in providing urban services and patronage, and had also begun to establish temporal rule in central Italy. Feeling threats from Byzantines, Lombards, and finally Muslims, the papacy sought alliances with the Franks. The propitious mission of Augustine of Canterbury, sent by Gregory to re-Christianize the British Isles, helped to attach the future of Christian Western Europe to the Anglo-Saxons as well.

Drawing on its roots in the later Roman world, Christian monasticism served as the primary agent in the continuing process of creating a uniquely Christian culture. The formalization of Western cenobitic monasticism in the Rule of Benedict created an institution, the monastery, which, along with the leadership of bishops in the remaining urban centers, would dominate intellectual culture through the entire early middle ages. Cassiodorus (*c.* 485–580) not only provided a model, later further elaborated upon by Isidore of Seville (*c.* 560–636), for monastic libraries and their attendant scriptoria (writing centers), but also articulated an intellectual program for monks in his *Institutes,* writing, "Read assiduously, diligently return to your reading, for constant and intent meditation is the mother of understanding." His contemporary, the philosopher and scholar of the quadrivium, Boethius (*c.* 480–524/5), ensured that Plato and a small portion of Aristotle would remain known in the West.

While the Celtic church converted by Saint Patrick would have a profound influence on early medieval culture, the conversion of the Anglo-Saxons (who migrated to Britain *c.* 450–600) begun by Augustine of Canterbury (597), as well as the mission of Columba (from 563) firmed up the foundation of Catholic Christianity in the West, allowing for a unified medieval Christian Europe to begin development. While the Synod of Whitby (664) would settle the question of Roman versus Celtic religious usage, the mission of Theodore (sent as Archbishop of Canterbury, 668–690) would re-invigorate Christian culture, leading to the creation of a brilliant monastic culture in Northumbria, particularly evident in the career of the Venerable Bede (673–735).

On the continent, the warlike Franks, led by the Merovingian dynasty, consolidated and then converted to Catholicism under the rule of Clovis (486–511). The kingdoms of his successors, although often feuding, provided enough stability for the Church to grow as the Franks blended with the Gallo-Romans. The Merovingian kings sought to maintain the traditions of Roman Rule and establish close ties with the Church. By the mid-eighth century, the Carolingians, a powerful aristocratic family, rose and challenged the position of the Merovingians. In 733, Charles Martel, the first prominent member of the family, led the Frankish armies that checked the Muslim advance into Europe at Tours/Poitiers. By 750, the Carolingian mayors of the palace possessed more power than the Merovingian kings, and in 751, Pippin III sought the recognition of Pope Zachary and became king. Pope Stephen anointed Pippin in 754, which both confirmed the sacral nature of his office and united and transformed Western Europe by sealing an alliance between Frankish kings and popes. This development both solidified Christendom and provided the basis for medieval political culture.

During his reign Charlemagne (786–814) united Western Europe and forged a political and cultural hegemony. Einhard's *Life of Charlemagne* explores the many aspects of this complex figure's long reign. Charlemagne restored the united Merovingian borders and expanded to create an empire stretching from northeastern Spain through northern Italy to Bavaria in the south and from Brittany to Denmark in the north. Institutionally, his kingdom created a court at Aachen, with attendant courtiers and annual assemblies of the warriors, which remained connected to the rest of the empire through a system of capitularies (circular legal letters) and the granting of benefices to loyal followers in return for obligations. In terms of religious institutions, Charlemagne maintained even closer ties with the papacy than had his predecessors. He extended the church hierarchy and promulgated capitularies aiming at uniformity in canon law, liturgy, and monastic practices. His reign continued the work of missionaries like Boniface, both solidifying the faith within the Frankish world and endeavoring to expand it into new areas. On Christmas day in the year 800, Pope Leo III crowned Charlemagne Roman Emperor. While this event helped to make even more formal the relationship between the Frankish ruler and the papacy, an idea of a universal imperial tradition, which combined the idea of the Franks as a "New Israel" with political Augustinianism culminating in the idea of a united Christendom, also emerged from it.

Much like their Merovingian predecessors, the Carolingians could not maintain political hegemony over the empire created by Charlemagne. Factors including family rivalries, complex regional problems, and the absence of a tradition of unified rule undermined efforts internally. Viking, Muslim, and Magyar attacks created disorder from the outside and dissolved the bonds of regions with the center leaving a militarized and localized society. Fortunately for Western Europe, the Carolingians did create an enduring culture.

The Carolingian Renaissance, a period of reform and revival of classical (Roman) and Christian (both biblical and patristic) culture, lasted from the reign of Charlemagne into the late ninth century. The leading scholar of Charlemagne's court, Alcuin (735–804), served as the principle advisor to Charlemagne in these efforts. Letters like *Epistolas de collendis* to Baugulf show the crucial role of schools to cultivate the seven liberal arts, particularly grammar, the essential key to interpreting scripture. This quickening of intellectual culture saw the creation or refurbishing of schools (under the leadership of skilled masters), libraries, and scriptoria. While these reforms primarily sought to make the clergy more effective, they reached the laity as well.

The movement combined the efforts of both monastic and cathedral schools (nascent in their development) and provided the firm basis for a common European intellectual and religious culture.

Developments in Anglo-Saxon England in many ways mirrored those on the continent. Plagued by Viking attacks and cultural stagnation, the reign of Alfred the Great (871–899) began the process of unification. More significantly, connection with the continent allowed for the transmission of cultural reforms leading to renewal and redefinition (as seen in Alfred's efforts to translate Latin works into the vernacular). Alfred's successors, using the effective organization of shires (local communities) and *fyrd* (military) service, proved more capable than the Carolingians in continuing political domination.

While the Capetian dynasty of Hugh Capet (987–996) would rise from the remnants of Carolingian rule in France, the Ottonian dynasty arose in Germany as both successors to the imperial title and close connections with the papacy. Successful in checking the advance of the Magyars at Lechfeld (955), Ottonian rulers sought to unite their Saxon homeland with the other German duchies. They accomplished this by keeping tight control of the church, particularly the appointment of bishops and abbots. Although this complicated the relationship between church and state, as did the coronation of Otto I as Holy Roman Emperor in 962, it also allowed for the development of cathedral schools. These trained future bishops and members of the imperial chancery.

The period known as the Early Middle Ages effectively ends in the transitional period around AD 1000. Although, like many attempts at periodization, a somewhat arbitrary date, by this time the Carolingian political world had broken down into the pieces that would become the kingdoms of the High Middle Ages. With the exception of Ottonian Germany, the intellectual culture created during the Carolingian Renaissance had lost momentum. The period around 1000 does, however, clearly mark a transition. The close connection with the Roman and early Christian periods are no longer as keenly felt, and a new medieval world, marked by self-consciously Christian kings and united in culture by the church, has emerged.

# THE BENEDICTINE RULE
## BENEDICT OF NURSIA (c. 480–543)

*Monasticism originated in the Egyptian desert in the late third century. Its scriptural basis was the story of the rich young man in the Gospels who asked Jesus what he needed to do to have eternal life. Jesus replied that he needed to keep the commandments; if he wished to be perfect, the young man should sell all he had, give it to the poor, and follow Him. Once the young man had departed, Jesus said to his disciples that those who left home, family, and possessions for His sake would be rewarded a hundredfold and have eternal life.*

*After Christianity was legalized and the possibility of being asked to give up one's life for Christ was consequently diminished, the monastic life began to be seen as the new form of martyrdom. The earliest monks were hermits, though they were not completely cut off from human contact since their reputation for holiness led many to seek them out for spiritual counsel. Communities of monks soon followed. Saint Basil the Great (330–379), father of Eastern monasticism, declared that living in a monastic community was preferable to living as a hermit because it was difficult to practice the virtue of charity if one had no neighbor.*

*In Gaul, the earliest monastic communities shared the extreme austerity that was characteristic of Eastern monasticism. In the sixth century, however, Saint Benedict of Nursia wrote a rule for monasteries, which, as Gregory the Great (540–604) pointed out, was "remarkable for its discretion." In his rule, based on the earlier, anonymous "Rule of the Master," Benedict prescribed a form of monastic life that required no rigorous physical hardships and could be adapted for communities of men or women in a wide variety of local conditions. Over time, the Benedictine Rule became the basis for most forms of the monastic life in the West.*

*To some degree, monasteries provided early medieval Europe with some of the urban functions of the old Roman cities. They kept alive*

"The Rule of Saint Benedict," translated by Oliver Joseph Thatcher, in *The Library of Original Sources* (Milwaukee, WI: University Extension Company, 1907), prologue, 130.

Oliver J. Thatcher and Edgar H. McNeal, *A Source Book for Mediaeval History* (New York: Scribners, 1905), 435–38, 440–46, 453–54, 456–57, 462–63, 467–68, 470, 478, 484–85.

*the intellectual heritage of Antiquity, preserving and copying many old manuscripts. This was especially true in economic terms, as the diligent and efficient monks, living under the principle "laborare est orare" (to work is to pray), cleared and put into production frontier land, often using the newest technology to do so. Ironically, these monasteries became places of wealth and power, causing Church reformers to found new monastic orders that would return to the primitive simplicity of the apostles. Such orders as the Cluniacs, Cistercians, Franciscans, and Dominicans showed the pattern of decadence and renewal in medieval Christendom.*

## Prologue

…Therefore we are constrained to found a school for the service of the Lord. In its organization we hope we shall ordain nothing severe, nothing burdensome; but if there should result anything a little irksome by the demands of justice for the correction of vices and the persevering of charity, do not therefore, through
5  fear, avoid the way of salvation, which cannot be entered upon save through a narrow entrance, but in which, as life progresses and the heart becomes filled with faith, one walks in the unspeakable sweetness of love; but never departing from His school, and persevering in His doctrine in the monastery until death, let us with patience share in the sufferings of Christ, that we may be worthy to
10  be partakers in His kingdom.…

## Chapter 2—The Qualities Necessary for an Abbot

The abbot who is worthy to rule over a monastery ought always to bear in mind by what name he is called and to justify by his life his title of superior. For he represents Christ in the monastery, receiving his name from the saying of the Apostle, "You have received the Spirit of adoption, whereby we cry, Abba,
15  Father."[1] Therefore the abbot should not teach or command anything contrary to the precepts of the Lord, but his commands and his teaching should be in accord with divine justice. He should always bear in mind that both his teaching and the obedience of his disciples will be inquired into on the dread day of judgment. For the abbot should know that the shepherd will have to bear
20  the blame if the Master finds anything wrong with the flock. Only in case the shepherd has displayed all diligence and care in correcting the fault of a restive and disobedient flock will he be freed from blame at the judgment of God, and be able to say to the Lord in the words of the prophet, "I have not hid Your

---

[1]Romans 8:15

righteousness within my heart; I have declared Your faithfulness and Your salvation;" but "they despising have scorned me."[2] Then shall the punishment fall upon the flock who scorned his care and it shall be the punishment of death.

The abbot ought to follow two methods in governing his disciples: teaching the commandments of the Lord to the apt disciples by his words, and to the obdurate and the simple by his deeds. And when he teaches his disciples that certain things are wrong, he should demonstrate it in his own life by not doing those things, lest when he has preached to others he himself should be a castaway,[3] and lest God should sometime say to him, a sinner, "What have you to do to declare My statutes, or that you should take My covenant in your mouth? Seeing that you hate instruction, and cast My words behind you," or "Why do you behold the mote that is in your brother's eye, but consider not the beam that is in your own eye?"[4] Let there be no respect of persons in the monastery. Let the abbot not love one more than another, unless it be one who excels in good works and in obedience. The freeman is not to be preferred to the one who comes into the monastery out of servitude, unless there be some other good reason. But if it seems right and fitting to the abbot, let him show preference to anyone of any rank whatsoever; otherwise let them keep their own places. For whether slave or free, we are all one in Christ and bear the same yoke of servitude to the one Lord, for there is no respect of persons with God.[5] For we have special favor in His sight only in so far as we excel others in all good works and in humility. Therefore, the abbot should have the same love toward all and should subject all to the same discipline according to their respective merits....

The abbot should always remember his office and his title, and should realize that as much is entrusted to him, so also much will be required from him. Let him realize how difficult and arduous a task he has undertaken, to rule the hearts and care for the morals of many persons, who require, one encouragements, another threats, and another persuasion. Let him so adapt his methods to the disposition and intelligence of each one that he may not only preserve the flock committed to him entire and free from harm, but may even rejoice in its increase.

Above all, the abbot should not be too zealous in the acquisition of earthly, transitory, mortal goods, forgetting and neglecting the care of the souls committed to his charge, but he should always remember that he has undertaken the government of souls of whose welfare he must render account....

---

[2]Psalm 40:10; Ezekiel 20:27
[3]I Corinthians 9:27
[4]Psalm 50:16–17; Matthew 7:3
[5]Galatians 3:28; Romans 2:11

### Chapter 3—Taking Counsel with the Brethren

Whenever important matters come up in the monastery, the abbot should call together the whole congregation and tell them what is under consideration. After hearing the advice of the brothers, he should reflect upon it and then do what seems best to him. We advise the calling of the whole congregation,
5    because the Lord often reveals what is best to one of the younger brothers. But let the brethren give their advice with all humility, and not defend their opinions too boldly; rather let them leave it to the decision of the abbot, and all obey him. But while the disciples ought to obey the master, he on his part ought to manage all things justly and wisely. Let everyone in the monastery obey the
10   rule in all things, and let no one depart from it to follow the desires of his own heart. Let no one of the brethren presume to dispute the authority of the abbot, either within or without the monastery; if anyone does so, let him be subjected to the discipline prescribed in the rule. But the abbot should do all things in the fear of the Lord, knowing that he must surely render account to God, the
15   righteous judge, for all his decisions. If matters of minor importance are to be considered, concerning the welfare of the monastery, let the abbot take counsel with the older brethren, as it is written: "Do all things with counsel, and after it is done you will not repent."[6]

### Chapter 5—Obedience

The first grade of humility is obedience without delay, which is becoming to
20   those who hold nothing dearer than Christ. So, when one of the monks receives a command from a superior, he should obey it immediately, as if it came from God Himself, being impelled thereto by the holy service he has professed and by the fear of hell and the desire of eternal life. Of such the Lord says, "As soon as he heard of Me, he obeyed Me;" and again to the Apostles, "He that
25   hears you, hears Me."[7] Such disciples, when they are commanded, immediately abandon their own business and their own plans, leaving undone what they were at work upon. With ready hands and willing feet they hasten to obey the commands of their superior, their act following on the heels of his command, and both the order and the fulfillment occurring, as it were, in the same
30   moment of time—such promptness does the fear of the Lord inspire.
     Good disciples who are inspired by the desire for eternal life gladly take up that narrow way of which the Lord said, "Narrow is the way which leads

---

[6]Sirach 32:24
[7]Psalm 17:44; Luke 10:16

unto life."[8] They have no wish to control their own lives or to obey their own will and desires, but prefer to be ruled by an abbot, and to live in a monastery, accepting the guidance and control of another. Surely such disciples follow the example of the Lord, who said, "I came not to do my own will, but the will of Him that sent me."[9] But this obedience will be acceptable to God and pleasing to men only if it be not given fearfully, or half-heartedly, or slowly, or with grumbling and protests. For the obedience which is given to a superior is given to God, as He Himself has said, "Who hears you, hears me."[10] Disciples ought to obey with glad hearts, "for the Lord loves a cheerful giver."[11] If the disciple obeys grudgingly and complains even within his own heart, his obedience will not be accepted by God, Who sees his unwilling heart; he will gain no favor for works done in that spirit, but, unless he does penance and mends his ways, he will rather receive the punishment of those that murmur against the Lord's commands.

## Chapter 7—Humility

Brethren, the holy Scripture says, "And whosoever shall exalt himself shall be abased; and he that shall humble himself shall be exalted."[12]... Therefore, brethren, if we wish to attain to the highest measure of humility and to that exaltation in heaven which is only to be gained by lowliness on earth, we must raise to heaven by our deeds such a ladder as appeared to Jacob in his dream, whereon he saw angels ascending and descending. For the meaning of that figure is that we ascend by humility of heart and descend by haughtiness.

And the ladder is our life here below which God raises to heaven for the lowly of heart. Our body and soul are the two sides of the ladder, in which by deeds consistent with our holy calling we insert steps whereby we may ascend to heaven.

Now the first step of humility is this, to escape destruction by keeping ever before one's eyes the fear of the Lord, to remember always the commands of the Lord, for they who scorn Him are in danger of hellfire, and to think of the eternal life that is prepared for them that fear Him. So a man should keep himself in every hour from the sins of the heart, of the tongue, of the eyes, of the hands, and of the feet. He should cast aside his own will and the desires of the flesh; he should think that God is looking down on him from heaven all the time, and that his acts are seen by God and reported to Him hourly by his angels....

---

[8]Matthew 7:14
[9]John 6:38
[10]Luke 10:16
[11]II Corinthians 9:7
[12]Matthew 23:12

The second step of humility is this, that a man should not delight in doing his own will and desires, but should imitate the Lord, who said, "I came not to do mine own will, but the will of him that sent me."[13]....

The fifth step of humility is this, that a man should not hide the evil thoughts
5   that arise in his heart or the sins which he has committed in secret, but should humbly confess them to his abbot....

The eighth step of humility is this, that the monk should follow in everything the common rule of the monastery and the examples of his superiors.

The ninth step of humility is this, that the monk should restrain his tongue
10  from speaking, and should keep silent even from questioning, as the Scripture says, "In a multitude of words there wants not sin" and "Let not an evil speaker be established in the earth."[14]

The tenth step of humility is this, that the monk should be not easily provoked to laughter, as it is written, "The fool raises his voice in laughter."[15]

15      The eleventh step of humility is this, that the monk, when he speaks, should do so slowly and without laughter, softly and gravely, using few words and reasonable, and that he should not be loud of voice; as it is written, "A wise man is known for his few words."

The twelfth step of humility is this, that the monk should always be humble
20  and lowly, not only in his heart, but in his bearing as well. Wherever he may be, in divine service, in the oratory, in the garden, on the road, in the fields, whether sitting, walking, or standing, he should always keep his head bowed and his eyes upon the ground. He should always be meditating upon his sins and thinking of the dread day of judgment, saying to himself as did that publican
25  of whom the gospel speaks, "Lord, I am not worthy, I a sinner, so much as to lift my eyes up to heaven;" and again with the prophet, "I am bowed down and humbled everywhere."[16]

Now when the monk has ascended all these steps of humility, he will arrive at that perfect love of God which casts out all fear.[17] By that love all those
30  commandments which he could not formerly observe without grievous effort and struggle, he will now obey naturally and easily, as if by habit; not in the fear of hell, but in the love of Christ and by his very delight in virtue. And thus the Lord will show the working of his Holy Spirit in this, His servant, freed from vices and sins.

---

[13]John 6:38

[14]Proverbs 10:19; Psalm 140:11

[15]Sirach 21:23

[16]Luke 18:13; Psalm 119:107

[17]I John 4:18

### Chapter 19—The Behavior of the Monks in the Services

We know, of course, that the divine presence is everywhere, and that "the eyes of the Lord look down everywhere upon the good and the evil," but we should realize this in its fullness, especially when we take part in divine worship. Remember the words of the prophet, "Serve the Lord in all fear," and again "Sing wisely," and yet again, "In the sight of the angels I will sing unto You."[18]  5 Let us then consider how we should behave in the sight of God and His angels, and let us so comport ourselves in the service of praise that our hearts may be in harmony with our voices.

### Chapter 20—The Reverence to be Shown in Prayer

When we have any request to make of powerful persons, we proffer it humbly and reverently; with how much greater humility and devotion, then, should we  10 offer our supplications unto God, the Lord of all. We should realize, too, that we are not heard for our much speaking, but for the purity and the contrition of our hearts. So when we pray, our prayer should be simple and brief, unless we are moved to speak by the inspiration of the Spirit. The prayer offered before the congregation also should be brief, and all the brothers should rise at the  15 signal of the superior.

### Chapter 28—Those who do not Mend their Ways after frequent Correction

If any brother has been frequently corrected and excommunicated, and still does not mend his ways, let the punishment be increased to the laying on of blows. But if he will not be corrected or if he attempts to defend his acts, then the abbot shall proceed to extreme measures as a wise physician will do; that  20 is, when the poultices and ointments, as it were, of prayer, the medicines of Scripture, and the violent remedies of excommunication and blows have all failed, he has recourse to the last means, prayer to God, the all-powerful, that He should work the salvation of the erring brother. But if he still cannot be cured, then the abbot shall proceed to the use of the knife, cutting out that evil  25 member from the congregation; as the Apostle says, "Put away from among yourselves that wicked person;" "If the unbelieving depart, let him depart;"[19] that the whole flock be not contaminated by one diseased sheep.

---

[18]Psalm 2:11; Psalm 47:7; Psalm 138:1
[19]I Corinthians 5:13; I Corinthians 7:15

## Chapter 29—Shall Brothers who have Left the Monastery be Received Back?

If a brother has left the monastery or has been cast out for his own fault, and shall wish to be taken back, he shall first of all promise complete reformation of that fault, and then shall be received into the lowest grade in the monastery to prove the sincerity of his humility. If he again departs, he shall be received back the third
5    time, knowing, however, that after that he shall never again be taken back.

## Chapter 30—The Manner of Correction for the Young

The forms of punishment should be adapted to every age and to every order of intelligence. So if children or youths, or those who are unable to appreciate the meaning of excommunication, are found guilty, they should be given heavy fasts and sharp blows for their correction.

## Chapter 33—Monks Should not Have Personal Property

10   The sin of owning private property should be entirely eradicated from the monastery. No one shall presume to give or receive anything except by the order of the abbot; no one shall possess anything of his own, books, paper, pens, or anything else; for monks are not to own even their own bodies and wills to be used at their own desire, but are to look to the father of the monastery for everything. So they
15   shall have nothing that has not been given or allowed to them by the abbot; all things are to be had in common according to the command of the Scriptures, and no one shall consider anything as his own property. If anyone has been found guilty of this most grievous sin, he shall be admonished for the first and second offence, and then if he does not mend his ways he shall be punished.

## Chapter 34—Whether All the Brothers are to be Treated Equally

20   It is written, "Distribution was made unto every man as he had need."[20] This does not mean that there should be respect of persons, but rather consideration for infirmities. The one who has less need should give thanks to God and not be envious; the one who has greater need should be humbled because of his infirmity, and not puffed up by the greater consideration shown him. Thus all
25   the members of the congregation shall dwell together in peace. Above all, let there be no complaint about anything, either in word or manner, and if anyone is guilty of this let him be strictly disciplined.

---

[20]Acts 4:35

## Chapter 39—The Amount of Food

Two cooked dishes, served either at the sixth or the ninth hour, should be sufficient for the daily sustenance. We allow two because of difference in taste, so that those who do not eat one may satisfy their hunger with the other, but two shall suffice for all the brothers, unless it is possible to obtain fruit or fresh vegetables, which may be served as a third. One pound of bread shall suffice 5 for the day, whether there be one meal or two. If the monks are to have supper as well as dinner, the cellarer shall cut off a third of the loaf of bread which is served at dinner and keep it for the later meal. In the case of those who engage in heavy labor, the abbot may at his discretion increase the allowance of food, but he should not allow the monks to indulge their appetites by eating or drinking 10 too much. For no vice is more inconsistent with the Christian character; as the Master says, "Take heed to yourselves lest at any time your hearts be overcharged with surfeiting."[21] A smaller amount of food shall be given to the youths than to their elders, and in general the rule should be to eat sparingly. All shall abstain from the flesh of four-footed beasts, except the weak and the sick. 15

## Chapter 48—The Daily Labor of the Monks

Idleness is the enemy of the soul; therefore the monks should always be occupied, either in manual labor or in holy reading.... But if the conditions of the locality or the needs of the monastery, such as may occur at harvest time, should make it necessary to labor longer hours, they shall not feel themselves ill-used, for true monks should live by the labor of their own hands, as did the 20 Apostles and the holy fathers. But the weakness of human nature must be taken into account in making these arrangements.... If any brother is negligent or lazy, refusing or being unable profitably to read or meditate at the time assigned for that, let him be made to work, so that he shall at any rate not be idle. The abbot shall have consideration for the weak and the sick, giving them tasks 25 suited to their strength, so that they may neither be idle nor yet be distressed by too heavy labor.

## Chapter 53—The Reception of Guests

All guests who come to the monastery are to be received in the name of Christ, who said, "I was a stranger and you took me in."[22] Honor and respect shall

---

[21]Luke 21:34
[22]Matthew 25:35

be shown to all, but especially to Christians and strangers. When a guest is announced the superior and the brothers shall hasten to meet him and shall give him the kindest welcome. At meeting, both shall say a short prayer and then they shall exchange the kiss of peace, the prayer being said first to frustrate the wiles of the devil. The manner of salutation shall be humble and devout; he who offers it to a guest shall bow his head or even prostrate his body on the ground in adoration of Christ, in whose name guests are received.... [Particular] honor shall be shown to the poor and to strangers, since it is in them that Christ is especially received; for the power of the rich in itself compels honor.

### Chapter 72—The Good Zeal Which Monks Should Have

There are two kinds of zeal: one that leads away from God to destruction, and one that leads to God and eternal life. Now these are the features of that good zeal which monks should cultivate: to honor one another; to bear with one another's infirmities, whether of body or mind; to vie with one another in showing mutual obedience; to seek the good of another rather than of oneself; to show brotherly love one to another; to fear God; to love the abbot devotedly; and to prefer the love of Christ above everything else. This is the zeal that leads us to eternal life.

### Chapter 73—This Rule Does Not Contain all the Measures Necessary for Righteousness

The purpose of this rule is to furnish a guide to the monastic life. Those who observe it will have at least entered on the way of salvation and will attain at least some degree of holiness. But he who aims at the perfect life must study and observe the teachings of all the holy fathers, who have pointed out in their writings the way of perfection. For every page and every word of the Bible, both the New and the Old Testament, is a perfect rule for this earthly life; and every work of the holy Catholic fathers teaches us how we may direct our steps to God. The Collations, the Institutes, the Lives of the Saints, and the rule of our father, Saint Basil, all serve as valuable instructions for monks who desire to live rightly and to obey the will of God. Their examples and their teachings should make us ashamed of our sloth, our evil lives, and our negligence. You who are striving to reach the heavenly land, first perfect yourself with the aid of Christ in this little rule, which is but the beginning of holiness, and then you may, under the favor of God, advance to higher grades of virtue and knowledge through the teaching of these greater works. Amen.

# THE ECCLESIASTICAL HISTORY OF THE ENGLISH PEOPLE
## BEDE (c. 672–735)

*The Venerable Bede lived as a monk of the Northumbrian abbeys of Wear-mouth and Jarrow from the age of seven. During his lifetime he contributed to the scholarly brilliance of what some scholars call the Northumbrian Renaissance, writing biblical commentaries, books on chronology, saints' lives, and at the end of his life, his most famous work,* The Ecclesiastical History of the English People.

*Bede modeled his* Ecclesiastical History *on that of Eusebius. As D. H. Farmer observed, "for each the history of the Church was simply a development of the story of the Acts of the Apostles. Just as Christ's apostles had worked, preached, and suffered to establish the Church in obedience to Christ, so did their successors in whatever time or place." In Book I, Bede recounted the story of the Roman mission headed by Augustine of Canterbury, which resulted in the conversion of the King of Kent and his people. Of particular interest to the modern reader is a letter Bede included in which Pope Gregory the Great explained how the missionaries should deal with pagan temples and holidays. Turning his attention to his own native region in Book II, Bede related the lengthy process by which King Edwin of Northumbria and his people accepted the Christian faith.*

*Bede concerned himself above all with demonstrating progress toward unity, so the centerpiece of his work is his account of the Synod of Whitby of 664. For nearly seventy years prior to that event, Roman Christians from Kent and Irish Christians from the island of Iona, off the western coast of Scotland, had worked separately to convert the Angles and Saxons. Because Ireland had never been part of the Roman Empire and was not in regular contact with other parts of the West, not only was the Irish church unusually structured, but its calendar and customs had developed independently of those of the universal Church. At the monastery of Streanaeshalch (renamed later by the Vikings as Whitby), Oswy, King of Northumbria, opted for unity rather than local diversity, a decision with which Bede wholeheartedly agreed.*

*Bede's Ecclesiastical History of England*, edited by A. M. Sellar (London: George Bell and Sons, 1907), 41–43, 45–48, 66–68, 102–5, 112–22, 192–201 [modernized].

## How the Britons,[1] being for a Time at Rest from Foreign Invasions, wore Themselves out by Civil Wars, And at the Same Time Gave Themselves Up to more Heinous Crimes

I§22In the meantime in Britain, there was some respite from foreign, but not from civil, war. The cities destroyed by the enemy and abandoned remained in ruins; and the natives who had escaped the enemy now fought against each other. Nevertheless, the kings, priests, private men, and the nobility, still remember-
5   ing the late calamities and slaughters, in some measure kept within bounds; but when these died, and another generation succeeded, which knew nothing of those times, and was only acquainted with the existing peaceable state of things, all the bonds of truth and justice were so entirely broken, that there was not only no trace of them remaining, but only very few persons seemed to
10  retain any memory of them at all. To other crimes beyond description, which their own historian, Gildas, mournfully relates, they added this—that they never preached the faith to the Saxons or English who dwelt amongst them. Nevertheless, the goodness of God did not forsake his people, whom He fore-knew, but sent to the aforesaid nation much more worthy heralds of the truth,
15  to bring it to the faith.

## How the Holy Pope Gregory sent Augustine, with other Monks, to Preach to the English Nation, And Encouraged them by a Letter of Exhortation not to Desist from their Labor

596

I§23In the year of our Lord 582, Maurice[2], the fifty-fourth from Augustus, as-cended the throne, and reigned twenty-one years. In the tenth year of his reign, Gregory,[3] a man eminent in learning and the conduct of affairs, was promoted to the Apostolic see of Rome, and presided over it thirteen years, six months,
20  and ten days. He, being moved by Divine inspiration, in the fourteenth year of the same Emperor, and about the one hundred and fiftieth after the coming of the English into Britain,[4] sent the servant of God, Augustine,[5] and with him divers other monks, who feared the Lord, to preach the Word of God to the English nation.

---

[1]The Britons were the Romano-British; "the enemy" Bede referred to in the second sentence of the chapter were the Saxons and the Angles, his own people.
[2]Flavius Mauricius Tiberius Augustus (539–602), Emperor at Byzantium (582–602)
[3]Gregory I the Great (c. 540–604), Pope (590–604)
[4]As his introduction to this chapter suggests, Bede was particularly interested in chronology; we owe to him the introduction into the West of dating from the Incarnation.
[5]Augustine, Prior of Saint Gregory's monastery in Rome prior to his dispatch to England

They having, in obedience to the Pope's commands, undertaken that work, when they had gone but a little way on their journey, were seized with craven terror, and began to think of returning home, rather than proceed to a barbarous, fierce, and unbelieving nation, to whose very language they were strangers; and by common consent they decided that this was the safer course. At once Augustine,          5
who had been appointed to be consecrated bishop, if they should be received by the English, was sent back, that he might, by humble entreaty, obtain of the blessed Gregory, that they should not be compelled to undertake so dangerous, toilsome, and uncertain a journey. The Pope, in reply, sent them a letter of exhortation, persuading them to set forth to the work of the Divine Word, and          10
rely on the help of God. The purport of which letter was as follows:

Gregory, the servant of the servants of God, to the servants of our Lord. Forasmuch as it had been better not to begin a good work than to think of desisting from one which has been begun, it behoves you, my beloved sons, to fulfill with all diligence the good work, which, by the help of the          15
Lord, you have undertaken. Let not, therefore, the toil of the journey, nor the tongues of evil-speaking men, discourage you; but with all earnestness and zeal perform, by God's guidance, that which you have set about; being assured that great labor is followed by the greater glory of an eternal reward. When Augustine, your Superior, returns, whom we          20
also constitute your abbot, humbly obey him in all things; knowing that whatsoever you shall do by his direction, will, in all respects, be profitable to your souls. Almighty God protect you with His grace, and grant that I may, in the heavenly country, see the fruits of your labor, inasmuch as, though I cannot labor with you, I shall partake in the joy of the reward,          25
because I am willing to labor. God keep you in safety, my most beloved sons. Given the 23rd of July, in the fourteenth year of the reign of our most religious lord, Mauritius Tiberius Augustus, the thirteenth year after the consulship of our lord aforesaid, and the fourteenth indiction.[6]

### How Augustine, Coming into Britain, First Preached in the Isle of Thanet to the King of Kent, And Having Obtained License from Him, Went into Kent, in Order to Preach Therein

597

I§25 Augustine, thus strengthened by the encouragement of the blessed Father          30
Gregory, returned to the work of the Word of God, with the servants of Christ

---

[6] *Indiction*—a cycle of fifteen years used for dating by the Roman and papal administrations. "The fourteenth indiction" meant the fourteenth year of the fifteen-year cycle.

who were with him, and arrived in Britain. The powerful Ethelbert was at that time King of Kent; he had extended his dominions as far as the boundary formed by the great river Humber, by which the Southern Saxons are divided from the Northern.... On this island landed the servant of the Lord,
5 Augustine, and his companions, being, as is reported, nearly forty men. They had obtained, by order of the blessed Pope Gregory, interpreters of the nation of the Franks, and sending to Ethelbert, signified that they were come from Rome, and brought a joyful message, which most undoubtedly assured to those that hearkened to it everlasting joys in heaven, and a kingdom that
10 would never end, with the living and true God. The King hearing this, gave orders that they should stay in the island where they had landed, and be furnished with necessaries, till he should consider what to do with them. For he had before heard of the Christian religion, having a Christian wife of the royal family of the Franks, called Bertha; whom he had received from her
15 parents, upon condition that she should be permitted to preserve inviolate the rites of her religion with the Bishop Liudhard, who was sent with her to support her in the faith.

Some days after, the King came into the island, and sitting in the open air, ordered Augustine and his companions to come and hold a conference
20 with him. For he had taken precaution that they should not come to him in any house, lest, by so coming, according to an ancient superstition, if they practiced any magical arts, they might impose upon him, and so get the better of him. But they came endowed with Divine, not with magic power, bearing a silver cross for their banner, and the image of our Lord and Savior painted
25 on a board; and chanting litanies, they offered up their prayers to the Lord for the eternal salvation both of themselves and of those to whom and for whom they had come. When they had sat down, in obedience to the King's commands, and preached to him and his attendants there present the Word of life, the King answered thus:
30 "Your words and promises are fair, but because they are new to us, and of uncertain import, I cannot consent to them so far as to forsake that which I have so long observed with the whole English nation. But because you are come from far as strangers into my kingdom, and, as I conceive, are desirous to impart to us those things which you believe to be true, and most beneficial,
35 we desire not to harm you, but will give you favorable entertainment, and take care to supply you with all things necessary to your sustenance; nor do we forbid you to preach and gain as many as you can to your religion."

Accordingly he gave them an abode in the city of Canterbury, which was the metropolis of all his dominions, and, as he had promised, besides supply-
40 ing them with sustenance, did not refuse them liberty to preach.

### How Saint Augustine in Kent Followed the Doctrine and Manner of Life of the Primitive Church, And Settled his Episcopal See in the Royal City

597

I§26As soon as they entered the dwelling-place assigned to them, they began to imitate the Apostolic manner of life in the primitive Church; applying themselves to constant prayer, watchings, and fastings; preaching the Word of life to as many as they could; despising all worldly things as in nowise concerning them; receiving only their necessary food from those they taught; living themselves in 5 all respects conformably to what they taught, and being always ready to suffer any adversity, and even to die for that truth which they preached. In brief, some believed and were baptized, admiring the simplicity of their blameless life, and the sweetness of their heavenly doctrine. There was on the east side of the city a church[7] dedicated of old to the honor of Saint Martin, built whilst the Romans 10 were still in the island, wherein the Queen, who, as has been said before, was a Christian, was wont to pray. In this they also first began to come together to chant the Psalms, to pray, to celebrate Mass, to preach, and to baptize till, when the King had been converted to the faith, they obtained greater liberty to preach everywhere and build or repair churches. 15

When he, among the rest, believed and was baptized, attracted by the pure life of these holy men and their gracious promises, the truth of which they established by many miracles, greater numbers began daily to flock together to hear the Word and, forsaking their heathen rites, to have fellowship, through faith, in the unity of Christ's Holy Church. It is told that the King, while he 20 rejoiced at their conversion and their faith, yet compelled none to embrace Christianity, but only showed more affection to the believers, as to his fellow citizens in the kingdom of Heaven. For he had learned from those who had instructed him and guided him to salvation that the service of Christ ought to be voluntary, not by compulsion. Nor was it long before he gave his teachers 25 a settled residence suited to their degree in his metropolis of Canterbury, with such possessions of divers sorts as were necessary for them.

### A Copy of the Letter which Pope Gregory sent to the Abbot Mellitus, then Going into Britain

601

I§30The aforesaid envoys having departed, the blessed Father Gregory sent after them a letter worthy to be recorded, wherein he plainly shows how carefully he watched over the salvation of our country. The letter was as follows: 30

---

[7]This church still stands and is in regular use. Its existence in Bede's day reminds us that Christianity had spread to Britain well before the Romans left in the early fifth century; it was the Angle and Saxon newcomers who had not yet been converted.

To his most beloved son, the Abbot Mellitus; Gregory, the servant of
the servants of God. We have been much concerned since the departure
of our people that are with you, because we have received no account
of the success of your journey. Howbeit, when Almighty God has led
you to the most reverend Bishop Augustine, our brother, tell him what
I have long been considering in my own mind concerning the matter of the English people; to wit, that the temples of the idols in that
nation ought not to be destroyed; but let the idols that are in them be
destroyed; let water be consecrated and sprinkled in the said temples,
let altars be erected, and relics placed there. For if those temples are
well built, it is requisite that they be converted from the worship of
devils to the service of the true God that the nation, seeing that their
temples are not destroyed, may remove error from their hearts, and
knowing and adoring the true God, may the more freely resort to the
places to which they have been accustomed.

And because they are used to slaughter many oxen in sacrifice to
devils, some solemnity must be given them in exchange for this, as
that on the day of the dedication, or the nativities of the holy martyrs,
whose relics are there deposited, they should build themselves huts of
the boughs of trees about those churches which have been turned to
that use from being temples, and celebrate the solemnity with religious
feasting, and no more offer animals to the Devil, but kill cattle and
glorify God in their feast, and return thanks to the Giver of all things
for their abundance; to the end that, whilst some outward gratifications
are retained, they may the more easily consent to the inward joys. For
there is no doubt that it is impossible to cut off everything at once from
their rude natures; because he who endeavors to ascend to the highest
place rises by degrees or steps, and not by leaps. Thus the Lord made
Himself known to the people of Israel in Egypt; and yet He allowed
them the use, in His own worship, of the sacrifices which they were
wont to offer to the Devil, commanding them in His sacrifice to kill
animals, to the end that, with changed hearts, they might lay aside
one part of the sacrifice, whilst they retained another; and although
the animals were the same as those which they were wont to offer, they
should offer them to the true God, and not to idols; and thus they
would no longer be the same sacrifices. This then, dearly beloved, it
behoves you to communicate to our aforesaid brother, that he, being
placed where he is at present, may consider how he is to order all things.
God preserve you in safety, most beloved son.

Given the 17<sup>th</sup> of June, in the nineteenth year of the reign of our most religious lord, Mauritius Tiberius Augustus, the eighteenth year after the consulship of our said lord, and the fourth indiction.

### Of the Reign of King Edwin,[8] and how Paulinus, Coming to Preach the Gospel, First Converted his Daughter and Others to the Mysteries of the Faith of Christ

615

II§9 At this time the nation of the Northumbrians, that is, the English tribe dwelling on the north side of the river Humber, with their King, Edwin, received the 5 Word of faith through the preaching of Paulinus, of whom we have before spoken. This King, as an earnest of his reception of the faith, and his share in the heavenly kingdom, received an increase also of his temporal realm[9], for he reduced under his dominion all the parts of Britain that were provinces either of the English or of the Britons, a thing which no English king had ever done before.... 10

The occasion of this nation's reception of the faith was the alliance by marriage of their aforesaid King with the Kings of Kent, for he had taken to wife Ethelberg, otherwise called Tata, daughter to King Ethelbert. When he first sent ambassadors to ask her in marriage of her brother Eadbald, who then reigned in Kent, he received the answer that it was not lawful to give a Christian 15 maiden in marriage to a pagan husband, lest the faith and the mysteries of the heavenly King should be profaned by her union with a king that was altogether a stranger to the worship of the true God. This answer being brought to Edwin by his messengers, he promised that he would in no manner act in opposition to the Christian faith which the maiden professed; but would give leave to her, 20 and all that went with her, men and women, bishops and clergy, to follow their faith and worship after the custom of the Christians. Nor did he refuse to accept that religion himself, if, being examined by wise men, it should be found more holy and more worthy of God.

So the maiden was promised, and sent to Edwin, and in accordance with the 25 agreement, Paulinus, a man beloved of God, was ordained bishop to go with her, and by daily exhortations, and celebrating the heavenly mysteries, to confirm her and her company, lest they should be corrupted by intercourse with the pagans.

Paulinus was ordained bishop by the Archbishop Justus on the 21<sup>st</sup> day of July, in the year of our Lord 625, and so came to King Edwin with the aforesaid 30 maiden as an attendant on their union in the flesh. But his mind was wholly bent upon calling the nation to which he was sent to the knowledge of truth;

---

[8] Edwin (c. 586–632), King of Northumbria (616–632)
[9] Bede took it for granted that a king's faith would, in general, be rewarded with earthly success.

according to the words of the Apostle, "To espouse her to the one true Husband, that he might present her as a chaste virgin to Christ."

Being come into that province, he labored much, not only to retain those that went with him, by the help of God, that they should not abandon the faith, but, if haply he might, to convert some of the pagans to the grace of the faith by his preaching. But, as the Apostle says, though he labored long in the Word, "The god of this world blinded the minds of them that believed not, lest the light of the glorious Gospel of Christ should shine unto them."

The next year there came into the province one called Eumer, sent by the King of the West-Saxons, whose name was Cuichelm, to lie in wait for King Edwin, in hopes at once to deprive him of his kingdom and his life. He had a two-edged dagger, dipped in poison, to the end that, if the wound inflicted by the weapon did not avail to kill the King, it might be aided by the deadly venom. He came to the King on the first day of the Easter festival, at the river Derwent, where there was then a royal township, and being admitted as if to deliver a message from his master, whilst unfolding in cunning words his pretended embassy, he started up on a sudden, and unsheathing the dagger under his garment, assaulted the King. When Lilla, the King's most devoted servant, saw this, having no buckler at hand to protect the King from death, he at once interposed his own body to receive the blow; but the enemy struck home with such force that he wounded the King through the body of the slaughtered thegn.[10] Being then attacked on all sides with swords, in the confusion he also slew impiously with his dagger another of the thegns, whose name was Forthhere.

On that same holy Easter night, the Queen had brought forth to the King a daughter, called Eanfled. The King, in the presence of Bishop Paulinus, gave thanks to his gods for the birth of his daughter; and the bishop, on his part, began to give thanks to Christ, and to tell the King that by his prayers to Him he had obtained that the Queen should bring forth the child in safety, and without grievous pain. The King, delighted with his words, promised that if God would grant him life and victory over the king by whom the murderer who had wounded him had been sent, he would renounce his idols, and serve Christ;[11] and as a pledge that he would perform his promise, he delivered up that same daughter to Bishop Paulinus, to be consecrated to Christ. She was the first to be baptized of the nation of the Northumbrians, and she received baptism on the holy day of Pentecost, along with eleven others of her house.

At that time, the King, being recovered of the wound which he had received, raised an army and marched against the nation of the West-Saxons and engag-

---

[10] *Thegn*—noble

[11] Early medieval warriors related to God as a victory-giver and Christ as a divine warrior battling the Devil for men's souls. This story has a number of contemporary and near-contemporary parallels.

ing in war, either slew or received in surrender all those of whom he learned that they had conspired to murder him. So he returned victorious into his own country, but he would not immediately and unadvisedly embrace the mysteries of the Christian faith, though he no longer worshipped idols, ever since he made the promise that he would serve Christ; but first took heed earnestly to     5
be instructed at leisure by the venerable Paulinus in the knowledge of faith, and to confer with such as he knew to be the wisest of his chief men, inquiring what they thought was fittest to be done in that case. And being a man of great natural sagacity, he often sat alone by himself a long time in silence, deliberating in the depths of his heart how he should proceed, and to which    10
religion he should adhere.

### How Edwin was Persuaded to Believe by a Vision
### which he had Once Seen when he was in Exile

625

II§12…But a heavenly vision, which the Divine Goodness was pleased once to reveal to this King when he was in banishment at the court of Redwald, King of the Angles, was of no little use in urging him to receive and understand the    15
doctrines of salvation. For when Paulinus perceived that it was a difficult task to incline the King's proud mind to the humility of the way of salvation and the reception of the mystery of the life-giving Cross, and at the same time was employing the word of exhortation with men and prayer to the Divine Goodness for the salvation of Edwin and his subjects; at length, as we may suppose, it was    20
shown him in spirit what the nature of the vision was that had been formerly revealed from Heaven to the King. Then he lost no time, but immediately admonished the King to perform the vow which he had made when he received the vision, promising to fulfill it if he should be delivered from the troubles of that time and advanced to the throne.    25

The vision was this. When Ethelfrid, his predecessor, was persecuting him, he wandered for many years as an exile, hiding in divers places and kingdoms, and at last came to Redwald, beseeching him to give him protection against the snares of his powerful persecutor. Redwald willingly received him, and promised to perform what was asked of him. But when Ethelfrid understood    30
that he had appeared in that province, and that he and his companions were hospitably entertained by Redwald, he sent messengers to bribe that King with a great sum of money to murder him, but without effect. He sent a second and a third time, offering a greater bribe each time, and, moreover, threatening to make war on him if his offer should be despised. Redwald, whether terrified by    35
his threats, or won over by his gifts, complied with this request, and promised either to kill Edwin or to deliver him up to the envoys. A faithful friend of his,

hearing of this, went into his chamber, where he was going to bed, for it was the first hour of the night; and, calling him out, told him what the King had promised to do with him, adding, "If, therefore, you are willing, I will this very hour conduct you out of this province, and lead you to a place where neither

5 Redwald nor Ethelfrid shall ever find you."

He answered, "I thank you for your good will, yet I cannot do what you propose, and be guilty of being the first to break the compact I have made with so great a King when he has done me no harm, nor shown any enmity to me; but, on the contrary, if I must die, let it rather be by his hand than by

10 that of any meaner man. For whither shall I now fly, when I have for so many long years been a vagabond through all the provinces of Britain, to escape the snares of my enemies?" His friend went away; Edwin remained alone without, and sitting with a heavy heart before the palace, began to be overwhelmed with many thoughts, not knowing what to do, or which way to turn.

15 When he had remained a long time in silent anguish of mind, consumed with inward fire, on a sudden in the stillness of the dead of night he saw approaching a person whose face and habit were strange to him, at sight of whom, seeing that he was unknown and unlooked for, he was not a little startled. The stranger coming close up, saluted him, and asked why he sat there in solitude

20 on a stone troubled and wakeful at that time, when all others were taking their rest, and were fast asleep. Edwin, in his turn, asked, what it was to him whether he spent the night within doors or abroad. The stranger, in reply, said, "Do not think that I am ignorant of the cause of your grief, your watching and sitting alone without. For I know of a surety who you are, and why you

25 grieve, and the evils which you fear will soon fall upon you. But tell me, what reward you would give the man who should deliver you out of these troubles and persuade Redwald neither to do you any harm himself, nor to deliver you up to be murdered by your enemies."

Edwin replied that he would give such an one all that he could in return

30 for so great a benefit. The other further added, "What if he should also assure you that your enemies should be destroyed, and you should be a king surpassing in power, not only all your own ancestors, but even all that have reigned before you in the English nation?" Edwin, encouraged by these questions, did not hesitate to promise that he would make a fitting return to him who

35 should confer such benefits upon him. Then the other spoke a third time and said, "But if he who should truly foretell that all these great blessings are about to befall you, could also give you better and more profitable counsel for your life and salvation than any of your fathers or kindred ever heard, do you consent to submit to him, and to follow his wholesome guidance?"

40 Edwin at once promised that he would in all things follow the teaching of

that man who should deliver him from so many great calamities, and raise him to a throne.

Having received this answer, the man who talked to him laid his right hand on his head saying, "When this sign shall be given you, remember this present discourse that has passed between us, and do not delay the performance of what 5 you now promise." Having uttered these words, he is said to have immediately vanished. So the King perceived that it was not a man, but a spirit, that had appeared to him.

Whilst the royal youth still sat there alone, glad of the comfort he had received, but still troubled and earnestly pondering who he was, and whence he 10 came, that had so talked to him, his aforesaid friend came to him, and greeting him with a glad countenance, "Rise," said he, "go in; calm and put away your anxious cares, and compose yourself in body and mind to sleep; for the King's resolution is altered, and he designs to do you no harm, but rather to keep his pledged faith; for when he had privately made known to the Queen his inten- 15 tion of doing what I told you before, she dissuaded him from it, reminding him that it was altogether unworthy of so great a king to sell his good friend in such distress for gold, and to sacrifice his honor, which is more valuable than all other adornments, for the love of money.

In short, the King did as has been said, and not only refused to deliver up the 20 banished man to his enemy's messengers, but helped him to recover his kingdom. For as soon as the messengers had returned home, he raised a mighty army to subdue Ethelfrid; who, meeting him with much inferior forces, (for Redwald had not given him time to gather and unite all his power) was slain.... Thus Edwin, in accordance with the prophecy he had received, not only escaped the danger 25 from his enemy, but, by his death, succeeded the King on the throne.

King Edwin, therefore, delaying to receive the Word of God at the preaching of Paulinus, and being wont for some time, as has been said, to sit many hours alone, and seriously to ponder with himself what he was to do, and what religion he was to follow, the man of God came to him one day, laid his right hand on his 30 head, and asked, whether he knew that sign? The King, trembling, was ready to fall down at his feet, but he raised him up, and speaking to him with the voice of a friend, said, "Behold, by the gift of God you have escaped the hands of the enemies whom you feared. Behold, you have obtained of His bounty the kingdom which you desired. Take heed not to delay to perform your third promise; accept 35 the faith, and keep the precepts of Him Who, delivering you from temporal adversity, has raised you to the honor of a temporal kingdom; and if, from this time forward, you shall be obedient to His will, which through me He signifies to you, He will also deliver you from the everlasting torments of the wicked, and make you partaker with Him of His eternal kingdom in heaven." 40

### Of the Council he Held with his Chief Men Concerning their Reception of the Faith of Christ, And how the High Priest Profaned his Own Altars

627

II§13'The King, hearing these words, answered that he was both willing and bound to receive the faith which Paulinus taught; but that he would confer about it with his chief friends and counselors, to the end that if they also were of his opinion, they might all together be consecrated to Christ in the font of
5   life. Paulinus consenting, the King did as he said; for, holding a council with the wise men, he asked of every one in particular what he thought of this doctrine hitherto unknown to them, and the new worship of God that was preached?

The chief of his own priests, Coifi, immediately answered him, "O King, consider what this is which is now preached to us; for I verily declare to you
10  what I have learnt beyond doubt that the religion which we have hitherto professed has no virtue in it and no profit. For none of your people has applied himself more diligently to the worship of our gods than I; and yet there are many who receive greater favors from you, and are more preferred than I, and are more prosperous in all that they undertake to do or to get. Now if the gods
15  were good for anything, they would rather forward me, who have been careful to serve them with greater zeal. It remains, therefore, that if upon examination you find those new doctrines, which are now preached to us, better and more efficacious, we hasten to receive them without any delay."

Another of the King's chief men, approving of his wise words and exhorta-
20  tions, added thereafter, "The present life of man upon earth, O King, seems to me, in comparison with that time which is unknown to us, like to the swift flight of a sparrow through the house wherein you sit at supper in winter, with your ealdormen and thegns, while the fire blazes in the midst, and the hall is warmed, but the wintry storms of rain or snow are raging abroad. The sparrow,
25  flying in at one door and immediately out at another, whilst he is within, is safe from the wintry tempest; but after a short space of fair weather, he immediately vanishes out of your sight, passing from winter into winter again. So this life of man appears for a little while, but of what is to follow or what went before we know nothing at all. If, therefore, this new doctrine tells us something more
30  certain, it seems justly to deserve to be followed." The other elders and King's counselors, by Divine prompting, spoke to the same effect.

But Coifi added that he wished more attentively to hear Paulinus discourse concerning the God Whom he preached. When he did so, at the King's command, Coifi, hearing his words, cried out, "This long time I have perceived
35  that what we worshipped was naught, because the more diligently I sought after truth in that worship, the less I found it. But now I freely confess that such truth evidently appears in this preaching as can confer on us the gifts of

life, of salvation, and of eternal happiness. For which reason my counsel is, O King, that we instantly give up to ban and fire those temples and altars which we have consecrated without reaping any benefit from them."

In brief, the King openly assented to the preaching of the Gospel by Pauli- 5 nus, and renouncing idolatry, declared that he received the faith of Christ. And when he inquired of the aforesaid high priest of his religion who should first desecrate the altars and temples of their idols, with the precincts that were about them, he answered, "I; for who can more fittingly than myself destroy those things which I worshipped in my folly, for an example to all others, through the wisdom which has been given me by the true God?" 10

Then immediately, in contempt of his vain superstitions, he desired the King to furnish him with arms and a stallion, that he might mount and go forth to destroy the idols; for it was not lawful before for the high priest either to carry arms, or to ride on anything but a mare. Having, therefore, girt a sword about him, with a spear in his hand, he mounted the King's stallion, and went his 15 way to the idols. The multitude, beholding it, thought that he was mad; but as soon as he drew near the temple he did not delay to desecrate it by casting into it the spear which he held; and rejoicing in the knowledge of the worship of the true God, he commanded his companions to tear down and set on fire the temple, with all its precincts.... 20

### How King Edwin and his Nation Became Christians; and Where Paulinus Baptized Them

627

I§14King Edwin, therefore, with all the nobility of the nation, and a large number of the common sort, received the faith, and the washing of holy regeneration, in the eleventh year of his reign, which is the year of our Lord 627, and about one hundred and eighty after the coming of the English into Britain.

He was baptized at York, on the holy day of Easter, being the 12th of April, 25 in the church of Saint Peter the Apostle, which he himself had built of timber there in haste, whilst he was a catechumen receiving instruction in order to be admitted to baptism. In that city also he bestowed upon his instructor and bishop, Paulinus, his episcopal see.... Paulinus, for the space of six years from this time, that is, till the end of the King's reign, with his consent and favor, 30 preached the Word of God in that country, and as many as were foreordained to eternal life believed and were baptized....

...So great was then the fervor of the faith, as is reported, and the desire for the laver of salvation among the nation of the Northumbrians that Pauli- nus at a certain time coming with the King and Queen to the royal township, 35 which is called Adgefrin, stayed there with them thirty-six days, fully occupied in catechizing and baptizing; during which days, from morning till night, he did nothing else but instruct the people resorting from all villages and places, in Christ's saving Word; and when they were instructed, he washed them with the water of absolution in the river Glen, which is close by....

### How the Province of the East Angles Received the Faith of Christ

627

5      I§15Edwin was so zealous for the true worship, that he likewise persuaded Earpwald, King of the East Angles, and son of Redwald, to abandon his idolatrous superstitions, and with his whole province to receive the faith and mysteries of Christ. And indeed his father Redwald had long before been initiated into the mysteries of the Christian faith in Kent, but in vain; for on
10    his return home, he was seduced by his wife and certain perverse teachers, and turned aside from the sincerity of the faith; and thus his latter state was worse than the former; so that, like the Samaritans of old, he seemed at the same time to serve Christ and the gods whom he served before; and in the same temple he had an altar for the Christian Sacrifice, and another small
15    one at which to offer victims to devils. Aldwulf, King of that same province, who lived in our time, testifies that this temple had stood until his time, and that he had seen it when he was a boy....

Earpwald, not long after he had embraced the Christian faith, was slain[12] by one Ricbert, a pagan; and from that time the province was in error for three
20    years, till Sigbert succeeded to the kingdom, brother to the same Earpwald, a most Christian and learned man, who was banished, and went to live in Gaul during his brother's life, and was there initiated into the mysteries of the faith, whereof he made it his business to cause all his province to partake as soon as he came to the throne. His exertions were nobly promoted by
25    Bishop Felix, who, coming to Honorius, the Archbishop, from the parts of Burgundy where he had been born and ordained, and having told him what he desired, was sent by him to preach the Word of life to the aforesaid nation of the Angles. Nor were his good wishes in vain; for the pious laborer in the spiritual field reaped therein a great harvest of believers, delivering all that
30    province (according to the inner signification of his name) from long iniquity and unhappiness, and bringing it to the faith and works of righteousness, and the gifts of everlasting happiness. He had the see of his bishopric appointed him in the city Dunwich, and having presided over the same province with pontifical authority seventeen years, he ended his days there in peace....

---

[12]Earpwald was probably killed because he had converted; Earpwald's fate demonstrates why it was so important that the King's decision to convert be linked to the conversion of his people.

## How the Question Arose about the Due Time of Keeping Easter with Those that Came out of Ireland

664

**III§25**At this time, a great and frequently debated question arose about the observance of Easter; those that came from Kent or Gaul affirming that the Irish celebrated Easter Sunday contrary to the custom of the universal Church. Among them was a most zealous defender of the true Easter, whose name was Ronan, an Irish by nation, but instructed in the rule of ecclesiastical truth in 5 Gaul or Italy. Disputing with Finan, he convinced many, or at least induced them to make a more strict inquiry after the truth; yet he could not prevail upon Finan, but, on the contrary, embittered him the more by reproof, and made him a professed opponent of the truth, for he was of a violent temper.

James, formerly the deacon of the venerable Archbishop Paulinus, as has 10 been said above, observed the true and Catholic Easter, with all those that he could instruct in the better way. Queen Eanfled and her followers also observed it as she had seen it practiced in Kent, having with her a Kentish priest who followed the Catholic observance, whose name was Romanus. Thus it is said to have sometimes happened in those times that Easter was twice celebrated in 15 one year; and that when the King, having ended his fast, was keeping Easter, the Queen and her followers were still fasting, and celebrating Palm Sunday.

Whilst Aidan lived, this difference about the observance of Easter was patiently tolerated by all men, for they well knew that though he could not keep Easter contrary to the custom of those who had sent him, yet he industriously 20 labored to practice the works of faith, piety, and love, according to the custom of all holy men; for which reason he was deservedly beloved by all, even by those who differed in opinion concerning Easter, and was held in veneration, not only by less important persons, but even by the bishops, Honorius of Canterbury, and Felix of the East Angles. 25

But after the death of Finan, who succeeded him, when Colman, who was also sent from Ireland, came to be bishop, a greater controversy arose about the observance of Easter, and other rules of ecclesiastical life. Whereupon this question began naturally to influence the thoughts and hearts of many who feared, lest haply, having received the name of Christians, they might run, or 30 have run, in vain. This reached the ears of the rulers, King Oswy and his son Alchfrid. Now Oswy, having been instructed and baptized by the Irish, and being very perfectly skilled in their language, thought nothing better than what they taught; but Alchfrid, having for his teacher in Christianity the learned Wilfrid, who had formerly gone to Rome to study ecclesiastical doctrine, and 35 spent much time at Lyons with Dalfinus, Archbishop of Gaul, from whom also he had received the crown of ecclesiastical tonsure, rightly thought that this

man's doctrine ought to be preferred before all the traditions of the Scots. For this reason he had also given him a monastery of forty families, at a place called Inhrypum; which place, not long before, he had given for a monastery to those that were followers of the Irish; but forasmuch as they afterwards, being left to
5　their choice, preferred to quit the place rather than alter their custom, he gave it to him whose life and doctrine were worthy of it.

Agilbert, Bishop of the West Saxons, above-mentioned, a friend of King Alchfrid and of Abbot Wilfrid, had at that time come into the province of the Northumbrians, and was staying some time among them; at the request of
10　Alchfrid, he made Wilfrid a priest in his aforesaid monastery. He had in his company a priest, whose name was Agatho. The question being raised there concerning Easter and the tonsure and other ecclesiastical matters, it was arranged that a synod should be held in the monastery of Streanaeshalch, which signifies the Bay of the Lighthouse, where the Abbess Hilda, a woman devoted
15　to the service of God, then ruled; and that there this question should be decided. The Kings, both father and son, came thither, and the bishops, Colman with his Irish clerks, and Agilbert with the priests Agatho and Wilfrid. James and Romanus were on their side; but the Abbess Hilda and her followers were for the Irish, as was also the venerable Bishop Cedd, long before ordained by
20　the Irish, as has been said above, and he acted in that council as a most careful interpreter for both parties.

King Oswy first made an opening speech, in which he said that it behoved those who served one God to observe one rule of life; and as they all expected the same kingdom in heaven, so they ought not to differ in the celebration of
25　the heavenly mysteries; but rather to inquire which was the truer tradition, that it might be followed by all in common; he then commanded his bishop, Colman, first to declare what the custom was which he observed, and whence it derived its origin. Then Colman said, "The Easter which I keep, I received from my elders, who sent me hither as bishop; all our forefathers, men beloved
30　of God, are known to have celebrated it after the same manner; and that it may not seem to any contemptible and worthy to be rejected, it is the same which the blessed John—the Evangelist, the disciple specially beloved of our Lord, with all the churches over which he presided, is recorded to have celebrated."

When he had said thus much, and more to the like effect, the King commanded
35　manded Agilbert to make known the manner of his observance and to show whence it was derived, and on what authority he followed it. Agilbert answered, "I beseech you, let my disciple, the priest Wilfrid, speak in my stead, because we both concur with the other followers of the ecclesiastical tradition that are here present, and he can better and more clearly explain our opinion in the
40　English language, than I can by an interpreter."

Then Wilfrid, being ordered by the King to speak, began thus: "The Easter which we keep, we saw celebrated by all at Rome, where the blessed Apostles, Peter and Paul, lived, taught, suffered, and were buried; we saw the same done by all in Italy and in Gaul, when we travelled through those countries for the purpose of study and prayer. We found it observed in Africa, Asia, Egypt, Greece,          5 and all the world, wherever the Church of Christ is spread abroad, among divers nations and tongues, at one and the same time; save only among these and their accomplices in obstinacy, I mean the Picts and the Britons, who foolishly, in these two remote islands of the ocean, and only in part even of them, strive to oppose all the rest of the world."          10

When he had so said, Colman answered, "It is strange that you choose to call our efforts foolish, wherein we follow the example of so great an Apostle, who was thought worthy to lean on our Lord's bosom, when all the world knows him to have lived most wisely."

Wilfrid replied, "Far be it from us to charge John with folly, for he literally          15 observed the precepts of the Mosaic Law, whilst the Church was still Jewish in many points, and the Apostles, lest they should give cause of offence to the Jews who were among the Gentiles, were not able at once to cast off all the observances of the Law which had been instituted by God, in the same way as it is necessary that all who come to the faith should forsake the idols which          20 were invented by devils. For this reason it was, that Paul circumcised Timothy, that he offered sacrifice in the temple, that he shaved his head with Aquila and Priscilla at Corinth; for no other advantage than to avoid giving offence to the Jews. Hence it was that James said to the same Paul, 'You see, brother, how many thousands of Jews there are which believe; and they are all zealous          25 of the Law.' And yet, at this time, when the light of the Gospel is spreading throughout the world, it is needless, nay, it is not lawful, for the faithful either to be circumcised, or to offer up to God sacrifices of flesh. So John, according to the custom of the Law, began the celebration of the feast of Easter, on the fourteenth day of the first month in the evening, not regarding whether the          30 same happened on a Saturday, or any other week-day. But when Peter preached at Rome, being mindful that our Lord arose from the dead, and gave to the world the hope of resurrection, on the first day of the week he perceived that Easter ought to be kept after this manner: he always awaited the rising of the moon on the fourteenth day of the first month in the evening, according to          35 the custom and precepts of the Law, even as John did. And when that came, if the Lord's day, then called the first day of the week, was the next day, he began that very evening to celebrate Easter, as we all do at the present time. But if the Lord's day did not fall the next morning after the fourteenth moon, but on the sixteenth, or the seventeenth, or any other moon till the twenty-first, he          40

waited for that, and on the Saturday before, in the evening, began to observe
the holy solemnity of Easter. Thus it came to pass that Easter Sunday was only
kept from the fifteenth moon to the twenty-first. Nor does this evangelical
and apostolic tradition abolish the Law, but rather fulfill it; the command be-
5    ing to keep the Passover from the fourteenth moon of the first month in the
evening to the twenty-first moon of the same month in the evening; which
observance all the successors of the blessed John in Asia, since his death, and
all the Church throughout the world, have since followed; and that this is the
true Easter, and the only one to be celebrated by the faithful, was not newly
10   decreed by the council of Nicaea, but only confirmed afresh, as the history of
the Church informs us."

    "Thus it is plain that you, Colman, neither follow the example of John, as
you imagine, nor that of Peter, whose tradition you oppose with full knowledge,
and that you neither agree with the Law nor the Gospel in the keeping of your
15   Easter. For John, keeping the Paschal time according to the decree of the Mosaic
Law, had no regard to the first day of the week, which you do not practice, seeing
that you celebrate Easter only on the first day after the Sabbath. Peter celebrated
Easter Sunday between the fifteenth and the twenty-first moon, which you do
not practice, seeing that you observe Easter Sunday from the fourteenth to the
20   twentieth moon; so that you often begin Easter on the thirteenth moon in the
evening, whereof neither the Law made any mention, nor did our Lord, the
Author and Giver of the Gospel, on that day either eat the old Passover in the
evening, or deliver the Sacraments of the New Testament, to be celebrated by
the Church, in memory of His Passion, but on the fourteenth. Besides, in your
25   celebration of Easter, you utterly exclude the twenty-first moon, which the Law
ordered to be specially observed. Thus, as I have said before, you agree neither
with John nor Peter, nor with the Law, nor the Gospel, in the celebration of
the greatest festival."

    To this Colman rejoined, "Did the holy Anatolius, much commended in the
30   history of the Church, judge contrary to the Law and the Gospel when he wrote
that Easter was to be celebrated from the fourteenth to the twentieth moon?
Is it to be believed that our most reverend Father Columba and his successors,
men beloved by God, who kept Easter after the same manner, judged or acted
contrary to the Divine writings? Whereas there were many among them whose
35   sanctity was attested by heavenly signs and miracles which they wrought; whom
I, for my part, doubt not to be saints, and whose life, customs, and discipline
I never cease to follow."

    "It is evident," said Wilfrid, "that Anatolius was a most holy, learned,
and commendable man; but what have you to do with him, since you do not
40   observe his decrees? For he undoubtedly, following the rule of truth in his Easter,

appointed a cycle of nineteen years, which either you are ignorant of, or if you know it, though it is kept by the whole Church of Christ, yet you despise it as a thing of naught.... Concerning your Father Columba and his followers, whose sanctity you say you imitate, and whose rule and precepts confirmed by signs from Heaven you say that you follow, I might answer, then when many, in the 5 day of judgment, shall say to our Lord that in His name they have prophesied, and have cast out devils, and done many wonderful works, our Lord will reply that He never knew them. But far be it from me to speak thus of your fathers, for it is much more just to believe good than evil of those whom we know not. Wherefore I do not deny those also to have been God's servants, and beloved 10 of God, who with rude simplicity, but pious intentions, have themselves loved Him. Nor do I think that such observance of Easter did them much harm, as long as none came to show them a more perfect rule to follow; for assuredly I believe that, if any teacher, reckoning after the Catholic manner, had come among them, they would have as readily followed his admonitions, as they are 15 known to have kept those commandments of God, which they had learned and knew."

"But as for you and your companions, you certainly sin if, having heard the decrees of the Apostolic see, nay, of the universal Church, confirmed, as they are, by Holy Scripture, you scorn to follow them; for, though your fathers were 20 holy, do you think that those few men, in a corner of the remotest island, are to be preferred before the universal Church of Christ throughout the world? And if that Columba of yours (and, I may say, ours also, if he was Christ's servant) was a holy man and powerful in miracles, yet could he be preferred before the most blessed chief of the Apostles, to whom our Lord said, 'You are Peter, and 25 upon this rock I will build my Church, and the gates of hell shall not prevail against it, and I will give unto you the keys of the kingdom of Heaven?'"

When Wilfrid had ended thus, the King said, "Is it true, Colman, that these words were spoken to Peter by our Lord?" He answered, "It is true, O King!" "Then," said he, "Can you show any such power given to your Columba?" 30

Colman answered, "None."

Then again the King asked, "Do you both agree in this, without any controversy, that these words were said above all to Peter, and that the keys of the kingdom of Heaven were given to him by our Lord?"

They both answered, "Yes." 35

Then the King concluded, "And I also say unto you that he is the doorkeeper, and I will not gainsay him, but I desire, as far as I know and am able, in all things to obey his laws, lest haply when I come to the gates of the kingdom of Heaven, there should be none to open them, he being my adversary who is proved to have the keys." 40

The King having said this, all who were seated there or standing by, both great and small, gave their assent, and renouncing the less perfect custom, hastened to conform to that which they had found to be better.

# LIFE OF CHARLEMAGNE
## EINHARD (*c.* 770–840)

*Einhard served Charlemagne (r. 768–814) and his successor, Louis the Pious (r. 813–840), from 791 until 830, at which time he retired to a monastery of his own foundation at Seligenstadt, in the Rhineland. Scholars disagree about his relationship with Louis the Pious and consequently about the dating of his biography of Charlemagne. He may have been attempting to hold up a mirror to Louis's own imperfections as a ruler, or he may, on the contrary, have been attempting to help Louis consolidate his position as ruler. Einhard's model for his* Life of Charlemagne *was Suetonius's* Augustus, *which influenced the length and ordering of the subject matter as well as some of the details.*

### Preface

Since I have taken upon myself to narrate the public and private life, and no small part of the deeds, of my lord and foster-father, the most excellent and most justly renowned King Charles, I have condensed the matter into as brief a form as possible. I have been careful not to omit any facts that could come to my knowledge, but at the same time not to offend by a prolix style those minds  5
that despise everything modern, if one can possibly avoid offending by a new work men who seem to despise also the masterpieces of antiquity, the works of most learned and luminous writers. Very many of them, I have no doubt, are men dedicated to a life of literary leisure, who feel that the affairs of the present generation ought not to be passed by, and who do not consider everything  10
done to-day as unworthy of mention and deserving to be given over to silence and oblivion, but are nevertheless seduced by lust of immortality to celebrate the glorious deeds of other times by some sort of composition rather than to deprive posterity of the mention of their own names by not writing at all.

Be this as it may, I see no reason why I should refrain from entering upon a  15
task of this kind, since no man can write with more accuracy than I of events that took place about me, and of facts concerning which I had personal knowledge,

*Einhard: Life of Charlemagne*, translated by Samuel Epes Turner (New York: American Book Company, 1880), 11–30, 40–67. 69–71 [modernized].

ocular demonstration, as the saying goes, and I have no means of ascertaining whether or not any one else has the subject in hand.

In any event, I would rather commit my story to writing, and hand it down to posterity in partnership with others, so to speak, than to suffer the most glorious life of this most excellent king, the greatest of all the princes of his day, and his illustrious deeds, hard for men of later times to imitate, to be wrapped in the darkness of oblivion.

But there are still other reasons, neither unwarrantable nor insufficient, in my opinion, that urge me to write on this subject, namely, the care that King Charles bestowed upon me in my childhood, and my constant friendship with himself and his children after I began to take up my abode at court. In this way he strongly endeared me to himself, and made me greatly his debtor as well in death as in life; so that were I, unmindful of the benefits conferred upon me, to keep silence concerning the most glorious and illustrious deeds of a man who claims so much at my hands, and suffer his life to lack due eulogy and written memorial, as if he had never lived, I should deservedly appear ungrateful, and be so considered, albeit my powers are feeble, scanty, next to nothing indeed, and not at all adapted to write and set forth a life that would tax the eloquence of a Cicero.

I submit the book. It contains the history of a very great and distinguished man; but there is nothing in it to wonder at besides his deeds, except the fact that I, who am a barbarian, and very little versed in the Roman language, seem to suppose myself capable of writing gracefully and respectably in Latin,[1] and to carry my presumption so far as to disdain the sentiment that Cicero is said in the first book of the "Tusculan Disputations" to have expressed when speaking of the Latin authors. His words are: "It is an outrageous abuse both of time and literature for a man to commit his thoughts to writing without having the ability either to arrange them or elucidate them, or attract readers by some charm of style." This dictum of the famous orator might have deterred me from writing if I had not made up my mind that it was better to risk the opinions of the world, and put my little talents for composition to the test, than to slight the memory of so great a man for the sake of sparing myself.

## Life of the Emperor Charles

The Merovingian family, from which the Franks used to choose their kings, is commonly said to have lasted until the time of Childeric, who was deposed, shaved, and thrust into the cloister by command of the Roman Pontiff Stephen.

---

[1]Einhard's disclaimer here is entirely conventional and not meant to be taken seriously.

But although, to all outward appearance, it ended with him, it had long since been devoid of vital strength, and conspicuous only from bearing the empty epithet Royal; the real power and authority in the kingdom lay in the hands of the chief officer of the court, the so-called Mayor of the Palace, and he was at the head of affairs. There was nothing left the King to do but to be content    5
with his name of King, his flowing hair, and long beard; to sit on his throne and play the ruler; to give ear to the ambassadors that came from all quarters, and to dismiss them, as if on his own responsibility, in words that were, in fact, suggested to him, or even imposed upon him. He had nothing that he could call his own beyond this vain title of King, and the precarious support allowed    10
by the Mayor of the Palace in his discretion, except a single country-seat, that brought him but a very small income. There was a dwelling-house upon this, and a small number of servants attached to it, sufficient to perform the neces- sary offices. When he had to go abroad, he used to ride in a cart, drawn by a yoke of oxen, driven, peasant-fashion, by a ploughman; he rode in this way to    15
the palace and to the general assembly of the people, that met once a year for the welfare of the kingdom, and he returned home in like manner.[2] The Mayor of the Palace took charge of the government, and of everything that had to be planned or executed at home or abroad.

At the time of Childeric's deposition, Pepin, the father of King Charles,    20
held this office of Mayor of the Palace, one might almost say, by hereditary right; for Pepin's father, Charles,[3] had received it at the hands of his father, Pepin, and filled it with distinction. It was this Charles that crushed the tyrants who claimed to rule the whole Frank land as their own, and that utterly routed the Saracens, when they attempted the conquest of Gaul, in two great battles—one    25
in Aquitania, near the town of Poitiers, and the other on the River Berre, near Narbonne—and compelled them to return to Spain. This honor was usually conferred by the people only upon men eminent from their illustrious birth and ample wealth. For some years, ostensibly under King Childeric, Pepin, the father of King Charles, shared the duties inherited from his father and grand-    30

---

[2]The Merovingian dynasty began with Clovis (481–510), the first Frankish king to practice orthodox Christianity, and ended with Childeric III, who was deposed in 751 by Pepin the Short, Charlemagne's father. The Merovingians were known as "the long-haired kings," since their long hair symbolized their power, hence Pepin caused Childeric to be tonsured as a monk when he deposed him. The Merovingian kings inherited their administrataive structures and much else from the Romans whom they succeeded as rulers of Gaul; for example, some late Roman provincial governors also used ox-carts for travelling around their provinces to be accessible to petitioners who wished to speak with them. Einhard's depiction of the weakness of the Merovingians is hyperbolized, though certainly by the mid-eighth century, the Carolingian Mayors of the Palace greatly surpassed them in power.
[3]Charles Martel (c. 688–741), Mayor of the Palace (715–741), son of Pepin of Herstal

father most amicably with his brother, Carloman. The latter, then, for reasons unknown, renounced the heavy cares of an earthly crown and retired to Rome. Here he exchanged his worldly garb for a cowl, and built a monastery on Mt. Oreste, near the Church of Saint Sylvester, where he enjoyed for several years
5   the seclusion that he desired, in company with certain others who had the same object in view. But so many distinguished Franks made the pilgrimage to Rome to fulfill their vows, and insisted upon paying their respects to him, as their former lord, on the way, that the repose which he so much loved was broken by these frequent visits, and he was driven to change his abode. Accordingly,
10   when he found that his plans were frustrated by his many visitors, he abandoned the mountain, and withdrew to the Monastery of Saint Benedict, on Monte Casino, in the province of Samnium, and passed the rest of his days there in the exercises of religion.

    Pepin, however, was raised, by decree of the Roman Pontiff,[4] from the rank
15   of Mayor of the Palace to that of King, and ruled alone over the Franks for fifteen years or more. He died of dropsy, in Paris, at the close of the Aquitanian war, which he had waged with William, Duke of Aquitania, for nine successive years, and left two sons, Charles and Carloman, upon whom, by the grace of God, the succession devolved.[5]

20     The Franks, in a general assembly of the people, made them both kings, on condition that they should divide the whole kingdom equally between them, Charles to take and rule the part that had belonged to their father, Pepin, and Carloman the part which their uncle, Carloman, had governed. The conditions were accepted, and each entered into possession of the share of the kingdom
25   that fell to him by this arrangement; but peace was only maintained between them with the greatest difficulty, because many of Carloman's party kept trying to disturb their good understanding, and there were some even who plotted to involve them in a war with each other. The event, however, showed the danger to have been rather imaginary than real, for at Carloman's death his widow fled
30   to Italy with her sons and her principal adherents, and without reason, despite her husband's brother, put herself and her children under the protection of Desiderius, King of the Lombards. Carloman had succumbed to disease after ruling two years in common with his brother, and at his death Charles was unanimously elected King of the Franks.

35     It would be folly, I think, to write a word concerning Charles's birth and infancy, or even his boyhood, for nothing has ever been written on the subject,

---

[4]Pope Zachary (r. 741–752)

[5]Pepin the Short died 24 September 768. The Franks elected Charles and Carloman joint kings on 9 October 768. The Franks, like the Romans in the fourth and fifth centuries, divided their kingdom among those they recognized as heirs of the previous king.

and there is no one alive now who can give information of it. Accordingly, I have determined to pass that by as unknown, and to proceed at once to treat of his character, his deeds, and such other facts of his life as are worth telling and setting forth, and shall first give an account of his deeds at home and abroad, then of his character and pursuits, and lastly of his administration and death, 5 omitting nothing worth knowing or necessary to know....

After bringing this war to an end and settling matters in Aquitania[6] (his associate in authority had meantime departed this life), he was induced, by the prayers and entreaties of Hadrian, Bishop of the city of Rome,[7] to wage war on the Lombards. His father before him had undertaken this task at the request of 10 Pope Stephen, but under great difficulties; for certain leading Franks, of whom he usually took counsel, had so vehemently opposed his design as to declare openly that they would leave the King and go home. Nevertheless, the war against the Lombard king, Astolf, had been taken up and very quickly concluded. Now, although Charles seems to have had similar, or rather just the same grounds 15 for declaring war that his father had, the war itself differed from the preceding one alike in its difficulties and its issue. Pepin, to be sure, after besieging King Astolf a few days in Pavia, had compelled him to give hostages, to restore to the Romans the cities and castles that he had taken, and to make oath that he would not attempt to seize them again: but Charles did not cease, after declaring 20 war, until he had exhausted King Desiderius by a long siege, and forced him to surrender at discretion; driven his son Adalgis, the last hope of the Lombards, not only from his kingdom, but from all Italy; restored to the Romans all that they had lost; subdued Hruodgaus, Duke of Friuli, who was plotting revolution; reduced all Italy to his power, and set his son Pepin as king over it. 25

At this point I should describe Charles's difficult passage over the Alps into Italy, and the hardships that the Franks endured in climbing the trackless mountain-ridges, the heaven-aspiring cliffs and ragged peaks, if it were not my purpose in this work to record the manner of his life rather than the incidents of the wars that he waged. Suffice it to say that this war ended with the subjection 30 of Italy, the banishment of King Desiderius for life, the expulsion of his son Adalgis from Italy, and the restoration of the conquests of the Lombard kings to Hadrian, the head of the Roman Church.

At the conclusion of this struggle, the Saxon war, that seems to have been only laid aside for the time, was taken up again. No war ever undertaken by 35 the Frank nation was carried on with such persistence and bitterness, or cost so much labor, because the Saxons, like almost all the tribes of Germany, were

---

[6]Charlemagne finished a war against Aquitania, a war begun during his father's reign. As a result of the war, he gained control of Aquitania and Gascony, large territories in southwestern Gaul.
[7]Hadrian I, Pope (r. 772–795)

a fierce people, given to the worship of devils, and hostile to our religion, and did not consider it dishonorable to transgress and violate all law, human and divine. Then there were peculiar circumstances that tended to cause a breach of peace every day. Except in a few places where large forests or mountain-ridges intervened and made the bounds certain; the line between ourselves and the Saxon passed almost in its whole extent through an open country, so that there was no end to the murders, thefts, and arsons on both sides. In this way the Franks became so embittered that they at last resolved to make reprisals no longer, but to come to open war with the Saxons. Accordingly war was begun against them, and was waged for thirty-three successive years with great fury, more, however, to the disadvantage of the Saxons than of the Franks. It could doubtless have been brought to an end sooner, had it not been for the faithlessness of the Saxons. It is hard to say how often they were conquered, and, humbly submitting to the King, promised to do what was enjoined upon them, gave without hesitation the required hostages, and received the officers sent them from the King. They were sometimes so much weakened and reduced that they promised to renounce the worship of devils, and to adopt Christianity; but they were no less ready to violate these terms than prompt to accept them, so that it is impossible to tell which came easier to them to do; scarcely a year passed from the beginning of the war without such changes on their part. But the King did not suffer his high purpose and steadfastness—firm alike in good and evil fortune—to be wearied by any fickleness on their part, or to be turned from the task that he had undertaken; on the contrary, he never allowed their faithless behavior to go unpunished, but either took the field against them in person, or sent his counts with an army to wreak vengeance and exact righteous satisfaction. At last, after conquering and subduing all who had offered resistance, he took ten thousand of those that lived on the banks of the Elbe, and settled them, with their wives and children, in many different bodies here and there in Gaul and Germany. The war that had lasted so many years was at length ended by their acceding to the terms offered by the King; which were renunciation of their national religious customs and the worship of devils, acceptance of the sacraments of the Christian faith and religion, and union with the Franks to form one people.[8]

---

[8]This sentence tells us a great deal about the way Charlemagne saw his own role. The terms of peace with the Saxons were religious; conversion to Christianity led to "union with the Franks to form one people." The Saxons did not cease to be Saxons and become Franks; rather, both Franks and Saxons shared a common Christian identity after the Saxons converted. Charlemagne, as ruler of this Christian people, did not see himself as a ruling a state with an established church; instead he saw himself as the secular head of Christendom. It was no coincidence that among the members of his palace school, Charlemagne's nickname was David.

Charles himself fought but two pitched battles in this war, although it was long protracted—one on Mount Osning, at the place called Detmold, and again on the bank of the river Hase, both in the space of little more than a month. The enemy were so routed and overthrown in these two battles that they never afterwards ventured to take the offensive or to resist the attacks of the King, unless they were protected by a strong position. A great many of the Frank as well as of the Saxon nobility, men occupying the highest posts of honor, perished in this war, which only came to an end after the lapse of thirty-two years. So many and grievous were the wars that were declared against the Franks in the meantime, and skillfully conducted by the King, that one may reasonably question whether his fortitude or his good fortune is to be more admired. The Saxon war began two years before the Italian war; but although it went on without interruption, business elsewhere was not neglected, nor was there any shrinking from other equally arduous contests. The King, who excelled all the princes of his time in wisdom and greatness of soul, did not suffer difficulty to deter him or danger to daunt him from anything that had to be taken up or carried through, for he had trained himself to bear and endure whatever came, without yielding in adversity, or trusting to the deceitful favors of fortune in prosperity....

Such are the wars, most skillfully planned and successfully fought, which this most powerful king waged during the forty-seven years of his reign. He so largely increased the Frank kingdom, which was already great and strong when he received it at his father's hands, that more than double its former territory was added to it. The authority of the Franks was formerly confined to that part of Gaul included between the Rhine and the Loire, the Ocean and the Balearic Sea; to that part of Germany which is inhabited by the so-called Eastern Franks, and is bounded by Saxony and the Danube, the Rhine and the Saale—this stream separates the Thuringians from the Sorabians; and to the country of the Alemanni and Bavarians. By the wars above mentioned he first made tributary Aquitania, Gascony, and the whole of the region of the Pyrenees as far as the River Ebro, which rises in the land of the Navarrese, flows through the most fertile districts of Spain, and empties into the Balearic Sea, beneath the walls of the city of Tortosa. He next reduced and made tributary all Italy from Aosta to Lower Calabria, where the boundary-line runs between the Beneventans and the Greeks, a territory more than a thousand miles long; then Saxony, which constitutes no small part of Germany, and is reckoned to be twice as wide as the country inhabited by the Franks, while about equal to it in length; in addition, both Pannonias, Dacia beyond the Danube, and Istria, Liburnia, and Dalmatia, except the cities on the coast, which he left to the Greek Emperor for friendship's sake, and because of the treaty that he had

made with him. In summary, he vanquished and made tributary all the wild and barbarous tribes dwelling in Germany between the Rhine and the Vistula, the Ocean and the Danube, all of which speak very much the same language, but differ widely from one another in customs and dress. The chief among them
5    are the Welatabians, the Sorabians, the Abodriti, and the Bohemians, and he had to make war upon these; but the rest, by far the larger number, submitted to him of their own accord.

He added to the glory of his reign by gaining the good-will of several kings and nations; so close, indeed, was the alliance that he contracted with Alphonso,
10   King of Galicia and Asturias, that the latter, when sending letters or ambassadors to Charles, invariably styled himself his man. His munificence won the kings of the Scots also to pay such deference to his wishes that they never gave him any other title than lord, or themselves than subjects and slaves: there are letters from them extant in which these feelings in his regard are expressed. His rela-
15   tions with Aaron, King of the Persians,[9] who ruled over almost the whole of the East, India excepted, were so friendly that this prince preferred his favor to that of all the kings and potentates of the earth, and considered that to him alone marks of honor and munificence were due. Accordingly, when the ambassadors sent by Charles to visit the most holy sepulchre and place of resurrection of our
20   Lord and Savior presented themselves before him with gifts, and made known their master's wishes, he not only granted what was asked, but gave possession of that holy and blessed spot. When they returned, he dispatched his ambassadors with them, and sent magnificent gifts, besides stuffs, perfumes, and other rich products of the Eastern lands. A few years before this, Charles had asked
25   him for an elephant, and he sent the only one that he had. The Emperors of Constantinople Nicephorus, Michael, and Leo made advances to Charles, and sought friendship and alliance with him by several embassies; and even when the Greeks suspected him of designing to wrest the empire from them, because of his assumption of the title of Emperor, they made a close alliance with him,
30   that he might have no cause of offence. In fact, the power of the Franks was always viewed by the Greeks and Romans[10] with a jealous eye, whence the Greek proverb "Have the Frank for your friend, but not for your neighbor."

This King, who showed himself so great in extending his empire and subduing foreign nations, and was constantly occupied with plans to that end,
35   undertook also very many works calculated to adorn and benefit his kingdom, and brought several of them to completion. Among these, the most deserving of mention are the basilica of the Holy Mother of God at Aix-la-Chapelle, built

---

[9]Harun al-Rashid, Abbasid Caliph (r. 786–809)
[10]The Byzantines referred to themselves as Roman.

in the most admirable manner, and a bridge over the Rhine at Mayence,[11] half a mile long, the breadth of the river at this point. This bridge was destroyed by fire the year before Charles died, but, owing to his death so soon after, could not be repaired, although he had intended to rebuild it in stone. He began two palaces of beautiful workmanship—one near his manor called Ingelheim, not far from Mayence; the other at Nimeguen, on the Waal, the stream that washes the south side of the island of the Batavians. But, above all, sacred edifices were the object of his care throughout his whole kingdom; and whenever he found them falling to ruin from age, he commanded the priests and fathers who had charge of them to repair them, and made sure by commissioners that his instructions were obeyed. He also fitted out a fleet for the war with the Northmen; the vessels required for this purpose were built on the rivers that flow from Gaul and Germany into the Northern Ocean. Moreover, since the Northmen continually overran and laid waste the Gallic and German coasts, he caused watch and ward to be kept in all the harbors, and at the mouths of rivers large enough to admit the entrance of vessels, to prevent the enemy from disembarking; and in the South, in Narbonensis and Septimania, and along the whole coast of Italy as far as Rome, he took the same precautions against the Moors, who had recently begun their piratical practices. Hence, Italy suffered no great harm in his time at the hands of the Moors, nor Gaul and Germany from the Northmen, save that the Moors got possession of the Etruscan town of Civita Vecchia by treachery, and sacked it, and the Northmen harried some of the islands in Frisia off the German coast.

Thus did Charles defend and increase as well as beautify his kingdom, as is well known; and here let me express my admiration of his great qualities and his extraordinary constancy alike in good and evil fortune. I will now forthwith proceed to give the details of his private and family life.

After his father's death, while sharing the kingdom with his brother, he bore his unfriendliness and jealousy most patiently, and, to the wonder of all, could not be provoked to be angry with him. Later he married a daughter of Desiderius, King of the Lombards, at the request of his mother; but he repudiated her at the end of a year for some reason unknown, and married Hildegard, a woman of high birth, of Suabian origin. He had three sons by her—Charles, Pepin, and Lewis—and as many daughters—Hruodrud, Bertha, and Gisela. He had three other daughters besides these—Theoderada, Hiltrud, and Ruodhaid—two by his third wife, Fastrada, a woman of East Frankish (that is to say, of German) origin, and the third by a concubine, whose name for the moment escapes me. At the death of Fastrada, he married Liutgard, an Alemannic woman, who bore

---

[11]Aix-la-Chapelle is now called Aachen; Mayence is Mainz.

him no children. After her death he had three concubines—Gersuinda, a Saxon, by whom he had Adaltrud; Regina, who was the mother of Drogo and Hugh; and Ethelind, by whom he had Theodoric. Charles's mother, Berthrada, passed her old age with him in great honor; he entertained the greatest veneration for her; and there was never any disagreement between them except when he divorced the daughter of King Desiderius, whom he had married to please her. She died soon after Hildegard, after living to see three grandsons and as many granddaughters in her son's house, and he buried her with great pomp in the Basilica of Saint Denis, where his father lay. He had an only sister, Gisela, who had consecrated herself to a religious life from girlhood, and he cherished as much affection for her as for his mother. She also died a few years before him in the nunnery where she had passed her life.

The plan that he adopted for his children's education was, first of all, to have both boys and girls instructed in the liberal arts, to which he also turned his own attention. As soon as their years admitted, in accordance with the custom of the Franks, the boys had to learn horsemanship, and to practice war and the chase, and the girls to familiarize themselves with cloth-making, and to handle distaff and spindle, that they might not grow indolent through idleness, and he fostered in them every virtuous sentiment. He only lost three of all his children before his death, two sons and one daughter: Charles, who was the eldest, Pepin, whom he had made King of Italy, and Hruodrud, his oldest daughter, whom he had betrothed to Constantine, Emperor of the Greeks. Pepin left one son, named Bernard, and five daughters, Adelaide, Atula, Guntrada, Berthaid, and Theoderada. The King gave a striking proof of his fatherly affection at the time of Pepin's death: he appointed the grandson to succeed Pepin, and had the granddaughters brought up with his own daughters. When his sons and his daughter died, he was not so calm as might have been expected from his remarkably strong mind, for his affections were no less strong, and moved him to tears. Again, when he was told of the death of Hadrian, the Roman Pontiff, whom he had loved most of all his friends, he wept as much as if he had lost a brother, or a very dear son. He was by nature most ready to contract friendships, and not only made friends easily, but clung to them persistently, and cherished most fondly those with whom he had formed such ties. He was so careful of the training of his sons and daughters that he never took his meals without them when he was at home, and never made a journey without them; his sons would ride at his side, and his daughters follow him, while a number of his body-guard, detailed for their protection, brought up the rear. Strange to say, although they were very handsome women, and he loved them very dearly, he was never willing to marry any of them to a man of their own nation or to a foreigner, but kept them all at home until his death, saying that he could not dispense with their society. Hence, though otherwise happy, he experienced the malignity of fortune as far as they were concerned; yet he concealed his knowledge of the rumors current in regard to them, and of the suspicions entertained of their honor.

By one of his concubines he had a son, handsome in face, but hunchbacked, named Pepin, whom I omitted to mention in the list of his children. When Charles was at war with the Huns, and was wintering in Bavaria, this Pepin shammed sickness, and plotted against his father in company with some of the leading Franks, who seduced him with vain promises of the royal authority. When his deceit was discovered, and the conspirators were punished, his head was shaved, and he was suffered, in accordance with his wishes, to devote himself to a religious life in the monastery of Prüm. A formidable conspiracy against Charles had previously been set on foot in Germany, but all the traitors were banished, some of them without mutilation, others after their eyes had been put out. Three of them only lost their lives; they drew their swords and resisted arrest, and, after killing several men, were cut down, because they could not be otherwise overpowered. It is supposed that the cruelty of Queen Fastrada was the primary cause of these plots, and they were both due to Charles's apparent acquiescence in his wife's cruel conduct, and deviation from the usual kindness and gentleness of his disposition. All the rest of his life he was regarded by every one with the utmost love and affection, so much so that not the least accusation of unjust rigor was ever made against him.

He liked foreigners, and was at great pains to take them under his protection. There were often so many of them, both in the palace and the kingdom, that they might reasonably have been considered a nuisance; but he, with his broad humanity, was very little disturbed by such annoyances, because he felt himself compensated for these great inconveniences by the praises of his generosity and the reward of high renown.

Charles was large and strong, and of lofty stature, though not disproportionately tall (his height is well known to have been seven times the length of his foot): the upper part of his head was round, his eyes very large and animated, nose a little long, hair fair, and face laughing and merry. Thus his appearance was always stately and dignified, whether he was standing or sitting; although his neck was thick and somewhat short, and his belly rather prominent; but the symmetry of the rest of his body concealed these defects. His gait was firm, his whole carriage manly, and his voice clear, but not so strong as his size led one to expect. His health was excellent, except during the four years preceding his death, when he was subject to frequent fevers; at the last he even limped a little with one foot. Even in those years he consulted rather his own inclinations than the advice of physicians, who were almost hateful to him, because they

wanted him to give up roasts, to which he was accustomed, and to eat boiled meat instead. In accordance with the national custom, he took frequent exercise on horseback and in the chase, accomplishments in which scarcely any people in the world can equal the Franks. He enjoyed the exhalations from natural
5   warm springs, and often practiced swimming, in which he was such an adept that none could surpass him; and hence it was that he built his palace at Aix-la-Chapelle, and lived there constantly during his latter years until his death. He used not only to invite his sons to his bath, but his nobles and friends, and now and then a troop of his retinue or body-guard, so that a hundred or more
10  persons sometimes bathed with him.

He used to wear the national, that is to say, the Frank, dress—next his skin a linen shirt and linen breeches, and above these a tunic fringed with silk; while hose fastened by bands covered his lower limbs, and shoes his feet, and he protected his shoulders and chest in winter by a close-fitting coat of otter
15  or marten skins. Over all he flung a blue cloak, and he always had a sword girt about him, usually one with a gold or silver hilt and belt; he sometimes carried a jeweled sword, but only on great feast-days or at the reception of ambassadors from foreign nations. He despised foreign costumes, however handsome, and never allowed himself to be robed in them, except twice in Rome, when he
20  donned the Roman tunic, chlamys, and shoes; the first time at the request of Pope Hadrian, the second to gratify Leo, Hadrian's successor. On great feast-days he made use of embroidered clothes, and shoes bedecked with precious stones; his cloak was fastened by a golden buckle, and he appeared crowned with a diadem of gold and gems: but on other days his dress varied little from
25  the common dress of the people.

Charles was temperate in eating, and particularly so in drinking, for he abominated drunkenness in anybody, much more in himself and those of his household; but he could not easily abstain from food, and often complained that fasts injured his health. He very rarely gave entertainments, only on great
30  feast-days, and then to large numbers of people. His meals ordinarily consisted of four courses, not counting the roast, which his huntsmen used to bring in on the spit; he was more fond of this than of any other dish. While at table, he listened to reading or music. The subjects of the readings were the stories and deeds of olden time: he was fond, too, of Saint Augustine's books, and
35  especially of the one entitled "The City of God." He was so moderate in the use of wine and all sorts of drink that he rarely allowed himself more than three cups in the course of a meal. In summer, after the midday meal, he would eat some fruit, drain a single cup, put off his clothes and shoes, just as he did for the night, and rest for two or three hours. He was in the habit of awaking and
40  rising from bed four or five times during the night. While he was dressing and

putting on his shoes, he not only gave audience to his friends, but if the Count of the Palace told him of any suit in which his judgment was necessary, he had the parties brought before him forthwith, took cognizance of the case, and gave his decision, just as if he were sitting on the judgment-seat. This was not the only business that he transacted at this time, but he performed any duty of the day whatever, whether he had to attend to the matter himself, or to give commands concerning it to his officers.

Charles had the gift of ready and fluent speech, and could express whatever he had to say with the utmost clearness. He was not satisfied with command of his native language merely, but gave attention to the study of foreign ones, and in particular was such a master of Latin that he could speak it as well as his native tongue; but he could understand Greek better than he could speak it. He was so eloquent, indeed, that he might have passed for a teacher of eloquence. He most zealously cultivated the liberal arts, held those who taught them in great esteem, and conferred great honors upon them. He took lessons in grammar of the deacon Peter of Pisa, at that time an aged man. Another deacon, Albin of Britain, surnamed Alcuin, a man of Saxon extraction, who was the greatest scholar of the day, was his teacher in other branches of learning. The King spent much time and labor with him studying rhetoric, dialectics, and especially astronomy; he learned to reckon, and used to investigate the motions of the heavenly bodies most curiously, with an intelligent scrutiny. He also tried to write, and used to keep tablets and blanks in bed under his pillow, that at leisure hours he might accustom his hand to form the letters; however, as he did not begin his efforts in due season, but late in life, they met with ill success.[12]

He cherished with the greatest fervor and devotion the principles of the Christian religion, which had been instilled into him from infancy. Hence it was that he built the beautiful basilica at Aix-la-Chapelle, which he adorned with gold and silver and lamps, and with rails and doors of solid brass. He had the columns and marbles for this structure brought from Rome and Ravenna, for he could not find such as were suitable elsewhere. He was a constant worshipper at this church as long as his health permitted, going morning and evening, even after nightfall, besides attending mass; and he took care that all the services there conducted should be administered with the utmost possible propriety, very often warning the sextons not to let any improper or unclean thing be brought into the building, or remain in it. He provided it with a great number of sacred vessels of gold and silver, and with such a quantity of clerical robes that not even the doorkeepers, who fill the humblest office in the church, were

---

[12]For most of the Middle Ages, reading and writing were not necessarily taught together; writing was closer to what we call calligraphy, and it was usually done by clerks. Hence Charlemagne's inability to learn to write tells us more about his fine motor control than his intellect.

obliged to wear their every-day clothes when in the exercise of their duties. He was at great pains to improve the church reading and psalmody, for he was well skilled in both, although he neither read in public nor sang, except in a low tone and with others.

5      He was very forward in succoring the poor, and in that gratuitous generosity which the Greeks call alms, so much so that he not only made a point of giving in his own country and his own kingdom, but when he discovered that there were Christians living in poverty in Syria, Egypt, and Africa, at Jerusalem, Alexandria, and Carthage, he had compassion on their wants, and used 10  to send money over the seas to them. The reason that he zealously strove to make friends with the kings beyond seas was that he might get help and relief to the Christians living under their rule. He cherished the Church of Saint Peter the Apostle at Rome above all other holy and sacred places, and heaped its treasury with a vast wealth of gold, silver, and precious stones. He sent great 15  and countless gifts to the popes; and throughout his whole reign the wish that he had nearest at heart was to re-establish the ancient authority of the city of Rome under his care and by his influence, and to defend and protect the Church of Saint Peter, and to beautify and enrich it out of his own store above all other churches. Although he held it in such veneration, he only repaired to 20  Rome to pay his vows and make his supplications four times during the whole forty-seven years that he reigned.

When he made his last journey thither, he had also other ends in view. The Romans had inflicted many injuries upon the Pontiff Leo, tearing out his eyes and cutting out his tongue, so that he had been compelled to call upon the 25  King for help. Charles accordingly went to Rome, to set in order the affairs of the Church, which were in great confusion, and passed the whole winter there. It was then that he received the titles of Emperor and Augustus, to which he at first had such an aversion that he declared that he would not have set foot in the Church the day that they were conferred, although it was a great feast-day, 30  if he could have foreseen the design of the Pope.[13] He bore very patiently with the jealousy which the Roman emperors showed upon his assuming these titles, for they took this step very ill; and by dint of frequent embassies and letters, in which he addressed them as brothers, he made their haughtiness yield to his magnanimity, a quality in which he was unquestionably much their superior.

---

[13] There are five separate accounts of the imperial coronation; only Einhard claims that Charlemagne was unaware of the pope's intention. However, the following March Charlemagne was still referring to himself as "Charles, by the grace of God, King of the Franks and of the Lombards, and Patrician of the Romans." By late May 801, he had reworked his title to add "most serene Augustus, crowned by God, great and pacific emperor governing the Roman empire."

It was after he had received the imperial name that, finding the laws of his people very defective (the Franks have two sets of laws, very different in many particulars), he determined to add what was wanting, to reconcile the discrepancies, and to correct what was vicious and wrongly cited in them. However, he went no further in this matter than to supplement the laws by a 5 few capitularies, and those imperfect ones; but he caused the unwritten laws of all the tribes that came under his rule to be compiled and reduced to writing. He also had the old rude songs that celebrate the deeds and wars of the ancient kings written out for transmission to posterity. He began a grammar of his native language. He gave the months names in his own tongue, in place of the 10 Latin and barbarous names by which they were formerly known among the Franks. He likewise designated the winds by twelve appropriate names; there were hardly more than four distinctive ones in use before....

Towards the close of his life, when he was broken by ill-health and old age, he summoned Lewis, King of Aquitania, his only surviving son by Hildegard, 15 and gathered together all the chief men of the whole kingdom of the Franks in a solemn assembly. He appointed Lewis, with their unanimous consent, to rule with himself over the whole kingdom, and constituted him heir to the imperial name; then, placing the diadem upon his son's head, he bade him be proclaimed Emperor and Augustus. This step was hailed by all present with great favor, for 20 it really seemed as if God had prompted him to it for the kingdom's good; it increased the King's dignity, and struck no little terror into foreign nations. After sending his son back to Aquitania, although weak from age he set out to hunt, as usual, near his palace at Aix-la-Chapelle, and passed the rest of the autumn in the chase, returning thither about the first of November. While wintering there, 25 he was seized, in the month of January, with a high fever, and took to his bed. As soon as he was taken sick, he prescribed for himself abstinence from food, as he always used to do in case of fever, thinking that the disease could be driven off, or at least mitigated, by fasting. Besides the fever, he suffered from a pain in the side, which the Greeks call pleurisy: but he still persisted in fasting, and 30 in keeping up his strength only by draughts taken at very long intervals. He died January twenty-eighth, the seventh day from the time that he took to his bed, at nine o'clock in the morning, after partaking of the holy communion, in the 72d year of his age and the 47$^{th}$ of his reign.

His body was washed and cared for in the usual manner, and was then car- 35 ried to the church, and interred amid the greatest lamentations of all the people. There was some question at first where to lay him, because in his lifetime he had given no directions as to his burial; but at length all agreed that he could nowhere be more honorably entombed than in the very basilica that he had built in the town at his own expense, for the love of God and our Lord Jesus 40

Christ and in honor of the Holy and Eternal Virgin, His Mother. He was buried there the same day that he died, and a gilded arch was erected above his tomb with his image and an inscription. The words of the inscription were as follows: "In this tomb lies the body of Charles, the Great and Orthodox Emperor, who
5    gloriously extended the kingdom of the Franks, and reigned prosperously for forty-seven yeas. He died at the age of seventy, in the year of our Lord 814, the 7<sup>th</sup> Indiction, on the 28<sup>th</sup> day of January."

# LETTER TO ABBOT BAUGULF

## CHARLEMAGNE (c. 742–814)
### KING OF THE FRANKS (r. 768–814)

*Charlemagne, King of the Franks, concerned with the education of clergy in his domains, dictated this circular letter. Addressed to Baugulf, Abbot of Fulda (r. 779–802), the king intended it to be copied and distributed to monasteries throughout his territories. Therefore, although formally addressed to a single monastic house, this missive illuminates the emphasis of Charlemagne's court on education and religious instruction throughout Christendom.*

*c. 780–800*

Be it known to your devotion, most pleasing in the sight of God, that We, along with Our faithful advisers, have deemed it useful that the bishoprics and monasteries which through the favor of Christ have been entrusted to Us to govern should, in addition to the way of life prescribed by their rule and practice of holy religion, devote their efforts to the study of literature and to 5 the teaching of it, each according to his ability, to those on whom God has bestowed the capacity to learn; that, just as the observance of a rule gives soundness to their conduct, so also an attention to teaching and learning may give order and adornment to their words, and those who seek to please God by living aright may not fail to please Him also by rightness in their 10 speaking. For it is written, "Either by your words shall you be justified, or by your words shall you be condemned."[1]

For although it is better to do what is right than to know it, yet knowledge comes before action. Thus each man must first learn what he wishes to carry out so that he will know in his heart all the more fully what he needs to do, 15 in order that his tongue may run on without stumbling into falsehood in the praise of Almighty God. For since falsehood is to be shunned by all men, how much more should it be avoided, as far as they are able, by those who have been chosen for this one purpose, that they should give special service to truth.

---

[1] Matthew 12:27

---

*Readings in Medieval History*, edited by Patrick J. Geary (New York: Broadview Press, 1989), 308–9. Copyright © Broadview Press Ltd. All rights reserved.

Letters have often been sent to Us in these last years from certain monasteries in which was set out what the brothers there living were striving to do for Us in their holy and pious prayers; and We found that in most of these writings their sentiments were sound, but their speech uncouth. Inwardly their pi-
5   ous devotions gave them a message of truth, but, because of their neglect of learning, their unskilled tongues could not express it without fault. And so it came about that We began to fear that their lack of knowledge of writing might be matched by a more serious lack of wisdom in the understanding of Holy Scripture. We all know well that, dangerous as are the errors of words,
10  yet much more dangerous are the errors of doctrine.

Wherefore We urge you not merely to avoid the neglect of the study of literature, but with a devotion that is humble and pleasing to God to strive to learn it, so that you may be able more easily and more rightly to penetrate the mysteries of the Holy Scriptures. For since there are figures of
15  speech, metaphors, and the like to be found on the sacred pages, there can be no doubt that each man who reads them will understand their spiritual meaning more quickly if he is first of all given full instruction in the study of literature. Let men be chosen for this work who have the will and ability to learn, and also the desire to instruct others; and let it be pursued with an
20  eagerness equal to Our devotion in prescribing it. For We want you, as befits the soldiers of the Church, to be inwardly devout and outwardly learned, pure in good living and scholarly in speech; so that whoever comes to see you in the name of God and for the inspiration of your holy converse, just as he is strengthened by the sight of you, so he may be instructed also by your
25  wisdom, both in reading and chanting, and return rejoicing, giving thanks to Almighty God. Therefore, if you wish to keep our favor, do not neglect to send copies of this letter to all your suffragans[2] and fellow bishops, and to all the monasteries.

---

[2] *Suffragans*—assistants

# LAWS
## ALFRED THE GREAT (847–899)
### KING OF WESSEX (871–899)

*Early medieval law differed significantly from the kind of Roman law we saw in the* Institutes *of Justinian, even in areas where local law was based on the Theodosian Code. Law was custom, an organic outgrowth of the life of the people of the community, transmitted for the most part orally, and enforced by community consensus. Lacking formal enactment and codification, customary law was flexible and adaptable to new situations, though changing it officially was a solemn act not undertaken lightly.*

Then I, King Alfred,[1] collected these together and ordered to be written many of them which our forefathers observed, those which I liked; and many of those which I did not like I rejected with the advice of my councilors, and ordered them to be differently observed. For I dared not presume to set in writing at all many of my own, because it was unknown to me what would please those who should come after us. But those which I found which seemed to me most just, either in the time of my kinsman, King Ine,[2] or of Offa, King of the Mercians,[3] or of Ethelbert,[4] who first among the English received baptism, I collected herein, and omitted the others. Then I, Alfred, King of the West Saxons, showed these to all my councilors, and they then said that they were all pleased to observe them.

1. First we direct, what is most necessary, that each man keep carefully his oath and pledge.

1.1 If anyone is wrongfully compelled to either of these, [to promise] treachery against his lord or any illegal aid, then it is better to leave it unfulfilled than to perform it.

---

[1] Alfred the Great, King of Wessex, is best known for having defeated the Vikings in 878, thereby putting an end to the gradual Danish conquest of England. In subsequent years, he and his successors pushed back the boundary of the area of Danish settlement, the Danelaw, and extended the rule of the Kings of Wessex until, by mid-tenth century, the King of Wessex was king of all England.

[2] Ine, King of Wessex (688–726)

[3] Offa, King of Mercia (757–796)

[4] Ethelbert, King of Kent (560–616)

---

From *English Historical Documents, c. 500–1042*, edited by Dorothy Whitelock, Second Edition, Volume I (London: Eyre Methuen, 1979), 408–16, *passim*. Reprinted by permission of Taylor & Francis Books UK.

1.2 [If, however, he pledges what is right for him to perform] and leaves it unfulfilled, let him with humility give his weapons and his possessions into his friends'
keeping and be 40 days in prison at a King's estate; let him endure there what
penance the bishop prescribes for him, and his kinsmen are to feed him if he has
no food himself.

1.3 If he has no kinsmen and has not the food, the King's reeve is to feed him.

1.4 If he has to be forced thither, and will not go otherwise, and he is bound,
he is to forfeit his weapons and his possessions.

1.5 If he is killed, he is to lie unpaid for.[5]

1.6 If he escapes before the end of the period, and he is caught, he is to be 40
days in prison, as he should have been before.

1.7 If he gets clear, he is to be outlawed, and to be excommunicated from all
the churches of Christ.

1.8 If, however, there is secular surety for him, he is to pay for the breach of surety
as the law directs him, and for the breach of pledge as his confessor prescribes
for him.

2.   If anyone for any guilt flees to any one of the monastic houses to which the
King's food-rent belongs, or to some other privileged community which is
worthy of honor, he is to have a respite of three days to protect himself, unless
he wishes to be reconciled.

2.1 If during that respite he is molested with slaying or binding or wounding, each
of those [who did it] is to make amends according to the legal custom, both with
wergild and with fine, and to pay to the community 120 shillings as compensation for the breach of sanctuary, and is to have forfeited his own [claim against
the culprit]....

4.   If anyone plots against the King's life, directly or by harboring his exiles or
his men, he is liable to forfeit his life and all that he owns.

4.1 If he wishes to clear himself, he is to do it by [an oath equivalent to] the
King's wergild.[6]

4.2 Thus also we determine concerning all ranks, both *ceorl* [7] and noble: he who
plots against his lord's life is to be liable to forfeit his life and all that he owns,
or to clear himself by his lord's wergild.

5.   Also we determine this sanctuary for every church which a bishop has consecrated: if a man exposed to a vendetta reaches it running or riding, no one
is to drag him out for seven days, if he can live in spite of hunger, unless he
himself fights [his way] out. If, however, anyone does so, he is liable to [pay

---

[5]The person who killed him will pay no *wergild* ("man price"). In many early medieval societies, a
murderer or his kindred paid a wergild, the amount based on the victim's social status, to satisfy the
obligation of the victim's kindred to pursue a vendetta against the murderer of their kinsman.

[6]*An oath equivalent to the King's wergild*—by finding oath-helpers whose total wergild was equivalent
to that of the king. The exact amount of the king's wergild at this time is uncertain, but it was at least
6,000 shillings, which would mean that five nobles, at 1,200 shillings each, could swear the oath.

[7]*Ceorl*—an ordinary freeman

for breach of] the King's protection and of the church's sanctuary—more, if he seizes more from there.

5.1 If the community have more need of their church, he is to be kept in another building, and it is to have no more doors than the church.

5.2 The head of that church is to take care that no one give him food during that period.

5.3 If he himself will hand out his weapons to his foes, they are to keep him for 30 days, and send notice about him to his kinsmen.

5.4 Further sanctuary of the church: if any man has recourse to the church on account of any crime which has not been discovered, and there confesses himself to God's name, it is to be half remitted.

5.5 Whoever steals on Sunday or at Christmas or Easter or on the Holy Thursday in Rogation days;[8] each of those we wish to be compensated doubly, as in the Lenten fast....

7. If anyone fights or draws his weapon in the King's hall, and he is captured, it is to be at the King's judgment whether he will grant him death or life.[9]...

10. If anyone lies with the wife of a man of a twelve-hundred wergild, he is to pay to the husband 120 shillings; to a man of a six-hundred wergild 100 shillings is to be paid; to a man of the *ceorl* class 40 shillings is to be paid....

22. If anyone brings up a charge in a public meeting before the King's reeve, and afterwards wishes to withdraw it, he is to make the accusation against a more likely person, if he can; if he cannot, he is to forfeit his compensation....

32. If anyone is guilty of public slander, and it is proved against him, it is to be compensated for with no lighter penalty than the cutting off of his tongue, with the proviso that it be redeemed at no cheaper rate than it is valued in proportion to the wergild....

34. Moreover, it is prescribed for traders: they are to bring before the King's reeve in a public meeting the men whom they take up into the country with them, and it is to be established how many of them there are to be; and they are to take with them men whom they can afterwards bring to justice at a public meeting; and whenever it may be necessary for them to have more men out with them on their journey, it is always to be announced, as often as it is necessary for them, to the King's reeve in the witness of the meeting....

40. Forcible entry into the King's residence shall be 120 shillings; into the Archbishop's, 90 shillings; into another bishop's or an ealdorman's, 60 shillings; into that of a man of a twelve-hundred wergild, 30 shillings; into that of a man of a six-hundred wergild, 15 shillings; forcible entry into a *ceorl*'s enclosure, five shillings.

40.1 If any of this happens when the army has been called out, or in the Lenten fast, the compensations are to be doubled.

---

[8] *Holy Thursday in Rogation days*—the Feast of the Ascension
[9] A crime committed in the King's hall, which was within the area protected by the King's Peace, carried a higher penalty than one committed outside that area. Over centuries, the protection of the King's Peace was gradually extended to roads, rivers, and ultimately, to the entire kingdom.

40.2 If anyone openly neglects the rules of the Church in Lent without permission, he is to pay 120 shillings compensation....

42.    Moreover we command that the man who knows his opponent to be dwelling at home is not to fight before he asks justice for himself.

42.1 If he has sufficient power to surround his opponent and besiege him there in his house, he is to keep him seven days inside and not fight against him, if he will remain inside; and then after seven days, if he will surrender and give up his weapons, he is to keep him unharmed for 30 days, and send notice about him to his kinsmen and his friends.

42.2 If he, however, reaches a church, it is then to be [dealt with] according to the privilege of the church, as we have said above.

42.3 If he [that attacker] has not sufficient power to besiege him in his house, he is to ride to the ealdorman and ask him for support; if he will not give him support, he is to ride to the king, before having recourse to fighting.

42.4 Likewise, if a man run across his opponent, and did not previously know him to be at home, if he will give up his weapons, he is to be kept for 30 days and his friends informed; if he will not give up his weapons, then he may fight against him. If he is willing to surrender, and to give up his weapons, and after that anyone fights against him, he [who does] is to pay wergild or compensation for wounds according to what he has done, and a fine, and is to have forfeited [the right to avenge] his kinsmen.

42.5 Moreover, we declare that a man may fight on behalf of his lord, if the lord is being attacked, without incurring a vendetta. Similarly the lord may fight on behalf of his man.

42.6 In the same way, a man may fight on behalf of his born kinsman, if he is being wrongfully attacked, except against his lord; that we do not allow.

42.7 And a man may fight without incurring a vendetta if he finds another man with his wedded wife, within closed doors or under the same blanket, or with his legitimate daughter or his legitimate sister, or with his mother who was given as a lawful wife to his father.

43.    These days are to be given to all freemen, but not to slaves or unfree laborers: 12 days at Christmas, and the day on which Christ overcame the devil, and the anniversary of Saint Gregory, and seven days at Easter and seven days after, and one day at the feast of Saint Peter and Saint Paul, and in harvest-time the whole week before the feast of Saint Mary, and one day at the feast of All Saints. And the four Wednesdays in the four Ember weeks[10] are to be given to all slaves, to sell to whomsoever they choose anything of what anyone has given them in God's name, or of what they can earn in any of their leisure moments.

---

[10] *Day on which Christ overcame the devil*—15 February; *anniversary of Saint Gregory*—12 March; *feast of Saint Peter and Saint Paul*—29 June; *feast of Saint Mary*—15 August; *feast of All Saints*—1 November; *Wednesdays in the four Ember weeks*—the Wednesdays following the first Sunday in Lent, Whitsunday (Pentecost), the Feast of the Finding of the Holy Cross (14 September), and the Feast of Saint Lucy (13 December)

# CORONATION OF OTTO I
## WIDUKIND OF CORVEY (925–c. 973)

*As Carolingian strength waned in East Francia in the late ninth and early tenth centuries, those who emerged as rulers were the tribal dukes, great landholders who consolidated their power over large regions. Although initially they preferred to elect a weak king, Magyar invasions from the east convinced them of the need for a strong leader. Henry the Fowler, Duke of Saxony (r. 919–936), founded a dynasty that ruled Germany until 1024. His son Otto I (r. 936–973) won a decisive victory over the Magyars at the Battle of the Lechfeld in 955, and in 962 was crowned emperor by Pope John XII (r. 955–964), whom he later deposed. Otto's conscious revival of Carolingian tradition is evident, not only in his designation as emperor—though of an empire that differed significantly from that of Charlemagne—but also in Widukind's richly detailed account of his coronation as king in 936.*

936

After the death of Henry, the father of his country and greatest and best of all kings, the Franks and Saxons chose as their prince his son Otto, who had already been designated king by his father. They ordered the coronation to be held at the palace in Aachen, the place of universal election....

And when they had arrived, the dukes and the great lords, with a force of the   5
chief vassals, gathered in the portico of the basilica of Charlemagne. They placed the new ruler on the throne that had been constructed there, giving him their hands and offering fealty; promising their help against all his enemies, they made him king according to their custom.

While this part of the ceremony was being carried out by the dukes and other   10
magistrates, Archbishop Hildibert of Mainz[1] awaited the procession of the new King with all the priestly order and the commoners in the basilica. The Archbishop awaited the procession of the King, holding the crozier[2] in his right hand and

---

[1]Hildibert, Archbishop of Mainz (927–937)
[2]*Crozier*—shepherd's staff, which symbolized a bishop's position as shepherd of Christ's flock

---

wearing the alb, the pallium, and the chasuble.[3] When the King came forward, he advanced to meet him, touching the King's right hand with his left. Then he led the King to the middle of the sanctuary and turned to the people standing about them (ambulatories[4] had been constructed above and below in that round basilica
5  so that all the people might have a good view).

"Lo," Hildibert said, "I bring before you Lord Otto, elected by God, formerly designated by Henry, now made King by all the princes. If this election pleases you, signify by raising your right hand to heaven." To this all the people raising their right hands on high loudly called down prosperity on the new ruler.
10  The King, dressed in a close-fitting tunic according to the Frankish custom, was escorted behind the altar, on which lay the royal insignia—sword with sword-belt, cloak with bracelets, staff with scepter and diadem....

When the question of who should crown the King arose, two bishops besides Hildibert were considered eligible: the Bishop of Trier because his city was the most
15  ancient and had been founded by Saint Peter, and the Bishop of Cologne because the place of coronation—Aachen—was in his diocese. But both of these men who would have enjoyed the honor deferred to the pre-eminence of Archbishop Hildibert.

Going to the altar and taking from it the sword with sword-belt and turning to the King, he said, "Accept this sword, with which you may chase out all the
20  adversaries of Christ, barbarians, and bad Christians, by the divine authority handed down to you and by the power of all the empire of the Franks for the most lasting peace of all Christians."

Then taking the bracelets and cloak, he clothed him saying, "These points [of the cloak] falling to the ground will remind you with what zeal of faith you should
25  burn and how you ought to endure in preserving peace to the end."

Then taking the scepter and staff, he said, "With these symbols you may be reminded that you should reproach your subjects with paternal castigation, but first of all you should extend the hand of mercy to ministers of God, widows, and orphans. And never let the oil of compassion be absent from your head in order
30  that you may be crowned with eternal reward in the present and in the future."

After having been sprinkled with holy oil and crowned with a golden diadem by the Bishops Hildibert and Wikfried [of Cologne] and all legal consecration having been completed, the King was led to the throne, to which he ascended by means of a spiral staircase. The throne of marvelous beauty had been constructed between
35  two marble pillars, and from there the King could see and be seen by all....

---

[3]*Alb, chasuble*—priestly vestments. The pallium was a long narrow strip of woolen cloth embroidered with crosses that rested on the shoulders; it was blessed at the tomb of Saint Peter and conferred on archbishops as a symbol of their office.

[4]An ambulatory was generally a walkway or processional route that circled behind the high altar of a large church or cathedral to allow pilgrims access to side chapels and saints' shrines without disturbing services. Here the word seems to refer to aisles or galleries built around the walls on two levels, perhaps to allow people to visit the tomb of Charlemagne without entering the sanctuary itself.

# VIII
# THE HIGH AND LATE
# MIDDLE AGES

Following the end of the first millennium, Western Europe experienced a period of population growth, technological advances, and social organization that enabled the rich political and intellectual culture characteristic of the Middle Ages to blossom. While the preceding period can no longer be regarded as the "Dark Ages," the period from 1000 to 1400 did see Europe more convincingly depart from its connections to classical Antiquity. The twelfth and thirteenth centuries, in particular, demonstrate an age of Christian civilization both comparable to the Patristic Age and novel in its particular features. Indeed, Charles Homer Haskins's characterization of the period as the Twelfth-Century Renaissance and Giles Constable's more recent label, the Reformation of the Twelfth Century, develop themes of both continuity and significant growth.

The world that emerged from the turbulent tenth-century raids of people like the Vikings and Magyars gave rise to a societal system foundational for the Middle Ages. The Saxon King Alfred the Great said that a kingdom needed men who fought, men who prayed, and men who worked. Authors like Aelfric (c. 955–c. 1020) extended this idea of three orders of society (*laboratores, oratores,* and *bellatores)* set in unity, all fulfilling their respective roles. Although the hard-working medieval peasant with his heavy iron plow and three-field system of agriculture did develop village communities that would last into the twentieth century and did provide the material sustenance for the entire civilization, the two remaining orders gave medieval society its political and intellectual character.

By the eleventh century, the leading families of Western Europe began to congeal to form the basis of a powerful group. The practice of primogeniture and attachment to estates of compact blocks of land allowed for long-term continuity. The members of this group monopolized both sacred and secular office-holding until medieval kings grew strong enough to promote others. These aristocrats ideally followed a specific code of conduct. This medieval warrior ethos, chivalry, inculcated virtues of prowess, courage, loyalty, and generosity.

The perceived domination of culture by medieval clergy, the *oratores*, lead to the High Middle Ages often being characterized as an age of faith. Because religious life offered prestige and a secure life, the clergy drew their leading members from the aristocracy. For this reason (among others), the distinction between secular and sacred should not be drawn very distinctly in this period.

Indeed, some of the many tensions experienced by this order of society stem directly from this close relationship.

Throughout the Middle Ages, monks and bishops struggled over leadership in the religious sphere. Because they both shared in the ordering of society, mainly by intellectual and cultural domination, but also by social and institutional connections, this tension between the ideals of contemplative and active life remained constant. Clerical thinkers both inherited the idea of a hierarchical society arranged from minor clerical orders all the way to the pope and promoted it to society at large.

Because of the introspective nature of Christian life and the Gospel admonition to reform, the clergy persistently sought to reform itself and the wider society. Following the founding of the Burgundian monastery of Cluny in 910 (free of all lay control and pledged to Saint Peter), reform based on a return to strict observance of the Benedictine rule spread throughout the monasteries of Europe. This first monastic reform movement ranged from a call for abandonment of the world to a call for more active engagement and produced popes like Gregory VII (*r.* 1073–1085), who would attempt to bring reform into the political realm. When the Cluniac movement began to wane, in the twelfth century, the Cistercians, led by charismatic figures like Bernard of Clairvaux (1090–1153) at the strict monastery at Citeaux, tried to create a more pure Benedictine ideal. Reform also affected the quite numerous regular canons (the resident clergy at cathedrals) and even extended to the military sphere with orders like the Templars and Hospitallers. These orders represent the effort to promote Christian ideas into the military aristocracy, much like attempts to regulate warfare such as the Peace of God and the Truce of God.

The social orders had a significant impact on medieval political traditions, but the overarching theme resides in a tendency toward one-man rule in a territorial state. This period witnessed tremendous growth in territory, the consolidation of territories into governable units, the growth of central institutions, and the emergence of governing classes. These developments occurred to varying degree in England, Germany, the Papacy, France, and Iberia.

In the eleventh century, Anglo-Saxon England experienced first a Danish conquest under Cnut (1016–1035), followed by the 1066 Norman conquest led by William the Conqueror (1066–1089). William sought to exert control of his kingdom through instruments like the Domesday Book, and later English kings like Henry II (*r.* 1154–1189) further developed the English (or in his case, Angevin) monarchy.

German Emperors, building on the success of the Ottonian rulers in using the Church to ensure regional control, weathered the turbulent storm over lay investiture. Growing out of Cluniac reform, clerics at both the local and universal level, called for moral reform of the clergy coupled with institutional reform of the Church. When a reform-minded pope, Gregory VII, took on Henry IV (r. 1084–1105), the ensuing fierce battle over the nature of rule permanently weakened the Empire. Only during the reign of Frederick Barbarossa (1152–1190) and then Frederick II (1212–1250) did the power of the Emperor recall earlier success and the image of the Emperor improve on the Ottonian ideology.

In comparison with its secular peers, the "Papal Monarchy" of the High Middle Ages was a triumph of organization and growing centralization. The rhetorically charged Investiture Controversy gives evidence of the Church's well-developed ecclesiology and ideology. Effective use of synods allowed for problems to be addressed at both the local and universal level. The development of the papal curia (particularly its chancellery), the College of Cardinals (often serving as papal legates), and the system of canon law allowed for the institutional church to maintain great influence throughout the kingdoms of Europe without needing frequent recourse to instruments like excommunication or the interdict. The power of this somewhat unconventional monarchy reached its zenith during the pontificate of Innocent III (1198–1216).

Despite suffering the most from the dissolution of the Carolingian Empire, the medieval French monarchy slowly overcame the powerful territorial principalities. The Capetian dynasty (987–1328) built on its base in the Île-de-France and continued the Carolingian tradition of royal rule with productive relations with the Church. Its great gains came at the expense of English rulers like John (r. 1199–1216). The French kings carefully incorporated newly won lands into their royal demesne controlled by their royal appointees, who were often not drawn from the aristocracy. By the thirteenth century, French kings like Louis IX (r. 1226–1270) and Philip IV "the Fair" (r. 1285–1314) had built an effective monarchy leading to their own problems with the Church. The crisis between Philip IV and Pope Boniface VIII (r. 1294–1303) wrestled with the rights of the king to tax the clergy and to bring clerics to justice. This contest allowed political theorists and rulers to imagine states having a core other than religion.

Although on the periphery of medieval Christendom, the Iberian kingdoms developed under the unique influence of the *Reconquista* and the interplay of Christian, Jewish, and Islamic cultures. The *Reconquista*, a long conflict that began in ninth century, lasted until Ferdinand and Isabella re-conquered Granada (1492). Three distinct kingdoms came to dominate the peninsula during this long period of conquest—Aragon, Castile, and Portugal. By the thirteenth century, Iberian monarchs played a decisive role in the western Mediterranean and promoted a brilliant court life.

Medieval culture blended Latin ecclesiastical culture based in monastic and cathedral schools with Jewish and Muslim thought and growing vernacular cultures. Within the liberal arts, the twelfth-century schools shifted the emphasis in the *Trivium* from grammar (ninth century) and rhetoric (eleventh century) to dialectic. Medieval scholars like Anselm of Canterbury (1033–1109) applied logic to issues ranging from eucharistic debates to the existence of God. Peter Abelard (1079–1142), the self-described leading scholar of his day, approached a range of such issue with dialectic in *Sic et Non*. This concentration on the third art of the *Trivium* led to the emergence of a new intellectual tradition, scholasticism, a formal method of reasoning and arguing best illustrated in the works of Thomas Aquinas (1225–1274). Growing out of the cathedral schools, like Chartres, a new institution, the university, developed where both masters and students applied the scholastic method. Although the first focus of universities remained the arts curriculum, scholars engaged fields of medicine, canon law (Gratian, *Decretum,* 1042), and theology (Peter Lombard, *Book of Sentences, c.* 1155). Perhaps the greatest Parisian master, Thomas Aquinas, in the *Summa Theologica* and the *Summa Contra Gentiles*, gave the final medieval statement on the long-contested question of the reconciliation of faith and reason.

Outside of the institutional church, medieval Christianity experienced a vibrancy reflected in a myriad of expressions. A quest for the *vita apostolica* drew men into a life of preaching and poverty, sometimes slipping into the heretical realms such as the Cathars (Albigensians) re-connected with older roots (Manichaean). More profitably, they offered a serious challenge to the contemplative ideal offered by monasticism. The Mendicant orders of Francis (1181–1226) and Dominic (1170–1221) transformed the religious landscape by combining traditional asceticism with work in the world particularly with the poor (the urban apostolate of the Franciscans) and in combating heresy through their exemplary lives and preaching (the apostolate of the Dominicans).

Finally, the Crusades represent a fusing of Christian mission with the chivalric ethos. These religious wars (1195–1291) demonstrate the full blossoming of a militant reformed Christianity marshaled by the pope. While the territorial gains could not be made permanent, the religious zeal elicited by the crusades would not reach a similar height until the religious wars of the sixteenth century.

The period after 1300, sometimes characterized as "the Waning of the Middle Ages," witnessed severe strains against the medieval scholastic synthesis and the uneasy political relationship between papacy and the developing kingdoms. While the strong central monarchies continued to grow in power, the Church suffered from the absence of widespread reforms, growing anti-clericalism, and the catastrophes of the Avignon papacy (1305–1378) and the Great Schism (1378–1417). Coupled with severe demographic and economic problems, such as severe famines (1315–1322) and the Black Death (1348–1349), Europe entered a new period ripe for change and renewal.

# THE INVESTITURE CONTROVERSY

*In the post-Carolingian period, laymen tended to dominate Church affairs in a variety of ways. If a landowner built a church for his tenants, he often believed he had a right to appoint the priest and take the revenues. If someone had a monastery on his lands, he might feel free to use it as a hunting lodge, a retirement home, or a dumping ground for unmarriageable children. Great noble families often viewed the bishoprics in the regions they dominated as family appointments, which meant bishops tended to share the values and lifestyle of the aristocracy. Prominent families in Rome used the papacy as a prize appointment for their younger sons.*

*In the early Church, bishops had been chosen by the "clergy and people" of their dioceses. Over time, the clergy of a particular diocese had come to be represented by some small group, perhaps the clergy of the cathedral or the monks of a particular monastery. Acclamation by the people had given way to selection by the king or local magnate. In Germany, the Emperor insisted upon the right to choose his own bishops for both practical and theoretical reasons. He depended on loyal, competent bishops as his administrators to keep power out of the hands of nobles who might wish to transform offices into hereditary possessions. But imperial theory, which stressed the Emperor's position as "anointed of the Lord, a God through grace, the supreme ruler, supreme shepherd, master, defender, and instructor of Holy Church, lord over his brothers, worthy to be adored by all men, chief and highest prelate," also provided a justification for the Emperor to take an active role in the selection of bishops and even popes, and to invest them with symbols of their spiritual authority. After deposing the scandalous Pope John XII in 964, Otto I (r. 962–973) had declared that no papal appointment could be made without imperial approval. In the mid-eleventh century, Henry III (r. 1039–1056), appalled by the existence of three men claiming to be pope at the same time, deposed them all and appointed the first of a series of reform-minded men to the papal office.*

*Around these popes emerged a group of uncompromising reformers, later called Gregorians after their most famous representative, Pope Gregory*

Ernest F. Henderson, *Select Historical Documents of the Middle Ages* (New York: George Bell and Sons, 1892), 372–73, 376–77, 394–405 [modernized].

*VII. The Gregorians viewed imperial meddling in the selection of popes and bishops as the most flagrant example of what was wrong with the Church, and upon the death (1056) of Henry III, they took advantage of the opportunity offered by the minority of his son and heir, Henry IV, to provide that the pope should henceforth be elected by the College of Cardinals. Their next move was to extend the reform downward to the level of the bishops by outlawing the practice of lay investiture, in which a secular ruler conferred on a bishop the ring that symbolized his marriage to the Church and the staff that represented his position as shepherd of Christ's flock. How, the Gregorians asked, did a layman think he had spiritual authority to give?*

*The ban on lay investiture led to an explosive conflict between Pope Gregory VII and King Henry IV, who wanted to appoint bishops who could help him restore the monarchy to the strength it had possessed in his father's time. This conflict was disastrous for the future of the Empire, for it brought civil war to Germany and resulted in the permanent strengthening of local rulers at the expense of the monarchy. But more important, it raised serious questions about the nature of a properly ordered Christian society and the liberty of the Church from secular interference.*

# LETTER

## Henry IV (1050–1106), KING OF THE ROMANS (1056–1084) TO Gregory VII (*c.* 1020–1085), POPE (1073–1085)

24 JANUARY 1076

Henry, King, not through usurpation, but through the holy ordination of God, to Hildebrand,[1] at present not Pope, but false monk.

Such greeting as this you have merited through your disturbances, inasmuch as there is no grade in the Church which you have omitted to make a partaker, not of honor, but of confusion; not of benediction, but of malediction. For, to mention few and special cases out of many, not only have you not feared to lay hands upon the rulers of the holy Church, the anointed of the Lord—namely, the archbishops, bishops and priests—but you have trodden them under foot like slaves ignorant of what their master is doing. You have won favor from the common herd by crushing them; you have looked upon all of them as knowing nothing, upon yourself alone, moreover, as knowing all things. This knowledge, however, you have used, not for edification, but for destruction; so that with reason we believe that Saint Gregory, whose name you have usurped for yourself, was prophesying concerning you when he said, "The pride of him who is in power increases the more, the greater the number of those subject to him; and he thinks that he himself can do more than all."

---

[1]Hildebrand was Gregory's name before becoming pope.

And we, indeed, have endured all this, being eager to guard the honor of the Apostolic See;[2] you, however, have understood our humility to be fear, and have not, accordingly, hesitated to rise up against the royal power conferred upon us by God, daring to threaten to divest us of it—as if we had received our kingdom from you! As if the Kingdom and the Empire were in your and not in God's hand! And, although our Lord Jesus Christ did call us to the kingdom, he did not, however, call you to the priesthood. For you have ascended by the following steps. Namely, by wiles, which the profession of monk abhors, you have achieved money; by money, favor; by the sword, the throne of peace. And from the throne of peace you have disturbed peace, inasmuch as you have armed subjects against those in authority over them; inasmuch as you, who were not called, have taught that our bishops called of God are to be despised; inasmuch as you have usurped for laymen the ministry over their priests, allowing them to depose or condemn those whom they themselves had received as teachers from the hand of God through the laying on of hands of the bishops.[3]

On me also who, although unworthy to be among the anointed, has nevertheless been anointed to the Kingdom, you have lain your hand; me who—as the tradition of the holy Fathers teaches, declaring that I am not to be deposed for any crime unless, which God forbid, I should have strayed from the faith—am subject to the judgment of God alone. For the wisdom of the holy Fathers committed even Julian the Apostate[4] not to themselves, but to God alone to be judged and to be deposed. For himself, the true Pope, Peter, also exclaims, "Fear God, honor the king."[5] But you who does not fear God, does dishonor in me, His appointed one. Wherefore Saint Paul, when he has not spared an angel of Heaven if he shall have preached otherwise, has not excepted you also who does teach otherwise upon earth. For he says, "If anyone, either I or an angel from heaven, should preach a gospel other than that which has been preached to you, he shall be damned."[6]

You, therefore, damned by this curse and by the judgment of all our bishops and by our own, descend and relinquish the apostolic chair which you have usurped. Let another ascend the throne of Saint Peter who shall not practice violence under the cloak of religion, but shall teach the sound doctrine of Saint Peter. I, Henry, King by the grace of God, do say unto you, together with all our bishops, Descend, descend, to be damned throughout the ages.

---

[2]Rome

[3]Gregory VII had urged laymen to withdraw obedience from bishops who had been guilty of simony, i.e, those who had purchased their offices. Simony was one of the evils the Gregorian reform movement attempted to eradicate.

[4]Julian (331–363), Roman Emperor (361–363) who attempted to revive Paganism

[5]I Peter 2:17

[6]Galatians 1:8

# Deposition of Henry IV
## Gregory VII (*c.* 1020–1085), Pope (1073–1085)

22 February 1076

O Saint Peter, chief of the apostles, incline to us, I beg, your holy ears, and hear me, your servant, whom you have nourished from infancy and whom, until this day, you have freed from the hand of the wicked, who have hated and do hate me for my faithfulness to you. You, and my lady, the mother of God, and your brother Saint Paul are witnesses for me among all the saints that your holy Roman church drew me to its helm against my will; that I had no thought of ascending your chair through force, and that I would rather have ended my life as a pilgrim than by secular means to have seized your throne for the sake of earthly glory.[1] And therefore I believe it to be through your grace and not through my own deeds that it has pleased and does please you that the Christian people, who have been especially committed to you, should obey me. And especially to me, as your representative and by your favor, has the power been granted by God of binding and loosing in Heaven and on earth.

On the strength of this belief therefore, for the honor and security of your church, in the name of Almighty God, Father, Son, and Holy Ghost, I withdraw, through your power and authority, from Henry the King, son of Henry the Emperor, who has risen against your church with unheard of insolence, the rule over the whole Kingdom of the Germans and over Italy. And I absolve all Christians from the bonds of the oath which they have made or shall make to him; and I forbid anyone to serve him as king.

For it is fitting that he who strives to lessen the honor of your church should himself lose the honor which belongs to him. And since he has scorned to obey as a Christian, and has not returned to God, Whom he had deserted—holding intercourse with the excommunicated; practicing manifold iniquities; spurning my commands which, as you bear witness, I issued to him for his own salvation; separating himself from your church and striving to rend it—I bind him in your stead with the chain of the anathema. And, leaning on you, I so bind him that the people may know and have proof that you are Peter, and above your rock the Son of the living God has built His church, and the gates of Hell shall not prevail against it.

---

[1] Gregory had been acclaimed by the Roman people as pope before the cardinals elected him. His opponents used this to question the validity of his election.

# LETTER

## Gregory VII (c. 1020–1085), Pope (1073–1085)

### to Hermann, Bishop of Metz (1072–1090)

15 March 1081

Bishop Gregory, servant of the servants of God, to his beloved brother in Christ, Hermann, Bishop of Metz, greeting and apostolic benediction.

It is doubtless owing to a dispensation of God that, as we learn, you are ready to bear labors and dangers in defense of the truth. For such is His ineffable grace and wonderful mercy that He never allows His chosen ones completely      5
to go astray—never permits them utterly to fall or to be cast down. For, after they have been afflicted by a time of persecution—a useful term of probation as it were—He makes them, even if they have passed through some trepidation, stronger than before. Since, moreover, manly courage impels one strong man to act more bravely than another and to press forward more boldly—even as      10
among cowards fear induces one to flee more disgracefully than another—we wish, beloved, with the voice of exhortation to impress this upon you: you should the more delight to stand in the army of the Christian faith among the first the more you are convinced that they are the most worthy and the nearest to God the victors.      15

Your demand, indeed, to be aided, as it were, by our writings and fortified against the madness of those who babble forth with unhallowed mouth that the authority of the holy and apostolic see had no right to excommunicate Henry—a man who despises the Christian law; a destroyer, namely, of the churches and of the Empire; a favorer of heretics and a partaker with them—or to absolve anyone      20
from the oath of fealty to him does not seem to us to be altogether necessary when so many and such absolutely certain proofs are to be found in the pages of Holy Scripture. Nor do we believe, indeed, that those who, heaping up for themselves damnation, impudently detract from the truth and run counter to it have joined these charges to the audacity of their defense so much from      25
ignorance as from a certain madness of wretched desperation. And no wonder. For it is the custom of the wicked to strive after protection from their iniquity and to defend those like to themselves; considering it of no importance that they incur perdition for lying.

For, to cite a few passages from among many, who does not know the      30
words of our Lord and Savior Jesus Christ who says in the gospel: "You are Peter and upon this rock will I build my church, and the gates of hell shall not prevail against it; and I will give unto you the keys of the kingdom of Heaven; and whatsoever you shall bind upon earth shall be bound also in Heaven, and

whatsoever you shall loose upon earth shall be loosed also in Heaven"?[1] Are kings excepted here, or do they not belong to the sheep which the Son of God committed to Saint Peter? Who, I ask, in this universal concession of the power of binding and loosing, can think that he is withdrawn from the authority of
5   Saint Peter, unless, perhaps, that unfortunate man who is unwilling to bear the yoke of the Lord and subjects himself to the burden of the devil, refusing to be among the number of Christ's sheep? It will help him little to his wretched liberty, indeed, that he shake from his proud neck the divinely granted power of Peter. For the more anyone, through pride, refuses to bear it, the more heavily
10   shall it press upon him unto damnation at the judgment.

    The holy fathers, indeed, as well in general councils as otherwise in their writings and doings, have called the Holy Roman Church the universal mother, accepting and serving with great veneration this institution founded by the divine will, this pledge of a dispensation to the church, this privilege handed
15   over in the beginning and confirmed to Saint Peter, the chief of the apostles. And even as they accepted its proofs in confirmation of their faith and of the doctrines of holy religion, so also they received its judgments—consenting in this, and agreeing as it were with one spirit and one voice: that all greater matters and exceptional cases, and judgments over all churches, ought to be
20   referred to it as to a mother and a head; that from it there was no appeal; that no one should or could retract or refute its decisions.

    Wherefore the blessed Pope Gelasius,[2] armed with the divine authority, when writing to the Emperor Anastasius[3] how and what he should think concerning the primacy of the holy and apostolic see, instructed him as follows:

25       Although before all priests in common who duly exercise divine functions it is right that the necks of the faithful should be bowed, by how much more should the Bishop of the Roman See be obeyed, whom both the supreme deity has willed to predominate over all priests and the subsequent piety of the whole Church in common has honored?
30       From which your prudence clearly sees that, with him whom the voice of Christ placed over all, and whom a venerable Church has always professed and devoutly holds as its primate, no one can, by any human device whatever, gain an equal privilege and be equally acknowledged.

35     Likewise Pope Julius,[4] when writing to the oriental bishops concerning the power of that same holy and apostolic see, said:

---

[1]Matthew 16:18–19

[2]Gelasius I, Pope (492–496)

[3]Anastasius I (*c.* 430–518), Emperor of Rome (491–518)

[4]Julius I, Pope (337–352). Because the Emperor and a number of the bishops in the East supported the Arians, certain prominent bishops from the East found themselves in exile

It would have become you, brethren, to choose your words and not to speak ironically against the Holy Roman and Apostolic Church, since our Lord Jesus Christ, addressing it as was fitting, said, "You are Peter, and upon this rock will I build my church, and the gates of hell shall not prevail against it; and I will give unto you the keys of the kingdom of Heaven." For it has the power, granted to it by a special privilege, of opening and closing for whom it will the gates of the kingdom of Heaven.

Is it not lawful, then, for him to whom the power of opening and closing Heaven is granted to exercise judgment upon earth? God forbid that it should not be! Remember what the most blessed apostle Paul says: "Know you not that we shall judge angels? How much more the things of earth!"[5]

The blessed Pope Gregory[6] also decreed that those kings should fall from their dignity who should dare to violate the statutes of the apostolic see, writing to a certain abbot, Senator, as follows:

But if any king, priest, judge, or secular person, disregarding this, the page of our decree, shall attempt to act counter to it, he shall lose the dignity of his power and honor. All shall know that he, in the sight of God, is guilty of committing a crime. And unless he restore the things which have been wrongfully removed by him, or unless he atone by fitting penance for his unlawful acts, he shall be kept away from the most sacred body and blood of our Lord and Savior Jesus Christ and shall undergo a stern vengeance at the eternal judgment.

But if the blessed Gregory, the most gentle of teachers, decreed that kings who should violate his decrees in the matter of a single hospice should not only be deposed, but also excommunicated and, at the last judgment, condemned, who, save one like to them, will blame us for having deposed and excommunicated Henry, who is not alone a scorner of the apostolic judgments but also, as far as in him lies, a treader under foot of Holy Mother Church herself and a most shameless robber and atrocious destroyer of the whole realm and of the churches.

As we have learned, through Saint Peter's teaching, from a letter concerning the ordination of Clement[7] in which it says:

---

in Rome. Julius held a synod which reaffirmed the Nicene position; he then wrote to those bishops who were supporting Arius—the letter Gregory here cited—arguing they should have brought the issue to him from the outset, since the Bishop of Rome could hear appeals from any part of the Church.

[5] I Corinthians 6:3
[6] Gregory I (c. 540–604), Pope (590–604)
[7] Clement, Pope (88–97)

If anyone shall be a friend to those with whom he [Clement] does not speak, he also is one of those who wish to exterminate the church of God; and while, with his body, he seems to be with us, he is with heart and soul against us. And such an enemy is far more dangerous than those

5      who are without and who are open enemies. For he, under the guise of friendship, does hostile acts, and rends and lays waste the church.

Mark well, beloved, if this Pope so severely judges the friend or companion of those with whom, on account of their actions he is angry, with what condemnation he will visit the man himself with whose actions he is displeased.

10     But to return to the matter in hand. Is not a dignity like this, founded by laymen—even by those who do not know God—subject to that dignity which the providence of God Almighty has, in His own honor, founded and given to the world? For His Son, even as He is undoubtingly believed to be God and man, so is He considered the highest priest, the head of all priests, sitting on

15     the right hand of the Father and always interceding for us. And He despised a secular kingdom, which makes the sons of this world swell with pride, and came of His own will to the priesthood of the cross.

Who does not know that kings and leaders are sprung from those who—ignorant of God—by pride, plunder, perfidy, murders—in a word by almost

20     every crime, the devil, who is the prince of this world, urging them on as it were—have striven with blind cupidity and intolerable presumption to dominate over their equals; namely, over men? To whom, indeed, can we better compare them, when they seek to make the priests of God bend to their footprints, than to him who is head over all the sons of pride and who, tempting

25     the Highest Pontiff Himself, the Head of priests, the Son of the Most High, and promising to Him all the kingdoms of the world, said: "All these I will give You if You will fall down and worship me?"[8]

Who can doubt but that the priests of Christ are to be considered the fathers and masters of kings and princes and of all the faithful? Is it not considered

30     miserable madness for a son to attempt to subject to himself his father, a pupil his master; and for one to bring into his power and bind with iniquitous bonds him by whom he believes that he himself can be bound and loosed not only on earth but also in Heaven? This the Emperor Constantine the Great, lord of all the kings and princes of nearly the whole world, evidently understood—as

35     the blessed Gregory reminds us in a letter to the Emperor Mauritius—when, sitting last after all the bishops in the holy council of Nicæa, he presumed to give no sentence of judgment over them, but, even calling them gods, decreed

---

[8]Matthew 4:9, Luke 4:6–7

that they should not be subject to his judgment but that he should be dependent upon their will.

Also the afore-mentioned Pope Gelasius, persuading the said Emperor Anastasius not to take offense at the truth which had been made clear to his senses, added this remark: "For, indeed, O august Emperor, there are two things    5
by which this world is chiefly ruled—the sacred authority of the pontiffs and the royal power; whereby the burden of the priests is by so much the heavier according as they, at the divine judgment of men, are about to render account for the kings themselves." And a little further on he says: "You know, therefore, that in these matters you are dependent on their judgment and that you are not    10
to wish to reduce them to do your will."

Very much of the pontiffs, accordingly, armed with such decrees and with such authorities, have ex-communicated—some of them kings; some, emperors. For, if any special example of the persons of such princes is needed—the blessed Pope Innocent excommunicated the Emperor Arcadius for consenting that Saint    15
John Chrysostom[9] should be expelled from his see. Likewise another Roman pontiff—Zachary, namely—deposed a King of the Franks,[10] not so much for his iniquities as for the reason that he was not fitted to exercise so great power. And he substituted Pipin, father of the Emperor Charles the Great, in his place—loosing all the Franks from the oath of fealty which they had sworn him. As, indeed,    20
the Holy Church frequently does by its authority when it absolves servitors from the fetters of an oath sworn to such bishops as, by apostolic sentence, are deposed from their pontifical rank. And the blessed Ambrose—who, although a saint, was not, indeed, bishop over the whole church—ex-communicated and excluded from the Church the Emperor Theodosius the Great for a fault which,    25
by other priests, was not regarded as very grave.[11] He shows, too, in his writings that, not by so much is gold more precious than lead as the priestly dignity is more lofty than the royal power; speaking thus towards the beginning of his

---

[9]John Chrysostom (*c.* 347–407), Patriarch of Constantinople from 398, made enemies at the imperial court because he demanded the moral reform of the clergy, criticized the Empress, and refused to co-operate with imperial religious policy. Emperor Arcadius (395–408) sent him into exile, where he died. Pope Innocent (401–417) excommunicated Arcadius in 406.

[10]Childeric III

[11]In 390, Theodosius, then in Milan, where Ambrose was Bishop, responded to the murder of a military commander in Thessalonica with an ill-considered order that resulted in a massacre. Ambrose wrote him, declaring it would be sacrilege to celebrate the Eucharist if the Emperor were present because he had blood on his hands; consequently, until Theodosius did public penance he would be excluded from the Christian community. When he next appeared at the door of the cathedral, Ambrose barred him from entering. Eventually Theodosius agreed that, in matters of the soul, he should obey his bishop, since ultimately he would not face God at the Judgment clad in imperial purple. This episode set a precedent that was cited repeatedly—for example, in this text—for more than a thousand years.

pastoral letter: "The honor and sublimity of bishops, brethren, is beyond all comparison. If one should compare them to resplendent kings and diademed princes it would be far less worthy than if one compared the base metal lead to gleaming gold. For, indeed, one can see how the necks of kings and princes

5    are bowed before the knees of priests; and how, having kissed their right hands, they believe themselves to be fortified by their prayers." And, after a little: "You should know, brethren, that we have thus mentioned all these things in order to show that nothing in this life can be found more lofty than priests or more sublime than bishops."

10    You, brother, should also remember that more power is granted to an exorcist when he is made a spiritual emperor for the casting out of demons than can be granted to any layman in the matter of secular dominion. Over all kings and princes of the earth who do not live religiously and do not, in their actions, fear God as they should, demons—alas, alas—hold sway, confounding them with a

15    wretched servitude. Such men desire to rule, not, induced by divine love, to the honor of God and for the saving of souls—like the priests of the church; but they strive to have dominion over others in order to show forth their intolerable pride and to fulfill the lusts of their heart. Concerning whom the blessed Augustine says in the first book on the Christian teaching: "For, indeed, whoever

20    strives to gain dominion even over those who are by nature his equals—that is, over men: his pride is altogether intolerable." Exorcists, then, have, as we have said, dominion from God over demons. How much more, therefore, over those who are subject to demons and member of demons? If, moreover, exorcists are so pre-eminent over these, how much the more so are priests!

25    Furthermore every Christian king, when he comes to die, seeks as a miserable suppliant the aid of a priest to the end that he may evade hell's prison, that he may pass from the shadows to the light, that, at the last judgment, he may appear absolved from the bonds of his sins. But what man—a layman even, not to speak of priests—has ever implored the aid of an earthly king for the

30    salvation of his soul when his last hour was near? And what king or emperor is able, by reason of the office imposed upon him, to snatch any Christian from the power of the devil through holy baptism, to number him among the sons of God, and to fortify him with the divine unction? And who of them—which is the greatest thing in the Christian religion—can with his own lips make the

35    body and blood of our Lord? Or who of them possesses the power of binding and loosing in Heaven and on earth? From which things it is clearly seen how greatly priests excel in power and dignity.

Or who of them can ordain anyone as clerk in the Holy Church—much less depose him for any fault? For in the matter of ecclesiastical grades a greater

40    power is needed to depose than to ordain. For bishops may ordain other bish-

ops, but by no means depose them without the authority of the Apostolic See. Who, therefore, that is even moderately intelligent, can doubt that priests are to be preferred to kings? But if kings are to be judged by priests for their sins, by whom should they be judged with more right than by the Roman Pontiff?

Finally, any good Christians whatever have much more right to be considered kings than have bad princes. For the former, seeking the glory of God, strenuously rule themselves; but the latter, enemies unto themselves, seeking the things which are their own and not the things which are God's, are tyrannical oppressors of others. The former are the body of the true king, Christ; the latter, of the devil. The former restrain themselves to the end that they may eternally reign with the supreme emperor; but the sway of the latter brings about this—that they shall perish in eternal damnation with the prince of darkness who is king over all the sons of pride.

Nor, indeed, is it much to be wondered at that wicked bishops are of one mind with a bad king whom—having wrongfully obtained honors from him—they love and fear. For they, simoniscally ordaining whom they please, sell God even for a paltry price. And as the good are indivisibly united with their head, so also the bad are pertinaciously banded together—chiefly against the good—with him who is the head of evil. But against them we ought surely not so much to hold discourse as to weep for them with tears and lamentations, to the end that God Almighty may snatch them from the nooses of Satan in which they are held captive and, after their great danger, bring them at length at some time to a knowledge of the truth.

We refer to kings and emperors who, too much swollen by worldly glory, rule not for God but for themselves. But, since it belongs to our office to distribute exhortation to each person according to the rank or dignity which he adorns, we take care, God impelling us, to provide weapons of humility just for emperors and kings and other princes, that they may be able to subdue the risings of the sea and the waves of pride. For we know that mundane glory and worldly cares usually do induce to pride, especially those who are in authority. They, in consequence, neglecting humility and seeking their own glory, always desire to dominate over their brothers. Wherefore to kings and emperors especially it is of advantage, when their mind tends to exalt itself and to delight in its own particular glory, to find out a means of humbling themselves and to be brought to realize that what they have been rejoicing in is the thing most to be feared. Let them, therefore, diligently consider how dangerous and how much to be feared the royal or imperial dignity is. For in it the fewest are saved; and those who, through the mercy of God, do come to salvation are not glorified in the Holy Church and in the judgment of the Holy Spirit to the same extent as many poor people. For, from the beginning of the world until these our

own times, in the whole of authentic history we do not find seven emperors
or kings whose lives were as distinguished for religion and as beautified by
significant portents as those of an innumerable multitude who despised the
world—although we believe many of them to have found mercy in the presence of God Almighty. For what emperor or king was ever honored by miracles
as were Saint Martin, Saint Antony, and Saint Benedict—not to mention the
apostles and martyrs? And what emperor or king raised the dead, cleansed lep-
ers, or healed the blind? See how the Holy Church praises and venerates the
Emperor Constantine of blessed memory, Theodosius and Honorius, Charles
and Louis as lovers of justice, promoters of the Christian religion, defenders
of the churches: it does not, however, declare them to have been resplendent
with so great a glory of miracles. Moreover, for how many kings or emperors
has the Holy Church ordered chapels or altars to be dedicated to their names,
or masses to be celebrated in their honor?

Let kings and other princes fear lest the more they rejoice at being placed
over other men in this life, the more they will be subjected to eternal fires. For of
them it is written, "The powerful shall powerfully suffer torments."[12] And they
are about to render account to God for as many men as they have had subjects
under their dominion. But if it be no little task for any private religious man
to guard his own soul: how much labor will there be for those who are rulers
over many thousands of souls? Moreover, if the judgment of the Holy Church
severely punishes a sinner for the slaying of one man, what will become of those
who, for the sake of worldly glory, hand over many thousands to death? And
such persons, although after having slain many the often say with their lips "I
have sinned," nevertheless rejoice in their hearts at having extended their fame
as it were. And they are unwilling not to have done what they have done, nor
do they grieve at having driven their brothers into Tartarus. And, so long as
they do not repent with their whole heart and are unwilling to let go what has
been acquired or retained through shedding of blood, their penitence before
God will remain without the worthy fruit of penitence. Surely, therefore, they
ought greatly to fear.

And it should frequently be recalled to their memory that, as we have said,
in the different kingdoms of the earth, from the beginning of the world, very
few of the innumerable multitude of kings are found to have been holy: whereas
in one see alone—the Roman one, namely—almost a hundred of the successive pontiffs since the time of Saint Peter the apostle are counted among the
most holy. Why, then, is this—except that the kings and princes of the earth,
enticed by vain glory, prefer, as has been said, the things that are their own to

---

[12]Book of Wisdom 6:7

the things that are spiritual; but the pontiffs of the church, despising vain glory, prefer to carnal things the things that are of God? The former readily punish those who sin against themselves and are indifferent to those who sin against God; the latter quickly pardon those who sin against themselves and do not lightly spare those who sin against God. The former, too much bent on earthly deeds, think slightingly of spiritual ones; the latter, sedulously meditating on heavenly things, despise the things which are of earth.

Therefore all Christians who desire to reign with Christ should be warned not to strive to rule through ambition of worldly power, but rather to keep in view what the blessed Gregory, most holy Pope, tells them to in his pastoral book when he says, "Among these things, therefore, what is to be striven for and what is to be feared except that he who surpasses in virtue shall be urged and shall come to rule, and that he who is without virtues shall not be urged and shall not come?" But if those who fear God come, when urged, with great fear to the apostolic chair, in which those who are duly ordained are made better by the merits of the apostle Saint Peter—with how much fear and trembling is the throne of the kingdom to be approached, where even the good and humble—as is shown in the case of Saul and David—become worse? For what we have said of the apostolic chair—we know it, too, by experience—is thus contained in the decrees of the blessed Pope Symmachus:[13] "He—Saint Peter, namely—has sent down to posterity a perennial gift of merits together with a heritage of innocence." And a little further on: "For who can doubt that he is holy who is raised by the apex of so great a dignity? And, if the goods acquired by merit are lacking, those which are furnished by his predecessor suffice. For either he [Saint Peter] exalts distinguished men to this summit, or he illumines those who are exalted."

Therefore let those whom Holy Church, of its own will and after proper counsel, not for transitory glory but for the salvation of many, calls to have rule or dominion, humbly obey. And let them always beware in that point as to which Saint Gregory, in that same pastoral book bears witness:

> Indeed, when a man disdains to be like to men, he is made like to an apostate angel. Thus Saul, after having possessed the merit of humility, came to be swelled with pride when at the summit of power. Through humility, indeed, he was advanced; through pride, reproved—God being witness who said: "When you were small in your own eyes, did I not make you head over the tribes of Israel?"[14]

---

[13]Symmachus, Pope (498–514)
[14]I Samuel 15:17

And a little further on: "Moreover, strange to say, when he was small in his own eyes he was great in the eyes of God; but when he seemed great in his own eyes he was small in the eyes of God." Let them also carefully retain what God says in the gospel: "I do not seek my glory"[15] and "He who wishes to be
5   the first among you shall be the servant of all."[16] Let them always prefer the honor of God to their own; let them cherish and guard justice by observing the rights of every man. Let them not walk in the counsel of the ungodly but, with an assenting heart, always consort with good men. Let them not seek to subject to themselves or to subjugate the Holy Church as a handmaid; but chiefly let
10  them strive, by recognizing the teachers and fathers, to honor in due form her eyes—namely the priests of God. For if we are ordered to honor our carnal fathers and mothers—how much more our spiritual ones! And if he who has cursed his carnal father or mother is to be punished with death—what does he merit who curses his spiritual father or mother? Let them not, enticed by carnal
15  love, strive to place one of their own sons over the flock for which Christ poured forth His blood, if they can find someone who is better and more useful than he, lest, loving their son more than God, they inflict the greatest detriment on the Holy Church. For he who neglects to provide to the best of his ability for such a want—and, as it were, necessity—of Holy Mother Church is openly
20  convicted of not loving God and his neighbor as a Christian should.

For if this virtue—namely, love—has been neglected, no matter what good any one does he shall be without every fruit of salvation. And so by humbly doing these things, and by observing the love of God and of their neighbor as they ought, they may hope for the mercy of Him who said: "Learn of Me,
25  for I am meek and lowly of heart."[17] If they shall have humbly imitated Him they shall pass from this servile and transitory kingdom to a true kingdom of liberty and eternity.

---

[15]John 8:50
[16]Mark 10:44
[17]Matthew 11:29

# POLICRATICUS
## JOHN OF SALISBURY (c. 1115–1180)

*John of Salisbury studied under many of the brilliant teachers of the early twelfth century, including Peter Abelard (1079–1142), who contributed to the intellectual revival then underway in the cathedral schools of Paris and Chartres. Returning to his native England, Salisbury became secretary to the Archbishop of Canterbury, a position that permitted him to pursue his scholarly interests, but that also brought him into contact with the leading political and religious figures of the day. He wrote* Policraticus *in 1159, five years after Henry II (r. 1154–1189) succeeded King Stephen (1135–1154), whose mild temperament and lack of strong leadership had exacerbated the instability caused by civil war. Henry, by contrast, had already demonstrated that he intended to rule with a firm hand and by his own will.*

*In* Policraticus, *John of Salisbury considered the contrast between good government and tyranny in terms that reflected his mastery of the classics, his familiarity with Roman law, and the influence of Gregorian ideas. His work was not simply theoretical, however; it had practical contemporary relevance. How did John describe a prince's relationship to the law? What did he mean by "liberty"? In his famous metaphor of the body politic, how did the various parts of the body interact, and what was their relationship to the head? What was the relationship of the prince to the Church? How did John define tyranny?*

1159

### Of the Difference Between a Prince and a Tyrant and of what is Meant by a Prince

IV§1 Between a tyrant and a prince there is this single or chief difference, that the latter obeys the law and rules the people by its dictates, accounting himself as but their servant. It is by virtue of the law that he makes good his claim to the foremost and chief place in the management of the affairs of the commonwealth and in the bearing of its burdens; and his elevation over others consists in this, 5

*The Statesman's Book of John of Salisbury*, translated by John Dickinson (New York: Russell & Russell, 1963), 3–11, 64–65, 198–200, 243–44, 335–36, 338–39, 350–57. ©Atheneum Publishers. All rights reserved.

453

that whereas private men are held responsible only for their private affairs, on the prince fall the burdens of the whole community. Wherefore deservedly there is conferred on him, and gathered together in his hands, the power of all his subjects, to the end that he may be sufficient unto himself in seeking and
5    bringing about the advantage of each individually, and of all; and to the end that the state of the human commonwealth may be ordered in the best possible manner, seeing that each and all are members one of another. Wherein we indeed but follow nature, the best guide of life; for nature has gathered together all the senses of her microcosm or little world, which is man, into the
10   head, and has subjected all the members in obedience to it in such wise that they will all function properly so long as they follow the guidance of the head, and the head remains sane.

Therefore the prince stands on a pinnacle which is exalted and made splendid with all the great and high privileges which he deems necessary for
15   himself. And rightly so, because nothing is more advantageous to the people than that the needs of the prince should be fully satisfied; since it is impossible that his will should be found opposed to justice. Therefore, according to the usual definition, the prince is the public power, and a kind of likeness on earth of the divine majesty. Beyond doubt a large share of the divine power is
20   shown to be in princes by the fact that at their nod men bow their necks and for the most part offer up their heads to the axe to be struck off, and, as by a divine impulse, the prince is feared by each of those over whom he is set as an object of fear.

And this I do not think could be, except as a result of the will of God.
25   For all power is from the Lord God, and has been with Him always, and is from everlasting. The power which the prince has is therefore from God, for the power of God is never lost, nor severed from Him, but He merely exercises it through a subordinate hand, making all things reach His mercy or justice. "Who, therefore, resists the ruling power, resists the ordinance of God,"[1] in
30   whose hand is the authority of conferring that power, and when He so desires, of withdrawing it again, or diminishing it. For it is not the ruler's own act when his will is turned to cruelty against his subjects, but it is rather the dispensation of God for His good pleasure to punish or chasten them.

Thus during the Hunnish persecution, Attila, on being asked by the rev-
35   erend bishop of a certain city who he was, replied, "I am Attila, the scourge of God." Whereupon it is written that the bishop adored him[2] as representing the divine majesty. "Welcome," he said, "is the minister of God," and "Blessed is he

---

[1]Romans 13:2
[2]*Adored him*—prostrated himself before Attila

that comes in the name of the Lord,"[3] and with sighs and groans he unfastened the barred doors of the church, and admitted the persecutor through whom he attained straightway to the palm of martyrdom.[4] For he dared not shut out the scourge of God, knowing that His beloved Son was scourged, and that the power of this scourge which had come upon himself was as naught except it came from God.

If good men thus regard power as worthy of veneration even when it comes as a plague upon the elect, who should not venerate that power which is instituted by God for the punishment of evil-doers and for the reward of good men, and which is promptest in devotion and obedience to the laws? To quote the words of the Emperor, "it is indeed a saying worthy of the majesty of royalty that the prince acknowledges himself bound by the Laws."[5] For the authority of the prince depends upon the authority of justice and law; and truly it is a greater thing than imperial power for the prince to place his government under the laws, so as to deem himself entitled to do nought which is at variance with the equity of justice.

## What the Law is; and that Although the Prince is not Bound by the Law, He is Nevertheless the Servant of the Law and of Equity, And Bears the Public Person, and Sheds Blood Blamelessly

IV§2Princes should not deem that it detracts from their princely dignity to believe that the enactments of their own justice are not to be preferred to the justice of God, whose justice is an everlasting justice, and His law is equity. Now equity, as the learned jurists define it, is a certain fitness of things which compares all things rationally, and seeks to apply like rules of right and wrong to like cases, being impartially disposed toward all persons, and allotting to each that which belongs to him. Of this equity the interpreter is the law, to which the will and intention of equity and justice are known.

Therefore Crisippus asserted that the power of the law extends over all things, both divine and human, and that it accordingly presides over all goods and ills, and is the ruler and guide of material things as well as of human beings. To which Papinian, a man most learned in the law, and Demosthenes, the great orator, seem to assent, subjecting all men to its obedience because all law is, as it were, a discovery, and a gift from God, a precept of wise men, the corrector

---

[3]Matthew 21:9
[4]Attila (406–453), leader of the Huns (4343–453), successfully invaded much of Western Europe.
[5]Justinian, *Codex* I:14§4

of excesses of the will, the bond which knits together the fabric of the state, and the banisher of crime; and it is therefore fitting that all men should live according to it who lead their lives in a corporate political body. All are accordingly bound by the necessity of keeping the law, unless perchance there is any who
5 can be thought to have been given the license of wrong-doing.

However, it is said that the prince is absolved from the obligations of the law; but this is not true in the sense that it is lawful for him to do unjust acts, but only in the sense that his character should be such as to cause him to practice equity not through fear of the penalties of the law but through love
10 of justice; and should also be such as to cause him from the same motive to promote the advantage of the commonwealth, and in all things to prefer the good of others before his own private will. Who, indeed, in respect of public matters can properly speak of the will of the prince at all, since therein he may not lawfully have any will of his own apart from that which the law or equity
15 enjoins, or the calculation of the common interest requires? For in these matters his will is to have the force of a judgment; and most properly that which pleases him therein has the force of law, because his decision may not be at variance with the intention of equity. "From your countenance," says the Lord, "let my judgment go forth, let your eyes look upon equity";[6] for the uncor-
20 rupted judge is one whose decision, from assiduous contemplation of equity, is the very likeness thereof.

The prince accordingly is the minister of the common interest and the bond-servant of equity, and he bears the public person in the sense that he punishes the wrongs and injuries of all, and all crimes, with evenhanded equity.
25 His rod and staff also, administered with wise moderation, restore irregularities and false departures to the straight path of equity, so that deservedly may the Spirit congratulate the power of the prince with the words, "Thy rod and thy staff, they have comforted me."[7] His shield, too, is strong, but it is a shield for the protection of the weak, and one which wards off powerfully the darts of the
30 wicked from the innocent. Those who derive the greatest advantage from his performance of the duties of his office are those who can do least for themselves, and his power is chiefly exercised against those who desire to do harm.

Therefore not without reason he bears a sword, wherewith he sheds blood blamelessly, without becoming thereby a man of blood, and frequently puts
35 men to death without incurring the name or guilt of homicide. For if we believe the great Augustine, David was called a man of blood not because of his wars, but because of Uriah. And Samuel is nowhere described as a man of

---

[6]Psalm 17:2
[7]Psalm 23:4
[8]I Samuel 15

blood or a homicide, although he slew Agag, the fat king of Amalech.[8] Truly the sword of princely power is as the sword of a dove, which contends without gall, smites without wrath, and when it fights, yet conceives no bitterness at all. For as the law pursues guilt without any hatred of persons, so the prince most justly punishes offenders from no motive of wrath but at the behest, and in accordance with the decision, of the passionless law. For although we see that the prince has lictors of his own, we must yet think of him as in reality himself the sole or chief lictor, to whom is granted by the law the privilege of striking by a subordinate hand. If we adopt the opinion of the Stoics, who diligently trace down the reason for particular words, *lictor* means *legis ictor*, or "hammer of the law," because the duty of his office is to strike those who the law adjudges shall be struck. Wherefore anciently, when the sword hung over the head of the convicted criminal, the command was wont to be given to the officials by whose hand the judge punishes evil-doers. "Execute the sentence of the law," or "Obey the law," to the end that the misery of the victim might be mitigated by the calm reasonableness of the words.

## That the Prince is the Minister of the Priests and Inferior to them; And of what Amounts to Faithful Performance of the Prince's Ministry

IV§3 This sword, then, the prince receives from the hand of the Church, although she herself has no sword of blood at all. Nevertheless she has this sword, but she uses it by the hand of the prince, upon whom she confers the power of bodily coercion, retaining to herself authority over spiritual things in the person of the pontiffs. The prince is, then, as it were, a minister of the priestly power, and one who exercises that side of the sacred offices which seems unworthy of the hands of the priesthood. For every office existing under, and concerned with the execution of, the sacred laws is really a religious office, but that is inferior which consists in punishing crimes, and which therefore seems to be typified in the person of the hangman. Wherefore Constantine, most faithful Emperor of the Romans, when he had convoked the council of priests at Nicaea, neither dared to take the chief place for himself nor even to sit among the presbyters, but chose the hindmost seat. Moreover, the decrees which he heard approved by them he reverenced as if he had seen them emanate from the judgment-seat of the divine majesty. Even the rolls of petitions containing accusations against priests which they brought to him in a steady stream, he took and placed in his bosom without opening them. And after recalling them to charity and harmony, he said that it was not permissible for him, as a man, and one who was subject to the judgment of priests, to examine cases touching gods, who cannot be judged save by God alone....

But if one who has been appointed prince has performed duly and faithfully the ministry which he has undertaken, as great honor and reverence are to be shown to him as the head excels in honor all the members of the body. Now he performs his ministry faithfully when he is mindful of his true status, and remembers that he bears the person of the *universitas* of those subject to him; and when he is fully conscious that he owes his life not to himself and to his own private ends, but to others, and allots it to them accordingly, with duly ordered charity and affection....

And so let him be both father and husband to his subjects, or, if he has known some affection more tender still, let him employ that; let him desire to be loved rather than feared, and show himself to him as such a man that they will out of devotion prefer his life to their own, and regard his preservation and safety as a kind of public life; and then all things will prosper well for him, and a small bodyguard will, in case of need, prevail by their loyalty against innumerable adversaries. For love is strong as death....

### What a Commonwealth is, According to Plutarch, And what Fills Therein the Place of the Soul and the Members

**V§2**...A commonwealth, according to Plutarch,[9] is a certain body which is endowed with life by the benefit of divine favor, which acts at the prompting of the highest equity, and is ruled by what may be called the moderating power of reason. Those things which establish and implant in us the practice of religion, and transmit to us the worship of God...fill the place of the soul in the body of the commonwealth. And therefore those who preside over the practice of religion should be looked up to and venerated as the soul of the body. For who doubts that the ministers of God's holiness are His representatives? Furthermore, since the soul is, as it were, the prince of the body, and has rulership over the whole thereof, so those whom our author calls the prefects of religion preside over the entire body....

The place of the head in the body of the commonwealth is filled by the prince, who is subject only to God and to those who exercise His office and represent Him on earth, even as in the human body the head is quickened and governed by the soul. The place of the heart is filled by the senate, from which proceeds the initiation of good works and ill. The duties of eyes, ears, and tongue are claimed by the judges and the governors of provinces. Officials and soldiers correspond to the hands. Those who always attend upon the prince are

---

[9]Book V of *Policraticus* is largely devoted to a discussion of a letter of instruction to the Emperor Trajan allegedly written by Plutarch. Most scholars agree that there was no such letter.

[10]*Husbandmen*—small farmers, many of whom would have been personally un-free in this period

likened to the sides. Financial officers and keepers…may be compared with the
stomach and intestines…. The husbandmen[10] correspond to the feet, which
always cleave to the soil, and need the more especially the care and foresight of
the head, since while they walk upon the earth doing service with their bodies,
they meet the more often with stones of stumbling, and therefore deserve aid    5
and protection all the more justly since it is they who raise, sustain, and move
forward the weight of the entire body….

### That the Soldiery of Arms is Necessarily Bound to Religion like that which is Consecrated to Membership in the Clergy and the Service of God; And that the Name of Soldier is One of Honor and Toil

VI§8Turn over in your mind the words of the oath itself, and you will find that
the soldiery of arms, not less than the spiritual soldiery, is bound by the requirements of its official duties to the sacred service and worship of God; for they owe   10
obedience to the prince and ever-watchful service to the commonwealth, loyally
and according to God. Wherefore, as I have said above, those who are neither
selected nor sworn, although they may be reckoned as soldiers in name, are in
reality no more soldiers than men are priests and clerics whom the Church has
never called into orders. For the name of soldier is one of honor, as it is one of   15
toil. And no man can take honor upon himself, but one who is called of God
glories in the honor which is conferred upon him.

Moses and the leaders of the faithful people, whenever it became needful
to fight the enemy, selected men who were brave and well-trained to war. For
these qualities are conditions prerequisite to selection. But the man who, without   20
being selected, yet forces his way into the service, provokes against himself the
sword which he usurps by his own rashness. For he runs against the everlasting
decree that he who takes up the sword shall perish by the sword.[11] Indeed if
we accept the authority of Cicero regarding such a man, he is rightly called not
a soldier but an assassin. For in the writings of the ancients men are called as-   25
sassins and brigands who follow the profession of arms without a commission
from the law. For the arms which the law does not itself use, can only be used
against the law.

The sacred Gospel narrative bears witness that two swords are enough[12]
for the Christian *imperium;* all others belong to those who with swords and   30
cudgels draw nigh to take Christ captive and seek to destroy His name. For
wherein do they partake of the character of the true soldier who, although they
may have been called, yet do not obey the law according to their oath, but

---

[11]Matthew 26:42
[12]Luke 22:38

deem the glory of their military service to consist in bringing contempt upon the priesthood, in cheapening the authority of the Church, in so extending the kingdom of man as to narrow the empire of Christ, and in proclaiming their own praises and flattering and extolling themselves with false commendations,
5    thus imitating the braggart soldier to the amusement of all who hear them? Their valor shines forth chiefly in stabbing with swords or tongues the clergy and the unarmed soldiery.

But what is the office of the duly ordained soldiery? To defend the Church, to assail infidelity, to venerate the priesthood, to protect the poor from inju-
10   ries, to pacify the province, to pour out their blood for their brothers (as the formula of their oaths instructs them), and, if need be, to lay down their lives. The high praises of God are in their throat, and two-edged swords are in their hands to execute punishment on the nations and rebuke upon the peoples, and to bind their kings in chains and their nobles in links of iron. But to what end?
15   To the end that they may serve madness, vanity, avarice, or their own private self-will? By no means. Rather to the end that they may execute the judgment that is committed to them to execute; wherein each follows not his own will but the deliberate decision of God, the angels, and men, in accordance with equity and the public utility. I say "to the end that they may execute," for as it
20   is for judges to pronounce judgment, so it is for these to perform their office by executing it. Verily, "this honor have all His saints." For soldiers that do these things are "saints," and are the more loyal to their prince in proportion as they more zealously keep the faith of God; and they advance the more successfully the honor of their own valor as they seek the more faithfully in all things the
25   glory of their God....

**VI§20** ... Then and then only will the health of the commonwealth be sound and flourishing, when the higher members shield the lower, and the lower respond faithfully and fully in like measure to the just demands of their superiors, so that each and all are as it were members one of another by a sort of reciprocity,
30   and each regards his own interest as best served by that which he knows to be most advantageous for the others.

### Wherein Consists the Difference Between a Tyrant and a True Prince....

**VIII§17** ...A tyrant, then, as the philosophers have described him, is one who oppresses the people by rulership based upon force, while he who rules in accordance with the laws is a prince. Law is the gift of God, the model of equity,
35   a standard of justice, a likeness of the divine will, the guardian of well-being, a bond of union and solidarity between peoples, a rule defining duties, a barrier

against the vices and the destroyer thereof, a punishment of violence and all wrong-doing. The law is assailed by force or by fraud, and, as it were, either wrecked by the fury of the lion or undermined by the wiles of the serpent. In whatever way this comes to pass, it is plain that it is the grace of God which is being assailed, and that it is God himself who in a sense is challenged to battle. The prince fights for the laws and the liberty of the people; the tyrant thinks nothing done unless he brings the laws to naught and reduces the people to slavery.

Hence the prince is a kind of likeness of divinity; and the tyrant, on the contrary, a likeness of the boldness of the Adversary, even of the wickedness of Lucifer, imitating him that sought to build his throne to the north and make himself like unto the Most High,[13] with the exception of His goodness. For had he desired to be like unto Him in goodness, he would never have striven to tear from Him the glory of His power and wisdom. What he most likely did aspire to was to be equal with him in authority to dispense rewards. The prince, as the likeness of the Deity, is to be loved, worshipped and cherished; the tyrant, the likeness of wickedness, is generally to be even killed. The origin of tyranny is iniquity, and springing from a poisonous root, it is a tree which grows and sprouts into a baleful pestilent growth, and to which the axe must by all means be laid. For if iniquity and injustice, banishing charity, had not brought about tyranny, firm concord and perpetual peace would have possessed the peoples of the earth forever, and no one would think of enlarging his boundaries. Then kingdoms would be as friendly and peaceful, according to the authority of the great father Augustine,[14] and would enjoy as undisturbed repose, as the separate families in a well-ordered state, or as different persons in the same family; or perhaps, which is even more credible, there would be no kingdoms at all, since it is clear from the ancient historians that in the beginning these were founded by iniquity as presumptuous encroachments against the Lord, or else were extorted from Him....

Therefore respect for the right and the just is either not sufficiently present or else is wholly wanting from the face of tyrants; and whether they are ecclesiastical or temporal tyrants, they desire for themselves power to do all things, despising what should precede and follow power. Still I would wish that both classes might be persuaded of this, that the divine judgment has not yet expired which was imposed on our first parents and their seed: namely that because they would not when they could, it was imposed upon them that they should not be able to obey justice even when they would willingly do so. For the proverb says, "He who will not when he may, when he wills he shall have nay." Of this

---

[13]Isaiah 14:12–14

[14]Augustine, *City of God*, IV§15

saying the great Basil is the author. For once when a poor woman besought him to intercede for her with the prince, he took her petition, and wrote thus upon it to the prince: "This poor woman has come to me because she thinks that I have some influence with you; if I have, please show it." And he gave back the paper to the woman, who went away and gave the letter to the prince. Reading it, the prince wrote back as follows: "Holy father, on your account I have wished to take pity on the poor woman, but I could not because she is subject to the tributes." The saint then wrote back to him, "If you would and could not, then well and good, no matter how the case stands; but if you could and would not, Christ will cause you to take your place among the needy so that when you will, you shall not be able." The Holy Truth, which is ever present to the elect, did not fail to confirm the words of its spokesman. For in a short space of time the same prince, having been tempted to disdain the Emperor, was led captive in fetters, thus by his own punishment making satisfaction for those whom he had unjustly oppressed. But on the sixth day as a result of the prayers of Basil he was freed from captivity, giving up his imperial pretensions, as the holy man had desired....

...[T]he commonwealth of the ungodly has also its head and members, and strives to correspond, as it were, to the civil institutions of a legitimate commonwealth. The tyrant who is its head is the likeness of the devil; its soul consists of heretical, schismatic, and sacrilegious priests, and, to use the language of Plutarch, prefects of religion who wage war on the law of the Lord; its heart of unrighteous counselors is like a senate of iniquity; its eyes, ears, tongue, and unarmed hand are unjust judges, laws and officials; its armed hand consists of soldiers of violence whom Cicero calls brigands; its feet are those who in the humbler walks of life go against the precepts of the Lord and His lawful institutions. All these can easily be restrained by their superiors....

### That Tyrants are the Ministers of God; and of what a Tyrant is....

**VIII§18**I do not, however, deny that tyrants are the ministers of God, who by His just judgment has willed them to be in the place of highest authority in one sphere or the other, that is to say over souls or over bodies, to the end that by their means the wicked may be punished, and the good chastened and exercised. For the sins of a people cause a hypocrite to reign over them, and, as the Book of Kings[15] bears witness, tyrants were brought into power over the people of Israel by the failings of the priests. For the earliest fathers and patriarchs followed nature, the best guide of life. They were succeeded by leaders, beginning with

---

[15]In the Vulgate, there are four books of Kings. The first two correspond to the two books of Samuel in modern editions of the Bible.

Moses, who followed the law, and judges who ruled the people by the authority of the law; and we read that the latter were priests. At last in the anger of the Lord, they were given kings, some good, but many bad. For Samuel had grown old, and when his sons did not walk in his ways, but followed after avarice and uncleanness, the people, who perchance had deserved that such priests should be in authority over them, forced God, whom they had despised, to give them a king. And so Saul was chosen, with the aforesaid right of a king, that he might take their sons and make them his charioteers, and take their daughters to bake his bread and cook his food, and take their fields and lands to distribute at his pleasure among his servants, and in short oppress the whole people under the yoke of slavery. None the less he was called the anointed of the Lord, and though practicing tyranny, did not therefore lose the honor of king. For God smote all with fear, so that they reverenced him as the minister of God and as in a sort bearing the likeness of God.

I will go further; even tyrants of the gentiles, who have been damned unto death from eternity, are the ministers of God and are called the anointed of the Lord. Therefore the prophet says, "Chieftains shall enter into the gates of Babylon," to wit Cirus and Darius; "for I have commanded my consecrated ones, and have summoned my mighty ones in mine anger, and them that exult in my glory."[16] Behold that He calls Medes and Persians "sanctified," not because they were holy men, but because they fulfilled the will of the Lord against Babylon. Elsewhere to the same effect: "Behold, I will bring on Nebuchadnezzar my servant, and because he served me well at Tyre, I will give unto him Egypt."[17]

Indeed all power is good since it is from Him from whom alone are all things and from whom comes only good. But at times it may not be good, but rather evil, to the particular individual who exercises it or to him upon whom it is exercised, though it is good from the universal standpoint, being the act of Him who uses our ills for His own good purposes. Just as in a painting, a black or smutty color or some other such feature, looked at by itself, is ugly, and yet considered as a part of the whole painting is pleasing; so things which separately examined seem foul and evil, yet when related to the whole appear good and fair, since He adapts all things to Himself whose works are all exceeding good.

Therefore even the rule of a tyrant, too, is good, although nothing is worse than tyranny. For tyranny is abuse of power entrusted by God to man. But this evil embraces a vast and varied use of things which are good. For it is clear that tyranny not only exists in the case of princes, but that everyone is a tyrant who abuses power that has been conferred upon him from above over those that are subjected to him. Further, if power falls to the lot of a wise man, who knows and

---

[16]Isaiah 13:3
[17]Ezekiel 29:18–19

has the proper use of all things, it is pleasing to all good men, and of advantage to all. But if it falls to the lot of a man who is foolish, then although it cannot be really evil to the good, for whom all things work together for good, it may nevertheless be temporarily very grievous unto them.

5      It is quite obvious that power may fall into the hands of men of either kind, though, because of the wickedness of our generation, who are continually provoking against ourselves the wrath of God, it more frequently happens that it comes into the hands of bad, that is to say of foolish, men. For what power in human history is anywhere recorded greater than that of the Roman Empire?
10   Yet if you run through the list of its rulers from the beginning you will find that, more often than not, power was in the hands of bad men. What man was ever more abominable or monstrous than Gaius Caligula, the third successor of Augustus, except Nero, who excelled all who went before and came after him in his infamy of life and unimaginable crimes?...

15      Whose ferocity, to be brief, was so great that he is reported to have ex-claimed: "Would that the Roman people had only one neck!" And because there was no foreign enemy, he set out with a great and incredible train to seek for one, and coursing through Germany and Gaul with an idle display of power, he halted by the shores of the Ocean almost in sight of Britain, and then re-
20   turned to Rome, all occasion for war being lacking, and having accomplished no other business beyond receiving the surrender of Belinus, son of the king of the Britains, whom his father had banished, along with a few companions. He fell into the bitterest hostility against the Jews and ordered the profanation of the sacred places of Jerusalem and that they should be filled with idols and that
25   he himself should be worshipped as a God. He harassed Pilate, the governor of Judea, with so much vexation that he sought a short way out of his misery by a speedy death at his own hand. His sisters, whom he had first shamefully defiled, he condemned to exile and afterwards commanded all the exiles together to be put to death. Finally he was himself slain by his own guards. Among his
30   private papers were found two little books containing the names of the most prominent citizens, whom he had marked for death; and one was headed "by the sword," the other "by the poniard." Besides, there was found a great chest of many diverse kinds of poisons, which, having been thrown into the sea by the command of Claudius Caesar, are said to have polluted all the waters with
35   a multitude of dead fish which bore witness to their deadly character.

Caligula was succeeded by his nephew Nero, after the intervening reign of Claudius; and he was a worthy successor to his wealth and his vices, surpassing him in both, and practicing capriciousness, lust, rankness, avarice and cruelty to the last degree of wickedness. For on the testimony of Orosius, he conceived
40   the whim of making a circuit of almost all the theaters of Greece and Italy, and

disgracing himself to the point of donning their motley attire, was often seen
to excel cornet-players, lute-players, tragedians and charioteers. Besides, he
was the prey of such furious lust that it is said that he did not refrain from his
own mother and sister or respect any tie of kinship, finally taking a man for his
wife, and being himself accepted as the wife of a man. His extravagance was so        5
unbridled that he fished with golden nets and purple twine; bathed in hot and
cold unguents; never wore the same garment twice, and is said never to have
traveled with less than a thousand carriages. At last he made a bonfire of the
city of Rome as a spectacle for his pleasure; for six days and seven nights the
blazing city delighted and terrified the eyes of the king. The warehouses built     10
of squared stones and the great "islands" of the ancients, which the ravenous
flames could not touch, were broken down and fired by the great engines which
had been formerly prepared for foreign war, the unhappy people being forced
to find lodging in the tombs and mansions of the dead.

Meanwhile he watched the spectacle from the top of the tower of Mecenas,        15
and rejoicing, as he said, in the beauty of the flames, declaimed in the garb of
a tragedian the ode of Heleifeles, and chanted the ritualistic hymns of the city
in which the splendor of the sun is celebrated. Moreover his avarice was so
headlong and violent that after this conflagration of the city, which Augustus
had boasted that he had changed from brick to marble, he would permit none      20
of the owners to approach the ruins of their property. Everything which had
in any way escaped the flames, he carried off for himself; he commanded the
Senate to confer upon him ten million sesterces annually; most of the senators
he despoiled of their property for no cause whatever; on a single day by the
application of torture he wrung from all the merchants their entire fortune.      25
His cruelty was so mad and furious that he put to death the greater part of the
Senate and almost annihilated the equestrian order. He did not even stop short
of parricide; his mother, his brother, his sister, his wife and all his other relatives
and connections he destroyed without hesitation.

This mountain of crime was augmented by his rash impiety against God.        30
For he was the first at Rome to condemn the Christians to torture and death,
and throughout all the provinces commanded them to suffer under the same
persecution. In this attempt to exterminate the very name itself, he put to death
the most blessed apostles of Christ, Peter by the cross, Paul by the sword. Shortly
thereafter the stricken city was visited by the most cruel calamities coming     35
from every side. For in the following autumn so great a pestilence settled upon
Rome that thirty thousand corpses went to swell the account of Libiciniana.
Hard upon this occurred a military disaster in Britain, in which the two chief
towns were captured with great loss and slaughter of citizens and allies. Then
in the East the great provinces of Armenia were lost, the Roman legions were    40

sent under the yoke by the Parthians, and Syria was hardly saved. In Asia three cities, namely Laodicie, Ierapolis, and Colose, were destroyed by an earthquake. Thus in substance Orosius; whose words and matter I use the more readily since I know that as a Christian, and a disciple of the great Augustine, he searched
5   diligently for the truth because of his devotion to our religion and faith.

     The same facts can be found set forth at greater length by other historical writers as well, who describe in greater detail the cruelties of tyrants and the wretched ends they came to. And if anyone should desire to investigate this matter more fully, let him read what Trogus Pompeius, Josephus, Egesippus,
10  Suetonius, Quintus Curtius, Cornelius Tacitus, Titus Livius, Serenus, and Tranquillus and other historians, whom it would be too long to enumerate, have included in their narratives. From which it will readily appear that it has always been lawful to flatter tyrants and to deceive them, and that it has always been an honorable thing to slay them if they can be curbed in no other way.
15  I am not now talking of tyrants in private life, but of those who oppress the commonwealth. For private tyrants can easily be restrained by the public laws which are binding upon the lives of all; but in the case of a priest, even though he acts the tyrant, it is not lawful to employ the material sword against him because of the reverence due to sacred things, unless perchance after he has
20  been unfrocked, he lifts a bloody hand against the Church of God; since the rule always prevails that there ought not to be double punishment of one man for the same offence. It does not seem beside the point to illustrate what has been said by a few examples....

## That by the Authority of the Divine Page it is a
## Lawful and Glorious Act to Slay Public Tyrants....

VIII§20 ...The histories teach, however, that none should undertake the death
25  of a tyrant who is bound to him by an oath or by the obligation of fealty. For we read that Sedechias, because he disregarded the sacred obligation of fealty, was led into captivity;[18] and that in the case of another of the kings of Judah whose name escapes my memory, his eyes were plucked out because, falling into faithlessness, he did not keep before his sight God, to whom the oath is taken;
30  since sureties for good behavior are justly given even to a tyrant.

     But as for the use of poison, although I see it sometimes wrongfully adopted by infidels, I do not read that it is ever permitted by any law. Not that I do not believe that tyrants ought to be removed from our midst, but it should be done without loss of religion and honor. For David, the best of all kings that I have

---

[18]II Kings 24–25

read of, and who, save in the incident of Uriah, walked blamelessly in all things, although he had to endure the most grievous tyrant, and although he often had an opportunity of destroying him, yet preferred to spare him, trusting in the mercy of God, within whose power it was to set him free without sin. He therefore determined to abide in patience until the tyrant should either suffer a change of heart and be visited by God with return of charity, or else should fall in battle, or otherwise meet his end by the just judgment of God. How great was his patience can be discerned from the fact that when he had cut off the edge of Saul's robe in the cave, and again when, having entered the camp by night, he rebuked the negligence of the sentinels, in both cases he compelled the king to confess that David was acting the juster part.

And surely the method of destroying tyrants which is the most useful and the safest is for those who are oppressed to take refuge humbly in the protection of God's mercy, and lifting up undefiled hands to the Lord, to pray devoutly that the scourge wherewith they are afflicted may be turned aside from them. For the sins of transgressors are the strength of tyrants. Wherefore Achior, the captain of all the children of Amon, gave this most wholesome counsel to Holofernes: "Inquire diligently, my lord," said he, "whether there be any iniquity of the people in the sight of their God, and then let us go up to them because their God will abandon them and deliver them to thee, and they shall be subdued beneath the yoke of thy power. But if there be no offence of this people in the sight of their God, we shall not be able to withstand them, because their God will defend them, and we shall be exposed to the reproach and scorn of all the earth."[19]...

---

[19]Judith 5:5, 24–25

# MAGNA CARTA

## JOHN (1167–1216), KING OF ENGLAND (1199–1216)

*Issued at Runnymede on 15 June 1215, Magna Carta was the outcome of
a dispute between King John of England and his barons, the great land-
owners. In part the dispute developed as a result of John's own failures—a
conflict with Pope Innocent III, which led to an interdict[1] lasting five years,
the loss of Normandy and other lands to King Philip II of France, and a
crushing defeat at the Battle of Bouvines (1214). But more fundamentally,
it reflected a growing discontent with the scope of royal government, which
had been expanding steadily for the past sixty years. The barons did not seek
to undermine royal authority, but instead to force the king to acknowledge
customary limits. They understood themselves to be speaking for the rest of
the community of the kingdom, and thus the provisions of Magna Carta
benefited not simply the barons, but all free men of England. Although the
pope annulled Magna Carta almost immediately on the grounds that an
oath made under duress was not binding, the regency government of John's
young successor, Henry III (1216–1272), reissued it after John's death. In
later years, disputes between the king and barons were often settled by the
confirmation of Magna Carta.*

15 JUNE 1215

John, by the grace of God, King of England, Lord of Ireland, Duke of Normandy
and Aquitaine, and Count of Anjou, to his arch-bishops, bishops, abbots, earls,
barons, justices, foresters, sheriffs, stewards, servants, and to all his officials and
loyal subjects, Greeting.

Know that before God, for the health of our soul and those of our ancestors 5
and heirs, to the honour of God, the exaltation of the holy Church, and the
better ordering of our kingdom, at the advice of our reverend fathers Stephen,
Arch-bishop of Canterbury, primate of all England, and cardinal of the holy
Roman Church; Henry, Arch-bishop of Dublin; William, Bishop of London;

[1] *Interdict*—an ecclesiastical penalty in which the churches in the affected area were closed
and no sacraments other than baptism and last rites were administered. Usually the idea
behind it was to encourage the inhabitants of the area to put pressure on their erring ruler.

From *Magna Carta*, Revised Edition, edited by G. R. C. Davis (London: British Library, 1985).

Peter, Bishop of Winchester; Jocelin, Bishop of Bath and Glastonbury; Hugh, Bishop of Lincoln; Walter, Bishop of Worcester; William, Bishop of Coventry; Benedict, Bishop of Rochester; Master Pandulf, sub-deacon and member of the papal household; Brother Aymeric, master of the knighthood of the Temple in England; William Marshal, Earl of Pembroke; William, Earl of Salisbury; William, Earl of Warren; William, Earl of Arundel; Alan de Galloway, Constable of Scotland; Warin FitzGerald; Peter FitzHerbert; Hubert de Burgh, seneschal of Poitou; Hugh de Neville; Matthew FitzHerbert; Thomas Basset; Alan Basset; Philip Daubeny; Robert de Roppeley; John Marshal; John FitzHugh; and other loyal subjects:

1. First, that we have granted to God, and by this present charter have confirmed for us and our heirs in perpetuity, that the English Church shall be free, and shall have its rights undiminished and its liberties[2] unimpaired. That we wish this so to be observed appears from the fact that of our own free will, before the outbreak of the present dispute between us and our barons, we granted and confirmed by charter the freedom of the Church's elections—a right reckoned to be of the greatest necessity and importance to it—and caused this to be confirmed by Pope Innocent III. This freedom we shall observe ourselves, and desire to be observed in good faith by our heirs in perpetuity.

To all free men of our kingdom we have also granted, for us and our heirs forever, all the liberties written out below, to have and to keep for them and their heirs, of us and our heirs.

2. If any earl, baron, or other person that holds lands directly of the Crown for military service shall die and at his death his heir shall be of full age and owe a relief,[3] the heir shall have his inheritance on payment of the ancient scale of relief. That is to say, the heir or heirs of an earl shall pay £100 for the entire earl's barony, the heir or heirs of a knight 100 shillings at most for the entire knight's fee, and any man that owes less shall pay less, in accordance with the ancient usage of fees.

3. But if the heir of such a person is under age and a ward,[4] when he comes of age he shall have his inheritance without relief or fine....

---

[2] In the Middle Ages, "liberties" referred to concrete privileges of a particular community, e.g., the Church, a town, or a guild. See also clauses 13 and 60 below.

[3] *Relief*—a sum of money paid by a free man's heir for the right to take possession of his lands

[4] Legal age was 21. The wardship of a minor heir and his lands was a highly prized right belonging to his father's lord, since it brought with it the income from the lands during the minority of the heir and often the right to arrange the heir's marriage to a bride of the lord's choice. The king often granted wardships belonging to him to those he wished to reward.

6. Heirs may be given in marriage, but not to someone of lower social standing. Before a marriage takes place, it shall be made known to the heir's next-of-kin.

7. At her husband's death, a widow may have her marriage portion[5] and inheritance at once and without trouble. She shall pay nothing for her dower, marriage portion, or any inheritance that she and her husband held jointly on the day of his death. She may remain in her husband's house for forty days after his death, and within this period her dower shall be assigned to her.

8. No widow shall be compelled to marry, so long as she wishes to remain without a husband. But she must give security that she will not marry without royal consent, if she holds her lands of the Crown, or without the consent of whatever other lord of whom she may hold them....

12. No scutage or aid[6] may be levied in our kingdom without its general consent, unless it is for the ransom of our person, to make our eldest son a knight, and (once) to marry our eldest daughter. For these purposes only a reasonable aid may be levied. Aids from the city of London are to be treated similarly.

13. The city of London shall enjoy all its ancient liberties and free customs, both by land and by water. We also will and grant that all other cities, boroughs, towns, and ports shall enjoy all their liberties and free customs.

14. To obtain the general consent of the realm for the assessment of an aid—except in the three cases specified above—or a scutage, we will cause the arch-bishops, bishops, abbots, earls, and greater barons to be summoned individually by letter. To those who hold lands directly of us we will cause a general summons to be issued, through the sheriffs and other officials, to come together on a fixed day (of which at least forty days notice shall be given) and at a fixed place. In all letters of summons, the cause of the summons will be stated. When a summons has been issued, the business appointed for the day shall go forward in accordance with the resolution of those present, even if not all those who were summoned have appeared.

15. In future we will allow no one to levy an aid from his free men, except to ransom his person, to make his eldest son a knight, and (once) to marry his eldest daughter. For these purposes only a reasonable aid may be levied.

---

[5]The marriage portion was the property a woman brought from her family to a marriage. She was also entitled to one-third of her husband's lands for the rest of her life; at her death this property, known as her dower, reverted to her husband's heir.

[6]*Scutage*—a monetary payment made in lieu of military service. *Aids*—sums levied from a man's tenants, both free and un-free, on certain occasions, customarily the three cases named here.

16. No man shall be forced to perform more service for a knight's fee, or other free holding of land, than is due from it.

17. Ordinary lawsuits shall not follow the royal court around, but shall be held in a fixed place....

20. For a trivial offence, a free man shall be fined only in proportion to the degree of his offence, and for a serious offence correspondingly, but not so heavily as to deprive him of his livelihood. In the same way, a merchant shall be spared his merchandise, and a villein the implements of his husbandry, if they fall upon the mercy of a royal court. None of these fines shall be imposed except by the assessment on oath of reputable men of the neighbourhood.

21. Earls and barons shall be fined only by their equals, and in proportion to the gravity of their offence.....

24. No sheriff, constable, coroners, or other royal officials are to hold lawsuits that should be held by the royal justices....

28. No constable or other royal official shall take corn[7] or other movable goods from any man without immediate payment, unless the seller voluntarily offers postponement of this.

29. No constable may compel a knight to pay money for castle-guard if the knight is willing to undertake the guard in person or, with reasonable excuse, to supply some other fit man to do it. A knight taken or sent on military service shall be excused from castle-guard for the period of this service.

30. No sheriff, royal official, or other person shall take horses or carts for transport from any free man without his consent.

31. Neither we nor any royal official will take wood for our castle, or for any other purpose, without the consent of the owner.

32. We will not keep the lands of people convicted of felony in our hand for longer than a year and a day, after which they shall be returned to the lords of the fees concerned.[8]...

35. There shall be standard measures of wine, ale, and corn (the London quarter) throughout the kingdom. There shall also be a standard width of

---

[7]*Corn*—grain

[8]Convicted felons forfeited their lands. As royal justice expanded at the expense of baronial and manorial courts, these forfeitures came to the king rather than to the felon's immediate lord, whose property rights were thereby infringed. This clause allows the king one-year's income from forfeited lands, presumably as compensation for court costs, while recognizing the property rights of the felon's lord.

dyed cloth, russet, and haberject,[9] namely two ells within the selvedges. Weights are to be standardised similarly....

38. In future no official shall place a man on trial upon his own unsupported statement, without producing credible witnesses to the truth of it.

39. No free man shall be seized or imprisoned, or stripped of his rights or possessions, or outlawed or exiled, or deprived of his standing in any other way, nor will we proceed with force against him, or send others to do so, except by the lawful judgement of his equals or by the law of the land.

40. To no one will we sell, to no one deny or delay right or justice.

41. All merchants may enter or leave England unharmed and without fear, and may stay or travel within it, by land or water, for purposes of trade, free from all illegal exactions, in accordance with ancient and lawful customs. This, however, does not apply in time of war to merchants from a country that is at war with us. Any such merchants found in our country at the outbreak of war shall be detained without injury to their persons or property, until we or our chief justice have discovered how our own merchants are being treated in the country at war with us. If our own merchants are safe they shall be safe too.

42. In future it shall be lawful for any man to leave and return to our kingdom unharmed and without fear, by land or water, preserving his allegiance to us, except in time of war, for some short period, for the common benefit of the realm. People that have been imprisoned or outlawed in accordance with the law of the land, people from a country that is at war with us, and merchants—who shall be dealt with as stated above—are excepted from this provision....

45. We will appoint as justices, constables, sheriffs, or other officials only men that know the law of the realm and are minded to keep it well....

54. No one shall be arrested or imprisoned on the appeal of a woman for the death of any person except her husband.[10]...

60. All these customs and liberties that we have granted shall be observed in our kingdom in so far as concerns our own relations with our subjects. Let all men of our kingdom, whether clergy or laymen, observe them similarly in their relations with their own men.

---

[9] *Quarter*—eight bushels; ruset, *haberject*—kinds of cloth

[10] An appeal was a formal accusation. In the trials by combat that were customary at this time, the appellor might be expected to fight the man he appealed; this expectation served to restrain him from making a frivolous accusation. Since a woman could not fight personally, she faced no similar risk. Her husband or another male relative therefore acted as her legal advocate.

61. Since we have granted all these things for God, for the better ordering of our kingdom, and to allay the discord that has arisen between us and our barons, and since we desire that they shall be enjoyed in their entirety, with lasting strength, forever, we give and grant to the barons the following security:

The barons shall elect twenty-five of their number to keep, and cause to be observed with all their might, the peace and liberties granted and confirmed to them by this charter.

If we, our chief justice, our officials, or any of our servants offend in any respect against any man, or transgress any of the articles of the peace or of this security, and the offence is made known to four of the said twenty-five barons, they shall come to us—or in our absence from the kingdom, to the chief justice—to declare it and claim immediate redress. If we, or in our absence abroad, the chief justice, make no redress within forty days, reckoning from the day on which the offence was declared to us or to him, the four barons shall refer the matter to the rest of the twenty-five barons, who may distrain upon and assail us in every way possible, with the support of the whole community of the land, by seizing our castles, lands, possessions, or anything else, saving only our own person and those of the queen and our children, until they have secured such redress as they have determined upon. Having secured the redress, they may then resume their normal obedience to us.

Any man who so desires may take an oath to obey the commands of the twenty-five barons for the achievement of these ends, and to join with them in assailing us to the utmost of his power. We give public and free permission to take this oath to any man who so desires, and at no time will we prohibit any man from taking it. Indeed, we will compel any of our subjects who are unwilling to take it to swear it at our command.

If one of the twenty-five barons dies or leaves the country, or is prevented in any other way from discharging his duties, the rest of them shall choose another baron in his place, at their discretion, who shall be duly sworn in as they were.

In the event of disagreement among the twenty-five barons on any matter referred to them for decision, the verdict of the majority present shall have the same validity as a unanimous verdict of the whole twenty-five, whether these were all present or some of those summoned were unwilling or unable to appear.

The twenty-five barons shall swear to obey all the above articles faithfully, and shall cause them to be obeyed by others to the best of their power.

We will not seek to procure from anyone, either by our own efforts or those of a third party, anything by which any part of these concessions or liberties might be revoked or diminished. Should such a thing be procured, it shall be null and void and we will at no time make use of it, either ourselves or through a third party. 5

62. We have remitted and pardoned fully to all men any ill-will, hurt, or grudges that have arisen between us and our subjects, whether clergy or laymen, since the beginning of the dispute. We have in addition remitted fully, and for our own part have also pardoned, to all clergy and laymen any offences committed as a result of the said dispute between Easter in 10 the sixteenth year of our reign and the restoration of peace.

In addition we have caused letters patent to be made for the barons, bearing witness to this security and to the concessions set out above, over the seals of Stephen, Arch-bishop of Canterbury, Henry, Arch-bishop of Dublin, the other bishops named above, and Master Pandulf. 15

63. It is accordingly our wish and command that the English Church shall be free, and that men in our kingdom shall have and keep all these liberties, rights, and concessions well and peaceably in their fullness and entirety for them and their heirs, of us and our heirs, in all things and all places forever. 20

Both we and the barons have sworn that all this shall be observed in good faith and without deceit. Witness the above-mentioned people and many others.

Given by our hand in the meadow that is called Runnymede, between Windsor and Staines, on the fifteenth day of June in the seventeenth year of our reign. 25

# FOURTH LATERAN COUNCIL

*The Fourth Lateran Council met in November 1215 under the leadership of Pope Innocent III (r. 1198–1216), who wished to promote Church reform in preparation for a new crusade to the Holy Land. Although the Council issued reform canons on a variety of subjects, its main concern was the quality of parish ministry. Heresy also concerned the Council, for as it met, an army composed primarily of French nobles was attempting to destroy the Albigensian heresy in the southern part of the Kingdom of France.*

*Innocent III was among the most powerful popes in history. In addition to calling the Albigensian crusade, he placed France under an interdict and thereby compelled King Philip II (r. 1180–1223) to reconcile with his wife; approved the founding of the Franciscan and Dominican orders; and turned King John (r. 1199–1216) of England into his vassal (and repudiated his signing of Magna Carta).*

1215

## Canon 1

We firmly believe and openly confess that there is only one true God, eternal and immense, omnipotent, unchangeable, incomprehensible, and ineffable, Father, Son, and Holy Ghost; three Persons indeed but one essence, substance, or nature absolutely simple; the Father (proceeding) from no one, but the Son from the Father only, and the Holy Ghost equally from both, always without      5
beginning and end. The Father begetting, the Son begotten, and the holy Ghost proceeding; consubstantial and co-equal, co-omnipotent and co-eternal, the one principle of the universe, Creator of all things invisible and visible, spiritual and corporeal, who from the beginning of time and by His omnipotent power made from nothing creatures both spiritual and corporeal, angelic, namely,      10
and mundane, and then human, as it were, common, composed of spirit and body. The devil and the other demons were indeed created by God good by nature but they became bad through themselves; man, however, sinned at the suggestion of the devil. This Holy Trinity in its common essence undivided and

in personal properties divided, through Moses, the holy prophets, and other servants gave to the human race at the most opportune intervals of time the doctrine of salvation.

5 And finally, Jesus Christ, the only begotten Son of God made flesh by the entire Trinity, conceived with the co-operation of the Holy Ghost of Mary, ever Virgin, made true man, composed of a rational soul and human flesh, one Person in two natures, pointed out more clearly the way of life. Who according to His divinity is immortal and impassable, according to His humanity was made passable and mortal, suffered on the cross for the salvation of the human 10 race, and being dead descended into Hell, rose from the dead, and ascended into Heaven. But He descended in soul, arose in flesh, and ascended equally in both; He will come at the end of the world to judge the living and the dead and will render to the reprobate and to the elect according to their works. Who all shall rise with their own bodies which they now have that they may receive 15 according to their merits, whether good or bad, the latter eternal punishment with the devil, the former eternal glory with Christ.

There is one universal Church of the faithful, outside of which there is absolutely no salvation. In which there is the same priest and sacrifice, Jesus Christ, whose body and blood are truly contained in the sacrament of the altar 20 under the forms of bread and wine; the bread being changed (*transsubstantiatio*) by divine power into the body, and the wine into the blood, so that to realize the mystery of unity we may receive of Him what He has received of us. And this sacrament no one can effect except the priest who has been duly ordained in accordance with the keys of the Church, which Jesus Christ Himself gave to 25 the Apostles and their successors.

But the sacrament of baptism, which by the invocation of each Person of the Trinity, namely, of the Father, Son, and Holy Ghost is effected in water, duly conferred on children and adults in the form prescribed by the Church by anyone whatsoever, leads to salvation. And should anyone after the reception of baptism 30 have fallen into sin, by true repentance he can always be restored. Not only virgins and those practicing chastity, but also those united in marriage, through the right faith and through works pleasing to God, can merit eternal salvation....

## Canon 18

No cleric may pronounce a sentence of death, or execute such a sentence, or be present at its execution. If anyone in consequence of this prohibition should 35 presume to inflict damage on churches or injury on ecclesiastical persons, let him be restrained by ecclesiastical censure. Nor may any cleric write or dictate letters destined for the execution of such a sentence. Wherefore, in the chanceries of the princes let this matter be committed to laymen and not to clerics. Neither may a cleric act as judge in the case of the Rottarii, archers, or other men of this kind devoted to the shedding of blood. No sub-deacon, deacon, or priest shall practice that part of surgery involving burning and cutting. Neither shall anyone in judicial tests or ordeals by hot or cold water or hot iron bestow any blessing; the earlier prohibitions in regard to dueling remain in force. 5

## Canon 21

All the faithful of both sexes shall after they have reached the age of discretion faithfully confess all their sins at least once a year to their own (parish) priest and perform to the best of their ability the penance imposed, receiving reverently at least at Easter the sacrament of the Eucharist, unless perchance at the advice of their own priest they may for a good reason abstain for a time from 10 its reception; otherwise they shall be cut off from the Church (ex-communicated) during life and deprived of Christian burial in death. Wherefore, let this salutary decree be published frequently in the churches, that no one may find in the plea of ignorance a shadow of excuse. But if anyone for a good reason should wish to confess his sins to another priest, let him first seek and obtain 15 permission from his own (parish) priest, since otherwise he (the other priest) cannot loose or bind him.

Let the priest be discreet and cautious that he may pour wine and oil into the wounds of the one injured after the manner of a skillful physician, carefully inquiring into the circumstances of the sinner and the sin, from the nature of 20 which he may understand what kind of advice to give and what remedy to apply, making use of different experiments to heal the sick one. But let him exercise the greatest precaution that he does not in any degree by word, sign, or any other manner make known the sinner, but should he need more prudent counsel, let him seek it cautiously without any mention of the person. He who dares to 25 reveal a sin confided to him in the tribunal of penance, we decree that he be not only deposed from the sacerdotal office but also relegated to a monastery of strict observance to do penance for the remainder of his life.

## Canon 42

As desirous as we are that laymen do not usurp the rights of clerics, we are no less desirous that clerics abstain from arrogating to themselves the rights of 30 laymen. Wherefore we forbid all clerics so to extend in the future their jurisdiction under the pretext of ecclesiastical liberty as to prove detrimental to secular justice; but let them be content with the laws and customs thus far approved, that the things that are Caesar's may be rendered to Caesar, and those that are God's may by a just division be rendered to God. 35

# SUMMA CONTRA GENTILES
## THOMAS AQUINAS (*c.* 1225–1274)

*In the late eleventh century, Saint Anselm of Bec (1033–1109) argued that a person of faith might use human reason to attempt to understand better what he knew from divine revelation to be true. Two generations later, Peter Abelard (1079–1142) began to apply dialectic, the art of reconciling apparently contradictory propositions through the use of logic, to the study of theology. Working only with Christian sources, these early Scholastics had an easy task by comparison with that of thirteenth-century thinkers such as Saint Thomas Aquinas (1225–1274).*

*In response to the demand of Western scholars for more texts, in the late twelfth-century Latin translations of Greek works began to arrive in Europe, initially from intellectual centers in Spain and Sicily that had close contact with the Islamic world. By the middle of the thirteenth century, the West had access to the complete works of Aristotle, who was regarded as such an authority that scholars referred to him as simply "The Philosopher," and the poet Dante described him as "the master of those who know." But Aristotle, for all his brilliance, was not a Christian, and consequently the recovery of his works raised a serious question: What was a Christian to do when the conclusions of human reason and the truths of divine revelation seemed to conflict with each other?*

*Aquinas's answer to this question was that such a conflict was, in fact, impossible. As he wrote in the first book of his greatest work, the* Summa Theologica, *"Grace does not destroy nature, but rather perfects it." Reason, properly used, could never reach a conclusion that was incompatible with divine revelation, since both were valid approaches to a single body of truth—an argument he developed in the* Summa Contra Gentiles. *How, then, could Aristotle have been so wrong about certain fundamental matters—the nature of God, the immortality of the soul, and the creation of the world, for example? For Aquinas, the answer was simple: Human reason was a reliable path to truth, but that path led only so far. When reason reached its limit, revelation was there to complete the journey.*

*c.* 1261

## On the Way in Which Divine Truth is to be Made Known

[§3]The way of making truth known is not always the same, and, as the Philosopher has very well said, "it belongs to an educated man to seek such certitude in each things as the nature of that thing allows."[1] The remark is also introduced by Boethius. But, since such is the case, we must first show what way is open

5   to us in order that we may make known the truth which is our object.

There is a two-fold mode of truth in what we profess about God. Some truths about God exceed all the ability of the human reason. Such is the truth that God is triune. But there are some truths which the natural reason also is able to reach. Such are that God exists, that He is one, and the like. In fact,

10  such truths about God have been proved demonstratively by the philosophers, guided by the light of the natural reason.

That there are certain truths about God that totally surpass man's ability appears with the greatest evidence. Since, indeed, the principle of all knowledge that the reason perceives about something is the understanding of the very sub-

15  stance of that being (for according to Aristotle "what a thing is" is the principle of demonstration), it is necessary that the way in which we understand the substance of a thing determines the way in which we know what belongs to it. Hence, if the human intellect comprehends the substance of something, for example, that of a stone or of a triangle, no intelligible characteristic belonging to that thing

20  surpasses the grasp of the human reason. But this does not happen to us in the case of God. For the human intellect is not able to reach a comprehension of the divine substance through its natural power. For, according to its manner of knowing in the present life, the intellect depends on the sense for the origin of knowledge; and so those things that do not fall under the senses cannot be

25  grasped by the human intellect except in so far as the knowledge of them is gathered from sensible things. Now, sensible things cannot lead the human intellect to the point of seeing in them the nature of the divine substance; for sensible things are effects that fall short of the power of their cause. Yet, beginning with sensible things, our intellect is led to the point of knowing about God that He

30  exists, and other such characteristics that must be attributed to the First Principle. There are, consequently, some intelligible truths about God that are open to the human reason; but there are others that absolutely surpass its power.

We may easily see the same point from the gradation of intellects. Consider the case of two persons of whom one has a more penetrating grasp of a

35  thing by his intellect than does the other. He who has the superior intellect understands many things that the other cannot grasp at all. Such is the case

---

[1]Aristotle, *Nichomachean Ethics*, 1.3

with a very simple person who cannot at all grasp the subtle speculations of philosophy. But the intellect of an angel surpasses the human intellect much more than the intellect of the greatest philosopher surpasses the intellect of the most uncultivated simple person; for the distance between the best philosopher and a simple person is contained within the limits of the human species, which the angelic intellect surpasses. For the angel knows God on the basis of a more noble effect than does man; and this by as much as the substance of an angel, through which the angel in his natural knowledge is led to the knowledge of God, is nobler than sensible things and even than the soul itself, through which the human intellect mounts to the knowledge of God. The divine intellect surpasses the angelic intellect much more than the angelic surpasses the human. For the divine intellect is in its capacity equal to its substance, and therefore it understands fully what it is, including all its intelligible attributes. But by his natural knowledge the angel does not know what God is, since the substance itself of the angel, through which he is led to the knowledge of God, is an effect that is not equal to the power of its cause. Hence, the angel is not able, by means of his natural knowledge, to grasp all the things that God understands in Himself; nor is the human reason sufficient to grasp all the things that the angel understands through his own natural power. Just as, therefore, it would be the height of folly for a simple person to assert that what a philosopher proposes is false on the ground that he himself cannot understand it, so (and even more so) it is the acme of stupidity for a man to suspect as false what is divinely revealed through the ministry of the angels simply because it cannot be investigated by reason.

The same thing, moreover, appears quite clearly from the defect that we experience every day in our knowledge of things. We do not know a great many of the properties of sensible things, and in most cases we are not to discover fully the natures of those properties that we apprehend by the sense. Much more is it the case, therefore, that the human reason is not equal to the task of investigating all the intelligible characteristics of that most excellent substance.

The remark of Aristotle likewise agrees with this conclusion. He says that "our intellect is related to the prime beings, which are most evident in their nature, as the eye of an owl is related to the sun."

Sacred Scripture also gives testimony to this truth. We read in Job: "Peradventure will you comprehend the steps of God, and find out the Almighty perfectly?"[2] And again: "Behold, God is great, exceeding our knowledge."[3] And Saint Paul: "We know in part."[4]

---

[2]Job 11:7
[3]Job 36:26
[4]I Corinthians 13:9

We should not, therefore, immediately reject as false, following the opinion of the Manicheans and many unbelievers, everything that is said about God even though it cannot be investigated by reason.

## That the Truth About God to Which the Natural Reason Reaches is Fittingly Proposed to Men for Belief

[§4]Since, therefore, there exists a two-fold truth concerning the divine being, one
5    to which the inquiry of the reason can reach, the other which surpasses the whole ability of the human reason, it is fitting that both of these truths be proposed to man divinely for belief. This point must first be shown concerning the truth that is open to the inquiry of the reason; otherwise, it might perhaps seem to someone that, since such a truth can be known by the reason, it was uselessly
10   given to men through a supernatural inspiration as an object of belief.

Yet, if this truth were left solely as a matter of inquiry for the human reason, three awkward consequences would follow.

The first is that few men would possess the knowledge of God. For there are three reasons why most men are cut off from the fruit of diligent inquiry
15   which is the discovery of truth. Some do not have the physical disposition for such work. As a result, there are many who are naturally not fitted to pursue knowledge; and so, however much they tried, they would be unable to reach the highest level of human knowledge which consists in knowing God. Others are cut off from pursuing this truth by the necessities imposed upon them
20   by their daily lives. For some men must devote themselves to taking care of temporal matters. Such men would not be able to give so much time to the leisure of contemplative inquiry as to reach the highest peak at which human investigation can arrive, namely, the knowledge of God. Finally, there are some who are cut off by indolence. In order to know the things that the reason can
25   investigate concerning God, a knowledge of many things must already be possessed. For almost all of philosophy is directed towards the knowledge of God, and that is why metaphysics, which deals with divine things, is the last part of philosophy to be learned. This means that we are able to arrive at the inquiry concerning the aforementioned truth only on the basis of a great deal of labor
30   spent in study. Now, those who wish to undergo such a labor for the mere love of knowledge are few, even though God has inserted into the minds of men a natural appetite for knowledge.

The second awkward effect is that those who would come to discover the above-mentioned truth would barely reach it after a great deal of time. The rea-
35   sons are several. There is the profundity of this truth, which the human intellect is made capable of grasping by natural inquiry only after a long training. Then,

there are many things that must be presupposed, as we have said. There is also the fact that, in youth, when the soul is swayed by the various movements of the passions, it is not in a suitable state for the knowledge of such lofty truth. On the contrary, "one becomes wise and knowing in repose." as it is said in the Physics. The result is this. If the only way open to us for the knowledge of God    5 were solely that of the reason, the human race would remain in the blackest shadows of ignorance. For then the knowledge of God, which especially renders men perfect and good, would come to be possessed only by a few, and these few would require a great deal of time in order to reach it.

The third awkward effect is this. The investigation of the human reason for    10 the most part has falsity present within it, and this is due partly to the weakness of our intellect in judgment, and partly to the admixture of images. The result is that many, remaining ignorant of the power of demonstration, would hold in doubt those things that have been most truly demonstrated. This would be particularly the case since they see that, among those who are reputed to be wise    15 men, each one teaches his own brand of doctrine. Furthermore, with the many truths that are demonstrated, there sometimes is mingled something that is false, which is not demonstrated but rather asserted on the basis of some probable or sophistical argument, which yet has the credit of being a demonstration. That is why it was necessary that the unshakeable certitude and pure truth concerning    20 divine things should be presented to men by way of faith.

Beneficially, therefore, did the divine Mercy provide that it should instruct us to hold by faith even those truths that the human reason is able to investigate. In this way, all men would easily be able to have a share in the knowledge of God, and this without uncertainty and error.    25

Hence it is written: "Henceforward you walk not as also the Gentiles walk in the vanity of their mind, having their understanding darkened."[5] And again: "All your children shall be taught of the Lord."[6]

### That the Truths Human Reason is Not Able to Investigate are Fittingly Proposed to Men for Belief

[§5]Now, perhaps some will think that men should not be asked to believe what the reason is not adequate to investigate, since the divine Wisdom provides in    30 the case of each thing according to the mode of its nature. We must therefore prove that it is necessary for man to receive from God as objects of belief even those truths that are above the human reason.

---

[5]Ephesians 4:17–18
[6]Isaiah 54:13

No one tends with desire and zeal towards something that is not already known to him. But, as we shall examine later on in this work, men are ordained by the divine Providence towards a higher good than human fragility can experience in the present life. That is why it was necessary for the human mind to be called to something higher than the human reason here and now can reach, so that it would thus learn to desire something and with zeal tend towards something that surpasses the whole state of the present life. This belongs especially to the Christian religion, which in a unique way promises spiritual and eternal goods. And so there are many things proposed to men in it that transcend human sense. The Old Law, on the other hand, whose promises were of a temporal character, contained very few proposals that transcended the inquiry of the human reason. Following this same direction, the philosophers themselves, in order that they might lead men from the pleasure of sensible things to virtue, were concerned to show that there were in existence other goods of a higher nature than these things of sense, and that those who gave themselves to the active or contemplative virtues would find much sweeter enjoyment in the taste of these higher goods.

It is also necessary that such truth be proposed to men for belief so that they may have a truer knowledge of God. For then only do we know God truly when we believe Him to be above everything that it is possible for man to think about Him; for, as we have shown, the divine substance surpasses the natural knowledge of which man is capable. Hence, by the fact that some things about God are proposed to man that surpass his reason, there is strengthened in man the view that God is something above what he can think.

Another benefit that comes from the revelation to men of truths that exceed the reason is the curbing of presumption, which is the mother of error. For there are some who have such a presumptuous opinion of their own ability that they deem themselves able to measure the nature of everything; I mean to say that, in their estimation, everything is true that seems to them so, and everything is false that does not. So that the human mind, therefore, might be freed from this presumption and come to a humble inquiry after truth, it was necessary that some things should be proposed to man by God that would completely surpass his intellect.

A still further benefit may also be seen in what Aristotle says in the *Ethics*. There was a certain Simonides who exhorted people to put aside the knowledge of divine things and to apply their talents to human occupations. He said that "he who is a man should know human things, and he who is mortal, things that are mortal." Against Simonides Aristotle says that "man should draw himself towards what is immortal and divine as much as he can." And so he says in the *De animalibus* that, although what we know of the higher substances is very little, yet that little is loved and desired more than all the knowledge that we have about less noble substances. He also says in the *De caelo et mundo* that when questions about the heavenly bodies can be given even a modest and merely plausible solution, he who hears this experiences intense joy. From all these considerations it is clear that even the most imperfect knowledge about the most noble realities brings the greatest perfection to the soul. Therefore, although the human reason cannot grasp fully the truths that are above it, yet, if it somehow holds these truths at least by faith, it acquires great perfection for itself.

Therefore it is written, "For many things are shown to you above the understanding of men."[7] Again, "So the things that are of God no man knows but the Spirit of God. But to us God has revealed them by His Spirit."[8]

### That to Give Assent to the Truths of Faith is Not Foolishness Even Though they are Above Reason

[§6]Those who place their faith in this truth, however, "for which the human reason offers no experimental evidence," do not believe foolishly, as though "following artificial fables."[9] For these "secrets of divine Wisdom"[10] the divine Wisdom itself, which knows all things to the full, has deigned to reveal to men. It reveals its own presence, as well as the truth of its teaching and inspiration, by fitting arguments; and in order to confirm those truths that exceed natural knowledge, it gives visible manifestation to works that surpass the ability of all nature. Thus, there are the wonderful cures of illnesses, there is the raising of the dead, and the wonderful immutation in the heavenly bodies; and what is more wonderful, there is the inspiration given to human minds, so that simple and untutored persons, filled with the gift of the Holy Spirit, come to possess instantaneously the highest wisdom and the readiest eloquence. When these arguments were examined, through the efficacy of the above-mentioned proof, and not the violent assault of arms or the promise of pleasures, and (what is most wonderful of all) in the midst of the tyranny of the persecutors, and innumerable throng of people, both simple and most learned, flocked to the Christian faith. In this faith there are truths preached that surpass every human intellect; the pleasures of the flesh are curbed; it is taught that the things of the world should be spurned. Now, for the minds of mortal men to assent to these things is the greatest of miracles, just as it is a manifest work of divine inspiration that,

---

[7]Sirach 3:23
[8]I Corinthians 2:10–11
[9]II Peter 1:16
[10]Hebrews 2:3–4

spurning visible things, men should seek only what is invisible. Now, that this has happened neither without preparation nor by chance, but as a result of the disposition of God, is clear from the fact that through many pronouncements of the ancient prophets God had foretold that He would do this. The books
5   of these prophets are held in veneration among us Christians, since they give witness to our faith.

The manner of this confirmation is touched on by Saint Paul: "Which," that is, human salvation, "having begun to be declared by the Lord, was confirmed unto us by them that hear Him: God also bearing them witness of signs, and
10   wonders, and divers miracles, and distributions of the Holy Ghost."[11]

This wonderful conversion of the world to the Christian faith is the clearest witness of the signs given in the past; so that it is not necessary that they should be further repeated, since they appear most clearly in their effect. For it would be truly more wonderful than all signs if the world had been led by simple and
15   humble men to believe such lofty truths, to accomplish such difficult actions, and to have such high hopes. Yet it is also a fact that, even in our own time, God does not cease to work miracles through His saints for the confirmation of the faith.

On the other hand, those who founded sects committed to erroneous doc-
20   trines proceeded in a way that is opposite to this. The point is clear in the case of Mohammed.[12] He seduced the people by promises of carnal pleasure to which the concupiscence of the flesh goads us. His teaching also contained precepts that were in conformity with his promises, and he gave free rein to carnal pleasure. In all this, as is not unexpected, he was obeyed by carnal men. As for proofs of
25   the truth of his doctrine, he brought forward only such as could be grasped by the natural ability of anyone with a very modest wisdom. Indeed, the truths that he taught he mingled with many fables and with doctrines of the greatest falsity. He did not bring forth any signs produced in a supernatural way, which alone fittingly gives witness to divine inspiration; for a visible action that can
30   be only divine reveals an invisibly inspired teacher of truth. On the contrary, Mohammed said that he was sent in the power of his arms—which are signs not lacking even to robbers and tyrants. What is more, no wise men, men trained in things divine and human, believed in him from the beginning. Those who believed in him were brutal men and desert wanderers, utterly ignorant of all
35   divine teaching, through whose numbers Mohammed forced others to become his followers by the violence of his arms. Nor do divine pronouncements on the part of preceding prophets offer him any witness. On the contrary, he perverts

---

[11]Hebrews 2:3–4
[12]Mohammed (c. 570–632), founder of Islam

almost all the testimonies of the Old and New Testaments by making them into fabrications of his own, as can be seen by anyone who examines his law. It was, therefore, a shrewd decision on his part to forbid his followers to read the Old and New Testaments, lest these books convict him of falsity. It is thus clear that those who place any faith in his words believe foolishly.                    5

### That the Truth of Reason is Not Opposed to the Truth of the Christian Faith

[§7]Now, although the truth of the Christian faith which we have discussed surpasses the capacity of the reason, nevertheless that truth that the human reason is naturally endowed to know cannot be opposed to the truth of the Christian faith. For that with which the human reason is naturally endowed is clearly most true; so much so, that it is impossible for us to think of such   10 truths as false. Nor is it permissible to believe as false that which we hold by faith, since this is confirmed in a way that is so clearly divine. Since, therefore, only the false is opposed to the true, as is clearly evident from an examination of their definitions, it is impossible that the truth of faith should be opposed to those principles that the human reason knows naturally.                    15

Furthermore, that which is introduced into the soul of the student by the teacher is contained in the knowledge of the teacher—unless his teaching is fictitious, which it is improper to say of God. Now, the knowledge of the principles that are known to us naturally has been implanted in us by God; for God is the Author of our nature. These principles, therefore, are also contained by the   20 divine Wisdom. Hence, whatever is opposed to them is opposed to the divine Wisdom, and, therefore, cannot come from God. That which we hold by faith as divinely revealed, therefore, cannot be contrary to our natural knowledge.

Again. In the presence of contrary arguments our intellect is chained, so that it cannot proceed to the knowledge of the truth. If, therefore, contrary   25 knowledges were implanted in us by God, our intellect would be hindered from knowing truth by this very fact. Now, such an effect cannot come from God.

And again. What is natural cannot change as long as nature does not. Now, it is impossible that contrary opinions should exist in the same knowing subject at the same time. No opinion or belief, therefore, is implanted in man by God   30 which is contrary to man's natural knowledge.

Therefore, the Apostle says, "The word is nigh thee, even in thy mouth and in thy heart. This is the word of faith, which we preach."[13] But because it overcomes reason, there are some who think that it is opposed to it: which is impossible.

---

[13]Romans 10:8

The authority of Saint Augustine also agrees with this. He writes as follows: "That which truth will reveal cannot in any way be opposed to the sacred books of the Old and the New Testament."

From this we evidently gather the following conclusion: whatever arguments are brought forward against the doctrines of faith are conclusions incorrectly derived from the first and self-evident principles imbedded in nature. Such conclusions do not have the force of demonstration; they are arguments that are either probable or sophistical. And so, there exists the possibility to answer them.

# ON KINGSHIP
## THOMAS AQUINAS (c. 1225–1274)

*In the two Summas, Aquinas dealt systematically and logically with both rational and revealed truth, drawing heavily on the Scriptures and Augustine as well as on Aristotle. In some areas, his views were seen as highly controversial, especially by Franciscans such as Saint Bonaventure (1221–1274). However, few contemporaries took issue with his political theory, which represented a dramatic shift away from the traditional Augustinian idea that government was the product of sin, toward Aristotle's view that human societies, and therefore civil governments, existed naturally because "man is by nature an animal destined to live in a polis."*

1267

### What is Meant by the Word "King"

I§1...Man has an end to which his whole life and all his actions are ordered; for man is an intelligent agent, and it is clearly the part of an intelligent agent to act in view of an end. Men also adopt different methods in proceeding towards their proposed end, as the diversity of men's pursuits and actions clearly indicates. Consequently man needs some directive principle to guide him towards his end. 5

To be sure, the light of reason is placed by nature in every man, to guide him in his acts towards his end. Wherefore, if man were intended to live alone, as many animals do, he would require no other guide to his end. Each man would be a king unto himself, under God, the highest King, inasmuch as he would direct himself in his acts by the light of reason given him from on high. 10 Yet it is natural for man, more than for any other animal, to be a social and political animal, to live in a group.

This is clearly a necessity of man's nature. For all other animals, nature has prepared food, hair as a covering, teeth, horns, claws as means of defense or at least speed in flight, while man alone was made without any natural provisions 15 for these things. Instead of all these, man was endowed with reason, by the use of which he could procure all these things for himself by the work of his hands.

Reprinted with permission from *On Kingship to the King of Cyprus*, translated by I. T. Eschmann (Toronto: Pontifical Institute of Mediaeval Studies, 1982), 3–29, 53–54, 63–67.

Now, one man alone is not able to procure them all for himself, for one man could not sufficiently provide for life, unassisted. It is therefore natural that man should live in the society of many.

Moreover, all other animals are able to discern, by inborn skill, what is
5    useful and what is injurious, even as the sheep naturally regards the wolf as his enemy. Some animals also recognize by natural skill certain medicinal herbs and other things necessary for their life. Man, on the contrary, has a natural knowledge of the things which are essential for his life only in a general fashion, inasmuch as he is able to attain knowledge of the particular things necessary
10   for human life by reasoning from natural principles. But it is not possible for one man to arrive at a knowledge of all these things by his own individual reason. It is therefore necessary for man to live in a multitude so that each one may assist his fellows, and different men may be occupied in seeking, by their reason, to make different discoveries—one, for example, in medicine, one in
15   this and another in that.

This point is further and most plainly evidenced by the fact that the use of speech is a prerogative proper to man. By this means, one man is able fully to express his conceptions to others. Other animals, it is true, express their feelings to one another in a general way, as a dog may express anger by barking and other
20   animals give vent to other feelings in various fashions. But man communicates with his kind more completely than any other animal known to be gregarious, such as the crane, the ant or the bee. With this in mind, Solomon says, "It is better that there be two than one; for they have the advantage of their company."[1]

If, then, it is natural for man to live in the society of many, it is necessary
25   that there exist among men some means by which the group may be governed. For where there are many men together and each one is looking after his own interest, the multitude would be broken up and scattered unless there were also an agency to take care of what appertains to the commonweal. In like manner, the body of a man or any other animal would disintegrate unless there were a
30   general ruling force within the body which watches over the common good of all members. With this in mind, Solomon says, "Where there is no governor, the people shall fall."[2]

Indeed it is reasonable that this should happen, for what is proper and what is common are not identical. Things differ by what is proper to each:
35   they are united by what they have in common. But diversity of effects is due to diversity of causes. Consequently, there must exist something which impels towards the common good of the many, over and above that which impels towards the particular good of each individual. Wherefore also in all things

---

[1]Ecclesiastes 4:9
[2]Proverbs 11:14

that are ordained towards one end, one thing is found to rule the rest. Thus in the corporeal universe, by the first body, i.e. the celestial body, the other bodies are regulated according to the order of Divine Providence; and all bodies are ruled by a rational creature. So, too, in the individual man, the soul rules the body; and among the parts of the soul, the irascible and the concupiscible parts 5 are ruled by reason. Likewise, among the members of a body, one, such as the heart or the head, is the principal and moves all the others. Therefore in every multitude there must be some governing power.

Now it happens in certain things which are ordained towards an end that one may proceed in a right way and also in a wrong way. So, too, in the government 10 of a multitude there is a distinction between right and wrong. A thing is rightly directed when it is led towards a befitting end; wrongly when it is led towards an unbefitting end. Now the end which befits a multitude of free men is different from that which befits a multitude of slaves, for the free man is one who exists for his own sake, while the slave, as such, exists for the sake of another. If, therefore, 15 a multitude of free men is ordered by the ruler towards the common good of the multitude, that rulership will be right and just, as is suitable to free men. If, on the other hand, a rulership aims, not at the common good of the multitude, but at the private good of the ruler, it will be an unjust and perverted rulership. The Lord, therefore, threatens such rulers, saying by the mouth of Ezekiel, "Woe to 20 the shepherds that feed themselves (seeking, that is, their own interest): should not the flocks be fed by the shepherd?"[3] Shepherds indeed should seek the good of their flocks, and every ruler, the good of the multitude subject to him.

If an unjust government is carried on by one man alone, who seeks his own benefit from his rule and not the good of the multitude subject to him, such a 25 ruler is called a tyrant—a word derived from strength—because he oppresses by might instead of ruling by justice. Thus among the ancients all powerful men were called tyrants. If an unjust government is carried on, not by one but by several, and if they be few, it is called an oligarchy, that is, the rule of a few. This occurs when a few, who differ from the tyrant only by the fact that they are 30 more than one, oppress the people by means of their wealth. If, finally, the bad government is carried on by the multitude, it is called a democracy, i.e., control by the populace, which comes about when the plebeian people by force of numbers oppress the rich. In this way the whole people will be as one tyrant.

In like manner we must divide just governments. If the government is 35 administered by many, it is given the name common to all forms of government, viz. polity, as for instance when a group of warriors exercise dominion over a city or province. If it is administered by a few men of virtue, this kind

---

[3]Ezekiel 34:8–10

of government is called an aristocracy, i.e. noble governance, or governance by noble men, who for this reason are called the optimates. And if a just government is in the hands of one man alone, he is properly called a king. Wherefore the Lord says by the mouth of Ezekiel, "My servant, David, shall be king over
5   them and all of them shall have one shepherd."[4]

From this it is clearly shown that the idea of king implies that he be one man who is chief and that he be a shepherd seeking the common good of the multitude and not his own.

Now since man must live in a group, because he is not sufficient unto
10  himself to procure the necessities of life were he to remain solitary, it follows that a society will be the more perfect the more it is sufficient unto itself to procure the necessities of life. There is, to some extent, sufficiency for life in one family of one household, namely, insofar as pertains to the natural acts of nourishment and the begetting of offering and other things of this kind. Self-
15  sufficiency exists, furthermore, in one street with regard to those things which belong to the trade of one guild. In a city, which is the perfect community, it exists with regard to all the necessities of life. Still more self-sufficiency is found in a province because of the need of fighting together and of mutual help against enemies. Hence the man ruling a perfect community, i.e., a city or a province,
20  is antonomastically called the king. The ruler of a household is called father, not king, although he bears a certain resemblance to the king, for which reason kings are sometimes called the fathers of their peoples.

It is plain, therefore, from what has been said, that a king is one who rules the people of one city or province, and rules them for the common good.
25  Wherefore Solomon says, "The king rules over all the land subject to him."[5]

## Whether it is More Expedient for a City or Province to be Ruled by One Man or By Many

I§2Having set forth these preliminary points we must now inquire what is better for a province or a city: whether to be ruled by one man or by many.

This question may be considered first from the viewpoint of the purpose of government. The aim of any ruler should be directed towards securing the
30  welfare of that which he undertakes to rule. The duty of the pilot, for instance, is to preserve his ship amidst the perils of the sea and to bring it unharmed to the port of safety. Now the welfare and safety of a multitude formed into a society lies in the preservation of its unity, which is called peace. If this is removed, the benefit of social life is lost and, moreover, the multitude in its

---

[4]Ezekiel 37:24
[5]Ecclesiastes 5:9

disagreement becomes a burden to itself. The chief concern of the ruler of a multitude, therefore, is to procure the unity of peace. It is not even legitimate for him to deliberate whether he shall establish peace in the multitude subject to him, just as a physician does not deliberate whether he shall heal the sick man encharged to him, for no one should deliberate about an end which he 5 is obliged to seek, but only about the means to attain that end. Wherefore the Apostle, having commended the unity of the faithful people, says, "Be careful to keep the unity of the spirit in the bond of peace."[6] Thus, the more efficacious a government is in keeping the unity of peace, the more useful it will be. For we call that more useful which leads more directly to the end. Now it is manifest 10 that what is itself one can more efficaciously bring about unity than several—just as the most efficacious cause of heat is that which is by its nature hot. Therefore the rule of one man is more useful than the rule of many.

Furthermore, it is evident that several persons could by no means preserve the stability of the community if they totally disagreed. For union is necessary 15 among them if they are to rule at all: several men, for instance, could not pull a ship in one direction unless joined together in some fashion. Now several are said to be united according as they come closer to being one. So one man rules better than several who come near being one.

Again, whatever is in accord with nature is best, for in all things nature 20 does what is best. Now, every natural governance is governance by one. In the multitude of bodily members there is one which is the principal mover, namely, the heart; and among the powers of the soul one power presides as chief, namely, the reason. Among bees there is one king bee and in the whole universe there is One God, Maker and Ruler of all things. And there is a reason for this. Every 25 multitude is derived from unity. Wherefore, if artificial things are an imitation of natural things and a work of art is better according as it attains a closer likeness to what is in nature, it follows that it is best for a human multitude to be ruled by one person.

This is also evident from experience. For provinces or cities which are not 30 ruled by one person are torn with dissensions and tossed about without peace, so that the complaint seems to be fulfilled which the Lord uttered through the Prophet, "Many pastors have destroyed my vineyard."[7] On the other hand, provinces and cities which are ruled under one king enjoy peace, flourish in justice, and delight in prosperity. Hence, the Lord by His prophets promises 35 to His people as a great reward that He will give them one head and that "one Prince will be in the midst of them."

---

[6]Ephesians 4:3
[7]Jeremiah 12:10

## That the Dominion of a Tyrant Is the Worst

[§3]Just as the government of a king is the best, so the government of a tyrant is the worst. For democracy stands in contrary opposition to polity, since both are governments carried on by many persons, as is clear from what has already been said; while oligarchy is the opposite of aristocracy, since both are governments
5    carried on by a few persons; and kingship is the opposite of tyranny since both are carried on by one person. Now, as has been shown above, monarchy is the best government. If, therefore, "it is the contrary of the best that is worst" it follows that tyranny is the worst kind of government.

Further, a united force is more efficacious in producing its effect than a
10   force which is scattered or divided. Many persons together can pull a load which could not be pulled by each one taking his part separately and acting individually. Therefore, just as it is more useful for a force operating for a good to be more united, in order that it may work good more effectively, so a force operating for evil is more harmful when it is one than when it is divided. Now,
15   the power of one who rules unjustly works to the detriment of the multitude, in that he diverts the common good of the multitude to his own benefit. Therefore, for the same reason that, in a just government, the government is better in proportion as the ruling power is one—thus monarchy is better than aristocracy, and aristocracy better than polity—so the contrary will be true of
20   an unjust government, namely, that the ruling power will be more harmful in proportion as it is more unitary. Consequently, tyranny is more harmful than oligarchy; and oligarchy more harmful than democracy.

Moreover, a government becomes unjust by the fact that the ruler, paying no heed to the common good, seeks his own private good. Wherefore the further
25   he departs from the common good the more unjust will his government be. But there is a greater departure from the common good in an oligarchy, in which the advantage of a few is sought, than in a democracy, in which the advantage of many is sought; and there is a still greater departure from the common good in a tyranny, where the advantage of only one man is sought. For a large number
30   is closer to the totality than a small number, and a small number than only one. Thus, the government of a tyrant is the most unjust.

The same conclusion is made clear to those who consider the order of Divine Providence, which disposes everything in the best way. In all things, good ensues from one perfect cause, i.e. from the totality of the conditions favorable
35   to the production of the effect, while evil results from any one partial defect. There is beauty in a body when all its members are fittingly disposed; ugliness, on the other hand, arises when any one member is not fittingly disposed. Thus ugliness results in different ways from many causes; beauty in one way from

one perfect cause. It is thus with all good and evil things, as if God so provided that good, arising from one cause, be stronger, and evil, arising from many causes, be weaker. It is expedient therefore that just government be that of one man only in order that it may be stronger; however, if the government should turn away from justice, it is more expedient that it be a government by many, so that it may be weaker and the many may mutually hinder one another. Among unjust governments, therefore, democracy is the most tolerable, but the worst is tyranny.

This same conclusion is also apparent if one considers the evils which come from tyrants. Since a tyrant, despising the common good, seeks his private interest, it follows that he will oppress his subjects in different ways according as he is dominated by different passions to acquire certain goods. The one who is enthralled by the passion of cupidity seizes the goods of his subjects; whence Solomon says, "A just king sets up the land; a covetous man shall destroy it."[8] If he is dominated by the passion of anger, he sheds blood for nothing; whence it is said by Ezekiel, "Her princes in the midst of her are like wolves ravening the prey to shed blood."[9] Therefore this kind of government is to be avoided, as the Wise man admonishes, "Keep far from the man who has the power to kill,"[10] because, forsooth, he kills not for justice' sake but by his power, for the lust of his will. Thus there can be no safety. Everything is uncertain when there is a departure from justice. Nobody will be able firmly to state: This thing is such and such, when it depends upon the will of another, not to say upon his caprice. Nor does the tyrant merely oppress his subjects in corporal things but he also hinders their spiritual good. Those who seek more to use, than to be of use to, their subjects prevent all progress, suspecting all excellence in their subjects to be prejudicial to their own evil domination. For tyrants hold the good in greater suspicion than the wicked, and to them the valor of others is always fraught with danger.

So the above-mentioned tyrants strive to prevent those of their subjects who have become virtuous from acquiring valor and high spirit in order that they may not want to cast off their iniquitous domination. They also see to it that there be no friendly relations among these so that they may not enjoy the benefits resulting from being on good terms with one another, for as long as one has no confidence in the other, no plot will be set up against the tyrant's domination. Wherefore they sow discords among the people, foster any that have arisen, and forbid anything which furthers society and co-operation among men, such as marriage, company at table and anything of like character, through which

---

[8]Proverbs 29:4
[9]Ezekiel 22:27
[10]Sirach 9:13

familiarity and confidence are engendered among men. They moreover strive to prevent their subjects from becoming powerful and rich since, suspecting these to be as wicked as themselves, they fear their power and wealth; for the subjects might become harmful to them even as they are accustomed to use
5   power and wealth to harm others. Whence in the Book of Job it is said of the tyrant, "The sound of dread is always in his ears and when there is peace" (that is, when there is no one to harm him), "he always suspects treason."[11]

It thus results that when rulers, who ought to induce their subjects to virtue, are wickedly jealous of the virtue of their subjects and hinder it as much as they
10  can, few virtuous men are found under the rule of tyrants. For, according to Aristotle's sentence, brave men are found where brave men are honored. And as Cicero says, "Those who are despised by everybody are disheartened and flourish but little." It is also natural that men, brought up in fear, should become mean of spirit and discouraged in the face of any strenuous and manly task.
15  This is shown by experience in provinces that have long been under tyrants. Hence the Apostle says to the Colossians, "Fathers, provoke not your children to indignation, lest they be discouraged."[12]

So, considering these evil effects of tyranny, King Solomon says, "When the wicked reign, men are ruined"[13] because, forsooth, through the wickedness
20  of tyrants, subjects fall away from the perfection of virtue. And again he says, "When the wicked shall bear rule the people shall mourn, as though led into slavery."[14] And again, "When the wicked rise up men shall hide themselves,"[15] that they may escape the cruelty of the tyrant. It is no wonder, for a man governing without reason, according to the lust of his soul, in no way differs from
25  the beast. Whence Solomon says, "As a roaring lion and a hungry bear, so is a wicked prince over the poor people."[16] Therefore men hide from tyrants as from cruel beasts and it seems that to be subject to a tyrant is the same thing as to lie prostrate beneath a raging beast.

## Why the Royal Dignity Is Rendered Hateful to the Subjects

[§4]Because both the best and the worst government are latent in monarchy, i.e.,
30  in the rule of one man, the royal dignity is rendered hateful to many people on account of the wickedness of tyrants. Some men, indeed, whilst they desire to

---

[11]Job 15:21
[12]Colossians 3:21
[13]Proverbs 28:12
[14]Proverbs 29:2
[15]Proverbs 28:28
[16]Proverbs 28:15

be ruled by a king, fall under the cruelty of tyrants, and not a few rulers exercise tyranny under the cloak of royal dignity.

A clear example of this is found in the Roman Republic. When the kings had been driven out by the Roman people, because they could not bear the royal, or rather tyrannical, arrogance, they instituted consuls and other magistrates by whom they began to be ruled and guided. They changed the kingdom into an aristocracy, and, as Sallust relates, "The Roman city, once liberty was won, waxed incredibly strong and great in a remarkably short time." For it frequently happens that men living under a king strive more sluggishly for the common good, inasmuch as they consider that what they devote to the common good, they do not confer upon themselves but upon another, under whose power they see the common goods to be. But when they see that the common good is not under the power of one man, they do not attend to it as if it belonged to another, but each one attends to it as if it were his own.

Experience thus teaches that one city administered by rulers, changing annually, is sometimes able to do more than some kings having, perchance, two or three cities; and small service exacted by kings weigh more heavily than great burdens imposed by the community of citizens. This held good in the history of the Roman Republic. The plebs were enrolled in the army and were paid wages for military service. Then when the common treasury was failing, private riches came forth for public uses, to such an extent that not even the senators retained any gold for themselves save one ring and the one bulla (the insignia of their dignity).

On the other hand, when the Romans were worn out by continual dissensions taking on the proportion of civil wars, and when by these wars the freedom for which they had greatly striven was snatched from their hands, they began to find themselves under the power of emperors who, from the beginning, were unwilling to be called kings, for the royal name was hateful to the Romans. Some emperors, it is true, faithfully cared for the common good in a kingly manner, and by their zeal the commonwealth was increased and preserved. But most of them became tyrants towards their subjects while indolent and vacillating before their enemies, and brought the Roman commonwealth to naught.

A similar process took place, also, among the Hebrew people. At first, while they were ruled by judges, they were ravished by their enemies on every hand, for each one "did what was good in his sight."[17] Yet when, at their own pressing, God gave them kings, they departed from the worship of the one God and were finally led into bondage, on account of the wickedness of their kings.

---

[17]Judges 21:25

Danger thus lurks on either side. Either men are held by the fear of a tyrant and they miss the opportunity of having that very best government which is kingship; or, they want a king and the kingly power turns into tyrannical wickedness.

## A Lesser Evil When a Monarchy Turns into a Tyranny than when an Aristocracy Becomes Corrupt

5    **I§5**When a choice is to be made between two things, from both of which danger impends, surely that one should be chosen from which the lesser evil follows. Now, lesser evil follows the corruption of a monarchy (which is tyranny) than from the corruption of an aristocracy.

Polyarchy most frequently breeds dissension. This dissension runs counter
10   to the good of peace, which is the principal social good. A tyrant, on the other hand, does not destroy this good, rather he obstructs one or the other individual interest of his subjects—unless, of course, there be an excess of tyranny and the tyrant rages against the whole community. Monarchy is therefore to be preferred to polyarchy, although either form of government might become dangerous.

15   Further, that from which great dangers may follow more frequently is, it would seem, the more to be avoided. Now, considerable dangers to the multitude follow more frequently from polyarchy than from monarchy. There is a greater chance that, where there are many rulers, one of them will abandon the intention of the common good than that it will be abandoned when there is but one
20   ruler. When any one among several rulers turns aside from the pursuit of the common good, danger of internal strife threatens the group because, when the chiefs quarrel, dissension will follow in the people. When, on the other hand, one man is in command, he more often keeps to governing for the sake of the common good. Should he not do so, it does not immediately follow that he also
25   proceeds to the total oppression of his subjects. This, of course, would be the excess of tyranny and the worst wickedness in government, as has been shown above. The dangers, then, arising from a polyarchy are more to be guarded against than those arising from a monarchy.

Moreover, in point of fact, a polyarchy deviates into tyranny not less but
30   perhaps more frequently than a monarchy. When, on account of there being many rulers, dissensions arise in such a government, it often happens that the power of one preponderates and he then usurps the government of the multitude for himself. This indeed may be clearly seen from history. There has hardly ever been a polyarchy that did not end in tyranny. The best illustration of this fact
35   is the history of the Roman Republic. It was for a long time administered by the magistrates but then animosities, dissensions and civil wars arose and it fell

into the power of the most cruel tyrants. In general, if one carefully considers what has happened in the past and what is happening in the present, he will discover that more men have held tyrannical sway in lands previously ruled by many rulers than in those ruled by one.

The strongest objection why monarchy, although it is the best form of    5
government, is not agreeable to the people is that, in fact, it may deviate into tyranny. Yet tyranny is wont to occur not less but more frequently on the basis of a polyarchy than on the basis of a monarchy. It follows that it is, in any case, more expedient to live under one king than under the rule of several men.

## How Provision Might Be Made that the King may not Fall into Tyranny

[86]Therefore, since the rule of one man, which is the best, is to be preferred,    10
and since it may happen that it be changed into a tyranny, which is the worst (all this is clear from what has been said), a scheme should be carefully worked out which would prevent the multitude ruled by a king from falling into the hands of a tyrant.

First, it is necessary that the man who is raised up to be king by those whom    15
it concerns should be of such condition that it is improbable that he should become a tyrant. Wherefore Daniel, commending the providence of God with respect to the institution of the king says, "The Lord has sought him a man according to his own heart, and the Lord has appointed him to be prince over his people."[18] Then, once the king is established, the government of the kingdom    20
must be so arranged that opportunity to tyrannize is removed. At the same time his power should be so tempered that he cannot easily fall into tyranny. How these things may be done we must consider in what follows.

Finally, provision must be made for facing the situation should the king stray into tyranny. Indeed, if there be not an excess of tyranny it is more expedient    25
to tolerate the milder tyranny for a while than, by acting against the tyrant, to become involved in many perils more grievous than the tyranny itself. For it may happen that those who act against the tyrant are unable to prevail and the tyrant then will rage the more. But should one be able to prevail against the tyrant, from this fact itself very grave dissensions among the people frequently    30
ensue: the multitude may be broken up into factions either during their revolt against the tyrant, or in process of the organization of the government, after the tyrant has been overthrown. Moreover, it sometimes happens that while the multitude is driving out the tyrant by the help of some man, the latter, having received the power, thereupon seizes the tyranny. Then, fearing to suffer from    35

---

[18]I Samuel 13:14

another what he did to his predecessor, he oppresses his subjects with an even more grievous slavery....

If the excess of tyranny is unbearable, some have been of the opinion that it would be an act of virtue for strong men to slay the tyrant and to expose
5   themselves to the danger of death in order to set the multitude free. An example of this occurs even in the Old Testament, for a certain Ehud slew Eglon, King of Moab, who was oppressing the people of God under harsh slavery, thrusting a dagger into his thigh; and he was made a judge of the people.[19]

But this opinion is not in accord with apostolic teaching. For Peter ad-
10   monishes us to be reverently subject to our masters, not only to the good and gentle but also the forward, "For if one who suffers unjustly bear his trouble for conscience' sake, this is grace."[20] Wherefore, when many emperors of the Romans tyrannically persecuted the faith of Christ, a great number both of the nobility and the common people were converted to the faith and were praised
15   for patiently bearing death for Christ. They did not resist although they were armed, and this is plainly manifested in the case of the holy Theban legion. Ehud, then, must be considered rather as having slain a foe than assassinated a ruler, however tyrannical, of the people. Hence in the Old Testament we also read that they who killed Jehoash, the king of Judah, who had fallen away
20   from the worship of God, were slain and their children spared according to the precept of the law.

Should private persons attempt on their own private presumption to kill the rulers, even though tyrants, this would be dangerous for the multitude as well as for their rulers. This is because the wicked usually expose themselves to
25   dangers of this kind more than the good, for the rule of a king, no less than that of a tyrant, is burdensome to them since, according to the words of Solomon, "A wise king scatters the wicked."[21] Consequently, by presumption of this kind, danger to the people from the loss of a good king would be more probable than relief through the removal of a tyrant. Furthermore, it seems that to proceed
30   against the cruelty of tyrants is an action to be undertaken, not through the private presumption of a few, but rather by public authority.

Should no human aid whatsoever against a tyrant be forthcoming, recourse must be had to God, the King of all, Who is a helper in due time in tribulation. For it lies in his power to turn the cruel heart of the tyrant to mildness. According
35   to Solomon, "The heart of the king is in the hand of the Lord, whithersoever He will He shall turn it."[22] He it was who turned into mildness the cruelty

---

[19]Judges 3:15–30
[20]I Peter 2:19
[21]Proverbs 20:26
[22]Proverbs 21:1

of King Ahasuerus, who was preparing death for the Jews. He it was who so filled the cruel King Nebuchadnezzar with piety that he became a proclaimer of the divine power. "Therefore," he said, "I, Nebuchadnezzar, do now praise and magnify and glorify the King of Heaven; because all His works are true and His ways judgments, and they that walk in pride He is able to abase."[23]  5
Those tyrants, however, whom he deems unworthy of conversion, he is able to put out of the way or to degrade, according to the words of the Wise Man, "God has overturned the thrones of proud princes and has set up the meek in their stead."[24] He it was who, seeing the affliction of his people in Egypt and hearing their cry, hurled Pharaoh, a tyrant over God's people, with all his  10
army into the sea. He it was who not only banished from his kingly throne the above-mentioned Nebuchadnezzar because of his former pride, but also cast him from the fellowship of men and changed him into the likeness of a beast. Indeed, His hand is not shortened that He cannot free His people from tyrants. For by Isaiah He promised to give his people rest from their labors and lashings  15
and harsh slavery in which they had formerly served; and by Ezekiel He says, "I will deliver my flock from their mouth," i.e., from the mouth of shepherds who feed themselves.

But to deserve to secure this benefit from God, the people must desist from sin, for it is by divine permission that wicked men receive power to rule as a  20
punishment for sin, as the Lord says by the Prophet Hosea, "I will give you a king in my wrath"[25] and it is said in Job that he "makes a man that is a hypocrite to reign for the sins of the people."[26] Sin must therefore be done away with in order that the scourge of tyrants may cease....

## On the Duties of a King

II§1 The next point to be considered is what the kingly office is and what quali-  25
ties the king should have. Since things which are in accordance with art are an imitation of the things which are in accordance with nature (from which we accept the rules to act according to reason), it seems best that we learn about the kingly office from the pattern of the regime of nature.

· In things of nature there is both a universal and a particular government.  30
The former is God's government Whose rule embraces all things and Whose providence governs them all. The latter is found in man and it is much like the divine government. Hence man is called a microcosmos. Indeed there is a

---

[23] Daniel 4:37
[24] Sirach 10:14
[25] Hosea 13:11
[26] Job 34:30

similitude between both governments in regard to their form; for just as the universe of corporeal creatures and all spiritual powers come under the divine government, in like manner the members of the human body and all the powers of the soul are governed by reason. Thus, in a proportionate manner, reason is to
5  man what God is to the world. Since, however, man is by nature a social animal living in a multitude, as we have pointed out above, the analogy with the divine government is found in him not only in this way that one man governs himself by reason, but also in that the multitude of men is governed by the reason of one man. This is what first of all constitutes the office of a king....
10      Therefore let the king recognize that such is the office which he undertakes, namely, that he is to be in the kingdom what the soul is in the body, and what God is in the world. If he reflect seriously upon this, a zeal for justice will be enkindled in him when he contemplates that he has been appointed to this position in place of God, to exercise judgment in his kingdom; further, he will
15  acquire the gentleness of clemency and mildness when he considers as his own members those individuals who are subject to his rule....

### That Regal Government Should be Ordained
### Principally to Eternal Beatitude

**II§4**As life by which men live well here on earth is ordained, as to its end, to that blessed life which we hope for in heaven, so too whatever particular goods are procured by man's agency—whether wealth, profits, health, eloquence, or
20  learning are ordained to the good life of the multitude. If, then, as we have said, the person who is charged with the care of our ultimate end ought to be over those who have charge of things ordained to that end, and to direct them by his rule, it clearly follows that, just as the king ought to be subject to the divine government administered by the office of priesthood, so he ought to preside
25  over all human offices, and regulate them by the rule of his government.
        ...Since the beatitude of heaven is the end of that virtuous life which we live at present, it pertains to the king's office to promote the good life of the multitude in such a way as to make it suitable for the attainment of heavenly happiness, that is to say, he should command those things which lead to the
30  happiness of Heaven and, as far as possible, forbid the contrary.
        What conduces to true beatitude and what hinders it are learned from the law of God, the teaching of which belongs to the office of the priest, according to the words of Malachi, "The lips of the priest shall guard knowledge and they shall seek the law from his mouth."[27] Wherefore the Lord prescribes in the Book
35  of Deuteronomy that "after he is raised to the throne of his kingdom, the king

---

[27]Malachi 2:7

shall copy out to himself the Deuteronomy of this law, in a volume, taking the copy of the priests of the Levitical tribe, he shall have it with him and shall read it all the days of his life, that he may learn to fear the Lord his God, and keep his words and ceremonies which are commanded in the law."[28] Thus the king, taught the law of God, should have for his principal concern the means by which the multitude subject to him may live well.

This concern is threefold: first of all, to establish a virtuous life in the multitude subject to him; second, to preserve it once established; and third, having preserved it, to promote its greater perfection.

...To establish virtuous living in a multitude three things are necessary. First of all, that the multitude be established in the unity of peace. Second, that the multitude thus united in the bond of peace, be directed to acting well. For just as a man can do nothing well unless unity within his members be presupposed, so a multitude of men lacking the unity of peace will be hindered from virtuous action by the fact that it is fighting against itself. In the third place, it is necessary that there be at hand a sufficient supply of the things required for proper living, procured by the ruler's efforts.

When virtuous living is set up in the multitude by the efforts of the king, it then remains for him to look to its conservation. Now there are three things which prevent the permanence of the public good. One of these arises from nature. The good of the multitude should not be established for one time only; it should be in a sense perpetual. Men, on the other hand, cannot abide Forever, because they are mortal. Even while they are alive they do not always preserve the same vigor, for the life of man is subject to many changes, and thus a man is not equally suited to the performance of the same duties throughout the whole span of his life. A second impediment to the preservation of the public good, which comes from within, consists in the perversity of the wills of men, inasmuch as they are either too lazy to perform what the commonweal demands, or, still further, they are harmful to the peace of the multitude because, by transgressing justice, they disturb the peace of others. The third hindrance to the preservation of the commonweal comes from without, namely, when peace is destroyed through the attacks of enemies and, as it sometimes happens, the kingdom or city is completely blotted out.

In regard to these three dangers, a triple charge is laid upon the king. First of all, he must take care of the appointment of men to succeed or replace others in charge of the various offices. Just as in regard to corruptible things (which cannot remain the same forever) the government of God made provision that through generation one would take the place of another in order that, in this

---

[28]Deuteronomy 17:18

way, the integrity of the universe might be maintained, so too the good of the multitude subject to the king will be preserved through his care when he sets himself to attend to the appointment of new men to fill the place of those who drop out. In the second place, by his laws and orders, punishments and rewards,

5   he should restrain the men subject to him from wickedness and induce them to virtuous deeds, following the example of God, Who gave His law to man and requires those who observe it with rewards, and those who transgress it with punishments. The king's third charge is to keep the multitude entrusted to him safe from the enemy, for it would be useless to prevent internal dangers

10  if the multitude could not be defended against external dangers.

Finally, for the proper direction of the multitude there remains the third duty of the kingly office, namely, that he be solicitous for its improvement. He performs this duty when, in each of the things we have mentioned, he corrects what is out of order and supplies what is lacking, and if any of them can be

15  done better he tries to do so. This is why the Apostle exhorts the faithful to be "zealous for the better gifts."[29]...

---

[29]I Corinthians 12:31

# IX
# THE RENAISSANCE

Most historical periods are in some sense false, labels and categories imposed by modern historians looking backward. In contrast, the men of the fourteenth and fifteenth centuries described their age and values as distinct from what had come before—they described themselves as living in the Renaissance. The middle of the fourteenth century saw tremendous intellectual and aesthetic changes in northern Italy, changes that mark the earliest stages of the Renaissance. The next three centuries saw sweeping political, religious, economic, social, and intellectual changes, all of which collectively describe and characterize the European Renaissance.

Politically, the Renaissance was characterized by both a growth in the actual power of monarchs and by an increasing interest in republican political ideas. Across Europe, the "New Monarchs" slowly extended their rule, gradually coming to possess both more theoretical authority and more actual power than their predecessors. For those monarchs sufficiently wealthy and far-sighted to exploit them, innovations in the technology and conduct of war permitted rulers to increase their power.

Medieval monarchs had, of necessity, relied as much on persuasion as compulsion to encourage obedience and service from their nobility. Among the many changes of the Renaissance, military service underwent significant evolution. The introduction of gunpowder weapons ended the supremacy of the heavily armored cavalry warrior. Muskets could be cheaply and rapidly produced, and learning to use a firearm was the work of days, not years. With no need for special training or high social status, an army could be composed of thousands of peasants—the only limitation on an army's size was the royal treasury. Castles no longer needed to be starved into surrender over the course of months; now an army could reduce them to rubble in short order. If sufficient money was available, then, these military innovations allowed any ruler to compel obedience from his subjects. Those same military resources also enabled the monarch better to root out pirates and robbers, to reduce internal tariffs, and impose uniform laws across wide areas.

In explaining and justifying the growth of monarchical power, Early-Modern observers looked backward, to the traditions of their nation and to classical antiquity. Much of the bureaucracy of the New Monarchs grew from

medieval traditions, adding new functions or increased authority to preexist-
ing institutions. The standing army, the apparatus of tax collection, the legal
system—all substantially increased the power of the Early-Modern soldier, tax
collector, or judge over his medieval counterpart while using medieval language
to emphasize continuity with the past. At the same time, those who approved of
the expanding royal power also appealed to antiquity to legitimate this growth.
In the ancient world, monarchs were necessary to curb the disorder of the late
Roman Republic, to reform or perfect the laws in the polis, and, above all,
monarchy was the form of government granted by God to the Hebrews.

   In 1494 the kings of France and Castile demonstrated the power of the
new military and political realities. France, claiming a right to the Kingdom of
Naples, invaded the peninsula. The artillery of the French King Charles VIII
(r. 1483–1498) quickly reduced the fortified cities of northern Italy and his
armies swept aside the medieval armies of the Italian states. The Castilian ruler
Ferdinand V (r. 1474–1516) intervened with his modern army, and a decade
of war followed. The result, formalized in a 1504 treaty, divided Italy between
France and Castile, ending the autonomy of the Italian city-states.

   The utter defeat of the Italian states sparked much discussion among Italians. The superiority of the new military system, irrefutably evident in the recent
wars, was acknowledged. The Castilian and French, however, had achieved
their military superiority through the rise of ever more powerful monarchs.
Thus, to many writers, political liberties had been sacrificed to gain military
and economic power. The question, however, remained whether those military
innovations *must* be tied to the political form of centralized monarchy. Perhaps,
Italians mused, there was another political system that could guarantee both
freedom from oppression within the state and protection against conquest
from abroad.

   Like their opponents, Renaissance writers who opposed the trend toward
centralized monarchy appealed to tradition and antiquity. They emphasized the
classical model of republics, exemplified in the polis and Republican Rome, as
the political form that would best prevent domestic tyranny while still ensuring
international viability.

   The life and works of Niccolò Machiavelli (1469–1527), the most famous
of these writers, amply illustrate these priorities. He began serving the government of Florence, his native city, in 1494, the year the French invaded Italy.
Serving as ambassador to both France and Castile, he witnessed at firsthand
the effectiveness of the New Monarchs and their methods. As commander of
the militia, he suffered a crushing military defeat at the hands of a Castilian
army, providing personal knowledge of the military innovations. The collapse
of his Florentine Republic as a consequence of the foreign interventions thrust

Machiavelli out of political power, and he began writing. His prominent works all address facets of the challenges facing Italy. *The Prince* (1513) explained how a ruler might seize and consolidate power in a manner similar to the New Monarchs; *The Discourses on Livy* (1517) examined the Roman philosopher for insight into contemporary Republicanism; *The Art of War* (1520) explored ways in which military innovation might not threaten Republican government.

The vast majority of Early-Modern Europeans conducted their economic activity at village or town markets, buying locally produced goods and selling their products to customers from the surrounding area. In this, the Renaissance differs not at all from the medieval and ancient worlds. Long-distance commerce, on the other hand, grew in scope, value, and complexity to levels unmatched since the height of the Roman Empire.

Within the continent of Europe, long-distance commerce centered on the movement of foods. The primary commodities of intra-European trade included olive oil, salt, wool, wines, and timber. Profits generated by this trade allowed commercial cities to import significant quantities of grain, by far the dominant commercial cargo, thus allowing those cities to grow to sizes unmatched in the past thousand years. Despite the devastation of the Black Death, Florence's population increased 60 percent during the Renaissance, reaching 140,000 inhabitants. Other major trading centers exhibited similar growth—Valencia's grain trade pushed its population to 60,000 (a 50 percent increase), Antwerp reached 100,000, Venice grew to 120,000, and Lyons' silk trade helped increase its population by at least 200 percent, to 80,000.

While intra-European commerce could be lucrative, the greatest profits came through transporting luxury goods across continents and oceans. The Far East offered exotic spices, including peppercorn, nutmeg, and cinnamon, as well as finished goods such as porcelain and silk. Despite the many middlemen involved in the overland trade from Asia, cities such as Genoa and Venice made enormous profits reselling these luxury goods. Once settled, the plantations of the western hemisphere harvested sugar, tobacco, and indigo, and the Spanish mines at Potosí and Guanajuato produced more than 50,000 tons of silver during the late Renaissance.

The lucrative long-distance trading routes both depended upon and encouraged the continuation of voyages of exploration. Naval innovations developed through the commercial transformations gave Europeans the technological capacity for voyages of very long distances, even global circumnavigations. A fervent desire to spread the Christian faith provided sincere religious motives for both states and individuals to find new lands. Successful discovery and colonization, moreover, offered opportunities to gain wealth, land, and resources at the expense of political rivals—another motivating factor. Many European monarchs, therefore, wished to underwrite voyages of discovery and, with their steadily increasing power and wealth, possessed the ability to do so.

As early as 1419, the Portuguese discovered the islands of Madeira 350 miles west of the African coast, marking the beginning of Europe's great push to explore and settle the globe. By the end of the fifteenth century, Europeans colonized numerous Atlantic islands, and established outposts along the African coasts. In 1498, Vasco da Gama (1460–1529) reached India, opening lucrative sea routes to Asia and intensifying competition among Europeans for commercial dominance. Ever-increasing expansion and competition in Asia, Africa, and the Americas characterized late-Renaissance Europe.

Throughout the Early-Modern period, including the Renaissance, European society defined itself in terms of *orders*. Unlike the modern conception of social classes, which views income as the most meaningful measure of identity, orders emphasized a man's independence and his social function as the defining characteristics of his social identity. Thus all clergy, whether wealthy and powerful bishops or poor rural priests, considered themselves part of the same social order because of their religious role. Likewise, a wealthy merchant would identify himself far more with a poorer merchant than with an equally wealthy craftsman.

Though rarely fully defined at law, Europeans implicitly understood their social hierarchies. Criminals, vagabonds, and beggars comprised the lowest orders, then came those honest laborers who worked for others, whether as renters, day-laborers, or apprentices. Still more prestigious were those independent (that is, self-employed) men who labored physically—farmers who owned their lands or craftsmen with their own shops, for example. The hierarchy continued upward from those who earned wages with their minds—lawyers or physicians—through those who lived on investments and rents (often called the gentry), ending with the nobility and, finally, royalty.

The existence of social hierarchies in no way impeded social mobility. Early-Modern Europeans, however, viewed social mobility in terms of their extended family, not as an individual goal. The entire family strove for advancement, which was expected to occur over generations. Disposable income could fund the education of a son or nephew, who might become a lawyer, surpassing his father's social position. That son, and his son after him, might cultivate their educations, their patrons, and their opportunities and, in time, a descendant might marry into a family of the lower gentry. Thus four generations or more might pass between the life of a wealthy artisan and his descendants' transformation into the better sort of people. Many characteristics associated with the Renaissance—the shift to a money economy, the expansion of trade, the spread of Humanism, the bureaucratization of the state—created and expanded opportunities for this sort of advancement through an ever-increasing demand for educated functionaries in both private enterprise and in government departments.

Changes in the nature and distribution of political power, economic growth, exploration of long-unknown lands, social expansion and mobility—all contributed to the emergence of Renaissance Humanism, the preeminent characteristic of the age. Emphasizing the centrality and uniqueness of humans in God's creation, Humanists sought to study human activity—which could include language, history, politics, and literature, for example. Studying those creatures made in the image of God, and their actions, one learns more of God Himself.

The highest and best achievements of man were evidenced in the classical world, so Renaissance Humanists embraced antiquity as the excellent standard by which everything should be judged. To consider a political form valid, it must be measured by classical models and weighed against classical authorities. Standards of aesthetic beauty derived from and reflected Greek and Roman architecture and sculpture. Excellent writing mirrored the form, style, and syntax of the ancients, especially that of Cicero and Quintilian. The Renaissance—literally *The Rebirth*—self-consciously sought to recreate ancient values and forms.

This permeation of classical antiquity throughout all intellectual discourse necessarily demanded scholars learn, and learn well, Latin and Greek. Not just an intellectual movement for isolated scholars, Humanism encompassed the political, social, religious, and economic elite of the age. Politically and socially powerful men expended great wealth amassing vast private libraries, often dispatching researchers to isolated monasteries and buying texts from monks fleeing Byzantium. Religious foundations restructured universities to emphasize the *studia humanitatis* (grammar, rhetoric, moral philosophy, poetry, and history), those studies best suited to understanding man as a creature of God. Merchants and wealthy artisans funded their sons' pursuit of this education, even though it contributed no material benefit to commercial life.

Humanism, though emphasizing knowledge and learning for ultimate ends, led to practical consequences as well. Civic Humanism emphasized action as the necessary complement to intellectual pursuits. As one increasingly apprehends truths of God's nature, laws, and desires, one will be impelled to act on those truths. Thus, one does not truly understand truth if one does not act on it. Thus the great figures of the Renaissance, though we may associate them with one particular endeavor, ranged broadly in the professional experiences. Machiavelli, as we have seen, commanded armies, conducted diplomacy, and wrote on the classics. In addition to his famous paintings and sculptures, Leonardo da Vinci (1452–1519) composed music, experimented with biology, planned inventions both practical and fanciful, and served in the military. Ximénez de Cisneros (1426–1517) served as Archbishop of Toledo and Chancellor of Castile, published a parallel Bible with six different translations and Greek, Aramaic, and Hebrew texts, and created and completely funded the University of Alcalá in Madrid. Giovanni Aurispa (1376–1459), in addition to bringing hundreds of previously unknown Greek texts to the West, variously served throughout his life as a professor, Apostolic Secretary, writer, and merchant.

# ON HIS OWN IGNORANCE
## PETRARCH (1304–1374)

*Petrarch (Francesco Petrarca) lived through most of the major upheavals of the fourteenth century: the great famine of 1315–1317, the opening phases of the Hundred Years' War, the Black Death and several of the subsequent outbreaks of plague, and the Avignonese papacy. A voracious reader of the classics from a young age, he developed many of the ideas that came to characterize Italian humanism, a literary movement that emphasized the study of subjects associated with human interaction, such as rhetoric, ethics, and history, as opposed to the theological and metaphysical concerns of the scholastics.*

*After discovering the private letters of Cicero in the cathedral library in Verona in 1345, Petrarch came to recognize in the Roman statesman and philosopher a man like himself, subject to error and human frailties, rather than the timeless authority whose works earlier thinkers mined for the bits of truth that might be found in them. He wanted to communicate with this Cicero across the intervening centuries, bemoaning the gulf—the dark age—that separated the two of them. In acknowledging that the ancients were humans who lived in a particular time and place separated from his own, Petrarch reasoned that to understand them fully, one had to study all their works in their entirety, in the original languages; taking statements out of context and reading works in translation introduced distortions that prevented the original authors from making themselves heard across that gap. He saw their works as offering a way forward out of the disorder that characterized his time. Cicero had argued that rhetoric should be studied with ethics so that eloquence might promote virtue by moving the will of the hearer; for Petrarch, this combination was essential, since the problems of the day required learned men to take action rather than to isolate themselves to ponder eternal truths.*

*Petrarch wrote* On His Own Ignorance and That of Many Others *in 1367. His pride had been stung by the patronizing comments of four second-rate scholastics who had criticized him for his failure to show proper reverence for Aristotle. In this, his response to their charges, he illustrated a number of these important differences between the humanist and the scholastic approaches to the works of the ancients.*

*The Renaissance Philosophy of Man*, edited by Ernst Cassirer et al. (Chicago: University of Chicago Press, 1948), 52–57, 60–67, 71–80, 86–88, 91. Reprinted with permission of University of Chicago Press; permission conveyed through Copyright Clearance Center, Inc.

…As had come to be their custom, there called on me these four friends whose names you need not be told, since you know them all. Moreover, an inviolable law of friendship forbids mentioning the names of friends when you are speaking
5   against them, even if they do not behave like friends in a particular case. They came in pairs, as equality of character or some chance bound them together. Occasionally all four of them came, and came with astonishingly winning manners, with a gay expression on their faces, and started an agreeable conversation. I have no doubt they came with good and pious intentions. However, through
10  some cracks an unfortunate grudge had crept into hearts that deserve a better guest. It is incredible, though it is true—if only it were not too true! The man whom they wish not only good health and happiness, whom they not only love but respect, honor by their visit and venerate, to whom they try with greatest effort to be not only kind but obedient and generous—this very same person is
15  the object of their envy. So full of patent and hidden frailties is human nature.

What is it that they envy me? I do not know, I must admit, and I am amazed when I try to find out. Certainly it is not wealth, for every single one of them surpasses me as much in wealth as "the British whale is bigger than the dolphin,"[1] as that man has said. Moreover, they wish me even greater wealth.
20  They know that what I have is moderate, not my own property but to be shared with others. It is not magnificent but very modest without haughtiness and pomp. They know that it really does not deserve any envy. They will not envy me my friends. The greater part of them death has taken from me, and I have the habit of sharing them willingly, just like everything else, with other friends.
25  They cannot envy me the shapeliness of my body. If there was ever such a thing, it has vanished entirely in the course of the years that vanquish all. By God's overflowing and preserving grace it is still quite satisfactory for my present age, but it has certainly long since ceased to be enviable. And if it were still as it was once, could I forget or could I then have forgotten the poetic sentence I drank
30  in as a small boy: "Shapeliness is a frail possession,"[2] or the words of Solomon in the book in which he teaches the young: "Gracefulness is deceitful and beauty is vain."[3] How should they then envy me what I do not have, what I held in contempt while I had it, and what I would despise now to the utmost were it given back to me, having learned and experienced how unstable it is?
35  They cannot even envy me learning and eloquence! Learning, they declare, I have absolutely none. Eloquence, if I had any, they despise according to the modern philosophic fashion. They reject it as unworthy of a man of letters. Thus

---

[1] Juvenal, *Satire* 10.12
[2] Ovid, *Ars Amaroia* II.113
[3] Proverbs 30:31

only "infantile inability to speak" and perplexed stammering, "wisdom" trying hard to keep one eye open and "yawning drowsily" as Cicero calls it, is held in good repute nowadays. They do not call to mind "Plato, the most eloquent of all men," and—let me omit the others—"Aristotle sweet and mild," but whom they made trite. From Aristotle's ways they swerve, taking eloquence to be an     5 obstacle and a disgrace to philosophy, while he considered it a mighty adorn-ment and tried to combine it with philosophy, "prevailed upon," it is asserted, "by the fame of the orator Isocrates."

Not even virtue can they envy me, though it is beyond doubt the best and most enviable of all things. To them it seems worthless—I believe because it     10 is not inflated and puffed up with arrogance. I should wish to possess it, and, indeed, they grant it to me unanimously and willingly. Small things they have denied me, and this very greatest possession they lavish upon me as a small gift. They call me a good man, even the best of men. If only I were not bad, not the worst in God's judgment! However, at the same time they claim that I am     15 altogether illiterate, that I am a plain uneducated fellow. This is just the opposite of what men of letters have stated when judging me, I do not care with how much truth. I do not make much of what these friends deprive me of, if only what they concede me were true. Most gladly should I divide between me and these brothers of mine the inheritance of Mother Nature and heavenly Grace, so     20 that they would all be men of letters and I a good man. I should wish to know nothing of letters or just so much as would be expedient for the daily praise of God. But, alas, I fear I shall be disappointed in this my humble desire just as they will be in their arrogant opinion. At any rate, they assert that I have a good character and am very faithful in my friendship, and in this last assertion     25 they are not mistaken, unless I am.

This, incidentally, is the reason why they count me among their friends. They are not prevailed upon to do so by my efforts in studying the honorable arts or the hope ever to hear and learn truth from me. Thus it comes plainly to what Augustine tells of his Ambrose, saying: "I began to love him, not as     30 a teacher of truth, but as a man who was kind to me"; or what Cicero feels about Epicurus—Cicero approves of his character in many passages, while he everywhere condemns his intellect and rejects his doctrine.

Since all this is the case, it may be doubtful what they envy me, though there is no doubt that they do envy me something. They do not well conceal it     35 and do not curb their tongues, which are urged by an inward impulse. In men otherwise neither unbalanced nor foolish this is nothing but a clear sign of undisciplined passion. Provided that they are envious of me as they obviously are, and that there is no other object of their envy—the latent virus is expand-ing by itself at any rate. For there is one thing, one empty thing, that they envy     40

me, however trifling it may be: my name and what fame I have already won within my lifetime—greater fame perhaps than would be due to my merits or in conformity with the common habit which but very rarely celebrates living men. It is upon this fame that they have fixed their envious eyes. If only I
5   could have done without it both now and often before! I remember that it has done me harm more often than good, winning me quite a few friends but also countless enemies. It has happened to me as to those who go into battle in a conspicuous helmet though with but little strength: they gain nothing from the dazzling brightness of this chimera except to be struck by more adversaries. Such
10  pestilence was once but too familiar to me during my more flourishing years; never was there one so troublesome as that which has now blazed up. I am now an anvil too soft for young men's wars and for assuming such burdens, and this pestilence revives unexpectedly from a quarter from which I do not deserve it and did not suspect it either, at a moment when it should have been long since
15  overcome by my moral conduct or consumed by the course of time.

But I will go on: They think they are great men, and they are certainly rich, all of them, which is the only mortal greatness nowadays. They feel, although many people deceive themselves in this respect, that they have not won a name and cannot hope ever to win one if their foreboding is right. Among such sorrows
20  they languish anxiously; and so great is the power of evil that they stick out their tongues and sharpen their teeth like mad dogs even against friends and wound those whom they love. Is this not a strange kind of blindness, a strange kind of fury? In just this manner the frantic mother of Pentheus tears her son to pieces and the raving Hercules his infant children. They love me and all that is mine,
25  with the single exception of my name—which I do not refuse to change. Let them call me Thersites or Choerilus, or whatever name they prefer, provided I thus obtain that this honest love suffers not the slightest restriction. They are all the more ablaze and aglow with a blind fire, since they are all such fervent scholars, working indefatigably all night long.

30  However, the first of them has no learning at all—I tell you only what you know—the second knows a little; the third not much; the fourth—I must admit—not a little but in such confused and undisciplined order and, as Cicero says, "with so much frivolity and vain boasting that it would perhaps be better to know nothing." For letters are instruments of insanity for many, of arrogance for
35  almost everyone, if they do not meet with a good and well-trained mind....

As the first point, they said that public renown supported me, but replied that it deserved little faith. So far they did not lie, since the vulgar mass very rarely sees the truth. Then they said that friendship with the greatest and most learned men, which has adorned my life—as I shall boast before the
40  Lord—stood against their verdict. For I have enjoyed close friendship with

many kings, especially with King Robert of Sicily,[4] who honored me in my younger years with frequent and clear testimonials of my knowledge and genius. They replied—and here I will not say their iniquity but their vanity evidently made them lie—that the king himself enjoyed great fame in literary matters but had no knowledge of them; and the others, however learned they were, did 5 not show a sufficiently perspicacious judgment concerning me, whether love of me or carelessness was the cause. They then made another objection against themselves, saying that the last three Roman popes had vied with each other in inviting me—in vain, it is true—to a high rank in their intimate household, and that Urban[5] himself, who is now at the head, was wont to speak well of 10 me and had already bestowed on me a most affable letter. Besides, it is known far and wide and doubted by no one that the present Roman Emperor[6]—for there has been no other legitimate emperor at this time—counts me among his dear familiars and has been wont to call me to him with the weight of daily requests and repeated messages and letters. In all this they feel that some people 15 find some proof that I must have a certain value. However, they resolve this objection too, maintaining that the Popes went astray together with the others, following the general opinion about me, or were induced to do so by my good moral behavior and not by my knowledge; and that the emperor was prevailed upon by my studies of the past and my historical works, for in this field they 20 do not deny me some knowledge.

Furthermore, they said, another objection against them was my eloquence. This I do not acknowledge altogether, by God not. They pretend that it is a rather effective means of persuasion. It might be the task of a rhetor or an orator to speak oppositely in order to persuade for a purpose, but many people without 25 knowledge had succeeded in persuading by mere phrases. Thus they attribute to luck what is a matter of art and bring forth the widespread proverb: "Much eloquence, little wisdom."[7] They do not take into account Cato's definition of the orator, which contradicts their false charge. Finally, it was said that the style of my writing is in opposition to their statement. They did not dare to blame 30 my style, not even to praise it too reservedly, and confessed that it is rather elegant and well chosen but without any learning. I do not understand how this can be, and I trust they did not understand it either. If they regain control of themselves and think over again what they have said, they will be ashamed of their silly ineptitude. For if the first statement were true—which I for my 35

---

[4]Robert the Wise (1277–1343), King of Naples (1309–1343), sponsored Petrarch's 1341 coronation as Poet Laureate in Rome.

[5]Urban V (r. 1362–1370)

[6]Charles IV (1316–1378), Holy Roman Emperor (1355–1378)

[7]Sallust, *Catilina* 5.4

part would neither assert nor make myself believe—I have no doubt that the second is wrong. How could the style of a person who knows nothing at all be excellent, since theirs amounts to nothing, though there is nothing they do not know? Do we so far suspect everything to be fortuitous that we leave no
5    room for reason?

What else do you want? Or what do you believe? I think you expect to hear the verdict of the judges. Well, they examined each point. Then, fixing their eyes on I know not what god—for there is no god who wants iniquity, no god of envy or ignorance, which I might call the twofold cloud-shrouding
10   truth—they pronounced this short final sentence: I am a good man without learning. Even if they have never spoken the truth and never shall speak it, may they have spoken it at least this once!

O bounteous, O saving Jesus, true God and true Giver of all learning and all intelligence, true "King of Glory" and "Lord of all powers of virtue," I now
15   pray to You on the knees of my soul: If You do not wish to grant me more, let it be my portion at least to be a good man. This I cannot be if I do not love You dearly and do not adore You piously. For this purpose I am born, not for learning. If learning happens to come along, it inflates, it tears down; it does not build up. It is a glittering shackle, a toilsome pursuit, and a resounding burden
20   for the soul. You know, O Lord, before whom all my desires and all my sighs are expanded. Whenever I have made a sober use of learning, I have sought in it nothing but to become good. It was not that I was confident that learning can achieve this or that anyone can achieve it beside You, although Aristotle and many others have promised just this. I believed that the road on which I
25   made my way would become more honorable and more clearly marked, and at the same time more pleasant with the aid of literary erudition, under the guidance of You and no one else. "You who looks into the hearts and reins,"[8] You know that it is as I say. I never was such a youth, never eager for fame to such a degree—though I do not deny I coveted it occasionally—that I should
30   not have wished to be good rather than learned. I desired to be both, I confess, since human longing is boundless and insatiable until it comes to rest in You, above Whom there is no place to which it could still rise.

I desired to be both good and learned. Now that the latter is wrenched from me or denied me, I am grateful to my judges for leaving me the better of
35   the two, provided they have not lied on this point also and granted me what they are not, intending to rob me of what they wanted to have. I was to find a comfort for my loss, though an empty one. They dealt with me after the fashion of envious women. When a woman is asked whether the woman next door is beautiful, she says that she is good and has good and decent manners. All good

8Psalm 7:9

qualities—just such as are not true—she allows her, because she wants to spoil her of the single and perhaps even true title, beauty. But You, my God, "Lord of Learning," "besides Whom there is no other god," You Whom I must and will prefer to Aristotle and all the philosophers and poets and all those who "boastingly make many haughty words,"[9] to learning and doctrines and to all  5 things whatsoever. You can grant me the true name of a good man which these four grant me untruly. I pray to You, grant it to me. I do not ask so much for the good name which Solomon prefers to "precious ointments";[10] I ask for the thing itself. I want to *be* good, to love You, and to deserve to be loved by You—for no one repays his lovers like You—to think of You, to be obedient to  10 You, to set my hope in You, and to speak of You. "Let all that is obsolete shrink back from my mouth; let all my thoughts be prepared unto You." For it is true: "The bow of the mighty man has been overcome and the weak have been girded with strength."[11] Happier by far is one of these feeble ones who believe in You than Plato, Aristotle, Varro, and Cicero, who with all their knowledge did not  15 know You. "Brought before You and put next to You Who are the Rock, their judges are overthrown and their learned ignorance has become manifest."

Therefore, let learning be the portion of those who take it away from me, or since it cannot be their portion, unless I am mistaken, let it be the portion of those who may have it. Let them keep their exorbitant opinion of everything that regards them, and the naked name Aristotle which delights many  20 ignorant people by its four syllables. Moreover, let them have the vain joy and the unfounded elation which is so near to ruin; in short, let them have all the profit people who are ignorant and puffed up earn from their errors in vague and easy credulity. My portion shall be humility and ignorance, knowledge of my own weakness, and contempt for nothing except the world and myself and  25 the insolence of those who are condemning me, and, furthermore, distrust in myself and hope in You. Finally, may God be my portion and what they do not envy me, illiterate virtue. They will burst into loud laughter when they hear this and will say that I speak piously without learning like any old women. People of their kind, tumid as they are with the fever of literary erudition, know nothing  30 so vile as piety; truly and soberly literate men love it above all things. For them it is written: "Piety is wisdom." However, my talking will confirm the others more and more in their opinion that I am "a good man without learning."

What shall we say now, my most faithful Donato? I speak to you, since the sting of their grudge has wounded you more than myself, whom it actually  35 stung. What shall we do, my friend? Shall we appeal to fairer judges or shall we keep silent and confirm their decision by our silence? I prefer the latter course.

---

[10]Ecclesiastes 7:1

[11]I Samuel 2:4

I want you to know that I do not in the least refuse to await the tenth day. This very moment I acquiesce in the verdict of any judge whomsoever. I implore you and everyone whom it may concern, all you who have passed a quite different sentence on me, to hold your hands up as I do and let their verdict become right
5    by patiently accepting it. I wish it were right on the point they concede me. Willingly I confess and freely I declare their verdict is right in what they deprive me of, though I emphatically deny that they are the right judges. Perhaps they will seek support in the law of which their god Aristotle speaks when he says: "Everybody judges well of what he knows and is a good judge in that matter;
10   it would not seem likely that anything can be better known than that in which he that judges abounds." Under such a pretext the most ignorant men would be best able to judge of ignorance. But it is not so.

It is the wise man who is entitled to judge of ignorance as well as of wisdom and of anything whatsoever—wise, of course, he must be in the specific matter
15   of which he is judging. Not as musicians judge of music and grammarians of grammar do the ignorant judge of ignorance. There are things of which it is extreme destitution to have plenty. Such things are better judged by anyone else than by him who is most affluent in them. None understands less of deformity than the deformed, who has become intimate with it and does not see what
20   must offend the eye of the beautiful. The same is true with all other defects. Nobody judges worse of ignorance than the ignorant. This I do not say because I intend to reject the court but because I want those who are ignorant to be ashamed of having pronounced a verdict—provided they can be ashamed. As for the rest, I accept the sentence in this matter, not only the verdict of friendly
25   envy, but just as readily that of hatred.

To sum up: Whoever calls me ignorant shares my own opinion. Sorrowfully and tacitly I recognize my ignorance, when I consider how much I lack of what my mind in its craving for knowledge is sighing for. But until the end of the present exile has come and terminated this our imperfection by which "we know
30   in part," I console myself with the consideration that this belongs to our common nature. I suppose it happens to all good and modest minds that they learn to know themselves and then find just this same consolation. It will certainly happen even to those who have obtained a vast knowledge—vast according to the character of human knowledge, which in itself is always trifling small and
35   becomes vast only when we take into account in what straits it is conceived and compare it with the knowledge of others. How infinitely small, I beseech you, is the greatest amount of knowledge granted to one single mind! Indeed, what a man knows, whosoever he may be, is nothing when compared—I will not say with God's knowledge—but with his own ignorance. The very men who
40   know most and understand most possess, I presume, in the highest degree this

knowledge of themselves and of their own imperfection, this knowledge which I have called their consolation. My judges are happy in their errors; they do not need such a consolation. They are happy, I say, not in their knowledge, but in their error and arrogant ignorance. They believe they lack nothing of having angelic knowledge, while without doubt much of human knowledge is lacking to everyone, and to many it is entirely lacking.... 5

I come back to my censors, of whom I have said so much already and must say more now; for I want nothing to remain hidden from you. I should not like to be called silly and stupid after having been called illiterate. Learning is an adventitious ornament; reason an inborn part of man. I should not be so much ashamed of lacking erudition as of lacking reason. I had enough reason to have avoided their snares. It would not have been so easy for them to catch me by their tricks. I was trapped in my own purity and caught in the most decent veil of friendship, which I believed to be true. It is but too easy to deceive one who is confiding in you. 15

I have told you before and now repeat it: Like many other citizens of that very beautiful and very great city, they used to come and see me, very often two at a time, occasionally also all four of them together. I was delighted and received them as though they were angels of God. I forgot everything besides them, since they occupied my mind entirely, cheering me up wonderfully. 20 Without delay we started long and various talks, as is the custom among friends. I paid no attention to what I said or how I said it. I had nothing else in mind than to show a joyful face and a still more joyful heart at the arrival of such guests. At times it was joy that forced me to keep silent; at times it was also a kind of reverence which told me not to block their strong desire to speak by 25 interrupting them, as happens in such cases, and from joy I said either nothing or mere commonplaces. I have not been taught to dress up or dissemble or feign anything in the company of friends. I am wont to carry my mind on my tongue and face and never to speak to friends in any other way than I would to myself. "Nothing is more pleasant," as Cicero says. 30

Why ought we to display ostentatiously our eloquence or our learning before friends who see our hearts, our affection, and our entire personality, provided they do not question us with the intention of putting us to the test but of learning from us? In the latter case no ostentation or embellishment is needed but a trustful sharing of knowledge and all other things, free from reserve and envy. 35 I therefore often wonder why so great a prince as the Emperor Augustus could take so much pains with trifles, amid such concern for important matters, that he never said a word without thorough deliberation and frequently preferred to address in written form, not only the people and the Senate, but even his wife and friends. Perhaps he did so in order to avoid letting slip by chance from 40

his mouth a superfluous or foolish word for which his heavenly speech could be denounced or criticized. He may have been justified in so acting when from the highest peak he was addressing his subjects in written form, in oracles as it were. I prefer a casual way of talking with friends and no elaborate sentences.
5    Goodbye to eloquence if it must be obtained with such constant effort! I had rather not be eloquent than always on my guard and pedantic. This was always my intention when with dear friends and intimates, especially when they were familiar with my powers.

Lately I have practiced it more than ever in the company of these four
10   friends, and in my friendly faith I inadvertently fell into the trap of hostile calumny. I said nothing that was carefully polished, nothing that was anxiously prepared. Whatever came to my mind sprang from my mouth before it even got there. They trapped me according to a pre-concerted plan and tested every single word of mine, taking whatever I said as if I had nothing better to say
15   and could not say it more elegantly. This they did once and again and again, until they found themselves easily confirmed in a sentence they wished to be true. Nothing is easier than to persuade people who want to be persuaded and already believe. This made them speak to me all the more confidently as to an ignorant fellow and to laugh at my ignorance, as I now believe. At the time I
20   did not suspect it in the least. As I took no precautions and was but a single man, I was entangled by the artifices of many and herded into the crowd of the ignorant without being aware of it.

They used to raise an Aristotelian problem or a question concerning animals. Then I was either silent or made a joke or began another subject. Some-
25   times I smiled and asked how on earth Aristotle could have known something for which there is no reason and which cannot be proved by experience. They were amazed and felt angry at me in silence. They looked at me as though I were a blasphemer to require anything beyond his authority in order to believe it. Thus we clearly ceased to be philosophers and eager lovers of wisdom
30   and became Aristotelians, or, more correctly, Pythagoreans. They revived the ridiculous habit of allowing no further question if "he" had said so. "He," as Cicero tells us, "was Pythagoras." I certainly believe that Aristotle was a great man who knew much, but he was human and could well be ignorant of some things, even of a great many things.
35   I should say more if those who are as much friends of truth as they are of sects permitted. By God, I am convinced and I have no doubt that "he went astray," as the saying goes, "the whole length of the way," not only in what is of little weight, where an error is unimportant and by no means dangerous, but in matters of the greatest consequence, and precisely in those regarding
40   supreme salvation. Of happiness he has indeed said a good deal in the beginning

and at the end of his *Ethics*. However, I will dare to say—and my censors may shout as loud as they please—he knew so absolutely nothing of true happiness that any pious old woman, any faithful fisherman, shepherd or peasant is—I will not say more subtle but happier in recognizing it. I am therefore all the more astonished that some of our Latin authors have so much admired that 5 Aristotelian treatise as to consider it almost a crime to speak of happiness after him and that they have borne witness of this even in writing.

It may perhaps be daring to say so, but it is true, unless I am mistaken: It seems to me that he saw of happiness as much as the night owl does of the sun, namely, its light and rays and not the sun itself. For Aristotle did not establish 10 happiness within its own boundaries and did not found it on solid ground, as a high building ought to be founded, but far away in foreign territory on a trembling site, and consequently did not comprehend two things, or, if he did, ignored them. These are the two things without which there can be absolutely no happiness: Faith and Immortality. I already regret saying that he did not 15 comprehend them or ignored them. For I ought to have said only one of the two phrases. Faith and immortality were not yet comprehended: he did not know of them, nor could he know of them or hope for them. The true light had not yet begun to shine, which lights every man who comes into this world.[12] He and all the others fancied what they wished and what by his very nature every man 20 wishes and whose opposite no one can wish: a happiness of which they sang as one sings of the absent beloved, and which they adorned with words. They did not see it. Like people made happy by a dram, they rejoiced in an absolute nothing. In fact, they were miserable and to be roused to their misery by the thunder of approaching death, to see with open eyes what that happiness really 25 is like, with which they had dealt in their dreams.

Some may believe that I have said all this out of my own imagination and therefore but too frivolously. Let them then read Augustine's thirteenth book on the Trinity. There they will find many weighty and acute discussions on this subject against those philosophers who—I use his words:—"shaped their happy 30 lives for themselves, just as it pleased each of them." This, I confess, I have said often before, and I will say it as long as I can speak, because I am confident that I have spoken the truth and shall speak it in the future, too. If they consider it a sacrilege, they may accuse me of violating religion, but then they must accuse Jerome too, "who does not care what Aristotle but what Christ said." I, on the 35 contrary, should not doubt that it is they who are impious and sacrilegious if they have a different opinion. God may take my life and whatever I love most dearly before I change this pious, true, and saving conviction or disown Christ from love of Aristotle.

---

[12]John 1:9

Let them certainly be philosophers and Aristotelians, though they are neither, but let them be both: I do not envy them these brilliant names of which
they boast, and even that wrongly. In return they ought not to envy me the
humble and true name of Christian and Catholic. But why do I ask for this?
5   I know they are willing to comply with this demand quite spontaneously and
will do what I ask. Such things they do not envy us; they spurn them as simple
and contemptible, inadequate for their genius and unworthy of it. We accept in
humble faith the secrets of nature and the mysteries of God, which are higher
still; they attempt to seize them in haughty arrogance. They do not manage
10  to reach them, not even to approach them; but in their insanity they believe
that they have reached them and strike heaven with their fists. They feel just
as if they had it in their grip, satisfied with their own opinion and rejoicing in
their error. They are not held back from their insanity—I will not say by the
impossibility of such an attempt, as is expressed in the words of the Apostle
15  to the Romans: "Who has known the mind of the Lord, or who has been His
counselor?"[13] Not even by the ecclesiastical and heavenly counsel: "Seek not
what is above you and search not out things above your strength; the things that
God has commanded to you, think thereupon always and be not inquisitive in
His many works; for it is not necessary for you to behold what is hidden." Of all
20  this I will not speak: indiscriminately they despise whatever they know has been
said from Heaven—yea, let me say, what is actually true—whatever has been
said from a Catholic point of view. However, there is at least a witty word not
ineptly said by Democritus: "No one looks at what is before his feet," he said;
"it is the regions of the sky they scrutinize." And there are very clever remarks
25  Cicero made to ridicule frivolous disputants who are heedlessly arguing and
arguing about nothing, "as if they just came from the council of the gods" and
had seen with their eyes what was going on there. And, finally, there are Homer's
more ancient and sharper words, by which Jupiter deters in grave sentences not
a mortal man, not any one of the common crowd of the gods, but Juno, his
30  wife and sister, the queen of the gods, from daring to investigate his intimate
secret or presumptuously believing it could be known to her at all.

But let us return to Aristotle. His brilliance has stunned many bleary and
weak eyes and made many a man fall into the ditches of error. I know, Aristotle
has declared himself for the rule of one, as Homer had done before him. For
35  Homer says thus, as far as it has been translated for us into our prose: "Multi-
dominion is not good; let one be the lord, one the supreme commander"; and
Aristotle says: "Plurality of rule is not good; let therefore one be the ruler."
Homer meant human rulership, Aristotle divine dominion; Homer was speaking of the principate of the Greek, the other of that of all men; Homer made

---

[13]Romans 11:34

Agamemnon the Atride king and ruler, Aristotle God—so far had the dazzling brightness of truth brought light to his mind. He did not know who this king is, I believe, nor did he know how great He is. He discussed the most trifling things with so much curiosity and did not see this one and greatest of things, which many illiterate people have seen, not by another light, but because it shed  5
a very different illumination. If these friends of mine do not see that this is the case, I see that they are altogether blind and bereft of eyesight; and I should not hesitate to believe that it must be visible to all who have sound eyes, just as it can be seen that the emerald is green, the snow white, and the raven black.

Our Aristotelians will bear my audacity in a more balanced mood when I  10
say that this is not merely my opinion of a single man, though I mention him alone. However ignorant I am, I do read, and I thought I understood something, before these people discovered my ignorance. I say, I do read; but in my more flourishing years I read even more assiduously. I still read the works of poets and philosophers, particularly those of Cicero, with whose genius and style I  15
have been particularly delighted since my early youth. I find much eloquence in them and the greatest elegance and power of words. What he says regarding the gods themselves, on whose nature he has published books under this title, and religion in general, sounds to me all the more like an empty fable the more eloquently it is presented. I thank God in silence that He gave me sluggish and  20
moderate gifts and a mind that does not saunter wantonly and "does not seek things above itself," not curious in scrutinizing what is difficult to investigate and pestiferous when discovered. I am grateful that I love Christ all the more and become all the firmer in the faith in Him, the more I hear sneering at His faith. My experience has been like that of one who has been rather lukewarm  25
in his love for his father and hears people now raise their voice against him. Then the love which seemed to be lulled to sleep flames up immediately; and this must necessarily happen if the son is a true and genuine son. Often, I call Christ Himself to witness, blasphemies uttered by heretics have turned me from a Christian into a most ardent Christian. For while the ancient pagans may tell  30
many fables about their gods, they do not, at any rate, blaspheme; they have no notion of the true God; they have not heard of Christ's name—and faith results from hearing. The voices of the Apostles were heard all over the earth, and their words spread unto the end of the world; but, when their words and doctrines were resounding all over the globe, these men were already dead and buried.  35
Thus they are to be pitied rather than culpable. Then envious soil had obstructed their ears, through which they might have drunk in the saving faith.

Of all the writings of Cicero, those from which I often received the most powerful inspiration are the three books which, as I said before, he entitled *On the Nature of the Gods*. There the great genius speaks of the gods and often  40 ridicules and despises them—not too seriously, it is true. It may be that he was afraid of capital punishment, which even the Apostles feared, before the Holy Ghost came to them. He ridicules them with very effective jokes, of which he has always so many at hand, to make it clear to everyone who understands how

5   he feels with regard to what he has undertaken to discuss. When I read these passages, I often have compassion for his fate and grieve in silent sorrow that this man did not know the true God. He died only a few years before the birth of Christ. Death had closed his eyes when, alas, the end of the error-stricken night and darkness, the first rise of truth, the dawn of true light and the sun

10   of justice were so near. In the countless books he wrote, Cicero, indeed, often falls short and speaks of "gods," engulfed by the torrent of vulgar error, as I said before; but at least he ridicules them, and even in his youth, when he wrote his book *About Invention*, he said that "those who have devoted their energies to philosophy do not believe there are gods." Now it is a fact that it is true and

15   supreme philosophy to know God, not "the gods"—always provided that such knowledge is accompanied by piety and faithful worship.

When the same Cicero in his later years, in the books he wrote *About the Gods*—not about God—gains control of himself, how is he lifted up by the wings of genius! At times you would think you were hearing not a pagan phi-

20   losopher but an Apostle. Thus he says, for instance in the first book, opposing Velleius, who is defending the doctrine of Epicurus: "You have censured those who beheld the world and its limbs: heaven, earth, the seas, and their insig-nia—the sun, the moon, and the stars—and found out how the seasons bring about maturation, alteration, and all kind of vicissitudes, and who thereupon

25   began to suspect from the magnificent and wonderful works produced that there is some excellent and outstanding nature that makes, moves, rules, and governs all this."…

His argument can be summed up more or less in this way: he puts before us almost all heavenly and earthly things, the spheres of heaven and the stars,

30   the stability and fertility of the earth, the usefulness of the sea and the streams, the variety of the seasons and the winds, herbs, plants, and trees and animate beings, the wonderful nature of birds, quadrupeds, and fishes, the manifold advantages derived from all these things, like food, handicraft, transportation, remedies against illness, hunting and fowling, architecture and navigation, and

35   innumerable arts—and all this devised either by ingenious minds or by nature. Furthermore, he points out the miraculously coherent structure and disposition of body, sense and limbs, and finally reason and sedulous activity. Everything he displays with great care and eloquence. I wonder whether any writer ever treated these matters with greater heed and keener insight. And all this he does merely

40   to lead us to this conclusion: whatever we behold with our eyes or perceive with

our intellect is made by God for the well-being of man and governed by divine providence and counsel. And even when he descends to individuals, when he mentions, if I am right, fourteen outstanding Roman leaders, Cicero adds: "We must believe that without the aid of God none of them was the man he was," and soon afterward: "Without divine inspiration no one was ever a great man." 5
And by inspiration a pious man can doubtless understand nothing but the Holy Ghost. Therefore, not to speak of his eloquence, which was unequaled among men, what would any Catholic author change in this sentence?

What shall we conclude from all this? Shall I count Cicero among Catholics? I wish I could. Were I but allowed to do so, if He who gave him such gifts 10 had but permitted him also to know Himself, as He granted permission to seek Him! Though the true God does not need our praise and mortal speech, we should now have hymns to the glory of God in our churches that would not be more true and holy, I presume—for this can neither be nor is it to be hoped for—but perhaps more melodious and more resounding. 15

However, far be it from me to espouse the genius of a single man in its totality because of one or two well-formulated phrases. Philosophers must not be judged from isolated words but from their uninterrupted coherence and consistency.[14] This I have learned from Cicero himself and from inborn reason. Who is so uncouth that he does not occasionally say a graceful word? But is that 20 enough? Often one word hides for the moment much ignorance; often bright eyes and fair hair veil ugly defects of the body. He who wants to be safe in praising the entire man must see, examine, and estimate the entire man. It happens that, side by side with what is pleasing, something else is hidden that offends as much or even more. Thus Cicero himself returns to his "gods" to the point 25 of nausea, in the very same book in which he has discussed many subjects most seriously and in a manner very closely resembling piety. He gives an account of the names and qualities of each of these gods, no longer intent on dealing with the providence of "God" but with that of "the gods." Listen, please, what he puts in: "We must venerate and worship these gods," he says, "and the best 30 and at the same time the most chaste form of worshiping the gods, that which is overflowing with piety, is adoring them with unabatedly pure, unpolluted, and uncorrupted mind and voice."

Alas, my dear Cicero, what did you say? So quickly have you forgotten the one God and yourself. Where did you leave that "outstanding Nature" and "that 35

[14]A significant difference between medieval and Renaissance humanists was their approach to classical authors. Medieval humanists viewed them as timeless authorities and looked for the truths contained in their works, whereas Renaissance humanists saw them as fellow human beings with whom they wished to communicate, albeit across a wide gulf. This meant that Medievals often took passages out of context, while Renaissance humanists saw the context as crucial to their understanding of what the author was trying to say.

Divine Being of most outstanding mind"? Where is now "the God who is better than man," and "the Maker of whatever cannot be made by human reason," "the Maker of all that is in heaven, and of the everlasting order we behold?" Where did you leave "the Inmate of the heavenly and divine mansion," moreover "the Ruler
5   and Supervisor and, as it were, Architect of this huge work"? You have almost driven Him out of the starry mansion you had allotted Him in that beautiful confession by giving Him such mean and unworthy companions, though He disdains them and proclaims through the voice of a prophet: "See ye that I alone am, and there is no other god besides me." Who are these new, these recent and infamous gods
10  whom you try to smuggle into the house of the Lord? Are they not those of whom another prophet says: "All gods of the nations are demons; it is the Lord who makes the heavens." Just now you spoke of that Maker and Creator of the heavens and all things, pleasing with good reason the ears and heart of a pious hearer. Thus quickly you group Him with rebellious creatures and impure spirits. With one
15  word you tear down whatever you seemed to say wisely and soberly....

     If I have said all this of my Cicero, whom I admire in many ways, what do you expect me to say of others? Many men have written many things in a subtle manner, some even in grave, pleasant, and eloquent form. But they have blended some false, dangerous, and ridiculous things with their words, as if they
20  were mixing poison with honey. A discussion of all this would take too much time and is not to the point here. Not in every case should I have the excuse Cicero had: not everyone is so alluring; and, though their subjects may also be sublime, they have not all his sweetness of speech. It happens often that one and the same song sounds pleasant or annoying according to the different persons
25  who sing it, and a different voice produces the same song very differently....

     But let me now at last, though late enough, return to where I started. For I have been driven off my course by the chain of related subjects. In this whole field Aristotle must be most carefully avoided, not because he committed more errors, but because he has more authority and more followers.
30       Forced by truth or by shame, they will perhaps confess that Aristotle did not see enough of divine and eternal things, since they are far removed from pure intellect. However, they will contend that he did foresee whatever is human and temporal. Thus we come back to what Macrobius says when he is disputing against this philosopher either jokingly or in earnest. "It seems to me that there
35  was nothing this great man could not know." Just the opposite seems to me true. I would not admit that any man had knowledge of all things through human study. This is why I am torn to pieces, and though envy has another root; this is what is claimed to be the reason: I do not adore Aristotle.
     But I have another whom to adore. He does not promise me empty and
40  frivolous conjectures of deceitful things which are of use for nothing and not

supported by any foundation. He promises me the knowledge of Himself. When He grants this to me, it will appear superfluous to busy myself with other things that are created by Him—one will see that it is easy to grasp them and, consequently, ridiculous to investigate them. It is He in whom I can trust, whom I must adore; it is He whom my judges ought to worship piously. If they did, they would know that philosophers have told many lies—those I mean who are philosophers by name, for true philosophers are wont to say nothing but what is true.[15] However, to their number Aristotle does not belong, nor even Plato, of whom our Latin philosophers have said that "he came nearer to truth than any one of the entire set of ancient philosophers."

These friends of ours, I have already said, are so captivated by their love of the mere name "Aristotle" that they call it a sacrilege to pronounce any opinion that differs from his on any matter. From this position they derive their crucial argument for my ignorance, namely, that I said something of virtue—I do not know what—otherwise than he did and did not say it in a sufficiently Aristotelian manner. It is very possible that I said something not merely different but even contradictory. I should not necessarily have said it badly, for I am "not bound to swear to the words of any master," as Horace says of himself. It is possible, too, that I said the same thing he said, though in other words, and that these friends of mine who judge of everything without understanding everything, had the impression that I said something else. The majority of the ignorant lot clings to words, as the shipwrecked do to a wooden plank, and believe that a matter cannot be better said and cannot be phrased otherwise: so great is the destitution of their intellect or of their speech, by which conceptions are expressed. I must confess, I have not too much delight in that man's style, as we have it; though I have learned from Greek witnesses and from Cicero's authority, long before I was condemned by the verdict of ignorance, that it is sweet and rich and ornate in his own tongue. It is due either to the rudeness or to the envious disposition of his interpreters that his style has come down to us so harsh and shabby. It cannot fully please our ears and does not stick to our memory. For this reason it is occasionally more agreeable for the hearer and more convenient for the speaker to express Aristotle's mind not in the words he used but in one's own.

Moreover, I do not dissemble what I have said very often to friends and must now write down here. I am well aware of the great danger threatening my fame and of the great new charge of ignorance brought against me. Nevertheless, I will write it down and will not fear the judgment of men: Let all hear me who are Aristotelians anywhere. You know how easily they will spit at the lonely

---

[15]Philosophy = *phil* + *sophia* = love of wisdom. "True philosophy," then, is the love of true wisdom, i.e., the love of God.

stranger, this tiny little booklet; they are a lot prone to insult. But for this the little book may take care itself. Let it look for a linen cloth to wipe itself clean; I shall be content if they do not spit at me. Let all the Aristotelians hear, I say, and since Greece is deaf to our tongue, let all those hear whom all Italy harbors
5   and France and contentious Paris with its noisy Straw Lane.[16]

I have read all Aristotle's moral books if I am not mistaken. Some of them I have also heard commented on. I seemed to understand something of them before this huge ignorance was detected. Sometimes I have perhaps become more learned through them when I went home, but not better, not so good
10  as I ought to be; and I often complained to myself, occasionally to others too, that by no facts was the promise fulfilled which the philosopher makes at the beginning of the first book of his *Ethics*, namely, that "we learn this part of philosophy not with the purpose of gaining knowledge but of becoming better." I see virtue, and all that is peculiar to vice as well as to virtue, egregiously
15  defined and distinguished by him and treated with penetrating insight. When I learn all this, I know a little bit more than I knew before, but mind and will remain the same as they were, and I myself remain the same. It is one thing to know, another to love; one thing to understand, another to will. He teaches what virtue is, I do not deny that; but his lesson lacks the words that sting and
20  set afire and urge toward love of virtue and hatred of vice or, at any rate, does not have enough of such power. He who looks for that will find it in our Latin writers, especially in Cicero and Seneca, and, what may be astonishing to hear, in Horace, a poet somewhat rough in style but most pleasing in his maxims.

However, what is the use of knowing what virtue is if it is not loved when
25  known? What is the use of knowing sin if it is not abhorred when it is known? If the will is bad, it can, by God, drive the lazy wavering mind toward the worse side, when the rigidity of virtue and the alluring ease of vice become apparent. Nor ought we to be astonished. Aristotle was a man who ridiculed Socrates, the father of this kind of philosophy, calling him—to use his own words—"a peddler
30  in morals, and despised him" if we believe Cicero, "though Socrates despised him no less."[17] No wonder that he is slow in rousing the mind and lifting it up to virtue. However, everyone who has become thoroughly familiar with our Latin authors knows that they stamp and drive deep into the heart the sharpest and most ardent stings of speech, by which the lazy are startled, the ailing are
35  kindled, and the sleepy aroused, the sick healed, and the prostrate raised, and those who stick to the ground lifted up to the highest thoughts and to honest desire. Then earthly things become vile; the aspect of vice stirs up an enormous

---

[16]Most classrooms of the University of Paris were located on Straw Lane.

[17]This remark is chronologically difficult; Socrates died in 399 BC and Aristotle was not born until 384. Perhaps Petrarch meant Plato.

hatred of vicious life; virtue and "the shape, and as it were, the face of honesty," are beheld by the inmost eye "and inspire miraculous love" of wisdom and of themselves, "as Plato says." I know but too well that all this cannot be achieved outside the doctrine of Christ and without His help: no one can become wise and good who has not drunk a large draught—not from the fabulous spring of Pegasus in the folds of Mount Parnassus—but from the true and unique source which has its origin in heaven, the source of the water that springs up in eternal life. Those who drink from it no longer thirst.[18] However, much is achieved also by the authors of whom I have just spoken. They are a great help to those who are making their way to this goal.

This is what many a man has thought of many of their writings, and Augustine professes such an opinion, explicitly naming Cicero's *Hortensius*, in grateful remembrance of what he experienced while reading it.[19] For though our ultimate goal does not lie in virtue, where the philosophers locate it, it is through the virtues that the direct way leads to the place where it does lie; and these virtues, I must add, must be not merely known but loved. Therefore, the true moral philosophers and useful teachers of the virtues are those whose first and last intention is to make hearer and reader good, those who do not merely teach what virtue and vice are and hammer into our ears the brilliant name of the one and the grim name of the other but sow into our hearts love of the best and eager desire for it and at the same time hatred of the worst and how to flee it. It is safer to strive for a good and pious will than for a capable and clear intellect. The object of the will, as it pleases the wise, is to be good; that of the intellect is truth. It is better to will the good than to know the truth. The first is never without merit; the latter can often be polluted with crime and then admits no excuse. Therefore, those are far wrong who consume their time in learning to know virtue instead of acquiring it, and, in a still higher degree, those whose time is spent in learning to know God instead of loving Him. In this life it is impossible to know God in His fullness; piously and ardently to love Him is possible. This love is a blessing at all times whatsoever; this knowledge sometimes makes us miserable—as does that knowledge the demons have, who tremble below in hell before Him they have learned to know. Things that are absolutely unknown are not loved; but, for those to whom more is not granted, it is sufficient to know God and virtue so far as to know that He is the most lucid, the most fragrant, the most delectable, the inexhaustible source of all that is good, from which, through which, and in which we are as good as we are, and to know that virtue is the best thing next to God Himself. When we know this, we shall love Him for His sake with our heart and marrows, and

---

[18]John 4:14
[19]Augustine, *Confessions*, VIII.17

virtue we shall love for His sake too. We shall revere Him as the unique author
of life, virtue we shall cultivate as its foremost adornment.

Since this is the case, it is perhaps not reprehensible, as my judges think, to
trust our own philosophers, although they are not Greek, particularly in matters
5    of virtue. If following them, and perhaps my own judgment too, I said something,
even if Aristotle has said it otherwise or said something different, I hope not to
lose my good reputation before fairer judges. Well known is the Aristotelian
habit, as it is expressed by Chalcidius in Plato's *Timaeus*: "In a manner peculiar
to him he picks out from a complete and perfect dogma what appears to him
10   to be right and neglects the rest in disdainful lack of interest." I may therefore
have said that he disdained to treat or neglected some matters or perhaps did
not think of them. I may really have said so; it is not incompatible with human
nature, though, if we follow our friends, that it does not agree with the fame of
the great man—provided I said something of the kind—for I do not remember
15   well what it was, and these men assail me with accusations that are not all too
sincere and not definite enough and make use of suspicions and murmured hints
instead. Is this, then, a sufficient reason for plunging me so deep into the floods
of ignorance and charging me with every error, because I was mistaken on one
single point—on a point on which I was perhaps not even wrong while they were?
20   Must I be condemned as always in error and knowing nothing whatever?

Here someone might say: What does all this mean? Do you snarl at Aristotle
too? At Aristotle not in the least but in behalf of the truth which I love though I
do not know it. I snarl at the stupid Aristotelians, who day by day in every single
word they speak do not cease to hammer into the heads of others Aristotle whom
25   they know by name only. He himself, I suppose, and their audience will at last
become sick and tired of it. For recklessly these people distort his words into a
wrong sense, even those which are right. Nobody loves and respects illustrious
men more than I. To genuine philosophers and particularly to true theologians
I apply what Ovid says: "Whenever poets were present, I believed gods were
30   there in person." I would not say all this of Aristotle if I did not know him to be
a very great man. He was a very great man, I know, but, as I have said, he was
human. I know that much can be learned from his books, but I am convinced
that outside of them much can be learned also; and I do not doubt that some men
knew a great deal before Aristotle wrote, before he studied, before he was born.
35   I will mention only Homer, Hesiodus, Pythagoras, Anaxagoras, Democritus,
Diogenes, Solon, and Socrates, and the prince of philosophy, Plato.

And who, they will say, has assigned this principate to Plato? I answer, not
I, but truth, as is said—that truth which he saw and to which he came nearer
than all the others, though he did not comprehend it. Moreover, there are many
40   authorities who assign this highest rank to him: first of all Cicero and Virgil—who

does not mention his name, it is true, but was a follower of his—then Pliny and Plotinus, Apuleius and Macrobius, Porphyry and Censorinus, Josephus, and among our Christian authors Ambrose, Augustine, and Jerome, and many others still. This could easily be proved if it were not known to everybody.

And who has not assigned this principate to him except the crazy and clamor-    5
ous set of Scholastics? That Averroes prefers Aristotle to all others comes from the fact that he undertook to comment upon his works and made them, as it were, his own property. These works deserve much praise, but the man who praises them is suspect. For it comes back to the old adage: "Every tradesman praises his own merchandise." There are people who do not dare to write anything of their    10
own. Eager to write, they become interpreters of the works of others. Like those who have no notion of architecture, they make it their profession to whitewash walls. They attempt to obtain the praise they cannot hope to acquire by them-selves, not even with the help of others, unless they praise above everyone else those authors and their books—the objects of their efforts—in an excited and    15
at the same time immoderate tone and always with great exaggeration. There are a great many people who comment upon the works of others—or, should I say, devastate them?—especially nowadays. More than any other work, the *Book of Sentences*[20] would bear witness to such devastation in a clear and complaining voice if it could speak: it has been the victim of thousands of such craftsmen.    20
And was there ever a commentator who did not praise the work he had adopted as though it were his own, or even more profusely than he would have extolled his own, since it is a token of refined manners to praise the work of another, while it betrays vanity and haughtiness to praise one's own product?

Let me omit those who chose entire books: one of them, or the most prominent    25
of them, is Averroes. It is well known what Macrobius, an eminent commenta-tor, but an eminent writer too, added at the end of his commentary, in which it was his purpose to interpret not even all the books of Cicero's *Republic* but only a part of one of them: "I must indeed declare," he says, "that there is nothing more perfect than this work: it contains the whole philosophy in its complete    30
and perfect state." Imagine, now, he spoke not of a part of a book but of all the books of all philosophers. Even with more words he could not have said more, for to a complete and perfect state only superfluous things can be added. Can therefore more than this complete perfection be contained in all the books that ever have been or will be written by philosophers—always provided that even    35
all books taken together could ever contain or will contain this perfection and that something is not missing in the first of them just as it will be missing in the very last?

---

[20]Peter Lombard's major work, *Four Books of Sentences*, served as the standard theological textbook in the Middle Ages.

So much for this matter. I know—as I have said before—that I am striking the hard rock of fame in not only mentioning such great philosophers but attempting to compare them with one another. The ignorance laid to my charge and never rejected will excuse my style, for ignorance is in the habit of making
5   people bold and loquacious. Orators are usually kept in check by the fear of losing their reputation or seeing it belittled. Of such fear I am relived by the verdict of my friends. What should I still fear? What I have lost cannot be lost a second time and can no longer be diminished. However I appraise it, it will amount to just what my friends figure it in their decision, or perhaps to a little
10  bit more: nothing can be less than nothing.

Having reached this point under the impulse of whatever kind of inspiration it may be, I shall at last try to find my way out as well as I can. I shall say what I remember having answered often enough to great men who asked me. If the question is raised, "Who was the greater and more brilliant man, Plato
15  or Aristotle?" my ignorance is not so great—though my friends attribute to me so much of it—that I should dare to pronounce a hasty judgment. We ought to keep our judgment under control and ponder it scrupulously even in matters of minor importance. Moreover, it does not slip from my memory how often a great dispute has broken out among learned men about learned men,
20  for instance, about Cicero and Demosthenes, or the same Cicero and Virgil, about Virgil and Homer, or Sallustius and Thucydides; finally about Plato and his schoolfellow Xenophon, and many others. In all these cases an inquiry is difficult to make and an appraisal would be questionable. Who will then sit in court and pass a judgment in the case Plato versus Aristotle? However, if the
25  question is asked, "Which of the two is more praised?" I would state without hesitation that in my opinion the difference between them is like that between two persons of whom one is praised by princes and nobles, the other by the entire mass of common people. Plato is praised by the greater men, Aristotle by the bigger crowd; and both deserve to be praised by great men as well as by many,
30  even by all men. Both have come as far in natural and human matters as one can advance with the aid of mortal genius and study. In divine matters Plato and the Platonists rose higher, though none of them could reach the goal he aimed at. But, as I have said, Plato came nearer to it. No Christian and particularly no faithful reader of Augustine's books will hesitate to confirm this, nor do the
35  Greeks deny it, however ignorant of letters they are in our time; in the footsteps of their forebears they call Plato "divine" and Aristotle "demonious."

On the other hand, I know quite well how strongly Aristotle has the habit of disputing against Plato in his books. Let him look to it, how honestly he does so and how remote from suspicion of envy he is. It is true that in some
40  passage he asserts that "Plato is his friend, but truth his better friend still," but

at the same time he ought to take to himself particularly the saying: "It is easy to quarrel with a dead man." Moreover, many very great men took up the defense of Plato after his death, especially on account of his Ideas, against which this eminently passionate disputant exerted every nerve of his genius so powerfully. Best known and very effective is the defense made by Augustine. I should believe that a pious reader will agree with him no less than with Aristotle or Plato.

Here I should like to insert only a word to refute the error of my judges and whoever agrees with them. It is their habit to form an opinion following closely the footsteps of the vulgar mass and insolently and ignorantly as well claiming that Aristotle wrote much. Not that they are wrong in saying this. There is no doubt that he wrote much, even more than they think; for there are some works which the Latin language does not possess as yet. However, they assert that Plato, whom they hate, whom they do not know, and whom they dislike, did not write anything except one or two small little books. This they would not say if they were as learned as they declare me to be unlearned. I am not versed in letters and am no Greek. Nevertheless, I have sixteen or more of Plato's books at home, of which I do not know whether they have ever heard the names. They will be amazed when they hear this. If they do not believe it, let them come and see. My library, which I left in your hand, is not illiterate, though it is the library of an illiterate man. It is not unknown to them. When they were testing me, they often set foot in it. Let them enter it now and test Plato, whether he, too, is famous without letters. They will find that it is as I say and will confess that I may be ignorant but am no liar, I expect. These most literate men will see not only several Greek writings of his but also some which are translated into Latin, all of which they have never seen elsewhere. They are free to judge of their value; of their number they will not dare to judge otherwise than I say and will not dispute it, however litigious they are. And how small a portion of Plato is this? I have seen many other works of his with my own eyes, especially in the hands of Barlaam the Calabrian, that modern example of Greek wisdom, who once began to teach me Greek. Though I am ignorant of Latin learning, and would perhaps have made me make good progress if death had not enviously bereaved me of him, thus obstructing the honest beginnings as is its custom.

Much too vagrantly am I rambling along at the heels of my ignorance, much too much am I indulging my mind and my pen. It is time to return. These and similar reasons brought me before the friendly and nevertheless unfair court of my friends—a strange combination of attributes! As far as I understand, none has so much weight as the fact that, though I am a sinner, I certainly am a Christian. It is true, I might well hear the reproach once launched at Jerome, as he himself reports: "You lie, you are a Ciceronian. For where your treasure

is, there is your heart also."[21] Then I shall answer: My incorruptible treasure and the superior part of my soul is with Christ; but, because of the frailties and burdens of mortal life, which are not only difficult to bear but difficult merely to enumerate, I cannot, I confess, lift up, however ardently I should wish, the
5    inferior parts of my soul, in which the irascible and concupiscible appetites are located, and cannot make them cease to cling to earth. I call upon Christ as witness and invoke Him: He alone knows how often I have tried again and again, sadly and indignantly and with the greatest effort, to drag them up from the ground and how much I suffer because I have not succeeded. Christ will perhaps
10  have compassion on me and lend me a helping hand in the sound attempt of my frail soul, which is weighed down and depressed by the mass of its sins.

In the meantime I do not deny that I am given to vain and injurious cares. But among these I do not count Cicero. I know that he has never done me harm; often has he brought me benefit. Nobody will be astonished to hear this
15  from me, when he hears Augustine assert that he has had a similar experience. I remember discussing this a little while ago and even more explicitly. Therefore, I shall now be content with this simple statement: I do not deny that I am delighted with Cicero's genius and eloquence, seeing that even Jerome—to omit countless others—was so fascinated by him that he could not free his own
20  style from that of Cicero, not even under the pressure of the terrible vision and of the insults of Rufinus. It always retained a Ciceronian flavor. He feels this himself, and in one place he apologizes for it.

Cicero, read with a pious and modest attitude, did no harm to him or to anybody else at any time. He was profitable to everybody, so far as eloquence is
25  concerned, to many others as regards living. This is especially true in Augustine's case, as I have already said. Augustine filled his pockets and his lap with the gold and silver of the Egyptians when he was about to depart from Egypt. Destined to be the great fighter for the Church, the great champion of Faith, he girded his loins with the weapons of the enemy, long before he went into battle. When
30  such weapons are in question, especially when eloquence is concerned, I confess, I admire Cicero as much or even more than all whoever wrote a line in any nation. However, much as I admire him, I do not imitate him. I rather try to do the contrary, since I do not want to be too much of an imitator of anybody and am afraid of becoming what I do not approve in others.

35  If to admire Cicero means to be a Ciceronian, I am a Ciceronian. I admire him so much that I wonder at people who do not admire him. This may appear a new confession of my ignorance, but this is how I feel, such is my amazement. However, when we come to think or speak of religion, that is, of supreme truth and true happiness, and of eternal salvation, then I am certainly not a Ciceronian,

---

[21]Matthew 6:21; Luke 12:34

or a Platonist, but a Christian. I even feel sure that Cicero himself would have been a Christian if he had been able to see Christ and to comprehend His doctrine. Of Plato, Augustine does not in the least doubt that he would have become a Christian if he had come to life again in Augustine's time or had foreseen the future while he lived. Augustine relates also that in his time most of the Platonists had become Christians and he himself can be supposed to belong to their number. If this fundament stands, in what way is Ciceronian eloquence opposed to the Christian dogma? Or how is it harmful to consult Cicero's writings, if reading the books of heretics does no harm, nay, is profitable, according to the words of the Apostle: "There must be heresies that they which are approved may be made manifest to you." Besides, any pious Catholic, however unlearned he may be, will find much more credit with me in this respect than Plato or Cicero.

These, then, are the more valid arguments for our ignorance. By God, I am so glad they are true that I wish them to become more true every day. Indeed, I agree perfectly with what certain eminent men have said—that these arrogant and ignorant people will charge any philosopher, however famous, and even their god Aristotle, with being rude and ignorant, as soon as they hear that one of them has come to life again and has become a Christian. In their arrogant ignorance they will look down on the same man to whom they before looked up in reverence, as if he had forgotten what he had learned just because he had turned away from the beclouded and loquacious ignorance of this world to the wisdom of God the Father: so rare is truth and so much is it hated. "Victorinus" was reputed to be such a brilliant man that he "deserved and got a statue in the Roman Forum," while he was still teaching rhetoric. I have no doubt that as soon as he professed Christ and the true Faith with clear and saving voice, he was considered dull and downright delirious by those arrogant demon-worshipers whom he feared so much to offend that, as Augustine reports in his *Confessions*, he delayed his conversion for quite a while. Just the same I suspect Augustine did himself. I suspect it all the more, because he was a more brilliant figure and his conversion was more conspicuous. The enemies of Christ and His Church were the more exasperated and grieved the more propitious and gratifying it was for the faithful when he resigned his chair of rhetoric in Milan—as he mentions in his same *Confessions*—grasped the heavenly wisdom under the guidance of Ambrose, that most faithful and holy herald of truth, and, ceasing to be a commentator of Cicero, was about to become a preacher of Christ.

Here let me tell what I once heard said of him, for I want you to understand how grave, how pestiferous, how deeply rooted this disease is. It happened that I once quoted some maxim of Augustine's to a man with a great name, and he took a deep breath and said, "What a pity that a genius like him was so deeply entangled in empty fables!"

I replied, "How miserable are you to say such a thing; most miserable if you really believe it."

But he smiled and retorted: "On the contrary, it is you who are stupid, if you believe what you say, though I hope better for you." What else might he hope 5 for me than that I should silently agree with him in his contempt of piety?

By all faith in God and men, in the judgment of such people nobody can be a man of letters unless he is also a heretic and a madman besides being impertinent and impudent, a two-legged animal disputing about four-legged animals and beasts everywhere in the streets and squares of every city. No wonder my 10 friends declare me not only ignorant but mad, since they doubtless belong to that sort of people who despise piety without regard to the attitude in which it is practiced and take diffidence to be a religious habit. They believe that a man has no great intellect and is hardly learned unless he dares to raise his voice against God and to dispute against the Catholic Faith, silent before Aristotle alone. The 15 more boldly a man ventures to attack Faith—for he will not be able to seize this fortress by the power of intelligence or by violence—the more these men think him highly gifted and learned. The more faithful and pious he proves to be when defending Faith, the more he is supposed to be slow of perception and unlearned, the more he is suspected of using Faith as a veil to cover and mask himself, in 20 consciousness of his ignorance. They act just as if the old fables they tell were not inconsistent and shaky and their silly talk empty and void; as if there could be had certain knowledge of ambiguous and unknown matters and not merely vague, loose, and uncertain opinions; as if knowledge of the true Faith were not the highest, most certain, and ultimately most beatifying of all knowledge. If one 25 deserts it, all other knowledge is not a path but a road with a dead end, not a goal but a disaster, not knowledge but error. However, these friends of our have a strange mentality and a peculiar way of forming their judgments. I am not sure whether the two philosophers of whom I have just now spoken, or others like them, would—I will not say: "have begun to displease the Jews, whom they 30 had pleased all the while before," as Jerome tells us in his interpretation of Paul's *Epistle to the Galatians*, but appear to these, our friends, just as raving mad as Paul appeared to the Pharisees and priests, since he had become a lamb instead of a wolf, an Apostle of Christ instead of a persecutor of the Christian name.

Therefore, it can be a comfort to me to be charged with ignorance. Even 35 were I charged with madness, it would be a comfort—since such great men are my companions. And it *is* a comfort to me: sometimes I am even delighted in my heart and happy to be accused, for honorable reasons, not only of ignorance, but even of madness....

# THE NEW EDUCATION
## PETRUS PAULUS VERGERIUS (1370–1444)

*Peter Paul Vergerius the Elder was an archetypical Renaissance man. As doctor of rhetoric, medicine, and canon law, he taught at universities in Padua, Bologna, and Florence. His wit and style revealed themselves in the earliest known Renaissance comedy,* Paulus, *which Vergerius wrote in 1390. A canon of the Cathedral of Ravenna, he played a part in the Ecumenical Council of Constance (1414–1418) and represented orthodox Catholicism against the Hussites at Prague (1420). His reputation for learning and wisdom led to his appointment as secretary to Sigismund, Holy Roman Emperor (r. 1433–1437) and King of Hungary (r. 1368–1437).*

*Employed by the Lord of Padua to educate his son, Ubertino, Vergerius wrote what became the preeminent Renaissance treatise on education,* On the Noble Character and Liberal Studies of Youth. *In this widely read work, Vergerius defined the proper subjects of study, and explained their benefits to students. Immensely influential, this work appeared in more than twenty editions by 1500, and was sold in every European capital.*

*c.* 1404

We call those studies liberal which are worthy of a free man; those studies by which we attain and practice virtue and wisdom; that education which calls forth, trains, and develops those highest gifts of body and of mind which ennoble men, and which are rightly judged to rank next in dignity to virtue only. For to a vulgar temper gain and pleasure are the one aim of existence, to 5 a lofty nature, moral worth and fame. It is, then, of the highest importance that even from infancy this aim, this effort, should constantly be kept alive in growing minds. For I may affirm with fullest conviction that we shall not have attained wisdom in our later years unless in our earliest we have sincerely entered on its search.... 10

Our youth of today, it is to be feared, is backward to learn; studies are accounted irksome. Boys hardly weaned begin to claim their own way, at a time when every art should be employed to bring them under control and attract

---

W. H. Woodward, *Vittorino da Feltre and other Humanist Educators* (Cambridge: Cambridge University Press, 1897), 102–10.

them to grave studies.... Or again, parents encourage their sons to follow a career traditional in their family, which may divert them from liberal studies: and the customary pursuits of the city in which we dwell exercise a decided influence on our choice.

5      In your own case, Ubertinus, you had before you the choice of training in Arms or in Letters. Either holds a place of distinction amongst the pursuits which appeal to men of noble spirit; either leads to fame and honor in the world. It would have been natural that you, the scion of a House ennobled by its prowess in arms, should have been content to accept your father's permission
10    to devote yourself wholly to that discipline. But to your great credit you elected to become proficient in both alike: to add to the career of arms traditional in your family, an equal success in that other great discipline of mind and character, the study of Literature....

Indeed the power which good books have of diverting our thoughts from
15    unworthy or distressing themes is another support to my argument for the study of letters. Add to this their helpfulness on those occasions when we find ourselves alone, without companions and without pre-occupations—what can we do better than gather our books around us? In them we see unfolded before us vast stores of knowledge, for our delight, it may be, or for our inspiration.
20    In them are contained the records of the great achievements of men; the wonders of Nature; the works of Providence in the past, the key to her secrets of the future. And, most important of all, this Knowledge is not liable to decay. With a picture, an inscription, a coin, books share a kind of immortality. In all these memory is, as it were, made permanent; although, in its freedom from
25    accidental risks, Literature surpasses every other form of record.

Literature indeed exhibits not facts alone, but thoughts, and their expression. Provided such thoughts be worthy, and worthily expressed, we feel assured that they will not die: although I do not think that thoughts without style will be likely to attract much notice or secure a sure survival. What greater charm can
30    life offer than this power of making the past, the present, and even the future, our own by means of literature? How bright a household is the family of books! we may cry, with Cicero. In their company is no noise, no greed, no self-will: at a word they speak to you, at a word they are still; to all our requests their response is ever ready and to the point. Books indeed are a higher-a wider, more
35    tenacious-memory, a store-house which is the common property of us all....

We come now to the consideration of the various subjects which may rightly be included under the name of "Liberal Studies." Amongst these I accord the first place to History, on grounds both of its attractiveness and of its utility, qualities which appeal equally to the scholar and to the statesman. Next in importance
40    ranks Moral Philosophy, which indeed is, in a peculiar sense, a "Liberal Art,"

in that its purpose is to teach men the secret of true freedom. History, then, gives us the concrete examples of the precepts inculcated by philosophy. The one shows what men should do, the other what men have said and done in the past, and what practical lessons we may draw therefrom for the present day. I would indicate as the third main branch of study, Eloquence, which indeed 5 holds a place of distinction amongst the refined Arts. By philosophy we learn the essential truth of things, which by eloquence we so exhibit in orderly adornment as to bring conviction to differing minds. And history provides the light of experienced cumulative wisdom fit to supplement the force of reason and the persuasion of eloquence. For we allow that soundness of judgment, wisdom of 10 speech, integrity of conduct are the marks of a truly liberal temper....

The Art of Letters, however, rests upon a different footing. It is a study adapted to all times and to all circumstances, to the investigation of fresh knowledge or to the re-casting and application of old. Hence the importance of grammar and of the rules of composition must be recognized at the outset, 15 as the foundation on which the whole study of Literature must rest: and closely associated with these rudiments, the art of disputation or logical argument....

Respecting the general place of liberal studies, we remember that Aristotle would not have them absorb the entire interests of life: for he kept steadily 20 in view the nature of man as a citizen, an active member of the State. For the man who has surrendered himself absolutely to the attractions of Letters or of speculative thought follows, perhaps, a self-regarding end and is useless as a citizen or as prince.

# Oration on the Dignity of Man
## Giovanni Pico (1463–1494)

*Unlike the humanists of the early Renaissance, Giovanni Pico, Count della Mirandola, was more concerned with philosophy than with rhetoric and ethics. He studied at the universities of Padua and Paris, and he had a great respect for the Scholastics. Pico's philosophical leanings were Neo-Platonist, as were those of a number of his contemporaries in Florence. Neo-Platonism emphasized the ideas of transcendent reality that the mind had the ability to understand, and a hierarchy of beings, all of which were related to one another through their participation in the hierarchy. Since man possessed spiritual, physical, and intellectual natures, he had the ability to move up or down this chain of being. Pico believed strongly that all philosophical schools contributed to one universal truth; he studied not only Greek and Latin thought, but also Jewish and Arabic philosophy, in their original languages, in keeping with the humanist insistence on going directly to the source.*

*Pico wrote the* Oration on the Dignity of Man *as an introductory speech for a disputation on 900 theses which he proposed to hold in January 1487. He never published the* Oration *because the disputation never took place; instead, Pope Innocent VIII (r. 1484–1492) appointed a commission to investigate the theses, some of which it declared to be heretical. In consequence, Pico was under suspicion for several years. As a result, at the end of his life he began to devote himself seriously to religion, becoming a follower of the controversial Florentine preacher Girolamo Savonarola (1452–1498).*

1486

I have read in the records of the Arabians, reverend Fathers, that Abdala the Saracen, when questioned as to what on this stage of the world, as it were, could be seen most worthy of wonder, replied, "There is nothing to be seen more wonderful than man." In agreement with this opinion is the saying of Hermes Trismegistus, "A great miracle, Asclepius, is man."

5

But when I weighed the reason for these maxims, the many grounds for the excellence of human nature reported by many men failed to satisfy me—that

---

*The Renaissance Philosophy of Man*, edited by Ernst Cassirer et al. (Chicago: University of Chicago Press, 1948), 223–25. Reprinted with permission of University of Chicago Press; permission conveyed through Copyright Clearance Center, Inc.

man is the intermediary between creatures, the intimate of the gods, the king of the lower beings, by the acuteness of his senses, by the discernment of his reason, and by the light of his intelligence the interpreter of nature, the interval between fixed eternity and fleeting time, and (as the Persians say) the bond,
5   nay, rather, the marriage song of the world, on David's testimony but little lower than the angels. Admittedly great though these reasons be, they are not the principal grounds, that is, those which may rightfully claim for themselves the privilege of the highest admiration. For why should we not admire more the angels themselves and the blessed choirs of heaven?
10   At last it seems to me I have come to understand why man is the most fortunate of creatures and consequently worthy of all admiration and what precisely is that rank which is his lot in the universal Chain of Being—a rank to be envied not only by brutes but even by the stars and by minds beyond this world. It is a matter past faith and a wondrous one. Why should it not be? For
15   it is on this very account that man is rightly called and judged a great miracle and a wonderful creature indeed.

God the Father, the supreme Architect, had already built this cosmic home we behold, the most sacred temple of His godhead, by the laws of His mysterious wisdom. The region above the heavens He had adorned with Intelligences, the
20   heavenly spheres He had quickened with eternal souls, and the excrementary and filthy parts of the lower world He had filled with a multitude of animals of every kind. But, when the work was finished, the Craftsman kept wishing that there were someone to ponder the plan of so great a work, to love its beauty, and to wonder at its vastness.

25   Therefore, when everything was done (as Moses and Timaeus bear witness), He finally took thought concerning the creation of man. But there was not among His archetypes that from which He could fashion a new offspring, nor was there in His treasure-houses anything which He might bestow on His new son as an inheritance, nor was there in the seats of all the world a place
30   where the latter might sit to contemplate the universe. All was now complete; all things had been assigned to the highest, the middle, and the lowest orders. But in its final creation it was not the part of the Father's power to fail as though exhausted. It was not the part of His wisdom to waver in a needful matter through poverty of counsel. It was not the part of His kindly love that he who
35   was to praise God's divine generosity in regard to others should be compelled to condemn it in regard to himself.

At last the best of artisans ordained that that creature to whom He had been able to give nothing proper to himself should have joint possession of whatever had been peculiar to each of the different kinds of being. He therefore took man
40   as a creature of indeterminate nature and, assigning him a place in the middle

of the world, addressed him thus: "Neither a fixed abode nor a form that is yours alone nor any function peculiar to yourself have We given you, Adam, to the end that according to your longing and according to your judgment you may have and possess what abode, what form, and what functions you yourself shall desire. The nature of all other beings is limited and constrained within the     5
bounds of laws prescribed by Us. You, constrained by no limits, in accordance with your own free will, in whose hand We have placed you, shall ordain for yourself the limits of your nature. We have set you at the world's center that you may from thence more easily observe whatever is in the world. We have made you neither of heaven nor of earth, neither mortal nor immortal, so that     10
with freedom of choice and with honor, as though the maker and molder of yourself, you may fashion yourself in whatever shape you shall prefer. You shall have the power to degenerate into the lower forms of life, which are brutish. You shall have the power, out of your soul's judgment, to be reborn into the higher forms, which are divine."                                             15

O supreme generosity of God the Father, O highest and most marvelous felicity of man! To him it is granted to have whatever he chooses, to be whatever he wills. Beasts as soon as they are born (so says Lucilius) bring with them from their mother's womb all they will ever possess. Spiritual beings, either from the beginning or soon thereafter, become what they are to be forever and ever. On     20
man when he came into life the Father conferred the seeds of all kinds and the germs of every way of life. Whatever seeds each man cultivates will grow to maturity and bear in him their own fruit. If they be vegetative, he will be like a plant. If sensitive, he will become brutish. If rational, he will grow into a heavenly being. If intellectual, he will be an angel and the son of God. And if,     25
happy in the lot of no created thing, he withdraws into the center of his own unity, his spirit, made one with God, in the solitary darkness of God, who is set above all things, shall surpass them all....

# POLITICAL THEORY
## NICCOLÒ MACHIAVELLI (1469–1527)

*Niccolò Machiavelli lived in Italy when that peninsula was divided into
more than a dozen warring states. While the* Art of War *was the only
major work published in his lifetime, he is best remembered for* The
Prince, *a 1513 guide written for the ruler who has recently seized power,
and the* Discourses, *a 1517 conversation about the nature and forms of
government.*

### THE PRINCE
1513

### Chapter 6—*Of New Principalities that Have Been Acquired by the Valor of the Prince*

...Those who by similar noble conduct become princes acquire their principalities with difficulty, but maintain them with ease; and the difficulties which they
experience in acquiring their principalities arise in part from the new ordinances
and customs which they are obliged to introduce for the purpose of founding
their state and their own security. We must bear in mind, then, that there is      5
nothing more difficult and dangerous, or more doubtful of success, than an
attempt to introduce a new order of things in any state. For the innovator has
for enemies all those who derived advantages from the old order of things, whilst
those who expect to be benefited by the new institutions will be but lukewarm
defenders. This indifference arises in part from fear of their adversaries who were    10
favored by the existing laws, and partly from the incredulity of men who have
no faith in anything new that is not the result of well-established experience.
Hence it is that, whenever the opponents of the new order of things have the
opportunity to attack it, they will do it with the zeal of partisans, whilst the
others defend it but feebly, so that it is dangerous to rely upon the latter.      15

If we desire to discuss this subject thoroughly, it will be necessary to examine
whether such innovators depend upon themselves, or whether they rely upon
others; that is to say, whether for the purpose of carrying out their plans they

*The Historical, Political and Diplomatic Writings of Niccolo Machiavelli*, translated by Christian E. Detmold (Boston: James R. Osgood and Company, 1882), 19–21, 27, 31–33,
51–59, 98–102, 122, 126–31, 134, 232–33, 319–23 [modernized].

have to resort to entreaties, or whether they can accomplish it by force. In the first case they always succeed badly, and fail to conclude anything; but when they depend upon their own strength to carry their innovations through, then they rarely incur any danger. Thence it was that all prophets who came with 5    arms in hand were successful, whilst those who were not armed were ruined. For besides the reasons given above, the dispositions of peoples are variable; it is easy to persuade them to anything, but difficult to confirm them in that belief. And therefore a prophet should be prepared, in case the people will not believe any more, to be able by force to compel them to that belief.

10        Neither Moses, Cyrus, Theseus, nor Romulus would have been able to make their laws and institutions observed for any length of time, if they had not been prepared to enforce them with arms. This was the experience of Brother Girolamo Savonarola,[1] who failed in his attempt to establish a new order of things so soon as the multitude ceased to believe in him; for he had not the 15    means to keep his believers firm in their faith, nor to make the unbelievers believe. And yet these great men experienced great difficulties in their course, and met danger at every step, which could only be overcome by their courage and ability. But once having surmounted them, then they began to be held in veneration; and having crushed those who were jealous of their great qualities, 20    they remained powerful, secure, honored, and happy....

### Chapter 7—Of New Principalities that Have Been Acquired by the Aid of Others and By Good Fortune

...Upon reviewing now all the actions of the Duke,[2] I should not know where to blame him; it seems to me that I should rather hold him up as an example (as I have said) to be imitated by all those who have risen to sovereignty, either by the good fortune or the arms of others. For being endowed with great cour- 25    age, and having a lofty ambition, he could not have acted otherwise under the circumstances; and the only thing that defeated his designs was the shortness of Alexander's life and his own bodily infirmity.

Whoever, then, in a newly-acquired state, finds it necessary to secure him- self against his enemies, to gain friends, to conquer by force or by cunning, to 30    make himself feared or beloved by the people, to be followed and revered by the soldiery, to destroy all who could or might injure him, to substitute a new for

---

[1]Girolamo Savonarola (1452–1498), Dominican priest who led Florence (1494–1498). After his strident moralism was condemned by Pope Alexander VI, Savonarola was arrested and executed.

[2]Cesare Borgia (1474–1507), Duke of Valentinois, illegitimate son of Pope Alexander VI. Alexander funded Cesare's attempt to found his own kingdom in northern Italy, an attempt cut short by the 1503 death of Alexander VI.

the old order of things, to be severe and yet gracious, magnanimous, and liberal, to disband a disloyal army and create a new one, to preserve the friendship of kings and princes, so that they may bestow benefits upon him with grace, and fear to injure him—such a one, I say, cannot find more recent examples than those presented by the conduct of the Duke Valentino....                    5

## Chapter 8—*Of Such as Have Acquired Sovereignty by Means of Crimes*

...Some may wonder how it was that Agathocles,[3] and others like him, after their infinite treason and cruelty, could live for any length of time securely in the countries whose sovereignty they had usurped, and even defend themselves successfully against external enemies, without any attempts on the part of their own citizens to conspire against them; whilst many others could not by means of   10
cruelty maintain their state even in time of peace, much less in doubtful times of war. I believe that this happened according as the cruelties were well or ill applied; we may call cruelty well applied (if indeed we may call that well which in itself is evil) when it is committed once from necessity for self-protection, and afterwards not persisted in, but converted as far as possible to the public   15
good. Ill-applied cruelties are those which, though at first but few, yet increase with time rather than cease altogether. Those who adopt the first practice may, with the help of God and man, render some service to their state, as had been done by Agathocles; but those who adopt the latter course will not possibly be able to maintain themselves in their state. Whence it is to be noted that in   20
taking possession of a state the conqueror should well reflect as to the harsh measures that may be necessary, and then execute them at a single blow, so as not to be obliged to renew them every day; and by thus not repeating them, to assure himself of the support of the inhabitants, and win them over to himself by benefits bestowed. And he who acts otherwise, either from timidity or from   25
being badly advised, will be obliged ever to be sword in hand, and will never be able to rely upon his subjects, who in turn will not be able to rely upon him, because of the constant fresh wrongs committed by him. Cruelties should be committed all at once, as in that way each separate one is less felt, and gives less offence; benefits, on the other hand, should be conferred one at a time, for   30
in that way they will be more appreciated. But above all a prince should live upon such terms with his subjects that no accident, either for good or for evil, should make him vary his conduct towards them. For when adverse times bring upon you the necessity for action, you will no longer be in time to do evil; and the good you may do will not profit you, because it will be regarded as having   35
been forced from you, and therefore will bring you no thanks....

---

[3]Agathocles, son of a potter, led an army to become tyrant of Syracuse (317–289 BC) and King of Sicily (304–289 BC).

### Chapter 9—*Of Civil Principalities*

…He who becomes prince by the aid of the nobles will have more difficulty in maintaining himself than he who arrives at that high station by the aid of the people. For the former finds himself surrounded by many who in their own opinion are equal to him, and for that reason he can neither command nor
5   manage them in his own way. But he who attains the principality by favor of the people stands alone, and has around him none, or very few, that will not yield him a ready obedience. Moreover, you cannot satisfy the nobles with honesty, and without wrong to others, but it is easy to satisfy the people, whose aims are ever more honest than those of the nobles; the latter wishing to oppress,
10   and the former being unwilling to be oppressed. I will say further, that a prince can never assure himself of a people who are hostile to him, for they are too numerous; the nobles on the other hand being but few, it becomes easy for a prince to make himself sure of them.

    The worst that a prince may expect of a people who are unfriendly to him
15   is that they will desert him; but the hostile nobles he has to fear, not only lest they abandon him, but also because they will turn against him. For they, being more far-sighted and astute, always save themselves in advance, and seek to secure the favor of him whom they hope may be successful.…

### Chapter 15—*Of the Means by Which Men, and Especially Princes, Win Applause or Incur Censure*

It remains now to be seen in what manner a prince should conduct himself
20   towards his subjects and his allies; and knowing that this matter has already been treated by many others, I apprehend that my writing upon it also may be deemed presumptuous, especially as in the discussion of the same I shall differ from the rules laid down by others. But as my aim is to write something that may be useful to him for whom it is intended, it seems to me proper to pursue
25   the real truth of the matter, rather than to indulge in mere speculation on the same; for many have imagined republics and principalities such as have never been known to exist in reality. For the manner in which men live is so different from the way in which they ought to live, that he who leaves the common course for that which he ought to follow will find that it leads him to ruin rather than
30   to safety. For a man who, in all respects, will carry out only his professions of good, will be apt to be ruined amongst so many who are evil. A prince therefore who desires to maintain himself must learn to be not always good, but to be so or not as necessity may require. Leaving aside then the imaginary things concerning princes, and confining ourselves only to the realities, I say that all
35   men when they are spoken of, and more especially princes, from being in a more

conspicuous position, are noted for some quality that brings them either praise or censure. Thus one is deemed liberal, another miserly (*misero*) to use a Tuscan expression (for avaricious is he who by rapine desires to gain, and miserly we call him who abstains too much from the enjoyment of his own). One man is esteemed generous, another rapacious; one cruel, another merciful; one faithless, and another faithful; one effeminate and pusillanimous, another ferocious and brave; one affable, another haughty; one lascivious, another chaste; one sincere, the other cunning; one facile, another inflexible; one grave, another frivolous; one religious, another skeptical; and so on.

I am well aware that it would be most praiseworthy for a prince to possess all of the above-named qualities that are esteemed good; but as he cannot have them all, nor entirely observe them, because of his human nature which does not permit it, he should at least be prudent enough to know how to avoid the infamy of those vices that would rob him of his state; and if possible also to guard against such as are likely to endanger it. But if that be not possible, then he may with less hesitation follow his natural inclinations. Nor need he care about incurring censure for such vices, without which the preservation of his state may be difficult. For, all things considered, it will be found that some things that seem like virtue will lead you to ruin if you follow them; whilst others, that apparently are vices, will, if followed, result in your safety and well-being.

## Chapter 16—*Of Liberality and Parsimoniousness*

To begin with the first of the above-named qualities, I say that it is well for a prince to be deemed liberal; and yet liberality, indulged in so that you will no longer be feared, will prove injurious. For liberality worthily exercised, as it should be, will not be recognized, and may bring upon you the reproach of the very opposite. For if you desire the reputation of being liberal, you must not stop at any degree of sumptuousness; so that a prince will in this way generally consume his entire substance, and may in the end, if he wishes to keep up his reputation for liberality, be obliged to subject his people to extraordinary burdens, and resort to taxation, and employ all sorts of measures that will enable him to procure money. This will soon make him odious with his people; and when he becomes poor, he will be contemned by everybody; so that having by his prodigality injured many and benefited few, he will be the first to suffer every inconvenience, and be exposed to every danger. And when he becomes conscious of this and attempts to retrench, he will at once expose himself to the imputation of being a miser.

A prince then, being unable without injury to himself to practice the virtue of liberality in such manner that it may be generally recognized, should not, when he becomes aware of this and is prudent, mind incurring the charge of parsimoniousness. For after a while, when it is seen that by his prudence and economy he makes his revenues suffice him, and that he is able to provide for his defense in case of war, and engage in enterprises without burdening his

5    people, he will be considered liberal enough by all those from whom he takes nothing, and these are the many; whilst only those to whom he does not give, and which are the few, will look upon him as parsimonious....

...And of all the things against which a prince should guard most carefully is the incurring the hatred and contempt of his subjects. Now, liberality will

10   bring upon you either the one or the other; there is therefore more wisdom in submitting to be called parsimonious, which may bring you blame without hatred, than, by aiming to be called liberal, to incur unavoidably the reputation of rapacity, which will bring upon you infamy as well as hatred.

### Chapter 17—*Of Cruelty and Clemency, and Whether it is Better to be Loved than Feared*

Coming down now to the other aforementioned qualities, I say that every prince

15   ought to desire the reputation of being merciful, and not cruel; at the same time, he should be careful not to misuse that mercy. Cesar Borgia was reputed cruel, yet by his cruelty he reunited the Romagna to his states, and restored that province to order, peace, and loyalty; and if we carefully examine his course, we shall find it to have been really much more merciful than the course of the people of Flor-

20   ence, who, to escape the reputation of cruelty, allowed Pistoja to be destroyed.[4] A prince, therefore, should not mind the ill repute of cruelty, when he can thereby keep his subjects united and loyal; for a few displays of severity will really be more merciful than to allow, by an excess of clemency, disorders to occur, which are apt to result in rapine and murder; for these injure a whole community, whilst

25   the executions ordered by the prince fall only upon a few individuals....

A prince, however, should be slow to believe and to act; nor should he be too easily alarmed by his own fears, and should proceed moderately and with prudence and humanity, so that an excess of confidence may not make him incautious, nor too much mistrust make him intolerant. This, then, gives rise

30   to the question "whether it be better to be beloved than feared, or "to be feared than beloved." It will naturally be answered that it would be desirable to be both the one and the other; but as it is difficult to be both at the same time, it is much more safe to be feared than to be loved, when you have to choose between the

---

[4]Pistoja, a subject city of Florence, was torn by civil war between Panciatichi and Cancellari factions in the late fifteenth century. Florence, preferring negotiation, refused military intervention, and the bloody violence continued for several years.

two. For it may be said of men in general that they are ungrateful and fickle, dissemblers, avoiders of danger, and greedy of gain. So long as you shower benefits upon them, they are all yours; they offer you their blood, their substance, their lives, and their children, provided the necessity for it is far off; but when it is near at hand, then they revolt. And the prince who relies upon their words, without 5 having otherwise provided for his security, is ruined; for friendships that are won by rewards, and not by greatness and nobility of soul, although deserved, yet are not real, and cannot be depended upon in time of adversity.

Besides, men have less hesitation in offending one who makes himself beloved than one who makes himself feared; for love holds by a bond of obligation 10 which, as mankind is bad, is broken on every occasion whenever it is for the interest of the obliged party to break it. But fear holds by the apprehension of punishment, which never leaves men. A prince, however, should make himself feared in such a manner that, if he has not won the affections of his people, he shall at least not incur their hatred; for the being feared, and not hated, can go 15 very well together, if the prince abstains from taking the substance of his subjects, and leaves them their women. And if you should be obliged to inflict capital punishment upon any one, then be sure to do so only when there is manifest cause and proper justification for it; and, above all things, abstain from taking people's property, for men will sooner forget the death of their fathers than the 20 loss of their patrimony. Besides, there will never be any lack of reasons for taking people's property; and a prince who once begins to live by rapine will ever find excuses for seizing other people's property. On the other hand, reasons for taking life are not so easily found, and are more readily exhausted....

To come back now to the question whether it be better to be beloved than 25 feared, I conclude that, as men love of their own free will, but are inspired with fear by the will of the prince, a wise prince should always rely upon himself, and not upon the will of others; but, above all, should he always strive to avoid being hated, as I have already said above.

### Chapter 18—*In What Manner Princes Should Keep Their Faith*

It must be evident to everyone that it is more praiseworthy for a prince always to 30 maintain good faith, and practice integrity rather than craft and deceit. And yet the experience of our own times has shown that those princes have achieved great things who made small account of good faith, and who understood by cunning to circumvent the intelligence of others; and that in the end they got the better of those whose actions were dictated by loyalty and good faith. You must know, 35 therefore, that there are two ways of carrying on a contest; the one by law, and the other by force. The first is practiced by men, and the other by animals; and as the first is often insufficient, it becomes necessary to resort to the second.

A prince, then, should know how to employ the nature of man, and that of the beasts as well. This was figuratively taught by ancient writers, who relate how Achilles and many other princes were given to Chiron the centaur to be nurtured, and how they were trained under his tutorship; which fable means nothing else than that their preceptor combined the qualities of the man and the beast; and that a prince, to succeed, will have to employ both the one and the other nature, as the one without the other cannot produce lasting results.

It being necessary then for a prince to know well how to employ the nature of the beasts, he should be able to assume both that of the fox and that of the lion; for whilst the latter cannot escape the traps laid for him, the former cannot defend himself against the wolves. A prince should be a fox, to know the traps and snares; and a lion, to be able to frighten the wolves; for those who simply hold to the nature of the lion do not understand their business.

A sagacious prince then cannot and should not fulfill his pledges when their observance is contrary to his interest, and when the causes that induced him to pledge his faith no longer exist. If men were all good, then indeed this precept would be bad; but as men are naturally bad, and will not observe their faith towards you, you must, in the same way, not observe yours to them; and no prince ever yet lacked legitimate reasons with which to color his want of good faith. Innumerable modern examples could be given of this; and it could easily be shown how many treaties of peace, and how many engagements, have been made null and void by the faithlessness of princes; and he who has best known how to play the fox has ever been the most successful.

But it is necessary that the prince should know how to color this nature well, and how to be a great hypocrite and dissembler. For men are so simple, and yield so much to immediate necessity, that the deceiver will never lack dupes. I will mention one of the most recent examples. Alexander VI[5] never did nor ever thought of anything but to deceive, and always found a reason for doing so. No one ever had greater skill in asseverating, or who affirmed his pledges with greater oaths and observed them less, than Pope Alexander; and yet he was always successful in his deceits, because he knew the weakness of men in that particular.

It is not necessary, however, for a prince to possess all the above-mentioned qualities; but it is essential that he should at least seem to have them. I will even venture to say, that to have and to practice them constantly is pernicious, but to seem to have them is useful. For instance, a prince should seem to be merciful, faithful, humane, religious, and upright, and should even be so in reality; but he should have his mind so trained that, when occasion requires it, he may know how to change to the opposite. And it must be understood that a prince,

[5]Pope Alexander VI (r. 1492–1503) represented the nadir of papal corruption.

and especially one who has but recently acquired his state, cannot perform all those things which cause men to be esteemed as good; he being often obliged, for the sake of maintaining his state, to act contrary to humanity, charity, and religion. And therefore is it necessary that he should have a versatile mind, capable of changing readily, according as the winds and changes for fortune bid   5 him; and, as has been said above, not to swerve from the good if possible, but to know how to resort to evil if necessity demands it.

A prince then should be very careful never to allow anything to escape his lips that does not abound in the above-named five qualities, so that to see and to hear him he may seem all charity, integrity, and humanity, all uprightness,   10 and all piety. And more than all else is it necessary for a prince to seem to possess the last quality; for mankind in general judge more by what they see and hear than by what they feel, every one being capable of the former, and but few of the latter. Everybody sees what you seem to be, but few really feel what you are; and these few dare not oppose the opinion of the many, who are protected by the   15 majesty of the state; for the actions of all men, and especially those of princes, are judged by the result, where there is no other judge to whom to appeal.

A prince then should look mainly to the successful maintenance of his state. The means which he employs for this will always be accounted honorable, and will be praised by everybody; for the common people are always taken by   20 appearances and by results, and it is the vulgar mass that constitutes the world. But a very few have rank and station, whilst the many have nothing to sustain them. A certain prince of our time, whom it is well not to name, never preached anything but peace and good faith; but if he had always observed either the one or the other, it would in most instances have cost him his reputation or   25 his state....

## THE DISCOURSES

1517

### *Of the Different Kinds of Republics, and of What Kind the Roman Republic Was*

I§2I will leave aside what might be said of cities which from their very birth have been subject to a foreign power, and will speak only of those whose origin has been independent, and which from the first governed themselves by their own laws, whether as republics or as principalities, and whose constitution and laws   30 have differed as their origin. Some have had at the very beginning, or soon after, a legislator, who, like Lycurgus with the Lacedæmonians, gave them by a single act all the laws they needed. Others have owed theirs to chance and to events, and have received their laws at different times, as Rome did. It is a great good fortune for a republic to have a legislator sufficiently wise to give her laws so   35

regulated that, without the necessity of correcting them, they afford security to those who live under them. Sparta observed her laws for more than eight hundred years without altering them and without experiencing a single dangerous disturbance. Unhappy, on the contrary, is that republic which, not having at the
5    beginning fallen into the hands of a sagacious and skillful legislator, is herself obliged to reform her laws. More unhappy still is that republic which from the first has diverged from a good constitution. And that republic is furthest from it whose vicious institutions impede her progress, and make her leave the right path that leads to a good end; for those who are in that condition can hardly
10   ever be brought into the right road. Those republics, on the other hand, that started without having even a perfect constitution, but made a fair beginning, and are capable of improvement—such republics, I say, may perfect themselves by the aid of events. It is very true, however, that such reforms are never effected without danger, for the majority of men never willingly adopt any new
15   law tending to change the constitution of the state, unless the necessity of the change is clearly demonstrated; and as such a necessity cannot make itself felt without being accompanied with danger, the republic may easily be destroyed before having perfected its constitution. That of Florence is a complete proof of this: re-organized after the revolt of Arezzo, in 1502, it was overthrown after
20   the taking of Prato in 1512.

Having proposed to myself to treat of the kind of government established at Rome, and of the events that led to its perfection, I must at the beginning observe that some of the writers on politics distinguished three kinds of government, viz. the monarchical, the aristocratic, and the democratic; and maintain
25   that the legislators of a people must choose from these three the one that seems to them most suitable. Other authors, wiser according to the opinion of many, count six kinds of governments, three of which are very bad, and three good in themselves, but so liable to be corrupted that they become absolutely bad. The three good ones are those which we have just named; the three bad ones
30   result from the degradation of the other three, and each of them resembles its corresponding original, so that the transition from the one to the other is very easy. Thus monarchy becomes tyranny; aristocracy degenerates into oligarchy; and the popular government lapses readily into licentiousness. So that a legislator who gives to a state which he founds, either of these three forms of
35   government, constitutes it but for a brief time; for no precautions can prevent either one of the three that are reputed good, from degenerating into its opposite kind; so great are in these the attractions and resemblances between the good and the evil.

Chance has given birth to these different kinds of governments amongst
40   men; for at the beginning of the world the inhabitants were few in number, and

lived for a time dispersed, like beasts. As the human race increased, the necessity for uniting themselves for defense made itself felt; the better to attain this object, they chose the strongest and most courageous from amongst themselves and placed him at their head, promising to obey him. Thence they began to know the good and the honest, and to distinguish them from the bad and vicious; for seeing a man injure his benefactor aroused at once two sentiments in every heart, hatred against the ingrate and love for the benefactor. They blamed the first, and on the contrary honored those the more who showed themselves grateful, for each felt that he in turn might be subject to a like wrong; and to prevent similar evils, they set to work to make laws, and to institute punishments for those who contravened them. Such was the origin of justice. This caused them, when they had afterwards to choose a prince, neither to look to the strongest nor bravest, but to the wisest and most just. But when they began to make sovereignty hereditary and non-elective, the children quickly degenerated from their fathers; and, so far from trying to equal their virtues, they considered that a prince had nothing else to do than to excel all the rest in luxury, indulgence, and every other variety of pleasure. The prince consequently soon drew upon himself the general hatred. An object of hatred, he naturally felt fear; fear in turn dictated to him precautions and wrongs, and thus tyranny quickly developed itself. Such were the beginning and causes of disorders, conspiracies, and plots against the sovereigns, set on foot, not by the feeble and timid, but by those citizens who, surpassing the others in grandeur of soul, in wealth, and in courage, could not submit to the outrages and excesses of their princes.

Under such powerful leaders the masses armed themselves against the tyrant, and, after having rid themselves of him, submitted to these chiefs as their liberators. These, abhorring the very name of prince, constituted themselves a new government; and at first, bearing in mind the past tyranny, they governed in strict accordance with the laws which they had established themselves; preferring public interests to their own, and to administer and protect with greatest care both public and private affairs. The children succeeded their fathers, and ignorant of the changes of fortune, having never experienced its reverses, and indisposed to remain content with this civil equality, they in turn gave themselves up to cupidity, ambition, libertinage, and violence, and soon caused the aristocratic government to degenerate into an oligarchic tyranny, regardless of all civil rights. They soon, however, experienced the same fate as the first tyrant; the people, disgusted with their government, placed themselves at the command of whoever was willing to attack them, and this disposition soon produced an avenger, who was sufficiently well seconded to destroy them. The memory of the prince and the wrongs committed by him being still fresh in their minds, and having overthrown the oligarchy, the people were not willing

to return to the government of a prince. A popular government was therefore resolved upon, and it was so organized that the authority should not again fall into the hands of a prince or a small number of nobles. And as all governments are at first looked up to with some degree of reverence, the popular state also
5   maintained itself for a time, but which was never of long duration, and lasted generally only about as long as the generation that had established it; for it soon ran into that kind of license which inflicts injury upon public as well as private interests. Each individual only consulted his own passions, and a thousand acts of injustice were daily committed, so that, constrained by necessity, or directed
10  by the counsels of some good man, or for the purpose of escaping from this anarchy, they returned anew to the government of a prince, and from this they generally lapsed again into anarchy, step by step, in the same manner and from the same causes as we have indicated.

Such is the circle which all republics are destined to run through. Seldom,
15  however, do they come back to the original form of government, which results from the fact that their duration is not sufficiently long to be able to undergo these repeated changes and preserve their existence. But it may well happen that a republic lacking strength and good counsel in its difficulties becomes subject after a while to some neighboring state, that is better organized than itself; and
20  if such is not the case, then they will be apt to revolve indefinitely in the circle of revolutions. I say, then, that all kinds of government are defective; those three which we have qualified as good because they are too short-lived, and the three bad ones because of their inherent viciousness. Thus sagacious legislators, knowing the vices of each of these systems of government by themselves, have
25  chosen one that should partake of all of them, judging that to be the most stable and solid. In fact, when there is combined under the same constitution a prince, a nobility, and the power of the people, then these three powers will watch and keep each other reciprocally in check....

### The Founders of a Republics, Monarchies, and Tyrannies

I§10Of all men who have been eulogized, those deserve it most who have been
30  the authors and founders of religions; next come such as have established republics or kingdoms....

### Of the Religion of the Romans

I§11...Numa, finding a very savage people, and wishing to reduce them to civil obedience by the arts of peace, had recourse to religion as the most necessary and assured support of any civil society; and he established it upon such foun-
35  dations that for many centuries there was nowhere more fear of the gods than

in that republic, which greatly facilitated all the enterprises which the Senate or its great men attempted. Whoever will examine the actions of the people of Rome as a body, or of many individual Romans, will see that these citizens feared much more to break an oath than the laws, like men who esteem the power of the gods more than that of men.... And whoever reads Roman history    5
attentively will see in how great a degree religion served in the command of the armies, in uniting the people and keeping them well-conducted, and in covering the wicked and shame.... In truth, there never was any remarkable lawgiver amongst any people who did not resort to divine authority, as otherwise his laws would not have been accepted by the people; for there are many good laws, the    10
importance of which is known to the sagacious lawgiver, but the reasons for which are not sufficiently evident to enable him to persuade others to submit to them; and therefore do wise men, for the purpose of removing this difficulty, resort to divine authority....

...I conclude that the religion introduced by Numa into Rome was one    15
of the chief causes of the prosperity of that city; for this religion gave rise to good laws, and good laws bring good fortune, and from good fortune results happy success in all enterprises. And as the observance of divine institutions is the cause of the greatness of republics, so the disregard of them produces their ruin; for where the fear of God is wanting, there the country will come to ruin,    20
unless it be sustained by the fear of the prince, which may temporarily supply the want of religion....

### *The Importance of Giving Religion a Prominent Influence in a State....*

1§12Princes and republics who wish to maintain themselves free from corruption must above all things preserve the purity of all religious observances, and treat them with proper reverence; for there is no greater indication of the ruin of a    25
country than to see religion contemned. And this is easily understood when we know upon what the religion of a country is founded; for the essence of every religion is based upon some one main principle. The religion of the Gentiles had for its foundation the responses of the oracles, and the tenets of the augurs and auspices; upon these alone depended all their ceremonies, rites, and sacri-    30
fices. For they readily believed that the deity which could predict their future good or ill was also able to bestow it upon them. Thence arose their temples, their sacrifices, their supplications, and all the other ceremonies; for the oracle of Delphos, the temple of Jupiter Ammon, and other celebrated oracles, kept the world in admiration and devoutness. But when these afterwards began to    35
speak only in accordance with the wishes of the princes, and their falsity was discovered by the people, then men became incredulous, and disposed to disturb all good institutions. It is therefore the duty of princes and heads of republics to

uphold the foundations of the religion of their countries, for then it is easy to keep their people religious, and consequently well-conducted and united. And therefore everything that tends to favor religion (even though it were believed to be false) should be received and availed of to strengthen it; and this should
5 be done the more, the wiser the rulers are, and the better they understand the natural course of things. Such was, in fact, the practice observed by sagacious men; which has given rise to the belief in the miracles that are celebrated in religions, however false they may be....

And certainly, if the Christian religion had from the beginning been
10 maintained according to the principles of its founder, the Christian states and republics would have been much more united and happy than what they are. Nor can there be a greater proof of its decadence than to witness the fact that the nearer people are to the Church of Rome, which is the head of our religion, the less religious are they. And whoever examines the principles upon which
15 that religion is founded, and sees how widely different from those principles its present practice and application are, will judge that her ruin or chastisement is near at hand. But as there are some of the opinion that the well-being of Italian affairs depends upon the Church of Rome, I will present such arguments against that opinion as occur to me; two of which are most important, and cannot
20 according to my judgment be controverted. The first is that the evil example of the court of Rome has destroyed all piety and religion in Italy, which brings in its train infinite improprieties and disorders; for as we may presuppose all good where religion prevails, so where it is wanting we have the right to suppose the very opposite. We Italians then owe to the Church of Rome and to her priests
25 our having become irreligious and bad; but we owe her a still greater debt, and one that will be the cause of our ruin, namely, that the Church has kept and still keeps our country divided. And certainly a country can never be united and happy except when it obeys wholly one government, whether a republic or a monarchy, as is the case in France and in Spain; and the sole cause why
30 Italy is not in the same condition, and is not governed by either one republic or one sovereign, is the Church; for having acquired and holding a temporal dominion, yet she has never had sufficient power or courage to enable her to seize the rest of the country and make herself sole sovereign of all Italy. And on the other hand she has not been so feeble that the fear of losing her temporal
35 power prevented her from calling in the aid of a foreign power to defend her against such others as had become too powerful in Italy. The Church, then, not having been powerful enough to be able to master all Italy, nor having permitted any other power to do so, has been the cause why Italy has never been able to unite under one head, but has always remained under a number
40 of princes and lords, which occasioned her so many dissensions and so much

weakness that she became a prey not only to the powerful barbarians, but of whoever chose to assail her. This we other Italians owe to the Church of Rome, and to none other....

### *The Romans Interpreted the Auspices According to Necessity....*

I§14 The system of auguries was not only, as we have said above, the principal basis of the ancient religion of the Gentiles, but was also the cause of the prosperity 5 of the Roman republic. Whence the Romans esteemed it more than any other institution, and resorted to it in their Consular Comitii, in commencing any important enterprise, in sending armies into the field, in ordering their battles, and in every other important civil or military action. Nor would they ever have ventured upon any expedition unless the augurs had first persuaded the soldiers 10 that the gods promised them victory. Amongst other auspices the armies were always accompanied by a certain class of soothsayers, termed *Pollari* (guardians of the sacred fowls), and every time before giving battle to the enemy, they required these *Pollari* to ascertain the auspices; and if the fowls ate freely, then it was deemed a favorable augury, and the soldiers fought confidently, but if the 15 fowls refused to eat, then they abstained from battle. Nevertheless, when they saw a good reason why certain things should be done, they did them anyhow, whether the auspices were favorable or not; but then they turned and interpreted the auguries so artfully, and in such manner, that seemingly no disrespect was shown to their religious belief.... 20

### *What Nations the Romans Had to Contend Against....*

II§2 ...Reflecting now as to whence it came that in ancient times the people were more devoted to liberty than in the present, I believe that it resulted from this, that men were stronger in those days, which I believe to be attributable to the difference of education, founded upon the difference of their religion and ours. For, as our religion teaches us the truth and the true way of life, it causes 25 us to attach less value to the honors and possessions of this world; whilst the Pagans, esteeming those things as the highest good, were more energetic and ferocious in their actions. We may observe this also in most of their institutions, beginning with the magnificence of their sacrifices as compared with the humility of ours, which are gentle solemnities rather than magnificent 30 ones, and have nothing of energy or ferocity in them. Besides this, the Pagan religion deified only men who had achieved great glory, such as commanders of armies and chiefs of republics, whilst ours glorifies more the humble and contemplative men than the men of action. Our religion, moreover, places the supreme happiness in humility, lowliness, and a contempt for worldly objects, 35 whilst the other, on the contrary, places the supreme good in grandeur of soul, strength of body, and all such other qualities as render men formidable; and if our religion claims of us fortitude of soul, it is more to enable us to suffer than to achieve great deeds.

5      These principles seem to me to have made men feeble, and caused them to become an easy prey to evil-minded men, who can control them more securely, seeing that the great body of men, for the sake of gaining Paradise, are more disposed to endure injuries than to avenge them. And although it would seem that the world has become effeminate and Heaven disarmed, yet this arises
10    unquestionably from the baseness of men, who have interpreted our religion according to the promptings of indolence rather than those of virtue. For if we were to reflect that our religion permits us to exalt and defend our country, we should see that according to it we ought also to love and honor our country, and prepare ourselves so as to be capable of defending her. It is this education, then,
15    and this false interpretation of our religion, that is the cause of there not being so many republics nowadays as there were anciently; and that there is no longer the same love and liberty amongst the people now as there was then....

### It is Necessary Frequently to Bring Religious Sects or Republics Back to their Original Principles

III§1There is nothing more true than that all the things of this world have a limit to their existence; but those only run the entire course ordained for them
20    by Heaven that do not allow their body to become disorganized, but keep it unchanged in the manner ordained, or if they change it, so do it that it shall be for their advantage, and not to their injury. And as I speak here of mixed bodies, such as republics or religious sects, I say that those changes are beneficial that bring them back to their original principles. And those are the best-constituted
25    bodies, and have the longest existence, which possess the intrinsic means of frequently renewing themselves, or such as obtain this renovation in consequences of some extrinsic accidents. And it is a truth clearer than light that, without such renovation, these bodies cannot continue to exist; and the means of renewing them is to bring them back to their original principles. For, as all
30    religious republic and monarchies must have within themselves some goodness, by means of which they obtain their first growth and reputation, and as in the process of time this goodness becomes corrupted, it will of necessity destroy the body unless something intervenes to bring it back to its normal condition. Thus, the doctors of medicine say, in speaking of the human body, that "every
35    day some ill humors gather which "must be cured."...

It is necessary then (as has been said) for men who live associated together under some kind of regulations often to be brought back to themselves, so to speak, either by external or internal occurrences. As to the latter, they are either the result of a law, that obliges the citizens of the association often to render an account of their conduct; or some man of superior character arises amongst them, whose noble example and virtuous actions will produce the same effect as such a law. This good then in a republic is due either to the excellence of some 5 one man, or to some law; and as to the latter, the institution that brought the Roman republic back to its original principles was the creation of the Tribunes of the people, and all the other laws that tended to repress the insolence and ambition of men. But to give life and vigor to those laws requires a virtuous citizen, who will courageously aid in their execution against the power of those 10 who transgress them....

In relation to this subject it was said by the magistrates who governed Florence from the year 1434 until 1494 that it was necessary every five years to resume the government, and that otherwise it would be difficult to maintain it. By "resuming the government" they meant to strike the people with the 15 same fear and terror as they did when they first assumed the government, and when they had inflicted the extremest punishment upon those who, according to their principles, had conducted themselves badly. But as the recollection of these punishments fades from men's minds, they become emboldened to make new attempts against the government, and to speak ill of it, and therefore it is 20 necessary to provide against this, by bringing the government back to its first principles. Such a return to first principles in a republic is sometimes caused by the simple virtues of one man, without depending upon any law that incites him to the infliction of extreme punishments; and yet his good example has such an influence that the good men strive to imitate him, and the wicked are 25 ashamed to lead a life so contrary to his example. Those particularly, who in Rome effected such beneficial results were Horatius Cocles, Scævola, Fabricius, the two Decii, Regulus Attilius, and some others, who by their rare and virtuous example produced the same effect upon the Romans as laws and institutions would have done. And certainly if at least some such signal punishments as 30 described above, or noble examples, had occurred in Rome every ten years, that city never would have become so corrupt; but as both became more rare, corruption increased more and more. In fact, after Marcus Regulus we find not a single instance of such virtuous example; and although the two Catos arose, yet there was so long an interval between Regulus and them, and between the one 35 Cato and the other, and they were such isolated instances, that their example could effect but little good; and especially the latter Cato found the citizens of Rome already so corrupt that he utterly failed to improve them by his example. Let this suffice so far as regards republics.

Now with regard to religions we shall see that revivals are equally necessary, and the best proof of this is furnished by our own, which would have
been entirely lost had it not been brought back to its pristine principles and
purity by Saint Francis and Saint Dominic; for by their voluntary poverty and
5    the example of the life of Christ, they revived the sentiment of religion in the
hearts of men, where it had become almost extinct. The new orders which they
established were so severe and powerful that they became the means of saving
religion from being destroyed by the licentiousness of the prelates and heads
of the Church. They continued themselves to live in poverty; and by means of
10   confessions and preachings they obtained so much influence with the people,
that they were able to make them understand that it was wicked even to speak
ill of wicked rulers, and that it was proper to render them obedience and to
leave the punishment of their errors to God. And thus these wicked rulers do
as much evil as they please, because they do not fear a punishment which they
15   do not see nor believe. This revival of religion then by Saint Francis and Saint
Dominic has preserved it and maintains it to this day. Monarchies also have
need of renewal, and to bring their institutions back to first principles. The
kingdom of France shows us the good effects of such renewals; for this monarchy more than any other is governed by laws and ordinances. The Parliaments,
20   and mainly that of Paris, are the conservators of these laws and institutions,
which are renewed by them from time to time, by executions against some of
the princes of the realm, and at times even by decisions against the king himself. And thus this kingdom has maintained itself up to the present time by its
determined constancy in repressing the ambition of the nobles; for if it were
25   to leave them unpunished, the disorders would quickly multiply, and the end
would doubtless be either that the guilty could no longer be punished without
danger, or that the kingdom itself would be broken up.

We may conclude, then, that nothing is more necessary for an association
of men, either as a religious sect, republic, or monarchy, than to restore to it
30   from time to time the power and reputation which it had in the beginning,
and to strive to have either good laws or good men to bring about such a result,
without the necessity of the intervention of any extrinsic force....

# X
# THE REFORMATION

The two centuries before the Reformation saw the Roman Catholic Church increasing in prestige. The Grand Duchy of Lithuania, the last pagan state in Europe, embraced Catholicism (1386) and the reconquest of Iberia from the Moors finished with the triumphant conquest of Granada (1492). The difficulties of the Avignon papacy (1309–1377) and the bitter period of two, and sometimes three, contending popes (1378–1417) were resolved. The Ecumenical Councils of Constance (1414–1418), Florence (1431–1445), and Lateran V (1512–1514) defined papal authority and brought (temporary) reconciliation between the Roman Catholic and Eastern Churches.

At the same time as the Church's institutional triumphs, common men and women across Europe became increasingly active in their religious devotion. The widespread use of the rosary, the explanation of the Beatific Vision, the formal proclamation of the doctrine of indulgence (1350), and the translation of the Bible into vernaculars all expressed the common man's concern with his salvation. Moreover, mysticism, actively seeking union with God in this life, marked these two centuries. Individuals, such as Catherine of Sienna (1347–1380) and Thomas à Kempis (1380–1471), as well as organizations of like-minded men, including the Brethren of the Common Life and the Friends of God, modeled and encouraged mystical union with God.

The emphasis on popular religious experience could, and did, lead to significant misunderstandings by the laity, sometimes culminating in heresy. The Fraticelli and the Michaelites, for example, declared wealthy clerics disqualified as clergy. The Waldensians, the Cathars, the Free Spirits, the Bogomils, the Lollard followers of John Wycliffe (1320–1384), and those who accepted the teachings of Jan Hus (1369–1415) all embraced some deviation from orthodox Catholic teaching, and their heresies led many to conclude that, to best protect orthodoxy, authority to interpret Scripture and doctrine must rest with the Catholic Church itself.

The emphasis on personal piety did not usually lead to heresy; most Christians could pursue personal devotion and remain faithful sons of the Church. A striking contrast, however, appeared between those passionately seeking God and the lifestyle of many clergy. The moral lapses of the clergy were, by far, the most common theme both of Renaissance vernacular literature and of the Church's edicts. Writers as geographically and chronologically diverse as Dante (1265–1321), Chaucer (c. 1343–1400), Erasmus (1466–1536), and Thomas More

(1478–1535) criticized the failings of the clergy. The Church, though clearly and thoroughly condemning the shortcomings of its priests, was unable wholly to eradicate those failings. Some bishops and abbots obtained their positions through purchase, rather than by merit and sincerity. Other clerics passed years without visiting their parishes or fulfilling their spiritual obligations. Some priests might possess multiple Church appointments simultaneously, unable adequately to perform their functions, even if they were so inclined. Other forms of moral laxity were often lampooned—priests with concubines, bishops extorting money, clerics playing cards or dice during the Mass.

Despite its shortcomings, it should be remembered that the Church was, though not perfect, strong and vibrant as the sixteenth century opened.

Martin Luther (1483–1546), son of a Saxon mine owner, reluctantly followed his father's wishes and prepared for a career in law. In 1505, after nearly being struck by lightning during a thunderstorm, Luther decided to follow his own calling. He withdrew from law school and became an Augustinian monk in Erfurt. Deeply troubled by a consciousness of his own sins, he frequently fasted, often prayed straight through the night, and even flagellated himself. At the same time, Luther demonstrated remarkable academic talents, and thus in 1508 received an assignment to the faculty at the recently established University of Wittenberg.

While teaching his courses on the Psalms, Hebrews, Romans, and Galatians, Luther concluded that the Catholic Church had lost sight of the biblical understanding of justification and righteousness. No works of penance, regardless of their number, could achieve righteousness, and justification was obtainable through faith alone (*sola fide*).

As Luther began teaching and preaching his beliefs, local events drew him into conflict with Church authorities. Johann Tetzel (1465–1519), a Dominican monk, was selling papal indulgences near Wittenberg. Tetzel offered complete remission of all punishment for sins, even those not yet committed or those of the dead, to anyone who "donated" to the construction of Saint Peter's Basilica in Rome. According to Catholic doctrine, an indulgence offers remission only to those purchasers who fully and sincerely repent of their sins, not to those who pay for the privilege. Tetzel, however, demanded no evidence of contrition or repentance; he seemed simply to sell forgiveness to anyone with ready cash.

Luther, disgusted with Tetzel's abuse of indulgences, wrote a list of ninety-five theses challenging the sale of indulgences, both in theory and in practice. Among other criticisms, Luther rejected the right of the pope to authorize indulgences, whether sold or freely dispensed. This rejection, in turn, rested on a denial of all papal authority to forgive sins and of the power of any penance in achieving righteousness. On 31 October 1517, Luther nailed his theses, written in Latin, to the door of Wittenberg Cathedral, offering to debate these propositions with any interested academic. Luther's theses were rapidly translated into German and, thanks to the new printing press, quickly distributed across Germany.

The Archbishop of Mainz forwarded the theses to Rome rather than address Luther himself. While the Church discussed his propositions, Luther further developed his theology. He rejected the apostolic succession, endorsed councils as the ultimate arbiter in matters of faith and doctrine, and asserted that nobles were as much church leaders as the ordained clergy. Finally, a year-and-a-half later, Pope Leo X (r. 1513–1521) responded with sharp criticism of Luther and summoned the wayward monk to Rome. Frederick III (r. 1486–1525), ruler of Saxony, intervened and arranged for Luther instead to meet the pope's representative at Augsburg.

After an inconclusive meeting, and Luther's refusal to cease preaching, Leo X formally excommunicated Luther in 1520 and appealed to Charles V (r. 1519–1556), the young Holy Roman Emperor, to enforce the edict. The Emperor, a devout Catholic, desired to obey the Church; at the same time, he did not want the pope to dictate his imperial policy. Charles therefore summoned Luther before the Imperial Diet (a type of parliament) at the city of Worms to defend himself. After three days of discussion, the Diet condemned Luther's writings and ordered him to renounce his beliefs. Luther refused, asserting that he must follow his conscience, and the Emperor in turn declared Luther an outlaw.

Frederick of Saxony (who never embraced Luther's ideas) quickly swept Luther into one of his castles, hiding the reformer from the Emperor's agents. During his year-long exile, Luther wrote and studied diligently. In early 1522, Luther emerged from hiding, returning to Wittenberg to reform church practices and moderate some of his more radical followers. As Luther's ideas spread across Germany, they were sometimes misunderstood and radicalized. The bloody Peasants' War (1524–1525), sparked by the radical Zwickau Prophets, sought to create an egalitarian society holding all property in common and abolishing all social distinctions.

Luther, for his part, continued as the guiding light of the German Reformation until his death. He wrote extensively, addressing a wide variety of theological concerns, many issues of church governance, and significant problems of the Christian life. He participated, for example, in the Marburg Colloquy (1529), a conference to find unity among divergent Protestant groups, and the following year collaborated with Philip Melanchthon (1497–1560) in writing the Augsburg Confession, the Lutheran statement of faith. By the time of his death, Luther left a widespread and well-established church.

Throughout his life, Luther emphasized respect for and obedience to the state. He did not claim individual Christians should make personal decisions about religious doctrine, but rather they ought to submit to the authorities established by God. His own ruler, the Elector of Saxony, endorsed and adopted his reforms; Luther did not attempt to impose them nor to subvert the authority of the prince. Lutheranism, then, spread across Germany and Scandinavia as it was adopted by rulers and princes, not as a movement of missionaries appealing to individual consciences. Some of those rulers were prompted by secular concerns—economic benefit from seizing Church lands, enhanced political power by excluding the authority of Rome, or increased prestige due the head of a Church. This should not obscure the fact, however, that other rulers acted from conviction—wrestling with the issues Luther raised and sincerely concluding he was right.

Luther sparked the Protestant movement in central Europe; the teachings of John Calvin (1509–1564) dominated Protestant thought and practice west of the Rhine. Son of a notary, Calvin studied Latin at the University of Paris and earned an M.A. in Theology; he earned his degree in law from the University of Orléans. In 1532, after his return to Paris to practice law, Calvin experienced a spiritual conversion. He became an active preacher, publically questioning Catholic doctrine until royal pressure forced him to flee.

His flight carried him to Basel, Switzerland, where he published his first great work, the *Institutes of the Christian Religion*, which became the definitive statement of Calvinist thought. After some wandering, he wound up in Geneva (1536), where the city fathers undertook a "new reformation of the faith." Within a few months, Calvin's learning and skill became apparent, and he was appointed pastor of a local church. The more conservative reformers eventually managed to force Calvin and his friends from the city, and they fled to Strasbourg, where Calvin served as a pastor for several years.

In 1541, Geneva's city council invited Calvin to return, and offered him authority to restructure political authority and power in the city along Protestant principles. While in Geneva, Calvin completed his final revision of *The Institutes*, the definitive statement of Reformed Protestant doctrine. Among Calvin's most significant institutional creations was the creation of a school for preachers, which drew students from across Europe. More significantly, it sent those same students back across Europe, fostering and nurturing Reformed Protestant movements in England, the Netherlands, Scotland, and France. In contrast to Luther, Calvin encouraged literate individuals to evaluate his theological claims for themselves, even if their rulers objected. In a world predicated on an organic conception of society, appeals to individual conscience seemed to reject social order and were, therefore, politically seditious. For this reason, Calvinism was always viewed as far more politically subversive than Lutheranism.

In England, the major reforming impulses of European Christianity met with explosive results. Christian Humanists demanded wayward clergy be brought into obedience with accepted practice, but explicitly affirmed Catholic doctrine. Adherents of Luther desired theological reforms in England along the lines that

German theologians followed. Followers of Calvin, on the other hand, sought a Protestantism emanating from Geneva. To complicate the situation further, members from many minor Protestant sects had fled to England, making theological discussions still more complex.

Henry VIII (r. 1509–1547) found himself in the midst of this complicated matrix. Well-educated and literate, he actively followed theological discussions on the continent, even winning the title "Defender of the Faith" from Pope Leo X for his condemnation of Luther. In addition to his genuine interest in theology, Henry was concerned with his political future. His father had seized the throne, terminating thirty years of intermittent civil war. As a consequence, Henry was not secure on the throne, and sought to consolidate his position in the person of his heir.

Henry's first wife, Catherine of Aragon (1485–1536), produced no sons that lived more than a few weeks. Henry sought an annulment of the marriage so that he might marry a more fertile wife, and began inquiries with the papacy. Catherine's nephew, Charles V, was the most powerful man in Christendom and would not permit the indignity of annulment for his aunt. Perceiving the pope would never grant his petition, Henry at last declared the English Church independent of Rome (1534).

A significant problem now confronted the English Church—following the break with Rome, which reformer's theology, if any, should the Church now follow? Over the next hundred years, the Anglican Church wrestled with this question, at times variously embracing Calvin's Reformed theology, Luther's beliefs, and Roman Catholic doctrine. Henry himself was generally unwilling to vary from Catholic doctrine, other than rejecting the primacy of Rome. The reign of his successor, Edward VI (r. 1547–1553), marked at first a clear Lutheran ascendancy, then increasing Calvinist preeminence. Edward's short reign was followed by his sister's. Mary I (r. 1553–1558) actively encouraged a return to Catholicism. In her turn, Mary was succeeded by her sister, Queen Elizabeth I (r. 1558–1603), who emphasized a moderate Protestantism, allowing much room for personal understanding of the vaguely worded doctrinal statements, so long as no one disturbed the peace of the kingdom. The English Reformation witnessed the deaths of many martyrs, both Catholic and Protestant. Sir Thomas More (1478–1535), William Tyndale (c. 1494–1536), Hugh Latimer (c. 1485–1555), Nicholas Ridley (d. 1555), Thomas Cranmer (1489–1556), and the Earl of Northumberland (1528–1572) number among the many who suffered martyrdom for their faith.

The Catholic response to laxity and disorder within the Church began before the Protestant Reformation, but was clearly quickened by the reformers and their complaints. Christian humanists had long agitated for changes to improve clerical discipline and education. In Castile, for example, the preeminent example of pre-Reformation Catholic reform was guided by Jiménez de Cisneros (1436–1517). As Archbishop of Toledo and confessor to Queen Isabel I (r. 1451–1504), Cisneros established seminaries for the nation's priests, demanded regular visits by bishops to their subordinate clergy, printed manuals of instruction and catechism, drove corrupt monks into conformity or exile, and produced the first multi-lingual Bible. His activities in reforming the clergy were models to Catholic states across Europe, and are typically cited to explain Protestantism's utter failure to penetrate Spain.

Most other European states, however, did not receive the farsighted and systematic Catholic reform Cisneros provided Castile. As a result, in much of Europe, the Catholic Church was faced with responding to the emerging Protestant challenges. The Church's institutional response, the Council of Trent (1545–1563), admitted, apologized for, and addressed many of the institutional abuses pointed out by Renaissance humanists and Protestant reformers. At the same time, the Council of Trent rejected Protestant theological claims and explicitly defined and explained Catholic dogma.

Believing many Protestants had embraced heresy through an incomplete or inaccurate understanding of Catholic doctrine, several new monastic orders were created specifically as educational orders. Some, like the Barnabites and Capuchins, focused on educating Catholics to prevent the spread of heresy. Others, like the Theatines, emphasized a role among Protestants, to win them back to the Church. The most famous of the new foundations, the Jesuits, gladly embraced both roles. Prominent individuals likewise labored to convert Protestants and educate Catholics. Cardinal Robert Bellarmine (1542–1621), for example, wrote *Concerning the Controversies of the Christian Faith Against the Heretics*, a persuasive defense of Catholic doctrine, and Francisco Suárez (1548–1617) wrote *The Defense of the Catholic Faith Against Anglican Errors* specifically to refute Protestant claims made by the James I (r. 1603–1625), King of England.

Despite the profound, and sometimes violent, disagreements among Catholics, Lutherans, and Calvinists, they all agreed in their condemnation of one group—Anabaptists, the most radical elements of the Protestant movement. Never a single group, Anabaptists did hold certain beliefs in common. Central among these beliefs, and the source of their name, Anabaptists believed in the necessity of adult baptism. Many of their other tenets marked them as socially marginal at best, revolutionary at worst. Their refusal to take oaths precluded them from most public service. Their emphatic pacifism further distanced them from the communities in which they resided. Their egalitarianism suggested a rejection of the very ideas of property and social order. Extremists, such as the murderous Zwickau Prophets, simply confirmed the fears of their detractors. To all other Christians, then, the Anabaptists were an example of reform run wild—an excess of zeal uncoupled from traditional authority and educated leaders—and were the most consistently persecuted group in every part of Europe.

# ADDRESS TO THE CHRISTIAN NOBILITY
## MARTIN LUTHER (1483–1546)

*By the beginning of the sixteenth century, most Christians generally agreed that the Church was in serious need of reform, as it had been from time to time in the past. The financial expedients to which the Avignon popes (1309–1377) had resorted to replace the traditional revenues they could not collect, together with the general perception that they were puppets of the Kings of France, had undermined confidence in the impartiality and integrity of the papal office. The unseemly scramble for support during and after the Great Schism (1378–1415), as well as the tendency of more recent popes to focus on the Papal States, had further eroded the papacy's credibility.*

*In some areas, pluralism (the holding of more than one Church office, especially more than one that involved pastoral duties) and worldly lifestyles among the clergy had led to a significant loss of respect among the ordinary faithful, for many of whom religious practice had become largely a matter of external observance. It was clearly time for some soul-searching, and thoughtful men of the day such as Desiderius Erasmus (c. 1466–1536), Sir Thomas More (1478–1535), and others brought the techniques of the new humanist scholarship to bear on the problems of the contemporary Church.*

*For a variety of reasons, the situation in the early sixteenth century differed from other periods that preceded major reform movements within the Church. Though still cherished by many, the ideal of a single Christian commonwealth had been declining for quite some time in the face of increasing loyalty to secular kingdoms. The growing diversity of lay religious experience meant the institutional Church no longer offered the only channel of access to God. The advent of paper in the fourteenth century and printing with movable type in the fifteenth made it possible for new ideas to circulate faster and more widely than ever before. But above all else, for the first time prominent reformers took issue with Church teaching more than with the conduct of the clergy. In a lecture on Galatians in 1535, Martin Luther wrote:*

*First Principles of the Reformation*, edited by Harry Wace and C. A. Buchheim (London: John Murray, 1883), 617–26.

If the papacy still had the sanctity and austerity of life that it had at the time of fathers like Jerome, Ambrose, Augustine, and others, when the clergy did not yet have an evil reputation for simony, extravagance, pleasures, wealth, adultery, sodomy, and countless other sins, but lived in accordance with the canons and decrees of the fathers, outwardly religious and holy, and even practiced celibacy—what, I ask you, would we have been able to do against the papacy?... But even if the religion and discipline of the papacy stood now as it did once, we would still have to follow the example of Paul, who attacked the false apostles despite their holy and virtuous fronts, and battle against the self-righteousness of the papal kingdom... Therefore we should pay attention not so much to the sinful lives of the papists as to their wicked doctrine and their hypocrisy, and this is what we chiefly attack. Let us suppose that the religion and the discipline of the ancient papacy were flourishing now and were being observed with the same rigor with which the hermits, Jerome, Augustine, Gregory, Bernard, Francis, Dominic, and many others observed it. We would still have to say, "If you have nothing to set against the wrath of God except your sanctity and the chastity of your lives, you are clearly sons of the slave woman, who must be cast out of the kingdom of heaven and condemned."... Therefore we are fighting today, not against the obvious wickedness and vice of the papacy but against its fictitious saints, who think that they lead an angelic life when they observe not only the commandments of God but also the counsels of Christ and works that are not required or works of supererogation. We say that this is a waste of time and effort, unless they have grasped that "one thing" which Christ says is the only thing "needful."

*Some twenty years before he delivered this lecture, Luther's study of the Scriptures had led him to a fundamentally new insight on the matter of justification, or how man entered into a right relationship with God: faith alone was necessary for salvation. In the light of this breakthrough, Luther rethought his views on the sacraments, the authority of the clergy and the Scriptures, the role of good works in the Christian life, and most other aspects of traditional Christianity.*

*The following two readings come from two of Luther's three great Reformation tracts of 1520. In* The Address to the Christian Nobility, *he called on the German princes to reform the Church, beginning with certain major issues to which Luther referred as "the three walls of the*

*Romanists." In this tract he explained the doctrine that came to be called*
*"the priesthood of all believers." Later the same year, he wrote* On Christian
Liberty, *which he dedicated to Pope Leo X, to set forth his view of the*
*relationship between faith and works in the Christian life.*

1520

The grace and might of God be with you, Most Serene Majesty! Most gracious,
well beloved gentlemen!

It is not out of mere arrogance and perversity that I, a single poor man, have
taken upon me to address your lordships. The distress and misery that oppress
all the Christian estates, more especially in Germany, have led not only myself,     5
but everyone else, to cry aloud and to ask for help, and have now forced me
too, to cry out and to ask, if God would give His Spirit to anyone, to reach a
hand to His wretched people. Councils have often put forward some remedy,
but through the cunning of certain men it has been adroitly frustrated, and
the evils have become worse; whose malice and wickedness I will now, by the     10
help of God, expose, so that, being known, they may henceforth cease to be so
obstructive and injurious. God has given us a young and noble sovereign, and
by this has roused hope in many hearts. Now it is right that we too should do
what we can, and make good use of time and grace.

The first thing that we must do is to consider the matter with great     15
earnestness and, whatever we attempt, not to trust in our own strength and
wisdom alone, even if the power of all the world were ours; for God will not
endure that a good work should be begun, trusting to our own strength and
wisdom. He destroys it; it is all useless: as we read in the 33rd Psalm. "There is
no king saved by the multitude of an host. A mighty man is not delivered by     20
much strength." And I fear it is for that reason that those beloved princes, the
Emperors Frederick the First and the Second, and many other German Emperors were, in former times, so piteously spurned and oppressed by the Popes,
though they were feared by all the world. Perchance they trusted rather in their
own strength than in God; therefore they could not but fall. And how would     25
the sanguinary tyrant Julius II[1] have risen to high in our own days but that, I
fear, France, the Germans, and Venice trusted to themselves? The children of
Benjamin slew forty-two thousand Israelites, for this reason that these trusted
to their own strength.

That it may not happen thus to us and to our noble Emperor Charles[2], we     30
must remember that in this matter we wrestle not against flesh and blood, but
against the rulers of the darkness of this world, who may fill the world with war

---

[1]Julius II, Pope (1503–1513)
[2]Charles V (1500–1558), Holy Roman Emperor (1519–1556) and King of all the Spains
(1516–1556)

and bloodshed, but cannot themselves be overcome thereby. We must renounce all confidence in our natural strength, and take the matter in hand with humble trust in God; we must seek God's help with earnest prayer, and have nothing before our eyes but the misery and wretchedness of Christendom, irrespective
5 of what punishment the wicked may deserve.... The greater the might of the foe, the greater is the misfortune if we do not act in the fear of God, and with humility. As Popes and Romanists have hitherto, with the Devil's help, thrown kings into confusion, so will they still do, if we attempt things with our own strength and skill, without God's help.

### The Three Walls of the Romanists

10 The Romanists have, with great adroitness, drawn three walls round themselves, with which they have hitherto protected themselves, so that no one could reform them, whereby all Christendom has fallen terribly.

Firstly, if pressed by the temporal power, they have affirmed and maintained that the temporal power has no jurisdiction over them, but, on the contrary,
15 that the spiritual power is above the temporal.

Secondly, if it were proposed to admonish them with the Scriptures, they objected that no one may interpret the Scriptures but the Pope.

Thirdly, if they are threatened with a Council, they pretend that no one may call a Council but the Pope....

### The First Wall

20 Let us, in the first place, attack the first wall. It has been devised that the Pope, bishops, priests, and monks are called the spiritual estate; princes, lords, artificers, and peasants are the temporal estate; which is a very fine, hypocritical device. But let no one be made afraid by it; and that for this reason: that all Christians are truly of the spiritual estate, and there is no difference among them, save of
25 office alone. As Saint Paul says, we are all one body, though each member does its own work to serve the others. This is because we have one baptism, one gospel, one faith, and are all Christians alike; for baptism, gospel, and faith, these alone make spiritual and Christian people.

As for the unction by a Pope or a bishop, tonsure, ordination, consecra-
30 tion, clothes differing from those of laymen—all this may make a hypocrite or an anointed puppet, but never a Christian or a spiritual man. Thus we are all consecrated as priests by baptism, as Saint Peter says, "You are a royal priest-hood, a holy nation"; and in the book of Revelations, "and has made us unto our God, kings and priests." For, if we have not a higher consecration in us
35 than Pope or bishop can give, no priest could ever be made by the consecration

of Pope or bishop; nor could he say the Mass, or preach, or absolve. Therefore the bishop's consecration is just as if in the name of the whole congregation he took one person out of the community, each member of which has equal power, and commanded him to exercise this power for the rest; in the same way as if ten brothers, co-heirs as king's sons, were to choose one from among them to    5 rule over their inheritance; they would, all of them, still remain kings and have equal power, although one is ordered to govern.

And to put the matter even more plainly; if a little company of pious Christian laymen were taken prisoners and carried away to a desert, and had not among them a priest consecrated by a bishop, and were there to agree to    10 elect one of them, married or un-married, and were to order him to baptize, to celebrate the Mass, to absolve and to preach; this man would as truly be a priest as if all the bishops and all the Popes had consecrated him. That is why in cases of necessity every man can baptize and absolve, which would not be possible if we were not all priests. This great grace and virtue of baptism and    15 of the Christian estate they have almost destroyed and made us forget by their ecclesiastical law. In this way the Christians used to choose their bishops and priests out of the community; these being afterwards confirmed by other bishops, without the pomp that we have now. So was it that Saints Augustine, Ambrose, Cyprian were bishops.    20

Since then the temporal power is baptized as we are, and has the same faith and gospel, we must allow it to be priest and bishop, and account its office an office that is proper and useful to the Christian community. For whatever issues from baptism may boast that it has been consecrated priest, bishop, and Pope, although it does not beseem everyone to exercise these offices. For, since    25 we are all priests alike, no man may put himself forward, or take upon himself, without our consent and election, to do that which we have all alike power to do. For, if a thing is common to all, no man may take it to himself without the wish and command of the community. And if it should happen that a man were appointed to one of these offices and deposed for abuses, he would be just    30 what he was before. Therefore a priest should be nothing in Christendom but a functionary; as long as he holds his office he has precedence of others; if he is deprived of it, he is a peasant and a citizen like the rest. Therefore a priest is verily no longer a priest after deposition. But now they have invented *characters indelebiles*, and pretend that a priest after deprivation still differs from a simple    35 layman. They even imagine that a priest can never be anything but a priest; that is, that he can never become a layman. All this is nothing but mere talk and ordinance of human invention.

It follows then, that between layman and priests, princes and bishops, or as they call it, between spiritual and temporal persons, the only real difference is    40

one of office and function, and not of estate, for they are all of the same spiritual estate, true priests, bishops, and Popes, though their functions are not the same, just as among priests and monks every man has not the same functions. And this Saint Paul says and Saint Peter, "we being many are one body in Christ, and
5   every one members one of another." Christ's body is not double or two-fold, one temporal, the other spiritual. He is one head, and he has one body.

We see then that just as those that we call spiritual, or priests, bishops, or Popes do not differ from other Christians in any other or higher degree, but in that they are to be concerned with the word of God, and the sacraments—that
10   being their work and office—in the same way the temporal authorities hold the sword and the rod in their hands to punish the wicked and to protect the good. A cobbler, a smith, a peasant—every man has the office and function of his calling, and yet all alike are consecrated priests and bishops, and every man in his office must be useful and beneficial to the rest, that so many kinds of
15   work may all be united into one community: just as the members of the body all serve one another.

Now see, what a Christian doctrine is this, that the temporal authority is not above the clergy and may not punish it. This is, as if one were to say, the hand may not help, though the eye is in grievous suffering. Is it not un-natural,
20   not to say un-Christian, that one member may not help another or guard it against harm? Nay, the nobler the member, the more the rest are bound to help it. Therefore I say forasmuch as the temporal power has been ordained by God for the punishment of the bad, and the protection of the good, therefore we must let it do its duty throughout the whole Christian body, without respect
25   of persons, whether it strike Popes, bishops, priests, monks, or nuns. If it were sufficient reason for fettering the temporal power that it is inferior among the officers of Christianity to the offices of priest or confessor, or to the spiritual estate—if this were so, then we ought to restrain tailors, cobblers, masons, carpenters, cooks, servants, peasants, and all secular workmen from providing
30   the Pope, or bishop, priests, and monks with shoes, clothes, houses, or victuals, or from paying them tithes. But if these laymen are allowed to do their work without restraint, what do the Romanist scribes mean by their laws? They mean that they withdraw themselves from the operation of temporal Christian power, simply in order that they may be free to do evil, and thus fulfill what Saint Peter
35   said, "There shall be false teachers among you…and through covetousness shall they with feigned words make merchandise of you."

Therefore the temporal Christian power must exercise its office without let or hindrance, without considering whom it may strike, whether Pope, or bishop, or priest; whoever is guilty, let him suffer for it. Whatever the ecclesiastical
40   law says in opposition to this is merely the invention of Romanist arrogance.

For this is what Saint Paul says to all Christians, "Let every soul" (I presume including the Popes) "be subject unto the higher powers, for he bears not the sword in vain. For he is the minister of God, a revenger to execute wrath upon him that does evil." Also Saint Peter, "Submit yourselves to every ordinance of man for the Lord's sake…for so is the will of God." He has also said that men would come who should despise government; as has come to pass through ecclesiastical law.…

### The Second Wall

The second wall is even more tottering and weak: that they alone pretend to be considered masters of the Scriptures; although they learn nothing of them all their life, they assume authority and juggle before us with impudent words, saying that the Pope cannot err in matters of faith, whether he be evil or good; albeit they cannot prove it by a single letter. That is why the canon law contains so many heretical and un-Christian, nay, un-natural laws; but of these we need not speak now. For whereas they imagine the Holy Ghost never leaves them, however unlearned and wicked they may be, they grow bold enough to decree whatever they like. But were this true, where were the need and use of the Holy Scriptures? Let us burn them, and content ourselves with the unlearned gentlemen at Rome, in whom the Holy Ghost dwells, who, however, can dwell in pious souls only. If I had not read it, I could never have believed that the Devil should have put forth such follies at Rome and find a following.

But not to fight them with our own words, we will quote Scriptures. Saint Paul says, "If anything be revealed to another that sits by, let the first hold his peace." What would be the use of this commandment if we were to believe him alone that teaches or has the highest seat? Christ Himself says, "And they shall be all taught of God." Thus it may come to pass that the Pope and his followers are wicked and not true Christians, and not being taught by God, have no true understanding, whereas a common man may have true understanding. Why should we then not follow him? Has not the Pope often erred? Who could help Christianity, in case the Pope errs, if we do not rather believe another who has the Scriptures for him?

Therefore it is a wickedly devised fable, and they cannot quote a single letter to confirm it, that it is for the Pope alone to interpret the Scriptures or to confirm the interpretation of them; they have assumed the authority of their own selves. And though they say that this authority was given to Saint Peter when the keys were given to him, it is plain enough that the keys were not given to Saint Peter alone, but to the whole community. Besides, the keys were not ordained for doctrine or authority, but for sin, to bind or loose; and what they claim besides this is mere invention. But what Christ said to Saint Peter, "I have

prayed for you, that your faith fail not," cannot relate to the Pope, inasmuch as there have been many Popes without faith, as they are themselves forced to acknowledge. Nor did Christ pray for Peter alone, but for all the Apostles and all Christians, as He says, "Neither pray I for these alone, but for them also which
5    shall believe on me through their word." Is not this plain enough?...

### The Third Wall

The third wall falls of itself, as soon as the first two have fallen; for if the Pope acts contrary to the Scriptures, we are bound to stand by the Scriptures to pun-ish and to constrain him, according to Christ's commandment; "Moreover if your brother shall trespass against you, go and tell him his fault between you
10   and him alone. If he shall hear you, you have gained your brother. But if he will not hear you, then take with you one or two more, that in the mouth of two or three witnesses every word may be established. And if he shall neglect to hear them, tell it unto the church. But if he neglect to hear the church, let him be unto you as an heathen man and a publican."... Moreover, they can
15   show nothing in the Scriptures giving the Pope sole power to call and confirm councils; they have nothing but their own laws; but these hold good only so long as they are not injurious to Christianity and the laws of God. Therefore, if the Pope deserves punishment, these laws cease to bind us, since Christendom would suffer if he were not punished by a council. Thus we read that the council
20   of the Apostles was not called by Saint Peter, but by all the Apostles and the elders.... Moreover if I consider the councils that the Pope has called, I do not find that they produced any notable results.

Therefore, when need requires and the Pope is a cause of offence to Chris-tendom, in these cases whoever can best do so, as a faithful member of the whole
25   body, must do what he can to procure a true free council. This no one can do so well as the temporal authorities, especially since they are fellow-Christians, fellow-priests, sharing one spirit, and one power in all things; and since they should exercise the office that they have received from God without hindrance, whenever it is necessary and useful that it should be exercised....

30   But as for their boasts of their authority, that no one must oppose it, this is idle talk. No one in Christendom has any authority to do harm, or to forbid others to prevent harm being done. There is no authority in the Church but for reformation. Therefore if the Pope wished to use his power to prevent the calling of a free council so as to prevent the reformation of the Church, we
35   must not respect him or his power; and if he should begin to excommunicate and fulminate, we must despise this as the ravings of a madman, and trusting in God, excommunicate and repel him as best we may. For this his usurped

power is nothing; he does not possess it, and he is at once overthrown by a text from the Scriptures. For Saint Paul says to the Corinthians, "That God has given us authority for edification and not for destruction." Who will set this text at naught?...

And now I hope we have laid the false, lying specter with which the 5 Romanists have long terrified and stupefied our consciences. And we have shown that, like all the rest of us, they are subject to the temporal sword; that they have no authority to interpret the Scriptures by force without skill; and that they have no power to prevent a council, or to pledge it in accordance with their pleasure, or to bind it beforehand and deprive it of its freedom; and that 10 if they do this, they are verily of the fellowship of Anti-Christ and the Devil, and have nothing of Christ but the name.

# ON CHRISTIAN LIBERTY
## MARTIN LUTHER (1483–1546)

1520

Christian faith has appeared to many an easy thing; nay, not a few even reckon it among the social virtues, as it were; and this they do because they have not made proof of it experimentally, and have never tasted of what efficacy it is. For it is not possible for any man to write well about it, or to understand well what is rightly written, who has not at some time tasted of its spirit under the 5 pressure of tribulation. While he who has tasted of it, even to a very small extent, can never write, speak, think, or hear about it sufficiently. For it is a living fountain, springing up unto eternal life, as Christ calls in the fourth chapter of Saint John.

Now, though I cannot boast of my abundance, and though I know how 10 poorly I am furnished, yet I hope that, after having been vexed by various temptations, I have attained some little drop of faith, and that I can speak of this matter, if not with more elegance, certainly with more solidity than those literal and too subtle disputants who have hitherto discoursed upon it without understanding their own words. That I may open, then, an easier way for the 15 ignorant—for these alone I am trying to serve—I first lay down these two propositions concerning spiritual liberty and servitude.

*A Christian man is the most free lord of all, and subject to none.*

*A Christian man is the most dutiful servant of all, and subject to everyone.*

Although these statements appear contradictory, yet when they are found to 20 agree together, they will be highly serviceable to my purpose. They are both the statements of Paul himself, who says, "Though I be free from all men, yet have I made myself servant unto all"[1] and "Owe no man anything, but to love one another."[2] Now love is by its own nature dutiful and obedient to the beloved object. Thus even Christ, though Lord of all things, was yet made of a woman; 25 made under the law; at once free and a servant; at once in the form of God and in the form of a servant.

---

[1] I Corinthians 9:19
[2] Romans 4:16

---

*First Principles of the Reformation*, edited by Henry Wace and C. A. Buchheim (London: John Murray, 1883), 634–47.

Let us examine the subject on a deep and less simple principle. Man is composed of a two-fold nature, a spiritual and a bodily. As regards the spiritual nature, which they name the soul, he is called the spiritual, inward, new man; as regards the bodily nature, which they name the flesh, he is called the fleshly,
5   outward, old man. The Apostle speaks of this, "Though our outward man perish, yet the inward man is renewed day by day."[3] The result of this diversity is that in the Scriptures opposing statements are made concerning the same man; the fact being that in the same man these two men are opposed to one another; the flesh lusting against the spirit, and the spirit against the flesh.

10   We first approach the subject of the inward man, that we may see by what means a man becomes justified, free, and a true Christian; that is, a spiritual, new, and inward man. It is certain that absolutely none among outward things, under whatever name they may be reckoned, has any weight in producing a state of justification and Christian liberty, nor, on the other hand, an unjustified state
15   and one of slavery. This can be shown by an easy course of argument.

What can it profit the soul, that the body should be in good condition, free, and full of life; that it should eat, drink, and act according to its pleasure; when even the most impious slaves of every kind of vice are prosperous in these matters? Again, what harm can ill-health, bondage, hunger, thirst, or any other
20   outward evil do the soul, when even the most pious of men, and the freest in the purity of their conscience, are harassed by these things? Neither of these states of things has to do with the liberty or the slavery of the soul....

And, to cast everything aside, even speculations, meditations, and whatever things can be performed by the exertions of the soul itself are of no profit. One
25   thing, and one alone, is necessary for life, justification, and Christian liberty, and that is the most holy word of God, the Gospel of Christ. As He says, "I am the resurrection and the life; he that believes in me shall not die eternally"[4]; and also "If the Son shall make you free, you shall be free indeed"[5]; and "Man shall not live by bread alone, but by every word that proceeds out of the mouth
30   of God."[6]

Let us therefore hold it for certain and firmly established that the soul can do without everything, except the word of God, without which none at all of its wants are provided for. But, having the word, it is rich and wants for nothing; since that is the word of life, of truth, of light, of peace, of justification,
35   of salvation, of joy, of liberty, of wisdom, of virtue, of grace, of glory, and of every good thing. It is on this account that the prophet in a whole psalm, and

---

[3]II Corinthians 4:16
[4]John 11:25
[5]John 8:36
[6]Matthew 4:4

in many other places, sighs for and calls upon the word of God with so many groanings and words....

But you will ask, "What is this word, and by what means is it to be used, since there are as many words of God?" I answer, the Apostle Paul explains what it is, namely the Gospel of God, concerning His son, incarnate, suffering, risen, and glorified through the Spirit, the sanctifier. To preach Christ is to feed the soul, to justify it, to set it free, and to save it, if it believes the preaching. For faith alone, and the efficacious use of the word God, bring salvation. "If you shall confess with your mouth the Lord Jesus, and shall believe in your heart that God has raised him from the dead, you shall be saved."[7] And again, "Christis the end of the law for righteousness to everyone that believes"[8]; and "The just shall live by faith."[9] For the word of God cannot be received and honored by any works, but by faith alone. Hence it is clear that as the soul needs the word alone for life and justification, so it is justified by faith alone and not by any works. For if it could be justified by any other means, it would have no need of the word, nor consequently of faith....

Since, then, this faith can reign only in the inward man, as it is said, "With the heart man believes unto righteousness;"[10] and since it alone justifies, it is evident that by no outward work of labor can the inward man be at all justified, made free, and saved; and that no works whatever have any relation to him. And so, on the other hand, it is solely by impiety and incredulity of heart that he becomes guilty, and a slave of sin, deserving condemnation; not by any outward sign or work. Therefore the first care of every Christian ought to be to lay aside all reliance on works and strengthen his faith alone more and more, and by it grow in the knowledge, not of works, but of Christ Jesus, who has suffered and risen again for him; as Peter teaches, when he makes no other work to be a Christian one. Thus Christ, when the Jews asked Him what they should do that they might work the works of God, rejected the multitude of works, with which He saw that they were puffed up, and commanded them one thing only, saying, "This is the work of God, that you believe on him whom He has sent, for him has God the Father sealed."[11]...

But you ask how it can be that the faith alone justifies and affords without works so great a treasure of good things, when so many works, ceremonies, and laws are prescribed to us in the Scriptures. I answer: before all things bear in

---

[7]Romans 10:9
[8]Romans 10:4
[9]Romans 1:17
[10]Romans 10:10
[11]A paraphrase of John 6:27–29

mind what I have said, that faith alone without works justifies, sets free, and saves, as I shall show more clearly below.

Meanwhile it is to be noted that the whole Scripture of God is divided into two parts—precepts and promises. The precepts certainly teach us what is good, but what they teach is not forthwith done. For they show us what we ought to do, but do not give us the power to do it. They were ordained, however, for the purpose of showing man to himself; that through them he may learn his own impotence for good, and may despair of his own strength. For this reason they are called the Old Testament, and are so....

Then comes in that other part of Scripture, the promises of God, which declare the glory of God, and say, "If you wish to fulfill the law and, as the law requires, not to covet, lo! Believe in Christ, in whom are promised to you grace, justification, peace, and liberty." All these things you shall have, if you believe, and shall be without them if you do not believe. For what is impossible for you by all the works of the law, which are many and yet useless, you shall fulfill in an easy and summary way through faith; because God the Father has made everything to depend on faith, so that whosoever has it has all things, and he who has it not has nothing. "For God has concluded them all in unbelief, that He might have mercy upon all."[12] Thus the promises of God give that which the precepts exact, and fulfill what the law commands; so that all is of God alone, both the precepts and their fulfillment. He alone commands. He alone also fulfills. Hence the promises of God belong to the New Testament; nay, are the New Testament.

Now since these promises of God are words of holiness, truth, righteousness, liberty, and peace, and are full of universal goodness; the soul, which cleaves to them with a firm faith, is so united to them—nay, thoroughly absorbed by them—that it not only partakes in, but is penetrated and saturated by, all their virtue. For if the touch of Christ was healing, how much more does that most tender spiritual touch, nay, absorption of the word, communicate to the soul all that belongs to the word. In this way, therefore, the soul, through faith alone, without works, is from the word of God justified, sanctified, endued with truth, peace, and liberty, and filled with every good thing, and is truly made the child of God; as it is said, "To them gave he power to become the sons of God, even to them that believe on his name."[13]

From all this it is easy to understand why faith has such great power, and why no good works, nor even all good works put together, can compare with it; since no work can cleave to the word of God, or be in the soul. Faith alone

---

[12]Romans 11:32
[13]John 1:12

and the word reign in it; and such as is the word, such is the soul made by it; just as iron exposed to fire glows like fire on account of its union with the fire. It is clear then that to a Christian man his faith suffices for everything, and that he has no need of works for justification. But if he has no need of works, neither has he need of the law; and, if he has no need of the law, he is certainly free from the law, and the saying is true, "The law is not made for a righteous man."[14] This is that Christian liberty, our faith, but that no one should need the law or works for justification and salvation.

Let us consider this as the first virtue of faith; and let us look also to the second. This also is an office of faith, that it honors with the utmost veneration and the highest reputation him in whom it believes, inasmuch as it holds him to be truthful and righteousness, with which we honor him in whom we believe. What higher credit can we attribute to anyone than truth and righteousness, and absolute goodness? On the other hand, it is the greatest insult to brand any one with the reputation of falsehood and unrighteousness, or to suspect him of these, as we do when we disbelieve him....

Thus the soul, in firmly believing the promises of God, holds Him to be true and righteous; and it can attribute to God no higher glory than the credit of being so. The highest worship of God is to ascribe to Him truth, righteousness, and whatever qualities we must ascribe to one in whom we believe. In doing this the soul shows itself prepared to do His whole will; in doing this it hallows His name, and gives itself up to be dealt with as it may please God. For it cleaves to His promises, and never doubts that He is true, just, and wise, and will do, dispose, and provide for all things in the best way. Is not such a soul, in this its faith, most obedient to God in all things? What commandment does there remain which has not been amply fulfilled by such an obedience? What fulfillment can be more full than universal obedience? Now this is not accomplished by works, but by faith alone....

[An] incomparable grace of faith is this, that it unites the soul to Christ, as the wife to the husband; by which mystery, as the Apostle teaches, Christ and the soul are made one flesh. Now if they are one flesh, and if a true marriage—nay, by far the most perfect of all marriages—is accomplished between them (for human marriages are but feeble types of this one great marriage), then it follows that all they have becomes theirs in common, as well good things as evil things; so that whatsoever Christ possesses, that the believing soul may take to itself and boast of as its own, and whatever belongs to the soul, that Christ claims as his.

---

[14]I Timothy 1:9

If we compare these possessions, we shall see how inestimable is the gain. Christ is full of grace, life, and salvation; the soul is full of sin, death, and condemnation. Let faith step in, and then sin, death, and hell will belong to Christ, and grace, life, and salvation to the soul. For, if he is a husband, he must needs

5    take to himself that which is his wife's, and, at the same time, impart to his wife that which is his. For, in giving her his own body and himself, how can he but give her all that is his? And, in taking to himself the body of his wife, how can he but take to himself all that is hers?...

Thus the believing soul, by the pledge of its faith in Christ, becomes free

10    from all sin, fearless of death, safe from hell, and endowed with the eternal righteousness, life, and salvation of its husband Christ. Thus he presents to himself a glorious bride, without spot or wrinkle, cleansing her with the washing of water by the word; that is, by faith in the word of life, righteousness, and salvation. Thus he betroths her unto himself "in faithfulness, in righteousness,

15    and in judgment, and in loving kindness, and in mercies...."

From all this you will again understand, why so much importance is attributed to faith, so that it alone can fulfill the law, and justify without any works. For you see that the first commandment, which says, "You shall worship one God only," is fulfilled by faith alone. If you were nothing but good works from

20    the soles of your feet to the crown of your head, you would not be worshipping God, nor fulfilling the first commandment, since it is impossible to worship God, without ascribing to Him the glory of truth and of universal goodness, as it ought in truth to be ascribed. Now this is not done by works, but only by faith of heart. It is not by working, but by believing, that we glorify God

25    and confess Him to be true. On this ground faith is the sole righteousness of a Christian man, and the fulfilling of all the commandments. For to him who fulfills the first, the task of fulfilling all the rest is easy.

Works, since they are irrational things, cannot glorify God; although they may be done to the glory of God, if faith be present. But at present we

30    are enquiring, not into the quality of the works done, but into him who does them, who glorifies God, and brings forth good works. This is faith of heart, the head and the substance of all our righteousness. Hence that is a blind and perilous doctrine which teaches that the commandments are fulfilled by works. The commandments must have been fulfilled, previous to any good works, and

35    good works follow their fulfillment, as we shall see....

And now let us turn...to the outward man. Here we shall give an answer to all those who, taking offence at the word of faith and at what I have asserted, say: "If faith does everything, and by itself suffices for justification, why then are good works commanded? Are we then to take our ease and do no works,

40    content with faith?" Not so, impious men, I reply; not so. That would indeed

really be the case, if we were thoroughly and completely inner and spiritual persons; but that will not happen until the last day, when the dead shall be raised. As long as we live in the flesh, we are but beginning and making advances in that which shall be completed in a future life. On this account the Apostle calls that which we have in this life, the first-fruits of the Spirit. In future we shall have the tenths, and the fullness of the Spirit. To this part belongs the fact I have stated before, that the Christian is the servant of all and subject to all. For in that part in which he is free, he does no works, but in that in which he is a servant, he does all works. Let us see on what principle this is so.

Although, as I have said, inwardly, and according to the spirit, a man is amply enough justified by faith, having all that he requires to have, except that this very faith and abundance ought to increase from day to day, even till the future life; still he remains in this mortal life upon earth, in which it is necessary that he should rule his own body, and have intercourse with men. Here then works begin; here he must not take his ease; here he must give heed to exercise his body by fastings, watchings, labor, and other moderate discipline, so that it may be subdued to the spirit, and obey and conform itself to the inner man and faith, and not rebel against them nor hinder them, as is its nature to do if it is not kept under. For the inner man, being conformed to God, and created after the image of God through faith, rejoices and delights itself in Christ, in whom such blessings have been conferred on it; and hence has only this task before it, to serve God with joy and for naught in free love....

These works, however, must not be done with any notion that by them a man can be justified before God—for faith, which alone is righteousness before God, will not bear with this false notion—but solely with this purpose, that the body may be brought into subjection, and be purified from its evil lusts, so that our eyes may be turned only to purging away those lusts. For when the soul has been cleansed by faith and made to love God, it would have all things to be cleansed in like manner; and especially its own body, so that all things might unite with it in the love and praise of God. Thus it comes that, from the requirements of his own body, a man cannot take his ease, but is compelled on its account to do many good works, that he may bring it into subjection. Yet these works are not the means of his justification before God; he does them out of disinterested love to the service of God; looking to no other end than to do what is well-pleasing to Him whom he desires to obey most dutifully in all things.

On this principle every man may easily instruct himself in what measure, and with what distinctions, he ought to chasten his own body. He will fast, watch, and labor, just as much as he sees to suffice for keeping down the wantonness and concupiscence of the body. But those who pretend to be justified

by works are looking, not to the mortification of their lusts, but only to the works themselves; thinking that, if they can accomplish as many works and as great ones as possible, all is well with them, and they are justified. Sometimes they even injure their brain, and extinguish nature, or at least make it useless.
5 This is enormous folly, and ignorance of Christian life and faith, when a man seeks, without faith, to be justified and saved by works....

A bishop, when he consecrates a church, confirms children, or performs any other duty of his office, is not consecrated as bishop by these works; nay, unless he had been previously consecrated as bishop, not one of those works would have
10 any validity; they would be foolish, childish, and ridiculous. Thus a Christian, being consecrated by his faith, does good works; but he is not by these works made a more sacred person, or more a Christian. That is the effect of faith alone; nay, unless he were previously a believer and a Christian, none of his works would have any value at all, they would really be impious and damnable sins.
15 True, then, are these two sayings: Good works do not make a good man, but a good man does good works. Bad works do not make a bad man, but a bad man does bad works. Thus it is always necessary that the substance or person should be good before any good works can be done, and that good works should follow and proceed from a good person. As Christ says: "A good
20 tree cannot bring forth evil fruit, neither can a corrupt tree bring forth good fruit."[15] Now it is clear that the fruit does not bear the tree, nor does the tree grow on the fruit; but, on the contrary, the trees bear the fruit and the fruit grows on the trees....

Since, then, works justify no man, but a man must be justified before he
25 can do any good work, it is most evident that it is faith alone which, by the mere mercy of God through Christ, and by means of His word, can worthily and sufficiently justify and save the person; and that a Christian man needs no work, no law, for his salvation; for by faith he is free from all law and in perfect freedom does gratuitously all that he does, seeking nothing either of profit or of
30 salvation—since by the grace of God he is already saved and rich in all things through his faith—but solely that which is well-pleasing to God.

So too no good work can profit an unbeliever to justification and salvation; and on the other hand no evil work makes him an evil and condemned person, but that unbelief, which makes the person and the tree bad, makes his works
35 evil and condemned. Wherefore, when any man is made good or bad, this does not arise from his works, but from his faith or unbelief....

Here is the truly Christian life; here is faith really working by love; when a man applied himself with joy and love to the works of that freest servitude, in

---

[15]Matthew 7:18

which he serves others voluntarily and for nought; himself abundantly satisfied in the fullness and riches of his own faith....

Thus from faith flow forth love and joy in the Lord, and from love a cheerful, willing, free spirit, disposed to serve our neighbor voluntarily, without taking any account of gratitude or ingratitude, praise or blame, gain or loss. Its object is not to lay men under obligations, nor does it distinguish between friends and enemies, or look to gratitude or ingratitude, but most freely and willingly spends itself and its goods, whether it loses them through ingratitude, or gains good will....

...There are very many persons, who, when they hear of this liberty of faith, straightway turn it into an occasion of license. They think that everything is now lawful for them, and do not choose to show themselves free men and Christians in any other way than by their contempt and reprehension of ceremonies, of traditions, of human laws; as if they were Christians merely because they refuse to fast on stated days, or eat flesh when others fast, or omit the customary prayers; scoffing at the precepts of men, but utterly passing over all the rest that belongs to the Christian religion. On the other hand, they are most pertinaciously resisted by those who strive after salvation solely by their observance of and reverence for ceremonies; as if they would be saved merely because they fast on stated days, or abstain from flesh, or make formal prayers; talking loudly of the precepts of the Church and of the Fathers, and not caring a straw about those things which belong to our genuine faith. Both these parties are plainly culpable, in that, while they neglect matters which are of weight and necessary for salvation, they contend noisily about such as are without weight and not necessary.

How much more rightly does the Apostle Paul teach us to walk in the middle path, condemning either extreme, and saying: "Let not him that eats despise him that eats not; and let not him who eats not judge him that eats."[16]...

It is not from works that we are set free by the faith of Christ, but from the belief in works, that is, from foolishly presuming to seek justification through works. Faith redeems our consciences, makes them upright and preserves them, since by it we recognize the truth that justification does not depend on our works, although good works neither can nor ought to be wanting to it; just as we cannot exist without food and drink and all the functions of this mortal body. Still it is not on them that our justification is based, but on faith; and yet they ought not on that account to be despised or neglected....

Since, then, we cannot live in this world without ceremonies and works; since the hot and inexperienced period of youth has need of being restrained

---

[16]Romans 14:3

and protected by such bonds; and since everyone is bound to keep under his own body by attention to these things; therefore the minister of Christ must be prudent and faithful in so ruling and teaching the people of Christ in all these matters that no root of bitterness may spring up among them, and so many be
5    defiled, as Paul warned the Hebrews; that is, that they may not lose the faith, and begin to be defiled by a belief in works, as the means of justification. This is a thing which easily happens, and defiles very many, unless faith be constantly inculcated along with works. It is impossible to avoid this evil, when faith is passed over in silence, and only the ordinances of men are taught, as has been
10  done hitherto by the pestilent, impious, and soul-destroying traditions of our pontiffs, and opinions of our theologians. An infinite number of souls have been drawn down to hell by these snares, so that you may recognize the work of Anti-Christ....

Hence in the Christian life ceremonies are to be no otherwise looked
15  upon than builders and workmen look upon those preparations for building or working which are not made with any view of being permanent or anything in themselves, but only because without them there could be no building and no work. When the structure is completed, they are laid aside. Here you see that we do not contemn these preparations, but set the highest value on them;
20  a belief in them we do contemn, because no one thinks that they constitute a real and permanent structure. If anyone were so manifestly out of his senses as to have no other object in life but that of setting up these preparations with all possible expense, diligence, and perseverance, while he never thought of the structure itself, but pleased himself and made his boast of these useless prepara-
25  tions and props; should we not all pity his madness, and think that, at the cost thus thrown away, some great building might have been raised?

# THE TWELVE ARTICLES

*To many German peasants and village priests, the Church hierarchy cooper-*
*ated with and formed part of what they saw as an oppressive ruling elite.*
*For these people, Luther's message of Gospel liberty became transformed into*
*a call for social revolution. Luther himself was appalled that anyone could*
*so misunderstand what he had been trying to say. For him, the freedom of*
*a Christian was spiritual, not physical, and revolt against the governing*
*authorities was revolt against God.*

1524

Peace to the Christian Reader and the Grace of God through Christ. There
are many evil writings put forth of late which take occasion, on account of the
assembling of the peasants, to cast scorn upon the Gospel, saying: Is this the
fruit of the new teaching, that no one should obey but all should everywhere
rise in revolt and rush together to reform or perhaps destroy altogether the    5
authorities, both ecclesiastic and lay? The articles below shall answer these godless
and criminal fault-finders, and serves in the first place to remove the reproach
from the word of God and in the second place to give a Christian excuse for
the disobedience or even the revolt of the entire peasantry....

*The Second Article*—According as the just tithe is established by the Old Testa-    10
ment and fulfilled in the New, we are ready and willing to pay the fair tithe[1] of
grain. The word of God plainly provides that in giving according to right to God
and distributing to His people, the services of a pastor are required. We will that
for the future our church provost, whomsoever the community may appoint,
shall gather and receive this tithe. From this he shall give to the pastor, elected    15
by the whole community.... The small tithes, whether ecclesiastical or lay, we
will not pay at all, for the Lord God created cattle for the free use of man. We
will not, therefore, pay farther an unseemly tithe which is of man's invention.

---

[1]Tithes were taxes, not voluntary offerings.

*Translations and Reprints from the Original Sources of European History: Reformation Number*
(Philadelphia: Department of History, University of Pennsylvania, 1897), III:18–23.

*The Third Article*—It has been the custom hitherto for men to hold us as their own property, which is pitiable enough, considering that Christ has delivered and redeemed us all, without exception, by the shedding of His precious blood, the lowly as well as the great. Accordingly, it is consistent with Scripture that
5    we should be free and wish to be so. Not that we would wish to be absolutely free and under no authority. God does not teach us that we should lead a disorderly life in the lusts of the flesh, but that we should love the Lord our God and our neighbor. We would gladly observe all this as God has commanded us in the celebration of the communion. He has not commanded us not to
10   obey the authorities, but rather that we should be humble, not only towards those in authority, but towards everyone. We are thus ready to yield obedience according to God's law to our elected and regular authorities in all proper things becoming to a Christian. We, therefore, take it for granted that you will release us from serfdom as true Christians, unless it should be shown us from
15   the Gospel that we are serfs....

*The Tenth Article*—In the tenth place, we are aggrieved by the appropriation by individuals of meadows and fields which at one time belonged to a community.[2] These we will take again into our own hands. It may, however, happen that the land was rightfully purchased. When, however, the land has unfortunately been
20   purchased in this way, some brotherly arrangement should be made according to circumstances.

*The Eleventh Article*—In the eleventh place we will entirely abolish the due called *Todfall*,[3] and will no longer endure it, nor allow widows and orphans to be thus shamefully robbed against God's will....

---

[2]In the Middle Ages, in many places it was long-standing custom that the tenants of a manor could graze their animals in the fields after harvest; in addition, villages often had meadows and other areas where the inhabitants had common grazing rights. In the fourteenth and fifteenth centuries, many landlords shifted from labor-intensive agriculture to stock-raising, often enclosing their fields and even at times evicting their tenants.

[3]*Todfall*—inheritance tax levied on un-free tenants; customarily the deceased tenant's best beast

# THE INSTITUTES
## JOHN CALVIN (1509–1564)

*John Calvin, born Jean Cauvin in the region of Picardy in northern France, was educated in theology and the law according to the tenets of French humanism. Calvin's father was a lawyer and, like Luther's father, wanted his son to be a lawyer. Instead, the young Calvin could not overcome his attraction to theology. Sometime between 1528 and 1533, he converted to Protestantism. In describing this experience, Calvin wrote, "God by a sudden conversion subdued and brought my mind to a teachable frame."*
*He first published* The Institutes of the Christian Religion *in 1536, when he was twenty-six years old. The work contains a systematic state-ment of Protestant theology from the Reformed tradition. Calvin re-issued it in revised and often expanded form four times before his death nearly thirty years later. The central principle of Calvinist theology is the absolute sovereignty of God; indeed, all his other teachings, including his famous doctrine of predestination, follow directly from that starting point. While it is correct to identify Calvin as one of the most important theologians of his or any day, his significance extends far more broadly because of the insights he offered into such areas as politics and society. Indeed, there is good reason to regard Calvin's ideas, as they appear in* The Institutes *and were interpreted and popularized by associates and successors over the years, as among the most influential bodies of thought to come out of the early-modern period of Western history. The selections that follow discuss primarily the nature of Christian liberty and polity. The dedication to Francis I of France (r. 1515–1547), one of the most illustrious of the Eu-ropean monarchs of that day, did not achieve Calvin's apparent objective of converting the king to Protestantism.*

1536

...This consideration constitutes true royalty, to acknowledge yourself in the government of your kingdom to be the minister of God. For where the glory of God is not made the end of the government it is not a legitimate sovereignty, but an usurpation. And he is deceived who expects lasting prosperity in that kingdom which is not ruled by the scepter of God, that is, His holy word; for          5

*Institutes of the Christian Religion by John Calvin*, edited by John Allen (Philadelphia: Presby-terian Board of Publications, 1921), I:22–23, II:63–75, 633–43.

that heavenly oracle cannot fail which declares that "where there is no vision, the people perish."[1] Nor should you be seduced from this pursuit by a contempt of our meanness. We are fully conscious to ourselves how very mean and abject we are, being miserable sinners before God, and accounted most despicable by men;
5    being (if you please) the refuse of the world, deserving of the vilest appellations that can be found; so that nothing remains for us to glory in before God, but His mercy alone, by which, without any merit of ours, we have been admitted to the hope of eternal salvation, and before men nothing but our weakness, the slightest confession of which is esteemed by them as the greatest disgrace. But
10   our doctrine must stand, exalted above all the glory, and invincible by all the power of the world, because it is not ours, but the doctrine of the living God, and of His Christ, Whom the Father has constituted King, that He may have dominion from sea to sea, and from the river even to the ends of the earth, with its strength of iron and with its splendor of gold and silver, smitten by the rod
15   of His mouth, may be broken to pieces like a potter's vessel;[2] for thus do the prophets foretell the magnificence of His kingdom....

**III§19**...Christian liberty, according to my judgment, consists of three parts. The first part is that the consciences of believers, when seeking an assurance of their justification before God, should raise themselves above the law, and forget all
20   the righteousness of the law. For since the law leaves no man righteous, either we must be excluded from all hope of justification, or it is necessary for us to be delivered from it, and that so completely as not to have any dependence on works. For he who imagines that in order to obtain righteousness he must produce any works, however small, can fix no limit or boundary, but renders
25   himself a debtor to the whole law. Avoiding, therefore, all mention of the law, and dismissing all thought of our own works in reference to justification, we must embrace the Divine mercy alone, and turning our eyes from ourselves, fix them solely on Christ. For the question is, not how we can be righteous, but how, though unrighteous and unworthy, we can be considered as righteous.
30   And the conscience that desires to attain any certainty respecting this must give no admission to the law. Nor will this authorize any one to conclude that the law is of no use to believers, whom it still continues to instruct and exhort, and stimulate to duty, although it has no place in their consciences before the tribunal of God. For these two things, being very different, require to be prop-
35   erly and carefully distinguished by us. The whole life of Christians ought to be an exercise of piety, since they are called to sanctification. It is the office of the law to remind them of their duty, and thereby to excite them to the pursuit of

---

[1]Proverbs 29:18
[2]Daniel 2:34, Isaiah 9:4, and Psalm 2:9

holiness and integrity. But when their consciences are solicitous how God may be propitiated, what answer they shall make, and on what they shall rest their confidence, if called to His tribunal, there must then be no consideration of the requisitions of the law, but Christ alone must be proposed for righteousness, who exceeds all the perfection of the law.... 5

The second part of Christian liberty, which is dependent on the first, is that their consciences do not observe the law as being under any legal obligation, but that, being liberated from the yoke of the law, they yield a voluntary obedience to the will of God. For being possessed with perpetual terrors as long as they remain under the dominion of the law, they will never engage with alacrity and 10 promptitude in the service of God unless they have previously received this liberty.... If they advert to the law, they see that every work they attempt or meditate is accursed. Nor is there the least reason for any person to deceive himself by concluding that an action is not necessarily altogether evil because it is imperfect, and that therefore the good part of it is accepted by God. For the law, requiring 15 perfect love, condemns all imperfection, unless its rigor be mitigated. Let him consider his work, therefore, which he wished to be thought partly good, and he will find that very work to be a transgression of the law, because it is imperfect.

See how all our works, if estimated according to the rigor of the law, are subject to its curse. How, then, could unhappy souls apply themselves with 20 alacrity to any work for which they could expect to receive nothing but a curse? On the contrary, if they are liberated from the severe exaction of the law, or rather from the whole of its rigor, and hear God calling them with paternal gentleness, then with cheerfulness and prompt alacrity they will answer to His call and follow His guidance. In short, they who are bound by the yoke of the 25 law are like slaves who have certain tasks appointed by their masters....

The third part of Christian liberty teaches us that we are bound by no obligation before God respecting external things, which in themselves are indifferent; but that we may indifferently sometimes use and at other times omit them. And the knowledge of this liberty also is very necessary for us; for 30 without it we shall have no tranquility of conscience, nor will there be any end of superstitions....

"I know," says Paul, "that there is nothing unclean of itself; but to him that esteems anything to be unclean, to him it is unclean."[3] In these words he makes all external things subject to our liberty, provided that our minds have regard to 35 this liberty before God. But if any superstitious notion cause to scruple, those things which were naturally pure become contaminated to us.... We see, in short, the tendency of this liberty, which is, that without any scruple of conscience or perturbation of mind we should devote the gifts of God to that use for which He

[3]Romans 14:4

has given them; by which confidence our souls may have peace with Him, and acknowledge His liberality towards us. For this comprehends all ceremonies, the observation of which is left free, that the conscience may not be bound by any obligation to observe them, but may remember that by the goodness of God it
5    may use them, or abstain from them, as shall be most conducive to edification.

Now, it must be carefully observed that Christian liberty is in all its branches a spiritual thing; all the virtue of which consists in appeasing terrified consciences before God, whether they are disquieted and solicitous concerning the remission of their sins, or are anxious to know if their works, which are imperfect
10   and contaminated by the defilements of the flesh, be acceptable to God; or are tormented concerning the use of things that are indifferent. Wherefore they are guilty of perverting its meaning who either make it the pretext of their irregular appetites, that they may abuse the Divine blessings to the purposes of sensuality, or who suppose that there is no liberty but what is used before men, and therefore
15   in the exercise of it totally disregard their weak brethren. The former of these sins is the more common in the present age. There is scarcely anyone, whom his wealth permits to be sumptuous, who is not delighted with luxurious splendor in his entertainments, in his dress, and in his buildings; who does not desire a pre-eminence in every species of luxury; who does not strangely flatter himself
20   on his elegance. And all these things are defended under the pretext of Christian liberty. They allege that they are things indifferent; this I admit, provided they be indifferently used.... But amidst an abundance of all things, to be immersed in sensual delights, to inebriate the heart and mind with present pleasures, and perpetually to grasp at new ones—these things are very remote from a legitimate
25   use of the Divine blessings. Let them banish, therefore, immoderate cupidity, excessive profusion, vanity, and arrogance that with a pure conscience they may make a proper use of the gifts of God. When their hearts shall be formed to this sobriety, they will have a rule for the legitimate enjoyment of them. On the contrary, without this moderation, even common and ordinary pleasures are charge-
30   able with excess.... Let all men, in their respective stations, whether of poverty, of competence, or of splendor, live in the remembrance of this truth, that God confers His blessings on them for the support of life, not for luxury....

Many persons err likewise in this respect, that, as if their liberty would not be perfectly secure unless witnessed by men, they make an indiscriminate and
35   imprudent use of it—a disorderly practice, which occasions frequent offense to their weak brethren. There are some to be found in the present day who imagine their liberty would be abridged if they were not to enter on the enjoyment of it by eating animal food on Friday. Their eating is not the subject of my reprehension; but their minds require to be divested of this false notion; for they
40   ought to consider that they obtain no advantage from their liberty before men,

but with God; and that it consists in abstinence as well as in use.... But they fall into a very pernicious error in disregarding the infirmity of their brethren, which it becomes us to bear, so as not rashly to do anything which would give them the least offense. But it will be said that it is sometimes right to assert our liberty before men. This I confess; yet the greatest caution and moderation 5 must be observed, lest we cast off all concern for the weak, whom God has so strongly recommended to our regards....

...That our liberty is not given us to be used in opposition to our weak neighbors, to whom charity obliges us to do every possible service; but rather in order that, having peace with God in our minds, we may also live peaceably 10 among men....

...Nothing can be plainer than this rule, that our liberty should be used, if it conduces to our neighbor's edification; but that if it be not beneficial to our neighbor, it should be abridged. There are some who pretend to imitate the prudence of Paul in refraining from the exercise of liberty, while they are 15 doing anything but exercising the duties of charity. For to promote their own tranquility, they wish all mention of liberty to be buried; whereas it is no less advantageous to our neighbors sometimes to use our liberty to their benefit and edification than at other times to moderate it for their accommodation. But a pious man considers this liberty in external things as granted him in order that 20 he may be the better prepared for all the duties of charity....

...It becomes us, indeed, to have regard to charity; but we must not offend God for the love of our neighbor. We cannot approve the intemperance of those who do nothing but in a tumultuous manner, and who prefer violent measures to lenient ones. Nor must we listen to those who, while they show themselves 25 the leaders in a thousand species of impiety, pretend that they are obliged to act in such a manner that they may give no offense to their neighbors; as though they are not at the same time fortifying the consciences of their neighbors in sin; especially since they are always sticking in the same mire without any hope of deliverance.... 30

Now, since the consciences of believers, being privileged with the liberty which we have described, have been delivered by the favor of Christ from all necessary obligation to the observance of those things in which the Lord has been pleased they should be left free, we conclude that they are exempt from all human authority. For it is not right that Christ should lose the acknowledge- 35 ments due to such kindness, or our consciences the benefit of it....

...Man is under two kinds of government—one spiritual, by which the conscience is formed to piety and the service of God; the other political, by which a man is instructed in the duties of humanity and civility, which are to be observed in an intercourse with mankind. They are generally, and not 40 improperly, denominated the spiritual and the temporal jurisdiction; indicating that the former species of government pertains to the life of the soul, and that the latter relates to the concerns of the present state; not only to the provision of food and clothing, but to the enactment of laws to regulate a man's life among his neighbors by the rules of holiness, integrity, and sobriety. For the former has its seat in the interior of the mind, whilst the latter only directs the external conduct: one may be termed a spiritual kingdom, and the other a political one. But these two, as we have distinguished them, always require to be considered separately; and while the one is under discussion, the mind must be abstracted from all consideration of the other. For man contains, as it were, two worlds, capable of being governed by various rulers and various laws. This distinction will prevent what the gospel inculcates concerning spiritual liberty from being mis-applied to political regulations; as though Christians were less subject to the external government of human laws because their consciences have been set at liberty before God; as though their freedom of spirit necessarily exempted them from all carnal servitude. Again, because even in those constitutions which seem to pertain to the spiritual kingdom, there may possibly be some deception, it is necessary to discriminate between these also; which are to be accounted legitimate, as according with the Divine word, and which, on the contrary, ought not to be received among believers....

Therefore, as works respect men, so conscience regards God; so that a good conscience is no other than inward integrity of heart. In which sense Paul says that "the end of the commandment is charity, out of a pure heart, and of a good conscience, and of faith unfeigned."[4] Afterwards also, in the same chapter, he shows how widely it differs from understanding, saying that "some, having put away a good conscience, concerning faith have made shipwreck."[5] For these words indicate that it is a lively inclination to the service of God, and a sincere pursuit of piety and holiness of life. Sometimes, indeed, it is likewise extended to men; as when the same apostle declares, "Herein do I exercise myself, to have always a conscience void of offense toward God and toward men."[6] But the reason of this assertion is that the fruits of a good conscience reach even to men. But in strict propriety of speech it has to do with God alone, as I have already observed. Hence it is that a law, which simply binds a man without relation to other men, or any consideration of them, is said to bind the conscience....

IV§20 ...For some men, when they hear that the gospel promises a liberty which acknowledges no king or magistrate among men, but submits to Christ alone, think they can enjoy no advantage of their liberty while they see any power

[4]I Timothy 1:5
[5]I Timothy 1:19
[6]Acts 24:16

exalted above them. They imagine, therefore, that nothing will prosper unless the whole world be modeled in a new form, without any tribunals, or laws, or magistrates, or anything of a similar kind, which they consider injurious to their liberty. But he who knows how to distinguish between the body and the soul, between this present transitory life and the future eternal one, will find 5 no difficulty in understanding, that the spiritual kingdom of Christ and civil government are things very different and remote from each other....

Yet this distinction does not lead us to consider the whole system of civil government as a polluted thing, which has nothing to do with Christian men. Some fanatics, who are pleased with nothing but liberty, or rather licentiousness 10 without any restraint, do indeed boast and vociferate that since we are dead with Christ to the elements of this world and, being translated into the kingdom of God, sit among the celestials, it is a degradation to us, and far beneath our dignity, to be occupied with those secular and impure cares which relate to things altogether uninteresting to a Christian man. Of what use, they ask, are laws without 15 judgments and tribunals? But what have judgments to do with a Christian man? And if it be unlawful to kill, of what use are laws and judgments to us? But as we have just suggested that this kind of government is distinct from that spiritual and internal reign of Christ, so it ought to be known that they are in no respect at variance with each other. For that spiritual reign, even now upon earth, com- 20 mences within us some preludes of the heavenly kingdom, and in this mortal and transitory life affords us some pre-libations of immortal and incorruptible blessedness; but this civil government is designed, as long as we live in this world, to cherish and support the external worship of God, to preserve the pure doctrine of religion, to defend the constitution of the Church, to regulate our lives in a 25 manner requisite for the society of men, to form our manners to civil justice, to promote our concord with each other, and to establish general peace and tranquility; all which I confess to be superfluous if the kingdom of God, as it now exists in us, extinguishes the present life. But if it is the will of God that while we are aspiring towards our true country, we be pilgrims on the earth, and if such aids 30 are necessary to our pilgrimage, they who take them from man deprive him of his human nature. They plead that there should be so much perfection in the Church of God that its order would suffice to supply the place of all laws; but they foolishly imagine a perfection which can never be found in any community of men. For since the insolence of the wicked is so great, and their iniquity so obstinate that it 35 can scarcely be restrained by all the severity of the laws, what may we expect they would do if they found themselves at liberty to perpetrate crimes with impunity, whose outrages even the arm of power cannot altogether prevent?

But for speaking of the exercise of civil polity, there will be another place more suitable. At present we only wish it to be understood that to entertain a 40 thought of its extermination is inhuman barbarism; it is equally as necessary to mankind as bread and water, light and air, and far more excellent. For it not only tends to secure the accommodations arising from all these things that men may breathe, eat, drink, and be sustained in life, though it comprehends all

5    these things while it causes them to live together, yet, I say, this is not its only tendency; its objects also are that idolatry, sacrileges against the name of God, blasphemies against His truth, and other offences against religion may not openly appear and be disseminated among the people; that the public tranquility may not be disturbed; that every person may enjoy his property without molesta-

10   tion; that men may transact their business together without fraud or injustice; that integrity and modesty may be cultivated among them; in short, that there may be a public form of religion among Christians, and that humanity may be maintained among men. Nor let anyone think it strange that I now refer to human polity the charge of the due maintenance of religion, which I may

15   appear to have placed beyond the jurisdiction of men. For I do not allow men to make laws respecting religion and the worship of God now, any more than I did before; though I approve of civil government, which provides that the true religion which is contained in the law of God, be not violated and polluted by public blasphemies, with impunity....

20       The Lord has not only testified that the function of magistrates has his approbation and acceptance, but has eminently commended it to us by dignifying it with the most honorable titles.... The authority possessed by kings and other governors over all things upon earth is not a consequence of the perverseness of men, but of the providence and holy ordinance of God, Who has been pleased

25   to regulate human affairs in this manner; forasmuch as He is present, and also presides among them, in making laws and in executing equitable judgments. This is clearly taught by Paul, when he enumerates governments among the gifts of God,[7] which, being variously distributed according to the diversity of grace, ought to be employed by the servants of Christ to the edification of the

30   Church.... Wherefore no doubt ought now to be entertained by any person that civil magistracy is a calling not only holy and legitimate, but far the most sacred and honorable in human life.

     Those who would wish to introduce anarchy reply that though in ancient times kings and judges presided over a rude people, that servile kind of government is now

35   quite incompatible with the perfection which accompanies the gospel of Christ. Here they betray not only their ignorance, but their diabolical pride, in boasting of perfection, of which not the smallest particle can be discovered in them.... In short, if they remember that they are the vice-gerents of God, it behooves them

---

[7]Romans 12:6–8

to watch with all care, earnestness, and diligence that in their administration they may exhibit to men an image, as it were, of the providence, care, goodness, benevolence, and justice of God. And they must constantly bear this in mind, that if in all cases "he be cursed that does the work of the Lord deceitfully,"[8] a far heavier curse awaits those who act fraudulently in a righteous calling.... 5

...I shall by no means deny that either aristocracy, or a mixture of aristocracy and democracy, far excels all others; and that indeed not of itself, but because it very rarely happens that kings regulate themselves so that their will is never at variance with justice and rectitude; or, in the next place, that they are endued with such penetration and prudence as in all cases to discover what is best. The 10 vice or imperfection of men therefore renders it safer and more tolerable for the government to be in the hands of many, that they may afford each other mutual assistance and admonition, and that if any one arrogate to himself more than is right, the many may act as censors and masters to restrain his ambition. That has always been proved by experience, and the Lord confirmed it by His 15 authority when He established a government of this kind among the people of Israel, with a view to preserve them in the most desirable condition till he exhibited in David a type of Christ. And as I readily acknowledge that no kind of government is more happy than this, where liberty is regulated with becoming moderation, and properly established on a durable basis, so also I consider those 20 as the most happy people who are permitted to enjoy such a condition; and if they exert their strenuous and constant efforts for its preservation and retention, I admit that they act in perfect consistence with their duty. And to this object the magistrates likewise ought to apply their greatest diligence that they suffer not the liberty, of which they are constituted guardians, to be in any respect 25 diminished, much less to be violated. If they are inactive and unconcerned about this, they are perfidious to their office, and traitors to their country. But if those to whom the will of God has assigned another form of government transfer this to themselves so as to be tempted to desire a revolution, the very thought will be not only foolish and useless, but altogether criminal.... For if it be His 30 pleasure to appoint kings over kingdoms, and senators or other magistrates over free cities, it is our duty to be obedient to any governors whom God has established over the places in which we reside.

Here it is necessary to state in a brief manner the nature of the office of magistracy, as described in the word of God and wherein it consists. If the Scrip- 35 ture did not teach that this office extends to both tables of the law, we might learn it from heathen writers; for not one of them has treated of the office of magistrates, of legislation, and civil government without beginning with religion

---

[8]Jeremiah 48:10

and Divine worship. And thus they have all confessed that no government can be happily constituted unless its first object be the promotion of piety and that all laws are preposterous which neglect the claims of God and merely provide for the interests of men. Therefore, as religion holds the first place among all the philosophers, and as this has always been regarded by the universal consent of all nations, Christian princes and magistrates ought to be ashamed of their indolence if they do not make it the object of their most serious care. We have already shown that this duty is particularly enjoined upon them by God; for it is reasonable that they should employ their utmost efforts in asserting and defending the honor of Him whose vice-gerents they are, and by whose favor they govern. And the principal commendations given in the Scripture to the good kings are for having restored the worship of God when it had been corrupted or abolished, or for having devoted their attention to religion, that it might flourish in purity and safety under their reigns.... We see, therefore, that they are constituted the protectors and vindicators of the public innocence, modesty, probity, and tranquility whose sole object it ought to be to promote the common peace and security of all. Of these virtues, David declares that he will be an example, when he shall be exalted to the royal throne.

> I will set no wicked thing before mine eyes. I will not know a wicked person. Whoso privily slanders his neighbor, him will I cut off: him that has a high look and a proud heart will I not suffer. Mine eyes shall be upon the faithful of the land, that they may dwell with me: he that walks in a perfect way, he shall serve me.[9]

But as they cannot do this unless they defend good men from the injuries of the wicked, and aid the oppressed by their relief and protection, they are likewise armed with power for the suppression of crimes and the severe punishment of malefactors, whose wickedness disturbs the public peace. For experience fully verifies the observation of Solon: "That all states are supported by reward and punishment; and that when these two things are removed, all the discipline of human societies is broken and destroyed." For the minds of many lose their regard for equity and justice unless virtue be rewarded with due honor; nor can the violence of the wicked be restrained unless crimes are followed by severe punishments. And these two parts are included in the injunction of the prophet to kings and other governors, to "execute judgment and righteousness."[10] *Righteousness* means the care, patronage, defense, vindication, and liberation of the innocent; *judgment* imports the repression of the audacity, the coercion of the violence, and the punishment of the crimes of the impious....

---

[9]Psalm 101:3–6
[10]Jeremiah 22:3

# ECCLESIASTICAL ORDINANCES
## JOHN CALVIN (1509–1564)

*John Calvin arrived in Geneva for the first time in 1536, the same year he published* The Institutes of the Christian Religion. *He stayed on at the request of the Protestant leader William Farel, who desired his assistance in reforming city governance and religious life. Calvin and Farel were both exiled from Geneva in 1538 after the city council denied them the power to excommunicate wayward church members. Calvin was welcomed back in 1541, however, after he defended Geneva's Protestants in a spirited response to Cardinal Sadoleto's open letter to the city council inviting Geneva to return to the Catholic fold. He would remain there until his death in 1564. In his reply to Sadoleto, Calvin wrote "there are three things on which the safety of the church is founded, viz., doctrine, discipline, and the sacraments, and to these a fourth is added, viz., ceremonies, by which to exercise the people in offices of piety...."*[1] *When the citizens of Geneva ceded to Calvin the authority to design and implement the structure of the church, he drafted the* Ecclesiastical Ordinances *almost immediately and they went into effect in November 1541. The Ordinances reflect Calvin's belief that the church needed to be disciplined and well-ordered to survive in the hostile environment of Reformation Europe. They endeavored to establish a church order based upon Calvin's understanding of the New Testament model. Although little is said about it in the excerpt below, the most distinctive feature of Calvin's system of church government was the Consistory, a body comprised of ministers and elders and charged with maintaining religious discipline. It is important to remember that these Ordinances were meant to prescribe church, not civil, government. Geneva had a city council and magistracy that wielded civil authority and meted out justice independently of church authority. Still, as one of his biographers has written, it may not be too much to suggest that, under the* Ecclesiastical Ordinances, *Geneva became Calvin's model city of God.*

---

[1] "Calvin's Reply to Sadoleto" (1 September 1539) in John C. Olin, ed., *A Reformation Debate: Sadoleto's Letter to the Genevans and Calvin's Reply* (Grand Rapids, MI: Baker Book House House, 1976), 63.

*The Protestant Reformation*, edited by Hans J. Hillberbrand (New York: Walker and Company, 1968): 173–78. Reprinted with permission of Walker & Company; permission conveyed through Copyright Clearance Center, Inc.

### Of the Frequency, Place and Time of Preaching

…Each Sunday, at daybreak, there shall be a sermon in Saint Peter's and Saint Gervaise's, also at the customary hour at Saint Peter, Magdalene, and Saint Gervaise. At three o'clock, as well, in all three parishes, the second sermon.

For purposes of catechetical instruction and the administration of the
5   sacraments, the boundaries of the parishes are to be observed as far as possible. Saint Gervaise is to be used by those who have done so in the past; likewise with Magdalene. Those who formerly attended Saint Germain, Holy Cross, the new church of Our Lady, and Saint Legier are to attend Saint Peter's.

On work days, besides the two sermons mentioned, there shall be preaching
10  three times each week, on Monday, Wednesday, and Friday. These sermons shall be announced for an early hour so that they may be finished before the day's work begins. On special days of prayer the Sunday order is to be observed.

To carry out these provisions and the other responsibilities pertaining to the ministry, five ministers and three co-adjutors will be needed. The latter will
15  also be ministers and help and reinforce the others as the occasion arises.

### Concerning the Second Order, Called Teachers

The proper duty of teachers is to instruct the faithful in sound doctrine so that the purity of the gospel is not corrupted by ignorance or evil opinions. We include here the aids and instructions necessary to preserve the doctrines and to keep the church from becoming desolate for lack of pastors and ministers.
20  To use a more familiar expression, we shall call it the order of the schools.

The order nearest to the ministry and most closely associated with the government of the church is that of lecturer in theology who teaches the Old and the New Testament.

Since it is impossible to profit by such instruction without first knowing
25  languages and the humanities, and also since it is necessary to prepare for the future in order that the church may not be neglected by the young, it will be necessary to establish a school to instruct the youth, to prepare them not only for the ministry but for government.

First of all, a proper place for teaching purposes must be designated, fit to
30  accommodate children and others who wish to profit by such instruction; to secure someone who is both learned in subject matter and capable of looking after the building, who can also read. This person is to be employed and placed under contract on condition that he provide under his charge readers in the languages and in dialectics, if it be possible. Also to secure men with bachelor degrees to
35  teach the children. This we hope to do to further the work of God.

These teachers shall be subject to the same ecclesiastical discipline as the ministers. There shall be no other school in the city for small children; the girls shall have their school apart, as before.

No one shall be appointed unless he is approved by the ministers, who will make their selection known to the authorities, after which he shall be presented 5 to the council with their recommendation. In any case, when he is examined, two members of the Little Council shall be present.

### The Third Order is that of Elders, those Commissioned or Appointed to the Consistory by the Authorities

Their office is to keep watch over the lives of everyone, to admonish in love those whom they see in error and leading disorderly lives. Whenever necessary they shall make a report concerning these to the ministers who will be designated to 10 make brotherly corrections and join with others in making such corrections.

If the church deems it wise, it will be well to choose two from the Little Council, four from the Council of Two Hundred, honest men of good demeanor, without reproach and free from all suspicion, above all fearing God and possessed of good and spiritual judgment. It will be well to elect them from every 15 part of the city so as to be able to maintain supervision over all. This we desire to be instituted.

This shall be the manner of their selection, inasmuch as the Little Council advises that the best men be nominated, and to call the minister so as to confer with them, after which those whom they suggest may be presented to the 20 Council of Two Hundred for their approval. If they are found worthy, after being approved, they shall take an oath similar to that required of the ministers. At the end of the year, after the election of the council, they shall present themselves to the authorities in order that it may be decided if they are to remain in office or be replaced. It will not be expedient to replace them often without cause, or 25 so long as they faithfully perform their duties.

### The Fourth Order, or the Deacons

There were two orders of deacons in the ancient church, the one concerned with receiving, distributing, and guarding the goods of the poor, their possessions, income, and pensions, as well as the quarterly offerings; the other, to take heed to and care for the sick and administer the pittance for the poor. This custom 30 we have preserved to the present. In order to avoid confusion, for we have both stewards and managers, one of the four stewards of the hospital is to act as receiver of all its goods and is to receive adequate remuneration that he may better exercise his office.

The number of four stewards shall remain as it is, of which number one shall be charged with the common funds, as directed, not only that there may be greater efficiency, but also that those who wish to make special gifts may be better assured that these will be distributed only as they desire. If the income
5   which the officials assign is not sufficient, or if some emergency should arise, the authorities shall instruct him to make adjustments according to the need.

The election of the managers, as well as of the stewards, is to be conducted as that of the elders; in their election the rule is to be followed which was delivered by Saint Paul respecting deacons.
10   Concerning the office and authority of stewards, we confirm the articles which have already been proposed, on condition that, in urgent matters, especially when the issue is no great matter and the expenditure involved is small, they not be required to assemble for every action taken, but that one or two of them may be permitted to act in the absence of the others, in a reasonable way.
15   It will be his task to take diligent care that the public hospital is well administered and that it is open not only to the sick but also to aged persons who are unable to work, to widows, orphans and other needy persons. Those who are sick are to be kept in a separate lodging, away from those who cannot work, old persons, widows, orphans, and other needy persons.
20   Also the care of the poor who are scattered throughout the city is to be conducted as the stewards may order.

Also, that another hospital is established for the transients who should be helped. Separate provision is to be made for any who are worthy of special charity. To accomplish this, a room is to be set aside for those who shall be
25   recommended by the stewards, and it is to be used for no other purpose.

Above all, the families of the managers are to be well-managed in an efficient and godly fashion, since they are to manage the houses dedicated to God.

The ministers and the commissioners or elders, with one of the syndics, for their part, are carefully to watch for any fault or negligence of any sort, in order
30   to beg and admonish the authorities to set it in order. Every three months they are to cause certain of their company, with the stewards, to visit the hospital to ascertain if everything is in order.

It will be necessary, also, for the benefit of the poor in the hospital and for the poor of the city who cannot help themselves, that a doctor and a competent
35   surgeon be secured from among those who practice in the city to have the care of the hospital and to visit the poor.

The hospital, for the pestilence in any case, is to be set apart; especially should it happen that the city is visited by this rod from God.

Moreover, to prevent begging, which is contrary to good order, it will be
40   necessary that the authorities delegate certain officers. They are to be stationed

at the doors of the churches to drive away any who try to resist and, if they act impudently or answer insolently, to take them to one of the syndics. In like manner, the heads of the precincts should always watch that the law against begging is well observed.

### The Persons Whom the Elders Should Admonish, and Proper Procedure in This Regard

If there shall be anyone who lays down opinions contrary to received doctrine, 5
he is to be summoned. If he recants, he is to be dismissed without prejudice. If he is stubborn, he is to be admonished from time to time until it shall be evident that he deserves greater severity. Then, he is to be excommunicated and this action reported to the magistrate.

If anyone is negligent in attending worship so that a noticeable offense is 10
evident for the communion of the faithful, or if anyone shows himself contemptuous of ecclesiastical discipline, he is to be admonished. If he becomes obedient, he is to be dismissed in love. If he persists, passing from bad to worse, after having been admonished three times, he is to be excommunicated and the matter reported to the authorities. 15

For the correction of faults, it is necessary to proceed after the ordinance of our Lord. That is, vices are to be dealt with secretly and no one is to be brought before the church for accusation if the fault is neither public nor scandalous, unless he has been found rebellious in the matter.

For the rest, those who scorn private admonitions are to be admonished 20
again by the church. If they will not come to reason nor recognize their error, they are to be ordered to abstain from communion until the improve.

As for obvious and public evil, which the church cannot overlook; if the faults merit nothing more than admonition, the duty of the elders shall be to summon those concerned, deal with them in love in order that they may be 25
reformed and, if they correct the fault, to dismiss the matter. If they persevere, they are to be admonished again. If, in the end, such procedure proves unsuccessful, they are to be denounced as contemptuous of God, and ordered to abstain from communion until it is evident that they have changed their way of life.

As for crimes that merit not only admonition but punitive correction; if 30
any fall into such error, according to the requirements of the case, it will be necessary to command them to abstain from communion so that they humble themselves before God and repent of their error.

If anyone by being contumacious or rebellious attempts that which is forbidden, the duty of the ministers shall be to reject him, since it is not proper 35
that he receive the sacrament.

Nevertheless, let all these measures be moderate; let there not be such a degree of rigor that anyone should be cast down, for all corrections are but medicinal, to bring back sinners to the Lord.

And let all be done in such a manner as to keep from the ministers any civil jurisdiction whatever, so that they use only the spiritual sword of the word of God as Saint Paul ordered them. Thus the consistory may in no wise take from the authority of the officers or of civil justice. On the contrary, the civil power is to be kept intact. Likewise, when it shall be necessary to exercise punishment or restraint against any party, the ministers and the consistory are to hear the party concerned, deal with them and admonish them as it may seem good, reporting all to the council which, for its part, shall deliberate and then pass judgment according to the merits of the case.

# THE THIRTY-NINE ARTICLES

*When Elizabeth I (r. 1558–1603) succeeded her sister Mary I (r. 1553–1558) on the throne of England, she faced a complicated religious situation. Many Englishmen had gladly returned to Roman Catholicism under Mary, but a significant number, strengthened in their Protestant beliefs by those who chose to accept death or exile under Mary, prayed that Elizabeth would reject what they called "popery" once and for all. She opted for what she termed a* Via Media *or "Middle Way," a compromise of sorts: a church that would be Catholic in liturgy and organization, but Protestant in theology. The Thirty-Nine Articles, originally issued by King Edward VI (r. 1547–1553) and revised by Elizabeth, became the definitive statement of the doctrine of the Church of England.*

1571

### Article 9—*Of Original or Birth Sin*

Original sin stands not in the following of Adam (as the Pelagians do vainly talk), but it is the fault and corruption of the nature of every man that naturally is engendered of the offspring of Adam, whereby man is very far gone from original righteousness, and is of his own nature inclined to evil, so that the flesh lusts always contrary to the spirit; and therefore in every person born into this 5 world, it deserves God's wrath and damnation. And this infection of nature does remain, yea, in them that are regenerated, whereby the lust of the flesh, called in Greek φρουημα σαρκοε (which some do expound the wisdom, some sensuality, some the affection, some the desire of the flesh), is not subject to the law of God. And although there is no condemnation for them that believe 10 and are baptized, yet the Apostle does confess that concupiscence and lust has of itself the nature of sin.

### Article 10—*Of Free Will*

The condition of man after the fall of Adam is such, that he cannot turn and prepare himself, by his own natural strength and good works, to faith and calling upon God. (§2) Wherefore we have no power to do good works pleasant and 15

*The Thirty-Nine Articles, Their History and Explanation*, edited by B. J. Kidd (London: Rivington's, 1899), 121–270, *passim* [modernized].

acceptable to God, without the grace of God by Christ preventing us that we may have a good will, and working with us when we have that good will.

### Article 11—*Of the Justification of Man*

We are accounted righteous before God, only for the merit of our Lord and Savior Jesus Christ by faith, and not for our own works or deservings. Wherefore
5   that we are justified by faith only is a most wholesome doctrine, and very full of comfort; as more largely is expressed in the Homily of Justification.

### Article 12—*Of Good Works*

Albeit that good works, which are the fruits of faith and follow after justification, cannot put away our sins and endure the severity of God's judgment, yet are they pleasing and acceptable to God in Christ, and do spring out necessarily of
10   a true and lively faith, insomuch that by them a lively faith may be as evidently known as a tree discerned by the fruit.

### Article 13—*Of Works Before Justification*

Works done before the grace of Christ and the inspiration of His Spirit, are not pleasant to God, forasmuch as they spring not of faith in Jesus Christ, neither do they make men meet to receive grace, or (as the School authors say) deserve
15   grace of congruity: yea, rather for that they are not done as God has willed and commanded them to be done, we doubt not but they have the nature of sin.

### Article 14—*Of Works of Supererogation*

Voluntary works besides, over, and above God's commandments, which they call works of supererogation, cannot be taught without arrogancy and impiety. For by them men do declare that they do not only render unto God as much
20   as they are bound to do, but that they do more for His sake than of bounden duty is required. Whereas Christ says plainly, When you have done all that are commanded to you, say, we be unprofitable servants.[1]

### Article 15—*Of Christ Alone Without Sin*

Christ in the truth of our nature was made like unto us in all things, sin only except, from which He was clearly void, both in His flesh and in His spirit. He
25   came to be the lamb without spot, Who by sacrifice of Himself once made, should take away the sins of the world: and sin, as Saint John says, was not in Him. But all we the rest, although baptized and born again in Christ, yet offend in many things: and if we say we have no sin, we deceive ourselves, and the truth is not in us.

---

[1]Luke 17:10

## Article 16—*Of Sin After Baptism*

Not every deadly sin willingly committed after baptism is sin against the Holy Ghost, and unpardonable. Wherefore the grant of repentance is not to be denied to such as fall into sin after baptism. After we have received the Holy Ghost, we may depart from grace given and fall into sin, and by the grace of God we may arise again and amend our lives. And therefore they are to be condemned, which say they can no more sin as long as they live here, or deny the place of forgiveness to such as truly repent.

## Article 17—*Of Predestination and Election*

Predestination to life is the everlasting purpose of God, whereby, before the foundations of the world were laid, He has constantly decreed by His counsel secret to us, to deliver from curse and damnation those whom He has chosen in Christ out of mankind, and to bring them by Christ to everlasting salvation as vessels made to honor. Wherefore they which be endowed with so excellent a benefit of God be called according to God's purpose by His Spirit working in due season; they through grace obey the calling; they be justified freely; they be made sons of God by adoption; they be made like the image of His only begotten Son Jesus Christ; they walk religiously in good works; and at length by God's mercy they attain to everlasting felicity.

As the godly consideration of Predestination and our Election in Christ is full of sweet, pleasant, and unspeakable comfort to godly persons and such as feel in themselves the working of the Spirit of Christ, mortifying the works of the flesh and their earthly members and drawing up their mind to high and heavenly things, as well because it does greatly establish and confirm their faith of eternal salvation to be enjoyed through Christ, as because it does fervently kindle their love towards God: so for curious and carnal persons, lacking the Spirit of Christ, to have continually before their eyes the sentence of God's Predestination is a most dangerous downfall, whereby the devil does thrust them either into desperation or into recklessness of most unclean living no less perilous than desperation.

Furthermore, we must receive God's promises in such wise as they be generally set forth to us in Holy Scripture; and in our doings that will of God is to be followed which we have expressly declared unto us in the word of God.

## Article 18—*Of Obtaining Eternal Salvation Only by the Name of Christ*

They also are to be had accursed that presume to say that every man shall be saved by the law or sect which he professes, so that he be diligent to frame his life according to that law and the light of nature. For Holy Scripture does set out to us only the name of Jesus Christ, whereby men must be saved.

### Article 19—*Of the Church*

The visible Church of Christ is a congregation of faithful men, in the which the pure word of God is preached and the sacraments be duly ministered according to Christ's ordinance in all those things that of necessity are requisite to the same. As the Church of Jerusalem, Alexandria, and Antioch have erred:
5   so also the Church of Rome has erred, not only in their living and manner of ceremonies, but also in matters of faith.

### Article 20—*Of the Authority of the Church*

The Church has power to decree rites or ceremonies and authority in controversies of faith; and yet it is not lawful for the Church to ordain anything contrary to God's word written, neither may it so expound one place of Scripture, that
10   it be repugnant to another. Wherefore, although the Church be a witness and a keeper of Holy Writ: yet, as it ought not to decree anything against the same, so besides the same ought it not to enforce anything to be believed for necessity of salvation.

### Article 21—*Of the Authority of General Councils*

General Councils may not be gathered together without the commandment
15   and will of princes. And when they be gathered together, forasmuch as they be an assembly of men, whereof all be not governed with the Spirit and word of God, they may err and sometime have erred, even in things pertaining unto God. Wherefore things ordained by them as necessary to salvation have neither strength nor authority, unless it may be declared that they be taken out of Holy
20   Scripture.

### Article 22—*Of Purgatory*

The Romish doctrine concerning Purgatory, pardons, worshipping and adoration as well of images as of relics, and also invocation of saints, is a fond thing vainly invented, and grounded upon no warranty of Scripture; but rather repugnant to the word of God.

### Article 23—*Of Ministering in the Congregation*

25   It is not lawful for any man to take upon him the office of public preaching or ministering the sacraments in the congregation before he be lawfully called and sent to execute the same. And those we ought to judge lawfully called and sent, which be chosen and called to this work by men who have public authority given unto them in the congregation to call and send ministers into
30   the Lord's vineyard.

### Article 24—*Of Speaking in the Congregation in Such a Tongue as the People Understands*

It is a thing plainly repugnant to the word of God and the custom of the primitive Church to have public prayer in the Church, or to minister the sacraments in a tongue not understood of the people.

### Article 25—*Of the Sacraments*

Sacraments ordained of Christ be not only badges or tokens of Christian men's profession, but rather they be certain sure witnesses and effectual signs of grace and God's good will towards us, by the which He does work invisibly in us, and does not only quicken, but also strengthen and confirm, our faith in Him. There are two sacraments ordained of Christ our Lord in the Gospel, that is to say, Baptism and the Supper of the Lord.

Those five commonly called sacraments, that is to say, confirmation, penance, orders, matrimony, and extreme unction, are not to be counted for sacraments of the Gospel, being such as have grown partly of the corrupt following of the Apostles, partly are states of life allowed in the Scriptures; but yet have not the like nature of sacraments with Baptism and the Lord's Supper, for that they have not any visible sign or ceremony ordained of God. The Sacraments were not ordained of Christ to be gazed upon or to be carried about, but that we should duly use them. And in such only as worthily receive the same, have they a wholesome effect or operation: but they that receive them unworthily, purchase to themselves damnation,[2] as Saint Paul says.

### Article 26—*Of the Unworthiness of the Ministers, Which Hinders Not the Effect of the Sacraments*

Although in the visible Church the evil be ever mingled with the good, and sometime the evil have chief authority in the ministration of the word and sacraments; yet, forasmuch as they do not the same in their own name, but in Christ's, and do minister by His commission and authority, we may use their ministry both in hearing the word of God and in the receiving of the sacraments. Neither is the effect of Christ's ordinance taken away by their wickedness, nor the grace of God's gifts diminished from such as by faith and rightly do receive the sacraments ministered unto them, which be effectual because of Christ's institution and promise, although they be ministered by evil men.

Nevertheless it appertains to the discipline of the Church that inquiry be made of evil ministers, and that they be accused by those that have knowledge of their offenses; and finally, being found guilty by just judgment, be deposed.

---

[2]I Corinthians 11:27

### Article 27—*Of Baptism*

Baptism is not only a sign of profession and mark of difference whereby Christian men are discerned from other that be not christened, but is also a sign of regeneration or new birth whereby, as by an instrument, they that receive baptism rightly are grafted into the Church; the promises of the forgiveness of
5    sin, and of our adoption to be the sons of God, by the Holy Ghost are visibly signed and sealed; faith is confirmed, and grace increased by virtue of prayer unto God. The baptism of young children is in any wise to be retained in the Church as most agreeable with the institution of Christ.

### Article 28—*Of the Lord's Supper*

The Supper of the Lord is not only a sign of the love that Christians ought to
10   have among themselves, one to another, but rather it is a sacrament of our redemption by Christ's death; insomuch that to such as rightly, worthily, and with faith receive the same, the bread which we break in a partaking of the body of Christ, and likewise the cup of blessing is a partaking of the blood of Christ.

Transubstantiation (or the change of the substance of bread and wine) in
15   the Supper of the Lord, cannot be proved by Holy Writ, but is repugnant to the plain words of Scripture, overthrows the nature of a sacrament, and has given occasion to many superstitions.

The body of Christ is given, taken, and eaten in the Supper only after an heavenly and spiritual manner. And the mean whereby the body of Christ is
20   received and eaten in the Supper is faith. The sacrament of the Lord's Supper was not by Christ's ordinance reserved, carried about, lifted up, or worshipped.

### Article 29—*Of the Wicked which do Not Eat the Body of Christ in the Use of the Lord's Supper*

The wicked and such as be void of a lively faith, although they do carnally and visibly press with their teeth (as Saint Augustine says) the sacrament of the body and blood of Christ, yet in nowise are they partakers of Christ, but rather to their
25   condemnation do eat and drink the sign or sacrament of so great a thing.

### Article 30—*Of Both Kinds*

The Cup of the Lord is not to be denied to the lay people; for both the parts of the Lord's sacrament, by Christ's ordinance and commandment, ought to be ministered to all Christian men alike.

### Article 31—*Of the One Oblation of Christ Finished Upon the Cross*

The offering of Christ once made is the perfect redemption, propitiation, and
30   satisfaction for all the sins of the whole world, both original and actual, and

there is none other satisfaction for sin but that alone. Wherefore the sacrifices of Masses, in the which it was commonly said that the priests did offer Christ for the quick and dead to have remission of pain or guilt, were blasphemous fables and dangerous deceits.

### Article 32—*Of The Marriage Of Priests*

Bishops, priests, and deacons are not commanded by God's laws either to vow 5 the estate of single life or to abstain from marriage. Therefore it is lawful also for them, as for all other Christian men, to marry at their own discretion, as they shall judge the same to serve better to godliness.

### Article 33—*Of Excommunicate Persons, How They are to be Avoided*

That person which by open denunciation of the Church is rightly cut off from the unity of the Church and excommunicated, ought to be taken of the whole 10 multitude of the faithful as an heathen and publican, until he be openly reconciled by penance and received into the Church by a judge that has authority thereto.

### Article 34—*Of the Traditions of the Church*

It is not necessary that traditions and ceremonies be in all places one or utterly alike; for at all times they have been diverse, and may be changed according to the diversity of countries, times, and men's manners, so that nothing be 15 ordained against God's word. Whosoever through his private judgment willingly and purposely does openly break the traditions and ceremonies of the Church which be not repugnant to the word of God, and be ordained and approved by common authority, ought to be rebuked openly that other may fear to do the like, as he that offends against the common order of the Church, and hurts the 20 authority of the magistrate, and wounds the conscience of the weak brethren. Every particular or national Church has authority to ordain, change, and abolish ceremonies or rites of the Church ordained only by man's authority, so that all things be done to edifying.

### Article 35—*Of Homilies*

The second Book of Homilies, the several titles whereof we have joined under this 25 Article, does contain a godly and wholesome doctrine and necessary for these times, as does the former Book of Homilies which were set forth in the time of Edward the Sixth. And therefore we judge them to be read in Churches by the ministers diligently and distinctly, that they may be understanded of the people.

### Article 36—*Of Consecration of Bishops and Ministers*

The Book of consecration of Archbishops and Bishops and ordering of Priests 30 and Deacons, lately set forth in the time of Edward the Sixth and confirmed

at the same time by authority of Parliament, does contain all things necessary to such consecration and ordering; neither has it anything that of itself is superstitious or ungodly. And therefore whosoever are consecrate or ordered according to the rites of that book, since the second year of the aforenamed
5    King Edward unto this time, or hereafter shall be consecrated or ordered according to the same rites, we decree all such to be rightly, orderly, and lawfully consecrate or ordered.

### Article 37—*Of the Civil Magistrates*

The Queen's Majesty has the chief power in this realm of England and other her dominions, unto whom the chief government of all estates of this realm,
10   whether they be ecclesiastical or civil, in all causes does appertain, and is not nor ought to be subject to any foreign jurisdiction.

Where we attribute to the Queen's Majesty the chief government, by which titles we understand the minds of some slanderous folks to be offended, we give not to our princes the ministering either of God's word or of sacraments,
15   the which thing the Injunctions also lately set forth by Elizabeth our Queen does most plainly testify: but only that prerogative which we see to have been given always to all godly princes in Holy Scriptures by God himself, that is, that they should rule all estates and degrees committed to their charge by God, whether they be ecclesiastical or temporal, and restrain with the civil sword the
20   stubborn and evil-doers.

The Bishop of Rome has no jurisdiction in this realm of England. The laws of the realm may punish Christian men with death for heinous and grievous offences. It is lawful for Christian men at the commandment of the Magistrate to wear weapons and serve in the wars.

### Article 38—*Of Christian Men's Goods Which are Not Common*

25   The riches and goods of Christians are not common, as touching the right, title, and possession of the same, as certain Anabaptists do falsely boast; notwithstanding every man ought of such things as he possesses liberally to give alms to the poor, according to his ability.

### Article 39—*Of a Christian Man's Oath*

As we confess that vain and rash swearing is forbidden Christian men by our
30   Lord Jesus Christ, so we judge that Christian religion does not prohibit but that a man may swear when the magistrate requires in a cause of faith and charity, so it be done according to the Prophet's teaching in justice, judgment, and truth.

# CANONS AND DECREES
## COUNCIL OF TRENT (1545–1563)

*Even before Protestant theologians had begun to pursue reformation in ways that led them to break with the medieval Church, Catholic critics of the status quo were demanding reform and renewal within the Church. However, owing largely to the political situation prevailing in early sixteenth-century Europe—in particular the Hapsburg-Valois wars, which made any possibility of reconciling the warring religious factions in the Empire decidedly unattractive to Francis I of France—the convocation of a council was delayed for many years. By the time the Council of Trent finally met in 1545, both sides in the religious conflict more or less agreed that the breach between them was irreparable, and this situation clearly influenced the tone of some of the canons and decrees. The Council achieved a major reform of the institutional operation of the Catholic Church. It also clarified Catholic teaching on many issues that were central to the sixteenth-century debates over religion.*

### Bull of Convocation

Paul, Bishop, servant of the servants of God, for a perpetual remembrance hereof:

Recognizing at the very beginning of our pontificate, which the divine providence of Almighty God, not for any merit of our own, but by reason of its own great goodness, has committed to us, to what troubled times and to how many distresses in almost all affairs our pastoral solicitude and vigilance were called, 5 we desired indeed to remedy the evils that have long afflicted and well-nigh overwhelmed the Christian commonwealth; but we also, as men compassed with infirmity, felt our strength unequal to take upon ourselves such a burden. For while we realized that peace was necessary to free and preserve the commonwealth from the many dangers that threatened it, we found all filled with 10 hatreds and dissensions, and particularly those princes, to whom God has entrusted almost the entire direction of affairs, at enmity with one another. Whilst we deemed it necessary for the integrity of the Christian religion and

*Canons and Decrees of the Council of Trent*, edited by H. J. Schroeder (Rockford, IL: Tan Books, 1979), 1–2, 8, 15–16, 17–19, 31–35, 51–52, 162–63, 215–17.

for the confirmation within us of the hope of heavenly things, that there be one fold and one shepherd for the Lord's flock, the unity of the Christian name was well-nigh rent and torn asunder by schisms, dissensions and heresies. Whilst we desired the commonwealth to be safe and protected against the arms and
5   insidious designs of the infidels, yet, because of our transgressions and the guilt of us all, indeed, because of the wrath of God hanging over us by reason of our sins, Rhodes had been lost, Hungary ravaged, war by land and sea intended and planned against Italy, and against Austria and Illyria, since the Turk, our godless and ruthless enemy, was never at rest and looked upon our mutual
10  enmities and dissensions as his fitting opportunity to carry out his designs with success. Wherefore, having been called, as we have said, in so great a tempest of heresies, discords and wars and in such restlessness of the waves to rule and pilot the bark of Peter, and not trusting sufficiently our own strength, we first of all cast our cares upon the Lord, that He might sustain us and provide our
15  soul with firmness and strength, our understanding with prudence and wisdom. Then, considering that our predecessors, endowed with admirable wisdom and sanctity, had often in the greatest dangers of the Christian commonwealth had recourse to ecumenical councils and general assemblies of bishops as the best and most suitable remedy, we also decided to hold a general council....
20      ...We announce, proclaim, convoke, ordain and decree a holy ecumenical and general council to be opened on the first day of November of the present year 1542 from the Incarnation of the Lord in the city of Trent, for all nations a commodious, free and convenient place, to be there begun and prosecuted and with the help of God concluded and completed to His glory and praise
25  and the welfare of the whole Christian people....

### Concerning the Symbol of Faith     4 FEBRUARY 1546

In the name of the holy and undivided Trinity, Father, Son, and Holy Ghost.

This holy, ecumenical, and general Council of Trent, lawfully assembled in the Holy Ghost... considering the magnitude of the matters to be dealt with, especially those comprised under the two heads, the extirpation of heresies and
30  the reform of morals, for which purposes it was chiefly assembled, and recognizing with the Apostle that its wrestling is not against flesh and blood, but against the spirits of wickedness in high places, exhorts with the same Apostle each and all above all things to be strengthened in the Lord and in the might of his power, in all things taking the shield of faith, wherewith they may be
35  able to extinguish all the fiery darts of the most wicked one, and to take the helmet of the hope of salvation and the sword of the spirit, which is the word of God. Wherefore, that this pious solicitude may begin and continue by the

grace of God, it ordains and decrees that before all else a confession of faith be set forth; following herein the examples of the Fathers, who in the more outstanding councils were accustomed at the beginning of their work to use this shield against heresies, with which alone they have at times drawn unbelievers to the faith, overcome heretics and confirmed the faithful. For this reason it 5 has thought it well that the symbol of faith which the holy Roman Church uses as the cardinal principle wherein all who profess the faith of Christ necessarily agree and as the firm and sole foundation against which the gates of hell shall never prevail, be expressed in the same words in which it is read in all the churches, which is as follows: 10

> I believe in one God the Father Almighty, creator of heaven and earth, of all things visible and invisible; and in one Lord Jesus Christ, the only begotten Son of God and born of the Father before all ages; God of God, light of light, true God of true God; begotten, not made, consubstantial with the Father, by whom all things were made; who for us 15 men and for our salvation descended from heaven, and was incarnate by the Holy Ghost of the Virgin Mary, and was made man; crucified also for us under Pontius Pilate, he suffered and was buried; and he arose on the third day according to the Scriptures, and ascended into heaven, sits at the right hand of the Father; and again he will come 20 with glory to judge the living and the dead; of whose kingdom there shall be no end; and in the Holy Ghost the Lord and giver of life, who proceeds from the Father and the Son; who with the Father and the Son together is adored and glorified; who spoke by the prophets; and in one holy Catholic and Apostolic Church. I confess one baptism for 25 the remission of sins; and I look for the resurrection of the dead, and the life of the world to come. Amen.

## Concerning the Canonical Scriptures    8 APRIL 1546

The holy, ecumenical and general Council of Trent, lawfully assembled in the Holy Ghost... keeps this constantly in view, namely, that the purity of the Gospel may be preserved in the Church after the errors have been removed. This 30 [Gospel], of old promised through the Prophets in the Holy Scriptures, our Lord Jesus Christ, the Son of God, promulgated first with His own mouth, and then commanded it to be preached by His Apostles to every creature as the source at once of all saving truth and rules of conduct. It also clearly perceives that these truths and rules are contained in the written books and in the unwritten 35 traditions, which, received by the Apostles from the mouth of Christ Himself, or from the Apostles themselves, the Holy Ghost dictating, have come down

to us, transmitted as it were from hand to hand. Following, then, the examples of the orthodox Fathers, it receives and venerates with a feeling of piety and reverence all the books both of the Old and New Testaments, since one God is the author of both; also the traditions, whether they relate to faith or to mor-
5   als, as having been dictated either orally by Christ or by the Holy Ghost, and preserved in the Catholic Church in unbroken succession....[1]

### Concerning the Edition and Use of the Sacred Books    8 APRIL 1546

...Furthermore, to check unbridled spirits, [the council] decrees that no one relying on his own judgment... shall, in matters of faith and morals pertaining to the edification of Christian doctrine, distorting the Holy Scriptures in accordance
10   with his own conceptions, presume to interpret them contrary to that sense which holy mother Church, to whom it belongs to judge of their true sense and interpretation, has held and holds, or even contrary to the unanimous teaching of the Fathers, even though such interpretations should never at any time be published. Those who act contrary to this shall be made known by the ordinaries
15   and punished in accordance with the penalties prescribed by the law.

And wishing, as is proper, to impose a restraint in this matter on printers also, who, now, without restraint, thinking what pleases them is permitted them, print without the permission of ecclesiastical superiors the books of the Holy Scriptures and the notes and commentaries thereon of all persons
20   indiscriminately, often with the name of the press omitted, often also under a fictitious press name, and what is worse, without the name of the author, and also indiscreetly have for sale such books printed elsewhere, [this council] decrees and ordains that in the future the Holy Scriptures, especially the old Vulgate edition, be printed in the most correct manner possible, and that it shall not be
25   lawful for anyone to print or to have printed any books whatsoever dealing with sacred doctrinal matters without the name of the author, or in the future to sell them, or even to have them in possession, unless they have first been examined and approved by the ordinary under penalty of anathema and fine....[2]

### Concerning Justification    13 JANUARY 1547
#### *The Necessity of Preparation for Justification in Adults, and Whence it Proceeds*

It is furthermore declared that in adults the beginning of that justification must
30   proceed from the predisposing grace of God through Jesus Christ, that is, from

---

[1] The decree then enumerates the sacred books of the canon: the Old Testament books of the Septuagint (i.e., the Hebrew canon), together with the deutero-canonical books (i.e., the Apocrypha) and the books of the New Testament.
[2] Realizing the crucial role played by the printing press in the rapid dissemination of ideas, both Catholic and Protestant authorities regulated the production and sale of books in areas under their control.

His vocation, whereby, without any merits on their part, they are called; that they who by sin had been cut off from God, may be disposed through His quickening and helping grace to convert themselves to their own justification by freely assenting to and co-operating with that grace; so that, while God touches the heart of man through the illumination of the Holy Ghost, man himself neither 5 does absolutely nothing while receiving that inspiration, since he can also reject it, nor yet is he able by his own free will and without the grace of God to move himself to justice in His sight. Hence, when it is said in the sacred writings: Turn to me, and I will turn to you, we are reminded of our liberty; and when we reply: Convert us, O Lord, to You, and we shall be converted; we confess 10 that we need the grace of God.

### The Manner of Preparation

Now they [the adults] are disposed to that justice when, aroused and aided by divine grace, receiving faith by hearing, they are moved freely toward God, believing to be true what has been divinely revealed and promised, especially that the sinner is justified by God by his grace, through the redemption that 15 is in Christ Jesus; and, when understanding themselves to be sinners, they, by turning themselves from the fear of divine justice, by which they are salutarily aroused, to consider the mercy of God, are raised to hope....

### In What the Justification of the Sinner Consists, and What are its Causes

This disposition or preparation is followed by justification itself, which is not only a remission of sins but also the sanctification and renewal of the inward 20 man through the voluntary reception of the grace and gifts whereby an unjust man becomes just and from being an enemy becomes a friend, that he may be an heir according to hope of life everlasting.... For though no one can be just except he to whom the merits of the passion of our Lord Jesus Christ are communicated, yet this takes place in that justification of the sinner, when by 25 the merit of the most holy Passion, the charity of God is poured forth by the Holy Ghost in the hearts of those who are justified and inheres in them; whence man through Jesus Christ, in whom he is ingrafted, receives in that justification, together with the remission of sins, all these infused at the same time, namely, faith, hope and charity. For faith, unless hope and charity be added to 30 it, neither unites man perfectly with Christ nor makes him a living member of His body. For which reason it is most truly said that faith without works is dead and of no profit, and in Christ Jesus neither circumcision avails anything nor un-circumcision, but faith that works by charity. This faith, conformably to Apostolic tradition, catechumens ask of the Church before the sacrament of 35 baptism, when they ask for the faith that gives eternal life, which without hope and charity faith cannot give. Whence also they hear immediately the word of Christ: If you would enter into life, keep the commandments....

### *How the Gratuitous Justification of the Sinner by Faith is to be Understood*

But when the Apostle says that man is justified by faith and freely, these words are to be understood in that sense in which the uninterrupted unanimity of the Catholic Church has held and expressed them, namely, that we are therefore said to be justified by faith, because faith is the beginning of human salvation, the foundation and root of all justification, without which, it is impossible to please God and to come to the fellowship of His sons; and we are therefore said to be justified gratuitously, because none of those things that precede justification, whether faith or works, merit the grace of justification. For, if by grace, it is not now by works, otherwise, as the Apostle says, grace is no more grace....

### On the Sacraments in General                     3 MARCH 1547

[1]If anyone says that the sacraments of the New Law were not all instituted by our Lord Jesus Christ, or that there are more or less than seven, namely, baptism, confirmation, Eucharist, penance, extreme unction, order and matrimony, or that any one of these seven is not truly and intrinsically a sacrament, let him be anathema....

[10]If anyone says that all Christians have the power to administer the Word and all the sacraments, let him be anathema....

### On the Sacrament of Order                        15 JULY 1563

[1]If anyone says that there is not in the New Testament a visible and external priesthood, or that there is no power of consecrating and offering the true Body and Blood of the Lord and of forgiving...sins, but only the office and bare ministry of preaching the Gospel; or that those who do not preach are not priests at all, let him be anathema....

[3]If anyone says that order or sacred ordination is not truly and properly a sacrament instituted by Christ the Lord, or that it is some human contrivance devised by men unskilled in ecclesiastical matters, or that it is only a certain rite for choosing ministers of the Word of God and of the sacraments, let him be anathema.

[4]If anyone says that by sacred ordination the Holy Ghost is not imparted and that therefore the bishops say in vain: *Receive ye the Holy Ghost,* or that by it a character is not imprinted, or that he who has once been a priest can again become a layman, let him be anathema.

[5]If anyone says that the holy unction which the Church uses in ordination is not only not required but is detestable and pernicious, as also are the other ceremonies of order, let him be anathema.

[6]If anyone says that in the Catholic Church there is not instituted a hierarchy by divine ordinance, which consists of bishops, priests, and ministers, let him be anathema.

[7]If anyone says that bishops are not superior to priests, or that they have not the power to confirm and ordain, or that the power which they have is common to them and to priests, or that orders conferred by them without the consent or call of the people or of the secular power are invalid, or that those who have been neither rightly ordained nor sent by ecclesiastical and canonical authority, but come from elsewhere, are lawful ministers of the Word and of the sacraments, let him be anathema.

### On the Invocation, Veneration, and Relics of Saints, and on Sacred Images      3–4 DECEMBER 1563

The holy council commands all bishops and others who hold the office of teaching and have charge of the *cura animarum*,[3] that in accordance with the usage of the Catholic and Apostolic Church, received from the primitive times of the Christian religion, and with the unanimous teaching of the holy Fathers and the decrees of sacred councils, they above all instruct the faithful diligently in matters relating to intercession and invocation of the saints, the veneration of relics, and the legitimate use of images, teaching them that the saints who reign together with Christ offer up their prayers to God for men, that it is good and beneficial suppliantly to invoke them and to have recourse to their prayers, assistance and support in order to obtain favors from God through His Son, Jesus Christ our Lord, who alone is our Redeemer and Savior; and that they think impiously who deny that the saints who enjoy eternal happiness in heaven are to be invoked, or who assert that they do not pray for men, or that our invocation of them to pray for each of us individually is idolatry, or that it is opposed to the word of God and inconsistent with the honor of the one mediator of God and men, Jesus Christ, or that it is foolish to pray vocally or mentally to those who reign in heaven. Also, that the holy bodies of the holy martyrs and of others living with Christ, which were the living members of Christ and the temple of the Holy Ghost, to be awakened by Him to eternal life and to be glorified, are to be venerated by the faithful, through which many benefits are bestowed by God on men....

Moreover, that the images of Christ, of the Virgin Mother of God, and of

---

[3]*Cura Animarum*—"Cure of souls," i.e., pastoral responsibilities

the other saints are to be placed and retained especially in the churches, and that due honor and veneration is to be given them; not, however, that any divinity or virtue is believed to be in them by reason of which they are to be venerated, or that something is to be asked of them, or that trust is to be placed in images, as

5   was done of old by the Gentiles who placed their hope in idols; but because the honor which is shown them is referred to the prototypes which they represent, so that by means of the images... we adore Christ and venerate the saints whose likeness they bear. That is what was defined by the decrees of the councils, especially of the Second Council of Nicaea, against the opponents of images.

10     Moreover, let the bishops diligently teach that by means of the stories of the mysteries of our redemption portrayed in paintings and other representations the people are instructed and confirmed in the articles of faith, which ought to be borne in mind and constantly reflected upon; also that great profit is derived from all holy images, not only because the people are thereby reminded of the

15   benefits and gifts bestowed on them by Christ, but also because through the saints the miracles of God and salutary examples are set before the eyes of the faithful, so that they may give thanks to God for those things, may fashion their own life and conduct in imitation of the saints and be moved to adore and love God and cultivate piety. But if anyone should teach or maintain anything

20   contrary to these decrees, let him be anathema. If any abuses shall have found their way into these holy and salutary observances, the holy council desires earnestly that they be completely removed, so that no representation of false doctrines and such as might be the occasion of grave error to the uneducated be exhibited. And if at times it happens, when this is beneficial to the illiterate,

25   that the stories and narratives of the Holy Scriptures are portrayed and exhibited, the people should be instructed that not for that reason is the divinity represented in picture as if it can be seen with bodily eyes or expressed in colors or figures. Furthermore, in the invocation of the saints, the veneration of relics, and the sacred use of images, all superstition shall be removed, all filthy quest

30   for gain eliminated, and all lasciviousness avoided, so that images shall not be painted and adorned with a seductive charm, or the celebration of saints and the visitation of relics be perverted by the people into boisterous festivities and drunkenness, as if the festivals in honor of the saints are to be celebrated with revelry and with no sense of decency. Finally, such zeal and care should be ex-

35   hibited by the bishops with regard to these things that nothing may appear that is disorderly or unbecoming and confusedly arranged, nothing that is profane, nothing disrespectful, since holiness becomes the house of God.[4]

---

[4]Psalm 92:5

# ACT OF SUPREMACY

## HENRY VIII (1491–1547), KING OF ENGLAND (1509–1547)

*While Henry VIII's desire to annul his marriage to Catherine of Aragon was the proximate cause for a rupture with Rome, there were long-term political and religious issues affecting the English body politic as well. With the kingdom having recently emerged from civil war and facing the future with only a daughter as heir, Henry had sincere concerns for the political stability of his kingdom. Moreover, there were equally long-standing concerns about the autonomy of the English church as well as the lifestyles of its members.*

*England's political and religious tensions would become invariably linked to the monarch's marital problems beginning in 1526 when the King met Anne Boleyn. After many years of negotiating, an English court headed by the Archbishop of Canterbury, Thomas Cranmer, finally annulled Henry's marriage to Catherine in 1533. Pope Clement VII subsequently excommunicated Henry, who, in turn, responded in 1534 with this Act of Parliament, which stated Henry's authority over the English church, possessing a power similar to that exercised by contemporary kings of France and Castile. Leaders of the Church and Parliament were ordered to give their consent to this document; Sir Thomas More's refusal led to his death.*

3 NOVEMBER 1534

Albeit the King's Majesty justly and rightfully is and owes to be the supreme head of the Church of England, and so is recognized by the clergy of this realm in their convocations, yet nevertheless for corroboration and confirmation thereof, and for increase of virtue in Christ's religion within this realm of England, and to repress and extirpate all errors, heresies, and other enormities and abuses 5 heretofore used in the same.

Be it enacted by authority of this present Parliament, that the King, our sovereign lord, his heirs, and successors, kings of this realm, shall be taken, accepted, and reputed the only supreme head on earth of the Church of England, called *Anglicana Ecclesia*, and shall have and enjoy, annexed and united to the 10

*Translations and Reprints from the Original Sources of European History* (Philadelphia: Department of History, University of Pennsylvania, 1900), I:17–18 [modernized].

imperial crown of this realm, as well the style and title thereof, as all honors, dignities, pre-eminences, jurisdictions, privileges, authorities, immunities, profits, and commodities, to the said dignity of supreme head of the same Church belonging and appertaining; and that our said sovereign lord, his heirs, and

5    successors, kings of this realm, shall have full power and authority from time to time to visit, repress, redress, reform, order, correct, restrain, and amend all such errors, heresies, abuses, offenses, contempts, and enormities, whatsoever they be, which by any manner spiritual authority or jurisdiction ought or may lawfully be reformed, repressed, ordered, redressed, corrected, restrained, or amended,

10   most to the pleasure of almighty God, the increase of virtue in Christ's religion, and for the conservation of the peace, unity and tranquility of this realm; any usage, custom, foreign laws, foreign authority, prescription, or any other thing or things to the contrary hereof notwithstanding.

# THE SCHLEITHEIM CONFESSION

*Although their theology was not as well developed as Melancthon or Calvin, the Anabaptists were the first Protestants to consolidate their beliefs into a Confession of Faith. Leaders of the Anabaptist movement, most of whom came from the lower orders of the Catholic clergy—parish priests and monks—met in the town of Schleitheim (Switzerland) in February of 1527. The meeting was presided over by Michael Sattler (c. 1495–1527), a former prior of a Benedictine monastery, who had joined the movement in 1525 and who would die a few years later.*

24 FEBRUARY 1527

The articles we have dealt with, and in which we have been united, are these: baptism, ban, the breaking of bread, separation from abomination, shepherds in the congregation, the sword, the oath.

1. Notice concerning baptism. Baptism shall be given to all those who have been taught repentance and the amendment of life and who believe truly    5
   that their sins are taken away through Christ, and to all those who desire to walk in the resurrection of Jesus Christ and be buried with Him in death, so that they might rise with Him; to all those who with such an understanding themselves desire and request it from us; hereby is excluded all infant baptism, the greatest and first abomination of the Pope. For this you have the    10
   reasons and the testimony of the writings and the practice of the apostles. We wish simply yet resolutely and with assurance to hold to the same.

2. We have been united as follows concerning the ban. The ban shall be employed with all these who have given themselves over to the Lord, to walk after Him in His commandments; those who have been baptized into the one body    15
   of Christ, and let themselves be called brothers or sisters, and still somehow slip and fall into error and sin, being inadvertently overtaken. The same shall be warned twice privately and the third time be publicly admonished before the entire congregation according to the command of Christ (Matthew 18). But this shall be done according to the ordering of the Spirit of God before    20
   the breaking of bread, so that we may all in one spirit and in one love break and eat from one bread and drink from one cup.

John H. Yoder, *The Legacy of Michael Sattler* (Scottdale, PA: Herald Press, 1973), 36–42. Reprinted with permission of Herald Press; permission conveyed through Copyright Clearance Center, Inc.

3. Concerning the breaking of bread, we have become one and agree thus: all those who desire to break the one bread in remembrance of the broken body of Christ and all those who wish to drink of one drink in remembrance of the shed blood of Christ, they must beforehand be united in the one body of Christ, that is the congregation of God, whose head is Christ, and that by baptism. For as Paul indicates, we cannot be partakers at the same time of the table of the Lord and the table of devils. Nor can we at the same time partake and drink of the cup of the Lord and the cup of devils. That is: all those who have fellowship with the dead works of darkness have no part in the light. Thus all who follow the devil and the world have no part with those who have been called out of the world unto God. All those who lie in evil have no part in the good. So it shall and must be that whoever does not share the calling of the one God to one faith, to one baptism, to one spirit, to one body together with all the children of God, may not be made one loaf together with them, as must be true if one wishes truly to break bread according to the command of Christ.

4. We have been united concerning the separation that shall take place from the evil and the wickedness which the devil has planted in the world, simply in this: that we have no fellowship with them, and do not run with them in the confusion of their abomination. So it is; since all who have not entered into the obedience of faith and have not united themselves with God so that they will to do His will are a great abomination before God, therefore nothing else can or really will grow or spring forth from them than abominable things. Now there is nothing else in the world and all creation than good or evil, believing and unbelieving, darkness and light, the world and those who are come out of the world, God's temple and idols, Christ and Belial, and none will have part with the other. To us, then, the commandment of the Lord is also obvious, whereby He orders us to be and to become separated from the evil one, and thus He will be our God and we shall be His sons and daughters. Further, He admonishes us therefore to go out from Babylon and from the earthly Egypt, that we may not be partakers in their torment and suffering, which the Lord will bring upon them. From all this we should learn that everything which has not been united with our God in Christ is nothing but an abomination which we should shun. By this are meant all popish and re-popish works and idolatry, gatherings, church attendance, winehouses, guarantees and commitments of unbelief, and other things of the kind, which the world regards highly, and yet which are carnal or flatly counter to the command of God, after the pattern of all the iniquity which is in the world. From all

this we shall be separated and have no part with such, for they are nothing but abominations, which cause us to be hated before our Christ Jesus, Who has freed us from the servitude of the flesh and fitted us for the service of God and the Spirit whom He has given us. Thereby shall also fall away from us the diabolical weapons of violence—such as sword, armor, and the like, and all of their use to protect friends or against enemies—by virtue of the word of Christ: "you shall not resist evil."

5. We have been united as follows concerning shepherds in the church of God. The shepherd in the church shall be a person according to the rule of Paul, fully and completely, who has a good report of those who are outside the faith. The office of such a person shall be to read and exhort and teach, warn, admonish, or ban in the congregation, and properly to preside among the sisters and brothers in prayer, and in the breaking of the bread, and in all things to take care of the body of Christ, that it may be built up and developed, so that the name of God might be praised and honored through us, and the mouth of the mocker be stopped. He shall be supported, wherein he has need, by the congregation which has chosen him, so that he who serves the Gospel can also live therefrom, as the Lord has ordered. But should a shepherd do something worthy of reprimand, nothing shall be done with him without the voice of two or three witnesses. If they sin they shall be publicly reprimanded, so that others might fear. But if the shepherd should be driven away or led to the Lord by the cross, at the same hour another shall be ordained to his place, so that the little folk and the little flock of God may not be destroyed, but be preserved by warning and be consoled.

6. We have been united as follows concerning the sword. The sword is an ordering of God outside the perfection of Christ. It punishes and kills the wicked, and guards and protects the good. In the law the sword is established over the wicked for punishment and for death, and the secular rulers are established to wield the same. But within the perfection of Christ, only the ban is used for the admonition and exclusion of the one who has sinned, without the death of the flesh, simply the warning and the command to sin no more. Now many, who do not understand Christ's will for us will ask whether a Christian may or should use the sword against the wicked for the protection and defense of the good, or for the sake of love. The answer is unanimously revealed: Christ teaches and commands us to learn from Him, for He is meek and lowly of heart and thus we shall find rest for our souls. Now Christ says to the woman who was taken in adultery, not that she should be stoned according to the law of His Father (and yet

He says, "what the Father commanded me, that I do") but with mercy and forgiveness and the warning to sin no more, says: "Go, sin no more." Exactly thus should we also proceed, according to the rule of the ban.

Second is asked concerning the sword, whether a Christian shall pass sentence in disputes and strife about worldly matters, such as the unbelievers have with one another. The answer: Christ did not wish to decide or pass judgment between brother and brother concerning inheritance, but refused to do so. So should we also do.

Third is asked concerning the sword, whether the Christian should be a magistrate if he is chosen thereto. This is answered thus: Christ was to be made king, but he fled and did not discern the ordinance of His Father. Thus we should also do as He did and follow after Him, and we shall not walk in darkness. For He Himself says, "Whoever would come after me, let him deny himself and take up his cross and follow me." He himself further forbids the violence of the sword when He says, "The princes of this world lord it over them etc., but among you it shall not be so." Further Paul says, "Whom God has foreknown, the same He has also predestined to be conformed to the image of His Son," etc. Peter also says, "Christ has suffered (not ruled) and has left us an example, that you should follow after in His steps."

Lastly, one can see in the following points that it does not befit a Christian to be a magistrate: the rule of the government is according to the flesh, that of the Christians according to the spirit. Their houses and dwelling remain in this world, that of the Christians is in Heaven. Their citizenship is in this world, that of the Christians is in Heaven. The weapons of their battle and warfare are carnal and only against the flesh, but the weapons of Christians are spiritual, against the fortification of the devil. The worldly are armed with steel and iron, but Christians are armed with the armor of God, with truth, righteousness, peace, faith, salvation, and with the Word of God. In sum: as Christ our Head is minded, so also must be minded the members of the body of Christ through Him, so that there be no division in the body, through which it would be destroyed. Since then Christ is as is written of Him, so must His members also be the same, so that His body may remain whole and unified for its own advancement and upbuilding. For any kingdom which is divided within itself will be destroyed.

7. We have been united as follows concerning the oath. The oath is a confirmation among those who are quarreling or making promises. In the law it is commanded that it should be done only in the name of God, truthfully and not falsely. Christ, who teaches the perfection of the law, forbids His followers all swearing, whether true nor false; neither by heaven nor by

earth, neither by Jerusalem nor by our head; and that for the reason which He goes on to give, "For you cannot make one hair white or black."[1] You see, thereby all swearing is forbidden. We cannot perform what is promised in swearing, for we are not able to change the smallest part of ourselves.

Now there are some who do not believe the simple commandment of God and who say, "But God swore by Himself to Abraham, because He was God (as He promised him that He would do good to him and would be his God if he kept His commandments). Why then should I not swear if I promise something to someone?" The answer: hear what Scripture says. "God, since He wished to prove over-abundantly to the heirs of His promise that His will did not change, inserted an oath so that by two immutable things we might have a stronger consolation (for it is impossible that God should lie)."[2] Notice the meaning of the passage: God has the power to do what He forbids you, for everything is possible to Him. God swore an oath to Abraham, Scripture says, in order to prove that His counsel is immutable. That means no one can withstand and thwart His will; thus He can keep His oath. But we cannot, as Christ said above, hold or perform our oath, therefore we should not swear.

Others say that swearing cannot be forbidden by God in the New Testament when it was commanded in the Old, but that it is forbidden only to swear by Heaven, earth, Jerusalem, and our head. Answer: hear the Scripture. He who swears by Heaven swears by God's throne and by Him who sits thereon. Observe: swearing by Heaven is forbidden, which is only God's throne; how much more is it forbidden to swear by God Himself. You blind fools, what is greater, the throne or He who sits upon it? Others say if it is then wrong to use God for truth, then the apostles Peter and Paul also swore. Answer: Peter and Paul only testify to that which God promised Abraham, Whom we long after have received. But when one testifies, one testifies concerning that which is present, whether it be good or evil. Thus Simeon spoke of Christ to Mary and testified, "Behold: this One is ordained for the falling and rising of many in Israel and to be a sign which will be spoken against."[3] Christ taught us similarly when He says your speech shall be yea, yea; and nay, nay; for what is more than that comes of evil. He says your speech or your word shall be yes and no, so that no one might understand that He had permitted it. Christ is simply yea and nay, and all those who seek Him simply will understand his Word. Amen.

---

[1]Matthew 5:36–37
[2]Hebrews 6:13–14
[3]Luke 2:34

# XI
# THE SCIENTIFIC
# REVOLUTION

Second only to the rise of Christianity itself, the Scientific Revolution stands as the single most important "event" in the Western Heritage. The famous historian Herbert Butterfield (1900–1979) seems to have coined the term "Scientific Revolution" when he first used it in 1948 to characterize the age of Copernicus and Newton during which modern science was born. Butterfield was unequivocal about the Scientific Revolution's importance when he insisted that "it outshines everything since the rise of Christianity and reduces the Renaissance and Reformation to the rank of mere episodes, mere internal displacements, within the system of medieval Christendom."

For good or ill, like it or not, modern science occupies a central position from which it touches everything in twenty-first-century society. Life and death, sickness and health—each is different today because of modern science. From medicine, technology, and communication, to food production, waste removal, and every mode of travel, modern science has displaced practices and perspectives that had prevailed for millennia. Our conceptions of the earth and of the heavens, indeed, even our understanding of human nature and what it means to say we "know" have been transformed by the power of science. Science has not just altered the way humans have succeeded—from conquering illnesses, curbing pain, diminishing hunger, and spreading wealth, to providing creature comforts and gadgetry of every sort—science has introduced new problems ranging from horrific weapons and killing procedures to new forms of pollution, waste, and destruction. And as science has added to our knowledge, it has changed and challenged many long-standing beliefs about the nature of human personhood, the viability of traditional ways of knowing, and even our conceptions of the good, the true, and the beautiful. So even as science has delivered on the promise that its knowledge will give power, that power has proven very dangerous and difficult to wield wisely.

Because the arrival of modern science has been such a mixed blessing and since its influence can be seen and felt everywhere, the student of the Western Heritage really must understand something of its origin and development. What were its sources and who were its creators? How did it arise? What ideas and practices set modern science apart from medieval and ancient notions of man and nature? Has modern science rendered all pre-modern beliefs obsolete, or just some of them? Does the story of modern science's birth provide any guidance about how to handle its mature contemporary forms? Did the rise of modern science demand changes and accommodations from politics or religion, from economics or the arts? Although complete answers to these questions are beyond the scope of this essay, it is nevertheless important that they be posed and considered. For such questions, among others, confront every student of Western Heritage who would contend successfully with the trials of ordering life in a world so prominently marked by science.

An obvious imprecision attaches to the historical business of labeling periods and assigning names to episodes of change, especially to those "events" extended over decades or even centuries. The Scientific Revolution of the sixteenth and seventeenth century is surely no exception. None of its leading figures identified himself as a "scientist"—a term that did not find wide currency until the nineteenth century. Some of them were mathematicians, others astronomers, church workers, medical doctors, or amateur practitioners. Their business was called *natural philosophy,* not science. Some were paid for their efforts. Many were not. The social categories, cultural conventions, and means of support that characterize the complex modern world of scientific research did not yet exist. So there is something almost anachronistic about transporting our contemporary notions of science and scientists to the Early-Modern period of European history.

Granting latitude for this imprecision, it is reasonable to situate the beginning of the Scientific Revolution in the first half of the sixteenth century and to associate it with three coincident publishing achievements of the late Renaissance. The year 1543 witnessed the publication of the first Latin translation of the complete works of the famed Greek mathematician Archimedes (*c.* 287–212 BC). That year also saw the printing of the spectacular anatomical treatise, *De Humani Corporis Fabrica* (*On the Fabric of the Human Body*) by Andreas Vesalius (1514–1564), a Belgian physician and anatomist. The third highly significant publication of 1543 appeared as its author neared death. It was *De revolutionibus orbium coelestium* (*On the Revolutions of the Heavenly Spheres*), the astronomical treatise of the Polish Church administrator and amateur astronomer Nicolaus Copernicus (1473–1543), whose conception of a moving Earth and stationary Sun would, more than any single idea, symbolize the Scientific Revolution's repudiation of the ancient and medieval world picture.

The following century and a half witnessed a most rare combination of creative genius, philosophical speculation, and raw intellectual drive, all fueled and inspired by wonder at the awful majesty of God's creation. A curious cast of unique characters with names such as Tycho Brahe (1546–1601), Johannes Kepler (1571–1630), Galileo Galilei (1564–1642), Francis Bacon (1561–1626),

René Descartes (1596–1650), William Harvey (1578–1657), Robert Boyle (1627–1691), and Isaac Newton (1642–1727), to name only a very few, began weaving the tapestry of modern science from remnant threads of both the Greco-Roman intellectual tradition and the Judeo-Christian philosophical and theological traditions. The creative process culminated in an entirely new world picture that replaced the vision of reality that had governed Western European minds for centuries. Most historians of science find the principal features of the new science in works of Isaac Newton, whose 1687 masterpiece *Philosophiae Naturalis Principia Mathematica* (*The Mathematical Principles of Natural Philosophy*) is widely regarded as the culmination of the Scientific Revolution. In view of this, there is some sense in placing the Scientific Revolution between the two symbolically significant dates 1543 and 1687, after which the culture of "Newtonianism" would fuel continued scientific efforts and spark a new Age of Reason or Enlightenment during the eighteenth century.

Prior to the acceptance of Copernicanism and the counterintuitive implications of a moving Earth, Western man situated himself in a cozy cosmos imaginatively derived from a well-crafted union between medieval Christianity and the nearly-but-never-fully-lost particulars of Greco-Roman science—especially those particulars most fully recovered by AD 1200 and derived from the mindset and empiricism of Aristotle (384–322 BC), the cosmology and technical astronomy of Ptolemy (AD 139–161), and the medicine, anatomy, and physiology of Galen (AD 130–201). Of course there had been other ancient authorities: Pythagoras in mathematics (582–500 BC), Plato in speculative natural philosophy (427–345 BC), Euclid in geometry (*fl.* 300 BC), and Hippocrates in Greek medicine (*c.* 460–*c.* 375 BC). Each had contributed his bits. The resulting Medieval Aristotelian-Ptolemaic-Christian World Picture presented a coherent synthesis, remarkable for its delightful splendor, sober hierarchy, and common sense, if not for its mathematical elegance. It was a comfortable image of one grand sphere containing inner-nested spheres with a stationary Earth at its center, and everything else—plants and animals, men and angels, saints and the damned, God and the Devil, planets, stars, and moon—ordered in its proper place. Heavenly bodies embedded in their own crystalline spheres were carried along around the Earth in perfect circular motion (befitting only of the heavens). Everything beneath the sphere of the moon was situated according to its terrestrial nature and typified by the imperfections of the sublunar realm. The whole scheme fit common sense perfectly as it "saved the phenomena" by reliably accounting for the motion of each heavenly body—at least those visible to the naked eye. It seemed eminently faithful to Scripture and Christian tradition. And it conformed to the settled opinion of all wise men in the new medieval universities. Its only weakness was that it was false. The medieval world picture presented a believable image. The achievement of the Scientific Revolution would be to turn this medieval picture into *The Discarded Image,* to borrow from the title of C. S. Lewis's fine book on the subject.

The process of dismantling and discarding the medieval image of the cosmos and of man's place in it was marked by no fewer than half a dozen themes, each of which became foundational to the new modern science. First, a fundamental achievement of modern science is the degree to which it has succeeded in fostering *the rejection of common sense* experience. Whatever its faults, the *geocentric* medieval world picture of a stationary Earth at the center of a world that revolved around it was a picture that matched common sense experience rather nicely. The Copernican *heliocentric* idea of the Earth rotating on its axis once each day while annually orbiting the Sun seemed self-evidently preposterous. Historians of science have sometimes remarked that with the birth of modern science "common sense was re-educated." No doubt, it was. But even as we speak of "sunrise" and "sunset" our daily language betrays our pre-modern common sense of things. If even the earliest varieties of modern science required a suspension of disbelief, how much more have the continued scientific achievements since the time of Galileo and Newton required the same? The sciences of electricity, magnetism, embryology, evolution, relativity, and quantum mechanics all have central ideas that defy common sense and whose comprehension demands imaginative and counterintuitive insight or sophisticated mathematical erudition.

The ability of modern science to re-educate common sense was, in no small part, linked to the second principal theme of the scientific revolution: *the substitution of a "quantitative" approach* to nature for the ancient "qualitative" approach. Pre-modern descriptions and explanations of phenomena again and again derived from inquiries into the qualities of the substances of which they were composed. Heavy things fell, explained Aristotle, because it was the nature of earthy things to seek the center, i.e., the Earth. Heavenly bodies moved in circular motion, insisted ancient and medieval astronomers, because heavenly perfection requires perfection of motion, which can only be attributed to the circle. Such reasoning, while potentially attractive, usually ignored what could be learned about nature through more rigorous mathematical analysis. To be sure, from Euclid to Ptolemy, from Archimedes to Leonardo da Vinci, ancient and medieval thinkers used mathematics. But the Scientific Revolution's achievement was to recognize and apply, as never before, the simple truth uttered by Galileo that "Mathematics is the language of nature." Johannes Kepler insisted that the God who created the heavens and the earth is "a geometer." For Kepler, the implication of this theological assertion was inescapable: When God thinks, he thinks geometric thoughts. When God creates, his universe embodies those thoughts. Man, made in the image of God, will be thinking the thoughts of God when he studies mathematically the universe that God has made. In short, Kepler understood science to be that mathematically charged quantitative enterprise of "thinking God's thoughts after him." Similarly, the confidence of Copernicus in the veracity of his new cosmology was grounded not in new observations, but in his certainty that truth would attach to his most mathematically elegant system. Even William Harvey's demonstration of the circulation of the blood rested, in no small part, upon his mathematical calculations of the volume and speed with which blood mechanically flowed through the heart and vessels.

As the new modern science embraced a mathematical approach to nature, it also began to think about nature itself according to a new overriding mechanical metaphor. If the qualitative medieval world picture tended, following Aristotle, to express its understanding of nature as if it were living and organic, modern science increasingly embraced a new "mechanical philosophy of nature" according to which the *concept of nature as a machine* became the governing metaphor. This was especially evident in the scientific work of such people as René Descartes, Robert Boyle, and Pierre Gassendi (1592–1655). Central to the developing modern science was their shared view that all observable phenomena were reducible to two universal principles: matter and motion. The mechanical philosophy of nature sought to expunge from science any reliance upon "occult" (mysterious) forces, mystical action at a distance, or unseen properties. Like a great machine, the cosmos and all its parts could, they hoped, be reduced to and explained ultimately in terms of the mechanistic interactions of its varied constituent material parts. Of course, the scientific program of reducing nature to a machine has met with uneven success. Even Isaac Newton abandoned such mechanical reductionism as he introduced "Force" as a third cardinal principle alongside matter and motion. If he did not claim to know the ultimate nature of gravitational force or understand why it functioned as it did, he at least succeeded in providing a rigorous mathematical description of how it acted upon bodies.

Indeed, Newton's universal law of gravitation reveals the fourth key theme of the scientific revolution. Science has been so successful, in part, because of its professed modesty of scope. Science tells *how* the world works, even if it cannot say *why* it behaves as it does. In the scientific revolution, natural philosophers abandoned hope for providing explanations in any ultimate sense. That is, science stopped asking *why questions* and began asking *how questions*. Put differently, scientists sought to *describe* nature and its behavior rather than to *explain* it in comprehensive terms. It sought proximate causes, not final causes.

Not surprisingly, this led to the fifth major theme of the Scientific Revolution, *the development of new methods*. As the natural philosophers began to frame their inquiry in different terms, their interrogation of nature took different shape.

Empirical evidence imaginatively suggested hypotheses that would, in turn, be subjected to rational scrutiny and critical test. Much has been made, since the days of Francis Bacon, of the so-called "Scientific Method." There really is no single method for having new ideas. The founders of modern science did not follow Bacon's philosophy, as Bacon dismissed most of their theories. Much of scientific "discovery" is a combination of informed hunches, elbow grease, sweat, and a pinch of luck. But it also requires asking the right questions. For example, Aristotle had begun with a false assumption that then prompted the wrong question. Concerning moving bodies (such as an archer's arrow, for example), Aristotle had asserted that every motion requires a mover. Therefore, he asked, "What keeps a body moving?" The concept of inertia would forever elude him. Galileo, on the other hand, asked a different question: "What causes a body ever to change its state of motion?" His question was fruitful in ways Aristotle's could never be.

To be sure all of these principal themes of the scientific revolution were conditioned by the sixth and fundamental theme—*a new astronomy* that demanded the *new heliocentric cosmology* to replace the geocentrism of the medieval world picture. If in fact the Earth did move, then Aristotelian physics would collapse and a new science of motion (mechanics) for both the heavens and the earth would be required. The old cosmology was grounded in a certainty that there was a radical distinction between the heavens (the realm beyond the sphere of the Moon) and the terrestrial "sublunar" realm. Each presumably had its own kind of motion, its own kind of matter, and its own fundamental nature that required a different "science" for each realm. With the new cosmology, this distinction between the lunar and the sublunar, between the heavens and the earth, was eliminated once and for all. Newton's law of universal gravitation was "universal" precisely because it applied to the motion of the planets in their orbits and to the falling of an apple to the surface of the Earth.

Thus by the beginning of the eighteenth century the birth of modern science had caused the rejection of common sense experience, installed a quantitative mathematical approach to nature, introduced the concept of nature as a machine, forced scientists to describe nature in terms answerable by *how* questions, developed new methods, and defended a new cosmology with its attendant implications for mechanics and astronomy.

Clearly, such changes rendered obsolete many pre-modern notions. The new world revealed by modern science demanded the surrender of many medieval concepts. Some intellectuals eventually insisted that the price of living in this new world was the abandonment of the old world's principal faith, traditional Christianity. Had science rendered the faith untenable? Some eventually thought so. For example, the early twenty-first century witnessed the publication of numerous books by such atheistic scientists and philosophers as Richard Dawkins and Daniel Dennett. These and their fellow-travelers confidently belched the opinion that science had rendered belief in God untenable. This custom of portraying science and religion as pitched in battle had a long pedigree stretching back to well before such nineteenth-century publications as John William Draper's *History of the Conflict between Religion and Science* (1874) and Andrew Dickson White's *A History of the Warfare of Science with Theology in Christendom* (1896). Even earlier, there were enlightenment skeptics and unbelievers in the eighteenth-century who imagined that the new science had destroyed traditional belief. But such assertions regarding the incompatibility of modern science with Christian faith betrayed a misunderstanding of the history and philosophy of science. Indeed, most of the principal founders of modern science were deeply committed Christians who understood their scientific work as harmonious extensions of their theological commitments, or at least, as benign pursuits posing no fundamental threat to orthodox belief. This was certainly true of such figures as Copernicus, Kepler, Galileo, Boyle, and Newton. For example, Kepler wrote, "Behold how through my effort God is being celebrated in astronomy."

Indeed, there remains the undeniable fact that modern science was born only once, and that was in the Christian civilization of Western Europe. Was this merely a coincidence, or did Christian civilization provide a congenial soil for the blossoming of modern science from its pre-modern antecedents? Think about the things that one must affirm philosophically before the scientific enterprise can even begin. Although the following notions may seem obvious, they have all been contested and rejected at one time by non-Christian cultures: To initiate scientific activity one must first believe that nature is real, that its study is a worthy pursuit, that the world is ordered according to laws, that the human mind is capable of discovering those laws, and that despite nature's law-abiding regularities, an element of chance remains—that is, because the world could be different than human reason predicts, experiment is necessary to find out how it really is. These somewhat abstract notions, if not derived explicitly from Christianity, are certainly compatible with the faith. There were other important and complicated ways that science and Christianity interacted during the Early-Modern period whose full story remains too rich and complex to tell here. Regardless, the lesson is clear. Despite its innovations and departures from the past, modern science did not render the Christian faith untenable. Of course, this does not require crediting Christianity for the birth of modern science either. Rather, it merely demands recognition of the fact that modern science grew from and remains compatible with key features of the two principal wellsprings of the Western heritage, the Judeo-Christian faith and Greco-Roman culture.

# THE REVOLUTIONS OF THE HEAVENLY SPHERES
## NICOLAUS COPERNICUS (1473–1543)

*In 1512, after completing his university training in canon law, mathematics, astronomy, and medicine, Nicolaus Copernicus settled into his position as canon at the Frauenburg cathedral in Poland near the Baltic Sea. Although Copernicus never took holy orders, he continued as a canonist (an official cathedral chapter staff member) for the rest of his life. Occupied with duties in finance, church law, politics, and various ecclesiastical affairs, Copernicus still found time for practicing medicine and, significantly, the work in mathematical astronomy that ultimately sparked a revolution in science.*

*Copernicus was committed to a heliostatic (stationary sun) conception of the universe. Such a model, to be true, would require the earth to rotate daily on its axis and to revolve annually about the sun, which Copernicus located near the center of the universe—hence the term heliocentric (sun-centered) is often used to indicate the Copernican departure from the dominate geocentric (earth-centered) view of the cosmos associated with the second-century (AD) astronomer Ptolemy. Copernicus's ideas were circulated first among friends in a brief treatise called* The Commentariolus *(1530).*

*Then, in 1543, the year of his death, his complete argument for the motion of the earth was published as* De revolutionibus orbium coelestium (On the Revolutions of the Heavenly Spheres). *The work's anonymous "Introduction" (reprinted here) seemed to indicate that Copernicus defended an instrumentalist view of his theory; that is, a view that conceived of heliocentrism as only a useful model for astronomical calculation, but not really a true picture of the cosmos. Copernicus did not write the introduction, however. Andreas Osiander (1498–1522), the Lutheran theologian who oversaw the book's publication, had written it. Copernicus clearly believed his heliocentric theory to be the accurate description of the real physical world. Because such a realist conception of his theory would likely be controversial,*

Robert Maynard Hutchins, Editor, *Great Books of the Western World* (Chicago: Encyclopaedia Britannica, Inc. 1952), XVI:505–9. Reprinted with permission from Great Books of the Western World ©1952, 1990 Encyclopaedia Britannica, Inc.

*Copernicus opened his volume with a dedication (also reprinted here) to Pope Paul III (r. 1534–1549), in which he argued that his heliocentric hypothesis was supported by some ancient thinkers and that those who were knowledgeable in mathematics would find his case compelling.*

*Since 1543 also saw, in addition to the work of Copernicus, the publication of a major new book on human anatomy,* On the Fabric of the Human Body *by Andreas Vesalius (1514–1564), as well as the first Latin translation of Archimedes' works, a compelling case can be made that this year (1543) marked the beginning of the Scientific Revolution.*

1543

## To the Reader Concerning the Hypotheses of this Work

Since the newness of the hypotheses of this work—which sets the earth in motion and puts an immovable sun at the centre of the universe—has already received a great deal of publicity, I have no doubt that certain of the savants have taken grave offense and think it wrong to raise any disturbance among

5   liberal disciplines which have had the right set-up for a long time now. If, however, they are willing to weigh the matter scrupulously, they will find that the author of this work has done nothing which merits blame. For it is the job of the astronomer to use painstaking and skilled observation in gathering together the history of the celestial movements, and then—since he cannot

10  by any line of reasoning reach the true causes of these movements—to think up or construct whatever causes or hypotheses he pleases such that, by the assumption of these causes, those same movements can be calculated from the principles of geometry for the past and for the future too. This artist is markedly outstanding in both of these respects: for it is not necessary that these

15  hypotheses should be true, or even probably; but it is enough if they provide a calculus which fits the observations—unless by some chance there is anyone so ignorant of geometry and optics as to hold the epicycle of Venus as probable and to believe this to be a cause why Venus alternately precedes and follows the sun at an angular distance of up to 40° or more. For who does not see that it

20  necessarily follows from this assumption that the diameter of the planet in its perigee should appear more than four times greater, and the body of the planet more than sixteen times greater, than in its apogee? Nevertheless the experience of all the ages is opposed to that. There are also other things in this discipline which are just as absurd, but it is not necessary to examine them right now. For

25  it is sufficiently clear that this art is absolutely and profoundly ignorant of the causes of the apparent irregular movements. And if it constructs and thinks up causes—and it has certainly thought up a good many—nevertheless it does not think them up in order to persuade anyone of their truth but only in order that they may provide a correct basis for calculation. But since for one and the same

movement varying hypotheses are proposed from time to time, as eccentricity or epicycle for the movement of the sun, the astronomer much prefers to take the one which is easiest to grasp. Maybe the philosopher demands probability instead; but neither of them will grasp anything certain or hand it on, unless it has been divinely revealed to him. Therefore let us permit these new hypotheses 5 to make a public appearance among old ones which are themselves no more probable, especially since they are wonderful and easy and bring with them a vast storehouse of learned observations. And as far as hypotheses go, let no one expect anything in the way of certainty from astronomy, since astronomy can offer us nothing certain, lest, if anyone take as true that which has been 10 constructed for another use, he go away from this discipline a bigger fool than when he came to it. Farewell.

## Preface and Dedication to Pope Paul III

I can reckon easily enough, Most Holy Father, that as soon as certain people learn that in these books of mine which I have written about the revolutions of the spheres of the world I attribute certain motions to the terrestrial globe, they 15 will immediately shout to have me and my opinion hooted off the stage. For my own works do not please me so much that I do not weigh what judgments others will pronounce concerning them. And although I realize that the conceptions of a philosopher are placed beyond the judgment of the crowd, because it is his loving duty to seek the truth in all things, in so far as God has granted that to 20 human reason; nevertheless I think we should avoid opinions utterly foreign to rightness. And when I considered how absurd this "lecture" would be held by those who know that the opinion that the Earth rests immovable in the middle of the heavens as if their centre had been confirmed by the judgments of many ages—if I were to assert to the contrary that the Earth moves; for a long time 25 I was in great difficulty as to whether I should bring to light my commentaries written to demonstrate the Earth's movement, or whether it would not be better to follow the example of the Pythagoreans and certain others who used to hand down the mysteries of their philosophy not in writing but by word of mouth and only to their relatives and friends—witness the letter of Lysis to Hipparchus. 30 They however seem to me to have done that not, as some judge, out of a jealous unwillingness to communicate their doctrines but in order that things of very great beauty which have been investigated by the loving care of great men should not be scorned by those who find it a bother to expend any great energy on letters—except on the money-making variety—or who are provoked by the 35 exhortations and examples of others to the liberal study of philosophy but on account of their natural stupidity hold the position among philosophers that drones hold among bees. Therefore, when I weighed these things in my mind, the scorn which I had to fear on account of the newness and absurdity of my opinion almost drove me to abandon a work already undertaken.

But my friends made me change my course in spite of my long-continued hesitation and even resistance. First among them was Nicholas Schonberg, Cardinal of Capua,[1] a man distinguished in all branches of learning; next to him was my devoted friend Tiedeman Giese, Bishop of Culm,[2] a man filled with the greatest zeal for the divine and liberal arts: for he in particular urged me frequently and even spurred me on by added reproaches into publishing this book and letting come to light a work which I had kept hidden among my things for not merely nine years, but for almost four times nine years. Not a few other learned and distinguished men demanded the same thing of me, urging me to refuse no longer—on account of the fear which I felt—to contribute my work to the common utility of those who are really interested in mathematics: they said that the absurder my teaching about the movement of the Earth now seems to very many persons, the more wonder and thanksgiving will it be the object of, when after the publication of my commentaries those same persons see the fog of absurdity dissipated by my luminous demonstrations. Accordingly I was led by such persuasion and by that hope finally to permit my friends to undertake the publication of a work which they had long sought from me.

But perhaps Your Holiness will not be so much surprised at my giving the results of my nocturnal study to the light—after having taken such care in working them out that I did not hesitate to put in writing my conceptions as to the movement of the Earth—as you will be eager to hear from me what came into my mind that in opposition to the general opinion of mathematicians and almost in opposition to common sense I should dare to imagine some movement of the Earth. And so I am unwilling to hide from Your Holiness that nothing except my knowledge that mathematicians have not agreed with one another in their researches moved me to think out a different scheme of drawing up the movements of the spheres of the world. For in the first place mathematicians are so uncertain about the movements of the sun and moon that they can neither demonstrate nor observe the unchanging magnitude of the revolving year. Then in setting up the solar and lunar movements and those of the other five wandering stars, they do not employ the same principles, assumptions, or demonstrations for the revolutions and apparent movements. For some make use of homocentric circles only, others of eccentric circles and epicycles, by means of which however they do not fully attain what they seek. For although those who have put their trust in homocentric circles have shown that various

---

[1]Nikolaus von Schönberg (1472–1537), Archbishop of Capua (1520–1536) and Cardinal
[2]Tiederman Giese (1480–1550), Bishop of Chelmno, Prussia (1538–1549)

different movements can be composed of such circles, nevertheless they have not been able to establish anything for certain that would fully correspond to the phenomena. But even if those who have thought up eccentric circles seem to have been able for the most part to compute the apparent movements numerically by those means, they have in the meanwhile admitted a great deal which    5
seems to contradict the first principles of regularity of movement. Moreover, they have not been able to discover or to infer the chief point of all, i.e., the form of the world and the certain commensurability of its parts. But they are in exactly the same fix as someone taking from different places hands, feet, head, and the other limbs—shaped very beautifully but not with reference to one    10
body and without correspondence to one another—so that such parts made up a monster rather than a man. And so, in the process of demonstration which they call "method," they are found either to have omitted something necessary or to have admitted something foreign which by no means pertains to the matter; and they would by no means have been in this fix, if they had followed    15
sure principles. For if the hypotheses they assumed were not false, everything which followed from the hypotheses would have been verified without fail; and though what I am saying may be obscure right now, nevertheless it will become clearer in the proper place.

Accordingly, when I had meditated upon this lack of certitude in the tradi-    20
tional mathematics concerning the composition of movements of the spheres of the world, I began to be annoyed that the philosophers, who in other respects had made a very careful scrutiny of the least details of the world, had discovered no sure scheme for the movements of the machinery of the world, which has been built for us by the Best and Most Orderly Workman of all. Wherefore I    25
took the trouble to reread all the books by philosophers which I could get hold of, to see if any of them even supposed that the movements of the spheres of the world were different from those laid down by those who taught mathematics in the schools. And as a matter of fact, I found first in Cicero that Nicetas thought that the Earth moved. And afterwards I found in Plutarch that there    30
were some others of the same opinion: I shall copy out his words here, so that they may be known to all:

Some think that the Earth is at rest; but Philolaus the Pythagorean says that it moves around the fire with an obliquely circular motion, like the sun and moon. Herakleides of Pontus and Ekphantus the Pythagorean    35
do not give the Earth any movement of locomotion, but rather a limited movement of rising and setting around its centre, like a wheel.

Therefore I also, having found occasion, began to meditate upon the mobility of the Earth. And although the opinion seemed absurd, nevertheless because I knew that others before me had been granted the liberty of constructing whatever circles they pleased in order to demonstrate astral phenomena, I thought that I too would be readily permitted to test whether or not, by the laying down that the Earth had some movement, demonstrations less shaky than those of my predecessors could be found for the revolutions of the celestial spheres.

And so, having laid down the movements which I attribute to the Earth farther on in the work, I finally discovered by the help of long and numerous observations that if the movements of the other wandering stars are correlated with the circular movement of the Earth, and if the movements are computed in accordance with the revolution of each plant, not only do all their phenomena follow from that but also this correlation binds together so closely the order and magnitudes of all the planets and of their spheres or orbital circles and the heavens themselves that nothing can be shifted around in any part of them without disrupting the remaining parts and the universe as a whole.

Accordingly, in composing my work I adopted the following order: in the first book I describe all the locations of the spheres or orbital circles together with the movements which I attribute to the earth, so that this book contains as it were the general set-up of the universe. But afterwards in the remaining books I correlate all the movements of the other planets and their spheres or orbital circles with the mobility of the Earth, so that it can be gathered from that how far the apparent movements of the remaining planets and their orbital circles can be saved by being correlated with the movements of the Earth. And I have no doubt that talented and learned mathematicians will agree with me, if—as philosophy demands in the first place—they are willing to give not superficial but profound thought and effort to what I bring forward in this work in demonstrating these things. And in order that the unlearned as well as the learned might see that I was not seeking to flee from the judgment of any man, I preferred to dedicate these results of my nocturnal study to Your Holiness rather than to anyone else; because, even in this remote corner of the earth where I live, you are held to be most eminent both in the dignity of your order and in your love of letters and even of mathematics; hence, by the authority of your judgment you can easily provide a guard against the bites of slanderers, despite the proverb that there is no medicine for the bite of a sycophant.

But if perchance there are certain "idle talkers" who take it upon themselves to pronounce judgment, although wholly ignorant of mathematics, and if by shamelessly distorting the sense of some passage in Holy Writ to suit their purpose, they dare to reprehend and to attack my work; they worry me so little that I shall even scorn their judgments as foolhardy. For it is not unknown that

Lactantius,[3] otherwise a distinguished writer but hardly a mathematician, speaks in an utterly childish fashion concerning the shape of the Earth when he laughs at those who have affirmed that the Earth has the form of a globe. And so the studious need not be surprised if people like that laugh at us. Mathematics is written for mathematicians; and among them, if I am not mistaken, my labors will be seen to contribute something to the ecclesiastical commonwealth, the principate of which Your Holiness now holds. For not many years ago under Leo X[4] when the Lateran Council was considering the question of reforming the Ecclesiastical Calendar, no decision was reached, for the sole reason that the magnitude of the year and the months and the movements of the sun and moon had not yet been measured with sufficient accuracy. From that time on I gave attention to making more exact observations of these things and was encouraged to do so by that most distinguished man, Paul, Bishop of Fossombrone,[5] who had been present at those deliberations. But what have I accomplished in this matter I leave to the judgment of Your Holiness in particular and to that of all other learned mathematicians. And so as not to appear to Your Holiness to make more promises concerning the utility of this book than I can fulfill, I now pass on to the body of the work.

---

[3]Lactantius (*c.* 240–*c.* 320)
[4]Leo XI (1475–1521), Pope (1513–1534)
[5]Paul of Middleburg (1445–1534), Bishop of Fossombrone (1494–1534)

# THE STARRY MESSENGER
## GALILEO GALILEI (1564–1642)

*Galileo Galilei was born in the same year as William Shakespeare and died in the year of Isaac Newton's birth. He emerged as one of the greatest figures in the history of science because of his original contributions to both physics and astronomy. Galileo spent his early academic career at Pisa before becoming a professor at the University of Padua, where he did important early research in physics. In 1610 he moved to Florence to become "Philosopher and First Mathematician to the Grand Duke of Tuscany." That year he also published his significant little volume called* Sidereus Nuncius (The Starry Messenger).

*The book reported the observations of the heavens that he had made with his homemade telescope during the preceding year. Although Galileo did not invent the telescope, he was the first to turn it toward the sky for astronomical purposes. Among the things he noted were the topographical details of the Moon's surface, sunspots, new stars, and the moons of Jupiter, which he shrewdly named the Medicean Planets after Tuscany's ruling family. Although Galileo was a convinced Copernican, he did not explicitly defend the heliocentric hypothesis in* The Starry Messenger. *Still, his book was a source of consternation and controversy for the day's leading scientists, because Galileo reported observations that contradicted long-respected Aristotelian notions regarding the perfection and immutability of the heavens. Accordingly, Galileo's slim volume implicitly defended Copernicanism by raising serious empirical questions regarding the viability of Aristotelian cosmology. The book quickly became a best-seller and suddenly converted its author from an obscure mathematician into a European celebrity.*

PADUA, 12 MARCH 1610

Revealing great, unusual, and remarkable spectacles, opening these to the consideration of every man, and especially of philosophers and astronomers; as observed by Galileo Galilei, Gentleman of Florence, Professor of Mathematics in the University of Padua, with the aid of a spyglass lately invented by him, in the surface of the Moon, in innumerable fixed stars, in nebulae, and above all 5

From *Discoveries and Opinions of Galileo* by Galileo Galilei, translated by Stillman Drake, copyright © 1957 by Stillman Drake. Used by permission of Doubleday, a division of Random House, Inc.

in four planets swiftly revolving about Jupiter at differing distances and periods, and known to no one before the author recently perceived them and decided that they should be named the Medicean Stars.

### To the Most Serene Cosimo II de'Medici, Fourth Grand Duke of Tuscany

Surely a distinguished public service has been rendered by those who have pro-
5   tected from envy the noble achievements of men who have excelled in virtue, and have thus preserved from oblivion and neglect those names which deserve immortality. In this way images sculptured in marble or cast in bronze have been handed down to posterity; to this we owe our statues, both pedestrian and equestrian; thus have we those columns and pyramids whose expense (as
10   the poet says) reaches to the stars; finally, thus cities have been built to bear the names of men deemed worthy by posterity of commendation to all the ages. For the nature of the human mind is such that unless it is stimulated by images of things acting upon it from without, all remembrance of them passes easily away.
15       Looking to things even more stable and enduring, others have entrusted the immortal fame of illustrious men not to marble and metal but to the custody of the Muses and to imperishable literary monuments. But why dwell upon these things as though human wit were satisfied with earthly regions and had not dared advance beyond? For, seeking further, and well understanding that
20   all human monuments ultimately perish through the violence of the elements or by old age, ingenuity has in fact found still more incorruptible monuments over which voracious time and envious age have been unable to assert any rights. Thus turning to the sky, man's wit has inscribed on the familiar and everlasting orbs of most bright stars the names of those whose eminent and godlike deeds
25   have caused them to be accounted worthy of eternity in the company of the stars. And so the fame of Jupiter, of Mars, of Mercury, Hercules, and other heroes by whose names the stars are called, will not fade before the extinction of the stars themselves.
      Yet this invention of human ingenuity, noble and admirable as it is, has
30   for many centuries been out of style. Primeval heroes are in possession of those bright abodes, and hold them in their own right. In vain did the piety of Augus-tus attempt to elect Julius Caesar into their number, for when he tried to give the name of "Julian" to a star which appeared in his time (one of those bodies which the Greeks call "comets" and which the Romans likewise named for their
35   hairy appearance), it vanished in a brief time and mocked his too ambitious wish. But we are able, most serene Prince, to read Your Highness in the heavens far more accurately and auspiciously. For scarce have the immortal graces of

your spirit begun to shine on earth when in the heavens bright stars appear as tongues to tell and celebrate your exceeding virtues to all time. Behold, then, four stars reserved to bear your famous name; bodies which belong not to the inconspicuous multitude of fixed stars, but to the bright ranks of the planets. Variously moving about most noble Jupiter as children of his own, they com- 5 plete their orbits with marvelous velocity—at the same time executing with one harmonious accord mighty revolutions every dozen years about the center of the universe; that is, the sun.

Indeed, the Maker of the stars himself has seemed by clear indications to direct that I assign to these new planets Your Highness's famous name in 10 preference to all others. For just as these stars, like children worthy of their sire, never leave the side of Jupiter by any appreciable distance, so (as indeed who does not know?) clemency, kindness of heart, gentleness of manner, splendor of royal blood, nobility in public affairs, and excellency of authority and rule have all fixed their abode and habitation in Your Highness. And who, I ask 15 once more, does not know that all these virtues emanate from the benign star of Jupiter, next after God as the source of all things good? Jupiter; Jupiter, I say, at the instant of Your Highness's birth, having already emerged from the turbid mists of the horizon and occupied the midst of the heavens, illuminating the eastern sky from his own royal house, looked out from that exalted throne 20 upon your auspicious birth and poured forth all his splendor and majesty in order that your tender body and your mind (already adorned by God with the most noble ornaments) might imbibe with their first breath that universal influence and power.

But why should I employ mere plausible arguments, when I may prove 25 my conclusion absolutely? It pleased Almighty God that I should instruct Your Highness in mathematics, which I did four years ago at that time of year when it is customary to rest from the most exacting studies. And since clearly it was mine by divine will to serve Your Highness and thus to receive from near at hand the rays of your surpassing clemency and beneficence, what wonder is it 30 that my heart is so inflamed as to think both day and night of little else than how I, who am indeed your subject not only by choice but by birth and lineage, may become known to you as most grateful and most anxious for your glory? And so, most serene Cosimo, having discovered under your patronage these stars unknown to every astronomer before me, I have with good right decided 35 to designate them by the august name of your family. And if I am first to have investigated them, who can justly blame me if I likewise name them, calling them the Medicean Stars, in the hope that this name will bring as much honor to them as the names of other heroes have bestowed on other stars? For, to say nothing of Your Highness's most serene ancestors, whose everlasting glory is 40

testified by the monuments of all history, your virtue alone, most worthy Sire, can confer upon these stars an immortal name. No one can doubt that you will fulfill those expectations, high though they are, which you have aroused by the auspicious beginning of your reign, and will not only meet but far surpass them.
5   Thus when you have conquered your equals you may still vie with yourself, and you and your greatness will become greater every day.

Accept then, most clement Prince, this gentle glory reserved by the stars for you. May you long enjoy those blessings which are sent to you not so much from the stars as from God, their Maker and their Governor.

### *Astronomical Message*

10   Which contains and explains recent observations made with the aid of a new spyglass concerning the surface of the moon, the Milky Way, nebulous stars, and innumerable fixed stars, as well as four planets never before seen, and now named the *Medicean Stars*.

Great indeed are the things which in this brief treatise I propose for ob-
15   servation and consideration by all students of nature. I say great, because of the excellence of the subject itself, the entirely unexpected and novel character of these things, and finally because of the instrument by means of which they have been revealed to our senses.

Surely it is a great thing to increase the numerous host of fixed stars previ-
20   ously visible to the unaided vision, adding countless more which have never before been seen, exposing these plainly to the eye in numbers ten times exceeding the old and familiar stars.

It is a very beautiful thing, and most gratifying to the sight, to behold the body of the moon, distant from us almost sixty earthly radii, as if it were no
25   farther away than two such measures—so that its diameter appears almost thirty times larger, its surface nearly nine hundred times, and its volume twenty-seven thousand times as large as when viewed with the naked eye. In this way one may learn with all the certainty of sense evidence that the moon is not robed in a smooth and polished surface but is in fact rough and uneven, covered
30   everywhere, just like the earth's surface, with huge prominences, deep valleys, and chasms.

Again, it seems to me a matter of no small importance to have ended the dispute about the Milky Way by making its nature manifest to the very senses as well as to the intellect. Similarly it will be a pleasant and elegant thing to
35   demonstrate that the nature of those stars which astronomers have previously called "nebulous" is far different from what has been believed hitherto. But what surpasses all wonders by far, and what particularly moves us to seek the attention of all astronomers and philosophers, is the discovery of four wandering

stars not known or observed by any man before us. Like Venus and Mercury, which have their own periods about the sun, these have theirs about a certain star that is conspicuous among those already known, which they sometimes precede and sometimes follow, without ever departing from it beyond certain limits. All these facts were discovered and observed by me not many days ago    5 with the aid of a spyglass which I devised, after first being illuminated by divine grace. perhaps other things, still more remarkable, will in time be discovered by me or by other observers with the aid of such an instrument, the form and construction of which I shall first briefly explain, as well as the occasion of its having been devised. Afterwards I shall relate the story of the observations I    10 have made.

About ten months ago a report reached my ears that a certain Fleming had constructed a spyglass by means of which visible objects, though very distant from the eye of the observer, were distinctly seen as if nearby. Of this truly remarkable effect several experiences were related, to which some persons gave    15 credence while others denied them. A few days later the report was confirmed to me in a letter from a noble Frenchman at Paris, Jacques Badovere, which caused me to apply myself wholeheartedly to inquire into the means by which I might arrive at the invention of a similar instrument. This I did shortly afterwards, my basis being the theory of refraction. First I prepared a tube of lead, at the ends    20 of which I fitted two glass lenses, both plane on one side while on the other side one was spherically convex and the other concave. Then placing my eye near the concave lens I perceived objects satisfactorily large and near, for they appeared three times closer and nine times larger than when seen with the naked eye alone. Next I constructed another one, more accurate, which represented    25 objects as enlarged more than sixty times. Finally, sparing neither labor nor expense, I succeeded in constructing for myself so excellent an instrument that objects seen by means of it appeared nearly one thousand times larger and over thirty times closer than when regarded with our natural vision.

It would be superfluous to enumerate the number and importance of the    30 advantages of such an instrument at sea as well as on land. But forsaking terrestrial observations, I turned to celestial ones, and first I saw the moon from as near at hand as if it were scarcely two terrestrial radii away. After that I observed often with wondering delight both the planets and the fixed stars, and since I saw these latter to be very crowded, I began to seek (and eventually found) a    35 method by which I might measure their distances apart.

Here it is appropriate to convey certain cautions to all who intend to undertake observations of this sort, for in the first place it is necessary to prepare quite a perfect telescope, which will show all objects bright, distinct, and free from any haziness, while magnifying them at least four hundred times    40 and thus showing them twenty times closer. Unless the instrument is of this kind it will be vain to attempt to observe all the things which I have seen in the heavens, and which will presently be set forth. Now in order to determine without much trouble the magnifying power of an instrument, trace on paper

5 the contour of two circles or two squares of which one is four hundred times as large as the other, as it will be when the diameter of one is twenty times that of the other. Then, with both these figures attached to the same wall, observe them simultaneously from a distance, looking at the smaller one through the telescope and at the larger one with the other eye unaided. This may be done

10 without inconvenience while holding both eyes open at the same time; the two figures will appear to be of the same size if the instrument magnifies objects in the desired proportion....

# LETTER TO THE GRAND DUCHESS
## GALILEO GALILEI (1564–1642) TO
### CHRISTINA (1565–1637), GRAND DUCHESS OF TUSCANY

*The Galileo affair, in which the noted Renaissance scientist clashed with the ecclesiastical powers of the Papal Inquisition in 1633, has been cited as a paradigmatic case of the warfare between science and religion. According to this interpretation, Galileo represents the scientific community, standing as the champion of objective free inquiry, while the Church and its leaders are cast in the mold of authoritarian, close-minded religious obscurantism. This interpretation is incorrect.*

*Neither was Galileo a spokesman for the scientific community, nor was the Church narrowly committed to a disproved cosmology despite evidence to the contrary. In fact, Galileo's real opponents had been the Aristotelian leaders of the scientific community who saw in Galileo a threat to their own standing. In short, the whole affair was much more complicated than science versus religion.*

*Keep in mind the conditioning fact that every player in the episode was a professed Christian committed to the truth of the Holy Bible. Indeed, one of the best interpretations of Galileo's difficulties emerges from viewing the affair as an intramural dispute within the Church over matters of biblical interpretation (hermeneutics).*

*In the years immediately following the publication of Galileo's* Starry Messenger, *many interested religious and political leaders discussed the implications of his astronomical findings for the interpretation of biblical passages that seemed to speak to scientific matters. In the midst of these deliberations, Galileo weighed in with his views on the way to relate Scripture to science. Written as a letter to the Grand Duchess Christina, Galileo's "Statement Regarding the Use of Biblical Quotations in the Matters of Science," as the letter came to be known, was widely circulated, although not actually published until 1636, three years after his trial by the Papal Inquisition.*

Some years ago, as Your Serene Highness well knows, I discovered in the heavens many things that had not been seen before our own age. The novelty of these things, as well as some consequences which followed from them in contradiction to the physical notions commonly held among academic philosophers, stirred up against me no small number of professors—as if I had placed these things in the sky with my own hands in order to upset nature and overturn the sciences. They seemed to forget that the increase of known truths stimulates the investigation, establishment, and growth of the arts; not their diminution or destruction.

    Showing a greater fondness for their own opinions than for truth, they sought to deny and disprove the new things which, if they had cared to look for themselves, their own senses would have demonstrated to them. To this end they hurled various charges and published numerous writings filled with vain arguments, and they made the grave mistake of sprinkling these with passages taken from places in the Bible which they had failed to understand properly, and which were ill suited to their purposes.

    These men would perhaps not have fallen into such error had they but paid attention to a most useful doctrine of Saint Augustine's, relative to our making positive statements about things which are obscure and hard to understand by means of reason alone. Speaking of a certain physical conclusion about the heavenly bodies, he wrote: "Now keeping always our respect for moderation in grave piety, we ought not to believe anything inadvisedly on a dubious point, lest in favor to our error we conceive a prejudice against something that truth hereafter may reveal to be not contrary in any way to the sacred books of either the Old or the New Testament."

    Well, the passage of time has revealed to everyone the truths that I previously set forth; and, together with the truth of the facts, there has come to light the great difference in attitude between those who simply and dispassionately refused to admit the discoveries to be true, and those who combined with their incredulity some reckless passion of their own. Men who were well grounded in astronomical and physical science were persuaded as soon as they received my first message. There were others who denied them or remained in doubt only because of their novel and unexpected character, and because they had not yet had the opportunity to see for themselves. These men have by degrees come to be satisfied. But some, besides allegiance to their original error, possess I know not what fanciful interest in remaining hostile not so much toward the things in question as toward their discoverer. No longer being able to deny them, these men now take refuge in obstinate silence, but being more than ever exasperated by that which has pacified and quieted other men, they divert their thoughts to other fancies and seek new ways to damage me.

I should pay no more attention to them than to those who previously contradicted me—at whom I always laugh, being assured of the eventual outcome—were it not that in their new calumnies and persecutions I perceive that they do not stop at proving themselves more learned than I am (a claim which I scarcely contest), but go so far as to cast against me imputations of 5 crimes which must be, and are, more abhorrent to me than death itself. I cannot remain satisfied merely to know that the injustice of this is recognized by those who are acquainted with these men and with me, as perhaps it is not known to others.

Persisting in their original resolve to destroy me and everything mine by 10 any means they can think of, these men are aware of my views in astronomy and philosophy. They know that as to the arrangement of the parts of the universe, I hold the sun to be situated motionless in the center of the revolution of the celestial orbs while the earth rotates on its axis and revolves about the sun. They know also that I support this position not only by refuting the arguments of 15 Ptolemy and Aristotle, but by producing many counterarguments; in particular, some which relate to physical effects whose causes can perhaps be assigned in no other way. In addition there are astronomical arguments derived from many things in my new celestial discoveries that plainly confute the Ptolemaic system while admirably agreeing with and confirming the contrary hypothesis. Possibly 20 because they are disturbed by the known truth of other propositions of mine which differ from those commonly held, and therefore mistrusting their defense so long as they confine themselves to the field of philosophy, these men have resolved to fabricate a shield for their fallacies out of the mantle of pretended religion and the authority of the Bible. These they apply, with little judgment, 25 to the refutation of arguments that they do not understand and have not even listened to.

First they have endeavored to spread the opinion that such propositions in general are contrary to the Bible and are consequently damnable and heretical. They know that it is human nature to take up causes whereby a man may oppress 30 his neighbor, no matter how unjustly, rather than those from which a man may receive some just encouragement. Hence they have had no trouble in finding men who would preach the damnability and heresy of the new doctrine from their very pulpits with unwonted confidence, thus doing impious and inconsiderate injury not only to that doctrine and its followers but to all mathematics 35 and mathematicians in general. Next, becoming bolder, and hoping (though vainly) that this seed which first took root in their hypocritical minds would send out branches and ascend to heaven, they began scattering rumors among the people that before long this doctrine would be condemned by the supreme authority. They know, too, that official condemnation would not only suppress 40 the two propositions which I have mentioned, but would render damnable all other astronomical and physical statements and observations that have any necessary relation or connection with these.

In order to facilitate their designs, they seek so far as possible (at least among the common people) to make this opinion seem new and to belong to me alone. They pretend not to know that its author, or rather its restorer and confirmer, was Nicholas Copernicus; and that he was not only a Catholic, but a priest and a canon. He was in fact so esteemed by the church that when the Lateran Council under Leo X took up the correction of the church calendar, Copernicus was called to Rome from the most remote parts of Germany to undertake its reform. At that time the calendar was defective because the true measures of the year and the lunar month were not exactly known. The Bishop of Fossombrone, then in charge of this matter, assigned Copernicus to seek more light and greater certainty concerning the celestial motions by means of constant study and labor. With Herculean toil he set his admirable mind to this task, and he made such great progress in this science and brought our knowledge of the heavenly motions to such precision that he became celebrated as an astronomer. Since that time not only has the calendar been regulated by his teachings, but tables of all the motions of the planets have been calculated as well.

Having reduced his system into six books, he published these at the instance of the Cardinal of Capua and the Bishop of Culm. And since he had assumed his laborious enterprise by order of the supreme pontiff, he dedicated this book *On the celestial revolutions* to Pope Paul III. When printed, the book was accepted by the holy Church, and it has been read and studied by everyone without the faintest hint of any objection ever being conceived against its doctrines. Yet now that manifest experiences and necessary proofs have shown them to be well grounded, persons exist who would strip the author of his reward without so much as looking at his book, and add the shame of having him pronounced a heretic. All this they would do merely to satisfy their personal displeasure conceived without any cause against another man, who has no interest in Copernicus beyond approving his teachings.

Now as to the false aspersions which they so unjustly seek to cast upon me, I have thought it necessary to justify myself in the eyes of all men, whose judgment in matters of religion and of reputation I must hold in great esteem. I shall therefore discourse of the particulars which these men produce to make this opinion detested and to have it condemned not merely as false but as heretical. To this end they make a shield of their hypocritical zeal for religion. They go about invoking the Bible, which they would have minister to their deceitful purposes. Contrary to the sense of the Bible and the intention of the holy Fathers, if I am not mistaken, they would extend such authorities until even in purely physical matters—where faith is not involved—they would have us altogether abandon reason and the evidence of our senses in favor of some biblical passage, though under the surface meaning of its words this passage may contain a different sense.

I hope to show that I proceed with much greater piety than they do, when I argue not against condemning this book, but against condemning it in the way they suggest—that is, without understanding it, weighing it, or so much as reading it. For Copernicus never discusses matters of religion or faith, nor does he use arguments that depend in any way upon the authority of sacred writings which he might have interpreted erroneously. He stand always upon physical conclusions pertaining to the celestial motions, and deals with them by astronomical and geometrical demonstration, founded primarily upon sense experiences and very exact observations. He did not ignore the Bible, but he knew very well that if his doctrine were proved, then it could not contradict the Scriptures when they were rightly understood. And thus at the end of his letter of dedication, addressing the pope, he said:

"If there should chance to be any exegetes ignorant of mathematics who pretend to skill in that discipline, and dare to condemn and censure this hypothesis of mine upon the authority of some scriptural passage twisted to their purpose, I value them not, but disdain their unconsidered judgment. For it is known that Lactantius—a poor mathematician though in other respects a worthy author—writes very childishly about the shape of the earth when he scoffs at those who affirm it to be a globe. Hence it should not seem strange to the ingenious if people of that sort should in turn deride me. But mathematics is written for mathematicians, by whom, if I am not deceived, these labors of mine will be recognized as contributing something to their domain, as also to that of the Church over which Your Holiness now reigns."

Such are the people who labor to persuade us that an author like Copernicus may be condemned without being read, and who produce various authorities from the Bible, from theologians, and from Church Councils to make us believe that this is not only lawful but commendable. Since I hold these to be of supreme authority, I consider it rank temerity for anyone to contradict them—when employed according to the usage of the holy Church. Yet I do not believe it is wrong to speak out when there is reason to suspect that other men wish, for some personal motive, to produce and employ such authorities for purposes quite different from the sacred intention of the holy Church.

Therefore I declare (and my sincerity will make itself manifest) not only that I mean to submit myself freely and renounce any errors into which I may fall in this discourse through ignorance of matters pertaining to religion, but that I do not desire in these matters to engage in disputes with anyone, even

on points that are disputable. My goal is this alone; that if, among errors that
may abound in these considerations of a subject remote from my profession,
there is anything that may be serviceable to the holy Church in making a decision concerning the Copernican system, it may be taken and utilized as seems
5   best to the superiors. And if not, let my book be torn and burnt, as I neither
intend nor pretend to gain from it any fruit that is not pious and Catholic. And
though many of the things I shall reprove have been heard by my own ears, I
shall freely grant to those who have spoken them that they never said them, if
that is what they wish, and I shall confess myself to have been mistaken. Hence
10  let whatever I reply be addressed not to them, but to whoever may have held
such opinions.

The reason produced for condemning the opinion that the earth moves
and the sun stands still is that in many places in the Bible one may read that
the sun moves and the earth stands still. Since the Bible cannot err, it follows as
15  a necessary consequence that anyone takes an erroneous and heretical position
who maintains that the sun is inherently motionless and the earth movable.

With regard to this argument, I think in the first place that it is very pious to
say and prudent to affirm that the holy Bible can never speak untruth—whenever its true meaning is understood. But I believe nobody will deny that it is
20  often very abstruse, and may say things which are quite different from what
its bare words signify. Hence in expounding the Bible if one were always to
confine oneself to the unadorned grammatical meaning, one might fall into
error. Not only contradictions and propositions far from true might thus be
made to appear in the Bible, but even grave heresies and follies. Thus it would
25  be necessary to assign to God feet, hands, and eyes, as well as corporeal and
human affections, such as anger, repentance, hatred, and sometimes even the
forgetting of things past and ignorance of those to come. These propositions
uttered by the Holy Ghost were set down in that manner by the sacred scribes
in order to accommodate them to the capacities of the common people, who
30  are rude and unlearned. For the sake of those who deserve to be separated from
the herd, it is necessary that wise expositors should produce the true senses of
such passages, together with the special reasons for which they were set down in
these words. This doctrine is so widespread and so definite with all theologians
that it would be superfluous to adduce evidence for it.
35  Hence I think that I may reasonably conclude that whenever the Bible has
occasion to speak of any physical conclusion (especially those which are very abstruse and hard to understand), the rule has been observed of avoiding confusion
in the minds of the common people which would render them contumacious
toward the higher mysteries. Now the Bible, merely to condescend to popular
40  capacity, has not hesitated to obscure some very important pronouncements,

attributing to God himself some qualities extremely remote from (and even contrary to) His essence. Who, then, would positively declare that this principle has been set aside, and the Bible has confined itself rigorously to the bare and restricted sense of its words, when speaking but casually of the earth, of water, of the sun, or of any other created thing? Especially in view of the fact that these things in no way concern the primary purpose of the sacred writings, which is the service of God and the salvation of souls—matters infinitely beyond the comprehension of the common people.

This being granted, I think that in discussions of physical problems we ought to begin not from the authority of scriptural passages, but from sense-experiences and necessary demonstrations; for the holy Bible and the phenomena of nature proceed alike from the divine Word, the former as the dictate of the Holy Ghost and the latter as the observant executrix of God's commands. It is necessary for the Bible, in order to be accommodated to the understanding of every man, to speak many things which appear to differ from the absolute truth so far as the bare meaning of the words is concerned. But Nature, on the other hand, is inexorable and immutable; she never transgresses the laws imposed upon her, or cares a whit whether her abstruse reasons and methods of operation are understandable to men. For that reason it appears that nothing physical which sense-experience sets before our eyes, or which necessary demonstrations prove to us, ought to be called in question (much less condemned) upon the testimony of biblical passages which may have some different meaning beneath their words. For the Bible is not chained in every expression to conditions as strict as those which govern all physical effects; nor is God any less excellently revealed in Nature's actions than in the sacred statements of the Bible. Perhaps this is what Tertullian meant by these words: "We conclude that God is known first through Nature, and then again, more particularly, by doctrine; by Nature in His works, and by doctrine in His revealed word."

From this I do not mean to infer that we need not have an extraordinary esteem for the passages of holy Scripture. On the contrary, having arrived at any certainties in physics, we ought to utilize these as the most appropriate aids in the true exposition of the Bible and in the investigation of those meanings which are necessarily contained therein, for these must be concordant with demonstrated truths. I should judge that the authority of the Bible was designed to persuade men of those articles and propositions which, surpassing all human reasoning, could not be made credible by science, or by any other means than through the very mouth of the Holy Spirit.

Yet even in those propositions which are not matters of faith, this authority ought to be preferred over that of all human writings which are supported only by bare assertions or probable arguments, and not set forth in a demonstrative way. This I hold to be necessary and proper to the same extent that divine wisdom surpasses all human judgment and conjecture.

But I do not feel obliged to believe that that same God who has endowed us with senses, reason, and intellect has intended to forge their use and by some 5 other means to give us knowledge which we can attain by them. He would not require us to deny sense and reason in physical matters which are set before our eyes and minds by direct experience or necessary demonstrations. This must be especially true in those sciences of which but the faintest trace (and that consisting of conclusions) is to be found in the Bible. Of Astronomy, for 10 instance, so little is found that none of the planets except Venus are so much as mentioned, and this only once or twice under the name of "Lucifer." If the sacred scribes had had any intention of teaching people certain arrangements and motions of the heavenly bodies, or had they wished us to derive such knowledge from the Bible, then in my opinion they would not have spoken of 15 these matters so sparingly in comparison with the infinite number of admirable conclusions which are demonstrated in that science. Far from pretending to teach us the constitution and motions of the heavens and the stars, with their shapes, magnitudes, and distances, the authors of the Bible intentionally forbore to speak of these things, though all were quite well known to them. Such 20 is the opinion of the holiest and most learned Fathers, and in Saint Augustine we find the following words:

"It is likewise commonly asked what we may believe about the form and shape of the heavens according to the Scriptures, for many contend much about these matters. But with superior prudence our authors have forborne to speak 25 of this, as in no way furthering the student with respect to a blessed life—and, more important still, as taking up much of that time which should be spent in holy exercises. What is it to me whether heaven, like a sphere, surrounds the earth on all sides as a mass balanced in the center of the universe, or whether like a dish it merely covers and overcasts the earth? Belief in Scripture is urged 30 rather for the reason we have often mentioned; that is, in order that no one, through ignorance of divine passages, finding anything in our Bibles or hearing anything cited from them of such a nature as may seem to oppose manifest conclusions, should be induced to suspect their truth when they teach, relate, and deliver more profitable matters. Hence let it be said briefly, touching the 35 form of heaven, that our authors knew the truth but the Holy Spirit did not desire that men should learn things that are useful to no one for salvation."

The same disregard of these sacred authors toward beliefs about the phenomena of the celestial bodies is repeated to us by Saint Augustine in his next chapter. On the question whether we are to believe that the heaven moves or 40 stands still, he writes thus:

"Some of the brethren raise a question concerning the motion of heaven, whether it is fixed or moved. If it is moved, they say, how is it a firmament? If it stands still, how do thee stars which are held fixed in it go round from east to west, the more northerly performing shorter circuits near the pole, so that heaven (if there is another pole unknown to us) may seem to revolve upon some axis, or (if there is no other pole) may be thought to move as a discus? To these men I reply that it would require many subtle and profound reasonings to find out which of these things is actually so; but to undertake this and discuss it is consistent neither with my leisure nor with the duty of those whom I desire to instruct in essential matters more directly conducing to their salvation and to the benefit of the holy Church."

From these things it follows as a necessary consequence that, since the Holy Ghost did not intend to teach us whether heaven moves or stands still, whether its shape is spherical or like a discus or extended in a plane, nor whether the earth is located at its center or off to one side, then so much the less was it intended to settle for us any other conclusion of the same kind. And the motion or rest of the earth and the sun is so closely linked with the things just named, that without a determination of the one, neither side can be taken in the other matters. Now if the Holy Spirit has purposely neglected to teach us propositions of this sort as irrelevant to the highest goal (that is, to our salvation), how can anyone affirm that it is obligatory to take sides on them, and that one belief is required by faith, while the other side is erroneous? Can an opinion be heretical and yet have no concern with the salvation of souls? Can the Holy Ghost be asserted not to have intended teaching us something that does concern our salvation? I would say here something that was heard from an ecclesiastic of the most eminent degree: "That the intention of the Holy Ghost is to teach us how one goes to heaven, not how heaven goes."

But let us again consider the degrees to which necessary demonstrations and sense experiences ought to be respected in physical conclusions, and the authority they have enjoyed at the hands of holy and learned theologians. From among a hundred attestations I have selected the following:

"We must also take heed, in handling the doctrine of Moses, that we altogether avoid saying positively and confidently anything which contradicts manifest experiences and the reasoning of philosophy or the other sciences. For since every truth is in agreement with all other truth, the truth of Holy Writ cannot be contrary to the solid reasons and experiences of human knowledge."

And in Saint Augustine we read: "If anyone shall set the authority of Holy Writ against clear and manifest reason, he who does this knows not what he has undertaken; for he opposes to the truth not the meaning of the Bible, which is beyond his comprehension, but rather his own interpretation; not what is in the Bible, but what he has found in himself and imagines to be there."

This granted, and it being true that two truths cannot contradict one another, it is the function of wise expositors to seek out the true senses of scriptural texts. These will unquestionably accord with the physical conclusions which manifest sense and necessary demonstrations have previously made certain to
5  us. Now the Bible, as has been remarked, admits in many places expositions that are remote from the signification of the words for reasons we have already given. Moreover, we are unable to affirm that all interpreters of the Bible speak by divine inspiration, for it that were so there would exist no differences between them about the sense of a given passage. Hence I should think it would be the
10  part of prudence not to permit anyone to usurp scriptural texts and force them in some way to maintain any physical conclusion to be true, when at some future time the senses and demonstrative or necessary reasons may show the contrary. Who indeed will set bounds to human ingenuity? Who will assert that everything in the universe capable of being perceived is already discovered and
15  known? Let us rather confess quite truly that "Those truths which we know are very few in comparison with those which we do not know."

We have it from the very mouth of the Holy Ghost that God delivered up the world to disputations, *so that man cannot find out the work that God has done from the beginning even to the end.*[1] In my opinion no one, in contradiction
20  to that dictum, should close the road to free philosophizing about mundane and physical things, as if everything had already been discovered and revealed with certainty. Nor should it be considered rash not to be satisfied with those opinions which have become common. No one should be scorned in physical disputes for not holding to the opinions which happen to please other people
25  best, especially concerning problems which have been debated among the greatest philosophers for thousands of years. One of these is the stability of the sun and mobility of the earth, a doctrine believed by Pythagoras and all his followers, by Heracleides of Pontus (who was one of them), by Philolaus the teacher of Plato, and by Plato himself according to Aristotle. Plutarch writes
30  in his *Life of Numa* that Plato, when he had grown old, said it was most absurd to believe otherwise. The same doctrine was held by Aristarchus of Samos, as Archimedes tells us; by Seleucus the mathematician, by Nicetas the philosopher (on the testimony of Cicero), and by many others. Finally this opinion has been amplified and confirmed with many observations and demonstrations by
35  Nicholas Copernicus. And Seneca, a most eminent philosopher, advises us in his book on comets that we should more diligently seek to ascertain whether it is in the sky or in the earth that the diurnal rotation resides.

Hence it would probably be wise and useful counsel if, beyond articles which concern salvation and the establishment of our Faith, against the stabil-

[1]Ecclesiastes 3:11

ity of which there is no danger whatever that any valid and effective doctrine can ever arise, men would not aggregate further articles unnecessarily. And it would certainly be preposterous to introduce them at the request of persons who, besides not being known to speak by inspiration of divine grace, are clearly seen to lack that understanding which is necessary in order to comprehend, let 5 alone discuss, the demonstrations by which such conclusions are supported in the subtler sciences. If I may speak my opinion freely, I should say further that it would perhaps fit in better with the decorum and majesty of the sacred writings to take measures for preventing every shallow and vulgar writer from giving to his compositions (often grounded upon foolish fancies) an air of authority by 10 inserting in them passages from the Bible, interpreted (or rather distorted) into senses as far from the right meaning of Scripture as those authors are near to absurdity who thus ostentatiously adorn their writings. Of such abuses many examples might be produced, but for the present I shall confine myself to two which are germane to thee astronomical matters. The first concerns those writ- 15 ings which were published against the existence of the Medicean planets recently discovered by me, in which many passages of holy Scripture were cited. Now that everyone has seen these planets, I should like to know what new interpretations those same antagonists employ in expounding the Scripture and excusing their own simplicity. My other example is that of a man who has lately published, in 20 defiance of astronomers and philosophers, the opinion that the moon does not receive its light from the sun but is brilliant by its own nature. He supports this fancy (or rather thinks he does) by sundry texts of Scripture which he believes cannot be explained unless his theory is true; yet that the moon is inherently dark is surely as plain as daylight. 25

It is obvious that such authors, not having penetrated the true senses of Scripture, would impose upon others an obligation to subscribe to conclusions that are repugnant to manifest reason and sense, if they had any authority to do so. God forbid that this sort of abuse should gain countenance and authority, for then in a short time it would be necessary to proscribe all the contemplative 30 sciences. People who are unable to understand perfectly both the Bible and the sciences far outnumber those who do understand. The former, glancing super-ficially through the Bible, would arrogate to themselves the authority to decree upon every question of physics on the strength of some word which they have misunderstood, and which was employed by the sacred authors for some different 35 purpose. And the smaller number of understanding men could not dam up the furious torrent of such people, who would gain the majority of followers simply because it is much more pleasant to gain a reputation for wisdom without effort or study than to consume oneself tirelessly in the most laborious disciplines. Let us therefore render thanks to Almighty God, who in His beneficence protects 40

us from this danger by depriving such persons of all authority, reposing the power of consultation, decision, and decree on such important matters in the high wisdom and benevolence of most prudent Fathers, and in the supreme authority of those who cannot fail to order matters properly under the guidance
5   of the Holy Ghost. Hence we need not concern ourselves with the shallowness of those men whom grave and holy authors rightly reproach, and of whom in particular Saint Jerome said, in reference to the Bible:

"This is ventured upon, lacerated, and taught by the garrulous old woman, the doting old man, and the prattling sophist before they have learned it. Others,
10  led on by pride, weigh heavy words and philosophize amongst women concerning holy Scripture. Others—oh, shame!—learn from women what they teach to men, and (as if that were not enough) glibly expound to others that which they themselves do not understand. I forbear to speak of those of my own profession who, attaining a knowledge of the holy Scriptures after mundane learning, tickle
15  the ears of the people with affected and studied expressions, and declare that everything they say is to be taken as the law of God. Not bothering to learn what the prophets and the apostles have maintained, they wrest incongruous testimonies into their own senses—as if distorting passages and twisting the Bible to their individual and contradictory whims were the genuine way of
20  teaching, and not a corrupt one."

I do not wish to place in the number of such lay writers some theologians whom I consider men of profound learning and devout behavior, and who are therefore held by me in great esteem and veneration. Yet I cannot deny that I feel some discomfort which I should like to have removed, when I hear them
25  pretend to the power of constraining others by scriptural authority to follow in a physical dispute that opinion which they think best agrees with the Bible, and then believe themselves not bound to answer the opposing reasons and experiences. In explanation and support of this opinion they say that since theology is queen of all the sciences, she need not bend in any way to accom-
30  modate herself to the teachings of less worthy sciences which are subordinate to her; these others must rather be referred to her as to their supreme empress, changing and altering their conclusions according to her statutes and decrees. They add further that if in the inferior sciences any conclusion should be taken as certain in virtue of demonstrations or experiences, while in the Bible another
35  conclusion is found repugnant to this, then the professors of that science should themselves undertake to undo their proofs and discover the fallacies in their own experiences, without bothering the theologians and exegetes. For, they say, it does not become the dignity of theology to stoop to the investigation of fallacies in the subordinate sciences; it is sufficient for her merely to determine the truth
40  of a given conclusion with absolute authority, secure in her inability to err.

Now the physical conclusions in which they say we ought to be satisfied by Scripture, without glossing or expounding it in senses different from the literal, are those concerning which the Bible always speaks in the same manner and which the holy Fathers all receive and expound in the same way. But with regard to these judgments I have had occasion to consider several things, and I shall set them forth in order that I may be corrected by those who understand more than I do in these matters—for to their decisions I submit at all times.

First, I question whether there is not some equivocation in failing to specify the virtues which entitle sacred theology to the title of "queen." It might deserve that name by reason of including everything that is learned from all the other sciences and establishing everything by better methods and with profounder learning. It is thus, for example, that the rules for measuring fields and keeping accounts are much more excellently contained in arithmetic and in the geometry of Euclid than in the practices of surveyors and accountants. Or theology might be queen because of being occupied with a subject which excels in dignity all the subjects which compose the other sciences, and because her teachings are divulged in more sublime ways.

That the title and authority of queen belongs to theology in the first sense, I think will not be affirmed by theologians who have any skill in the other sciences. None of these, I think, will say that geometry, astronomy, music, and medicine are much more excellently contained in the Bible than they are in the books of Archimedes, Ptolemy, Boethius, and Galen. Hence it seems likely that regal pre-eminence is given to theology in the second sense; that is, by reason of its subject and the miraculous communication of divine revelation of conclusions which could not be conceived by men in any other way, concerning chiefly the attainment of eternal blessedness.

Let us grant then that theology is conversant with the loftiest divine contemplation, and occupies the regal throne among sciences by dignity. But acquiring the highest authority in this way, if she does not descend to the lower and humbler speculations of the subordinate sciences and has no regard for them because they are not concerned with blessedness, then her professors should not arrogate to themselves the authority to decide on controversies in professions which they have neither studied nor practiced. Why, this would be as if an absolute despot, being neither a physician nor an architect but knowing himself free to command, should undertake to administer medicines and erect buildings according to his whim—at grave peril of his poor patients' lives, and the speedy collapse of his edifices.

Again, to command that the very professors of astronomy themselves see to the refutation of their own observations and proofs as mere fallacies and sophisms is to enjoin something that lies beyond any possibility of accomplishment.

For this would amount to commanding that they must not see what they see and must not understand what they know, and that in searching they must find the opposite of what they actually encounter. Before this could be done they would have to be taught how to make one mental faculty command another,
5    and the inferior powers the superior, so that the imagination and the will might be forced to believe the opposite of what the intellect understands. I am referring at all times to merely physical propositions, and not to supernatural things which are matters of faith.

I entreat those wise and prudent Fathers to consider with great care the
10   difference that exists between doctrines subject to proof and those subject to opinion. Considering the force exerted by logical deductions, they may ascertain that it is not in the power of the professors of demonstrative sciences to change their opinions at will and apply themselves first to one side and then to the other. There is a great difference between commanding a mathematician or a
15   philosopher and influencing a lawyer or a merchant, for demonstrated conclusions about things in nature or in the heavens cannot be changed with the same facility as opinions about what is or is not lawful in a contract, bargain, or bill of exchange. This difference was well understood by the learned and holy Fathers, as proven by their having taken great pains in refuting philosophical
20   fallacies. This may be found expressly in some of them; in particular, we find the following words of Saint Augustine: "It is to be held as an unquestionable truth that whatever the sages of this world have demonstrated concerning physical matters is in no way contrary to our Bibles; hence whatever the sages teach in their books that is contrary to the holy Scriptures may be concluded without any
25   hesitation to be quite false. And according to our ability let us make this evident, and let us keep the faith of our Lord, in whom are hidden all the treasures of wisdom, so that we neither become seduced by the verbiage of false philosophy nor frightened by the superstition of counterfeit religion."

From the above words I conceive that I may deduce this doctrine: That in
30   the books of the sages of this world there are contained some physical truths which are soundly demonstrated, and others that are merely stated; as to the former, it is the office of wise divines to show that they do not contradict the holy Scriptures. And as to the propositions which are stated but not rigorously demonstrated, anything contrary to the Bible involved by them must be held
35   undoubtedly false and should be proved so by every possible means.

Now if truly demonstrated physical conclusions need not be subordinated to biblical passages, but the latter must rather be shown not to interfere with the former, then before a physical proposition is condemned it must be shown to be not rigorously demonstrated—and this is to be done not by those who
40   hold the proposition to be true, but by those who judge it to be false. This

seems very reasonable and natural, for those who believe an argument to be false may much more easily find the fallacies in it than men who consider it to be true and conclusive. Indeed, in the latter case it will happen that the more the adherents of an opinion turn over their pages, examine the arguments, repeat the observations, and compare the experiences, the more they will be confirmed in that belief. And Your Highness knows what happened to the late mathematician of the University of Pisa who undertook in his old age to look into the Copernican doctrine in the hope of shaking its foundations and refuting it, since he considered it false only because he had never studied it. As it fell out, no sooner had he understood its grounds, procedures, and demonstrations than he found himself persuaded, and from an opponent he became a very staunch defender of it. I might also name other mathematicians who, moved by my latest discoveries, have confessed it necessary to alter the previously accepted system of the world, as this is simply unable to subsist any longer.

If in order to banish the opinion in question from the world it were sufficient to stop the mouth of a single man—as perhaps those men persuade themselves who, measuring the minds of others by their own, think it impossible that this doctrine should be able to continue to find adherents—then that would be very easily done. But things stand otherwise. To carry out such a decision it would be necessary not only to prohibit the book of Copernicus and the writings of other authors who follow the same opinion, but to ban the whole science of astronomy. Furthermore, it would be necessary to forbid men to look at the heavens, in order that they might not see Mars and Venus sometimes quite near the earth and sometimes very distant, the variation being so great that Venus is forty times and Mars sixty times as large at one time as another. And it would be necessary to prevent Venus being seen round at one time and forked at another, with very thin horns; as well as many other sensory observations which can never be reconciled with the Ptolemaic system in any way, but are very strong arguments for the Copernican. And to ban Copernicus now that his doctrine is daily reinforced by many new observations and by the learned applying themselves to the reading of his book, after this opinion has been allowed and tolerated for those many years during which it was less followed and less confirmed, would seem in my judgment to be a contravention of truth, and an attempt to hide and suppress her the more as she revealed herself the more clearly and plainly. Not to abolish and censure his whole book, but only to condemn as erroneous this particular proposition, would (if I am not mistaken) be a still greater detriment to the minds of men, since it would afford them occasion to see a proposition proved that it was heresy to believe. And to prohibit the whole science would be but to censure a hundred passages of holy Scripture which teach us that the glory and greatness of Almighty God are marvelously discerned in all his works and divinely read in the open book of heaven. For let no one believe that reading the lofty concepts written in that book leads to nothing further than the mere seeing of the splendor of the sun and the stars and their rising and setting, which is as far as the eyes of brutes and of the vulgar can penetrate. Within its pages are couched mysteries so profound and concepts so sublime that the vigils, labors, and studies of hundreds upon hundreds of the most acute minds have still not pierced them, even after continual investigations for thousands of years. The eyes of an idiot perceive little by beholding the external appearance of a human body, as compared with the wonderful contrivances which a careful and practiced anatomist or philosopher discovers in that same body when he seeks out the use of all those muscles, tendons, nerves, and bones; or when examining the functions of the heart and the other principal organs, he seeks the seat of the vital faculties, notes and observes the admirable structure of the sense organs, and (without ever ceasing in his amazement and delight) contemplates the receptacles of the imagination, the memory, and the understanding. Likewise, that which presents itself to mere sight is as nothing in comparison with the high marvels that the ingenuity of learned men discovers in the heavens by long and accurate observation. And that concludes what I have to say on this matter....

# APHORISMS
## FRANCIS BACON (1561–1626)

*Since the seventeenth century the term Baconianism has evolved into a synonym for the supposed method of modern scientific discovery marked by robust empiricism and inductive logic. It is ironic, therefore, that Francis Bacon, the architect of this new philosophy of science was not a scientist, never followed his own method, and made no scientific discoveries or contributions. But he did manage to doubt or criticize the substantial scientific efforts of such early modern natural philosophers as Nicolaus Copernicus, William Harvey, Johannes Kepler, William Gilbert, and Galileo Galilei. Does this mean that Bacon's iconic standing is undeserved and his contribution to the Western intellectual heritage immaterial? No. But it does mean that his place in the Scientific Revolution was not that of the investigator of nature but that of the philosopher-prophet. In his writings Bacon preached about the possibility and power of scientific knowledge as the ground for human progress.*

*Francis Bacon was a contemporary of Galileo and Shakespeare and the son of Sir Nicholas Bacon, England's senior legal officer. The younger Bacon attended Trinity College, Cambridge, where he studied law with the aim of pursuing politics and the legal profession. His political career reached its highest and lowest points in the same year, 1618, when he became Lord High Chancellor and then confessed to taking bribes, a crime for which he spent time in the Tower of London. His only defense was that the bribes had not influenced his political decisions. Following his brief incarceration he turned his attention to the philosophy of science.*

*His bold and ultimately unfinished project was a six-part work called* The Great Instauration, *which aimed to underscore the utility and nobility of the sciences. An expanded and revised version of his 1605 work,* The Advancement of Learning, *was its first part. The second part, published in 1620, was* The New Organon, *from which this reading is taken. Bacon sought to release science from its servitude to Aristotle's deductive logic and*

*The Works of Francis Bacon*, edited by James Spedding (London: Longmans, 1858), IV: 47–55, 79–80, 99–100.

*to scholastic bookishness. The* Organon *was the name given to the body of Aristotle's works. Hence Bacon's title was explicit in its bid to replace "The Philosopher." Bacon believed that scientific knowledge, to the degree it was empirical, inductive, and experimental, would be powerful, useful, and progressive. He urged a new philosophy of science that would overcome the various dogmas and distortions—he called them "Idols"—that inhibit genuine scientific knowledge. That he failed to appreciate the achievements of his contemporaries and underestimated the power of mathematics is, perhaps, not surprising. That he has become famous, despite the fact that his method has never produced a single discovery, shows the force of his utopian conviction that the modern mind would one day equate science with both knowledge and power.*

1620

1. Man, being the servant and interpreter of Nature, can do and understand so much and so much only as he has observed in fact or in thought of the course of nature. Beyond this he neither knows anything nor can do anything.

2. Neither the naked hand nor the understanding left to itself can effect much. It is by instruments and helps that the work is done, which are as much wanted for the understanding as for the hand. And as the instruments of the hand either give motion or guide it, so the instruments of the mind supply either suggestions for the understanding, or cautions.

3. Human knowledge and human power meet in one; for where the cause is not known, the effect cannot be produced. Nature to be commanded must be obeyed; and that which in contemplation is as the cause is in operation as the rule.

4. Toward the effecting of works, all that man can do is to put together or put asunder natural bodies. The rest is done by nature working within.

5. The study of nature with a view to works is engaged in by the mechanic, the mathematician, the physician, the alchemist, and the magician; but by all (as things now are) with slight endeavor and scanty success.

6. It would be an unsound fancy and self-contradictory to expect that things which have never yet been done can be done except by means which have never yet been tried.

7. The productions of the mind and hand seem very numerous in books and manufactures. But all this variety lies in an exquisite subtlety and derivations from a few things already known, not in the number of axioms.

8. Moreover, the works already known are due to chance and experiment rather than to sciences; for the sciences we now possess are merely systems for the

nice ordering and setting forth of things already invented, not methods of invention or directions for new works....

12. The logic now in use serves rather to fix and give stability to the errors which have their foundation in commonly received notions than to help the search after truth. So it does more harm than good....

19. There are and can be only two ways of searching into and discovering truth. The one flies from the senses and particulars to the most general axioms, and from these principles, the truth of which it takes for settled and immovable, proceeds to judgment and to the discovery of middle axioms. And this way is now in fashion. The other derives axioms from the senses and particulars, rising by a gradual and unbroken ascent, so that it arrives at the most general axioms last of all. This is the true way, but as yet untried.

20. The understanding left to itself takes the same course (namely, the former) which it takes in accordance with logical order. For the mind longs to spring up to positions of higher generality, that it may find rest there, and so after a little while wearies of experiment. But this evil is increased by logic, because of the order and solemnity of its disputations.

23. There is a great difference between the Idols of the human mind and the Ideas of the divine. That is to say, between certain empty dogmas, and the true signatures and marks set upon the works of creation as they are found in nature.

24. It cannot be that axioms established by argumentation should avail for the discovery of new works, since the subtlety of nature is greater many times over than the subtlety of argument. But axioms duly and orderly formed from particulars easily discover the way to new particulars, and thus render sciences active....

30. Though all the wits of all the ages should meet together and combine and transmit their labors, yet will no great progress ever be made in science by means of anticipations; because radical errors in the first concoction of the mind are not to be cured by the excellence of functions and subsequent remedies.

31. It is idle to expect any great advancement in science from the superinducing and engrafting of new things upon old. We must begin anew from the very foundations, unless we would revolve forever in a circle with mean and contemptible progress....

33. This must be plainly avowed: no judgment can be rightly formed either of my method or of the discoveries to which it leads, by means of anticipa-

tions (that is to say, of the reasoning which is now in use); since I cannot be called on to abide by the sentence of a tribunal which is itself on trial....

36. One method of delivery alone remains to us which is simply this: we must lead men to the particulars themselves, and their series and order; while men on their side must force themselves for a while to lay their notions by and begin to familiarize themselves with facts....

38. The idols and false notions which are now in possession of the human understanding, and have taken deep root therein, not only so beset men's minds that truth can hardly find entrance, but even after entrance is obtained, they will again in the very instauration of the sciences meet and trouble us, unless men being forewarned of the danger fortify themselves as far as may be against their assaults.

39. There are four classes of Idols which beset men's minds. To these for distinction's sake I have assigned names, calling the first class *Idols of the Tribe*; the second, *Idols of the Cave*; the third, *Idols of the Market Place*; the fourth, *Idols of the Theater*.

40. The formation of ideas and axioms by true induction is no doubt the proper remedy to be applied for the keeping off and clearing away of idols. To point them out, however, is of great use; for the doctrine of Idols is to the interpretation of nature what the doctrine of the refutation of sophisms is to common logic.

41. The *Idols of the Tribe* have their foundation in human nature itself, and in the tribe or race of men. For it is a false assertion that the sense of man is the measure of things. On the contrary, all perceptions as well of the sense as of the mind are according to the measure of the individual and not according to the measure of the universe. And the human understanding is like a false mirror, which, receiving rays irregularly, distorts and discolors the nature of things by mingling its own nature with it.

42. The *Idols of the Cave* are the idols of the individual man. For everyone (besides the errors common to human nature in general) has a cave or den of his own, which refracts and discolors the light of nature, owing either to his own proper and peculiar nature; or so his education and conversation with others; or to the reading of books, and the authority of those whom he esteems and admires; or to the differences of impressions, accordingly as they take place in a mind preoccupied and predisposed or in a mind indifferent and settled; or the like. So that the spirit of man (according as it is meted out to different individuals) is in fact a thing variable and full of perturbation, and governed as it were by chance. Whence it was well

observed by Heraclitus that men look for sciences in their own lesser worlds, and not in the greater or common world.

43. There are also Idols formed by the intercourse and association of men with each other, which I call *Idols of the Market Place*, on account of the commerce and consort of men there. For it is by discourse that men associate, and words are imposed according to the apprehension of the vulgar. And therefore the ill and unfit choice of words wonderfully obstructs the understanding. Nor do the definitions or explanations wherewith in some things learned men are wont to guard and defend themselves, by any means set the matter right. But words plainly force and overrule the understanding, and throw all into confusion, and lead men away into numberless empty controversies and idle fancies.

44. Lastly, there are Idols which have immigrated into men's minds from the various dogmas of philosophies, and also from wrong laws of demonstration. These I call *Idols of the Theater*, because in my judgment all the received systems are but so many stage plays, representing worlds of their own creation after an unreal and scenic fashion. Nor is it only of the systems now in vogue, or only of the ancient sects and philosophies, that I speak; for many more plays of the same kind may yet be composed and in like artificial manner set forth; seeing that errors the most widely different have nevertheless causes for the most part alike. Neither again do I mean this only of entire systems, but also of many principles and axioms in science, which by tradition, credulity, and negligence have come to be received.

But of these several kinds of Idols I must speak more largely and exactly, that the understanding may be duly cautioned....

81. Again there is another great and powerful cause why the sciences have made but little progress, which is this. It is not possible to run a course aright when the goal itself has not been rightly placed. Now the true and lawful goal of the sciences is none other than this, that human life be endowed with new discoveries and powers. But of this the great majority have no feeling, but are merely hireling and professorial, except when it occasionally happens that some workman of neuter wit and covetous of honor applies himself to a new invention; which he mostly does at the expense of his fortunes. But in general, so far are men from proposing to themselves to augment the mass of arts and sciences, that from the mass already at hand they neither take nor look for anything more than what they may turn to use in their lectures, or to gain, or to reputation, or to some similar advantage. And if any one out of all the multitude court science with honest affection and for her own sake, yet even with him the object will be found

to be rather the variety of contemplations and doctrines than the severe and rigid search after truth. And if by chance there be one who seeks after truth in earnest, yet even he will propose to himself such a kind of truth as shall yield satisfaction to the mind and understanding in rendering causes for things long since discovered, and not the truth which shall lead to new assurance of works and new light of axioms. If then the end of the sciences has not as yet been well placed, it is not strange that men have erred as to the means....

109. Another argument of hope may be drawn from this—that some of the inventions already known are such as before they were discovered it could hardly have entered any man's head to think of; they would have been simply set aside as impossible. For in conjecturing what may be men set before them, the example of what has been, and divine of the new with an imagination pre-occupied and colored by the old; which way of forming opinions is very fallacious; for streams that are drawn from the springheads of nature do not always run in the old channels.

If, for instance, before the invention of ordnance a man had described the thing by its effects, and said that there was a new invention, by means of which the strongest towers and walls could be shaken and thrown down at a great distance, men would doubtless have begun to think over all the ways of multiplying the force of catapults and mechanical engines by weights and wheels and such machinery for ramming and projecting; but the notion of a fiery blast suddenly and violently expanding and exploding would hardly have entered into any man's imagination or fancy, being a thing to which nothing immediately analogous had been seen, except perhaps in an earthquake or in lightning, which as magnolia or marvels of nature, and by man not imitable, would have been immediately rejected.

In the same way, if, before the discovery of silk, anyone had said that there was a kind of thread discovered for the purposes of dress and furniture which far surpassed the thread of linen or of wool in fineness and at the same time in strength, and also in beauty and softness; men would have begun immediately to think of some silky kind of vegetable, or of the finer hair of some animal, or of the feathers and down of birds; but of a web woven by a tiny worm, and that in such abundance and renewing itself yearly, they would assuredly never have thought. Nay, if anyone had said anything about a worm, he would no doubt have been laughed at as dreaming of a new kind of cobwebs.

So again, if, before the discovery of the magnet, anyone had said that a certain instrument had been invented by means of which the quarters and

points of the heavens could be taken and distinguished with exactness, men would have been carried by their imagination to a variety of conjectures concerning the more exquisite construction of astronomical instruments; but that anything could be discovered agreeing so well in its movements with the heavenly bodies, and yet not a heavenly body itself, but simply a     5
substance of metal or stone, would have been judged altogether incredible. Yet these things and others like them lay for so many ages of the world concealed from men, nor was it by philosophy or the rational arts that they were found out at last, but by accident and occasion; being indeed, as I said, altogether different in kind and as remote as possible from anything   10
that was known before; so that no pre-conceived notion could possibly have led to the discovery of them.

There is therefore much ground for hoping that there are still laid up in the womb of nature many secrets of excellent use, having no affinity or parallelism with anything that is now known, but lying entirely out of the   15
beat of the imagination, which have not yet been found out. They, too, no doubt will some time or other, in the course and revolution of many ages, come to light of themselves, just as the others did; only by the method of which we are now treating they can be speedily and suddenly and simultaneously presented and anticipated....                                      20

# PRINCIPIA
## SIR ISAAC NEWTON (1642–1727)

*With the publication in 1687 of his* Philosophiae Naturalis Principia
Mathematica (The Mathematical Principles of Natural Philosophy),
*usually called simply the* Principia, *Isaac Newton gained wide recognition
as having made the culminating contribution to the Scientific Revolution and thereby established himself as the foremost scientific mind of the
English-speaking world. Accordingly, the term "Newtonian" came to define
the modern, rational, and scientific age that emerged from the shadow of
his genius.*

*Not just a scientist and mathematician, Newton, like the vast majority
of seventeenth-century Englishmen, was deeply concerned with theological topics. Indeed, as a natural philosopher—the word* scientist, *with its
restricted application, had not yet come into fashion—Newton sought to
understand nature as God's creation. Accordingly, he believed the universe
was ordered because he knew God had created it. It comes as little surprise,
then, that from time to time Newton made theological references in his
scientific works, such as the "General Scholium" of the* Principia.

*It is important to recognize, however, that Newton professed a deep
commitment to particular rules of reasoning in experimental philosophy,
and was wary of speculative hypotheses, like Descartes' cosmology of vortices,
that could not fully account for nature's phenomena. He began his "General
Scholium" with a discussion of this problem. Moreover, the* Principia *opens
with Newton's list of carefully enumerated "Rules of Reasoning in Philosophy." Even his "General Scholium" is known for its famous, if puzzling
and often misinterpreted, phrase—hypotheses non fingo, "I frame no
hypotheses." Surely Newton did frame hypotheses; he insisted that hypotheses that cannot be reconciled with the results of empirical investigation
must ultimately be discarded or modified. This remains among the central
canons of modern science.*

*Sir Isaac Newton's Mathematical Principles of Natural Philosophy and His System of the World,*
translated by Andrew Motte (Berkeley: University of California Press, 1934), 398–400,
543–47. Reprinted with permission of University of California Press; permission conveyed
through Copyright Clearance Center, Inc.

1687

### Rules of Reasoning in Philosophy

#### *Rule I*

We are to admit no more causes of natural things than such as are both true and sufficient to explain their appearances. To this purpose the philosophers say that Nature does nothing in vain, and more is in vain when less will serve; for Nature is pleased with simplicity, and affects not the pomp of superfluous causes.

#### *Rule II*

5 Therefore to the same natural effects we must, as far as possible, assign the same causes. As to respiration in a man and in a beast; the descent of stones in Europe and in America; the light of our culinary fire and of the sun; the reflection of light in the earth, and in the planzets.

#### *Rule III*

The qualities of bodies, which admit neither intensification nor remission of
10 degrees, and which are found to belong to all bodies within the reach of our experiments, are to be esteemed the universal qualities of all bodies whatsoever.

For since the qualities of bodies are only known to us by experiments, we are to hold for universal all such as universally agree with experiments; and such as are not liable to diminution can never be quite taken away. We are certainly not
15 to relinquish the evidence of experiments for the sake of dreams and vain fictions of our own devising; nor are we to recede from the analogy of Nature, which is wont to be simple, and always consonant to itself. We no other way know the extension of bodies than by our senses, nor do these reach it in all bodies; but because we perceive extension in all that are sensible, therefore we ascribe
20 it universally to all others also. That abundance of bodies are hard, we learn by experience; and because the hardness of the whole arises from the hardness of the parts, we therefore justly infer the hardness of the undivided particles not only of the bodies we feel but of all others. That all bodies are impenetrable, we gather not from reason, but from sensation. The bodies which we handle
25 we find impenetrable, and thence conclude impenetrability to be an universal property of all bodies whatsoever. That all bodies are movable, and endowed with certain powers (which we call the inertia) of persevering in their motion, or in their rest, we only infer from the like properties observed in the bodies which we have seen. The extension, hardness, impenetrability, mobility, and inertia of
30 the whole, result from the extension, hardness, impenetrability, mobility, and inertia of the parts; and hence we conclude the least particles of all bodies to be also all extended, and hard and impenetrable, and movable, and endowed with their proper inertia. And this is the foundation of all philosophy. Moreover, that the divided but contiguous particles of bodies may be separated from one

another, is matter of observation; and, in the particles that remain undivided, our minds are able to distinguish yet lesser parts, as is mathematically demonstrated. But whether the parts so distinguished, and not yet divided, may, by the powers of Nature, be actually divided and separated from one another, we cannot certainly determine. Yet, had we the proof of but one experiment that any undivided particle, in breaking a hard and solid body, suffered a division, we might by virtue of this rule conclude that the undivided as well as the divided particles may be divided and actually separated to infinity.

Lastly, if it universally appears, by experiments and astronomical observations, that all bodies about the earth gravitate towards the earth, and that in proportion to the quantity of matter which they severally contain; that the moon likewise, according to the quantity of its matter, gravitates towards the earth; that, on the other hand, our sea gravitates towards the moon; and all the planets one towards another; and the comets in like manner towards the sun; we must, in consequence of this rule, universally allow that all bodies whatsoever are endowed with a principle of mutual gravitation. For the argument from the appearances concludes with more force for the universal gravitation of all bodies than for their impenetrability; of which, among those in the celestial regions, we have no experiments, nor any manner of observation. Not that I affirm gravity to be essential to bodies: by their *vis insita* I mean nothing but their inertia. This is immutable. Their gravity is diminished as they recede from the earth.

### *Rule IV*

In experimental philosophy we are to look upon propositions inferred by general induction from phenomena as accurately or very nearly true, not withstanding any contrary hypotheses that may be imagined, till such time as other phenomena occur, by which they may either he made more accurate, or liable to exceptions. This rule we must follow that the argument of induction may not be evaded by hypotheses.

## General Scholium

The hypothesis of vortices is pressed with many difficulties. That every planet by a radius drawn to the sun may describe areas proportional to the times of description, the periodic times of the several parts of the vortices should observe the square of their distances from the sun; but that the periodic times of the planets may obtain the $3/_2^{th}$ power of their distances from the sun, the periodic times of the parts of the vortex ought to be as the $3/_2^{th}$ power of their distances. That the smaller vortices may maintain their lesser revolutions about Saturn, Jupiter, and other planets, and swim quietly and undisturbed in the greater vortex of the sun, the periodic times of the parts of the sun's vortex should be equal; but the rotation of the sun and planets about their axes, which ought to correspond with the motions of their vortices, recede far from all these proportions. The motions of the comers are exceedingly regular, are governed by the same laws with the motions of the planets, and can by no means be accounted

5   for by the hypothesis of vortices; for comets are carried with very eccentric motions through all parts of the heavens indifferently, with a freedom that is incompatible with the notion of a vortex.

Bodies projected in our air suffer no resistance but from the air. Withdraw the air, as is done in Mr. Boyle's vacuum, and the resistance ceases; for in this void

10  a bit of fine down and a piece of solid gold descend with equal velocity. And the same argument must apply to the celestial spaces above the earth's atmosphere; in these spaces, where there is no air to resist their motions, all bodies will move with the greatest freedom; and the planets and comets will constantly pursue their revolutions in orbits given in kind and position, according to the laws

15  above explained; but though these bodies may, indeed, continue in their orbits by the mere laws of gravity, yet they could by no means have at first derived the regular position of the orbits themselves from those laws.

The six primary planets are revolved about the sun in circles concentric with the sun, and with motions directed towards the same parts, and almost in

20  the same plane. Ten moons are revolved about the earth, Jupiter, and Saturn, in circles concentric with them, with the same direction of motion, and nearly in the planes of the orbits of those planets; but it is not to be conceived that mere mechanical causes could give birth to so many regular motions, since the comets range over all parts of the heavens in very eccentric orbits; for by that

25  kind of motion they pass easily through the orbs of the planets, and with great rapidity; and in their aphelions, where they move the slowest, and are detained the longest, they recede to the greatest distances from each other, and hence suffer the least disturbance from their mutual attractions. This most beautiful system of the sun, planets, and comets, could only proceed from the counsel

30  and dominion of an intelligent and powerful Being. And if the fixed stars are the centers of other like systems, these, being formed by the like wise counsel, must be all subject to the dominion of One; especially since the light of the fixed stars is of the same nature with the light of the sun, and from every system light passes into all the other systems: and lest the systems of the fixed stars should,

35  by their gravity, fall on each other, he hath placed those systems at immense distances from one another.

This Being governs all things, not as the soul of the world, but as Lord over all; and on account of his dominion he is wont to be called Lord God παντοκρὸτωρ Universal Ruler, for God is a relative word, and has a respect

40  to servants; and Deity is the dominion of God not over his own body, as those

imagine who fancy God to be the soul of the world, but over servants. The
Supreme God is a Being eternal, infinite, absolutely perfect; but a being, however
perfect, without dominion, cannot be said to be Lord God; for we say, my God,
your God, the God of Israel, the God of Gods, and Lord of Lords; but we do
not say, my Eternal, your Eternal, the Eternal of Israel, the Eternal of Gods; we      5
do not say, my Infinite, or my Perfect: these are titles which have no respect to
servants. The word God usually signifies Lord; but every lord is not a God. It is
the dominion of a spiritual being which constitutes a God: a true, supreme, or
imaginary dominion makes a true, supreme, or imaginary God. And from his
true dominion it follows that the true God is a living, intelligent, and powerful      10
Being; and, from his other perfections, that he is supreme, or most perfect. He
is eternal and infinite, omnipotent and omniscient; that is, his duration reaches
from eternity to eternity; his presence from infinity to infinity; he governs all
things, and knows all things that are or can be done. He is not eternity and
infinity, but eternal and infinite; he is not duration or space, but he endures      15
and is present. He endures forever, and is everywhere present; and, by existing
always and everywhere, he constitutes duration and space. Since every particle
of space is [always], and every indivisible moment of duration is [everywhere],
certainly the Maker and Lord of all things cannot be [never] and [nowhere].
Every soul that has perception is, though in different times and in different      20
organs of sense and motion, still the same indivisible person. There are given
successive parts in duration, coexistent parts in space, but neither the one nor
the other in the person of a man, or his thinking principle; and much less can
they be found in the thinking substance of God. Every man, so far as he is a
thing that has perception, is one and the same man during his whole life, in all      25
and each of his organs of sense. God is the same God, always and everywhere.
He is omnipresent not [virtually] only, but also [substantially]; for virtue cannot subsist without substance. In him are all things contained and moved; yet
neither affects the other: God suffers nothing from the motion of bodies; bodies
find no resistance from the omnipresence of God. It is allowed by all that the      30
Supreme God exists necessarily; and by the same necessity he exists [always]
and [everywhere]. Whence also he is all similar, all eye, all ear, all brain, all
arm, all power to perceive, to understand, and to act; but in a manner not at
all human, in a manner not at all corporeal, in a manner utterly unknown to
us. As a blind man has no idea of colors, so have we no idea of the manner by      35
which the all-wise God perceives and understands all things. He is utterly void
of all body and bodily figure, and can therefore neither be seen, nor heard, nor
touched; nor ought he to be worshiped under the representation of any corporeal
thing. We have ideas of his attributes, but what the real substance of anything
is we know not. In bodies, we see only their figures and colors, we hear only      40

the sounds, we touch only their outward surfaces, we smell only the smells, and taste the savors; but their inward substances are not to be known either by our senses, or by any reflex act of our minds: much less, then, have we any idea of the substance of God. We know him only by his most wise and excellent

5   contrivances of things, and final causes; we admire him for his perfections, but we reverence and adore him on account of his dominion: for we adore him as his servants; and a god without dominion, providence, and final causes, is nothing else but Fate and Nature. Blind metaphysical necessity, which is certainly the same always and everywhere, could produce no variety of things. All that

10  diversity of natural things which we find suited to different times and places could arise from nothing but the ideas and will of a Being necessarily existing. But, by way of allegory, God is said to see, to speak, to laugh, to love, to hate, to desire, to give, to receive, to rejoice, to be angry, to fight, to frame, to work, to build; for all our notions of God are taken from the ways of mankind by

15  a certain similitude, which, though not perfect, has some likeness, however. And thus much concerning God; to discourse of whom from the appearances of things, does certainly belong to Natural Philosophy.

Hitherto we have explained the phenomena of the heavens and of our sea by the power of gravity, but have not yet assigned the cause of this power. This

20  is certain, that it must proceed from a cause that penetrates to the very centers of the sun and planets, without suffering the least diminution of its force; that operates not according to the quantity of the surfaces of the particles upon which it acts (as mechanical causes used to do), but according to the quantity of the solid matter which they contain, and propagates its virtue on all sides

25  to immense distances, decreasing always as the inverse square of the distances. Gravitation towards the sun is made up out of the gravitations towards the several particles of which the body of the sun is composed; and in receding from the sun decreases accurately as the inverse square of the distances as far as the orbit of Saturn, as evidently appears from the quiescence of the aphelion

30  of the planets; nay, and even to the remotest aphelion of the comets, if these aphelions are also quiescent. But hitherto I have not been able to discover the cause of those properties of gravity from phenomena, and I frame no hypotheses; for whatever is not deduced from the phenomena is to be called an hypothesis; and hypotheses, whether metaphysical or physical, whether of occult qualities

35  or mechanical, have no place in experimental philosophy. In this philosophy particular propositions are inferred from the phenomena, and afterwards rendered general by induction. Thus it was that the impenetrability, the mobility, and the impulsive force of bodies, and the laws of motion and of gravitation, were discovered. And to us it is enough that gravity does really exist, and

act according to the laws which we have explained, and abundantly serves to account for all the motions of the celestial bodies, and of our sea.

And now we might add something concerning a certain most subtle spirit which pervades and lies hid in all gross bodies; by the force and action of which spirit the particles of bodies attract one another at near distances, and cohere, if 5 contiguous; and electric bodies operate to greater distances, as well repelling as attracting the neighboring corpuscles; and light is emitted, reflected, refracted, inflected, and heats bodies; and all sensation is excited, and the members of animal bodies move at the command of the will, namely, by the vibrations of this spirit, mutually propagated along the solid filaments of the nerves, from 10 the outward organs of sense to the brain, and from the brain into the muscles. But these are things that cannot be explained in few words, nor are we furnished with that sufficiency of experiments which is required to an accurate determination and demonstration of the laws by which this electric and elastic spirit operates. 15

# ON THE MOTION OF THE HEART AND BLOOD

## WILLIAM HARVEY (1587–1657)

*Key among the ingredients to the scientific revolution's so-called "new experimental philosophy" stand an emphasis upon experimental investigation and the stress upon quantitative measurement. Each of these components of the new science figured prominently in the discovery of the circulation of the blood by the English physician William Harvey. Although sixteenth-century investigations had provided much new information regarding the function of the heart and blood, it was not until the 1620s that William Harvey combined these insights in the context of careful quantitative experimentation to provide a scientific demonstration of the blood's circulation. After studying at Cambridge and Padua, Harvey moved to London where he practiced medicine and undertook his studies of the circulatory system. The following selection comes from Harvey's famous treatise* De Motu Cordis et sanguinis in animalibus, *in which he carefully described his experiments that demonstrated the circulation of the blood in animals. It remains a classic account of the scientific revolution's "new experimental philosophy" in practice.*

LONDON, 1628

Most Illustrious Prince! The heart of animals is the foundation of their life, the sovereign of everything within them, the sun of their microcosm, that upon which all growth depends, from which all power proceeds. The king, in like manner, is the foundation of his kingdom, the sun of the world around him, the heart of the republic, the fountain whence all power, all grace does flow. What I have 5 here written of the motions of the heart I am the more emboldened to present to Your Majesty, according to the custom of the present age, because almost all things human are done after human examples, and many things in a king are after the pattern of the heart. The knowledge of his heart, therefore, will not be useless to a prince, as embracing a kind of Divine example of his functions—and 10 it has still been usual with men to compare small things with great. Here, at all events, best of princes, placed as you are on the pinnacle of human affairs, you

*Exercitatio Anatomica de Motu Cordis et Sanguinis in Animalibus*, translated by Chauncey D. Leak (Springfield, IL: Charles C. Thomas, 1970), 3, 73–104. Text & illustrations reprinted with permission of Charles C. Thomas, Publisher; permission conveyed through Copyright Clearance Center, Inc.

may at once contemplate the prime mover in the body of man, and the emblem of your own sovereign power. Accept, therefore, with your wonted clemency, I most humbly beseech you, illustrious Prince, this, my new treatise on the heart; you, who are yourself the new light of this age, and, indeed, its very heart; a prince abounding in virtue and in grace, and to whom we gladly refer all the blessings which England enjoys, all the pleasure we have in our lives.

### Chapter 9—*The Circulation of the Blood is Proved by a Prime Consideration*

If anyone says these are empty words, broad assertions without basis, or innovations without just cause, there are three points coming for proof, from which I believe the truth will necessarily follow, and be clearly evident.

First, blood is constantly being transmitted from the vena cava to the arteries by the heart beat in such amounts that it cannot be furnished by the food consumed, and in such a way that the total quantity must pass through the heart in a short time. Second, blood is forced by the pulse in the arteries continually and steadily to every part of the body in a much greater amount than is needed for nutrition or than the whole mass of food could supply. And likewise third, the veins continually return this blood from every part of the body to the heart. These proved, I think it will be clear that the blood circulates, passing away from the heart to the extremities and then returning back to the heart, thus moving in a circle.

Let us consider, arbitrarily or by experiment, that the left ventricle of the heart when filled in diastole, contains two or three ounces, or only an ounce and a half. In a cadaver I have found it holding more than three ounces. Likewise let us consider how much less the ventricle contains when the heart contracts or how much blood it forces into the aorta with each contraction, for, during systole, everyone will admit something is always forced out, as shown in Chapter III, and apparent from the structure of the valves. As a reasonable conjecture suppose a fourth, fifth, sixth, or even an eighth part is passed into the arteries. Then we may suppose in man that a single heart beat would force out either a half ounce, three drams, or even one dram of blood, which because of the valvular block could not flow back that way into the heart.

The heart makes more than a thousand beats in a half hour, in some two, three, or even four thousand. Multiplying by the drams, there will be in half an hour either 3,000 drams, 2,000 drams, five hundred ounces, or some other such proportionate amount of blood forced into the arteries by the heart, but always a greater quantity than is present in the whole body. Likewise in a sheep or dog, suppose one scruple goes out with each stroke of the heart, then in half an hour 1,000 scruples or about three and a half pounds of blood would be pumped out. But as I have determined in the sheep, the whole body does not contain more than four pounds of blood.

On this assumption of the passage of blood, made as a basis for argument, and from the estimation of the pulse rate, it is apparent that the entire quantity of blood passes from the veins to the arteries through the heart, and likewise     5
through the lungs.

But suppose this would not occur in half an hour, but rather in an hour, or even in a day, it is still clear that more blood continually flows through the heart than can be supplied by the digested food or be held in the veins at any one time.     10

It cannot be said that the heart in contracting sometimes pumps and sometimes doesn't, or that it propels a mere nothing or something imaginary. This point has been settled previously, and besides, it is contrary to common sense. If the ventricles must be filled with blood in cardiac dilatation, something must always be pushed out in contraction, and not a little amount either, since     15
the passages are not small nor the contractions few. This quantity expelled is some proportion of the contents of the ventricle, a third, a sixth, or an eighth, and an equivalent amount of blood must fill it up in diastole, so that there is a relation between the ventricular capacity in contraction and in dilatation. Since the ventricles in dilating do not become filled with nothing, or with something     20
imaginary, so in contracting they never expel nothing or something imaginary, but always blood in an amount proportionate to the contraction.

So it may be inferred that if the heart in a single beat in man, sheep, or ox, pumps one dram, and there are 1,000 beats in half an hour, the total amount pumped in that time would be ten pounds five ounces; if two drams at a single     25
stroke, then twenty pounds ten ounces; if half an ounce, then forty-one pounds eight ounces; and if one ounce, then a total of eighty-three pounds four ounces, all of which would be transferred from the veins to the arteries in half an hour.

The amount pumped at a single beat, and the factors involved in increasing or diminishing it, may perhaps be more carefully studied later from many     30
observations of mine.

Meanwhile I know and state to all that the blood is transmitted sometimes in a larger amount, other times in a smaller, and that the blood circulates sometimes rapidly, sometimes slowly, according to temperament, age, external or internal causes, normal or abnormal factors, sleep, rest, food, exercise, mental     35
condition, and such like.

But suppose even the smallest amount of blood be transmitted through the lungs and heart at a single beat, a greater quantity would eventually be pumped into the arteries and the body than could be furnished by the food consumed, unless by constantly making a circuit and returning.     40

The matter is obvious in animal experimentation. If an opening be cut not only in the aorta, but even in a small artery, as Galen claims, in man, the whole blood content may be drained from the entire body, from veins as well as arteries, in almost half an hour's time.

5      Butchers can also well enough confirm this point. In killing an ox by cutting the arteries of the neck, the whole mass of blood may be drained off and all the vessels emptied in less than a quarter of an hour. We know how quickly an excessive hemorrhage may occur in removing a tumor or in an amputation.

The force of this argument would not be lost by saying that blood flows
10    equally if not more from veins than from arteries, in butchering or amputating. The contrary of this really holds. Because they collapse, and have no power to propel blood, and because there is a block where the valves are placed, as shall be shown later, the veins really pour out little blood. The arteries, however, squirt it out in quantities, with force, as if ejected from a syringe. The matter may be
15    tested by cutting the artery in the neck of a sheep or dog, but leaving the vein alone, and it will easily be seen with how much force, in what amounts, and how quickly all the blood in the body is drained, from veins as well as arteries. The arteries receive blood from the veins in no other way than by transmission through the heart, as previously said. So by ligating the aorta close to the heart,
20    there need be no uncertainty about finding the arteries empty if they be opened in the neck or elsewhere, and the veins filled.

The reason is now apparent why so much blood is found in the veins in anatomical dissection, and so little in the arteries, so much in the right side of the heart, so little in the left. This fact probably led the ancients to believe that arter-
25    ies contained only spirits during an animal's life. The reason for the difference is probably as follows. There is no other passage from the veins to the arteries except through the heart and lungs, so when an animal expires and the lungs stop moving, the blood is prevented from passing from the pulmonary artery to the pulmonary vein and then into the left ventricle of the heart. This is like what was noted previ-
30    ously in the embryo, where the transit is prevented by the lack of motion in the lungs and the opening and closing of its tiny pores. The heart, however, does not stop at the same time as the lungs, but outlives them and continues to beat. The left ventricle and the arteries continue to send blood to the rest of the body and into the veins, but, receiving none from the lungs, they soon become empty.

35     This fact awakens not a little belief in our position, since it can be ascribed to no other reason than what we have proposed.

It further appears that the greater or more vehemently the arteries pulsate, the quicker will the body be exhausted of its blood in a hemorrhage. Hence in fainting or alarm, when the heart beats slowly and feebly, a hemorrhage is
40    reduced or stopped.

This is also why one cannot draw forth by any effort more than half the blood by cutting the jugular or femoral veins or arteries in a dead body after the heart stops beating. Nor may a butcher succeed in bleeding an ox after hitting it on the head and stunning it, if he does not cut its throat before the heart stops beating.

5

Finally, it may now be suspected why no one so far has said anything to the point on the place, manner, or purpose of the anastomosis of veins and arteries. I shall now discuss this point.

### Chapter 10—*The First Proposition, Concerning the Amount of Blood Passing from Veins to Arteries During the Circulation, Is Freed from Objections, and Confirmed by Experiments*

Whether the matter be referred to calculation or to experiment and dissection, the important proposition has been established that blood is continually poured into the arteries in a greater amount than can be supplied by the food. Since it all flows past in so short a time, it must be made to flow in a circle.

10

Someone may say here that a great amount may flow out without any necessity for a circulation and that it all may come from the food. An example might be given in the rich milk supply of the mammae. A cow may give three or four, or even seven and more gallons of milk daily, and a mother two or three pints when nursing a baby or twins, all of which must obviously come from the food. It may be replied that the heart, by computation, does more in an hour or less.

15

Not yet persuaded, one may still insist that cutting an artery opens a very abnormal passage through which blood may forcibly pour, but that nothing like this happens in the intact body, with no outlet made. With the arteries filled, in their natural state, so large an amount cannot pass in so short a time as to make a return necessary. It may be replied that from the computation and reasons already given, the excess contained in the dilated heart in comparison with the constricted must be in general pumped out with each beat and this amount must be transmitted, as long as the body is intact and in a natural state.

20

25

In serpents and certain fishes by ligating the veins a little below the heart, you will see the space between the ligature and the heart quickly become empty. So, unless you deny what you see, you must admit the blood returns to the heart. This will be clear later in discussing the second proposition.

30

We may close here with a single conclusive example, by which anyone may be convinced by his own eyes.

If a live snake be cut open, the heart may be seen quietly and distinctly beating for more than an hour, moving like a worm and propelling blood when

35

it contracts longitudinally, for it is oblong. It becomes pale in systole, the reverse in diastole, and almost all the other things we have mentioned as proving the truth may be clearly observed, for here all happens slower and more distinctly. This especially may be seen more clearly than the midday sun. The vena cava
5    enters at the lower part of the heart, the artery leaves at the upper. Now, pinching off the vena cava with a forceps or between finger and thumb, the course of blood being intercepted some distance below the heart, you will see that the space between the finger and the heart is drained at once, the blood being emptied by the heart beat. At the same time, the heart becomes much paler
10   even in distention, smaller from lack of blood, and beats more slowly, so that it seems to be dying. Immediately on releasing the vein, the color and size of the heart returns to normal.

On the other hand, leaving the vein alone, if you ligate or compress the artery a little distance above the heart, you will see the space between the
15   compression and the heart, and the latter also, become greatly distended and very turgid, of a purple or livid color, and, choked by the blood, it will seem to suffocate. On removing the block, the normal color, size, and pulse return.

This is evidence of two kinds of death, failure from a lack, and suffocation from excess. In these examples of both, one may find proof before his eyes of
20   the truth spoken about the heart.

## Chapter 11—*The Second Proposition is Proven*

Our second proposition may appear more clearly by considering certain experiments from which it is obvious that blood enters a limb through the arteries and returns through the veins, that the arteries are the vessels carrying blood from the heart and the veins the channels returning it to the heart, and that,
25   in the extremities, blood passes from arteries to veins directly by anastomosis or indirectly through pores in the flesh, as discussed before in regard to its transfer from veins to arteries in the heart and thorax. From this it may be clear that it moves in a circle from the center to the extremities and back from the extremities to the center.
30   Then, making certain calculations, it will also be clear that the quantity may neither be supplied from the food taken in nor necessarily be required for nutrition.

These experiments will also clear up some points regarding ligatures: why they may cause swelling, which is neither by heat nor suction nor any reason
35   yet known; what uses and advantages may be obtained from them in practice; how they may either suppress or provoke hemorrhage; how they may cause gangrene in the limbs, and what their function may be in castrating animals or removing fleshy tumors.

Because no one has understood the rationale of these matters, it has happened that almost everyone recommends ligatures in treating disease on the authority of the ancients, and very few use them properly or get any benefit from them.

Some ligatures are tight, others middling. I call a ligature tight when it is pulled so firmly about a limb that the beat of the artery cannot be felt beyond it. We use this kind in amputations to control bleeding. This kind is also used in castrating animals and removing tumors, where we see the testicles and tumors dying and dropping off because the ligature keeps out heat and nourishment.

I call a ligature middling, which compresses a limb on all sides, but without pain, so that the artery may still pulsate somewhat beyond the ligature. This type is used for "drawing," in bloodletting. The proper ligature for phlebotomy is applied above the elbow in such a manner that the artery at the wrist may still be felt beating slightly.

Now, let an experiment be made on a man's arm, using a bandage as in blood-letting, or grasping tightly with the hand. The best subject is one who is lean, with large veins, warm after exercise when more blood is going to the extremities and the pulse is stronger, for then all will be more apparent.

Under these conditions, place on a ligature as tightly as the subject can stand. Then it may be observed that the artery does not pulsate beyond the bandage, in the wrist or elsewhere. Next, just above the ligature the artery is higher in diastole and beats more strongly, swelling near the ligature as if trying to break through and flood past the barrier. The artery at this place seems abnormally full. The hand, however, retains its natural color and appearance. In a little time it begins to cool a bit, but nothing is "drawn" into it.

After this bandage has been on for some time, loosen it to the medium tightness used, as I said, in blood-letting. You will see the whole hand at once become suffused and distended, and its veins become swollen and varicosed. After ten or fifteen beats of the artery you will see the hand become impacted and gorged with a great amount of blood "drawn" by this medium tight ligature, but without pain, heat, horror of a vacuum or any other cause so far proposed.

If one will place a finger on the artery as it beats at the edge of the bandage, the blood may be felt to flow under it at the moment of loosening. The subject, also, on whose arm the experiment is made, clearly feels, as the ligature is slackened, warmth and blood pulsing through, as though an obstacle has been removed. And he is conscious of it following the artery and diffusing through the hand, as it warms and swells.

In the case of the tight bandage, the artery is distended and pulsates above it, not below; in the mediumly tight one, however, the veins become turgid and the arteries shrink below the ligature, never above it. Indeed, in this case, unless you compress these swollen veins very strongly, you will scarcely be able to force any blood above the ligature or cause the veins there to be filled.

From these facts any careful observer may easily understand that blood enters a limb through the arteries. A tight bandage about them "draws" noth-
5　ing, the hand keeps its color, nothing flows into it, neither is it distended. With a little slackening, as in a mediumly tight ligature, it is clear that the blood is instantly and strongly forced in, and the hand made to swell. When they pulsate, blood flows through them into the hand, as when a medium bandage is used, but otherwise not, with a tight ligature, except above it. Meanwhile, the
10　veins being compressed, nothing can flow through them. This is indicated by the fact that they are much more swollen below the bandage than above it, or than is usual with it removed, and that while compressed they carry nothing under the ligature to the parts above. So it is clear that the bandage prevents the return of blood through the veins to the parts above it and keeps those
15　below it engorged.

The arteries, however, for the simple reason that they are not blocked by the moderate ligature, carry blood beyond it from the inside of the body by the power and impulse of the heart. This is the difference between a tight and medium bandage; the former not only blocks the flow of blood in the veins but
20　also in the arteries, the latter does not impede the pulsating force from spreading beyond the ligature and carrying blood to the extremities of the body.

One may reason as follows. Below a medium bandage we see the veins become swollen and gorged and the hand filled with blood. This must be caused by blood passing under the ligature either in veins, arteries or tiny pores. It
25　cannot come through the veins, certainly not through invisible ducts, so it must flow through the arteries, according to what has been said. It obviously cannot flow through the veins since the blood cannot be squeezed back above the ligature unless it is completely loosened. Then we see the veins suddenly collapse, discharging themselves to the part above, the hand loses its flush, and
30　the stagnant blood and swelling quickly fade away.

Further, he whose arm has been bound for some time with a medium bandage, and whose hand has been rendered somewhat swollen and cold, feels, as the ligature is loosened, something cold creeping up with the returning blood to the elbow or armpit. I think this cold blood returning to the heart,
35　after removing the bandage in blood-letting, is a cause of fainting, which we sometimes see even in robust persons, usually when the ligature is removed, or, as is commonly said, when the blood turns.

Moreover, immediately on loosening a tight bandage to a medium one, we see the veins below it, but not the arteries, swollen with blood continu-
40　ally carried in by the arteries. This indicates that blood passes from arteries to

veins, not the reverse, and that there is either an anastomosis of these vessels or pores in the flesh and solid parts permeable to blood. It also indicates that the veins inter-communicate, since, with a medium ligature above the elbow, they all swell up at the same time, and, if even a single venule be cut with a lancet, they all quickly shrink, giving up their blood to this one, and subside 5 almost together.

Anyone may understood from this the reasons for the "drawing" power exist-ing in ligatures, and perhaps in all fluxes. It is clear how the blood cannot escape from the hand when the veins are compressed with what I call a medium bandage, but being driven in by the heart beat through the arteries, and not being able to 10 escape anywhere, the part must necessarily become gorged and swollen.

How can it be otherwise? Heat, pain, and the suction of a vacuum have a certain "drawing" power to fill a part, but not to distend or swell it abnormally, nor to overcome it so suddenly and powerfully by impact of blood that the flesh and vessels are in danger of being torn or ruptured. It is neither believable nor 15 demonstrable that heat, pain, or the *vis vacui* can do this.

Furthermore, this "drawing" power occurs in a ligature without pain, heat, or the suction of a vacuum. If pain happens to "draw" any blood, with the arm tied above the elbow, how may the hand and fingers and their veins become swollen below the ligature, since because of its pressure, blood cannot get there 20 through the veins? And why is neither swelling, nor sign of venous filling or engorgement, nor any vestige of "drawing" apparent above the ligature?

The obvious cause of the "drawing" or abnormal swelling in the hand and fingers below the bandage is the forceful and copious influx of blood which cannot escape. Indeed, is not the cause of all tumors and oppressive swellings, 25 what Avicenna says, that the way in is open but the way out closed, so there must be an engorgement or tumor?

May not this happen in boils? As long as the swelling is increasing and has not come to a final state, a full pulse may be felt in the area, especially in more acute tumors in which the swelling is sudden. But these are for later investiga- 30 tion. However, this happened in an accident I experienced. I was thrown once from a carriage and struck my head at a place where an arterial branch crosses the temporal region. Immediately I felt, in the space of about twenty pulsa-tions, a tumor the size of an egg but without either heat or great pain. It seems the blood was pushed out with an unusual amount and speed because of the 35 nearness of the artery to the place of injury.

Now it also appears why, in phlebotomy, if we wish the blood to flow longer and with greater force, we ligate above the cut, not below. If such a flow would come through the veins above, the ligature would not only be of no aid, but would positively hinder it, for if blood flowed downwards from the upper 40

part of an extremity through the veins, it would more properly be tied below the cut so the impeded blood would escape through the cut more abundantly. But since it is forced elsewhere through arteries into the veins lower down, from which return is prevented by the ligature, the veins swell, and being
5   under tension can eject their contents through the opening to some distance with unusual force. When the bandage is loosened, and the returning channels opened, the flow sinks to not more than a drop at a time. Everyone knows in performing phlebotomy that if you either loosen the bandage, tie below the cut, or bind the limb too tightly, the blood will escape without force, because
10  in the latter the influx of blood through the arteries is blocked by the tightness of the ligature, while in the former the venous return is not properly checked because of its looseness.

### Chapter 12—*That There is a Circulation of the Blood Follows from the Proof of the Second Proposition*

Since these things are so, it establishes the proof of what I said previously, that blood continually passes through the heart. For we have seen that blood
15  spreads from the arteries to the veins, not from veins to arteries; we have seen further that almost the total amount of blood can be taken from an arm if a single cutaneous vein be opened with a lancet and a bandage properly applied, and we have seen still further, that there is so much force behind it, and so sufficient a flow that the blood may easily and quickly be withdrawn not only in
20  the amount present in the arm below the ligature before the cut was made, but in the whole arm, and in the entire body, arteries as well as veins.

So it must be admitted, first, that blood is supplied with force and impetus to push it beneath the ligature, for it escapes with vigor, which is derived from the pumping action of the heart and from this alone. Likewise, it must be further
25  admitted that this flow comes from the heart, and by way of the heart, by a transfer accomplished from the great veins, since it passes through the arteries beneath the ligature, not through veins, and arteries never receive blood from veins except by way of the left ventricle of the heart. Nor could any such an amount be drawn from a single vein anywhere, a bandage being applied above
30  it, especially with such force, such an amount,, or so easily and quickly, except by the beating power of the heart in the manner described.

If these things are so, we may very readily compute the amount of blood and come to some conclusion on its circular motion. If, for instance, in phlebotomy, one were to let the blood flow with its usual force and rate for a half
35  hour, there is no doubt but that the greater part of it would be drained off, practically emptying not only arteries but also the great veins, and that fainting

and syncope would follow. It is reasonable to assume that as great an amount of blood as is lost in this half hour's time, passed from the great veins through the heart to the aorta. Further, if you figure how many ounces of blood flow through a single arm, or pass under a medium bandage in twenty or thirty heart-beats, you will have a basis for estimating how much flows through the   5 other arm in the same time, or through both sides of the neck, or through both legs, and through all the other arteries and veins of the body. Since all these are continually supplied with fresh blood, which must flow through the lungs and ventricles of the heart, from the veins, it must be accomplished in a circuit, since the amount involved is much more than can be furnished from the food   10 consumed, or than is needed for the nourishment of the parts.

It is further to be observed that this truth is often demonstrated in blood-letting. Though you properly bandage the arm, and puncture the vein correctly with a lancet, if a fainting state of mind comes on through fear or any other cause, and the heart beats more sluggishly, blood will escape only a drop at a   15 time, especially if the ligature be made a little more tight. The reason is that the feeble beat in the compressed artery, with the weaker propelling power, cannot force the blood under the bandage. For the same reason the feeble and languid heart cannot force the normal amount of blood through the lungs or transfer it from the veins to the arteries. In the same way and for the same reasons, it   20 happens that the menses of women and all types of hemorrhages are checked. If the opposite occurs, the patient recovering his mind, and losing his fear, you will see the arteries at once beat more powerfully, even in the bound-off part, so the blood gushes from the opening and flows steadily.

### Chapter 13—*The Third Proposition is Proven, and the Circulation of the Blood is Demonstrated from It*

So far we have considered the amount of blood flowing through the heart and   25 lungs in the body cavity, and similarly from the arteries to the veins in the periphery. It remains for us to discuss how blood from the extremities gets back to the heart through the veins, and whether or not these are the only vessels serving this purpose. This done we may consider the three basic propositions proving the circulation of the blood so well established, so plain and obvious,   30 as to force belief.

This proposition will be perfectly clear from a consideration of the valves found in the venous cavities, from their functions, and from experiments demonstrable with them.

The celebrated anatomist, Hieronymus Fabricius of Aquapendente, or,   35 instead of him, Jacobus Sylvius, as Doctor Riolan wishes it, first described

membranous valves in the veins, of sigmoid or semilunar shape, and being very delicate eminences on the inner lining of these vessels. They are placed differently in different individuals, but are attached to the sides of the veins, and they are directed upwards toward the main venous trunks. As there are usually two
5    together, they face and touch each other, and their edges are so apt to join or close that they prevent anything from passing from the main trunks or larger veins to the smaller branches. They are so arranged that the horns of one set are opposite the hollow part of the preceding set, and so on alternately.

The discoverer of these valves and his followers did not rightly appreciate
10   their function. It is not to prevent blood from falling by its weight into areas lower down, for there are some in the jugular vein which are directed downwards, and which prevent blood from being carried upwards. They are thus not always looking upwards, but more correctly, always towards the main venous trunks and the heart. Others as well as myself have sometimes found them in the milky
15   veins and in the venous branches of the mesentery directed towards the vena cava and portal vein. To this may be added that there are none in the arteries, and that one may note that dogs, oxen, and all such animals have valves at the branches of the crural veins at the top of the sacrum, and in branches from the haunches, in which no such weight effect of an erect stature is to be feared.
20   Nor, as some say, are the valves in the jugular veins to prevent apoplexy, since the head is more likely to be influenced by what flows into it through the carotid arteries. Nor are they present to keep blood in the smaller branches, not permitting it to flow entirely into the larger more open trunks, for they are placed where there are no branches at all, although I confess they are more
25   frequently seen where there are branchings. Nor are they present for slowing the flow of blood from the center of the body, for it seems likely it would flow slowly enough anyway, as it would then be passed from larger to smaller branches, become separated from the source and mass, and be moved from warmer to cooler places.
30   The valves are present solely that blood may not move from the larger veins into the smaller ones lest it rupture or varicose them, and that it may not advance from the center of the body into the periphery through them, but rather from the extremities to the center. This latter movement is facilitated by these delicate valves, the contrary completely prevented. They are so situated that
35   what may pass the horns of a set above is checked by those below, for whatever may slip past the edges of one set is caught on the convexity of those beyond, so it may not pass farther.

I have often noticed in dissecting veins, that no matter how much care I take, it is impossible to pass a probe from the main venous trunks very far into
40   the smaller branches on account of the valvular obstructions. On the contrary

it is very easy to push it in the opposite direction, from the branches toward the larger trunks. In many places a pair of valves are so placed that when raised they join in the middle of the vein, and their edges are so nicely united that one cannot perceive any crack along their junction. On the other hand, they yield to a probe introduced from without inwards and are easily released in   5 the manner of flood-gates opposing a river flow. So they intercept, and when tightly closed, completely prevent in many places a flow of blood back from the heart and vena cava. They are so constituted that they can never permit blood to move in the veins from the heart upwards to the head, downwards toward the feet, or sidewise to the arms. They oppose any movement of blood from   10 the larger veins toward the smaller ones, but they favor and facilitate a free and open route starting from the small veins and ending in the larger ones.

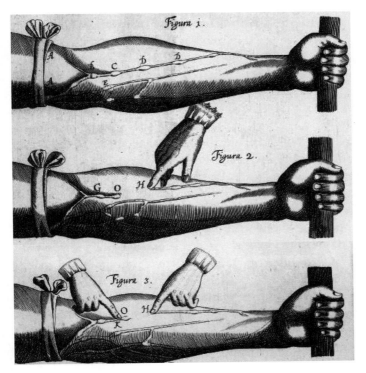

This fact may be more clearly shown by tying off an arm of a subject as if for blood-letting (A,A, figure 1). There will appear at intervals (especially in rustics) knots, or swellings, like nodules (B, C, D, E, F), not only where there is   15 branching (E, F), but also where none occurs (C, D). These are caused by the valves, appearing thus on the surface of the hand and arm. If you will clear the blood away from a nodule or valve by pressing a thumb or finger below it (H,

figure 2), you will see that nothing can flow back, being entirely prevented by the valve, and that the part of the vein between the swelling and the finger (H, O, figure 2), disappears, while above the swelling or valve it is well distended (O, G). Keeping the vein thus empty of blood, if you will press downwards
5   against the valve, (O, figure 3) by a finger of the other hand on the distended upper portion (K, figure 3), You will note that nothing can be forced through the valve. The greater effort you make the more the vein is distended toward the valve, but you will observe that it stays empty below it (H, O, figure 3). From many such experiments it is evident that the function of the valves in the
10   veins is the same as that of the three sigmoid valves placed at the opening of the aorta and pulmonary artery, to prevent, when they arc tightly closed, the reflux of blood passing over them.

      Further, with the arm bound as before and the veins swollen, if you will press on a vein a little below a swelling or valve (L, figure 4) and then squeeze
15   the blood upwards beyond the valve (N) with another finger (M), you will see that this part of the vein stays empty, and that no back flow can occur through the valve (as in H, O, figure 2). But as soon as the finger (H) is removed, the vein is filled from below (as in D, C, figure 1). Thus it is clearly evident that blood moves through the veins toward the heart, from the periphery inwards,
20   and not in the opposite direction. The valves in some places, either because they do not completely close, or because they occur singly, do not seem adequate to block a flow of blood from the center, but the majority certainly do. At any rate, wherever they seem poorly made, they appear to be compensated for in some way, by the greater frequency or better action of the succeeding valves. So, as
25   the veins are the wide open passages for returning blood to the heart, they are adequately prevented from distributing it from the heart.

      Above all, note this. With the arm of your subject bound, the veins distended, and the nodes or valves prominent, apply your thumb to a vein a little below a valve so as to stop the blood coming up from the hand, and then with
30   your finger press the blood from that part of the vein up past the valve, as was said before. Remove your thumb, and the vein at once fills up from below (as in D, C, figure 1). Again compress with your thumb, and squeeze the blood out in the same way as before, and do this a thousand times as quickly as possible. By careful reckoning, of course, the quantity of blood forced up beyond
35   the valve by a single compression may be estimated, and this multiplied by a thousand gives so much blood transmitted in this way through a single portion of the veins in a relatively short time, that without doubt you will be very easily convinced by the quickness of its passage of the circulation of the blood.

      But you may say this experiment of mine violates natural conditions. Then
40   if you will take as long a distance from the valve as possible, observing how

quickly, on releasing your thumb, the blood wells up and fills the vein from below, I do not doubt but that you will be thoroughly convinced.

### Chapter 14—*Conclusion of the Demonstration of the Circulation of the Blood*

Briefly let me now sum up and propose generally my idea of the circulation of the blood.

It has been shown by reason and experiment that blood by the beat of the ventricles flows through the lungs and heart and is pumped to the whole body. There it passes through pores in the flesh into the veins through which it returns from the periphery everywhere to the center, from the smaller veins into the larger ones, finally coming to the vena cava and right auricle. This occurs in such an amount, with such an outflow through the arteries, and such a reflux through the veins, that it cannot be supplied by the food consumed. It is also much more than is needed for nutrition. It must therefore be concluded that the blood in the animal body moves around in a circle continuously, and that the action or function of the heart is to accomplish this by pumping. This is the only reason for the motion and beat of the heart.

# XII
# THE EARLY-MODERN
# BODY POLITIC

The "modern era" of the history of the Western world is distinct for a number of reasons. Compared with the Middle Ages, in particular, modernity places a greater emphasis on the things of this world, on human reason and science as instruments and paths to truth, and on the capacity of man to improve or even perfect himself. Consistent with these attitudes have been the remarkable advances of more recent centuries toward democratic government, social egalitarianism, and higher and higher material standards of living based upon the fruits of technology.

From the earliest stirrings of this new historical epoch in the latter phases of the Middle Ages, a distinctive form of polity began to emerge as well: the "modern state." Medieval kingdoms were characterized by authority that tended to be stronger at the local level than at the "national" level—if anyone were even inclined to conceive of politics in national terms. Medieval "lords" wielded authority in personal terms and treated their own territories as if they were personal possessions. Kings, while owed fealty by such lords, were often powerless to impose royal authority on their subordinates or in their subordinates' territories. As a consequence, medieval polities were not at all unified or consolidated entities. Within medieval France, for example, scores of different legal regimes and independent customs units prevailed, and the king himself actually governed only the territory immediately surrounding Paris. The "modern state," by contrast, represents a polity in which the authority of the state is exercised more or less uniformly and effectively throughout the entire territorial expanse of the state, and more commonly by way of impersonal agencies. In his penetrating essay *On the Medieval Origins of the Modern State,* the historian Joseph R. Strayer encapsulated the character of the transition to this new polity in the following terms: "[W]hat we are looking for is the appearance of political units persisting in time and fixed in space, the development of permanent, impersonal institutions, agreement on the need for an authority which can give final judgments, and acceptance of the idea that this authority should receive the basic loyalty of its subjects." Strayer identified the time frame for this development as the period between 1100 and 1600, but the evolution of this new kind of state did not stop in 1600; rather it has been ongoing. Still, by the beginning of the seventeenth century, it is clear that a fundamental transition had occurred, and the tell-tale signs of the "modern state" were easiest to see in France and England.

If the mark of the new body politic was going to be strong, uniform authority to which subjects throughout the state would be expected to give their "basic loyalty," it should come as no surprise that debates would arise concerning where the chief power of the state should reside. More explicitly, the most prominent argument that accompanied the development of the modern state pertained to the question of *sovereignty.* "Sovereignty" is a power that cannot be overruled; *Webster's Seventh New Collegiate Dictionary* defines it as "supreme power, especially over a body politic." All modern states possess it, or they are not states worthy of the name. Within every state, however, there are numerous possible places where sovereignty might reside. Modern-day Americans, no doubt recalling the first three words of the United States Constitution, like to believe that sovereignty lies with "the people." In fact, our federal system, which provides checks and balances within the national government, divides sovereignty within our polity along vertical (as between state and national governments) and horizontal (as among the executive, legislative, and judicial branches of the national government) lines. During the sixteenth and seventeenth centuries, the principal competitors for sovereignty were monarchs, on the one hand, and parliamentary bodies claiming to speak for the most important segments of society, such as nobilities, church, and common people, on the other. In both France and England, it would take decades of contention and, on occasion, bloody civil wars finally to resolve the question of who possessed sovereignty. As this contention played itself out, great philosophical tracts appeared endorsing one kind of sovereignty or the other. Each one of the selections in this chapter is of sixteenth- or seventeenth-century origin and offers a defense of either monarchical or parliamentary/popular sovereignty, and is itself the product of a national state in the midst of an effort to resolve this great political question.

In France, monarchical sovereignty, also known as "royal absolutism," prevailed as the organizing principle of the Early-Modern body politic. But, this outcome was not confirmed until France had passed through one of the darkest chapters of its uniquely bloody history—the so-called "wars of religion" of the sixteenth century—and the alternative to monarchical sovereignty had proven itself utterly incapable of providing coherent leadership for the country. French kings had been endeavoring to consolidate their personal authority over more and more elements of government for centuries prior to the tumultuous and deadly decades that followed upon the untimely death of Henry II in 1559. Henry II (*r.* 1547–1559) had been a strong king, and although each of his three sons succeeded him in their turns, none was mature, competent, or long-lived enough to rule effectively. Weakness on the throne, when compounded by religious division between the Catholic majority and a small but resolute and powerful Huguenot (Protestant) minority, caused the country to fall apart. Powerful factions contended violently for power, and while the most prominent of these groups were the Catholics and Protestants, the "wars of religion" actually amounted to a protracted contest for power over the state. Historians have numbered no fewer than nine civil wars in the four final decades of the sixteenth century, but the common thread in all of them was the pursuit of political supremacy by some faction. Moreover, what allowed this mayhem to happen was, in the words of Robert R. Palmer and Joel Colton, "the absence of government." No doubt the most infamous moment of these civil wars came in 1572, when thousands of Huguenots were murdered in cold blood on orders of the Queen-Mother Catherine de Medici (1519–1589) in the massacre of Saint Bartholomew's Day. *The Defense of Liberty Against Tyrants*, composed by an anonymous French Protestant seven years later, not surprisingly endorses the idea of popular sovereignty, and holds that kings should understand themselves to be subordinate to the people and, therefore, function as their servants. This idea, needless to say, proved ahead of its time, but remains an important marker in the ongoing discourse on this issue. Jean Bodin (1530–1596), "the first thinker to develop the modern theory of sovereignty," produced *Six Books of the Commonwealth* in 1576 as his own prescription of a definitive remedy for his country's political ills. He offered, in this work, a spirited defense of monarchical sovereignty.

With the ascension to the throne of Henry IV (r. 1589–1610) in 1589, the wars of religion began to subside, largely because the new king, born a Protestant, ultimately converted to Catholicism but soon thereafter, in the 1598 Edict of Nantes, decreed a policy of official toleration for the Huguenot minority. Furthermore, Henry IV ruled as if he possessed sovereignty. When numerous *parlements*, law courts that traditionally claimed the power to register (thereby officially sanctioning) or not to register (thereby negating) all royal edicts, refused to endorse the Edict of Nantes, the king simply forced the policy of toleration into effect. So it was, as Palmer and Colton attest, that "under Henry IV, the foundations of the later royal absolutism…were laid down."

But, Henry IV was assassinated in 1610, leaving a young son Louis XIII (r. 1610–1643) to inherit the throne under the regency of the Queen-Mother. Fractious elements among the clergy and nobility that the deceased ruler had held in check tried anew to assert their own bid for a share of ruling authority. The means they chose for this was to force the child-king to convene the Estates-General, an assembly of representatives of the three separate orders of French society—clergy, nobility, and commoners. The meeting of this body in

1614–1615 revealed that the other would-be possessors of sovereignty were so contentious and mutually distrustful that, as if by default, the king came away with his supreme power intact. During the next 175 years, the Estates-General never convened again, and successive French kings brought the theory of royal absolutism to its fullest flowering. Louis XIV's (*r.* 1643–1715) much celebrated utterance, "I am the State," captures the essence of this doctrine as no other expression could. The fact that these monarchs understood their power to come solely from God connects the absolutism of France with the "divine right" theory of monarchy that was expressed by James VI of Scotland (*r.* 1567–1625) (who became James I of England in 1603) in *The Trew Law of Free Monarchies.*

When Elizabeth I (*r.* 1558–1603), the last Tudor monarch, died without issue in 1603, the throne passed to James Stuart, the son of her cousin Mary, Queen of Scots. Arriving in London as a foreigner, James I was not familiar with the relationship his predecessors had worked out with Parliament. In fact, the common articulation of this "Tudor Compromise" was that the monarch ruled "in Parliament." Although this arrangement had worked remarkably well for decades, James I's absolutist leanings would not allow him to accept it unquestioningly. The "wisest fool in Christendom," as James was known, lived up to his billing as he constantly challenged or defied Parliament's authority and sought to enhance the monarch's prerogative.

When Charles I (*r.* 1625–1649) succeeded his father in 1625, the royal quarrel with Parliament intensified. Between 1629 and 1640, the king refused to call the body into session and committed almost every imaginable offense against what Parliament took to be its own liberties. Forced by his own need for money to reconvene the Lords and Commons in 1640, Charles confronted Members determined to fight back against his own absolutist pretensions. In fact, both parties to the escalating contest over sovereignty raised troops, and in 1642, these armies went to war against each other. As in France, there was a religious dimension to the political struggle: Many Members of the House of Commons were Puritans, or reformed Protestants, and the king's support-ers tended to be more orthodox Anglicans. But the principal issue at stake in the English Civil War of the 1640s was whether the monarch would have to share meaningful power in the state with the Lords and Commons, or be free to possess sovereignty himself.

The defeat of the royal army, and the trial and execution of the king that followed in 1649, definitely gave Parliament the upper hand. Ironically, however, the most famous political tract to emerge in the immediate aftermath of the events—*Leviathan,* published by Thomas Hobbes (1588–1679) in 1651—

argued for the absolutist case, on the grounds that human beings are so unruly by nature that they need an irresistibly strong, or "sovereign," authority over them. The winners of the English Civil War actually tried to rule for eleven years without a king. What may have appeared to be the sovereignty of the Parliament, however, turned out to be a dictatorship vested in Oliver Cromwell (1599–1658). By 1660, the situation had become untenable, and a newly elected Parliament invited the son of the executed king to come and reign as Charles II (r. 1660–1685). At the moment of the Restoration, it was declared that the government of England was to be by "Kings, Lords, and Commons." Although such language sought to heal the divisions from the Civil War, it did not definitively settle the question of who would possess the upper hand.

Charles II had plenty of his own arguments with Parliament over the extent of the royal prerogative, but he knew enough from his father's brutal fate not to push such disagreements too far. Upon the restored king's death, however, his younger brother ascended the throne as James II (r. 1685–1688) and the tension between monarch and Parliament heated to dangerous levels. The new king guaranteed his own unpopularity by systematically violating laws that discriminated against Catholics, long a suspect group in England as a result of hostility spawned of the Reformation and the Tudors' creation of a national Protestant church. None too secretly, James II was a Catholic himself, and in the spring of 1688, he and his second wife (also a Catholic) produced a son and heir and had him baptized in the Roman Church. In June of that same year, leaders of Parliament invited William (1650–1702), Prince of Orange, and husband of James's daughter Mary (1662–1694) from an earlier Protestant marriage, to take the English throne with his wife and avert a Catholic succession. Since neither James II nor any significant force acting on his behalf contested this move, the revolution was dubbed "Glorious" for being accomplished without bloodshed. (Ample bloodshed would come in ensuing years, but most of the Jacobite violence occurred outside of England.)

In view of the fact that Parliament had dethroned a legitimate king and enthroned his successor, a prima facie case appears to have been made that the "Glorious Revolution" of 1688 vested sovereignty with that body. The following year, Parliament further diminished the royal prerogative and elevated its own by requiring the monarch to sign a Bill of Rights that guaranteed specific parliamentary and popular liberties and forever outlawed a Catholic succession in England. One who had sided with the Parliament against the Stuart kings in their long-standing duel over the extent of each other's authority was John Locke (1632–1704). His *Two Treatises of Civil Government* were written while Charles II was still on the throne, but were not published until 1690. For this reason,

Locke's views on the role of government, natural rights, the social contract, popular sovereignty, and the legitimacy of revolution are inextricably linked with the resolution of England's own violent and protracted struggle over these fundamental questions of the Early-Modern body politic.

# DEFENSE OF LIBERTY AGAINST TYRANTS
## ANONYMOUS

*The Defense of Liberty Against Tyrants* was written by an anonymous
French Protestant, and appeared seven years after the infamous Massacre
of Saint Bartholomew's Day, on which day large numbers of Huguenots
(French Calvinists) were murdered as both political and religious threats
to the French monarchy.

1579

### The First Question:
### Whether Subjects are Bound to Obey Princes if
### they Command that which is Against the Law of God

This question may seem at the first view to be altogether superfluous and unprofitable, for it seems to make a doubt of an axiom always held infallible amongst
Christians, confirmed by many testimonies in Holy Scripture, divers examples
of the histories of all ages, and by the death of all the holy martyrs. For it may be
well demanded why Christians have endured so many afflictions unless they were          5
always persuaded that God must be obeyed simply and absolutely, and kings, unless they command not that which is repugnant to the law of God. On the other
hand, why should the apostles have answered that God must rather be obeyed
than men, and also seeing that only the will of God is always just, and that of
men may be, and often is, unjust, who can doubt that we must always obey God's          10
commandments without any exception, and men's ever with limitation?

But there are in our day many princes calling themselves Christians who
arrogantly assume an unlimited power, over which God Himself has no command, and they have no want of flatterers who adore them as gods upon earth,
many others also who, from fear or by constraint, either seem or do believe          15
that princes ought to be obeyed in all things, and by all men…. These princes
exceed their bounds, not contenting themselves with that authority which the
almighty and all-good God has given them, but seek to usurp that sovereignty
which He has reserved to Himself over all men; not content to command the
bodies and goods of their subjects at their pleasure, they assume license to enforce          20

---

Junius Brutus, *Vindiciae Contra Tyrannos: A Defense of Liberty Against Tyrants* (London, 1689)
[modernized].

consciences, which appertains chiefly to Jesus Christ. Holding the earth not great enough for their ambition, they will climb and conquer heaven itself....

## The Second Question:
### Whether it is Lawful to Resist a Prince who Infringes the Law of God, or Ruins His Church.
### By Whom, How, and to What Extent it is Lawful

This question seems at first view to be of a high and difficult nature, since there is small occasion to speak to princes that fear God. On the contrary, there will be
5    much danger to trouble the ears of those who acknowledge no other sovereign but themselves, for which reason few or none have meddled with it, and if any have at all touched it, it has been only in passing. The question is—Is it lawful to resist a prince violating the law of God, or ruinating the church, or hindering the restoring of it? If we hold ourselves to the tenor of the Holy Scripture,
10   it will resolve us. For, if it was lawful for the Jewish people (the which may be easily gathered from the books of the Old Testament); yea, since it had been enjoined them, I believe it will not be denied that the same must be allowed to the whole people of any Christian kingdom or country whatsoever....

But I see well an objection will be made here. What will you say? That a
15   whole people, that beast of many heads, must they run in a mutinous dis-order to order the business of the commonwealth? What address or direction is there in an unruly and unbridled multitude? What counsel or wisdom, to manage the affairs of state?

When we speak of all the people, we understand by that only those who
20   hold their authority from the people—to wit, the magistrates—who are inferior to the king and whom the people have substituted or established, as it were, consorts in the empire, and with a kind of tribunicial authority to restrain the encroachments of sovereignty and to represent the whole body of the people. We understand also the assembly of the estates, which is nothing else but an
25   epitome, or brief collection of the kingdom, to whom all public affairs have special and absolute reference; such were the seventy ancients in the kingdom of Israel, amongst whom the high priest was, as it were, president...

## The Third Question:
### Whether it is Lawful to Resist a Prince Who Oppresses or Ruins a Public State, And how far such Resistance may be Extended.
### By Whom, How, and by What Right or Law it is Permitted

Since we must here discuss the lawful authority of a lawful prince, I am confident that this question will be the less acceptable to tyrants and wicked princes; for it is no marvel if those who receive no law but what their own will and fancy dictate unto them be deaf unto the voice of that law which is grounded upon reason. But I persuade myself that good princes will willingly entertain this discourse, insomuch as they know that all magistrates, be they of ever so high a rank, are but an animated and speaking law. Nothing, therefore, that may be 5 pressed home against the bad can fall within any inference against good kings or princes, since good and bad princes are opposite and contrary. Therefore, that which shall be urged against tyrants is so far from detracting anything from kings; on the contrary, the more tyrants are laid open in their proper colors, the more glorious does the true worth and dignity of kings appear; neither can 10 the vicious imperfections of the one be laid open without giving addition of perfections and respect to the honor of the other.

But for tyrants, let them say and think what they please; that shall be the least of my care, for it is not to them, but against them, that I write. Kings, I believe, will readily consent to that which is propounded, for by true proportion 15 of reason they ought as much to hate tyrants and wicked governors as shepherds hate wolves, physicians, poisoners, true prophets, false doctors. It must necessarily occur that reason infuses into good kings as much hatred against tyrants as nature imprints in dogs against wolves, for as the one lives by rapine and spoil, so the other is born or bred to redress and prevent all such outrages.... 20

We have shown before that it is God Who appoints kings, Who chooses them, Who gives the kingdom to them. Now we say that the people establish kings, puts the scepter into their hands, and who with their suffrages approves the election. God would have it done in this manner, so that kings should acknowledge that, after God, they hold their power and sovereignty from the 25 people, and that it might the rather induce them to apply and address the utmost of their care and thoughts for the profit of the people, without being puffed with any vain ideas that they were formed of any matter more excellent than other men... But let them remember and know that they are of the same mold and condition as others, raised from the earth by the voice and 30 acclamations, as it were, upon the shoulders of the people unto their thrones, that they might afterwards bear on their own shoulders the greatest burdens of the commonwealth....

Since no one was ever born with a crown on his head and scepter in his hand, and since no man can be a king by himself nor reign without people—on 35 the contrary, the people may subsist of themselves, and did long before they had any kings—it must of necessity follow that kings were at first constituted by the people....

To conclude in a word, all kings at first were elected, and those who at this day seem to have their crowns and royal authority by inheritance have, or 40

should have, first and principally their confirmation from the people. Briefly, although the people of some countries have been accustomed to choose their kings of a lineage which for some notable merits have worthily deserved it, yet we must believe that they choose the stock itself, and not every branch that
5    proceeds from it; neither are they so tied to that election that, if the successor degenerate, they may not choose another more worthy…

Now, seeing that the people choose and establish their kings, it follows that the whole body of the people is above the king; for it is a thing most evident that he who is established by another is accounted under him who
10   has established him, and he who receives his authority from another is less than he from whom he derives his power. Potiphar the Egyptian set Joseph over all his house; Nebuchadnezar, Daniel over the province of Babylon; Darius, the six score governors over the kingdom…. So it is that for the ship's voyage, the owner appoints a pilot over her, who sits at the helm and
15   ensures she keeps her course, nor runs upon any dangerous shelf. The pilot, doing his duty, is obeyed by the mariners; still, the pilot is a servant as well as the least in the ship, from whom he only differs in this, that he serves in a better place than they do.

In a commonwealth, commonly compared to a ship, the king holds the
20   place of pilot, the people in general are owners of the vessel, obeying the pilot while he is careful of the public good. This pilot neither is, nor ought to be, esteemed other than servant to the public; as a judge or general in war differs little from other officers but that he is bound to bear greater burdens and expose himself to more dangers…. Furthermore, there is an infinite sort
25   of people who live without a king, but we cannot imagine a king without people….

For truly neither are subjects, as it is commonly said, the king's slaves or bondsmen, being neither prisoners taken in the wars nor bought for money. But, as considered in one entire body, they are lords, as we have formerly
30   proved; so each of them in particular ought to be held as the king's brothers and kinsmen. And to avoiding thinking this strange, let us hear what God Himself says when He prescribes a law to kings—that they lift not their heart above their brethren from amongst whom they were chosen…. The almighty and all-good God, of whose great gentleness and mercy we are
35   daily partakers, and very seldom feel His severity, although we justly deserve it, yet is it always mercifully mixed with compassion; whereby He teaches princes, His lieutenants, that subjects ought rather to be held in obedience by love than by fear….

## The Fourth Question:
### Whether Neighbor Princes May, or are Bound by Law to, Aid the Subjects of other Princes Persecuted for True Religion, or Oppressed by Manifest Tyranny

We have one other question to discuss.... We have already sufficiently proved that all tyrants, whether those who seek to captivate the minds and souls of the people with an erroneous and superstitious opinion in matter of religion, or those who would enthrall their bodies and estates with miserable servitude and excessive impositions, may justly by the people be both suppressed 5 and expelled. But, since tyrants are for the most part so cunning and subjects seldom so cautious that the disease is hardly known or, at the least, not carefully observed before the remedy prove almost desperate, nor think of their own defense before they are brought to those straits that they are unable to defend themselves, but compelled to implore the assistance of others. Our question 10 therefore is if Christian princes lawfully may, and ought to, succor those subjects who are afflicted for true religion, or oppressed by unjust servitude, and whose sufferings are either for the kingdom of Christ, or for the liberty of their own state? There are many, who, hoping to advance their own ends and encroach on others' rights, will readily embrace the afflicted and proclaim the lawfulness of 15 it; but the hope of gain is the certain and only aim of their purposes....

...Briefly, to epitomize what has been said, if a prince outrageously overpass the bounds of piety and justice, a neighbor prince may justly and religiously leave his own country, not to invade and usurp another's, but to contain the other within the limits of justice and equity. And if he neglect or omit his duty 20 herein, he shows himself a wicked and unworthy magistrate....

Finally, as there have ever been tyrants scattered here and there, so also all histories testify that there have been neighboring princes to oppose tyranny and maintain the people in their right. The princes of these times, by imitating so worthy examples, should suppress the tyrants both of bodies and souls, 25 and restrain the oppressors both of the commonwealth and of the church of Christ. Otherwise, they themselves may most deservedly be branded with that infamous title of tyrant.

And to conclude this discourse in a word, piety commands that the law and church of God be maintained. Justice requires that tyrants and destroyers 30 of the commonwealth be compelled to reason. Charity challenges the right of relieving and restoring the oppressed. Those who make no account of these things do as much as in them lies to drive piety, justice, and charity out of this world, that they may never more be heard of.

# THE TRUE LAW OF FREE MONARCHIES
## JAMES VI (1566–1625), KING OF SCOTLAND (1567–1625)

*James VI of Scotland was the son of Mary, Queen of Scots, and Henry,
Lord Darnley. As the closest kinsman of Queen Elizabeth I, he became
King James I of England at her death in 1603. Until it happened, however, his accession was by no means a sure thing. James wrote this treatise
in 1598 as an expression of his views on the relationship between a ruler
and his subjects.*

1598

Accept, I pray you (my dear countrymen) as thankfully this pamphlet that I
offer unto you as lovingly it is written for your well-being. I would be loath
both to be faschious and feckless, and therefore, if it be not sententious[1], at
least it is short. It may be you miss many things that you look for in it. But for
excuse thereof, consider rightly that I only lay down herein the true grounds      5
to teach you the right way, without wasting time upon refuting the adversaries.
And yet I trust, if you will take narrow tent,[2] you shall find most of their great
guns paid home again[3], either with contrary conclusions or tacit objections,
suppose in a dairned form[4] and indirectly. For my intention is to instruct and
not irritate, if I may eschew it. The profit I would wish you to make of it is as   10
well so to frame all your actions according to these grounds as may confirm you
in the course of honest and obedient subjects to your king in all times coming,
as also when you shall fall in purpose[5] with any that shall praise or excuse the
by-past rebellions that broke forth either in this country or in any other, you
shall herewith be armed against their siren songs, laying their particular examples  15
to the square of[6] these grounds. Whereby you shall soundly keep the course
of righteous judgment, discerning wisely of every action only according to the
quality thereof, and not according to your pre-judged conceits[7] of the commit-

---

[1] *Faschious*—troublesome; *feckless*—worthless; *sententious*—pithy
[2] *Take narrow tent*—pay careful attention
[3] *Paid home again*—refuted; turned back on them
[4] *Suppose in a dairned form*—subtly
[5] *Fall in purpose*—fall into conversation
[6] *Laying…to the square of*—measuring against
[7] *Conceits*—opinions

---

*The Political Works of James I*, edited by Charles Howard McIlwain (Cambridge: Harvard
University Press, 1918), 53–56, 62–63 [modernized].

ters; so shall you, by reaping profit to yourselves, turn my pain[8] into pleasure. But lest the whole pamphlet run out at the gaping mouth of this preface, if it were any more enlarged, I end, with committing you to God, and me to your charitable censures.

5     As there is not a thing so necessary to be known by the people of any land, next the knowledge of their God, as the right knowledge of their allegiance, according to the form of government established among them, especially in a monarchy (which form of government, as resembling the Divinity, approaches nearest to perfection, as all the learned and wise men from the beginning have 10 agreed upon, unity being the perfection of all things), so has the ignorance and (which is worse) the seduced opinion of the multitude blinded by them, who think themselves able to teach and instruct the ignorant, procured the wreck and overthrow of sundry flourishing commonwealths, and heaped heavy calamities, threatening utter destruction upon others. And the smiling success that 15 unlawful rebellions have often times had against princes in ages past (such have been the misery and iniquity of the time) have by way of practice strengthened many in their error; albeit there cannot be a more deceptive argument than to judge the justness of the cause by the outcome thereof, as hereafter shall be proved more at length. And, among others, no commonwealth that ever has 20 been since the beginning has had greater need of the true knowledge of this ground than this, our so-long dis-ordered and distracted commonwealth, has. The mis-knowledge hereof being the only spring from whence have flowed so many endless calamities, miseries, and confusions, as is better felt by many, than the cause thereof well known and deeply considered.

25     The natural zeal therefore, that I bear to this, my native country, with the great pity I have to see the so-long disturbance thereof, for lack of the true knowledge of this ground (as I have said before) has compelled me at last to break silence, to discharge my conscience to you, my dear countrymen, herein, that knowing the ground from whence these, your many endless troubles, have 30 proceeded, as well as you have already too-long tasted the bitter fruits thereof, you may, by knowledge and eschewing of the cause, escape and divert the lamentable effects that ever necessarily follow thereupon.

    I have chosen, then, only to set down in this short treatise the true grounds of the mutual duty and allegiance betwixt a free and absolute monarchy and his 35 people; not to trouble your patience with answering the contrary propositions, which some have not been ashamed to set down in writ, to the poisoning of infinite number of simple souls, and their own perpetual and well-deserved infamy. For by answering them, I could not have eschewed whiles[9] to pick and

---

[8] *Pain*—effort

[9] *Whiles*—from time to time

bite well saltly[10] their persons; which would rather have bred contentiousness among the readers (as they had liked or mis-liked) than sound instruction of the truth. Which I protest to Him that is the searcher of all hearts, is the only mark that I shoot at herein.

First then, I will set down the true grounds whereupon I am to build, out of the Scriptures, since monarchy is the true pattern of Divinity, as I have already said. Next, from the fundamental laws of our own kingdom, which nearest must concern us. Thirdly, from the law of nature, by diverse similitudes drawn out of the same, and will conclude thereafter by answering the most weighty and appearing incommodities that can be objected.

The prince's duty to his subjects is so clearly set down in many places of the Scriptures, and so openly confessed by all the good princes, according to their oath in their coronation, as not needing to be long therein, I shall as shortly as I can run through it.

Kings are called gods by the prophetical King David,[11] because they sit upon God's throne in the earth, and have the account of their administration to give unto him. Their office is to minister justice and judgment to the people, as the same David says, to advance the good, and punish the evil; as he likewise says, to establish good laws to his people, and procure obedience to the same, as diverse good Kings of Judah did. To procure the peace of the people, as the same David says. To decide all controversies that can arise among them, as Solomon did. To be the minister of God for the wealth of them that do well and, as the minister of God, to take vengeance upon them that do evil, as Saint Paul says. And finally, as a good pastor, to go out and in before his people, as is said in the first of Samuel, that through the prince's prosperity, the people's peace may be procured, as Jeremiah says.[12]

And therefore in the coronation of our own kings, as well as of every Christian monarchy, they give their oath, first to maintain the religion presently professed within their country, according to their laws, whereby it is established, and to punish all those that should press to alter or disturb the profession thereof. And next to maintain all the lowable[13] and good laws made by their predecessors; to see them put in execution, and the breakers and violators thereof to be punished, according to the tenor of the same. And lastly, to maintain the whole country, and every estate therein, in all their ancient privileges and liberties, as well against all foreign enemies as among themselves. And, in short, to procure the good

---

[10] *To pick and bite well saltly*—to attack sharply

[11] Psalm 82:6

[12] Psalm 101; II Kings 18:3, 22:2, 23:3; II Chronicles 29:2, 34:2, 35:26–27; Psalm 72:7; I Kings 3:9; Romans 13:4; I Samuel 8:19–20; Jeremiah 29:7

[13] *Lowable*—desirable, permissible

and flourishing of his people, not only in maintaining and putting to execution the old allowable laws of the country, and by establishing of new (as necessity and evil manners will require), but by all other means possible to foresee and present all dangers that are likely to fall upon them, and to maintain concord,

5 wealth, and civility among them, as a loving father and careful watchman, caring for them more than for himself, knowing himself to be ordained for them, and they not for him; and therefore accountable to that great God, who placed him as his lieutenant over them, upon the peril of his soul to procure the wealth of both souls and bodies, as far as in him lies, of all them that are committed to his

10 charge. And this oath in the coronation is the clearest, civil, and fundamental law whereby the king's office is properly defined.

By the law of nature, the king becomes a natural father to all his lieges at his coronation. And as the father of his fatherly duty is bound to care for the nourishing, education, and virtuous government of his children, even so is the

15 king bound to care for all his subjects. As all the toil and pain that the father can take for his children will be thought light and well bestowed by him, so that the effect thereof redound to their profit and wealth, so ought the prince to do towards his people. As the kindly father ought to foresee all inconvenience and dangers that may arise towards his children, and though with the hazard of his

20 own person press to prevent the same, so ought the king towards his people. As the father's wrath and correction upon any of his children that offends ought to be by a fatherly chastisement seasoned with pity, as long as there is any hope of amendment in them, so ought the king towards any of his lieges that offend in that measure. And shortly, as the father's chief joy ought to be in procuring

25 his children's welfare, rejoicing at their wealth, sorrowing and pitying at their evil, to hazard for their safety, travel for their rest, wake for their sleep, and, in a word, to think that his earthly felicity and life stands and lives more in them than in himself; so ought a good prince think of his people....

And according to these fundamental laws already alleged, we daily see that

30 in the Parliament (which is nothing else but the head court of the king and his vassals) the laws are but craved by his subjects, and only made by him at their rogation[14] and with their advice. For albeit the king make daily statutes and ordinances, enjoining such pains thereto as he thinks meet, without any advice of Parliament or estates; yet it lies in the power of no Parliament to make

35 any kind of law or statute unless his scepter give to it the force of a law. And although diverse changes have been in other countries of the blood royal and kingly house, the kingdom being reft by conquest from one to another, as in our neighbor country in England (which was never in ours), yet the same ground of

---

[14]*Rogation*—formal request

the king's right over all the land and subjects thereof remains alike in all other free monarchies as well as in this. For when the Bastard of Normandy[15] came into England and made himself king, was it not by force, and with a mighty army? Where he gave the law, and took none, changed the laws, inverted the order of government, set down the strangers, his followers, in many of the old possessors' rooms, as at this day well appears a great part of the gentlemen in England, being come of the Norman blood and their old laws, which to this day they are ruled by, are written in his language, and not in theirs. And yet his successors have, with great happiness, enjoyed the Crown to this day; whereof the like was also done by all them that conquered them before.

And for conclusion of this point, that the king is over-lord over the whole lands, it is likewise daily proved by the law of our hordes, of want of heirs, and of bastardies. For if a hoard be found under the earth, because it is no more in the keeping or use of any person, it of the law pertains to the king. If a person, inheritor of any lands or goods, die without any sort of heirs, all his lands and goods return to the king. And if a bastard die un-rehabited[16] without heirs of his body (which rehabiting only lies in the king's hands), all that he has likewise returns to the king. And as you see it manifest that the king is over-lord of the whole land, so is he master over every person that inhabits the same, having power over the life and death of every one of them. For although a just prince will not take the life of any of his subjects without a clear law; yet the same laws whereby he takes them are made by himself, or his predecessors; and so the power flows always from himself. As by daily experience we see, good and just princes will from time to time make new laws and statutes, adjoining the penalties to the breakers thereof, which before the law was made had been no crime to the subject to have committed. Not that I deny the old definition of a king, and of a law, which makes the king to be a speaking law, and the law a dumb king, for certainly a king that governs not by his law can neither be countable to God for his administration nor have a happy and established reign. For albeit it be true that I have at length proved that the king is above the law, as both the author and giver of strength thereto; yet a good king will not only delight to rule his subjects by the law, but even will conform himself in his own actions thereunto, always keeping that ground, that the health of the common-wealth be his chief law. And where he sees the law doubtsome or rigorous, he may interpret or mitigate the same, lest otherwise *summum ius* be *summa iniuria*. And therefore general laws, made publicly in Parliament, may upon known respects to the king by his authority be mitigated and suspended upon causes only known to him....

---

[15]William I, King of England (1066–1087) and Duke of Normandy (1035–1087)

[16]*Un-rehabited*—not having been declared legitimate in the eyes of the law

# THE PETITION OF RIGHT

*Charles I, King of England (1625–1649), and his Parliaments were at odds from the moment of his accession. Charles married a foreign Catholic princess, collected taxes and forced loans without the explicit consent of Parliament, and arrested critics by special command without formally charging them, all while badly prosecuting a war against both France and Spain. Galvanized into unity by Charles's behavior and decisions, Parliament presented this* Petition of Right *to the king. Confronted by the rare solidarity of Parliament, and desperately short of money, King Charles formally accepted the Petition on 7 June 1628.*

7 JUNE 1628

TO THE KING'S MOST EXCELLENT MAJESTY.

Humbly show unto our Sovereign Lord the King, the Lords Spiritual and Temporal, and Commons in Parliament assembled, that whereas it is declared and enacted by a statute made in the time of the reign of King Edward the First, commonly called *Statutum de Tallagio non concedendo*, that no tallage or aid shall be laid or levied by the King or his heirs in this realm without the goodwill and 5 assent of the archbishops, bishops, earls, barons, knights, burgesses, and other the freemen of the commonalty of this realm; and by authority of Parliament holden in the five and twentieth year of the reign of King Edward the Third it is declared and enacted that from thenceforth no person shall be compelled to make any loans to the King against his will, because such loans were against 10 reason and the franchise of the land; and by other laws of this realm it is provided that none should be charged by any charge or imposition, called a benevolence, or by such like charge, by which the statutes before-mentioned, and other the good laws and statutes of this realm, your subjects have inherited this freedom, that they should not be compelled to contribute to any tax, tallage, aid, or other 15 like charge, not set by common consent in Parliament.

Yet nevertheless, of late divers commissions directed to sundry commissioners in several counties with instructions have issued, by means whereof your people have been in divers places assembled and required to lend certain

*The Constitutional Documents of the Puritan Revolution, 1625–1660*, edited by Samuel Gardiner (Oxford: Clarendon, 1906), 66–70.

sums of money unto Your Majesty, and many of them upon their refusal so to do have had an oath administered unto them, not warrantable by the laws or statutes of this realm, and have been constrained to become bound to make appearance and give attendance before your Privy Council and in other places,

5  and others of them have been therefore imprisoned, confined, and sundry other ways molested and disquieted; and divers other charges have been laid and levied upon your people in several counties by lords lieutenants, deputy-lieutenants, commissioners for musters, justices of peace, and others, by command or direction from Your Majesty or your Privy Council, against the laws

10  and free customs of this realm.

And where also by the statute called *The Great Charter of the Liberties of England* it is declared and enacted that no freeman may be taken or imprisoned, or be disseised of his freeholds or liberties or his free customs, or be outlawed or exiled, or in any manner destroyed, but by the lawful judgment of his peers,

15  or by the law of the land.

And in the eight and twentieth year of the reign of King Edward the Third, it was declared and enacted by authority of Parliament that no man of what estate or condition that he be, should be put out of his lands or tenements, nor taken, nor imprisoned, nor disherited, nor put to death, without being brought

20  to answer by due process of law.

Nevertheless, against the tenor of the said statutes, and other the good laws and statutes of your realm, to that end provided, divers of your subjects have of late been imprisoned without any cause showed, and when for their deliverance they were brought before your justices by Your Majesty's writs of *habeas corpus*,

25  there to undergo and receive as the Court should order, and their keepers commanded to certify the causes of their detainer; no cause was certified but that they were detained by Your Majesty's special command, signified by the Lords of your Privy Council, and yet were returned back to several prisons, without being charged with anything to which they might make answer according to

30  the law.

And whereas of late great companies of soldiers and mariners have been dispersed into divers counties of the realm, and the inhabitants against their wills have been compelled to receive them into their houses, and there to suffer them to sojourn, against the laws and customs of this realm, and to the great

35  grievance and vexation of the people.

And whereas also by authority of Parliament, in the twenty-fifth year of the reign of King Edward the Third, it is declared and enacted that no man shall be forejudged of life or limb against the form of the Great Charter, and the law of the land; and by the said Great Charter and other the laws and statutes of this

40  your realm, no man ought to be adjudged to death but by the laws established in

this your realm, either by the customs of the same realm or by acts of Parliament; and whereas no offender of what kind soever is exempted from the proceedings to be used, and punishments to be inflicted by the laws and statutes of this your realm, nevertheless of late divers commissions under Your Majesty's Great Seal have issued forth, by which certain persons have been assigned and appointed commissioners with power and authority to proceed within the laud, according to the justice of martial law against such soldiers and mariners, or other dissolute persons joining with them, as should commit any murder, robbery, felony, mutiny, or other outrage or misdemeanour whatsoever, and by such summary course and order, as is agreeable to martial law and is used in armies in time of war, to proceed to the trial and condemnation of such offenders, and them to cause to be executed and put to death, according to the law martial.

By pretext whereof, some of Your Majesty's subjects have been by some of the said commissioners put to death, when and where, if by the laws and statutes of the land they had deserved death, by the same laws and statutes also they might, and by no other ought to have been adjudged and executed:

And also sundry grievous offenders by colour thereof, claiming an exemption, have escaped the punishments due to them by the laws and statutes of this your realm, by reason that divers of your officers and ministers of justice have unjustly refused, or forborne to proceed against such offenders according to the same laws and statutes, upon pretence that the said offenders were punishable only by martial law, and by authority of such commissions as aforesaid, which commissions, and all other of like nature, are wholly and directly contrary to the said laws and statutes of this your realm:

They do therefore humbly pray Your Most Excellent Majesty that no man hereafter be compelled to make or yield any gift, loan, benevolence, tax, or such like charge, without common consent by act of Parliament; and that none be called to make answer, or take such oath, or to give attendance, or be confined, or otherwise molested or disquieted concerning the same, or for refusal thereof; and that no freeman, in any such manner as is before-mentioned, be imprisoned or detained; and that Your Majesty will be pleased to remove the said soldiers and mariners, and that your people may not be so burdened in time to come; and that the foresaid commissions for proceeding by martial law may be revoked and annulled; and that hereafter no commissions of like nature may issue forth to any person or persons whatsoever, to be executed as aforesaid, lest by colour of them any of Your Majesty's subjects be destroyed or put to death, contrary to the laws and franchise of the land.

All which they most humbly pray of Your Most Excellent Majesty, as their rights and liberties according to the laws and statutes of this realm: and that Your Majesty would also vouchsafe to declare that the awards, doings, and proceedings to the prejudice of your people, in any of the premises, shall not be drawn hereafter into consequence or example. And that Your Majesty would be also graciously pleased, for the further comfort and safety of your people, to declare your royal will and pleasure, that in the things aforesaid all your officers and ministers shall serve you, according to the laws and statutes of this realm, as they tender the honour of Your Majesty, and the prosperity of this kingdom.

# DENIAL OF PARLIAMENTARY JURISDICTION
## CHARLES I (1600–1649), KING OF ENGLAND (1625–1649)

*England experienced a civil war (1642–1648) as Charles I and Parliament struggled to determine which would be the locus of the nation's political and religious authority. Parliament ultimately triumphed on the battlefield and captured the king. In the fall of 1648, the Treaty of Newport was negotiated, which outlined a distribution of shared power between the monarchy and legislature. The Parliamentarian army, however, dominated by English Puritans and led by Oliver Cromwell, was mistrustful of those who wished to compromise with the king. The army, therefore, on 6 December 1648 purged Parliament, forcibly prohibiting many Members of the House of Commons from taking their seats; 83 of the 489 elected Members retained their seats.*

*The now-reduced Rump Parliament indicted the king for treason on 2 January 1649, beginning his trial. The House of Lords rejected this indictment, leading to their complete abolition by Commons. When brought before the Parliamentary court, Charles I refused to enter a plea. Instead, he offered this speech, which both defended his royal authority and rejected that of the Rump Parliament. A week later, Charles was convicted of treason. He was beheaded in London on 30 January 1649.*

21 JANUARY 1649

Having already made my protestations, not only against the illegality of this pretended court, but also that no earthly power can justly call me, who am your King, in question as a delinquent, I would not any more open my mouth upon this occasion more than to refer myself to what I have spoken were I in this case alone concerned; but the duty I owe to God in the preservation of 5 the true liberty of my people will not suffer me at this time to be silent. For how can any free-born subject of England call life or anything he possesses his own if power without right daily make new, and abrogate the old fundamental laws of the land, which I now take to be the present case? Wherefore when

*The Constitutional Documents of the Puritan Revolution, 1625–1660*, edited by Samuel Gardiner (Oxford: Clarendon, 1906), 374–76.

I came hither, I expected that you would have endeavoured to have satisfied me concerning these grounds which hinder me to answer to your pretended impeachment. But since I see that nothing I can say will move you to it, though negatives are not so naturally proved as affirmatives, yet I will show you the
5  reason why I am confident you cannot judge me, nor indeed the meanest man in England, for I will not, like you, without showing a reason seek to impose a belief upon my subjects.

There is no proceeding just against any man but what is warranted either by God's laws or the municipal laws of the country where he lives. Now I am
10  most confident this day's proceeding cannot be warranted by God's laws; for, on the contrary, the authority of obedience unto Kings is clearly warranted and strictly commanded in both the Old and New Testament, which, if denied, I am ready instantly to prove.

And for the question now in hand, there it is said that "where the word of
15  a King is, there is power; and who may say unto him, what dost thou?"[1] Then for the law of this land, I am no less confident that no learned lawyer will affirm that an impeachment can lie against the King, they all going in his name; and one of their maxims is that the King can do no wrong. Besides, the law upon which you ground your proceedings must either be old or new—if old, show
20  it; if new, tell what authority, warranted by the fundamental laws of the land, has made it, and when. But how the House of Commons can erect a Court of Judicature, which was never one itself (as is well known to all lawyers) I leave to God and the world to judge. And it were full as strange that they should pretend to make laws without King or Lords' House, to any that have heard
25  speak of the laws of England.

And admitting, but not granting, that the people of England's commission could grant your pretended power, I see nothing you can show for that, for certainly you never asked the question of the tenth man in the kingdom, and in this way you manifestly wrong even the poorest ploughman if you demand
30  not his free consent; nor can you pretend any colour for this your pretended commission without the consent at least of the major part of every man in England of whatsoever quality or condition, which I am sure you never went about to seek, so far are you from having it.

Thus you see that I speak not for my own right alone, as I am your King,
35  but also for the true liberty of all my subjects, which consists not in the power of government, but in living under such laws, such a government as may give themselves the best assurance of their lives and property of their goods; nor in this must or do I forget the privileges of both Houses of Parliament, which this

---

[1]Ecclesiastes 8:4

day's proceedings do not only violate, but likewise occasion the greatest breach of their public faith that (I believe) ever was heard of, with which I am far from charging the two Houses; for all the pretended crimes laid against me bear date long before this Treaty at Newport, in which I having concluded as much as in me lay, and hopefully expecting the Houses' agreement thereunto, I was sud- 5 denly surprised and hurried from thence as a prisoner; upon which account I am against my will brought hither, where since I am come, I cannot but to my power defend the ancient laws and liberties of this kingdom, together with my own just right. Then for anything I can see, the higher House is totally excluded; and for the House of Commons, it is too well known that the major part of them 10 are detained or deterred from sitting; so as if I had no other, this were sufficient for me to protest against the lawfulness of your pretended Court.

Besides all this, the peace of the kingdom is not the least in my thoughts; and what hope of settlement is there so long as power reigns without rule or law, changing the whole frame of that government under which this kingdom 15 has flourished for many hundred years? Nor will I say what will fall out in case this lawless, unjust proceeding against me do go on. And believe it, the Commons of England will not thank you for this change; for they will remember how happy they have been of late years under the reigns of Queen Elizabeth, the King my father, and myself, until the beginning of these unhappy troubles, 20 and will have cause to doubt that they shall never be so happy under any new; and by this time it will be too sensibly evident that the arms I took up were only to defend the fundamental laws of this kingdom against those who have supposed my power has totally changed the ancient government.

Thus, having showed you briefly the reasons why I cannot submit to your 25 pretended authority without violating the trust which I have from God for the welfare and liberty of my people, I expect from you either clear reasons to convince my judgment, showing me that I am in an error (and then truly I will answer) or that you will withdraw your proceedings.

# LEVIATHAN
## THOMAS HOBBES (1588–1679)

*Thomas Hobbes, fearing war was about to erupt in England, went into self-imposed exile in 1641 and returned ten years later. While in France, he wrote* Leviathan, *a secular defense of monarchy based on his understanding of the emerging scientific revolution.*

1651

### Of the Interior Beginnings of Voluntary Motions

I§6 …That which men desire, they are also said to *love*: and to *hate* those things for which they have aversion. So that desire and love are the same thing; save that by desire, we always signify the absence of the object; by love, most commonly the presence of the same. So also by aversion, we signify the absence; and by hate, the presence of the object.                                   5

Of appetites and aversions, some are born with men; as appetite of food, appetite of excretion, and exoneration, which may also and more properly be called aversions, from somewhat they feel in their bodies; and some other appetites, not many. The rest, which are appetites of particular things, proceed from experience, and trial of their effects upon themselves or other men. For of things   10
we know not at all, or believe not to be, we can have no further desire, than to taste and try. But aversion we have for things, not only which we know have hurt us, but also that we do not know whether they will hurt us, or not.…

And because the constitution of a man's body is in continual mutation, it is impossible that all the same things should always cause in him the same   15
appetites and aversions: much less can all men consent in the desire of almost any one and the same object.

But whatsoever is the object of any man's appetite or desire, that is it which he for his part calls *good*; and the object of his hate and aversion, *evil*; and of his contempt, *vile* and *inconsiderable*. For these words of good, evil, and con-   20
temptible are ever used with relation to the person that uses them, there being nothing simply and absolutely so, nor any common rule of good and evil to be taken from the nature of the objects themselves, but from the person of the

*The English Works of Thomas Hobbes of Malmesbury*, edited by Sir William Molesworth (London: John Bohn, 1839), III:40–41, 61, 74, 85–87, 93, 110–21, 130–31, 145–47, 151, 153–54, 157–61, 162, 163, 169, 170, 186, 194–98, 199–200, 203, 206, 208, 250, 251, 252, 253–54, 256–57, 310–11, 335–36, 355–56, 427, 537, 538, 577

man, where there is no commonwealth; or, in a commonwealth, from the person that represents it; or from an arbitrator or judge, whom men disagreeing shall by consent set up, and make his sentence the rule thereof....

### Of the Virtues Commonly Called Intellectual

I§8...The passions that most of all cause the difference of wit are principally the
5   more or less desire of power, or riches, of knowledge, and of honor. All which may be reduced to the first, that is, desire of power. For riches, knowledge, and honor are but several sorts of power.

And therefore, a man who has no great passion for any of these things, but is, as men term it, indifferent, though he may be so far a good man as to
10   be free from giving offence, yet he cannot possibly have either a great fancy or much judgment. For the thoughts are to the desires as scouts and spies to range abroad and find the way to the things desired....

### Of Power, Worth, Dignity, Honor, and Worthiness

I§10...The greatest of human powers, is that which is compounded of the powers of most men, united by consent, in one person, natural, or civil, that
15   has the use of all their powers depending on his will; such as is the power of a commonwealth....

### Of the Difference of Manners

I§11...The felicity of this life consists not in the repose of a mind satisfied. For there is no such *finis ultimus*, utmost aim, nor *summum bonum*, greatest good, as is spoken of in the books of the old moral philosophers. Nor can a man any
20   more live whose desires are at an end than he whose senses and imaginations are at a stand. Felicity is a continual progress of the desire from one object to another; the attaining of the former being still but the way to the latter. The cause whereof is that the object of man's desire is not to enjoy once only, and for one instant of time, but to assure forever the way of his future desire. And
25   therefore the voluntary actions and inclinations of all men tend, not only to the procuring, but also to the assuring of a contented life; and differ only in the way, which arises partly from the diversity of passions in diverse men and partly from the difference of the knowledge, or opinion, each one has of the causes which produce the effect desired.

30   So that in the first place, I put for a general inclination of all mankind a perpetual and restless desire of power after power, that ceases only in death. And the cause of this is not always that a man hopes for a more intensive delight than he has already attained to, or that he cannot be content with a moderate

power, but because he cannot assure the power and means to live well which he has present without the acquisition of more. And from hence it is that kings, whose power is greatest, turn their endeavors to the assuring it at home by laws, or abroad by wars. And when that is done, there succeeds a new desire; in some, of fame from new conquest; in others, of ease and sensual pleasure; in others, of admiration, or being flattered for excellence in some art, or other ability of the mind.

Competition of riches, honor, command, or other power inclines to contention, enmity, and war because the way of one competitor to the attaining of his desire is to kill, subdue, supplant, or repel the other. Particularly, competition of praise inclines to a reverence of antiquity. For men contend with the living, not with the dead; to these ascribing more than due, that they may obscure the glory of the other.

Desire of ease and sensual delight disposes men to obey a common power, because by such desires a man does abandon the protection that might be hoped for from his own industry and labor. Fear of death and wounds disposes to the same, and for the same reason. On the contrary, needy men and hardy, not contented with their present condition, as also all men that are ambitious of military command, are inclined to continue the causes of war, and to stir up trouble and sedition, for there is no honor military but by war, nor any such hope to mend an ill game as by causing a new shuffle.

Desire of knowledge and arts of peace inclines men to obey a common power. For such desire contains a desire of leisure, and consequently protection from some other power than their own....

And they that make little or no inquiry into the natural causes of things, yet from the fear that proceeds from the ignorance itself of what it is that has the power to do them much good or harm, are inclined to suppose and feign unto themselves several kinds of powers invisible, and to stand in awe of their own imaginations, and in time of distress to invoke them, as also in the time of an expected good success to give them thanks, making the creatures of their own fancy, their gods. By which means it has come to pass that from the innumerable variety of fancy, men have created in the world innumerable sorts of gods. And this fear of things invisible is the natural seed of that which everyone in himself calls religion, and in them that worship or fear that power otherwise than they do, superstition.

And this seed of religion, having been observed by many, some of those that have observed it have been inclined thereby to nourish, dress, and form it into laws, and to add to it of their own invention any opinion of the causes of future events, by which they thought they should be best able to govern others, and make unto themselves the greatest use of their powers....

## Of the Natural Condition of Mankind

I§13Nature has made men so equal in the faculties of the body and mind as that though there be found one man sometimes manifestly stronger in body or of quicker mind than another, yet when all is reckoned together, the difference between man and man is not so considerable as that one man can thereupon
5 claim to himself any benefit to which another may not pretend as well as he. For as to the strength of body, the weakest has strength enough to kill the strongest, either by secret machination, or by confederacy with others, that are in the same danger with himself.

And as to the faculties of the mind, setting aside the arts grounded upon
10 words, and especially that skill of proceeding upon general and infallible rules, called science, which very few have, and but in few things, as being not a native faculty born with us, nor attained, as prudence, while we look after somewhat else, I find yet a greater equality amongst men than that of strength. For prudence is but experience, which equal time equally bestows on all men in those
15 things they equally apply themselves unto. That which may perhaps make such equality incredible is but a vain conceit of one's own wisdom, which almost all men think they have in a greater degree than the vulgar; that is, than all men but themselves and a few others, whom by fame, or for concurring with themselves, they approve. For such is the nature of men that howsoever they may acknowledge
20 many others to be more witty, or more eloquent, or more learned, yet they will hardly believe there be many so wise as themselves, for they see their own wit at hand and other men's at a distance. But this proves rather that men are in that point equal than unequal. For there is not ordinarily a greater sign of the equal distribution of anything than that every man is contented with his share.

25 From this equality of ability arises equality of hope in the attaining of our ends. And therefore if any two men desire the same thing, which nevertheless they cannot both enjoy, they become enemies; and in the way to their end, which is principally their own conservation, and sometimes their delectation only, endeavor to destroy or subdue one another....

30 And from this diffidence of one another, there is no way for any man to secure himself so reasonable as anticipation; that is, by force or wiles to master the persons of all men he can, so long till he see no other power great enough to endanger him. And this is no more than his own conservation requires and is generally allowed....

35 Again, men have no pleasure but, on the contrary, a great deal of grief in keeping company where there is no power able to over-awe them all. For every man looks that his companion should value him at the same rate he sets upon himself; and upon all signs of contempt or undervaluing naturally endeavors, as far as he dares, (which amongst them that have no common power to keep

them in quiet, is far enough to make them destroy each other) to extort a greater value from his contemners by damage, and from others by the example.

So that in the nature of man we find three principal causes of quarrel. First, competition; secondly, diffidence; thirdly, glory.

The first makes men invade for gain; the second, for safety; and the third, for reputation. The first use violence to make themselves masters of other men's persons, wives, children, and cattle; the second, to defend them; the third, for trifles, as a word, a smile, a different opinion, and any other sign of undervalue, either direct in their persons or by reflection in their kindred, their friends, their nation, their profession, or their name.

Hereby it is manifest that during the time men live without a common power to keep them all in awe, they are in that condition which is called war, and such a war as is of every man against every man. For war consists not in battle only, or the act of fighting, but in a tract of time wherein the will to contend by battle is sufficiently known; and therefore the notion of *time* is to be considered in the nature of war as it is in the nature of weather. For as the nature of foul weather lies not in a shower or two of rain, but in an inclination thereto of many days together, so the nature of war consists not in actual fighting, but in the known disposition thereto during all the time there is no assurance to the contrary. All other time is *peace*.

Whatsoever therefore is consequent to a time of war, where every man is enemy to every man, the same is consequent to the time wherein men live without other security than what their own strength and their own invention shall furnish them withal. In such condition there is no place for industry, because the fruit thereof is uncertain. And consequently no culture of the earth; no navigation, nor use of the commodities that may be imported by sea; no commodious building; no instruments of moving, and removing, such things as require much force; no knowledge of the face of the earth; no account of time; no arts; no letters; no society; and which is worst of all, continual fear and danger of violent death; and the life of man, solitary, poor, nasty, brutish, and short.

It may seem strange to some man that has not well weighed these things that nature should thus dissociate and render men apt to invade and destroy one another. And he may therefore, not trusting to this inference made from the passions, desire perhaps to have the same confirmed by experience. Let him therefore consider with himself, when taking a journey, he arms himself and seeks to go well-accompanied; when going to sleep, he locks his doors; when even in his house he locks his chests; and this when he knows there be laws, and public officers, armed, to revenge all injuries shall be done him; what opinion he has of his fellow-subjects when he rides armed; of his fellow citizens when he locks his doors; and of his children and servants when he locks his chests. Does he not there

as much accuse mankind by his actions as I do by my words? But neither of us accuse man's nature in it. The desires and other passions of man are in themselves no sin. No more are the actions that proceed from those passions till they know a law that forbids them, which, till laws be made, they cannot know; nor can any
5   law be made till they have agreed upon the person that shall make it.

It may peradventure be thought there was never such a time nor condition of war as this, and I believe it was never generally so over all the world. But there are many places where they live so now. For the savage people in many places of America, except the government of small families, the concord whereof depends
10   on natural lust, have no government at all, and live at this day in that brutish manner, as I said before. Howsoever, it may be perceived what manner of life there would be where there were no common power to fear, by the manner of life, which men that have formerly lived under a peaceful government use to degenerate into a civil war.

15   But though there had never been any time wherein particular men were in a condition of war one against another, yet in all times kings and persons of sovereign authority, because of their independency, are in continual jealousies, and in the state and posture of gladiators, having their weapons pointing, and their eyes fixed on one another; that is, their forts, garrisons, and guns upon
20   the frontiers of their kingdoms, and continual spies upon their neighbors, which is a posture of war. But because they uphold thereby the industry of their subjects, there does not follow from it that misery which accompanies the liberty of particular men.

To this war of every man against every man this also is consequent, that
25   nothing can be unjust. The notions of right and wrong, justice and injustice have there no place. Where there is no common power, there is no law. Where no law, no injustice. Force and fraud are in war the two cardinal virtues. Justice and injustice are none of the faculties neither of the body nor mind. If they were, they might be in a man that were alone in the world, as well as his senses and
30   passions. They are qualities that relate to men in society, not in solitude. It is consequent also to the same condition that there be no propriety, no dominion, no *mine* and *thine* distinct, but only that to be every man's that he can get, and for so long as he can keep it. And thus much for the ill condition which man by mere nature is actually placed in, though with a possibility to come out of
35   it, consisting partly in the passions, partly in his reason.

The passions that incline men to peace are fear of death, desire of such things as are necessary to commodious living, and a hope by their industry to obtain them. And reason suggests convenient articles of peace, upon which men may be drawn to agreement. These articles are they which otherwise are called the Laws of
40   Nature, whereof I shall speak more particularly, in the two following chapters.

## Of the First and Second Natural Laws, and of Contracts

[§14]The right of nature, which writers commonly call *jus naturale*, is the liberty each man has to use his own power as he will himself for the preservation of his own nature—that is to say, of his own life—and consequently of doing anything which in his own judgment and reason he shall conceive to be the aptest means thereunto.

By *liberty* is understood, according to the proper signification of the word, the absence of external impediments. Which impediments may oft take away part of a man's power to do what he would, but cannot hinder him from using the power left him according as his judgment and reason shall dictate to him.

A *law of nature*, *lex naturalis*, is a precept or general rule found out by reason by which a man is forbidden to do that which is destructive of his life, or takes away the means of preserving the same, and to omit that by which he thinks it may be best preserved. For though they that speak of this subject use to confound *jus* and *lex*, *right* and *law*, yet they ought to be distinguished, because *right* consists in liberty to do or to forbear, whereas *law* determines and binds to one of them, so that law and right differ as much as obligation and liberty, which in one and the same matter are inconsistent.

And because the condition of man, as has been declared in the precedent chapter, is a condition of war of every one against every one, in which case everyone is governed by his own reason, and there is nothing he can make use of that may not be a help unto him in preserving his life against his enemies, it follows that in such a condition every man has a right to everything, even to one another's body. And therefore, as long as this natural right of every man to everything endures, there can be no security to any man, how strong or wise soever he be, of living out the time which nature ordinarily allows men to live. And consequently it is a precept, or general rule of reason, *that every man ought to endeavor peace, as far as he has hope of obtaining it; and when he cannot obtain it, that he may seek and use all helps and advantages of war.* The first branch of which rule contains the first and fundamental law of nature, which is *to seek peace and follow it.* The second, the sum of the right of nature, which is *by all means we can to defend ourselves.*

From this fundamental law of nature, by which men are commanded to endeavor peace, is derived this second law, *that a man be willing, when others are so too, as far-forth as for peace and defense of himself he shall think it necessary to lay down this right to all things, and be contented with so much liberty against other men as he would allow other men against himself.* For as long as every man holds this right of doing anything he likes, so long are all men in the condition of war. But if other men will not lay down their right as well as he, then there is no reason for anyone to divest himself of his. For that were to expose himself to prey, which no man is bound to, rather than to dispose himself to peace. This is that law of the Gospel, *whatsoever you require that others should do to you, that do to them.* And that law of all men, *guod tibi fieri non vis, alteri ne feceris.*

To *lay down* a man's *right* to anything is to *divest* himself of the *liberty* of
5   hindering another of the benefit of his own right to the same....

Whensoever a man transfers his right, or renounces it, it is either in consideration of some right reciprocally transferred to himself, or for some other good he hopes for thereby. For it is a voluntary act, and of the voluntary acts of every man the object is some *good to himself.* And therefore there be some rights
10   which no man can be understood by any words or other signs to have abandoned or transferred. As first a man cannot lay down the right of resisting them that assault him by force to take away his life, because he cannot be understood to aim thereby, at any good to himself. The same may be said of wounds and chains and imprisonment, both because there is no benefit consequent to such patience,
15   as there is to the patience of suffering another to be wounded or imprisoned, as also because a man cannot tell when he sees men proceed against him by violence whether they intend his death or not. And lastly the motive and end for which this renouncing and transferring of right is introduced is nothing else but the security of a man's person in his life, and in the means of so preserving life, as
20   not to be weary of it. And therefore if a man by words or other signs seem to despoil himself of the end for which those signs were intended, he is not to be understood as if he meant it or that it was his will, but that he was ignorant of how such words and actions were to be interpreted.

The mutual transferring of right is that which men call *contract.*
25   There is difference between transferring of right to the thing and transferring, or tradition, that is delivery of the thing itself. For the thing may be delivered together with the translation of the right, as in buying and selling with ready-money, or exchange of goods or lands, and it may be delivered some time after.

Again, one of the contractors may deliver the thing contracted for on his
30   part, and leave the other to perform his part at some determinate time after, and in the meantime be trusted; and then the contract on his part is called *pact* or *covenant.* Or both parts may contract now to perform hereafter, in which cases he that is to perform in time to come being trusted, his performance is called *keeping of promise* or faith, and the failing of performance, if it be voluntary,
35   *violation of faith....*

### Of Other Laws of Nature

[§15]From that law of nature by which we are obliged to transfer to another such rights as being retained hinder the peace of mankind, there follows a third, which is this, *that men perform their covenants made*, without which covenants are in vain and but empty words, and the right of all men to all things remaining, we are still in the condition of war.

And in this law of nature consists the fountain and original of *justice*. For where no covenant has preceded, there has no right been transferred, and every man has right to everything, and consequently, no action can be unjust. But when a covenant is made, then to break it is *unjust*, and the definition of *injustice* is no other than *the not performance of covenant*. And whatsoever is not unjust is *just*....

The laws of nature are immutable and eternal; for injustice, ingratitude, arrogance, pride, iniquity, acception of persons, and the rest can never be made lawful. For it can never be that war shall preserve life, and peace destroy it.

The same laws, because they oblige only to a desire and endeavor, I mean an unfeigned and constant endeavor, are easy to be observed. For in that they require nothing but endeavor, he that endeavors their performance fulfills them; and he that fulfills the law is just.

And the science of them is the true and only moral philosophy. For moral philosophy is nothing else but the science of what is *good* and *evil* in the conversation and society of mankind. *Good* and *evil* are names that signify our appetites and aversions, which in different tempers, customs, and doctrines of men are different. And diverse men differ not only in their judgment on the senses of what is pleasant and unpleasant to the taste, smell, hearing, touch, and sight, but also of what is conformable or disagreeable to reason in the actions of common life. Nay, the same man, in diverse times, differs from himself, and one time praises, that is, calls good, what another time he dispraises and calls evil. From whence arise disputes, controversies, and at last war. And therefore so long as a man is in the condition of mere nature, which is a condition of war, as private appetite is the measure of good and evil. And consequently all men agree on this, that peace is good, and therefore also the way, or means of peace, which, as I have showed before, are *justice, gratitude, modesty, equity, mercy*, and the rest of the laws of nature are good; that is to say, *moral virtues*; and their contrary *vices*, evil....

These dictates of reason, men used to call by the name of laws, but improperly, for they are but conclusions or theorems concerning what conduces to the conservation and defense of themselves; whereas law, properly, is the word of him that by right has command over others. But yet if we consider the same theorems as delivered in the word of God that by right commands all things, then are they properly called laws.

## Of Persons, Authors, and Things Personated

**I§16**…A multitude of men are made *one* person when they are by one man, or one person, represented; so that it be done with the consent of every one of that multitude in particular. For it is the *unity* of the representer, not the *unity* of the represented, that makes the person *one*. And it is the representer that bears the person,
5 and but one person; and *unity* cannot otherwise be understood in multitude.

And because the multitude naturally is not *one*, but *many*, they cannot be understood for one, but many, authors of everything their representative says or does in their name, every man giving their common representer authority from himself in particular, and owning all the actions the representer does, in
10 case they give him authority without stint. Otherwise, when they limit him in what and how far he shall represent them, none of them owns more than they gave him commission to act.

And if the representative consist of many men, the voice of the greater number must be considered as the voice of them all. For if the lesser number
15 pronounce, for example, in the affirmative, and the greater in the negative, there will be negatives more than enough to destroy the affirmatives; and thereby the excess of negatives, standing un-contradicted, are the only voice the representative has.…

## Of the Causes, Generation, and Definition of a Commonwealth

**II§17**The final cause, end, or design of men, who naturally love liberty and
20 dominion over others, in the introduction of that restraint upon themselves in which we see them live in commonwealths is the foresight of their own preservation and of a more contented life thereby; that is to say, of getting themselves out from that miserable condition of war, which is necessarily consequent, as has been shown in Chapter XIII, to the natural passions of men when there is
25 no visible power to keep them in awe and tie them by fear of punishment to the performance of their covenants and observation of those laws of nature set down in the fourteenth and fifteenth chapters.

For the laws of nature, as *justice, equity, modesty, mercy*, and, in sum, *doing to others as we would be done to*, of themselves, without the terror of some
30 power to cause them to be observed, are contrary to our natural passions that carry us to partiality, pride, revenge, and the like. And covenants, without the sword, are but words and of no strength to secure a man at all. Therefore, notwithstanding the laws of nature, which everyone has then kept, when he has the will to keep them, when he can do it safely; if there be no power erected,
35 or not great enough for our security, every man will and may lawfully rely on his own strength and art for caution against all other men.…

The only way to erect such a common power as may be able to defend them from the invasion of foreigners, and the injuries of one another, and thereby to secure them in such sort as that by their own industry, and by the fruits of the earth, they may nourish themselves and live contentedly is to confer all their power and strength upon one man, or upon one assembly of men, that may reduce all their wills, by plurality of voices, unto one will. Which is as much as to say, to appoint one man, or assembly of men, to bear their person, and everyone to own and acknowledge himself to be author of whatsoever he that so bears their person shall act, or cause to be acted, in those things which concern the common peace and safety; and therein to submit their wills, everyone to his will, and their judgments to his judgment. This is more than consent or concord; it is a real unity of them all in one and the same person, made by covenant of every man with every man, in such manner as if every man should say to every man, *I authorize and give up my right of governing myself to this man, or to this assembly of men, on this condition, that you give up the right to him, and authorize all his actions in like manner.*

This done, the multitude so united in one person is called a COMMONWEALTH, in Latin *civitas*. This is the generation of that great LEVIATHAN, or rather, to speak more reverently, of that *mortal god* to which we owe, under the *immortal God*, our peace and defense. For by this authority, given him by every particular man in the commonwealth, he has the use of so much power and strength conferred on him that by terror thereof he is enabled to perform the wills of them all to peace at home, and mutual aid against their enemies abroad. And in him consists the essence of the commonwealth; which, to define it, is *one person, of whose acts a great multitude, by mutual covenants one with another, have made themselves every one the author, to the end he may use the strength and means of them all, as he shall think expedient, for their peace and common defense.*

And he that carries this person is called SOVEREIGN, and said to have *sovereign power*. And everyone besides, his SUBJECT.

The attaining to this sovereign power is by two ways. One, by natural force; as when a man makes his children to submit themselves and their children to his government, as being able to destroy them if they refuse; or by war subdues his enemies to his will, giving them their lives on that condition. The other is when men agree amongst themselves to submit to some man, or assembly of men, voluntarily, on confidence to be protected by him against all others. This latter may be called a political commonwealth, or commonwealth by *institution*; and the former, a commonwealth by *acquisition*. And first, I shall speak of a commonwealth by institution.

### Of the Rights of Sovereigns by Institution

II§18A *commonwealth* is said to be *instituted* when a *multitude* of men do agree and *covenant, every one with every one,* that to whatsoever *man,* or *assembly of men,* shall be given by the major part the *right* to *present* the person of them all, that is to say, to be their *representative;* everyone, as well he that *voted for it* as he 5 that *voted against it,* shall *authorize* all the actions and judgments of that man, or assembly of men, in the same manner as if they were his own, to the end to live peaceably amongst themselves, and be protected against other men.

From this institution of a commonwealth are derived all the *rights* and *faculties* of him, or them, on whom sovereign power is conferred by the consent 10 of the people assembled.

First, because they covenant, it is to be understood, they are not obliged by former covenant to anything repugnant hereunto. And consequently they that have already instituted a commonwealth, being thereby bound by covenant to own the actions and judgments of one, cannot lawfully make a new covenant 15 amongst themselves to be obedient to any other, in anything whatsoever, without his permission. And therefore, they that are subjects to a monarch cannot without his leave cast off monarchy and return to the confusion of a dis-united multitude; nor transfer their person from him that bears it to another man, or other assembly of men. For they are bound, every man to every man, to own 20 and be reputed author of all that he that already is their sovereign, shall do and judge fit to be done. So that any one man dissenting, all the rest should break their covenant made to that man, which is injustice. And they have also every man given the sovereignty to him that bears their person; and therefore if they depose him, they take from him that which is his own, and so again it is injus-25 tice. Besides, if he that attempts to depose his sovereign be killed or punished by him for such attempt, he is author of his own punishment, as being by the institution author of all his sovereign shall do. And because it is injustice for a man to do anything for which he may be punished by his own authority, he is also upon that title unjust. And whereas some men have pretended for their 30 disobedience to their sovereign a new covenant, made, not with men, but with God; this also is unjust, for there is no covenant with God but by mediation of somebody that represents God's person, which none does but God's lieutenant, who has the sovereignty under God. But this pretence of covenant with God is so evident a lie, even in the pretenders' own consciences, that it is not only an 35 act of an unjust, but also of a vile and unmanly disposition....

...The opinion that any monarch receives his power by covenant, that is to say, on condition, proceeds from want of understanding this easy truth, that covenants being but words and breath have no force to oblige, contain, constrain, or protect any man but what it has from the public sword; that is, from the untied hands of that man, or assembly of men, that has the sovereignty and whose actions are avouched by them all, and performed by the strength of them all, in him united....

...And whether he be of the congregation or not, and whether his consent 5 be asked or not, he must either submit to their decrees, or be left in the condition of war he was in before; wherein he might without injustice be destroyed by any man whatsoever....

...No man that has sovereign power can justly be put to death, or otherwise in any manner by his subjects punished. For seeing every subject is another of 10 the actions of his sovereign, he punishes another for the actions committed by himself....

...And as the power, so also the honor of the sovereign ought to be greater than that of any or all the subjects. For in the sovereignty is the fountain of honor. The dignities of lord, earl, duke, and prince are his creatures. As in the 15 presence of the master the servants are equal and without any honor at all, so are the subjects in the presence of the sovereign. And though they shine some more, some less, when they are out of his sight, yet in his presence they shine no more than the stars in the presence of the sun.

But a man may here object that the condition of subjects is very miserable... 20 Not considering that the state of man can never be without some incommodity or other; and that the greatest that in any form of government can possibly happen to the people in general is scarce sensible, in respect of the miseries and horrible calamities, that accompany a civil war, or that dissolute condition of masterless men, without subjection to laws and a coercive power to tie their 25 hands from rapine and revenge. Nor considering that the greatest pressure of sovereign governors proceeds not from any delight or profit they can expect in the damage or weakening of their subjects, in whose vigor consists their own strength and glory, but in the restiveness of themselves that unwillingly contributing to their own defense, make it necessary for their governors to draw from 30 them what they can in time of peace, that they may have means on any emergent occasion or sudden need to resist or take advantage on their enemies....

## Of Dominion Paternal and Despotical

**II§20**...But the rights and consequences of sovereignty are the same in both. His power cannot, without his consent, be transferred to another. He cannot forfeit it. He cannot be accused by any of his subjects of injury. He cannot be 35 punished by them. He is judge of what is necessary for peace, and judge of doctrines. He is sole legislator, and supreme judge of controversies, and of the times and occasions of war and peace. To him it belongs to choose magistrates, counselors, commanders, and all other officers and ministers, and to determine of rewards and punishments, honor, and order....

5 So that it appears plainly to my understanding, both from reason and Scripture, that the sovereign power, whether placed in one man, as in monarchy, or in one assembly of men, as in popular and aristocratic commonwealths, is as great as possibly men can be imagined to make it. And though of so unlimited a power, men may fancy many evil consequences, yet the consequences of the want of it, which is perpetual war of every man against his neighbor, are much

10 worse. The condition of man in this life shall never be without inconveniences, but there happens in no commonwealth any great inconvenience but what proceeds from the subject's disobedience and breach of those covenants from which the commonwealth has its being. And whosoever thinking sovereign power too great will seek to make it less must subject himself to the power that

15 can limit it; that is to say, to a greater.

The greatest objection is that of the practice; when men ask where and when such power has by subjects been acknowledged. But one may ask them again, when or where has there been a kingdom long free from sedition and civil war. In those nations whose commonwealths have been long-lived, and not been

20 destroyed but by foreign war, the subjects never did dispute of the sovereign power. But howsoever, an argument from the practice of men that have not sifted to the bottom, and with exact reason weighed the causes and nature of commonwealths, and suffer daily those miseries that proceed from the ignorance thereof, is invalid. For though in all places of the world, men should lay the

25 foundation of their houses on the sand, it could not thence be inferred that so it ought to be. The skill of making, and maintaining, commonwealths consists in certain rules, as does arithmetic and geometry; not, as tennis-play, on practice only. Which rules neither poor men have the leisure, nor men that have had the leisure have hitherto had the curiosity or the method to find out.

## Of the Liberty of Subjects

30 **II§21**Liberty, or freedom, signifies, properly, the absence of opposition; by opposition I mean external impediments of motion, and may be applied no less to irrational and inanimate creatures than to rational. For whatsoever is so tied, or environed, as it cannot move but within a certain space, which space is determined by the opposition of some external body, we say it has not liberty to

35 go further. And so of all living creatures, whilst they are imprisoned or restrained with walls or chains; and of the water while it is kept in by banks or vessels that otherwise would spread itself into a larger space, we use to say they are not at liberty to move in such manner as without those external impediments they

would. But when the impediment of motion is in the constitution of the thing itself, we use not to say it wants the liberty, but the power, to move, as when a stone lies still, or a man is fastened to his bed by sickness.

And according to this proper and generally received meaning of the word, a FREEMAN *is he that in those things which by his strength and wit he is able to do, is* 5 *not hindered to do what he has a will to.* But when the words *free* and *liberty* are applied to anything but bodies, they are abused; for that which is not subject to motion is not subject to impediment. And therefore, when it is said, for example, the way is free, no liberty of the way is signified, but of those that walk in it without stop. And when we say a gift is free, there is not meant any liberty 10 of the gift, but of the giver, that was not bound by any law or covenant to give it. So when we speak freely, it is not the liberty of voice or pronunciation, but of the man, whom no law has obliged to speak otherwise than he did. Lastly, from the use of the word free-will, no liberty can be inferred of the will, desire, or inclination, but the liberty of the man; which consists in this, that he finds 15 no stop in doing what he has the will, desire, or inclination to do.

Fear and liberty are consistent; as when a man throws his goods into the sea for *fear* the ship should sink, he does it nevertheless very willingly, and may refuse to do it if he will. It is therefore the action of one that was *free*. So a man sometimes pays his debt only for *fear* of imprisonment, which, because 20 nobody hindered him from detaining, was the action of a man at *liberty*. And generally all actions which men do in commonwealths for *fear* of the law, are actions which the doers had *liberty* to omit.

*Liberty* and *necessity* are consistent, as in the water that has not only liberty, but a necessity consistent of descending by the channel; so likewise in the ac- 25 tions which men voluntarily do. Which, because they proceed from their will, proceed from liberty; and yet, because every act of man's will, and every desire, and inclination proceeds from some cause, and that from another cause, in a continual chain, whose first link is in the hand of God the first of all causes, proceed from *necessity*.... 30

But as men, for the attaining of peace and conservation of themselves thereby, have made an artificial man, which we call a commonwealth; so also have they made artificial chains, called *civil laws*, which they themselves, by mutual covenants, have fastened at one end to the lips of that man, or assembly, to whom they have given the sovereign power, and at the other end to their own 35 ears. These bonds, in their own nature but weak, may nevertheless be made to hold, by the danger, though not by the difficulty, of breaking them....

...The laws are of no power to protect them without a sword in the hands of a man, or men, to cause those laws to be put in execution. The liberty of a subject lies therefore only in those things which, in regulating their actions, the 40 sovereign has prætermitted, such as is the liberty to buy and sell, and otherwise contract with one another; to choose their own abode, their own diet, their own trade of life, and institute their children as they themselves think fit; and the like.

5 Nevertheless we are not to understand that by such liberty the sovereign power of life and death is either abolished, or limited. For it has already been shown that nothing the sovereign representative can do to a subject, on what pretence soever, can properly be called injustice or injury, because every subject is author of every act the sovereign does; so that he never wants right to any-
10 thing otherwise than as he himself is the subject of God, and bound thereby to observe the laws of nature....

To come now to the particulars of the true liberty of a subject; that is to say, what are the things which, though commanded by the sovereign, he may nev-ertheless, without injustice, refuse to do; we are to consider what rights we pass
15 away when we make a commonwealth; or, which is all one, what liberty we deny ourselves by owning all the actions, without exception, of the man, or assembly, we make our sovereign. For in the act of our *submission* consists both our *obliga-tion* and our *liberty*; which must therefore be inferred by arguments taken from thence, there being no obligation on any man which arises not from some act
20 of his own; for all men equally are by nature free. And because such arguments must either be drawn from the express words, *I authorize all his actions*, or from the intention of him that submits himself to his power, which intention is to be understood by the end for which he so submits; the obligation and liberty of the subject is to be derived either from those words, or others equivalent; or else
25 from the end of the institution of sovereignty, namely, the peace of the subjects within themselves, and their defense against a common enemy....

As for other liberties, they depend on the silence of the law. In cases where the sovereign has prescribed no rule, there the subject has the liberty to do, or forbear, according to his own discretion. And therefore such liberty is in some
30 places more, and in some less; and in some times more, in other times less, ac-cording as they that have the sovereignty shall think most convenient....

The obligation of subjects to the sovereign is understood to last as long, and no longer, than the power lasts, by which he is able to protect them. For the right men have by nature to protect themselves when none else can protect
35 them can by no covenant be relinquished. The sovereignty is the soul of the commonwealth, which once departed from the body, the members do no more receive their motion from it. The end of obedience is protection; which, where-soever a man sees it, either in his own or in another's sword, nature applies his obedience to it, and his endeavors to maintain it. And though sovereignty, in
40 the intention of them that make it, be immortal; yet is it in its own nature not

only subject to violent death by foreign war; but also through the ignorance and passions of men; it has in it, from the very institution, many seeds of a natural mortality by intestine discord....

## Of Civil Laws

II§26By civil laws, I understand the laws that men are therefore bound to observe because they are members, not of this or that commonwealth in particular, but of a commonwealth. For the knowledge of particular laws belongs to them that profess the study of the laws of their several countries; but the knowledge of civil law in general, to any man....

And first it is manifest that law in general is not counsel, but command; nor a command of any man to any man, but only of him whose command is addressed to one formerly obliged to obey him....

Which considered, I define civil law in this manner. CIVIL LAW *is to every subject those rules which the commonwealth has commanded him, by word, writing, or other sufficient sign of the will, to make use of for the distinction of right and wrong; that is to say, of what is contrary and what is not contrary to the rule....*

The legislator in all commonwealths is only the sovereign, be he one man, as in a monarchy, or one assembly of men, as in a democracy or aristocracy. For the legislator is he that makes the law. And the commonwealth only prescribes and commands the observation of those rules which we call law; therefore the commonwealth is the legislator. But the commonwealth is no person, nor has capacity to do anything but by the representative, that is, the sovereign; and therefore the sovereign is the sole legislator. For the same reason, none can abrogate a law made but the sovereign, because a law is not abrogated but by another law that forbids it to be put in execution.

The sovereign of a commonwealth, be it an assembly or one man, is not subject to the civil laws. For having power to make and repeal laws, he may when he pleases free himself from that subjection by repealing those laws that trouble him and making of new, and consequently he was free before....

The law of nature, therefore, is a part of the civil law in all commonwealths of the world. Reciprocally also, the civil law is a part of the dictates of nature. For justice, that is to say, performance of covenant and giving to every man his own, is a dictate of the law of nature. But every subject in a commonwealth has convenanted to obey the civil law; either one with another, as when they assemble to make a common representative, or with the representative itself one by one, when subdued by the sword they promise obedience that they may receive life; and therefore obedience to the civil law is part also of the law of nature. Civil and natural law are not different kinds, but different parts of law; whereof one part being written is called civil, the other unwritten, natural....

...It is not that *juris prudentia*, or wisdom of subordinate judges, but the reason of this, our artificial man, the commonwealth, and his command that makes law. And the commonwealth being in their representative but one person, there cannot easily arise any contradiction in the laws; and when there does, the same reason is able, by interpretation or alteration, to take it away. In all courts of justice, the sovereign, which is the person of the commonwealth, is he that judges. The subordinate judge ought to have regard to the reason which moved his sovereign to make such law, that his sentence may be according thereunto; which then is his sovereign's sentence; otherwise it is his own, and an unjust one....

### Of Those Things that Weaken or Tend to the Dissolution of a Commonwealth

**II§29**...The *diseases* of a commonwealth that proceed from the poison of seditious doctrines, whereof one is *That every private man is judge of good and evil actions*. This is true in the condition of mere nature, where there are no civil laws; and also under civil government in such cases as are not determined by the law. But otherwise it is manifest that the measure of good and evil actions is the civil law; and the judge the legislator, who is always representative of the commonwealth. From this false doctrine men are disposed to debate with themselves and dispute the commands of the commonwealth; and afterwards to obey or disobey them as in their private judgments they shall think fit; whereby the commonwealth is distracted and *weakened*.

Another doctrine repugnant to civil society is that *whatsoever a man does against his conscience is sin*; and it depends on the presumption of making himself judge of good and evil. For a man's conscience and his judgment is the same thing, and as the judgment, so also the conscience may be erroneous. Therefore, though he that is subject to no civil law sins in all he does against his conscience because he has no other rule to follow but his own reason; yet it is not so with him that lives in a commonwealth, because the law is the public conscience, by which he has already undertaken to be guided. Otherwise in such diversity as there is of private consciences, which are but private opinions, the commonwealth must needs be distracted, and no man dare to obey the sovereign power further than it shall seem good in his own eyes....

### Of the Office of the Sovereign Representative

**II§30**...To the care of the sovereign belongs the making of good laws. But what is a good law? By a good law I mean not a just law, for no law can be unjust. The law is made by the sovereign power, and all that is done by such power is warranted and owned by every one of the people; and that which every man will have so, no man can say is unjust. It is in the laws of a commonwealth, as in the laws of gaming; whatsoever the gamesters all agree on is injustice to none of them. A good law is that which is *needful* for the good *of the people*, and withal *perspicuous*.                                                                 5

For the use of laws, which are but rules authorized, is not to bind the people from all voluntary actions, but to direct and keep them in such a motion as not to hurt themselves by their own impetuous desires, rashness, or indiscretion; as hedges are set, not to stop travelers, but to keep them in their way. And therefore a law that is not needful, having not the true end of a law, is not good. A    10 law may be conceived to be good when it is for the benefit of the sovereign, though it be not necessary for the people; but it is not so. For the good of the sovereign and people cannot be separated. It is a weak sovereign that has weak subjects; and a weak people whose sovereign wants power to rule them at his will. Unnecessary laws are not good laws, but traps for money, which, where    15 the right of sovereign power is acknowledged, are superfluous; and where it is not acknowledged, insufficient to defend the people....

## Of the Kingdom of God by Nature

**II§31**...But seeing a commonwealth is but one person, it ought also to exhibit to God but one worship; which then it does when it commands it to be exhibited by private men publicly. And this is public worship; the property whereof is to    20 be *uniform*. For those actions that are done differently by different men cannot be said to be a public worship. And therefore, where many sorts of worship be allowed, proceeding from the different religions of private men, it cannot be said there is any public worship, nor that the commonwealth is of any religion at all....                                                                          25

...And because a commonwealth has no will, nor makes no laws, but those that are made by the will of him or them that have the sovereign power, it follows that those attributes which the sovereign ordains in the worship of God, for signs of honor, ought to be taken and used for such by private men in their public worship....                                                                   30

## Of the Word of God, and of Prophets

**III§36**...For when Christian men take not their Christian sovereign for God's prophet, they must either take their own dreams for the prophecy they mean to be governed by and the tumor of their own hearts for the Spirit of God, or they must suffer themselves to be led by some strange prince, or by some of their fellow-subjects that can bewitch them by slander of the government    35 into rebellion, without other miracle to confirm their calling than sometimes an extraordinary success and impunity; and by this means destroying all laws, both divine and human, reduce all order, government, and society to the first chaos of violence and civil war....

## Of Power Ecclesiastical

5   **III§42**...The right of judging what doctrines are fit for peace and to be taught the subjects is in all commonwealths inseparably annexed, as has been already proved, to the sovereign power civil, whether it be in one man or in one assembly of men. For it is evident to the meanest capacity that men's actions are derived from the opinions they have of the good or evil, which from those
10   actions redound unto themselves; and consequently men that are once possessed of an opinion that their obedience to the sovereign power will be more hurtful to them than their disobedience will disobey the laws, and thereby overthrow the commonwealth and introduce confusion and civil war; for the avoiding whereof, all civil government was ordained....
15     ...And therefore Christian kings are still the supreme pastors of their people, and have power to ordain what pastors they please to teach the Church; that is, to teach the people committed to their charge....
    ...They depend only on the sovereign, which is the soul of the commonwealth; which failing, the commonwealth is dissolved into a civil war, no one
20   man so much as cohering to another for want of a common dependence on a known sovereign; just as the members of the natural body dissolve into earth for want of a soul to hold them together. Therefore there is nothing in this similitude from whence to infer a dependence of the laity on the clergy, or of the temporal officers on the spiritual, but of both on the civil sovereign, which
25   ought indeed to direct his civil commands to the salvation of souls; but is not therefore subject to any but God himself....

# SECOND TREATISE OF CIVIL GOVERNMENT
## JOHN LOCKE (1632–1704)

*Reading widely across disciplines, John Locke earned a degree in medicine from Oxford University, corresponded with the leading European scholars, and was active in English political life in the seventeenth century. He wrote his Second Treatise of Civil Government in 1681, but published it in 1689 in the aftermath of the Glorious Revolution. A justification of moderate representative polities, the Second Treatise formed the foundation for classical liberal ideas of government for the next two hundred years. Locke's insistence that the individual possessed God-given rights of which no government could deprive him is echoed in the first paragraph of the Declaration of Independence.*

1689

**II§1**...Political Power, then, I take to be a right of making laws with penalties of death, and consequently all less penalties, for the regulating and preserving of property, and of employing the force of the community in the execution of such laws, and in the defense of the commonwealth from foreign injury, and all this only for the public good....

5

### Of the State of Nature

**II§2**...We must consider what state all men are naturally in, and that is a state of perfect freedom to order their actions, and dispose of their possessions and persons, as they think fit, within the bounds of the law of nature, without asking leave or depending upon the will of any other man.

A state also of equality, wherein all the power and jurisdiction is recipro-   10
cal, no one having more than another; there being nothing more evident than that creatures of the same species and rank, promiscuously born to all the same advantages of nature, and the use of the same faculties, should also be equal one amongst another without subordination or subjection....

The state of nature has a law of nature to govern it which obliges every-   15
one. And reason, which is that law, teaches all mankind who will but consult

---

John Locke, *The Works of John Locke, Esquire* (London: John Churchill, 1714), II:159–62, 164–68, 172–75, 178, 180, 182–86, 191–202, 205–6, 215, 217, 219–22, 226–27 [modernized].

it that being all equal and independent, no one ought to harm another in his life, health, liberty, or possessions, for men being all the workmanship of one omnipotent and infinitely wise Maker. All the servants of one sovereign Master, sent into the world by his order, they are his property whose workmanship they are, made to last during his, not one another's pleasure. And being furnished with like faculties, sharing all in one community of nature, there cannot be supposed any such subordination among us that may authorize us to destroy one another, as if we were made for one another's uses as the inferior ranks of creatures are for ours. Every one as he is bound to preserve himself and not to quit his station willfully, so by the like reason, when his own preservation comes not in competition, ought he, as much as he can, to preserve the rest of mankind, and may not unless it be to do justice on an offender, take away or impair the life, or what tends to the preservation of the life, the liberty, health, limb, or goods of another....

And that all men may be restrained from invading others' rights, and from doing hurt to one another, and the law of nature be observed which wills the peace and preservation of all mankind, the execution of the law of nature is in that state, put into every man's hands, whereby everyone has a right to punish the transgressors of that law to such a degree as may hinder its violation....

And thus in the state of nature, one man comes by a power over another; but yet no absolute or arbitrary power to use a criminal, when he has got him in his hands, according to the passionate heats or boundless extravagancy of his own will, but only to retribute to him, so far as calm reason and conscience dictate, what is proportionate to his transgression, which is so much as may serve for reparation and restraint. For these two are the only reasons why one man may lawfully do harm to another, which is that we call punishment. In transgressing the law of nature, the offender declares himself to live by another rule than that of common reason and equity, which is that measure God has set to the actions of men for their mutual security; and so he becomes dangerous to mankind....

...Civil government is the proper remedy for the inconveniences of the state of nature, which must certainly be great, where men may be judges in their own case.... How much better it is than the state of nature, where one man commanding a multitude has the liberty to be judge in his own case, and may do to all his subjects whatever he pleases without the least question or control of those who execute his pleasure? And in whatsoever he does, whether led by reason, mistake, or passion, must be submitted to? Which men in the state of nature are not bound to do one to another. And if he that judges, judges amiss in his own, or any other case, he is answerable for it to the rest of mankind....

## Of the State of War

**II§3** ...Men living together according to reason without a common superior on earth with authority to judge between them is properly the state of nature. But force, or a declared design of force upon the person of another where there is no common superior on earth to appeal to for relief is the state of war.... Want of a common judge with authority puts all men in a state of nature. Force without right upon a man's person makes a state of war, both where there is and is not a common judge.... 5

To avoid this state of war (wherein there is no appeal but to Heaven, and wherein every the least difference is apt to end, where there is no authority to decide between the contenders) is one great reason of mens putting themselves 10 into society, and quitting the state of nature. For where there is an authority, a power on earth from which relief can be had by appeal, there the continuance of the state of war is excluded, and the controversy is decided by that power....

## Of Slavery

**II§4** The natural liberty of man is to be free from any superior power on earth, and not to be under the will or legislative authority of man, but to have only 15 the law of nature for his rule. The liberty of man in society is to be under no other legislative power but that established by consent in the commonwealth, nor under the dominion of any will or restraint of any law but what that legislative shall enact according to the trust put in it.... Freedom of men under government is to have a standing rule to live by common to every one of that 20 society, and made by the legislative power erected in it; a liberty to follow my own will in all things where that rule prescribes not, and not to be subject to the inconstant, uncertain, unknown, arbitrary will of another man, as freedom of nature is to be under no other restraint but the law of nature.

This freedom from absolute, arbitrary power is so necessary to and closely 25 joined with a man's preservation that he cannot part with it but by what forfeits his preservation and life together. For a man not having the power of his own life cannot, by compact or his own consent, enslave himself to anyone, nor put himself under the absolute, arbitrary power of another to take away his life when he pleases....

## Of Property

**II§5** ...Though the earth and all inferior creatures be common to all men, yet every 30 man has a property in his own person. This nobody has any right to but himself. The labor of his body, and the work of his hands, we may say, are properly his.

Whatsoever then he removes out of the state that nature has provided and left it in, he has mixed his labor with, and joined to it something that is his own, and thereby makes it his property. It being by him removed from the common state nature has placed it in, it has by this labor something annexed to it that excludes the common right of other men. For this labor being the unquestionable property of the laborer, no man but he can have a right to what that is once joined to, at least where there is enough and as good left in common for others...

...'Tis allowed to be his goods who has bestowed his labor upon it, though before it was the common right of everyone....

...The same law of nature that does by this means give us property does also bound that property too. God has given us all things richly (I Timothy 6:12) is the voice of reason confirmed by inspiration. But how far has he given it us? To enjoy. As much as anyone can make use of to any advantage of life before it spoils; so much he may by his labor fix a property in. Whatever is beyond this is more than his share, and belongs to others. Nothing was made by God for man to spoil or destroy....

...As much land as a man tills, plants, improves, cultivates, and can use the product of, so much is his property. He by his labor does, as it were, enclose it from the common....

...The measure of property nature has well set by the extent of men's labor and the conveniencies of life. No man's labor could subdue or appropriate all; nor could his enjoyment consume more than a small part, so that it was impossible for any man this way to entrench upon the right of another, or acquire to himself a property to the prejudice of his neighbor, who would still have room for as good and as large a possession (after the other had taken out his) as before it was appropriated. Measure did confine every man's possession to a very moderate proportion.... The same rule of propriety, that every man should have as much as he could make use of, would hold still in the world without straitening anybody, since there is land enough in the world to suffice double the inhabitants, had not the invention of money, and the tacit agreement of men to put a value on it, introduced (by consent) larger possessions, and a right to them....

...It is plain that men have agreed to a disproportionate and unequal possession of the earth, they having by a tacit and voluntary consent, found out a way how a man may fairly possess more land than he himself can use the product of, by receiving in exchange for the overplus gold and silver, which may be hoarded up without injury to anyone, these metals not spoiling or decaying in the hands of the possessor. This partage of things in an inequality of private possessions, men have made practicable out of the bounds of society, and without compact only by putting a value on gold and silver, and tacitly agreeing in the use of money. For in governments, the laws regulate the right of property, and the possession of land is determined by positive constitutions....

## Of Paternal Power

**II§6**...Though I have said that all men by nature are equal, I cannot be supposed to understand all sorts of equality; age or virtues may give men a just precedency. Excellency of parts and merit may place others above the common 5 level. Birth may subject some, and alliance or benefits others, to pay an observance to those to whom nature, gratitude, or other respects may have made it due; and yet all this consists with the equality which all men are in, in respect of jurisdiction or dominion, one over another; which was the equality I there spoke of as proper to the business in hand, being that equal right that every 10 man has to his natural freedom, without being subjected to the will or authority of any other man....

...Law, in its true notion, is not so much the limitation as the direction of a free and intelligent agent to his proper interest, and prescribes no farther than is for the general good of those under that law. Could they be happier without 15 it, the law, as an useless thing, would of itself vanish, and that ill deserves the name of confinement which hedges us in only from bogs and precipices. So that, however it may be mistaken, the end of law is not to abolish or restrain, but to preserve and enlarge freedom. For in all the states of created beings capable of laws where there is no law, there is no freedom. For liberty is to be free from 20 restraint and violence from others; which cannot be where there is no law. But freedom is not, as we are told, a liberty for every man to do what he lists: (For who could be free when every other man's humor might domineer over him?) But a liberty to dispose and order as he lists his person, actions, possessions, and his whole property, within the allowance of those laws under which he is, 25 and therein not to be subject to the arbitrary will of another, but freely follow his own....

...The freedom, then, of man, and liberty of acting according to his own will, is grounded on his having reason, which is able to instruct him in that law he is to govern himself by, and make him know how far he is left to the 30 freedom of his own will. To turn him loose to an unrestrained liberty before he has reason to guide him is not the allowing him the privilege of his nature to be free, but to thrust him out amongst brutes and abandon him to a state as wretched, and as much beneath that of a man, as theirs....

...There being always annexed to the enjoyment of land a submission to the 35 government of the country of which that land is a part, it has been commonly supposed that a father could oblige his posterity to that government of which he himself was a subject, and that his compact held them; whereas, it being only a

necessary condition annexed to the land and the inheritance of an estate which
is under that government, reaches only those who will take it on that condition, and so is no natural tie or engagement, but a voluntary submission. For
every man's children being by nature as free as himself, or any of his ancestors
5   ever were, may, whilst they are in that freedom, choose what society they will
join themselves to, what commonwealth they will put themselves under. But if
they will enjoy the inheritance of their ancestors, they must take it on the same
terms their ancestors had it, and submit to all the conditions annexed to such a
possession. By this power indeed fathers oblige their children to obedience to
10   themselves, even when they are past minority, and most commonly too subject
them to this or that political power....

## Of Political or Civil Society

II§7God having made man such a creature that, in his own judgment, it was
not good for him to be alone, put him under strong obligations of necessity,
convenience, and inclination to drive him into society, as well as fitted him
15   with understanding and language to continue and enjoy it....

Because no political society can be nor subsist without having in itself the
power to preserve the property and, in order thereunto, punish the offences of
all those of that society; there, and there only, is political society, where every one
of the members has quitted this natural power, resigned it up into the hands of
20   the community in all cases that exclude him not from appealing for protection
to the law established by it. And thus all private judgment of every particular
member being excluded, the community comes to be umpire by settled standing
rules, indifferent and the same to all parties; and by men having authority from
the community, for the execution of those rules, decides all the differences that
25   may happen between any members of that society concerning any matter of
right; and punishes those offences which any member has committed against
the society, with such penalties as the law has established; whereby it is easy to
discern who are, and who are not, in political society together. Those who are
united into one body, and have a common established law and judicature to
30   appeal to, with authority to decide controversies between them, and punish
offenders, are in civil society one with another. But those who have no such
common appeal, I mean on earth, are still in the state of nature, each being,
where there is no other, judge for himself, and executioner; which is, as I have
before showed it, the perfect state of nature.... He has given a right to the
35   commonwealth to employ his force for the execution of the judgments of the
commonwealth, whenever he shall be called to it; which indeed are his own
judgments, they being made by himself or his representative. And herein we

have the original of the legislative and executive power of civil society, which is to judge by standing laws....

Wherever, therefore, any number of men are so united into one society as to quit every one his executive power of the law of nature and to resign it to the public, there and there only is a political or civil society. And this is done, wherever any number of men, in the state of nature, enter into society to make one people, one body politic, under one supreme government; or else when anyone joins himself to and incorporates with any government already made. For hereby he authorizes the society, or which is all one, the legislative thereof, to make laws for him as the public good of the society shall require; to the execution whereof his own assistance (as to his own decrees) is due. And this puts men out of a state of nature into that of a commonwealth, by setting up a judge on earth with authority to determine all the controversies and redress the injuries that may happen to any member of the commonwealth; which judge is the legislative, or magistrates appointed by it. And wherever there are any number of men, however associated, that have no such decisive power to appeal to, there they are still in the state of nature....

...The end of civil society being to avoid and remedy those inconveniencies of the state of nature which necessarily follow from every man's being judge in his own case, by setting up a known authority to which everyone of that society may appeal upon any injury received, or controversy that may arise, and which every one of the society ought to obey....

...In absolute monarchies indeed, as well as other governments of the world, the subjects have an appeal to the law, and judges to decide any controversies and restrain any violence that may happen betwixt the subjects themselves, one amongst another.... For if it be asked what security, what fence is there in such a state against the violence and oppression of this absolute ruler? The very question can scarce be born. They are ready to tell you that it deserves death only to ask after safety. Betwixt subject and subject, they will grant, there must be measures, laws, and judges for their mutual peace and security. But as for the ruler, he ought to be absolute, and is above all such circumstances; because he has power to do more hurt and wrong, 'tis right when he does it. To ask how you may be guarded from harm or injury on that side where the strongest hand is to do it is presently the voice of faction and rebellion. As if when men quitting the state of nature entered into society, they agreed that all of them but one should be under the restraint of laws, but that he should still retain all the liberty of the state of nature, increased with power, and made licentious by impunity. This is to think that men are so foolish that they take care to avoid what mischiefs may be done them by pole-cats or foxes, but are content, nay think it safety, to be devoured by lions....

## Of the Beginning of Political Societies

II§8Men being, as has been said, by nature all free, equal, and independent, no one can be put out of this estate and subjected to the political power of another without his own consent. The only way whereby anyone divests himself of his natural liberty and puts on the bonds of civil society is by agreeing with other
5   men to join and unite into a community for their comfortable, safe, and peaceable living one amongst another, in a secure enjoyment of their properties, and a greater security against any that are not of it….

For when any number of men have, by the consent of every individual, made a community, they have thereby made that community one body, with
10  a power to act as one body, which is only by the will and determination of the majority….

And thus every man, by consenting with others to make one body politic under one government, puts himself under an obligation to every one of that society to submit to the determination of the majority, and to be concluded by
15  it; or else this original compact, whereby he with others incorporates into one society, would signify nothing, and be no compact, if he be left free and under no other ties than he was in before in the state of nature….

…For where the majority cannot conclude the rest, there they cannot act as one body, and consequently will be immediately dissolved again.
20  Whosoever therefore out of a state of nature unite into a community must be understood to give up all the power necessary to the ends for which they unite into society to the majority of the community, unless they expressly agreed in any number greater than the majority. And this is done by barely agreeing to unite into one political society, which is all the compact that is, or needs be,
25  between the individuals that enter into or make up a commonwealth….

…The son cannot ordinarily enjoy the possession of his father but under the same terms his father did—by becoming a member of the society; whereby he puts himself presently under the government he finds there established, as much as any other subject of that commonwealth….
30  …There is a common distinction of an express and a tacit consent which will concern our present case. Nobody doubts but an express consent of any man, entering into any society, makes him a perfect member of that society, a subject of that government. The difficulty is what ought to be looked upon as a tacit consent, and how far it binds; *i.e.*, how far anyone shall be looked on
35  to have consented, and thereby submitted, to any government where he has made no expressions of it at all. And to this I say that every man that has any possessions or enjoyment of any part of the dominions of any government does thereby give his tacit consent, and is as far forth obliged to obedience to the laws

of that government, during such enjoyment, as anyone under it; whether this his possession be of land, to him and his heirs forever, or a lodging only for a week; or whether it be barely traveling freely on the highway; and in effect, it reaches as far as the very being of anyone within the territories of that government....

...So that whenever the owner who has given nothing but such a tacit        5
consent to the government will, by donation, sale, or otherwise, quit the said possession, he is at liberty to go and incorporate himself into any other commonwealth; or to agree with others to begin a new one, *in vacuis locis*, in any part of the world they can find free and unpossessed. Whereas he that has once, by actual agreement and any express declaration, given his consent to        10
be of any commonweal, is perpetually and indispensably obliged to be and remain unalterably a subject to it, and can never be again in the liberty of the state of nature, unless, by any calamity, the government he was under comes to be dissolved, or else by some public act cuts him off from being any longer a member of it....        15

...Nothing can make any man so but his actually entering into it by positive engagement and express promise and compact....

## Of the Ends of Political Society and Government

**II§9**If Man in the state of nature be so free as has been said, if he be absolute lord of his own person and possessions, equal to the greatest and subject to nobody, why will he part with his freedom? Why will he give up this empire        20
and subject himself to the dominion and control of any other power? To which 'tis obvious to answer that though in the state of nature he has such a right, yet the enjoyment of it is very uncertain, and constantly exposed to the invasion of others. For all being kings as much as he, every man his equal and the greater part no strict observers of equity and justice, the enjoyment of the property he        25
has in this state is very unsafe, very unsecure. This makes him willing to quit this condition, which however free, is full of fears and continual dangers: And 'tis not without reason that he seeks out and is willing to join in society with others who are already united, or have a mind to unite, for the mutual preservation of their lives, liberties, and estates, which I call by the general name, property.        30

The great and chief end therefore, of men's uniting into commonwealths and putting themselves under government is the preservation of their property. To which in the state of nature there are many things wanting.

First, there wants an established, settled, known law, received and allowed by common consent to be the standard of right and wrong, and the common        35
measure to decide all controversies between them. For though the law of nature be plain and intelligible to all rational creatures, yet men being biased by their

interest, as well as ignorant for want of study of it, are not apt to allow of it as a law binding to them in the application of it to their particular cares.

Secondly, in the state of nature there wants a known and indifferent judge with authority to determine all differences according to the established law. For everyone in that state being both judge and executioner of the law of nature, men being partial to themselves, passion and revenge is very apt to carry them too far, and with too much heat, in their own cases, as well as negligence and unconcernedness to make them too remiss in other men's.

Thirdly, in the state of nature there often wants power to back and support the sentence when right, and to give it due execution. They who by any injustice offended will seldom fail, where they are able, by force to make good their injustice; such resistance many times makes the punishment dangerous, and frequently destructive, to those who attempt it....

The first power, viz., of doing whatsoever he thought fit for the preservation of himself and the rest of mankind, he gives up to be regulated by laws made by the society, so far forth as the preservation of himself and the rest of that society shall require; which laws of the society in many things confine the liberty he had by the law of nature.

Secondly, the power of punishing he wholly gives up and engages his natural force (which he might before employ in the execution of the law of nature, by his own single authority, as he thought fit) to assist the executive power of the society, as the law thereof shall require....

But though men when they enter into society give up the equality, liberty, and executive power they had in the state of nature into the hands of the society, to be so far disposed of by the legislative as the good of the society shall require; yet it being only with an intention in everyone the better to preserve himself his liberty and property (for no rational creature can be supposed to change his condition with an intention to be worse), the power of the society, or legislative constituted by them, can never be supposed to extend farther than the common good, but is obliged to secure everyone's property by providing against those three defects above-mentioned that made the state of nature so unsafe and uneasy. And so whoever has the legislative or supreme power of any commonwealth is bound to govern by established standing laws, promulgated and known to the people, and not by extemporary decrees; by indifferent and upright judges, who are to decide controversies by those laws; and to employ the force of the community at home only in the execution of such laws, or abroad to prevent or redress foreign injuries and secure the community from inroads and invasion. And all this to be directed to no other end but the peace, safety, and public good of the people....

## Of the Extent of the Legislative Power

II§11 The great end of men's entering into society being the enjoyment of their properties in peace and safety, and the great instrument and means of that being the laws established in that society, the first and fundamental positive law of all commonwealths is the establishing of the legislative power; as the first and fundamental natural law, which is to govern even the legislative itself, is the preservation of the society and (as far as will consist with the public good) of every person in it. This legislative is not only the supreme power of the commonwealth, but sacred and unalterable in the hands where the community have once placed it; nor can any edict of anybody else, in what form soever conceived, or by what power soever backed, have the force and obligation of a law which has not its sanction from that legislative which the public has chosen and appointed. For without this the law could not have that which is absolutely necessary to its being a law, the consent of the society, over whom nobody can have a power to make laws but by their own consent and by authority received from them.... Though it be the supreme power in every commonwealth; yet,

First, it is not, nor can possibly be, absolutely arbitrary over the lives and fortunes of the people.... The legislative power... the utmost bounds of it, is limited to the public good of the society. It is a power that has no other end but preservation, and therefore can never have a right to destroy, enslave, or designedly to impoverish the subjects....

Secondly, the legislative or supreme authority cannot assume to itself a power to rule by extemporary arbitrary decrees, but is bound to dispense justice, and decide the rights of the subjects by promulgated standing laws, and known authorized judges.... Men give up all their natural power to the society which they enter into, and the community put the legislative power into such hands as they think fit, with this trust, that they shall be governed by declared laws, or else their peace, quiet, and property will still be at the same uncertainty, as it was in the state of nature....

Thirdly, the supreme power cannot take from any man any part of his property without his own consent. For the preservation of property being the end of government, and that for which men enter into society, it necessarily supposes and requires that the people should have property.... Hence it is a mistake to think that the supreme or legislative power of any commonwealth can do what it will, and dispose of the estates of the subject arbitrarily, or take any part of them at pleasure....

...Governments cannot be supported without great charge, and 'tis fit everyone who enjoys his share of the protection should pay out of his estate his proportion for the maintenance of it. But still it must be with his own consent; *i.e.*, the consent of the majority, giving it either by themselves or their representatives chosen by them....

Fourthly, the legislative cannot transfer the power of making laws to any other hands. For it being but a delegated power from the people, they who have it cannot pass it over to others....

These are the bounds which the trust that is put in them by the society, and the law of God and nature, have set to the legislative power of every commonwealth, in all forms of government.

First, they are to govern by promulgated established laws, not to be varied in particular cases, but to have one rule for rich and poor, for the favorite at court, and the country man at plough.

Secondly, these laws also ought to be designed for no other end ultimately but the good of the people.

Thirdly, they must not raise taxes on the property of the people without the consent of the people, given by themselves or their deputies. And this property concerns only such governments where the legislative is always in being, or at least where the people have not reserved any part of the legislative to deputies, to be from time to time chosen by themselves.

Fourthly, the legislative neither must nor can transfer the power of making laws to anybody else, or place it anywhere but where the people have.

## Of the Legislative, Executive, and Federative Power of the Commonwealth

II§12 The legislative power is that which has a right to direct how the force of the commonwealth shall be employed for preserving the community and the members of it. But because those laws which are constantly to be executed, and whose force is always to continue, may be made in a little time, therefore there is no need that the legislative should be always in being, not having always business to do. And because it may be too great a temptation to human frailty apt to grasp at power for the same persons who have the power of making laws to have also in their hands the power to execute them, whereby they may exempt themselves from obedience to the laws they make and suit the law, both in its making and execution, to their own private advantage, and thereby come to have a distinct interest from the rest of the community, contrary to the end of society and government....

But because the laws that are at once and in a short time made have a constant and lasting force, and need a perpetual execution or an attendance thereunto, therefore 'tis necessary there should be a power always in being which should see to the execution of the laws that are made and remain in force. And thus the legislative and executive power come often to be separated.

There is another power in every commonwealth... the whole community is one body in the state of nature, in respect of all other states or persons out of its community....

This therefore contains the power of war and peace, leagues and alliances, and all the transactions with all persons and communities without the commonwealth, and may be called federative....

These two powers, executive and federative, though they be really distinct in themselves, yet one comprehending the execution of the municipal laws of the society within itself upon all that are parts of it, the other the management of the security and interest of the public without, with all those that it may receive benefit or damage from, yet they are always almost united. And though this federative power in the well or ill management of it be of great moment to the commonwealth, yet it is much less capable to be directed by antecedent, standing, positive laws than the executive, and so must necessarily be left to the prudence and wisdom of those whose hands it is in, to be managed for the public good....

...It is almost impracticable to place the force of the commonwealth in distinct, and not subordinate hands; or that the executive and federative power should be placed in persons that might act separately, whereby the force of the public would be under different commands, which would be apt sometime or other to cause disorder and ruin.

## Of the Subordination of the Powers of the Commonwealth

II§13 Though in a constituted commonwealth, standing upon its own basis and acting according to its own nature, that is, acting for the preservation of the community, there can be but one supreme power, which is the legislative, to which all the rest are and must be subordinate, yet the legislative being only a fiduciary power to act for certain ends, there remains still in the people a supreme power to remove or alter the legislative when they find the legislative act contrary to the trust reposed in them. For all power given with trust for the attaining an end, being limited by that end, whenever that end is manifestly neglected or opposed the trust must necessarily be forfeited, and the power devolve into the hands of those that gave it, who may place it anew where they shall think best for their safety and security. And thus the community perpetually retains a supreme power of saving themselves from the attempts and designs of anybody, even of their legislators, whenever they shall be so foolish, or so wicked, as to lay and carry on designs against the liberties and properties of the subject. For no man or society of men, having a power to deliver up their preservation or consequently the means of it, to the absolute will and arbitrary dominion of another; when ever anyone shall go about to bring them into such a slavish condition, they will always have a right to preserve what they have not a power to part with; and to rid themselves of those who invade this fundamental, sacred, and unalterable law of self-preservation, for which they entered into society. And thus the community may be said in this respect to be always the supreme

5  power, but not as considered under any form of government, because this power of the people can never take place till the government be dissolved....

...Allegiance being nothing but an obedience according to law, which when he violates, he has no right to obedience, nor can claim it otherwise than as the public person vested with the power of the law, and so is to be considered

10  as the image, phantom, or representative of the commonwealth, acted by the will of the society, declared in its laws; and thus he has no will, no power but that of the law. But when he quits this representation, this public will, and acts by his own private will, he degrades himself and is but a single private person without power and without will that has any right to obedience; the members

15  owing no obedience but to the public will of the society....

...Using force upon the people without authority, and contrary to the trust put in him that does so, is a state of war with the people who have a right to reinstate their legislative in the exercise of their power. For having erected a legislative with an intent they should exercise the power of making laws,

20  either at certain set times or when there is need of it, when they are hindered by any force from what is so necessary to the society, and wherein the safety and preservation of the people consists, the people have a right to remove it by force. In all states and conditions the true remedy of force without authority is to oppose force to it. The use of force without authority always puts him that

25  uses it into a state of war as the aggressor, and renders him liable to be treated accordingly....

## Of Prerogative

II§14...And where the body of the people, or any single man, is deprived of their right or is under the exercise of a power without right, and have no appeal on earth, then they have a liberty to appeal to Heaven whenever they judge the

30  cause of sufficient moment. And therefore though the people cannot be judge so as to have by the constitution of that society any superior power to determine and give effective sentence in the case, yet they have by a law antecedent and paramount to all positive laws of men reserved that ultimate determination to themselves which belongs to all mankind, where there lies no appeal on earth;

35  viz., to judge whether they have just cause to make their appeal to Heaven. And this judgment they cannot part with, it being out of a man's power so to submit himself to another as to give him a liberty to destroy him; God and nature never allowing a man so to abandon himself as to neglect his own preservation. And

since he cannot take away his own life, neither can he give another power to take it. Nor let anyone think this lays a perpetual foundation for disorder; for this operates not till the inconveniency is so great that the majority feel it, and are weary of it, and find a necessity to have it amended....

## Of Paternal, Political, and Despotical Power

**II§15**...May the commands then of a prince be opposed? May he be resisted as      5
often as anyone shall find himself aggrieved, and but imagine he has not right done him? This will unhinge and overturn all polities, and instead of government and order, leave nothing but anarchy and confusion.

To this I answer: that force is to be opposed to nothing but to unjust and unlawful force....                                                                                     10

## Of the Dissolution of Government

**II§19**...That which makes the community, and brings men out of the loose state of nature into one politic society, is the agreement which everyone has with the rest to incorporate and act as one body, and so be one distinct commonwealth. The usual, and almost only, way whereby this union is dissolved is the inroad of foreign force making a conquest upon them.... Whenever the society is dis-     15
solved, 'tis certain the government of that society cannot remain....

...When the legislative is altered. Civil society being a state of peace amongst those who are of it, from whom the state of war is excluded by the umpirage, which they have provided in their legislative, for the ending all differences that may arise amongst any of them, 'tis in their legislative that the members of a     20
commonwealth are united and combined together into one coherent living body. This is the soul that gives form, life, and unity to the commonwealth. From hence the several members have their mutual influence, sympathy, and connection. And therefore when the legislative is broken or dissolved, dissolution and death follows. For the essence and union of the society consisting in     25
having one will, the legislative, when once established by the majority, has the declaring and, as it were, keeping of that will....

There is one way more whereby such a government may be dissolved, and that is when he who has the supreme executive power neglects and abandons that charge, so that the laws already made can no longer be put in execution.     30
This is demonstratively to reduce all to anarchy, and so effectually to dissolve the government.... and the people become a confused multitude, without order or connection.... Where the laws cannot be executed, it is all one, as if there were no laws, and a government without laws is, I suppose, a mystery in politics, unconceivable to human capacity, and inconsistent with human society.     35

In these and the like cases, when the government is dissolved, the people are at liberty to provide for themselves by erecting a new legislative, differing from the other by the change of persons or form, or both, as they shall find it most for their safety and good....

5    There is therefore secondly another way whereby governments are dissolved, and that is when the legislative or the prince either of them act contrary to their trust.... when they endeavor to invade the property of the subject and to make themselves, or any part of the community, masters or arbitrary disposers of the lives, liberties, or fortunes of the people....

10    ...By this breach of trust they forfeit the power the people had put into their hands for quite contrary ends, and it devolves to the people, who have a right to resume their original liberty and, by the establishment of a new legislative (such as they shall think fit) provide for their own safety and security, which is the end for which they are in society....

15    ...The people generally ill treated, and contrary to right, will be ready upon any occasion to ease themselves of a burden that fits heavy upon them....

...Such revolutions happen not upon every little mis-management in public affairs. Great mistakes in the ruling part, many wrong and inconvenient laws, and all the slips of human frailty will be borne by the people without mutiny or
20    murmur. But if a long train of abuses, prevarications, and artifices, all tending that same way, make the design visible to the people, and they cannot but feel what they lie under, and see whither they are going, 'tis not to be wondered that they should then rouse themselves and endeavor to put the rule into such hands which may secure to them the ends for which government was at first erected; and without
25    which ancient names and specious forms are so far from being better that they are much worse than the state of nature, or pure anarchy; the inconveniencies being all as great and as near, but the remedy farther off and more difficult....

But is they who say it lays a foundation for rebellion mean that it may occasion civil wars or intestine broils to tell the people they are absolved from
30    obedience when illegal attempts are made upon their liberties or properties, and may oppose the unlawful violence of those who were their magistrates when they invade their properties contrary to the trust put in them; and that there-fore this doctrine is not to be allowed, being too destructive to the peace of the world. They may as well say upon the same ground that honest men may not
35    oppose robbers or pirates, because this may occasion disorder or bloodshed. If any mischief come in such cases, it is not to be charged upon him who defends his own right, but on him that invades his neighbor's....

...'Tis true such men may stir, whenever they please, but it will be only to their own just ruin and perdition. For till the mischief be grown general, and
40    the ill designs of the rulers become visible, or their attempts sensible to the

greater part, the people, who are more disposed to suffer than right themselves by resistance, are not apt to stir. The examples of particular injustice or oppression of here and there an unfortunate men moves them not....

...The common question will be made, Who shall be judge whether the prince or legislative act contrary to their trust? This, perhaps, ill-affected and factious men may spread among the people when the prince only makes use of his due prerogative. To this I reply the people shall be judge; for who shall be judge whether his trustee or deputy acts well and according to the trust reposed in him but he who deputes him, and must, by having deputed him, have still a power to discard him when he fails in his trust?...

If a controversy arise betwixt a prince and some of the people in a matter where the law is silent or doubtful, and the thing be of great consequence, I should think the proper umpire in such a case should be the body of the people....

To conclude, the power that every individual gave the society when he entered into it can never revert to the individuals again as long as the society lasts, but will always remain in the community; because without this there can be no community, no commonwealth, which is contrary to the original agreement. So also when the society has placed the legislative in any assembly of men to continue in them and their successors, with direction and authority for providing such successors, the legislative can never revert to the people whilst that government lasts. Because having provided a legislative with power to continue forever, they have given up their political power to the legislative, and cannot resume it. But if they have set limits to the duration of their legislative, and made this supreme power in any person or assembly only temporary. Or else, which by the miscarriages of those in authority, it is forfeited; upon the forfeiture, or at the determination of the time set, it reverts to the society, and the people have a right to act as supreme and continue the legislative in themselves; or erect a new form, or under the old form place it in new hands, as they think good.

# ABSOLUTISM

## JACQUES–BENIGNE BOSSUET (1624–1704), BISHOP OF MEAUX

*The most articulate and widely read proponent of absolutist theory was Jacques-Benigne Bossuet, a French bishop, tutor to the crown prince of France, and one of the most prominent orators of the seventeenth century. He published a work defending absolutism,* Politics Drawn from the Very Words of Holy Scripture, *from which this extract is taken.*

1679

We have already seen that all power is of God. The ruler, adds Saint Paul, "is the minister of God to you for good. But if you do that which is evil, be afraid; for he bears not the sword in vain, for he is the minister of God, a revenger to execute wrath upon him that does evil."

Rulers, then, act as the ministers of God and as His lieutenants on earth. 5 It is through them that God exercises His empire. Think you "to withstand the kingdom of the Lord in the hand of the sons of David"? Consequently, as we have seen, the royal throne is not the throne of a man, but the throne of God Himself.

Moreover, that no one may assume that the Israelites were peculiar in having 10 kings over them who were established by God, note what is said in Ecclesiasticus: "God has given every people its ruler, and Israel is manifestly reserved to Him." He therefore governs all peoples and gives them their kings, although He governed Israel in a more intimate and obvious manner. It appears from all this that the person of the king is sacred, and that to attack him in any way is 15 sacrilege. Kings should be guarded as holy things, and whosoever neglects to protect them is worthy of death....

But kings, although their power comes from on high, as has been said, should not regard themselves as masters of that power to use it at their pleasure; they must employ it with fear and self-restraint, as a thing coming from God 20 and of which God will demand an account. "Hear, O kings, and take heed; understand, judges of the earth; lend your ears, you who hold the peoples under your sway, and delight to see the multitude that surround you. It is God who

---

*Readings in Modern European History*, edited by James Harvey Robinson and Charles A. Beard (Boston: Ginn and Company, 1908), I:5–8.

gives you the power. Your strength comes from the Most High, Who will question your works and penetrate the depths of your thoughts, for, being ministers of His kingdom, you have not given righteous judgments nor have you walked according to His will. He will straightway appear to you in a terrible manner, for to those who command is the heaviest punishment reserved. The humble and the weak shall receive mercy, but the mighty shall be mightily tormented. For God fears not the power of anyone, because He made both great and small and He has care for both."

Kings should tremble, then, as they use the power God has granted them; and let them think how horrible is the sacrilege if they use for evil a power which comes from God. We behold kings seated upon the throne of the Lord, bearing in their hand the sword which God Himself has given them. What profanation, what arrogance, for the unjust king to sit on God's throne, to render decrees contrary to His laws, and to use the sword which God has put in his hand for deeds of violence and to slay his children!…

The royal power is absolute. With the aim of making this truth hateful and insufferable, many writers have tried to confound absolute government with arbitrary government. But no two things could be more unlike, as we shall show when we come to speak of justice.

The prince need render account of his acts to no one. Without this absolute authority the king could neither do good nor repress evil. It is necessary that his power be such that no one can hope to escape him and, finally, the only protection of individuals against the public authority should be their innocence. This conforms with the teaching of Saint Paul, "Will you then not be afraid of the power? Do that which is good."

I do not call majesty that pomp which surrounds kings or that exterior magnificence which dazzles the vulgar. That is but the reflection of majesty and not majesty itself. Majesty is the image of the grandeur of God in the prince.

God is infinite, God is all. The prince, as prince, is not regarded as a private person; he is a public personage; all the state is in him; the will of all the people is included in his. As all perfection and all strength are united in God, so all the power of individuals is united in the person of the prince. What grandeur that a single man should embody so much!

The power of God makes itself felt in a moment from one extremity of the earth to another. Royal power works at the same time throughout all the realm. It holds all the realm in position, as God holds the earth. Should God withdraw His hand, the earth would fall to pieces; should the king's authority cease in the realm, all would be in confusion.

Look at the prince in his cabinet. Thence go out the orders which cause the magistrates and the captains, the citizens and the soldiers, the provinces and the armies on land and on sea, to work in concert. He is the image of God, Who, seated on this throne high in the heavens, makes all nature move....

Finally, let us put together the things so great and so august which we have said about royal authority. Behold an immense people united in a single person; behold this holy power, paternal and absolute; behold the secret cause    5 which governs the whole body of the state, contained in a single head: you see the image of God in the king, and you have the idea of royal majesty. God is holiness itself, goodness itself, and power itself. In these things lies the majesty of God. In the image of these things lies the majesty of the prince.

So great is this majesty that it cannot reside in the prince as its source; it is    10 borrowed from God, who gives it to him for the good of the people, whom it is desirable to check by a superior force. Something of divinity itself is attached to princes and inspires fear in the people. The king should not forget this. "I have said"—it is God who speaks—"I have said, 'you are gods; and all of you are children of the Most High.' But you shall die like men, and fall like one of the    15 princes." "I have said, 'you are gods'"; that is to say, you have in your authority, and you bear on your forehead, a divine imprint. "You are the children of the Most High"; it is He who has established your power for the good of mankind. But, O gods of flesh and blood, gods of clay and dust, "you shall die like men, and fall like princes." Grandeur separates men for a little time, but a common    20 fall makes them all equal at the end.

O kings, exercise your power, then, boldly, for it is divine and salutary for human kind, but exercise it with humility. You are endowed with it from without. Know that it leaves you feeble, it leaves you mortal, it leaves you sinners, and charges you before God with a very heavy account.                              25

# ENGLISH BILL OF RIGHTS

*Following the flight of her father in 1688, Mary and her husband William were offered the Throne of England, if they accepted a Parliamentary statement of fundamental rights. They agreed to Parliament's declaration of rights, and were crowned in April 1689. Late that same year, the declaration to which the sovereigns agreed, the* Bill of Rights, *was formally recognized as a fundamental law of England and remains a constitutional foundation for much of the English-speaking world.*

16 DECEMBER 1689

Whereas the Lords Spiritual and Temporal and Commons assembled at Westminster, lawfully, fully, and freely representing all the estates of the people of this realm, did upon the thirteenth day of February in the year of our Lord one thousand six hundred eighty-eight present unto Their Majesties, then called and known by the names and style of William and Mary, Prince and Princess of Orange, being present in their proper persons, a certain declaration in writing made by the said Lords and Commons in the words following, viz:                                     5

Whereas the late King James the Second, by the assistance of divers evil counselors, judges, and ministers employed by him, did endeavour to subvert and extirpate the Protestant religion and the laws and liberties of this Kingdom:       10

By assuming and exercising a power of dispensing with and suspending of laws, and the execution of laws without consent of Parliament;

By committing and prosecuting divers worthy prelates for humbly petitioning to be excused from concurring to the said assumed power;

By issuing, and causing to be executed a commission under the Great Seal       15
for erecting a court, called "The Court of Commissioners for Ecclesiastical Causes;"

By levying money for and to the use of the Crown by pretence of prerogative, for other time and in other manner than the same was granted by Parliament;                                                                                   20

By raising and keeping a standing army within this Kingdom in time of peace, without consent of Parliament, and quartering of soldiers contrary to law;

---

"Bill of Rights," *1 William and Mary, Session 2, Chapter 2* (1688)

By causing several good subjects, being Protestants, to be disarmed, at the same time when Papists were both armed and employed contrary to law;

By violating the freedom of election of Members to serve in Parliament;

By prosecutions in the Court of King's Bench for matters and causes cognizable only in Parliament; and by divers other arbitrary and illegal courses;

And whereas, of late years partial, corrupt, and unqualified persons have been returned and served on juries in trials; and particularly divers jurors in trials for high treason which were not freeholders;

And excessive bail has been required of persons committed in criminal cases to elude the benefit of the laws made for the liberty of the subjects;

And excessive fines have been imposed;

And illegal and cruel punishments inflicted;

And several grants and promises made of fines and forfeitures, before any conviction or judgment against the persons upon whom the same were to be levied;

All which are utterly and directly contrary to the known laws and statutes and freedom of this realm.

And whereas the said late King James the Second having abdicated the government, and the throne being thereby vacant:

His Highness the Prince of Orange (whom it has pleased Almighty God to make the glorious instrument of delivering this Kingdom from Popery and arbitrary power) did (by the advice of the Lords Spiritual and Temporal, and divers principal persons of the Commons) cause letters to be written to the Lords Spiritual and Temporal being Protestants, and other letters to the several counties, cities, universities, boroughs, and Cinque Ports for the choosing of such persons to represent them as were of right to be sent to Parliament, to meet and sit at Westminster upon the two and twentieth day of January in this year 1688, in order to such an establishment as that their religion, laws, and liberties might not again be in danger of being subverted.

Upon which letters, elections having been accordingly made:

And thereupon the said Lords Spiritual and Temporal and Commons, pursuant to their respective letters and elections, being now assembled in a full and free representative of this nation, taking into their most serious consideration the best means for attaining the ends aforesaid, do in the first place (as their ancestors in like case have usually done), for the vindicating and asserting their ancient rights and liberties, declare,

That the pretended power of suspending of laws, or the execution of laws, by regal authority without consent of Parliament, is illegal.

That the pretended power of dispensing with laws, or the execution of laws, by regal authority, as it has been assumed and exercised of late, is illegal.

That the commission for erecting the late Court of Commissioners for Eccle- 5
siastical Causes, and all other commissions and courts of like nature, are illegal and pernicious.

That levying of money for or to the use of the Crown by pretence of preroga- tive, without grant of Parliament, for longer time, or in other manner than the same is or shall be granted, is illegal. 10

That it is the right of the subject to petition the King; and all commitments and prosecutions for such petitioning are illegal.

That the raising and keeping a standing army within this Kingdom in time of peace, unless it be with consent of Parliament, is against law.

That the subjects which are Protestants may have arms for their defence, suit- 15
able to their condition, and as allowed by law.

That election of Members of Parliament ought to be free.

That the freedom of speech and debates, or proceedings in Parliament, ought not to be impeached or questioned in any court or place out of Parliament.

That excessive bail ought not to be required, nor excessive fines imposed, nor 20
cruel and unusual punishments inflicted.

That jurors ought to be duly impaneled and returned; and jurors which pass upon men in trials for high treason ought to be freeholders.

That all grants and promises of fines and forfeitures of particular persons before conviction are illegal and void. 25

And that for redress of all grievances, and for the amending, strengthening, and preserving of the laws, Parliaments ought to be held frequently.

And they do claim, demand, and insist upon all and singular the premises, as their undoubted rights and liberties; and that no declarations, judgments, do- ings, or proceedings to the prejudice of the people in any of the said premises, 30
ought in any wise to be drawn hereafter into consequence or example.

To all which demand of their rights they are particularly encouraged by the declaration of His Highness the Prince of Orange as being the only means for obtaining a full redress and remedy therein.

Having, therefore, an entire confidence that his said Highness the Prince of 35
Orange will perfect the deliverance so far advanced by him, and will still preserve

them from the violation of their rights which they have here asserted, and from all other attempts upon their religion, rights, and liberties:

The said Lords Spiritual and Temporal and Commons, assembled at Westminster, do resolve that William and Mary, Prince and Princess of Orange, be and be
5   declared King and Queen of England, France, and Ireland, and the dominions thereunto belonging; to hold the Crown and royal dignity of the said kingdoms and dominions, to them the said Prince and Princess, during their lives, and the life of the survivor of them; and that the sole and full exercise of the regal power be only in, and executed by, the said Prince of Orange, in the names of
10   the said Prince and Princess, during their joint lives; and after their deceases, the said crown and royal dignity of the said kingdoms and dominions to be to the heirs of the body of the said Princess; and for default of such issue, to the Princess Anne of Denmark and the heirs of her body; and for default of such issue, to the heirs of the body of the said Prince of Orange.

15   And the said Lords Spiritual and Temporal and Commons do pray the said Prince and Princess of Orange to accept the same accordingly....

Upon which their said Majesties did accept the Crown and royal dignity of the kingdoms of England, France, and Ireland, and the dominions thereunto belonging, according to the resolution and desire of the said Lords and Commons
20   contained in the said declaration.

And thereupon Their Majesties were pleased that the said Lords Spiritual and Temporal and Commons, being the two Houses of Parliament, should continue to sit, and with Their Majesties' royal concurrence make effectual provision for the settlement of the religion, laws, and liberties of this Kingdom, so that the
25   same for the future might not be in danger again of being subverted, to which the said Lords Spiritual and Temporal and Commons did agree, and proceed to act accordingly.

Now in pursuance of the premises the said Lords Spiritual and Temporal and Commons in Parliament assembled for the ratifying, confirming, and establishing
30   the said declaration and the articles, clauses, matters, and things therein contained by the force of law made in due form by authority of Parliament, do pray that it may be declared and enacted that all and singular the rights and liberties asserted and claimed in the said declaration are the true, ancient, and indubitable rights and liberties of the people of this kingdom, and so shall be esteemed, allowed,
35   adjudged, deemed, and taken to be; and that all and every the particulars aforesaid shall be firmly and strictly holden and observed as they are expressed in the said declaration, and all officers and ministers whatsoever shall serve Their Majesties and their successors according to the same in all time to come....